新中国六十五年

New China in 65 Years

中华人民共和国国家统计局 编
National Bureau of Statistics of China

中国统计出版社
China Statistics Press

图书在版编目（ＣＩＰ）数据

新中国 65 年 ：汉英对照 / 中华人民共和国国家统计局编. -- 北京 ：中国统计出版社，2014.9
ISBN 978-7-5037-7281-8

Ⅰ. ①新… Ⅱ. ①中… Ⅲ. ①统计资料—中国—1949～2014—汉、英 Ⅳ. ①C832

中国版本图书馆 CIP 数据核字 (2014) 第 208743 号

新中国 65 年
New China in 65 Years

作　　者 / 中华人民共和国国家统计局
责任编辑 / 叶礼奇　郭　栋　王振宇　佘竞雄　李　冲
装帧设计 / 张　冰　黄　晨　李雪燕　李　静　王　芳
出版发行 / 中国统计出版社
通信地址 / 北京市丰台区西三环南路甲 6 号　邮政编码 /100073
电　　话 / 邮购（010）63376909　书店（010）68783171
网　　址 /http://csp.stats.gov.cn
印　　刷 / 北京画中画印刷有限公司
经　　销 / 新华书店
开　　本 /880mm×1230mm　1/16
字　　数 /600 千字
印　　张 /20.5
版　　别 /2014 年 9 月第 1 版
版　　次 /2014 年 9 月第 1 次印刷
定　　价 /280.00 元

图片提供：中国新闻图片社

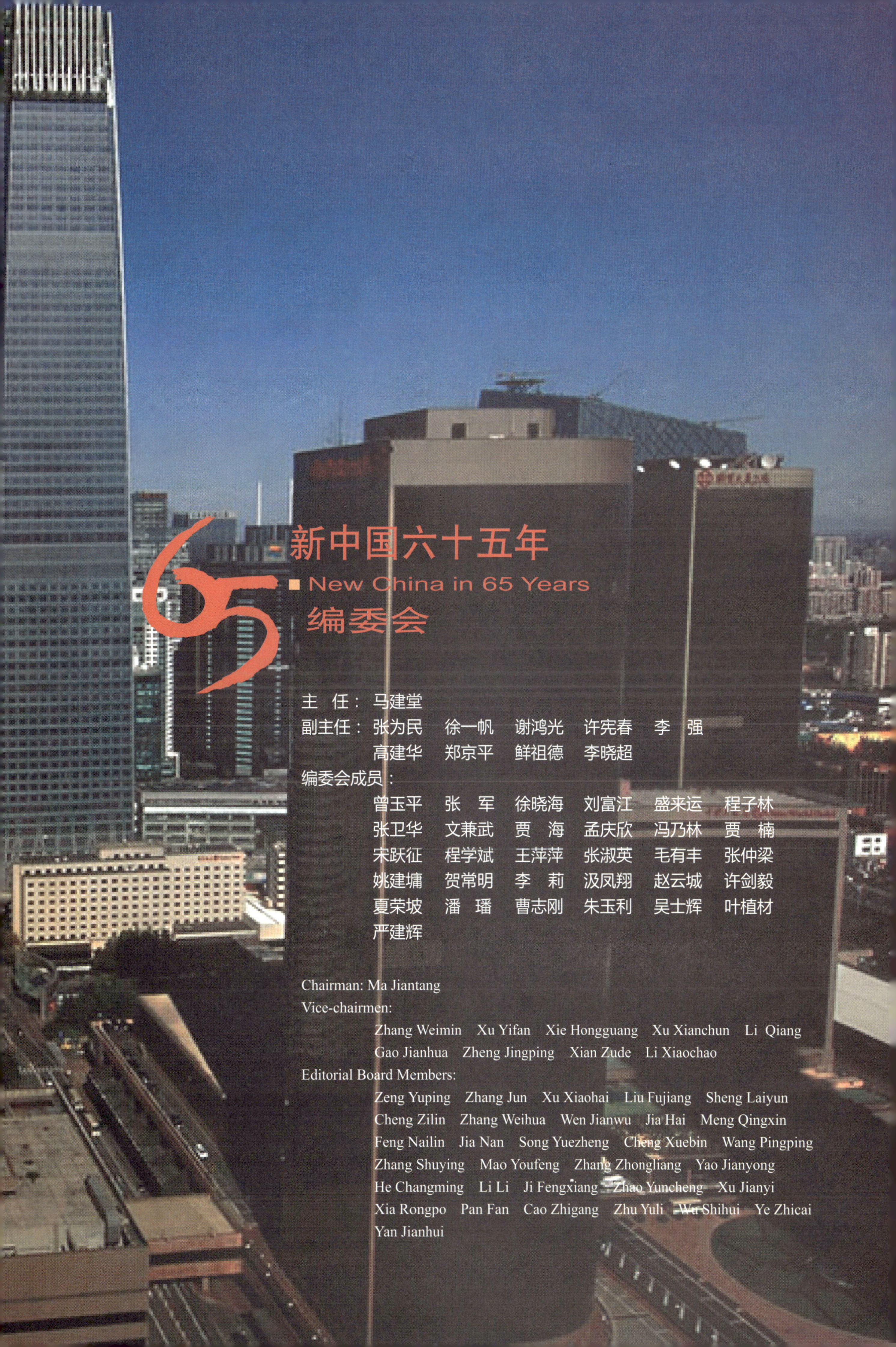

新中国六十五年
New China in 65 Years
编委会

65 新中国六十五年

New China in 65 Years

编辑部成员

编辑部主任：

盛来运　严建辉

编辑部副主任：

王文波　钟守洋　张　军　刘国宁

执行编辑：

赵国华　叶礼奇

编　辑：付凌晖　江明清　刘爱华　林京兴　张　蕾　卞丽华
石毅华　郁　红　王冠华　周　平　黄　涛　黄永山
许小乐　贾占华　董　辉　胡婷婷　俞炳彬　贺飞燕
郭　栋　王振宇

资料整理与提供（以姓氏笔画为序）：

于卫宁　于弘文　万忠兵　王青青　王挺漳　韦　革
申孟宜　邢明发　朱　虹　任宝莹　刘　畅　刘立青
刘旭玲　刘晓燕　严先溥　李　胤　李　嵩　李桂芝
李燕丽　杨　波　杨红军　肖　宁　肖　丽　谷亚丽
宋勇军　张　刚　张　昕　张　敏　张延华　张会英
陈　希　范小玉　郑云玉　赵利婧　侯　锐　俞家红
饶志刚　宫少军　夏　萍　殷国俊　栾尽晖　高　毅
唐　平　常文莉　韩　峰　覃　丹　路亚南　阚小清

责任编辑：

叶礼奇　郭　栋　王振宇　佘竞雄　李　冲

装帧设计：

张　冰　黄　晨　李雪燕　李　静　王　芳

数据见证历史　成就奠基未来

STATISTICS AS A WITNESS TO HISTORY ACHIEVEMENTS LAY A FOUNDATION FOR FUTURE

国家统计局局长
Commissioner
National Bureau of Statistics
Ma Jiantang

当丰收的馨香溢满神州大地，我们迎来中华人民共和国成立65周年的喜庆日子。65年来，在中国共产党的正确领导下，全国各族人民同心同德，艰苦奋斗，战胜各种艰难曲折和风险考验，不断夺取新中国建设、改革开放伟大胜利，将几代人矢志追求的现代化宏伟目标和民族伟大复兴梦想不断变为现实和向前推进。65载不平凡历程，犹如一幅气势磅礴而绚丽多彩的画卷，必将载入中华民族自强不息、顽强奋进的光辉史册，永远镌刻在人类发展进步的历史丰碑上。

值此共和国65年华诞之际，由国家统计局组织编辑的大型历史资料书籍《新中国六十五年》正式出版发行。该书以翔实的统计数据和丰富的文字资料，从经济、社会、文化、生态等多个方面，全方位、系统性地展示了新中国成立65年取得的辉煌成就。书中汇集的一笔笔鲜活的数据，一张张生动的图表，勾画出新中国不断走向进步、日益繁荣富强的壮丽征程，凝聚着中国共产党对改革和建设事业的持续探索，饱含着全体中国人民的不懈奋斗。与建国初期经济社会一穷二白状况相比，2013年我国国内生产总值达到57万亿元，位居世界第二位，综合国力和国际影响力显著提升；粮食产量连续多年稳定在1万亿斤以上，不仅有效解决了13亿中国人的吃饭问题，也为世界粮食安全做出重要贡献；工业生产能力和竞争力不断增强，主要工业产品产量跃居世界前列，“中国制造”逐步享誉全球；货物进出口总额突破4万亿美元，跃居世界第一位；城乡居民生活发生翻天覆地的变化，实现了从基本消除贫困到总体小康再到向全面小康迈进的连续跨越；教育、科技、文化、卫生、体育、环保等各项社会事业全面繁荣进步，经济社会发展的协调性、可持续性大为增强。

序

Preface

可以毫不夸张地说，近代以来，中国的国力从来不曾如此强大，百姓的生活从来不曾如此富足，人民的精神面貌从来不曾如此昂扬，一个生机盎然、蒸蒸日上的社会主义中国已经巍然屹立于世界东方。65 年光辉历程已经证明并将继续证明：只有社会主义才能救中国，只有改革开放才能发展中国、发展社会主义、发展马克思主义。

百尺竿头须进步，民族复兴歌未央。65 年艰苦卓绝的奋斗历程，奠定了中华民族伟大复兴的牢固基石。展望未来，我国仍处在可以大有作为的重要战略机遇期，工业化、信息化、城镇化、农业现代化持续推进，发展潜力巨大，我们对建设一个更加强大的中国充满信心。但也要看到，进入发展新阶段，可以预见和难以预见的风险和挑战增多，统筹稳增长、促改革、调结构的难度更大，需要我们更加锐意改革、开拓进取、勇于创新。让我们紧密团结在以习近平同志为总书记的党中央周围，进一步坚定道路自信、理论自信、制度自信，以 65 年辉煌成就为新的起点，迎难而上，奋力实干，在全面深化改革、全面建成小康社会的新征程上交出优异答卷，续写实现中华民族伟大复兴中国梦的新辉煌!

As the fragrance of the annual harvest spreads across the vast land of China, we celebrate the joyous day marking the 65th anniversary of the founding of the People's Republic of China (PRC). From that proud moment, during 65 years, under the correct leadership of the Communist Party of China, the people of all nationalities have been united in working hard to overcome various difficulties and setbacks and cope with various risks and challenges to constantly achieve great victories in the construction of New China and the ongoing reform and opening up. They have constantly turned into reality the grand goal of modernization that has been pursued by generations and the dream of a great rejuvenation of the Chinese nation and put the goal and the dream forward. The marvelous course of 65 years is just like a magnificent and colorful scroll painting revealing a glorious history of the Chinese people's continuous self-improvement and tenacious striving for progress that will forever engraved on the monument of human development.

To mark the occasion of the 65th anniversary of the founding of the PRC, under the organization of the NBS, this historic book "New China in 65 Years" is published. Through full and accurate statistics and abundant text, its purpose is to comprehensively and systematically reveal the remarkable achievements New China has made since its founding in numerous aspects including economy, society, culture and ecology. The fresh statistics and vivid charts collected in the book provide a clear outline of the nation's grand journey of constant progress and growing prosperity, embodying the continuous exploration of reform and construction by the Communist Party of China, fully illustrating the unremitting efforts of the Chinese people. In the early days of the PRC, the economy and society were mired in abject poverty. However, by 2013, GDP had reached 57 trillion yuan, ranking second in the world, greatly improving China's comprehensive national strength and international influence. Grain output has exceeded 500 billion kilograms for many years, not only solving the food problems of 1.3 billion Chinese people, but also making an important contribution to world food safety. China's capacity and competitiveness in industrial production have constantly expanded, so that output of major industrial products has moved to the forefront in the world, and the label "Made in China" has come to enjoy a high reputation in the world. In 2013, China's total import and export trade exceeded US$4 trillion, ranking first in the world. Great changes have taken place in the life of both urban and rural residents, as the nation has moved from "basically eliminating poverty" to "building a generally well-off society" and now on to "striving to create a moderately prosperous society in all respects". Social undertakings such as education, science and technology, culture, health, sports and environmental protection have all seen significant progress. The coordination and sustainability of socio-economic development have been greatly enhanced. It is no exaggeration to say that, in modern times, China's national strength has never been so strong, the life of its people has never been so prosperous and the Chinese people have never been so high-spirited. A vibrant and thriving China has risen majestically in the East. The glorious journey of 65 years has proved and will continue to prove that only socialism can save China, and only the reform and opening up can develop China and its cause of socialism and Marxism.

There is still some way to go to achieve every aspect of the dream of national rejuvenation. However, the Chinese people's arduous struggle for the past 65 years has laid a solid foundation for fully achieving the set goals. The nation is still in an important period of taking full advantage of the strategic opportunities offered. Industrialization, informatization, urbanization and agricultural modernization have been constantly promoted and retain great potential for further development. We are fully confident of building a more powerful China. It should be noted, however, that we still face many risks, some that can be predicted and others that remain hidden, and these pose many challenges at this present new stage of development. It is more difficult to coordinate between ensuring steady growth, advancing reform and adjusting the structure. It requires us to continue to show keen determination in reform, make pioneering efforts to advance and have the courage to innovate. Let us rally closely around the Party Central Committee with Comrade Xi Jinping as General Secretary, further consolidate our confidence in China's socialist path, theory and system. From a new starting point after 65 years of glorious achievement, we must boldly advance to meet all difficulties, work hard and continue to make remarkable progress in comprehensively deepening reform and building a moderately prosperous society in all respects, and continue to create new glory in realizing the Chinese dream of great national rejuvenation.

目录

Contents

序 Preface

数据见证历史 成就奠基未来 马建堂
STATISTICS AS A WITNESS TO HISTORY
ACHIEVEMENTS LAY A FOUNDATION FOR FUTURE

第一部分：六十五载峥嵘路 砥砺奋进谱华章
CHINA'S 65-YEAR JOURNEY USHERS IN GREAT DEVELOPMENT

一、从一穷二白到世界第二大经济体，综合国力和国际影响力实现了举世瞩目的历史性跨越
I. From a poor and backward state to the second-largest world economy, the combined power of the state and its international influence have achieved a remarkable historic leap.

3 （一）国民经济快速增长，综合国力显著增强。
Rapid growth of the national economy and significant strengthening of the integrated power of the state.

7 （二）经济发展水平不断提高，国际影响力持续攀升。
The continuous rise in the level of economic development and the steady growth of international influence.

二、从单一失衡到百业兴旺，经济结构的协调性逐步增强
II. From imbalance to numerous thriving businesses, coordination within the economic structure has gradually advanced.

22 （一）产业结构逐步升级，以农业为主到以工业为主并正向服务业主导型经济转变。
Gradual upgrading of the industrial structure; changes from agricultural-based to industrial-based and service-oriented economy.

28 （二）所有制结构深刻变化，实现由单一公有制到多种所有制经济共同发展的转变。
Profound changes in the ownership system structure have achieved the transformation from a single public ownership economy to a diversified-ownership economy.

32 （三）分配结构不断调整，从绝对平均主义转变为以按劳分配为主、多种分配方式并存。
Continuous adjustment of income distribution structure has produced a transition from absolute egalitarianism to the main form of work-based that coexists with other forms of distribution.

36 （四）城镇化稳步推进，城乡统筹协调发展趋势明显。
Steady urbanization, clear trends of coordinated urban and rural development.

41 （五）区域发展协调性显著增强，各具特色、良性互动的区域发展格局正在形成。
Coordination of regional development has been significantly enhanced, forming a pattern of positive interaction between regions.

三、从短缺匮乏到丰富充裕，商品和服务供给能力极大提高

III. Shift from a supply deficit to a rich abundance of goods and services.

49 （一）农业综合生产能力稳步提高，成功解决了占世界五分之一人口的吃饭问题。
Steady improvement in overall agricultural production capacity has successfully resolved the problem of providing food for one fifth of the world's population.

56 （二）工业生产能力迅速提升，工业品供给实现了从严重依赖进口到满足世界需求的历史性跨越。
A rapid increase in industrial production capacity has led to an historic leap from heavy dependence on imports for industrial supplies to satisfying world demand.

59 （三）服务业发展方兴未艾，对经济社会的支撑和带动作用日益突出。
Service industry development is rising, playing an increasingly prominent role in the support and promotion of economic and social development.

四、从"瓶颈"制约到优势支撑，基础设施和基础产业实现跨越式大发展

IV. From "bottleneck" constraints to the advantages of support, infrastructure and foundational industries achieved huge leaps in development

68 （一）农业基础设施投入增加，农业生产条件不断改善。
Increase in investments in agricultural infrastructure and improvements in agricultural production conditions.

71 （二）能源产品产量大幅增加，基础保障作用显著增强。
Energy production output sharply increased, basic safety functions significantly enhanced.

78 （三）交通运输建设突飞猛进，由铁路、公路、民用航空、水运和管道组成的综合运输网络四通八达。
The transportation network has advanced by leaps and bounds with an integrated network of railways, highways, civil airways, waterways, and pipelines.

五、从封闭半封闭到全方位开放，对外开放取得举世公认的伟大成就

V.China has made universally-acknowledged achievements on its path from a closed and semi-closed economy to one open to the outside world.

87 （一）货物贸易规模不断扩大，进出口总额跃居世界第一。
Scale of trade in goods expanded, and import and export volumes rank first in the world.

93 （二）服务贸易从无到有，成为对外贸易的重要组成部分。
Trade in services grows from nothing to become an important part of China's foreign trade.

95 （三）积极参与经济全球化进程，从大规模"引进来"到大踏步"走出去"。
China adopts "drawing in" and "moving outward" strategies to guide its active participation in economic globalization.

102 （四）国际经济文化交流与合作日趋多样化，互利共赢新格局初步形成。
A win-win framework has been established thanks to increasingly diverse international economic and cultural exchange and cooperation.

六、从温饱不足到向全面小康迈进，人民生活水平发生翻天覆地的变化

VI. China makes the leap from a society lacking basic necessities to a peaceful and prosperous society. People's living standards see earth-shaking changes.

107 （一）就业规模不断扩大，就业结构逐步改善。
The scope of employment has widened and employment structure has been optimized.

112 （二）城乡居民收入大幅增加，生活水平显著提高。
The income of urban and rural residents sees sharp increase and people's

living standards improve by a large margin.
124 （三）社会保障不断完善，扶贫工作取得举世瞩目的成就。
China has improved its social security and attained poverty relief achievements that have attracted world-wide attention.

七、从文盲大国到人力资源大国，从受制于人到引领未来，教育和科技事业成就辉煌

VII. Transformed from a largely illiterate country to a nation rich in human resources, China has become a leader of the future, no longer restricted by others. China has made splendid achievements in its educational, scientific, and technological undertakings.

131 （一）教育事业取得巨大进步，人口素质大幅提高。
Tremendous progress has been made in education and the basic skills of the population have greatly improved.
138 （二）科技事业快速发展，科研成果硕果累累。
The pursuit of science and technology has moved ahead quickly and has seen many research achievements.

八、从相对落后到全面繁荣，文化卫生体育环保等社会事业取得长足进步。

VIII. From relative backwardness to full prosperity, culture, health, sports, environmental protection and other social sectors have made a big step forward.

149 （一）文化事业繁荣发展，经济效益不断提高。
The prosperous development of the cultural sector and the constant improvement of economic efficiency.
153 （二）医疗卫生事业成绩斐然，人民健康水平显著提高。
Impressive achievements in medicine and health care have resulted in a significant increase in the level of human health.
158 （三）体育事业全面进步，竞技体育不断取得历史性突破。
Physical education gets all-round development, and historic breakthroughs have continually been reached in physical fitness and athletics.
162 （四）环境保护稳步推进，成效逐渐显现。
Nature and environmental protection steadily improve and gradually begin to show results.

第二部分：统计表

Statistical Data

165 表 1 全国自然状况和自然资源
Basic Condition and Natural Resources
166 表 2 全国行政区划（年底数）
Divisions of Administrative Areas in China (at Year-end)
168 表 3 全国人口状况
Population
170 表 4 人口年龄结构和抚养比
Age Composition and Dependency Ratio of Population
171 表 5 全国就业人员和城镇登记失业人员
Employment and Unemployment
173 表 6 全国城镇单位就业人员数和平均工资
Number of Staff and Workers and Average Wage
175 表 7 国内生产总值
Gross Domestic Product
177 表 8 国内生产总值构成
Composition of Gross Domestic Product
179 表 9 国内生产总值指数（上年 =100)
Indices of Gross Domestic Product(preceding year=100)
181 表 10 国内生产总值指数 (1952 年 =100)
Indices of Gross Domestic Product(year of 1952=100)
183 表 11 支出法国内生产总值
Gross Domestic Product by Expenditure Approach
185 表 12 全国居民消费水平及指数
Household Consumption and Its Indices
187 表 13 全社会固定资产投资
Total Investment in Fixed Assets
189 表 14 按资金来源分全社会固定资产投资和房屋建筑面积
Total Investment in Fixed Assets by Source of Funds and Floor Space of Buildings
190 表 15 全国房地产开发情况
Floor Space of Buildings and Real Estate Development of China
191 表 16 国家财政收支总额及增长速度
Government Revenue and Expenditure and Their Increase Rates
193 表 17 全国各项税收
Taxes
195 表 18 国家财政主要支出项目
Main Government Expenditure by Item
197 表 19 国家财政债务还本付息支出
Government Payment for the Principal and Interest of Debts
198 表 20 中央财政债务余额情况
Balance of Debts of National Government Finance

199 表 21 全国外债余额
Balance of Foreign Debts
200 表 22 各种价格总指数
Price Indices
202 表 23 各种价格定基指数
Fixed-base Price Indices
203 表 24 全国城乡居民人均收支和恩格尔系数
Per Capita Annual Income, Expenditure and Engel Coefficient of Urban and Rural Households
204 表 25 全国城乡居民住房面积和储蓄存款余额
Resident Buildings, Savings Deposit in Urban and Rural Areas
206 表 26 全国城乡居民平均每百户年末主要耐用消费品拥有量
Durable Consumer Goods Owned Per 100 Households at Year-end
208 表 27 全国城市公用事业
Basic Statistics on Urban Public Utilities
214 表 28 全国城市设施水平
Level of National Municipal Public Facilities
216 表 29 全国环境保护基本情况
Basic Statistics on Environmental Protection
217 表 30 全国农林牧渔业总产值和构成
Gross Output Value and Composition of Farming, Forestry, Animal Husbandry and Fishery
219 表 31 全国农林牧渔业总产值指数
Indices of Gross Output Value of Farming, Forestry, Animal Husbandry and Fishery
221 表 32 全国农业生产条件
Production Condition for Agriculture
223 表 33 全国主要农业产品产量
Yield of Major Farm Crops, Forest Products, Livestock Products and Aquatic Products
227 表 34 全国受灾和成灾面积
Areas Covered and Affected by Natural Disaster
229 表 35 全国工业企业主要经济指标
Main Indicators of Industrial Enterprises
231 表 36 全国工业企业主要经济效益指标
Main Indicators on Economic Benefit of Industrial Enterprises
232 表 37 全国主要工业产品产量
Output of Major Industrial Products
240 表 38 全国能源生产总量及构成
Total Production of Energy and Its Composition
242 表 39 全国能源消费总量及构成
Total Consumption of Energy and Its Composition
244 表 40 全国分品种能源消费量
Consumption of Energy by Type

245 表 41 全国人均生活能源消费量
Annual Per Capita Energy Consumption for Non-Production Purpose
246 表 42 全国建筑业企业概况
Main Indicators on Construction Enterprises
248 表 43 全国运输线路长度
Length of Transport Routes
250 表 44 全国客运量
Passenger Traffic
252 表 45 全国旅客周转量
Passenger-Kilometers
254 表 46 全国货运量
Freight Traffic
256 表 47 全国货物周转量
Freight Ton-Kilometers
258 表 48 全国民用汽车拥有量
Number of Civil Vehicles Owned
260 表 49 全国邮电业务量
Postal and Telecommunication Services
266 表 50 全国社会消费品零售总额
Total Retail Sale of Consumer Goods
267 表 51 全国进出口贸易总额
Total Value of Imports and Exports
269 表 52 按贸易方式和商品类别分全国进出口贸易总额
Total Value of Imports and Exports by Trading Form and by Category of Commodities
270 表 53 全国实际利用外资
Uitilization of Foreign Capital
271 表 54 对外经济合作
Economic Cooperation with Foreign Countries or Regions
272 表 55 全国国际旅游情况
International Tourism
273 表 56 全国国内旅游情况
Statistics of Domestic Tourism
274 表 57 全国金融机构人民币业务基本情况
General Statistics of Financial Institutions of RMB
276 表 58 全国金融机构法定存款利率
Official Deposits Rates in Financial Institutions
277 表 59 全国金融机构法定贷款利率
Official Lending Rates in Financial Institutions
278 表 60 全国证券市场基本情况
General Statistics on Securities Markets
279 表 61 全国保险业基本情况
General Statistics on Insurance
280 表 62 黄金和外汇储备

Gold and Foreign Exchange Reserves
281 表 63 国际收支概况
General Statistics on Balance of Payments
282 表 64 全国各级各类学校数
Number of School by Level and Type of School
284 表 65 全国各级各类学校专任教师数
Number of Full-Time Teachers by Level and Type of School
286 表 66 全国各级各类学校在校学生数
Number of Students Enrollment by Level and Type of School
288 表 67 全国各级各类学校招生数
Number of New Students Enrollment by Level and Type of School
290 表 68 全国各级各类学校毕业生数
Number of Graduates by Level and Type of School
292 表 69 研究生和留学人员数
Number of Postgraduates and Students Studying Abroad
294 表 70 全国各级学校平均在校生数、升学率和入学率
Student Enrollment, Percentage of Graduates Entering Higher Level Schools by Level and Percentage of School-Age Children Enrolled
296 表 71 教育经费情况
Basic Statistics on Educational Funds
297 表 72 全国科技活动发展情况
Basic Statistics on Scientific and Technological Activities
298 表 73 全国文化事业机构数
Number of Cultural Institutes
300 表 74 图书、期刊和报纸出版
Number of Books, Magazines and Newspaper Published
302 表 75 运动员获世界冠军情况
World Championships Won by Chinese Athletes
303 表 76 全国各类医疗卫生机构数
Health Institutions by Kind
305 表 77 全国各类卫生机构人员数
Number of Employed Personnel in Health Institutions
307 表 78 全国医疗卫生机构床位
Number of Beds in Health Care Institutions
309 表 79 养老机构及提供住宿的社会服务床位数
Institution for the Aged and Beds of Social Welfare Institutions with Accommodations
310 表 80 全国社会保障基本情况
Basic Statistics for Social Security of China

六十五载峥嵘路 砥砺奋进谱华章

——新中国成立 65 周年我国经济社会发展成就辉煌

CHINA'S 65-YEAR JOURNEY USHERS IN GREAT DEVEIOPMENT

Economic and social achievements 65 years after the anniversary of the founding of the People's Republic of China

1949 年 10 月 1 日，毛泽东同志向全世界庄严宣告中华人民共和国成立。这一彪炳史册的历史时刻，宣告了一个旧时代的终结，标志着中华民族从此迈向伟大复兴的新纪元。如今，伟大祖国即将迎来 65 周年华诞。65 年，在漫漫历史长河中不过短暂一瞬，但对于中国和中国人民来说，却是一段不平凡的峥嵘历程。65 年来，中国共产党团结带领全国各族人民，自强不息，砥砺奋进，经受了一次次严峻考验，战胜了一个个艰难险阻，把一个积贫积弱、满目疮痍、百废待兴的旧中国建设成了一个团结统一、繁荣富强、蒸蒸日上的新兴大国，谱写了中华民族发展史和人类发展史上的华彩乐章。

On October 1, 1949, Comrade Mao Zedong solemnly proclaimed the foundation of the People's Republic of China to the world. This historic moment crowned by eternal glory put an end to the old era. From that point on, the Chinese people began a new era of great revival. Today, the Great Motherland is approaching its 65th anniversary. From a historical point of view, 65 years is a very short period of time, yet this period has been a long and challenging path for China and the Chinese people. During these 65 years, the Chinese Communist Party (CCP) has managed to unite and lead all the peoples of the country. The CCP continued to strengthen, withstanding difficult tests and overcoming obstacles one after another. The Party turned a poor, weak, and completely devastated old China that was in need of restoration into a unified and prosperous nation that is growing and becoming more prosperous day by day. In so doing, the Party has composed a magnificent final movement in the symphony of the history of the Chinese people and the history of mankind.

1 从一穷二白到世界第二大经济体，综合国力和国际影响力实现了举世瞩目的历史性跨越

From a poor and backward state to the second-largest world economy, the combined power of the state and its international influence have achieved a remarkable historic leap.

新中国成立以来的65年，是我国经济大踏步前进、彻底告别积弱积贫的65年，是成功由低收入国家迈入上中等收入国家行列的65年，也是综合国力和国际影响力不断提升、实现历史性跨越的65年。

During the 65 years since the founding of the PRC, the country's economic development has progressed by leaps and bounds. It successfully transformed from a low-income country into an upper middle income country. The combined power of the state and its international influence are continuously increasing, so that the last 65 years have amounted to a historic leap for China.

（一）国民经济快速增长，综合国力显著增强。

建国以来，我国经济发展尽管经历曲折与艰难，但总体上保持较快发展，特别是 1978 年党的十一届三中全会做出了改革开放的历史抉择，实现了新中国发展史上具有深远意义的伟大转折，我国经济发展驶入快车道，经济总量不断扩大，国家财力显著增强。

国内生产总值年均增长 8.2%。1953-2013 年，我国国内生产总值按不变价计算增加了 122 倍，年均增长 8.2%，平均每 9 年翻一番；其中 1979-2013 年年均增长 9.8%，而同期世界经济年均增速只有 2.7%。我国高速增长期持续的时间和增长速度都超过了经济起飞时期的日本和亚洲“四小龙”，堪称人类经济发展史上的奇迹。近几年随着我国进入转型发展新阶段，经济增长由高速向中高速换挡，经济增速维持在 7%-8% 的区间平稳运行，增长的稳定性进一步增强。

经济总量连续跨上新台阶。1952 年，我国国内生产总值只有 679 亿元，到 1978 年增加到 3645 亿元，之后连续跨越，2013 年已经接近 60 万亿元，为 568845 亿元。其中，从 1978 年上升到 1986 年的 1 万亿元用了 8 年时间；上升到 1991 年的 2 万亿元用了 5 年时间；此后 10 年平均每年上升近 1 万亿元，2001 年超过 10 万亿元大关；此后 5 年平均每年上升 2 万亿元，2006 年超过 20 万亿元；之后每两年上升 10 万亿元，2008 年超过 30 万亿元，2010 年超过 40 万亿元，2012 年超过 50 万亿元。扣除价格因素，2013 年我国每 3 天所创造的财富量，就相当于 1952 年全年创造的财富量。

(1) Rapid growth of the national economy and significant strengthening of the integrated power of the state.

Since the founding of the state, the Chinese economy has undergone a general trend of rapid development in spite of complications and difficulties. This was especially made possible by the historic choice to adopt reform and an open door policy at the third plenary session of the 11th CPC Central Committee in 1978. It was a great turning point that had far-reaching significance for the recent history of the development of China. China's economic development has entered the fast lane, total economic volume is continuously increasing, and the financial power of the state has been greatly strengthened.

The average annual GDP growth rate is 8.2%. Over the period from 1953 to 2013, China's GDP increased 122 times at constant prices, with an average annual growth rate of 8.2%, and a doubling of GDP has taken place approximately every 9 years. In the period of 1979-2013, the average annual growth of the Chinese economy was 9.8%, while the average annual growth rate of the world economy was only 2.7%. China has surpassed Japan and the "Four Asian Tigers" in terms of the length of the period of its continuous economic development and the rate of its economic growth. China is now considered to be the foremost "economic miracle" in the history of mankind. In recent years, as China has entered a new period of economic transformation, rates of economic growth have changed from high to medium-high within the range of 7-8%, and the stability of economic growth continues to strengthen.

The country's total economic volume reached new heighs continuously. In 1952, China's GDP was only 67.9 billion yuan. It increased to 364.5 billion yuan in 1978, and since then it has been growing continuously, it has been close to 60 trillion yuan, reaching 56.8845 trillion yuan in 2013. It took China 8 years to grow its GDP to 1 trillion yuan between 1978 and 1986, but it only took 5 years to double GDP to 2 trillion yuan in 1991. Over the following 10 years, GDP growth reached around 1 trillion yuan a year, and the 10 trillion yuan mark was hit in 2001. Annual growth amounted to 2 trillion yuan over the next 5 years, and the total economic volume reached 20 trillion yuan in 2006. Then, every two years, growth reached 10 trillion yuan, and in 2008 the 30 trillion yuan mark was conquered. In 2010, 40 trillion yuan was reached, and in 2012, 50 trillion yuan was reached. After adjusting for inflation factors, the amount of wealth generated in three days in 2013 was equal to the amount produced during a whole year in 1952.

ASCOTT

国内生产总值

国内生产总值被许多经济学家称为 20 世纪的伟大发明，它是指在一定时期内（一个季度或一年），一个国家或地区的经济中所生产出的全部最终产品和劳务的价值。国内生产总值有三种表现形态，即价值形态、收入形态和产品形态。从价值形态看，它是所有常住单位在一定时期内所生产的全部货物和服务价值超过同期投入的全部非固定资产货物和服务价值的差额，即所有常住单位的增加值之和；从收入形态看，它是所有常住单位在一定时期内所创造并分配给常住单位和非常住单位的初次分配收入之和；从产品形态看，它是最终使用的货物和服务减去进口货物和服务。正如任何指标反映客体都会有局限性一样，国内生产总值无法反映经济增长的所付出的代价特别是环境方面的损失，也无法反映社会福利的改善，但与其他指标相比，它是公认反映一个国家的经济表现和经济实力比较好的综合性指标。

Gross Domestic Product (GDP)

Gross domestic product, called as a great invention of the twentieth century by many economists, refers to the market value of all final goods and services produced within a country or a region in a given period of time (usually a quarter or a year). GDP has three forms, namely, the forms of value, income and product. From the perspective of value form, it means the difference between all goods and services value produced by a resident unit in a given period of time and the input of all the unfixed asset and services value during the same period, namely the sum of the added value of all resident units. From the perspective of income form, it refers to the sum of the primary distribution of income created by resident units in a given period and assigned to the resident units and non-resident units. From the perspective of product form, it is the ultimate use of goods and services minus the import of goods and services. Any indicators reflecting the object cannot escape from limitations, and GDP is no exception. It cannot reflect the cost of economic growth, especially environmental loss, nor can it reflect the improvement of social welfare. However, compared with other indicators, it is universally recognized as a good comprehensive indicator to reveal the economic performance and economic strength of a country.

图 1　1952-2013 年国内生产总值
Gross Domestic Product, 1952-2013

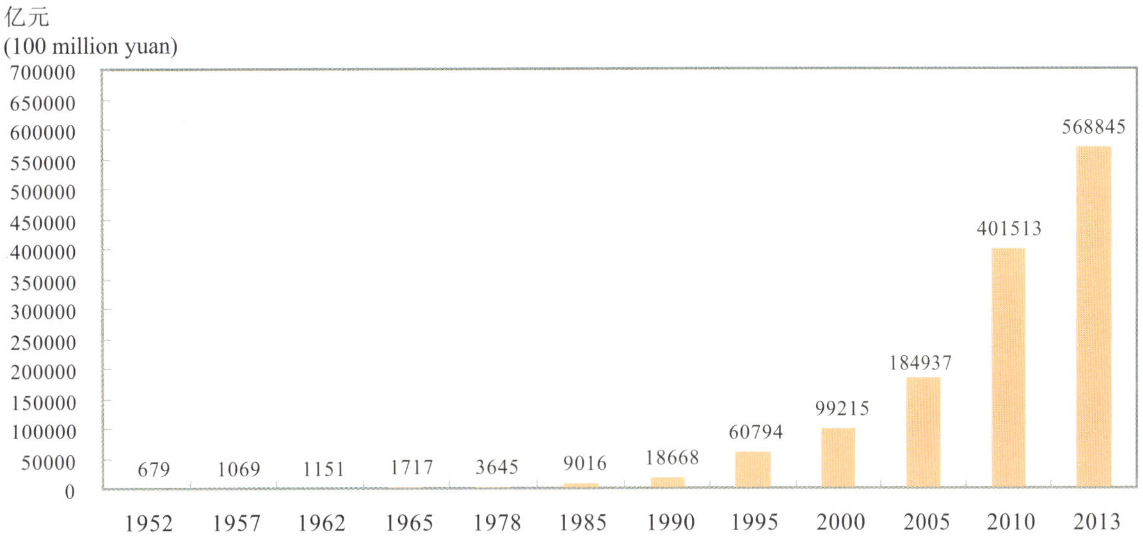

图 2 1950-2013 年财政收入
National Government Revenue, 1950-2013

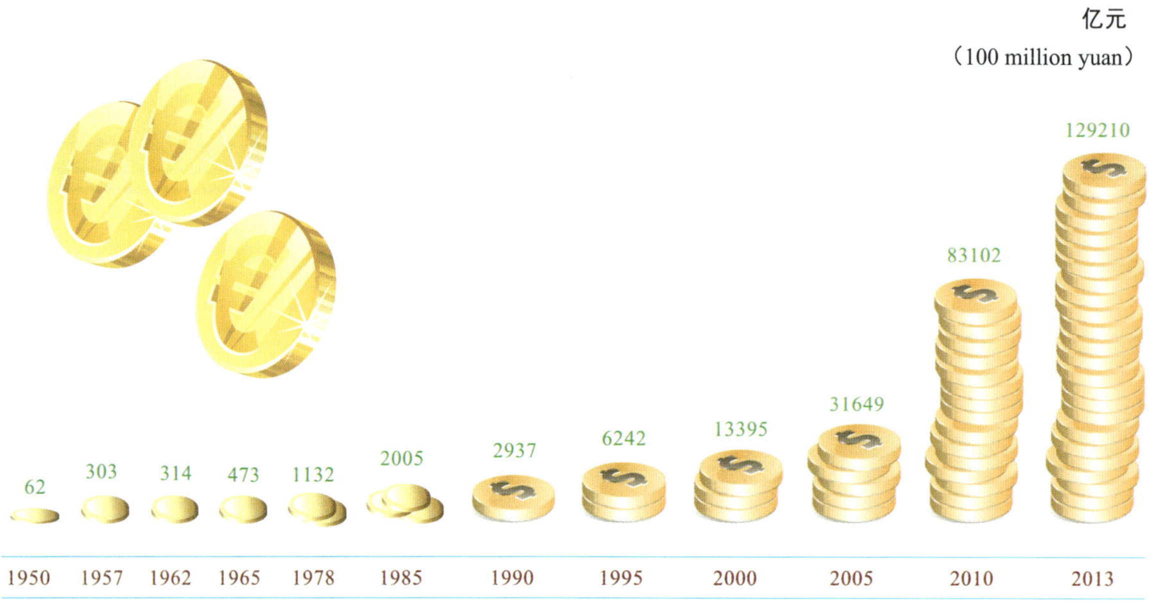

财政收入大幅增加。1950 年我国财政收入只有 62 亿元，1978 年上升到 1132 亿元，1999 年超过 1 万亿元，达到 11444 亿元，2007 年超过 5 万亿元，达到 51322 亿元，2011 年超过 10 万亿元，达到 103874 亿元，2013 年进一步扩大到 129210 亿元，1951-2013 年年均增长 12.9%。财政实力的增强为政府促进经济社会发展、改善经济运行中的薄弱环节、有效应对来自国内外的风险和挑战提供了有力的资金保障。

A substantial increase in financial income. In 1950, China's fiscal revenue accounted for only 6.2 billion yuan, but by 1978, revenue had risen to 113.2 billion yuan, and in 1999 it exceeded 1 trillion yuan to reach 1.1444 tillion yuan. In 2007, fiscal revenue exceeded 5 trillion yuan and reached 5.1322 trillion yuan, in 2011 it surpassed 10 trillion yuan and reached 10.3874 trillion yuan, and in 2013 a further step was made to the amount of 12.921 trillion yuan. Between 1951 and 2013, the average annual growth rate was 12.9%. Strengthening financial stability provided the government with strong social guarantees to promote the development of an economic society, improve weaknesses in the framework of economic expansion, and effectively resist foreign and internal challenges and risks.

（二）经济发展水平不断提高，国际影响力持续攀升。

65 年来，我国经济总量、人均国民总收入居世界的位次大幅上升，外汇储备迅速增加，主要工农业产品产量名列前茅，对世界经济增长的贡献不断提高，国际影响持续扩大。

经济总量跃居世界第二位。建国之初，我国经济总量占世界的比重较低，经过近 30 年的发展，1978 年才达到 1.7%，居世界第 10 位；2000 年超过意大利，居世界第 6 位；2005 年超过法国，居世界第 5 位；2006 年超过英国，居世界第 4 位；2008 年超过德国，居世界第 3 位；2010 年超过日本，成为仅次于美国的世界第二大经济体。根据世界银行数据，2013 年，我国国内生产总值约为 92403 亿美元，相当于美国的 55.0%，占世界的份额达到 12.3%，比 1978 年提高 10.6 个百分点。伴随着经济总量居世界位次稳步提升，我国对世界经济增长的贡献不断提高，2008-2013 年我国对世界经济增长的贡献率超过 30%。

(2)The continuous rise in the level of economic development and the steady growth of international influence.

Within 65 years, the total economic volume of China and GNI per capita have risen significantly higher in world rankings. Foreign currency reserves are rapidly increasing, China's major industrial and agricultural products and outputs rank among the world's best, the country's contribution to global economic growth is continuously growing, and its global influence is steadily increasing.

The second largest economy in the world. When the People's Republic of China was first founded, China's total economic volume was fairly low in relation to the rest of the world, but after nearly 30 years of development, in 1978 it barely reached 1.7% share and was the 10th largest economy in the world. In 2000, China positioned itself ahead of Italy and won sixth place in the world; in 2005 it bypassed France, finishing fifth in the world; in 2006, China exceeded England, ranking the fourth in the world; in 2008 China's economy surpassed Germany's, rising to third place; and in 2010 China left behind Japan, thus becoming the second-largest economic entity in the world, preceded only by the United States. According to the World Bank, China's GDP was 9.2403 trillion dollars, amounting to 55.0% of the USA's GDP and comprising 12.3% of world GDP, an increase of 10.6% since 1978. As the total economic volume of China has steadily risen in the world rankings, China has increased its contribution to the world's economic growth. From 2008 to 2013 China's contribution to the growth of the world economy was more than 30% annually.

表 1　1978–2013 年 GDP 排名前十位的国家

GDP of Top Ten Countries, 1978 and 2013

单位：亿美元　　100 million US$

排名 Ranking	1978				2013			
	国家	Country	经济总量 GDP	占世界比重 Percentage of the World (%)	国家	Country	经济总量 GDP	占世界比重 Percentage of the World (%)
1	美国	USA	23566	27.6	美国	USA	168000	22.4
2	日本	Japan	9967	11.7	中国	China	92403	12.3
3	德国	Germany	7166	8.4	日本	Japan	49015	6.5
4	法国	France	5001	5.9	德国	Germany	36348	4.9
5	英国	United Kingdom	3251	3.8	法国	France	27349	3.7
6	意大利	Italy	3036	3.6	英国	United Kingdom	25223	3.4
7	加拿大	Canada	2183	2.6	巴西	Brazil	22457	3.0
8	巴西	Brazil	2008	2.4	俄罗斯	Russia	20968	2.8
9	西班牙	Spain	1558	1.8	意大利	Italy	20713	2.8
10	中国	China	1482	1.7	印度	India	18768	2.5

资料来源：世界银行数据库。　Source: World Bank WDI Database.

成功由低收入国家迈进上中等收入国家行列。1952年，我国人均国内生产总值只有119元，到1978年也只有381元，改革开放后人均国内生产总值不断跃上新台阶，2013年突破4万元大关，达到41908元（约合6767美元），扣除价格因素，比1952年增长50.5倍，年均增长6.7%，其中1979-2013年年均增长8.7%。与此同时，人均国民总收入也实现快速增长。根据世界银行数据，我国人均国民总收入由1962年的70美元上升至2013年的6560美元，按照世界银行的划分标准，已经由低收入国家跃升至上中等收入国家。对于我国这样一个经济发展起点低、人口基数大的国家，能够取得这样的进步实在是难能可贵。

Successful transition from a low-income country to an upper middle income country. In 1952, per capita GDP in China was only 119 yuan, while in 1978 it had reached 381yuan. After the adoption of reform and the open door policy, GDP per capita began growing rapidly, and reached a new level in 2013 when it hit 40,000 yuan, reaching 41,908 yuan (about US$ 6,767). After deducting inflation factors, current GDP per capita is 50.5 times higher than the GDP per capita in 1952. The average annual GDP growth rate increased by 6.7%, reaching 8.7% during the period between 1979 and 2013. At the same time, GNI per capita also experienced rapid growth. According to the World Bank, GNI per capita increased from US$70 to US$6560 from 1962 to 2013, allowing China to make the leap from a low-income country to an upper middle income country as defined by the World Bank. Such progress is very valuable for China, a state with such a low economic starting point and such a huge population.

中等收入国家

按照世界银行的标准，通常按人均国民总收入对世界各国经济发展水平分成四组，即低收入国家、中等偏下收入国家、中等偏上收入国家和高收入国家。其中，中等偏下收入国家和中等偏上收入国家合称为中等收入国家。由于经济发展水平不断提高，加上价格变化，划分标准也要随之不断进行调整。2014年7月世界银行新制定的划分标准为：人均国民收入小于1045美元，为低收入组；人均国民收入介于1046和4125美元之间，为下中等收入组；人均国民收入介于4126和12745美元之间，为上中等收入组；人均国民收入大于12746美元，为高收入组。需要指出的是，尽管从经济总规模上看，我国已经是世界第二，但如果按人均水平划分，我国仍然是中等收入国家，与美国、德国、日本等高收入国家仍有比较大的差距。

Middle-Income Countries

According to the standards of World Bank, the economic development level of each country is divided into four groups in accordance with the gross national income per capita of countries,namely low-income, lower-middle income, upper-middle income and high-income countries, among which the lower- and upper-middle income countries are generally referred to as the middle-income countries. Due to the constantly increasing economy as well as the price change, the classification standards also need to be adjusted accordingly. In July, 2014, the World Bank set a new standard as follows: countries with national income per capita less than $1,045 falls into the low-income group, countries with national income per capita between $1,046 and $4,125, the lower-middle-income group, countries with national income per capita between $4,126 and $12,745, the upper-middle-income group, and countries with national income per capita of exceeding $12,746, the high-income group. It should be noted that, viewed from the total economy scale, China already ranks the second in the world, but it still remains a middle-income country ranked by per capita income, lagging much behind the high- income countries like the United States, Germany and Japan.

图 3　1952-2013 年人均国内生产总值
GDP Per Capita, 1952-2013

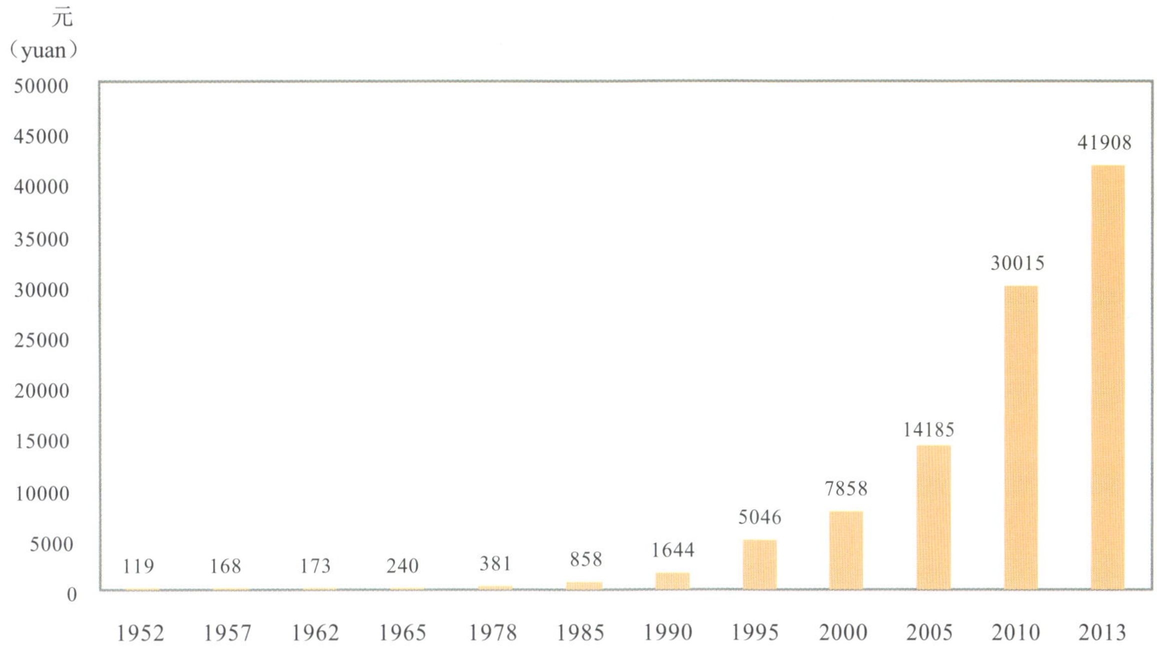

图 4　2013 年世界主要国家人均国民总收入
GNI Per Capita of Main Countries in the World, 2013

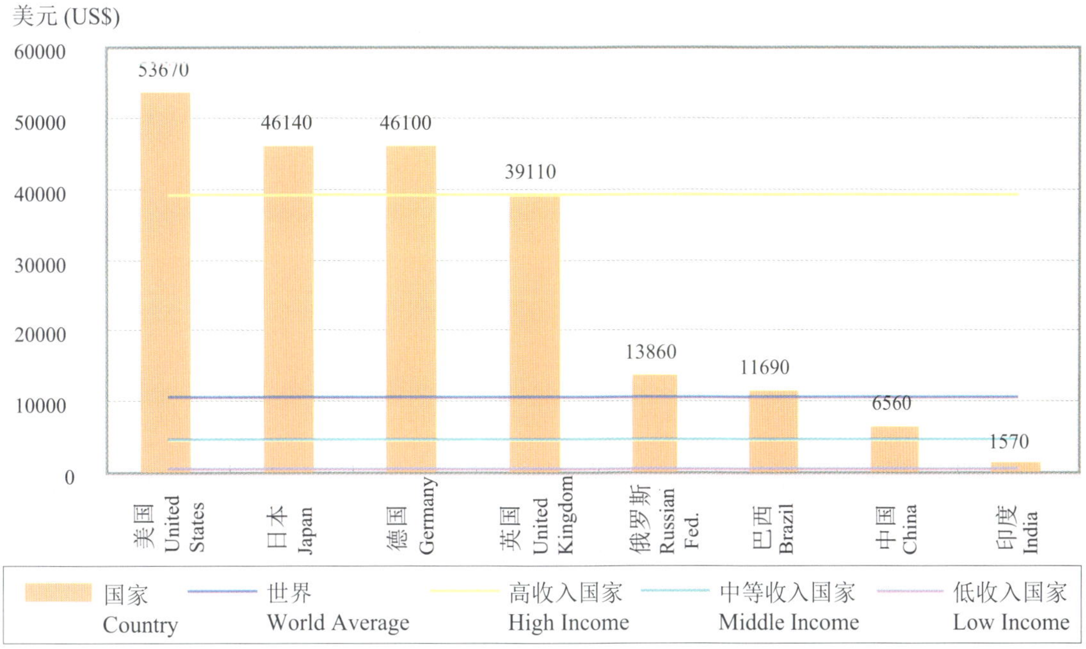

资料来源：世界银行数据库。　Source: World Bank WDI Database.

外汇储备由短缺到世界第一。1952年末，我国外汇储备只有1.39亿美元，到1978年末只增加到1.67亿美元，人均只有0.17美元，折合成人民币不足1块钱。改革开放以来，我国对外经济逐渐发展壮大，经常项目贸易盈余不断积累，外汇储备的短缺迅速成为历史。1990年外汇储备超过百亿美元，年末达到111亿美元，1996年超过千亿美元，年末达到1050亿美元，2001年加入WTO后外汇储备迅速增加，2006年突破1万亿美元，年末达到10663亿美元，超过日本位居世界第一位，2009年、2011年又相继突破2万亿美元和3万亿美元大关，2013年末达到38213亿美元，连续八年稳居世界第一位。

Foreign exchange reserves: from deficit to first place in the world. In 1952, China's foreign exchange reserves amounted to only US$ 139 million. In 1978, they had increased to US$ 167 million , which was only 0.17 USD per capita, or less than RMB 1 yuan. Since the adoption of reform and the open door policy, China's foreign-linked economy gradually began to grow and develop, and the export surplus generated by current operations has continued to accumulate, making a lack of foreign exchange reserves a thing of the past. In 1990, foreign exchange reserves exceeded US$10 billion, reaching US$11.1 billion, and in 1996, reserves reached US$105 billion. Foreign exchange reserves have increased dramatically since 2001 when China joined the WTO, and in 2006 the country met the USD $1 trillion mark, reaching $ 1.0663 trillion, overtaking Japan to stand in first place in the world. In 2009 and 2011, respectively, reserves broke through the 2 and 3 trillion USD marks, and the 2013 figure was 3.8213 trillion USD. China has ranked first in the world in amount of foreign exchange reserves for 8 consecutive years.

图5　1952-2013年年末外汇储备余额
Foreign Exchange Reserves at the Year-end, 1952-2013

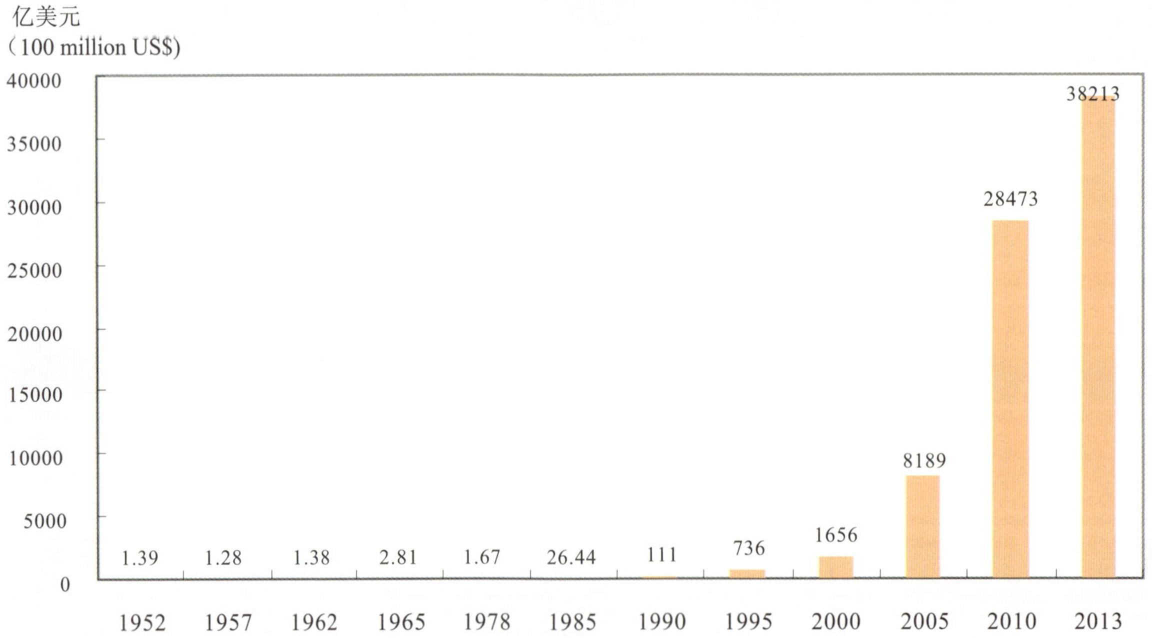

外汇储备

外汇储备是指一国政府所持有的国际储备资产中的外汇部分，即一国政府保有的以外币表示的债权，是一个国家货币当局持有并可以随时兑换外国货币的资产。一定的外汇储备是一国进行经济调节、实现内外平衡的重要手段。当国际收支出现逆差时，动用外汇储备可以促进国际收支的平衡；当国内宏观经济不平衡，出现总需求大于总供给时，可以动用外汇组织进口，从而调节总供给与总需求的关系，促进宏观经济的平衡。当汇率出现波动时，可以利用外汇储备干预汇率，使之趋于稳定。因此，外汇储备是实现经济均衡稳定的一个必不可少的手段，特别是在经济全球化不断发展，一国经济更易于受到其他国家经济影响的情况下，更是如此。外汇储备并不是越多越好，从我国情况看，外汇储备必须有相应的基础货币对应，实际上加大了货币政策的操作难度。

Foreign Exchange Reserve

Foreign exchange reserve refers to the foreign part of international reserve assets held by a government, namely, the creditor' right denominated in foreign currencies and held by a government, or the asset held by the national monetary authority and can be exchanged at any time. A certain amount of foreign exchange reserve is one of the important means for economic adjustment, and the internal and external balance. When the deficit of payments balance occurs, the use of foreign exchange reserve can enhance the balance of international payments; When domestic macro-economy becomes imbalanced, total demand is bigger than the total supply, foreign exchange reserve can be used for import, thus to regulate the relationship between aggregate supply and demand, and promote the macroeconomic equilibrium. Foreign exchange reserve can be used to intervene in the exchange rate and stabilize the economy in case of the exchange rate fluctuation. Therefore, the foreign exchange reserve is an indispensable means for economic equilibrium and stability, especially under the circumstance that a country's economy is vulnerable to the influences from other countries especially as the economy is increasingly globalized. Many foreign exchange reserves do not equal to a sound economy. In view of the situation in China, foreign exchange reserves must have corresponding monetary base, which actually makes the monetary policy operation more difficult.

主要工农业产品产量位居世界前列。新中国成立时，我国是个贫穷落后的农业国，生产力水平极低，特别是工业生产比较落后，与发达国家差距很大。65 年来，伴随着工业化进程持续推进和农业基础不断夯实，主要工农业产品产量先后跃居世界前列。2013 年，我国粗钢、煤、发电量、水泥、棉布产量均位列世界第一位，原油产量位居世界第四位；谷物、籽棉、花生产量稳居世界第一位，油菜籽、甘蔗、大豆产量分列第二、四、四位。

China's major industrial and agricultural products stand in first place in world rankings. At the time of its foundation, China was a poor and backward country with a very low level of productivity, especially in the field of industrial production, and the economic gap between China and developed countries was very large. During the 65 years since the founding of the People's Republic of China, the output of major industrial and agricultural industries began to occupy top spots in world rankings as the process of industrialization and the constant strengthening of the country's agricultural base continued to advance. In 2013, China ranked first in the world in the production of crude steel, coal, electricity, cement, fertilizer and cotton. China was also the fourth-largest oil producer, the first-largest producer of peanuts, tea and fruit, the second-largest producer of rapeseed, fourth-largest sugarcane producer, and fourth-largest soybean producer.

表 2 我国主要经济指标和主要工农业产品产量居世界位次
Ranking of China in the World in Terms of Main Economic Indicators and Industrial and Agricultural Products

指 标 Item	1978 年	1990 年	2000 年	2005 年	2010 年	2013 年
国内生产总值 Gross Domestic Product	10	11	6	5	2	2
人均国民总收入① Per Capita GNI①	175(188)	178(200)	141(207)	128(208)	120(215)	109(214)
外汇储备 Foreign Exchange Reserves	38	7	2	2	1	1
主要工业产品产量 Output of Major Industrial Products						
粗 钢 Crude Steel	5	4	2	1	1	1
煤 Coal	3	1	1	1	1	1
原 油 Crude Oil	8	5	5	5	4	4
发电量 Amount of Electric Power Generation//Electricity	7	4	2	2	1	1
水 泥 Cement	4	1	1	1	1	1
化 肥 Fertilizer	3	3	1	1	1	
棉 布 Woven Cotton Fabrics	1	1	2	2	1	1
主要农业产品产量 Volume of Production of Major Agricultural Products						
谷 物 Cereals	2	1	1	1	1	1
肉 类② Meat②	3	1	1	1	1	
籽 棉 Seed Cotton	3	1	1	1	1	1
大 豆 Soybean	3	3	4	4	4	4
花 生 Peanuts	2	2	1	1	1	1
油菜籽 Rapeseeds	2	1	1	1	1	2
水 果③ Fruits③	9	4	1	1	1	

注：①括号中为参加排序的国家和地区数。② 1990 年以前为猪、牛、羊肉产量的位次。③不包括瓜类。
资料来源：联合国粮农组织数据库、联合国《统计月报》数据库及世界银行数据库。

① The number in parentheses indicates the number of countries or territories which the ranking is based on. ② Before 1990, it refered to the rank of Pork, Beef and Mutton. ③ Exludes melons.

Sources: FAO database, UN Monthly Statistics database and World Bank database.

图 6　主要工业产品产量世界前 10 位
Output of Major Industrial Products of Top Ten Countries

资料来源：联合国统计月报数据库、联合国粮农组织数据库、国际汽车制造商协会。
Source: UN Monthly Bulletin of Statistics Database; UN FAO Database; The International Organization of Motor Vehicle Manufacturers.

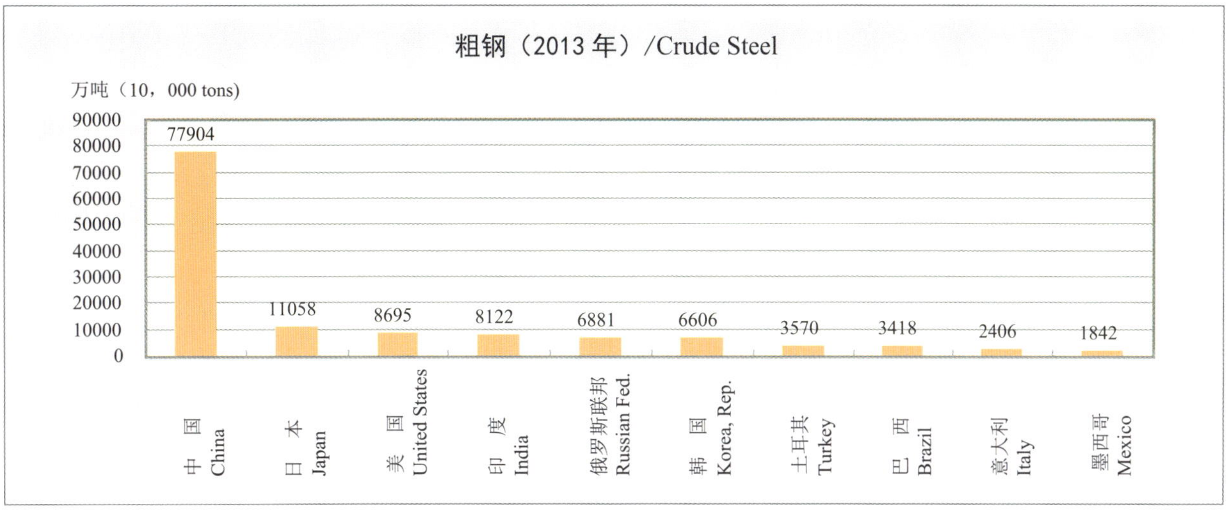

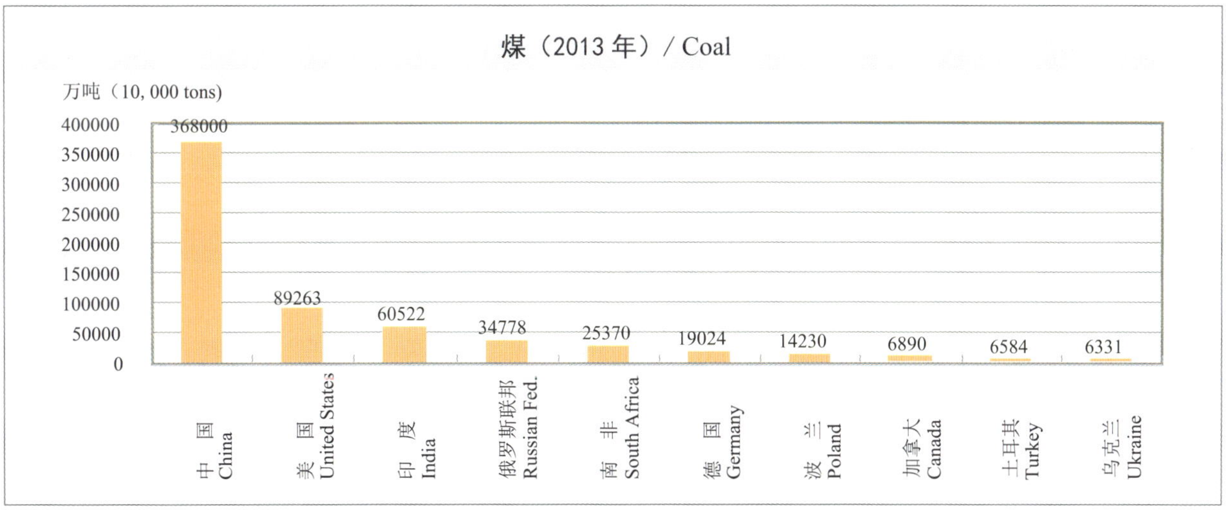

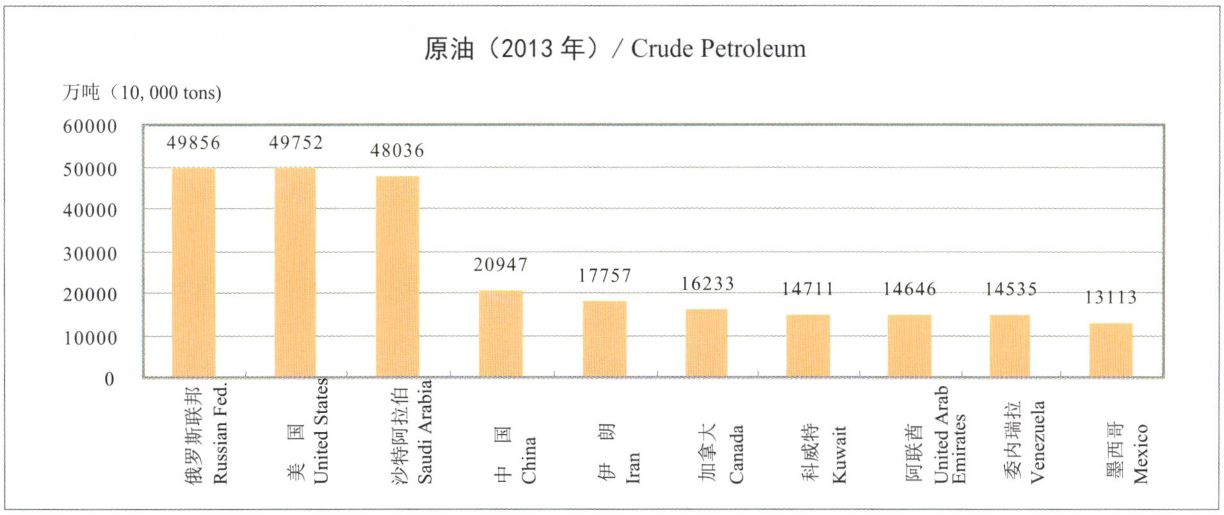

发电量（2013 年）/Electricity

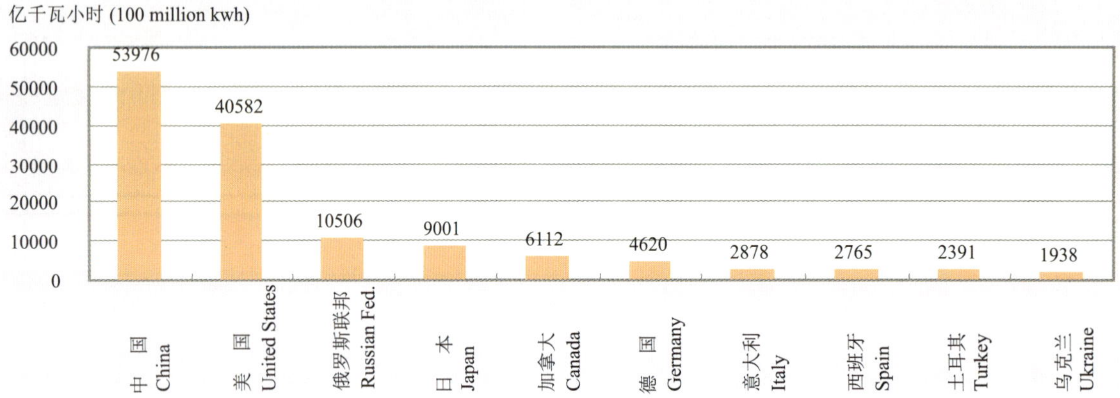

汽车（2013 年）/Motor Vehicles

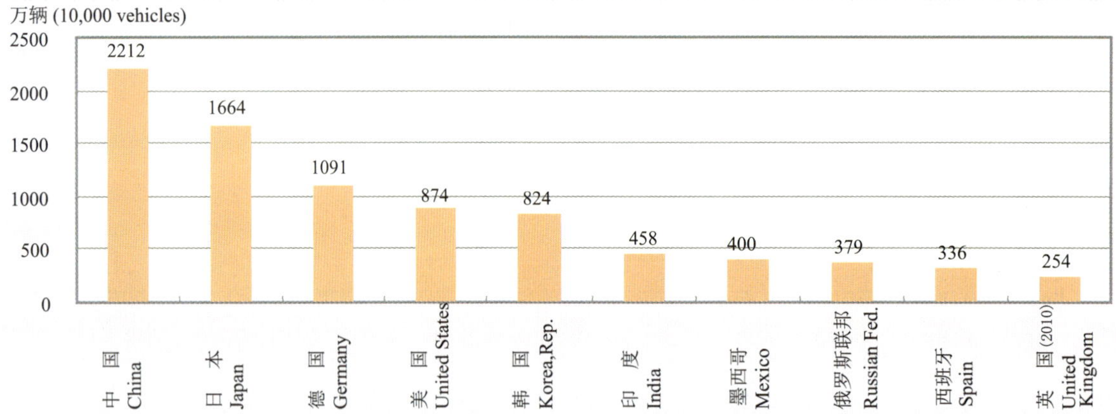

化肥（2011 年）/Fertilizer

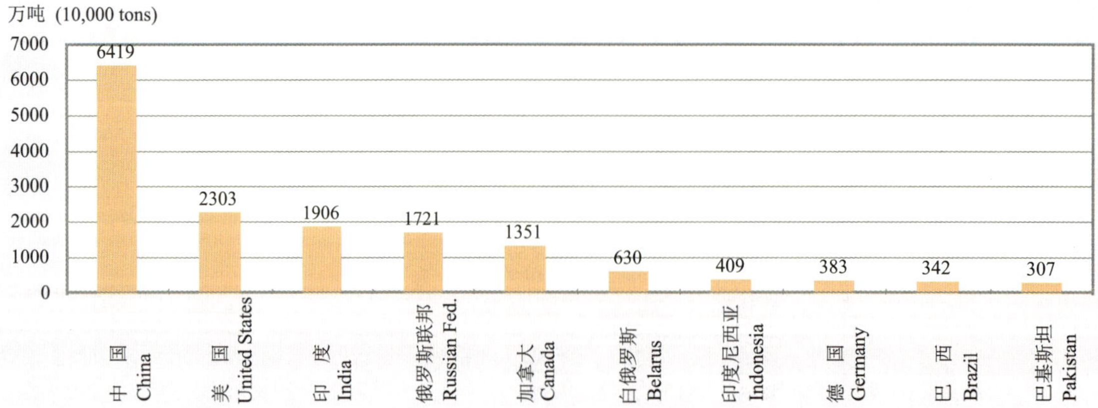

图 7　主要农产品产量世界前 10 位
Production of Major Farm Crops of Top Ten Countries

资料来源：联合国 FAO 数据库。
Source: FAO Database.

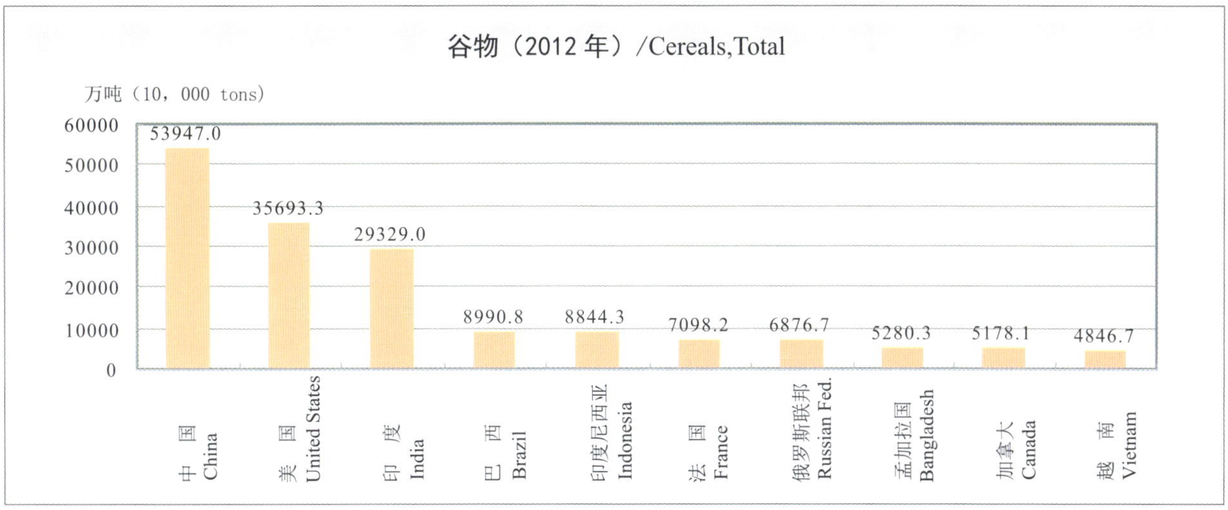

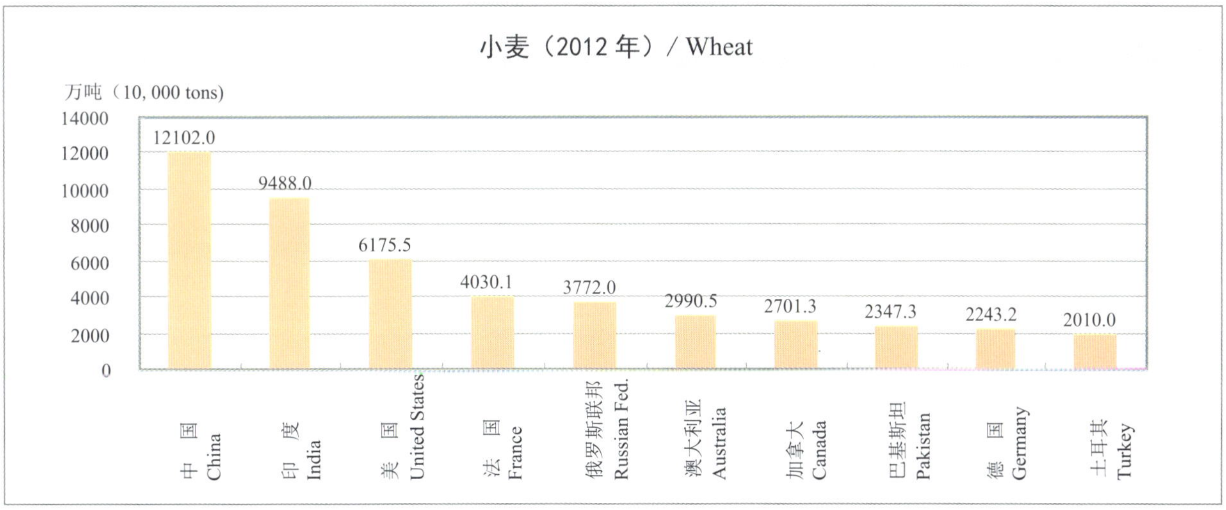

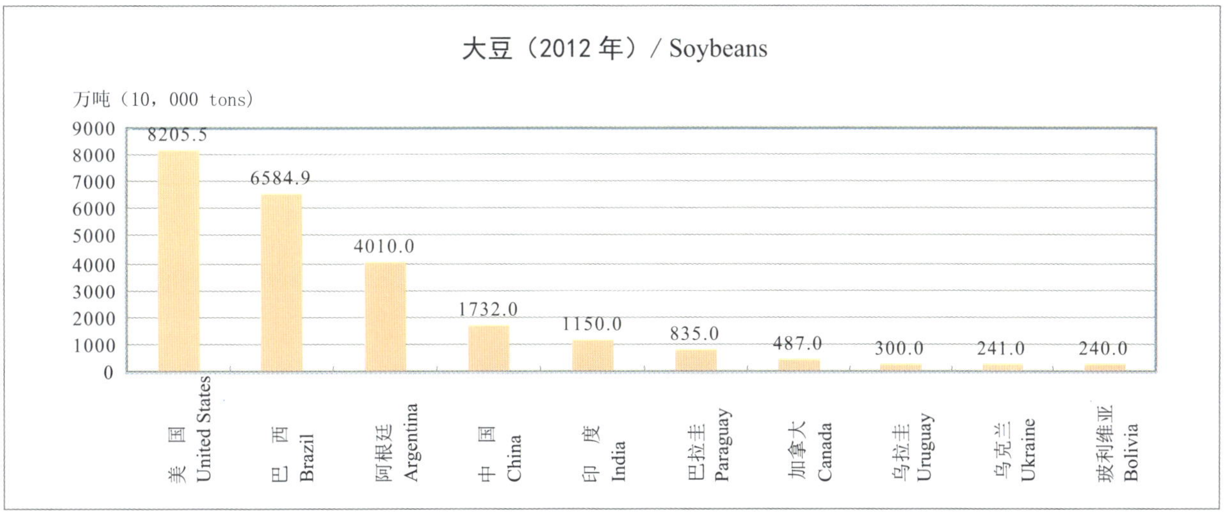

花生（2012 年）/Groundnuts, with Shell

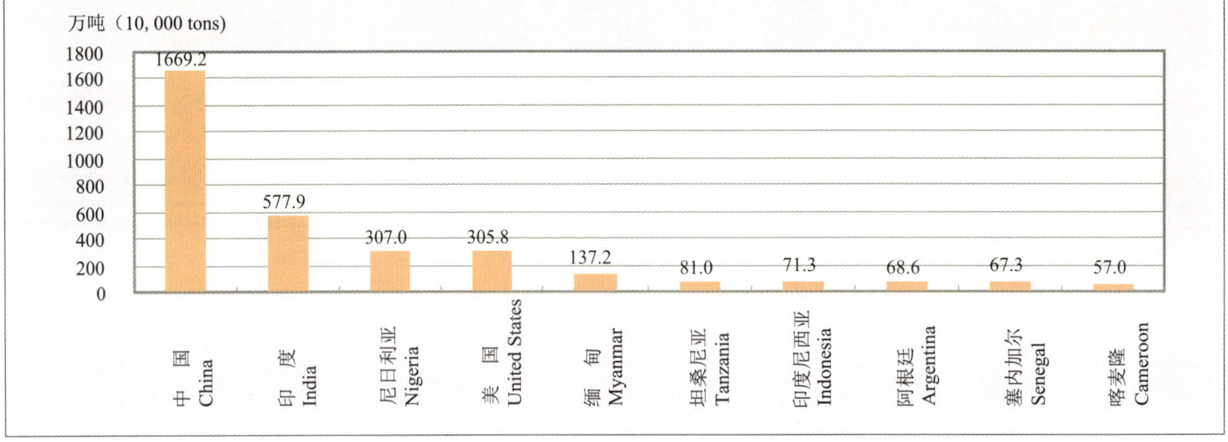

油菜籽（2012 年）/ Rapeseed

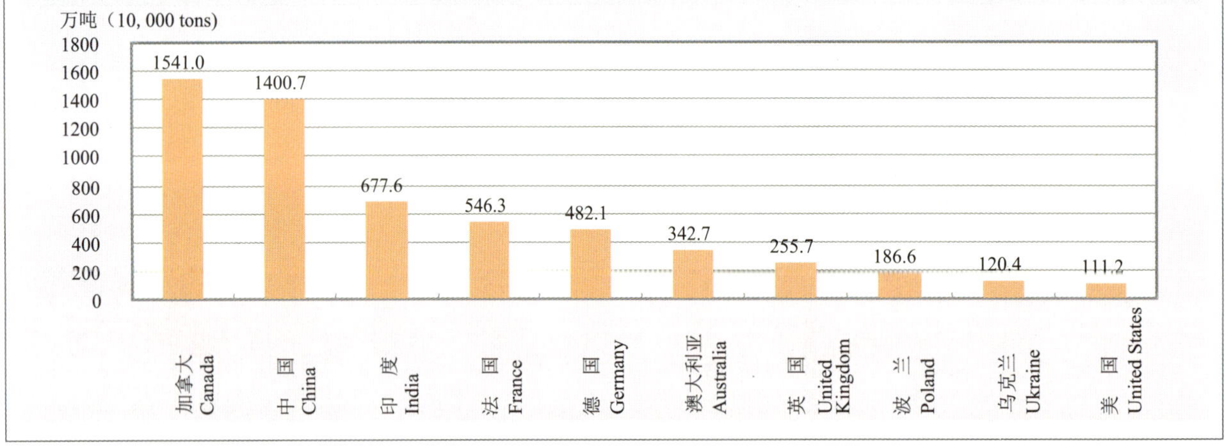

籽棉（2012 年） /Seed Cotton

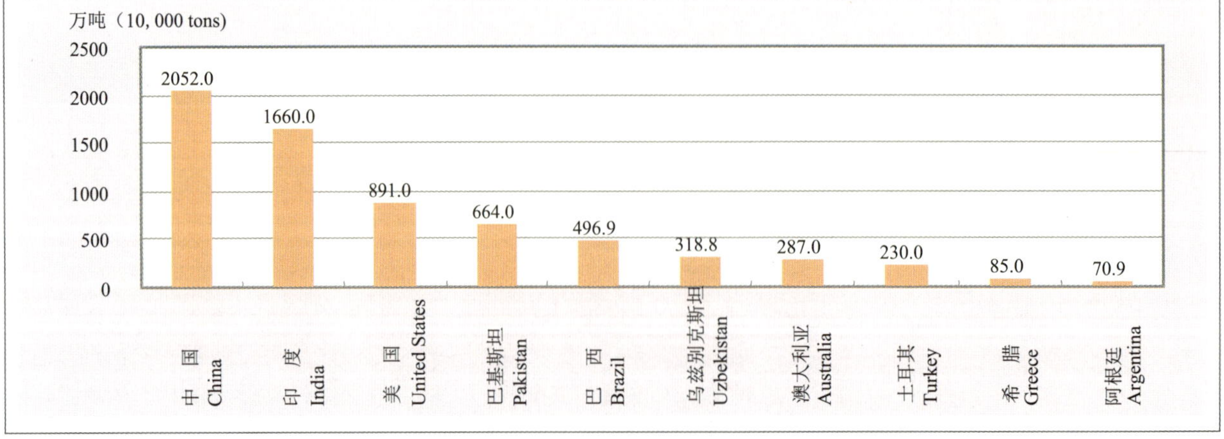

甘蔗（2012 年）/Sugar Cane

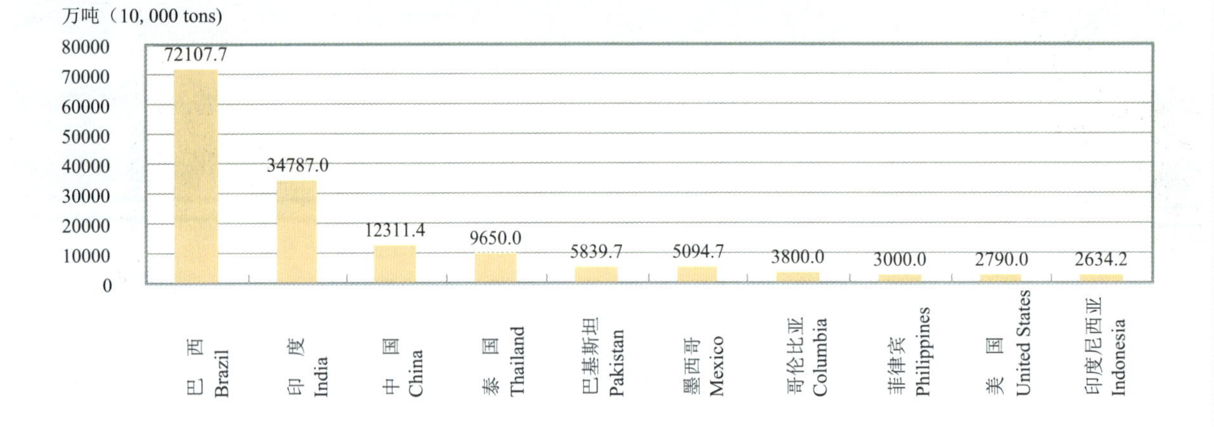

茶叶（2012 年）/ Tea

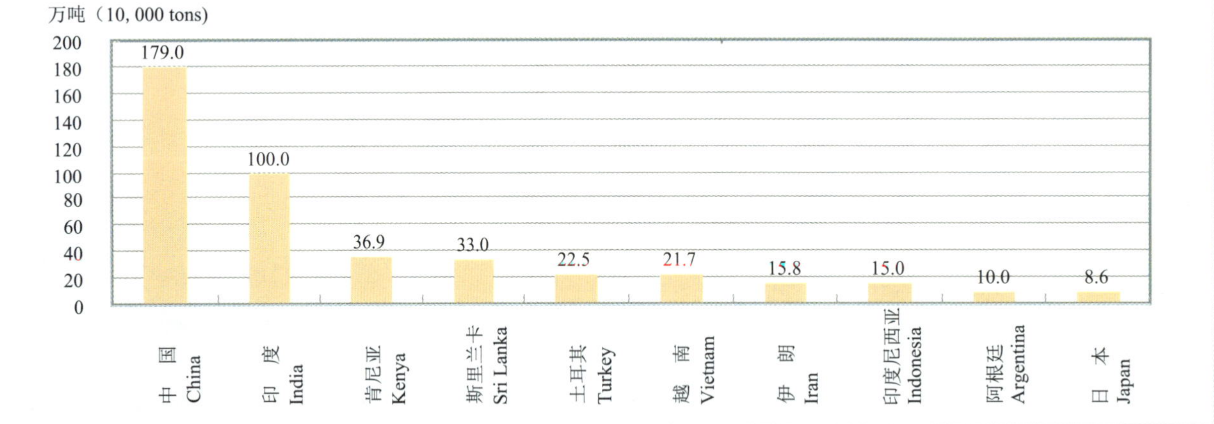

水果（不包括瓜类）（2012 年）/Fruit excl. Melons

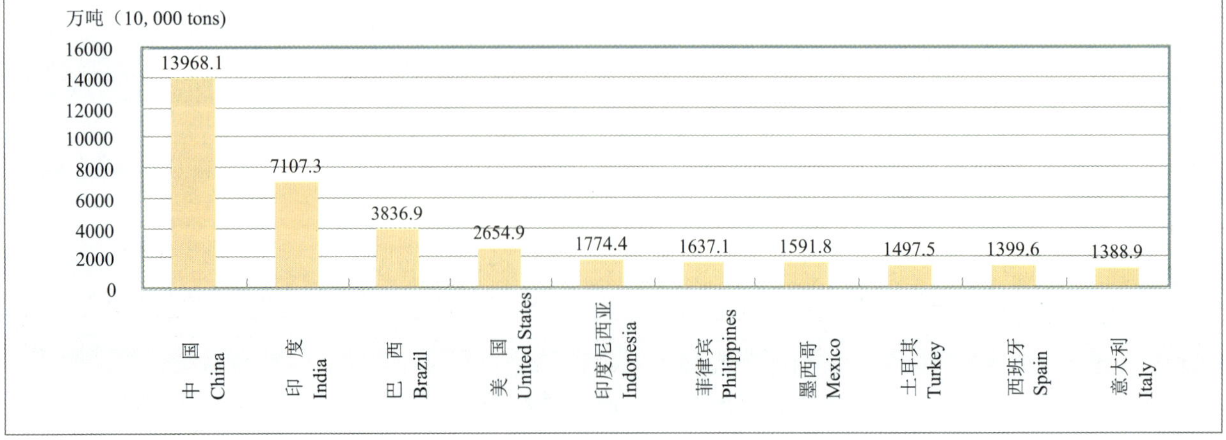

2 从单一失衡到百业兴旺 经济结构的协调性逐步增强

From imbalance to numerous thriving businesses, coordination within the economic structure has gradually advanced.

新中国成立以来的65年，是我国对经济结构调整重要性认识不断深化的65年，是经济结构在经济快速成长中逐步调整优化的65年，也是经济发展的全面性、协调性和可持续性日益增强的65年。

The 65 years since the founding of PRC have witnessed 65 years of the continuous deepening of understanding of the importance of economic structural adjustment, 65 years of the revision and optimization of the economic structure in the process of rapid economic growth, and 65 years of the comprehensive coordination and increasing sustainability of economic development.

（一）产业结构逐步升级，以农业为主到以工业为主并正向服务业主导型经济转变。

建国初期，农业在我国国民经济中居于主要地位，工业门类不全、基础薄弱，服务业发展滞后。从建国到1978年，在优先发展工业战略带动下，我国逐步建立

(1) Gradual upgrading of the industrial structure; changes from agricultural-based to industrial-based and service-oriented economy.

In the early years of the PRC, agriculture was the most important sector of the national economy. Industrial categories were incomplete, infrastructure was weak, and the development of China's service industry lagged far behind that of developed nations. From the founding of the PRC through 1978, China gradually established a relatively complete industrial system

优先发展重工业战略

新中国成立初期，工业基础极为薄弱，不仅难以满足经济建设和国防需要，甚至连基本的生活用品也难以完全满足，工业水平亟待提高。为了保障国家政治独立和国防安全，尽快改变我国工业十分落后的面貌，同时受苏联工业化道路成功的带动，我国政府确立了优先发展重工业的战略。

1953年，全国开始执行发展国民经济的第一个五年计划，基本任务是"集中主要力量发展重工业，建立国家工业化和国防现代化的初步基础"。"一五"计划期间，国家集中力量先后对数百个工业项目进行了建设，包括鞍山钢铁公司、长春第一汽车制造厂、沈阳第一机床厂、武汉长江大桥等在内的多个重大项目建成投产，飞机、汽车、发电设备、重型机器、新式机床、精密仪表、电解铝、无缝钢管、合金钢、塑料、无线电等工业从无到有地建设起来。"一五"时期我国的工业建设取得了举世瞩目的巨大成就，工业残缺不全的状况得到明显改观，基本建立起独立的工业体系，为社会主义工业化奠定了初步基础。事实证明，优先发展重工业战略符合当时我国的国情，不仅是正确的，也是十分必要的。

Strategy of Prioritizing Heavy Industry Development

China, in its early and newly-founded stage, had very weak industrial foundation. It could hardly meet the needs of economic construction and national defense, and could barely satisfy the demand for daily necessities. The industrial level was in much need of improvements. In order to safeguard the political independence and defense safety and change our backward industry as soon as possible, as well as guided by the successful way of Soviet Union industrialization, the Chinese government set the priority strategy of developing heavy industry.

In 1953, China started to implement the first Five-Year Plan for the development of national economy, with the basic task of "focusing much strength on heavy industry, laying the foundation for the national industrialization and national defense modernization." During the first Five-Year Plan, China focused on constructing hundreds of industrial projects, including Anshan Iron and Steel Company, Changchun First Automobile Factory, Shenyang First Machine Tool Plant, Wuhan Yangtze River Bridge and other major projects. Such industries as airplane, automobile, power equipment, heavy machinery, junior machine, precision meter, electrolytic aluminums, seamless steel tube, alloy steel, plastics, wireless were all established from the scratch. Chinese industrial construction made great and internationally amazing achievements during the first Five-Year Plan. The fragmentary industrial situation was obviously improved, and an independent industrial system set up by and large, which laid a preliminary basis for the socialist industrialization. It was approved that the priority strategy of developing heavy industry in accordance with the national conditions of that time is correct and necessary.

起比较完整的工业体系。改革开放以来工业化进程不断加快，工业得到长足发展，工业增加值占国内生产总值的比重不断上升。近年来随着我国经济发展阶段的变化，服务业发展明显加快，对经济增长的贡献上升，三次产业协同发展的基本格局初步形成。

产业结构由以农业为主转变为以工业为主。1952 年，三次产业增加值占国内生产总值的比重分别为 51.0%、20.9% 和 28.2%。针对工业发展落后的状况，建国以来确立了优先发展工业的战略，推动了工业的快速发展，工业比重迅速提高。1978 年，三次产业比重调整为 28.2:47.9:23.9，第一、三产业比重分别比 1952 年下降了 22.8 和 4.3 个百分点，第二产业比重提高了 27.0 个百分点。改革

which benefitted from the prioritization of secondary industry. The industrialization process continuously accelerated after the implementation of reform and opening-up policy, industry rapidly developed, and the industrial value-added of gross domestic product continued to rise. In recent years, service industry's development significantly accelerated along with the overall changes in China's economic development, contributing to the rising economic growth and the collaborative development of three economic sectors.

Industrial structure had changed from agricultural-based to industrial-based. In 1952, the value added output of primary, secondary, and tertiary sectors respectively accounted for 51.0 percent, 20.9 percent, and 28.2 percent of GDP. Since the PRC's founding, a strategy of prioritizing industrial development has been established in response to slow economic development, promoting the rapid development of industry and increasing its proportion of overall GDP. By 1978, the three sectors' proportions of GDP changed to 28.2, 47.9, and 23.9, respectively. Primary and tertiary sectors' proportions of GDP declined by 22.8 percent and 4.3 percent respectively compared to the 1952 data, while the proportion of secondary industry's value increased by 27.0 percent. Since the beginning of reform and opening up,

开放以来，我国积极承接国际产业转移，工业化发展不断深入，工业实力和竞争力进一步增强，“中国制造”逐步享誉全球。根据世界银行数据，目前我国制造业增加值占世界的比重超过20%。我国用60多年的时间实现了从落后的农业国到世界制造业大国的历史跨越，几乎走完了发达国家200-300年的工业化历程。

工业结构由门类单一到齐全、由低端制造向中高端制造迈进。建国初期，我国工业部门比较单一，经过65年的建设，目前已拥有41个工业大类、201个中类、581个小类，包含联合国工业行业分类中所有的类别，一个行业比较齐全的工业体系已经形成。与此同时，随着工业化水平的不断提高，我国工业发展由侧重于价值链低端的劳动密集型产业逐渐向中高端迈

China undertook international industrial transfer, continuously deepening the development of industrialization and enhancing industrial strength and competitiveness, gradually making “Made in China” known worldwide. According to World Bank data, China’s manufacturing industry’s value added output accounted for more than 20 percent of total global production at present. In just over 60 years, China has achieved an historic change from an agricultural country that lagged behind many others to a global manufacturing country, completing an industrialization process that developed countries completed in 200 to 300 years.

Industrial structure has developed from a simple to complete, from low-end manufacturing to high-end manufacturing. In the early days of the PRC, the country’s industrial sector was relatively simple. But after 65 years of construction, China now has 41 industrial sections, 201 divisions and 581 groups, including all the categories in the United Nations Industrial Classification, forming a relatively complete industrial system. With the continuous increase in its level of industrialization, China shifted its focus away from low-end labor-intensive industry, gradually progressing to high-end industry. A series of major breakthroughs have been made in fields such as space technology, high performance computer technology, CNC

进，在航天技术、高性能计算机技术、数控机床制造技术、通信技术等领域实现了一系列重大突破，电子信息、航空航天、生物医药、新能源、新材料等高技术产业从无到有，蓬勃发展，成为带动工业结构转型升级的重要因素。2004-2013 年，我国高技术产业增加值年均增长 15.8%，装备制造业增加值年均增长 16.3%。

近年来产业发展呈现由工业主导型向服务业主导型转变的新趋势。伴随着工业化、城镇化的深入推进，研发、设计、营销、

manufacturing technology, and communication technology. Electronic information, aerospace, bio-medicine, new energy, new materials, and other high-tech industries are flourishing, becoming important factors driving the transformation and upgrading of China's industrial structure. From 2004 to 2013, China's high-tech industry's value-added annual average growth rate was 15.8 percent, and in the equipment manufacturing field it was 16.3 percent.

Industrial development present new trends from the industry-led to service-oriented in recent years. Industrialization and urbanization have led to a rapid growth in demand for research and development, design, marketing, logistics, and other production services. In addition, the growth of residents' consumer structure accelerated, significantly increasing demand

物流等生产性服务需求增长较快，加之居民消费结构升级加快，对养老、医疗、教育、家政等生活性服务需求明显增加，服务业发展势头良好。2013年，第三产业增加值达到262204亿元，比1978年实际增长34.4倍，年均增长10.7%，快于国内生产总值增速0.9个百分点。特别是2013年我国三次产业结构出现了历史性的积极变化，第三产业现价增加值占国内生产总值的比重上升到46.1%，首次超过第二产业，比第二产业比重高2.2个百分点。2014年上半年，第三产业比重进一步提高到46.6%，比第二产业高0.6个百分点。这一变化标志着我国经济发展将进入由工业主导型经济向服务业主导型经济转变的新阶段。

for consumer services, including pensions, healthcare, education, and housekeeping, adding momentum to the development of the service industry. In 2013, the value-added output of China's tertiary industry reached 26.2204 trillion yuan, 34.4 times higher than its output in 1978; average annual growth in tertiary industry reached 10.7 percent, 0.9 percentage points higher than the GDP growth rate. Especially in 2013, China's three industries structure showed positive historic changes: tertiary industry's value-added output at current price comprised 46.1 percent of GDP, surpassing that of secondary industry, by 2.2 percent, for the first time. In the first half of 2014, tertiary industry's proportion of GDP further increased to 46.6 percent, making it 0.6 percent higher than that of secondary industry. These changes indicate that China's economic development entered a new phase of transition, from an industrial-led economy to a service-based economy.

图8 1994-2011年中国制造业增加值占世界制造业比重

The Share of Value-added of China's Manufacturing Industry of Total Global Production, 1994-2011

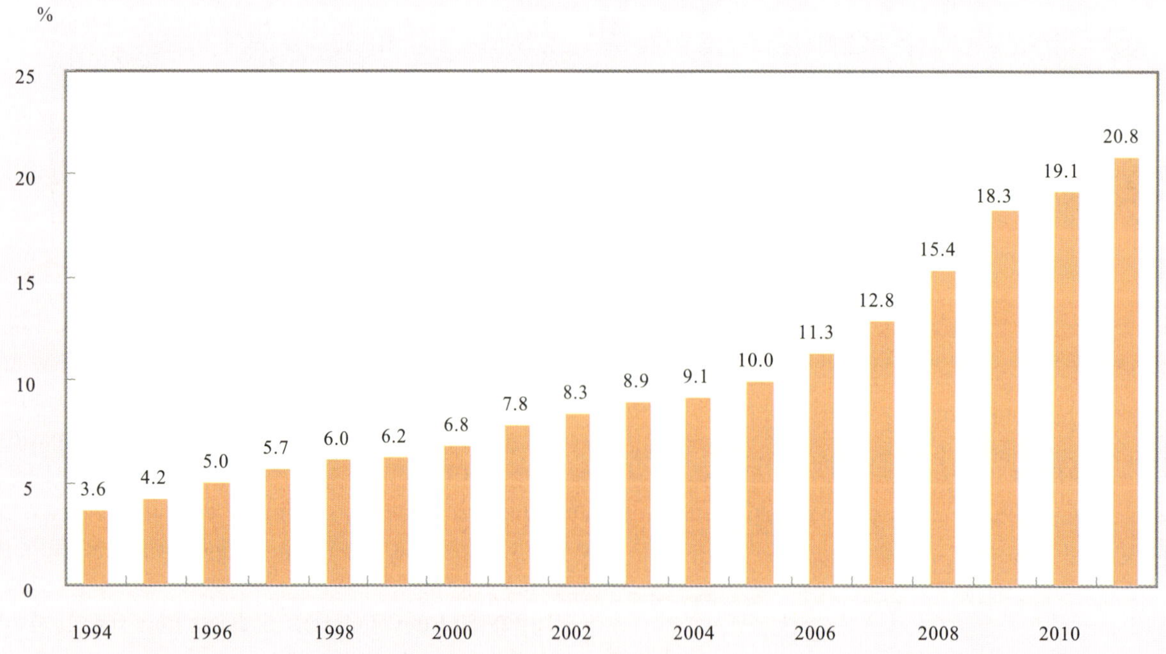

资料来源：世界银行数据库。 Source: World Bank WDI Database.

服务业主导型经济的新特征

2013年，我国三次产业结构出现了历史性的积极变化，第三产业现价增加值占国内生产总值比重上升到46.1%，首次超过第二产业。这一变化标志我国经济发展进入了由工业主导型向服务业主导型转变的新阶段。与工业主导型经济相比，服务业主导型经济具有如下新特征：一是经济增长可能放缓。与工业相比，服务业的产业链条相对较短，投资的强度相对较低，劳动生产率增长总体上也慢于工业，因此服务业发展在短期内难以完全弥补工业增速下行的影响，带来经济增速的放缓。二是经济增长稳定性相对较高。服务业主要是满足国内消费需求，受国际市场波动和汇率等变化的影响相对较小，同时消费增长本身的稳定性较高，因而服务业主导下的经济增长将更趋稳定。三是经济增长的就业弹性趋于提升。服务业多为劳动密集型行业，对就业的吸纳能力较强，经济增长的就业弹性趋于提升。四是有利于促进居民收入增长。服务业由于劳动密集程度较高，服务业增加值中分配给劳动力的份额通常也较高，在服务业主导型经济下，劳动者报酬在社会财富中的分配比例将趋于提高，有利于改善收入分配结构。五是有利于改善投资和消费的关系。服务业主要是满足消费需求，有利于提高消费倾向和释放消费潜力，带来消费率的提升。

New Characteristics of Service Industry-Oriented Economy

In 2013, the historic and positive changes took place in the third industry structure in China, the added value of present price of the third industry rose to 46.1% of the total GDP, surpassing the second industry for the first time. This change marks the new stage of entering into service industry-oriented economy from industry-oriented economy. Compared with the industry-oriented economy, Service-oriented economy has the following new features: the first is the possible slow economic growth. Compared with the industry-oriented economy, service industry-oriented economy has a relatively short industry chain, low investment intensity, and the slower growth of labor productivity in general. Therefore, the development of service industry is difficult to fully compensate for the effects of industrial growth rate downward in the short term, which will bring the economic slowdown. The second is the rather stable economic growth. Service industry mainly meets domestic consumption demand, less influenced by global market volatility and exchange rate. At the same time, the stability of consumption growth is high itself, thus the economic growth dominated by the service industry will be more stable. The third is the increased employment elasticity of economic growth. Service industry is labor-intensive industries, with strong employability, thus leading to the rise of employment elasticity of economic growth. The forth is the contribution of service industry-oriented economy to promoting the income growth. Because of high labor intensity, the proportion allocated to labor in the service added value is usually high in the service industry, leading economy and laborers remuneration in the allocation of social wealth will tend to increase, thus refining the income distribution structure. The fifth is the improved relationship between investment and consumption by service industry-oriented economy. Service industry is mainly to meet the consumer demand, increasing the propensity to consume and releasing of the consumption potential, thus it can bring the growth of consumption rate.

图 9　1952–2013 年三次产业结构
Structure of the Value-added of Three Industries, 1952-2013

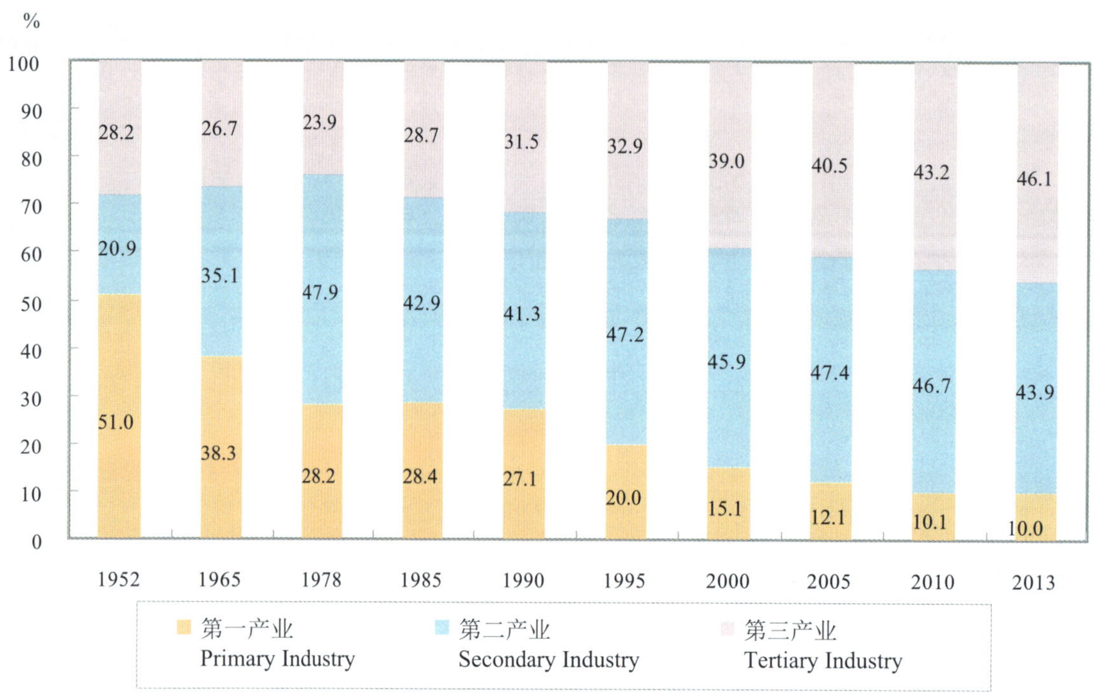

（二）所有制结构深刻变化，实现由单一公有制到多种所有制经济共同发展的转变。

改革开放前，我国所有制结构主要是单一的公有制经济，全民所有制经济和集体所有制经济占绝对优势。改革开放后，随着我国对社会主义初级阶段理论及所有制理论认识的不断深化，非公有制经济得到迅速发展壮大，在整体经济中的地位不断上升。到目前，多种所有制经济共同发展、相得益彰的格局逐步形成。

(2) Profound changes in the ownership system structure have achieved the transformation from a single public ownership economy to a diversified-ownership economy.

Before reform and opening up, China's economic ownership structure was mainly unitary public ownership and the dominant ownership was the state ownership, and collective ownership. After China's reform and opening up, while the understanding of the theory of the primary stage of socialism and the ownership theory of ownership has deepened, the non-public economy sector has been rapidly expanding and raising its status in the national economy. Various forms of ownership have developed, gradually forming pattern which complement each other.

公有制主体地位巩固，继续保持控制力和影响力。1978 年，全民所有制企业数量占工业企业的 24.0%，实现产值占工业总产值的 77.6%；集体所有制企业数量占工业企业的 76.0%，实现产值占工业总产值的 22.4%。改革开放以后，伴随着非公经济的发展壮大，国有企业数量占比有所下降，但从总体规模和经营效益来看，依然保持对经济的控制力和影响力。2013 年，国有及国有控股和集体控股企业的资产占全部规模以上工业的 41.9%，实现主营业务收入占 27.5%，实现利润占 26.1%。在关系国家命脉的重要行业和关键领域，公有制经济一直占据主导地位。2013 年，在石油和天然气开采业、电力热力生产和供应业、石油加工炼焦及核燃料加工业、煤炭开采和洗选业、汽车制造业、铁路船舶航空航天和其他运输设备制造业现价工业总产值中，国有及国有控股企业产值所占比重分别达到 87.8%、93.0%、67.8%、53.0%、41.1% 和 39.0%。

Public ownership has consolidated its dominant position, continuing to maintain control and influence. In 1978, state-owned enterprises accounted for 24.0 percent of industrial enterprises, and their output accounted for 77.6 percent of industrial output by value; the number of collective enterprises accounted for 76.0 percent of industrial enterprises, and their output value accounted for 22.4 percent of total industrial output. After the implementation of reform and opening up policies, the number of state-owned enterprises started to decline with the development and growth of the non-public economy, but from the perspective of overall size and operating efficiency, state-owned enterprises maintained control and influence over the economy. In 2013, the combined assets of state-owned enterprises, state-held enterprises, and collective-held industrial enterprises accounted for 41.9 percent of China's industrial enterprises above designated size, achieving main business revenues of 27.5 percent and profits of 26.1 percent. The public economy has taken the dominant position in important industries and key areas of national economic dependence. In 2013, the gross industrial output value of state-owned enterprises and state-held enterprises in the extraction of petroleum and natural gas, production and supply of electric power and heat power, processing of petroleum, coking and processing of nuclear fuel, mining and washing of coal, manufacture of automobiles, manufacture of railway, ship, aerospace and other transport equipments reached 87.8 percent, 93.0 percent, 67.8 percent, 53.0 percent, 41.4 percent and 39.0 percent at current prices respectively.

非公有制经济政策变迁

建国以来特别是改革开放以来，党在开创和发展中国特色社会主义过程中，不断深化对非公有制经济地位和作用的认识，不断创新发展非公有制经济理论政策。

1987 年，党的十三大提出私营经济是公有制经济必要和有益的补充，要以公有制为主体、大力发展有计划的商品经济，非公有制经济开始得到恢复和发展。1992 年，党的十四大明确提出建立社会主义市场经济体制，实行多种经济成分长期共同发展，非公有制经济开始蓬勃发展。1997 年，党的十五大提出"以公有制为主体，多种所有制经济共同发展，是社会主义初级阶段的一项基本经济制度"，从基本制度上确立了非公有制经济在社会主义市场经济中的地位。2002 年，党的十六大强调毫不动摇地巩固和发展公有制经济，毫不动摇地鼓励、支持和引导非公有制经济发展。2005 年，国务院《关于鼓励支持和引导个体私营等非公有制经济发展的若干意见》正式下发，对于推动非公有制经济跨入历史发展的新阶段、实现更快更好的发展，具有重要的现实意义和深远的历史影响。2007 年，党的十七大在"两个毫不动摇"的基础上提出，坚持平等保护物权，形成各种所有制经济平等竞争、相互促进新格局。2012 年，党的十八大进一步提出保证各种所有制经济依法平等使用生产要素、公平参与市场竞争、同等受到法律保护。2013 年，党的十八届三中全会《决定》明确提出公有制经济和非公有制经济都是社会主义市场经济的重要组成部分，都是我国经济社会发展的重要基础。这是党的文件第一次将公有制经济与非公有制经济这样并列提出，是我们党对中国特色社会主义规律认识不断深化的结果。

经过多年的探索和实践，我国以公有制为主体、多种所有制经济共同发展的所有制结构已经建立并不断得到完善，特别是个体、私营等非公有制经济在政策扶持和引导下得到长足发展，在繁荣城乡经济、增强财政收入、扩大社会就业、改善人民生活、优化经济结构等方面发挥了重要作用。

the Policy Change of Non-public Economy

Since the founding of new China, especially since the reform and opening up, the CPC Party in the process of launching and developing socialism with Chinese characteristics has deepened the understanding of the non-public economic status and role, continuing to innovate and develop the theory of the non-public economic policy.

In 1987, the 13th National Congress of the Party put forward that the private economy is a necessary and useful complement to the public ownership economy, we should focus on public ownership, develop a planned commodity economy, and then the non-public sectors of the economy began to recover and develop. In 1992, the 14th Party Congress explicitly proposed that we should establish the socialist market economy system, various economic elements should be commonly developed for long term, as a result non-public economy began to flourish. In 1997, the 15th Party Congress put forward "taking the public ownership as the main body and developing the multi ownership economy is a basic economic system in the primary stage of socialism", establishing the position of non-public ownership economy in the socialist market economy from the basic system. In 2002, the 16th Party Congress stressed that we should unswervingly consolidate and develop the public sector of the economy, and unswervingly encourage, support and guide non-public economic development. In 2005, the State Council issued "opinions about encouraging, supporting and guiding the individual private and other non-public sectors of the economy development" formally, it is of important practical significance and far-reaching historical influence to promote the non-public owned economy entering a new stage and achieving faster and better development. In 2007, the 17th Party Congress, on the basis of two "unwavering", put forward that we should ensure equal protection of property rights to form new pattern that various ownership economy are equally competed and mutually promoted. In 2012, the 18th Party Congress further ensured that various ownership economy equally use the production factors in accordance with the law, fairly engage in the market competition, equally protected by law. In 2013, Third Plenary Session of the 18th Party Congress issued "decision", which clearly put forward that the public sector of the economy and the non-public sector of the economy both are an important component of the socialist market economy, serving as an important foundation for China's economic and social development. This is first time the Party's documents put forward public ownership economy and the non-public ownership economy at the same time, which represents our Party's deepening understanding of the laws of socialist Chinese characteristics

After years of exploration and practice, the structure of ownership with the public ownership as the main body, common development of multi ownership economy has been established and improved, especially the individual, private and other non-public economic development has made great achievements under support and guidance of the policy, which plays an important role in the prosperity of urban and rural economic, strengthening the financial income, increasing employment, improving people's lives, optimizing the economic structure.

非公有制经济快速发展，在促进增长、扩大就业和激发市场活力等方面发挥越来越重要的作用。在各项政策的扶持和引导下，非公有制经济从无到有，飞速发展，已经成为社会主义市场经济的重要组成部分。从企业数量看，2013年，规模以上非公企业数量达34.26万个，占全部规模以上工业企业数的92.6%，其中私人控股企业占76.0%，外商及港澳台商投资控股企业占12.6%。从产值看，2013年，规模以上非公企业实现产值占规模以上工业总产值的73.8%，其中私人控股企业占51.3%，外商及港澳台商投资控股企业占17.8%。从就业看，2013年，城镇国有和集体单位从业人员仅占全部城镇从业人员的18.1%，而改革开放初期城镇从业人员几乎全部集中在公有制企业。从投资看，2013年，全社会民间投资同比增长22.3%，快于全社会固定资产投资3.2个百分点，占全社会固定资产投资的比重达到63.5%。

Rapid development of non-public economy sector has played an increasingly important role in promoting growth, expanding employment, and stimulating market vitality. With political support and guidance, the non-public economy rapidly developed from scratch to become an important part of the socialist market economy. In 2013, the number of non-public enterprises above designated size reached 342.6 thousand, representing 92.6 percent of all industrial enterprises above designated size, among which private enterprises accounted for 76.0 percent, and enterprises with investment from foreign sources, Hong Kong, Macao and/or Taiwan accounted for 12.6 percent. From the perspective of production levels, the output value of non-public enterprises above designated size accounted for 73.8 percent of the total output value of industrial enterprises above designated size, among which private enterprises accounted for 51.3 percent, and enterprises with investment from foreign sources, Hong Kong, Macao and/or Taiwan accounted for 17.8 percent. From the perspective of employment, in 2013, the urban employees in state-owned and collectively-owned enterprises accounted for only 18.1 percent of all urban employees, while almost all employees in the cities that first implemented reform and opening up policies were concentrated in the public sector. From an investment perspective, in 2013, private investment grew by 22.3 percent, 3.2 percentage points faster than total investment in fixed assets in the whole country, and accounting for 63.5 percent of investment in fixed assets in the whole country.

图 10 2013年按注册类型分的城镇就业人员构成
Composition of Employed Persons in Urban Units by Status of Registration, 2013

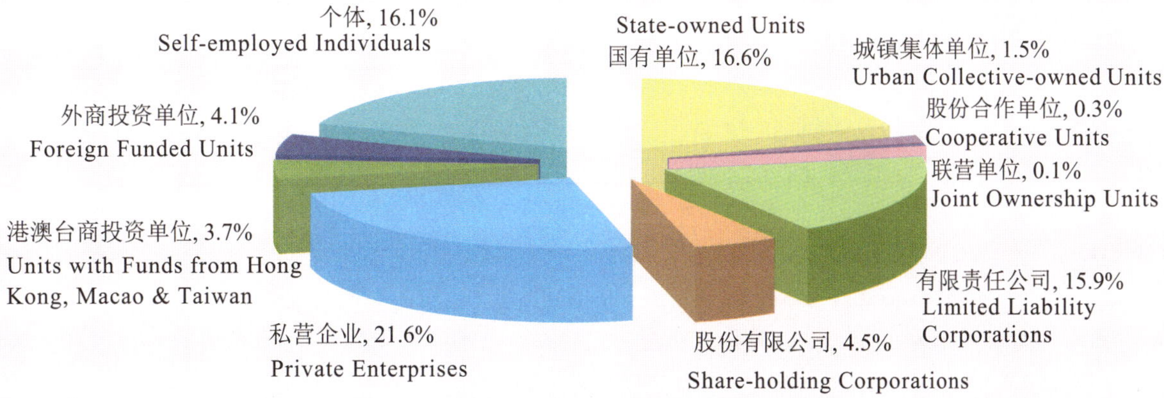

（三）分配结构不断调整，从绝对平均主义转变为以按劳分配为主、多种分配方式并存。

建国初期到改革开放前，国家、企业、居民三者分配关系表现为“国家得大头、企业得中头，个人得小头”，居民收入分配则实行绝对平均主义。改革开放以来，我国不断调整和完善收入分配制度，坚决打破平均主义“大锅饭”，把按劳分配和按生产要素分配结合起来，确立了劳动、资本、技术、土地等生产要素按贡献参与分配的原则，极大地调动了广大人民群众的积极性，解放和发展了社会生产力。

国家、企业和居民三者分配关系逐步调整。改革开放以来，国家在分配政策上做出了一系列重大调整，农村实行家庭联产承包责任制，城市实行“放权

(3) Continuous adjustment of income distribution structure has produced a transition from absolute egalitarianism to the main form of work-based that coexists with other forms of distribution.

In the period from the founding of the PRC until the implementation of reform and opening up, the income distribution relationship that existed among the state, enterprises, and residents was represented by the expression “the state gets the largest share, enterprises get the medium share, individuals get the small share. ” Absolute egalitarianism was implemented to distribute residents’ income. Since the initiation of reform and opening up, China has been continuously adjusting and improving the income distribution system to break down the egalitarianism of the “eating from the same big pot,” integrating work-based distribution and production factors-based distribution. China established labor, capital, technology, land, and other production factors as parameters for distribution, and greatly mobilized enthusiasm of the masses, unleashing and developing society’s productive power.

Gradual adjustment of distribution among state, enterprises, and residents. Since the adoption of reform and opening up policy, the state has made a series of major adjustments to income distribution policies and implemented the household contract responsibility system in rural areas and a system characterized by

让利”的“经营责任制”，同时采取多种放开搞活的措施，促进个体、私营、外资经济发展。国家、企业和居民三者的初次分配关系从1978年的33.9%、11.1%和55.0%变为2011年的15.4%、23.9%和60.7%，国家收入比重下降了18.5个百分点，企业收入和居民收入比重分别上升了12.8和5.7个百分点。近年来随着我国进入转型发展的新阶段，党中央、国务院更加重视改善收入分配结构，千方百计增加居民收入，特别是不失时机地推进有利于扩大就业和增加居民收入的服务业发展，保障了居民收入增长和经济发展基本实现同步。2013年，全国居民人均可支配收入同比实际增长8.1%，快于国内生产总值7.7%的增速；2014年上半年实际增长8.3%，快于国内生产总值7.4%的增速。

“decentralization of power management responsibility” in urban areas. It has also taken various measures to advance the economic development of residents, private enterprises, and foreign investment. The initial proportion of distribution among the state, enterprises, and residents changed distribution relationship from 33.9 percent, 11.1 percent, and 55.0 percent respectively in 1978 had changed to 15.4 percent, 23.9 percent, and 60.7 percent by in 2011. The proportion of income distributed to the State income proportion dropped by 18.5 percent, whereas the proportion of income distributed to enterprises and residents inhabitants income proportion rose by 12.8 and 5.7 percent, respectively. In recent years, as China has entered a new phase of restructuring and development, the Communist Party of China’s Central Committee and State Council have put more emphasis on improving the country’s income distribution structure and doing everything possible to increase income. In particular, they have focused on seizing opportunities for the development of service industry in order development to expand employment and increase residents’ incomes, achieving the synchronization of income growth and economic development. In 2013, national per capita disposable income increased by 8.1 percent, faster than the GDP growth rate of 7.7 percent.; in the first half of 2014, real income growth rate accounted reached for 8.3 percent, faster higher than the 7.4 percent of GDP growth rate.

居民收入来源日益多元化。改革开放前，工资性收入几乎是城镇居民收入唯一来源，农村居民收入的主要来源为从集体所得的工分收入。改革开放后，随着农村家庭联产承包责任制的推行、私营经济的快速发展、市场化水平的不断提高，以及政府转移支付的力度加大，城乡居民收入来源逐渐趋向多元。从城镇居民看，表现为工资性收入尽管仍是主体，但比重在逐步降低，经营净收入、财产性收入和转移性收入的比重均不同程度提高。2013 年，城镇居民人均总收入中，工资性收入占比为 64.1%，比 1978 年下降了 28.5 个百分点；经营净收入从无到有，

Increased diversification of residents' income sources. Before the implementation of reform and opening up, wages were almost the only source of income for urban residents, while the main source of income for rural residents was from work in collective labor. After the start of reform and opening up, the implementation of the rural household contract responsibility system, rapid development of the private economic sector, the increase in the level of the market economy, and efforts to intensify government transfer payments led to the gradual diversification of income sources for urban and rural residents. For urban residents, wages remained the main source of income, but their proportion gradually reduced; the proportions of net income from household operations, income from property, and transfer income increased to varying degrees. In 2013, per capita wage income accounted for 64.1 percent of the total income of urban residents, 28.5 percentage points lower than in 1978; net income from household operations accounted

占比达到9.5%，1981年仅占0.05%；财产性收入占2.7%，1981年仅占0.5%；转移性收入占23.7%，比1964年提高19.2个百分点。从农村居民看，随着农村剩余劳动力大量外出务工，工资性收入成为农民收入的重要来源，占比快速提高。2013年，在农村居民人均纯收入中，工资性收入占比为45.2%，比1985年提高27.2个百分点；家庭经营收入占比为42.6%，下降31.8个百分点；财产性收入、转移性收入从无到有，持续增加，占比分别达到3.3%和8.8%。

for 9.5 percent, whereas in 1981 this accounted for only 0.05 percent of total income; property income accounted for 2.7 percent, whereas in 1981 it accounted for just 0.5 percent; transfer income accounted for 23.7 percent, 19.2 percentage points higher than in 1964. For rural residents, along with a large number of rural surplus labor moving out for work, wage income has become farmers an important source of income. The proportions rapidly increased. In 2013, per capita net income of rural residents, the wage income accounted for 45.2 percent, 27.2 percentage points higher than in 1985; net income from household operation accounted for 42.6 percent, 31.8 percentage points lower than in 1985; property income and transfer income have continued to increase from scratch, accounting for 3.3 percent and 8.8 percent, respectively.

表3　农村居民收入结构的变化
Proportion of Income of Rural Residents

单位：%　　　　(%)

收入项目	Item	1990年	1995年	2000年	2005年	2010年	2013年
纯收入	Net Income of Rural Residents	100.0	100.0	100.0	100.0	100.0	100.0
工资性收入	Wage Income	20.2	22.4	31.2	36.1	41.1	45.2
家庭经营收入	Net Income from Houshold Operations	75.6	71.4	63.3	56.7	47.9	42.6
财产性收入	Porperty Income	4.2	2.6	2.0	2.7	3.4	3.3
转移性收入	Transfer Income		3.6	3.5	4.5	7.7	8.8

表4　城镇居民收入结构的变化
Proportion of Income of Urban Residents

单位：%　　　　(%)

收入项目	Item	1990年	1995年	2000年	2005年	2010年	2013年
总收入	Total Income of Urban Residents	100.0	100.0	100.0	100.0	100.0	100.0
工资性收入	Wage Income	75.8	78.9	71.2	68.9	65.2	64.1
经营净收入	Net Income from Houshold Operations	1.5	1.8	3.9	6.0	8.1	9.5
财产性收入	Porperty Income	1.0	2.1	2.0	1.7	2.5	2.7
转移性收入	Transfer Income	21.7	17.1	22.9	23.4	24.2	23.7

（四）城镇化稳步推进，城乡统筹协调发展趋势明显。

新中国成立后，由于传统的计划体制和严格的户籍制度的限制，城乡之间生产要素不能自由流动，工农业产品不能平等交易，大量农村富余劳动力无法转移到城市，城乡二元体制逐步形成并不断强化。改革开放以来，城乡发展进入新的历史阶段。一方面，城镇化进程的加快，打破城乡间劳动力、土地、资本等要素市场的隔离；另一方面，社会主义新农村建设扎实推进，以工促农、以城带乡机制逐步形成，有力地促进了城乡二元结构的改变。

城镇化水平不断提高。1949-2013 年，城市数量由 132 个发展到 658 个。根据第六次全国人口普查数据，1978-2010 年，

(4) Steady urbanization, clear trends of coordinated urban and rural development.

After the founding of the PRC, restrictions in the traditional planning system and strict household registration system limited the free flow of production factors between urban and rural areas: industrial and agricultural products could not be freely traded, and most of the rural surplus labor force was unable to move to cities. An urban-rural binary system formed and continued to strengthen. After the reform and opening up policy was implemented, urban and rural development entered an historic new stage. The urbanization process accelerated, breaking the division between urban and rural labor, land, capital, and other market factors. The building of a new socialist countryside was promoted in order to promote agriculture and to form a system in which urban areas assist rural areas, effectively promoting changes in the urban-rural dual system.

Continuous increase in the level of urbanization. From 1949 to 2013, the number of cities in China grew from 132 to 658. According to the sixth national census data, from

1000 万人口城市由 0 个增加到 6 个，500 万 -1000 万人口城市由 2 个增加到 10 个，300 万 -500 万人口城市由 2 个增加到 21 个，100 万 -300 万人口城市由 25 个增加到 103 个，50 万 -100 万人口城市由 35 个增加到 138 个，50 万以下城市由 129 个增加到 380 个。城镇化率稳步提升。1949 年，城镇人口占总人口的比重仅为 10.64%，1978 年提高到 17.92%，2011 年突破 50%，达到 51.27%，2013 年进一步上升到 53.73%，比 1949 年提高 43.09 个百分点，年平均上升 0.66 个百分点，其中 1979-2013 年年平均上升 1.02 个百分点。城镇吸纳就业的能力不断增强，城镇就业人员占全国的比重从 1952 年的 12.0% 上升到 2013 年的 49.7%。

1978 to 2010, the number of cities of 10 million population increased from 0 to 6, the number of cities with populations of 5 to 10 million population increased from 2 to 10, the number of cities with populations of 3 to 5 million population increased from 2 to 21, the number of cities with populations of 1 to 3 million population increased from 25 to 103, the number of cities with populations of 0.5 to 1 million population increased from 35 to 138, the number of cities with a population of less than 0.5 million rose from 129 to 380. The level of urbanization has been steadily advancing. In 1949, the urban population accounted for only 10.64 percent of China's total population, increasing to 17.92 percent in 1978, 51.27 percent in 2011, and 53.73 percent in 2013, a 43.09 percent increase over the urban population in 1949; the annual average growth rate of cities reached 0.66 percent, which rose by an average 1.02 percentage every year from 1979 to 2013. The ability to create jobs in cities has continued to grow as urban employment's proportion of total national employment rose from 12.0 percent in 1952 to 49.7 percent in 2013.

图 11　1949-2013 年城镇人口占总人口的比重
Proportion of Urban Population to Total Population, 1949-2013

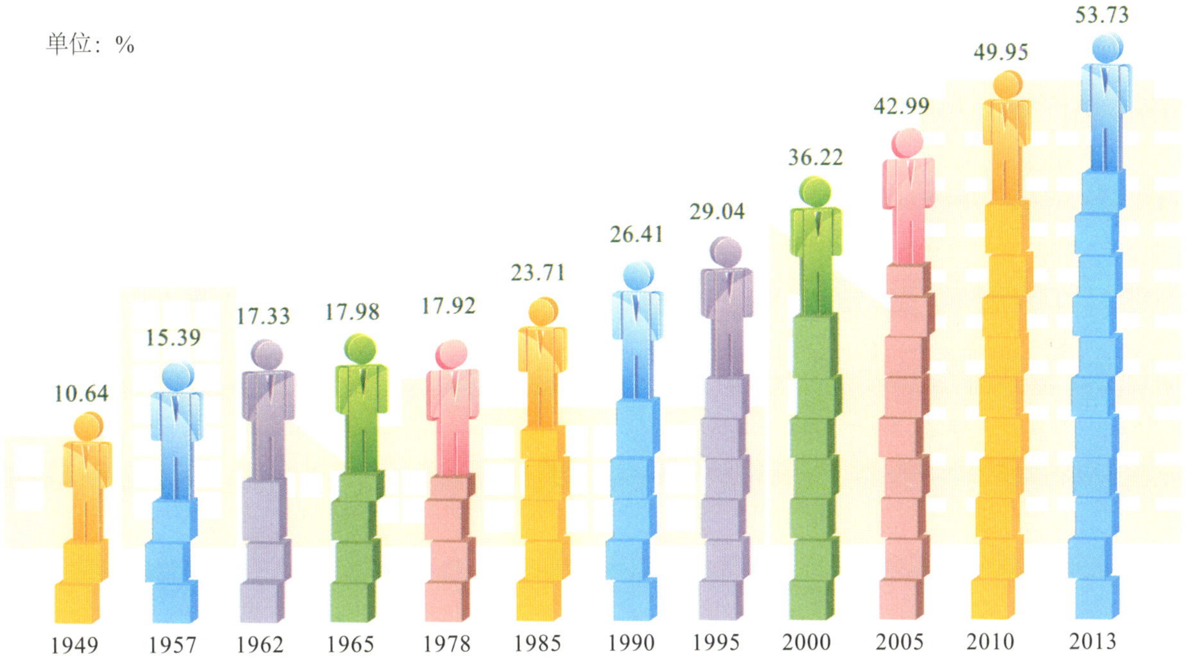

城镇化率

城镇化率是国际上衡量城镇化水平的通行指标。我国城镇化率有两种统计口径。一种是常住人口的城镇化率，即城镇常住人口占全部人口的比重，由国家统计局负责统计和发布。所谓常住人口是指实际经常居住在某地区一定时间（指半年以上）的人口，既包括有户籍且实际在住的人口（即〞户籍常住人口〞），也包括无户籍但实际在住的人口（即〞外来人口〞和〞本地其他行政区域流入人口〞）。这个概念和口径在国际上是可比的。另外一种是户籍人口城镇化率，是依据公安部门的户籍资料计算的城镇化水平。户籍人口是指公民依照《中华人民共和国户口登记条例》，已在其经常居住地的公安户籍管理机关登记了常住户口的人。这类人口不管其是否外出，也不管外出时间长短，只要在某地注册有常住户口，则为该地区的户籍人口。

2013 年，我国常住人口的城镇化率为 53.73%，户籍人口的城镇化率为 35% 左右。造成两个数据差异的根本原因是城乡二元结构和户籍制度的束缚。下一步要加快推进以人为本的新型城镇化，特别要加快农民工市民化进程，努力实现 1 亿左右农业转移人口和其他常住人口在城镇落户。

Urbanization Rate

The urbanization rate is a popular index to measure the urbanization level in the world. China's urbanization rate has two kinds of statistic caliber. One is the urbanization rate of the resident population, namely permanent urban population proportion of the total population, censored and released by the National Bureau of Statistics. The resident population refers to the population who actually often stay in one area (of more than half a year), including the domicile and the actual living population (i.e. "domicile resident population"), non-registered but actually lived population ("floating population" and "local administrative region of the inflow of population"). The concept and the diameter are comparable in the world. Another one is the household register population urbanization rate, a level of urbanization calculated on the basis of police stations of the household registration data. The household register population refers to the citizens of the People's Republic of China who has registered permanent residence of people in their regular place of residence in public security stations of household control in accordance with the "Household Registration Ordinance", This kind of population are identified as the household registered population of the area regardless of presence or absence for long or short time, and so long as registered for permanent residence.

In 2013, the urbanization rate of China's population is 53.73%, and the urbanization rate is about 35%. The cause of the differences between the two rates is the fetter of two structures in urban and rural areas as well as the household registration system. The next step is to accelerate the new urbanization based on the human resources, especially to speed up the process of urbanization of migrant workers, and to strive to achieve the transfer of 100 million of agricultural population and other resident population settling in the towns.

农村面貌发生翻天覆地的变化。在积极推进城镇化发展的同时，党中央、国务院高度重视“三农”问题，坚持工业反哺农业、城市支持农村和“多予少取放活”方针，特别是新世纪以来不断加大强农惠农富农政策力度，着力改善农村生产生活条件，大力加强农村水、电、燃气、通讯等基础设施建设，农村面貌发生了翻天覆地的变化。国家财政对“三农”的投入由1978年的151亿元增加到2012年的12388亿元，增长了81倍。农业基础设施条件大为改善。2013年，我国农村公路里程为378万公里，比1978年增长了5.4倍；通公路的乡（镇）占全国乡（镇）总数的99.97%，通公路的建制村占全国建制村

Incredible changes in rural areas. While actively promoting urbanization, the CPC's Central Committee and the State Council have attached great importance to the "Three Rural Issues about rural areas, agriculture and farmers" , insisting on industry's support of agriculture, on cities' support of the countryside, and on the "giving more, taking less, and loosening control" policy.In the 21st century, the government has continued to increase support for boosting agriculture, benefitting farmers and increasing rural prosperity, making efforts to improve rural production and living conditions, vigorously strengthening construction of water, electricity, gas, telecommunications, and other infrastructure facilities, and making many incredible changes in rural areas. State financial investment in the "Three Rural Issues about rural areas, agriculture and farmers" increased from 15.1 billion yuan in 1978 to 1.2388 trillion yuan in 2012, increasing by 81 times. Agricultural infrastructure has been greatly improved. In 2013, China's rural highway mileage reached 3.78 million kilometers, 5.4 times the mileage that existed in 1978; 99.97 percent of all towns have highways

总数的 99.7%；已通电话的行政村比重达 100%；通邮的行政村比重达 99.20%。移动电话、计算机、摩托车等耐用消费品在农村普及的速度明显加快。2013 年末，农村固定电话用户达到 8242 万户，比 1978 年增长 111 倍。2012 年，农村居民家庭平均每百户移动电话、计算机、摩托车拥有量分别为 197.8 部、21.4 部、62.2 辆，分别比 2000 年增长 1.8、44.5 和 44.8 倍。

passing through them; 99.7 percent of all national administrative villages have with highways passing through them; the proportion of villages with a telephone connection reached 100 percent; and the proportion of villages with postal service reached 92.20 percent. The growth of the popularity of mobile phones, computers and motorcycles, etc. durable consumer goods in rural areas has accelerated. By the end of 2013, the number of rural subscribers to fixed telephone connections reached 82.42 million, 111 times the number of subscribers in 1978. In 2012, there were 197.8, 21.4 and 62.2 mobile phones, computers and motorcycles respectively per 100 rural households, an increase of 1.8, 44.5 and 44.8 times compared with 2000.

“村村通”工程

〝村村通〞工程是我国构建和谐社会、支持新农村建设的一项重大民生工程，包括农村公路〝村村通〞工程、农村电力〝村村通〞工程、农村广播电视〝村村通〞工程、农村通信〝村村通〞工程，涵盖公路、电力、生活和饮用水、电话网、有线电视网、互联网等各个方面。

〝村村通〞工程的实施取得积极成果，全国具备条件的所有乡镇和建制村基本通公路，9 亿农民的出行难题基本得到解决；2005 年底基本实现了村村通电；基本构建了农村广播电视公共服务体系，20 户以上已通电的自然村全部通广播电视；基本实现了全国〝村村通电话，乡乡能上网〞，村村通宽带也进展顺利。总之，〝村村通工程〞极大地改善了农村道路、通信等基础设施条件，方便了农村居民生产生活，丰富了农民的精神文化生活。

Project of “All Village Access"

As a major livelihood project aiming at constructing a harmonious society in China and supporting the new rural construction, "All Village Access" project includes "All Village Road Access" project, "All Village Electricity Access" project, "All Village Radio & TV Access" project, "All Village Tele-Communication Access", covering engineering, road, electricity, drinking water, telephone network, cable network, the Internet and other aspects.

The implementation of the "All Village Access" project achieved positive results. All geographically qualified towns and administrative villages have roads, basically solving the travel problems of 900 million farmers. By the end of 2005, the basic power coverage to every village has been achieved; The rural radio and TV public service system has been completed of basic construction, the electrified villages of more than 20 households have access to radios and televisions; the "All Village Telephone Access" has come true, and "All Village Broadband Access" is under way smoothly. In a word, "All Village Access"project has greatly improved the rural roads, communication and other infrastructure, facilitating the production as well as the living of rural residents and enriching the cultural life of farmers.

（五）区域发展协调性显著增强，各具特色、良性互动的区域发展格局正在形成。

我国区域发展经历了不同的历史阶段。建国之初，为改变旧中国遗留下来的工业基础薄弱、沿海与内地布局严重不平衡的局面，以及考虑到当时特殊的国际国内政治环境需要，我国在区域布局上侧重加强中西部发展，通过“三线建设”，建成了一批铁路、石油、机械、电力项目，推动中西部地区经济比重上升。1978 年以来，按照小平同志提出的“让一部分地区、一部分人先富起来，逐步实现共同富裕”和“两个大局”的战略构想，东部地区作为改革开放的先行地区和前沿地带率先发展起来。上世纪 90 年代，面对我国地区发展差距不断扩大，

(5) Coordination of regional development has been significantly enhanced, forming a pattern of positive interaction between regions.

China's regional development experienced different historical stages. At the time of the founding of the People's Republic of China, the country focused on strengthening the development of central and western parts of the country in order to change the old China's legacy, which was characterized by a weak industrial base and a serious imbalance between coastal and inland areas, and in order to address the needs of the international and domestic political environment at that time. In the "Third Line Construction", the country built a system of railways and established petroleum, machinery and electricity generation projects to promote the rise of the central and western Chinese economy. Since 1978, following the Deng Xiaoping's proposal "encouraging part of the region, some people to get rich first, and drive and help other regions, other people, and gradually achieve common prosperity" and Deng's presentation of the "two overall situations" strategic vision, eastern China became the first region to implement reform and opening up policy, becoming the front-line for development. In the 1990s, faced with a widening gap in regional development, the CPC Central Committee and the State Council took stock of the development

党中央、国务院审时度势，相继做出了西部大开发、振兴东北地区等老工业基地、促进中部地区崛起等重大战略决策，有力地促进区域协调发展，并逐步形成新的发展特点。

东部地区率先发展，引领带动作用突出。东部地区在我国经济社会发展中具有举足轻重的作用。1952 年，东部地区工业总产值占全国的比重为 68.3%，1978 年，这一比例仍然高达 59.2%。改革开放以来，东部地区率先发展起来，辐射带动了全国的改革开放和发展，创造了大量就业岗位和社会财富，为财政增收、综合国力增强做出了突出贡献。2013 年，东部地区生产总值占全国的 55.4%，比 1978 年上升 5.4 个百分点；全社会固定资产投资占全国的 45.8%，上升 7.2 个百分点；进出口总额占全国的 83.7%，上升 9.3 个百分点。近年来，面

situation by closely following western China's development, reviving northeast China's old industrial base, promoting the rise of central China, and other major strategic decisions, effectively promoting coordinated regional development and gradually forming new development patterns.

Eastern region leads the development process, playing a prominent role. China's eastern region has played a decisive role in the nation's economic and social development. In 1952, the eastern region's industrial output accounted for 68.3 percent of the country's total industrial output; in 1978, this proportion remained as high as 59.2 percent. Following the start of the reform and opening up process, the eastern region began developing first, leading the whole country's development under the reform and opening up process, creating a large number of jobs and increasing social wealth, providing additional income for public finances and making an outstanding contribution to the rise of overall national strength. In 2013, the eastern region's GDP accounted for 55.4 percent of national GDP, showing an increase of 5.4 percent over 1978; total investment in fixed assets in the eastern region accounted for 45.8 percent of the national total, showing an increase of 7.2 percent; the total amount of the eastern region's exports and imports accounted for 83.7 percent of the national total, showing an increase of 9.3 percent. In recent years, faced with a slowdown in economic growth and transformative pressure created by various structural

改革开放的排头兵——深圳经济特区

作为我国改革开放的总设计师邓小平亲自倡导设立的第一个经济特区，深圳经济特区一直被视为我国改革开放的排头兵和试验场。1980 年 8 月，深圳经济特区正式建立。特区实行不同于内地的管理体制，以中外合资、合作经营企业、外商独资企业为主，多种所有制经济并存。

深圳经济特区成立以来，敢闯敢试验、敢为天下先，勇于突破传统束缚，率先进行市场取向的经济改革，创下了物价改革、企业产权转让、住房制度改革等众多“中国第一”。1983 年，深圳首家股份制企业诞生；1986 年，深圳探索国企股份制改造新路；1990 年，深圳证券交易所成立，成为内地两大证券交易所之一；1997 年，深圳基本完成了从计划经济到社会主义市场经济的过渡；2006 年，《深圳市实施“走出去”战略规划纲要》出台，首次把“走出去”列入城市重点发展战略；2009 年，深圳证券交易所创业板开市交易，我国多层次资本市场进一步完善；2010 年，国务院批准深圳经济特区范围扩大到深圳全市，深圳正式迈进大特区时代。

经过 30 多年不懈努力，深圳迅速从一个边陲小镇发展成为一座现代化大城市，综合经济实力跃居全国大中城市前列，创造了世界工业化、现代化、城市化发展史上的奇迹，在全国改革开放和经济发展中具有引领和带动作用。

The Shenzhen Special Economic Zone ——Vanguard of Reform and Opening up

As the first Special Economic Zone advocated and designed personally by Deng Xiaoping, the general designer of China’s Reform and Opening-up, Shenzhen Special Economic Zone has been regarded as the vanguard and the test field of China's Reform and Opening-up. In August 1980, the Shenzhen Special Economic Zone was established officially. The management system in Special Economic Zone was dominated by Sino-foreign joint ventures, cooperative enterprises, wholly foreign-owned enterprises, various ownership economy coexisting, being different from that on the mainland.

Since its establishment, Shenzhen Special Economic Zone, with the courage to break through the traditional fetter, took the lead in the market oriented economic reform, set a record of "Number Ones in China" like price reform, enterprise property rights transfer, and the reform of the housing system. In 1983, Shenzhen's first joint-stock enterprise came into being. In 1986, Shenzhen explored the new path of transforming state-owned joint-stock enterprises. In 1990, Shenzhen stock exchange was established to be one of the mainland's two largest stock exchanges. In 1997, Shenzhen has basically completed the transition from planned economy to socialist market economy. In 2006, "Shenzhen’s implementation of the ‘Going Out’ strategy plan" was published, putting "going out" as the key strategy of the development of city for the first time. In 2009, the GEM trading took place in Shenzhen stock exchange, which represented that the multi-level capital market in China further improved. In 2010, the State Council approved the expansion of Shenzhen Special Economic Zone to the city of Shenzhen, Shenzhen formally entered the SAR era.

After the unremitting efforts of more than 30 years, Shenzhen has rapidly developed from a small border town into a modern city, whose comprehensive economic strength ranks the forefront of the national large and medium-sized city, creating a miracle in the world industrialization, modernization, as well as city development history and playing a leading role in the country's reform and opening up and economic development.

全面改革的试验田——中国（上海）自由贸易试验区

2013 年 9 月 29 日，中国（上海）自由贸易试验区在上海正式挂牌成立。试验区的范围涵盖上海外高桥保税区、上海外高桥保税物流园区、洋山保税港区和上海浦东机场综合保税区等 4 个海关特殊监管区域，总面积约 28.78 平方公里。上海自贸区将重点在投资管理、贸易监管、金融开放创新、事中事后监管和拓展改革新领域等 5 个方面先行先试，进行制度探索，形成可复制、可推广的经验，发挥示范带动、服务全国的积极作用，促进各地区共同发展。

上海自贸区制度创新的一大亮点是以"负面清单"为核心的投资管理模式创新。所谓"负面清单管理模式"是指政府规定哪些经济领域不开放，除了清单上的禁区，其他行业、领域和经济活动都许可。上海自贸区借鉴国际通行规则，对外商投资试行准入前国民待遇，研究制订试验区外商投资与国民待遇等不符的负面清单，改革外商投资管理模式。负面清单管理可以简化对外资进入的审批管理，在外资准入方面更加透明，对于增强外资信心，鼓励、吸引外商投资都将起到积极作用。从"正面清单"到"负面清单"，一字之差，却是政府管理思维的巨大转变。

The China (Shanghai) Free Trade Pilot Zone
——the Testing Ground for Overall Reform

On September 29, 2013, China (Shanghai) Free Trade Pilot Zone was formally established in Shanghai. The scope of the pilot area covers Shanghai Waigaoqiao Bonded Zone, Shanghai Waigaoqiao Bonded Logistics Park, Yangshan Bonded Port and Shanghai Pudong Airport Comprehensive Bonded Zone under special customs supervision, taking up a total area of about 28.78 square kilometers. Shanghai Free Trade Pilot Zone will focus on the following 5 aspects: investment management, trade regulation, financial innovation, supervision during and after business, and the expansion of the reform in new areas. The Free Trade Zone will take the initiative to explore the new system, getting experience that can be duplicated and popularized. The Free Trade zone will play a demonstrative and active role in driving and serving the whole country in order to promote the common development of all regions.

One of the highlights of the innovations of Shanghai Free Trade Pilot Zone is the innovation of investment management mode with the "Negative List" as the core. The so-called "Negative List Management Mode" refers to the mode that government designates which areas of the economy are not open. Except from the negative areas on the list, other industries, areas and economic activities are all permitted. Shanghai Free Trade Pilot Zone draws lessons from the popular international rules with the implementation of the Pre-Establishment National Treatment to foreign investments, studying and formulating the negative list for the inconsistency between the foreign investments and national treatment, reforming the investment management mode for foreign investment. The negative list management can simplify the approval and management of the entry of foreign investment, making the permission for foreign investment more transparent. These will play a positive role in reinforcing the confidence of the foreign investment, encouraging and attracting foreign investment. The transition from the "positive list" to the "negative list", even though only one word is changed, reflects the huge change in the government's management thinking.

对经济增长趋缓和各种结构性矛盾带来的转型压力，东部地区率先调整，在技术创新、产业升级、开拓国际市场和资源方面先行先试，涌现出一大批具有高科技含量的产业和企业，转型引领作用明显。

中西部地区加快发展，后发优势明显。1952 年，中、西部地区工业总产值占全国的比重分别为 21.3% 和 10.4%，1978 年分别上升到 25.1% 和 15.7%。随后由于东部地区较快发展，中西部经济所占比重有所下降。新世纪以来，中西部地区凭借资源、劳动力等优势大力承接东部地区产业转移，后发优势不断发挥，投资大幅增加，经济发展明显加快。2000–2013

contradictions, the eastern region took the lead in making adjustments to its economy, taking the first steps in technological innovation, industrial upgrading, opening of international markets and resource development. These steps made the emergence of a large number of high-tech industries and enterprises possible, playing a key role in leading China's economic transformation.

Acceleration of the central and western region's development shows the advantages of late development. In 1952, the central region's industrial output accounted for 21.3 percent of the national total industrial output, and the western region's output accounted for 10.4 percent of national output; in 1978, the proportions of the regions' outputs in the national total had risen to 25.1 and 15.7 percent, respectively. Afterwards, due to the rapid development of the eastern region, the central and western region's proportions declined somewhat. In the 21st century, the central and western regions have relied on their resources, labor force and other advantages, to accept an industrial shift from the eastern region. Late-development

图 12 1952–2013 年东中西部地区工业总产值结构
Structure of Industrial Output by Eastern, Central and Western Regions, 1952-2013

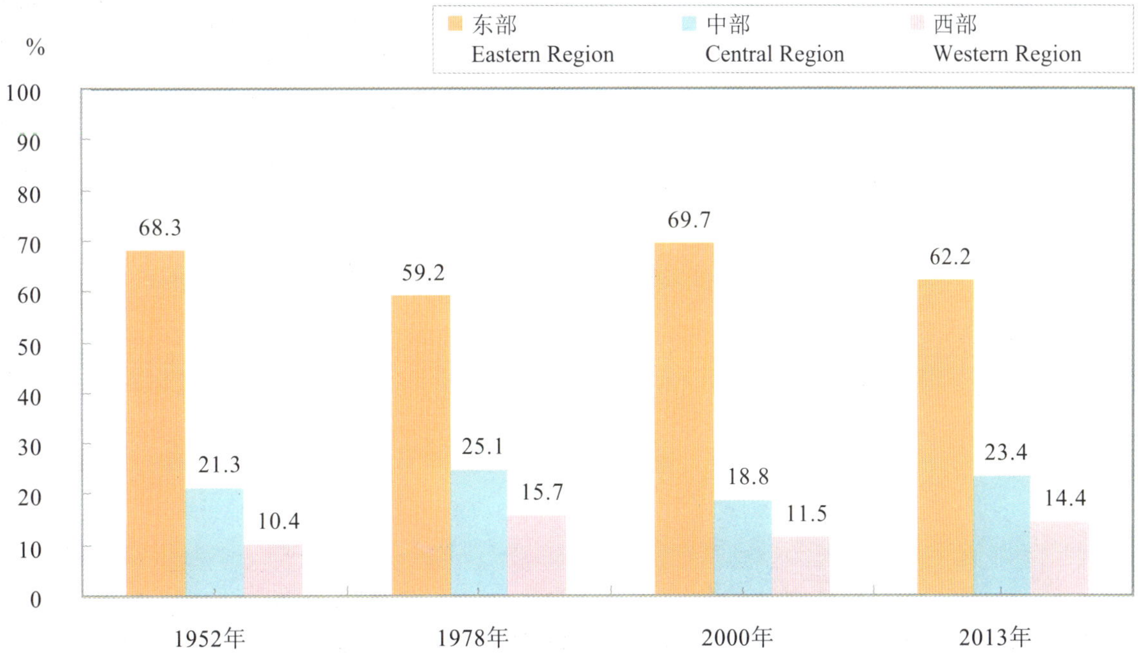

年，中部地区全社会固定资产投资年均增长 24.2%，西部地区年均增长 23.8%，分别比东部地区快 4.8 和 4.4 个百分点。2013 年，中部地区全社会固定资产投资占全国的比重为 28.5%，比 1999 年提高 7.7 个百分点；西部地区占 24.5%，提高 6.3 个百分点。相应地，中西部经济增速已经接近或快于东部地区。2000-2013 年，西部地区生产总值年均实际增长 12.3%，快于东部 0.5 个百分点；中部地区生产总值年均实际增长 11.6%，接近东部 11.8% 的增速。

advantages continued to play a part, and a substantial increase in investment has noticeably accelerated economic development in the central and western regions. Between 2000 and 2013, the average annual growth rate of investment in fixed assets in the central region was 24.2 percent, while in the western region it was 23.8 percent, faster than that of the eastern region by 4.8 percent and 4.4 percent respectively. In 2013, total investment in the fixed assets of the country's central region accounted for 28.5 percent of total investment in the whole country's fixed assets, 7.7 percent more than in 1999; total investment in fixed assets in the western region accounted for 24.5 percent of the whole country's, 6.3 percent more than in 1999. Accordingly, economic growth in the central and western regions was also clearly faster than in the eastern region. From 2000 to 2013, the western regions' average annual GDP growth rates were 12.3 percent, faster than the eastern region's GDP growth rate by 0.5 percent, the central regions' average annual GDP growth rates were 11.6 percent, close to the 11.8 percent growth rate of the eastern region.

西部大开发战略

西部大开发是中共中央贯彻邓小平同志关于我国现代化建设〝两个大局〞战略思想、面向新世纪做出的重大战略决策，在我国区域协调发展总体战略中具有重要地位。

1999 年 9 月，中共十五届四中全会明确提出要实施西部大开发战略。2000 年 1 月，国务院西部地区开发领导小组召开西部地区开发会议，研究加快西部地区发展的基本思路和战略任务，对实施西部大开发战略的重点工作进行全面部署。2001 年 3 月，〝十五〞计划对实施西部大开发战略再次进行了具体部署。西部地区特指陕西、甘肃、宁夏、青海、新疆、四川、重庆、云南、贵州、西藏、广西、内蒙古 12 个省、自治区和直辖市。整个西部地区面积约占全国国土总面积的 71%，1999 年末人口约占全国的 29%，其中少数民族人口占全国的 75%左右。实施西部大开发，就是要依托亚欧大陆桥、长江水道、西南出海通道等交通干线，发挥中心城市作用，以线串点，以点带面，逐步形成西部有特色的西陇海兰新线、长江上游、南（宁）贵、成昆（明）等跨行政区域的经济带，带动其他地区发展，有步骤、有重点地推进西部大开发。2006 年 12 月，国务院常务会议审议并原则通过《西部大开发〝十一五〞规划》。

西部大开发战略的实施使西部大地焕发出勃勃生机，西部地区的经济增长速度一改滞后的局面，2000–2013 年西部地区 GDP 年均增长 12.3%，分别比东部、中部地区快 0.5 和 0.7 个百分点，2013 年西部地区 GDP 占全国的比重上升至 20.0%，比 1999 年提高 2.1 个百分点。投资保持较快增长，基础设施建设取得突破性进展，大大改变了西部地区闭塞落后的面貌。2000–2013 年，西部地区全社会固定资产投资年均增长 23.8%，比东部地区快 4.4 个百分点，青藏铁路、西气东输、西电东送等一批标志性工程相继建成。人民生活水平明显提高，群众得到更多实惠。2013 年，西部地区城镇居民人均可支配收入 22710 元，农村居民人均纯收入 6834 元。

The West Development Strategy

The West Development Strategy is the significant strategic decision for the Chinese Communist Party (CPC) to carry out the "Two Overall Situation" strategic thinking and major strategic decisions in face of the new century raised by comrade Deng Xiaoping, holding an important position in China's strategy for regional coordinative development.

In September 1999, the West Development Strategy was put forward at the 4th Plenary Session of the 15th Central Committee of the Chinese Communist Party in September. In January 2000, the conference about the development in western region was held by the leading group for western development in State Council, studying the basic idea and strategic task to accelerate the development of the western regions and fully deploying the key tasks in the process of implementing the West Development Strategy. In March 2001, the 10th Five-Year Plan redeployed the implementation of the West Development Strategy. The western region specifically refers to such provinces, autonomous regions, and municipalities directly under the central government as Shaanxi, Gansu, Ningxia, Qinghai, Xinjiang, Sichuan, Chongqing, Yunnan, Guizhou, Tibet, Guangxi, and Inner Mongolia. The entire western region accounts for about 71% of total national territorial area. By the end of 1999, the population accounted for about 29% of the country. The minority population in western region accounted for about 75% of the country's total. The implementation of the West Development Strategy relies upon the arterial traffic, such as the Eurasian Continental Bridge, the Yangtze River Waterway and the Southwest Sea Channel, playing the role of the central city. The traffic connects the region closely and gradually forms such distinctive cross-regional economic belts as Western Longhai-Lanxin railway, the upper reaches of the Yangtze River, the South (Ning) Gui, Cheng Kun (Ming), stimulating the development of the other regions and promoting the development of the western region in a gradual and focused manner. In December 2006, the executive meeting of the State Council reviewed and approved the West Development in the 11th Five-year Plan in principle.

The implementation of the West Development Strategy brought vitality to the west region, the western region's economic growth rate accelerated from lagging behind. The GDP in western region achieved the average annual growth of 12.3% during 2000 to 2013, 0.5 percent faster than eastern region and 0.7 percent faster than the central region respectively. In 2013, the GDP of the western region increased the proportion against the country's total GDP accounted for 20.0%, 2.1 percentage points higher than in 1999. Investment maintains a rapid growth and the infrastructure construction has made breakthroughs, changing the face of poverty and backward in western regions dramatically. From 2000 to 2013, the total investment in fixed assets achieved an average annual growth rate of 23.8%, 4.4% faster than the eastern region. The Qinghai-Tibet railway, the West-East natural gas transmission, West-East power transmission and a number of landmark projects have been completed. The people's living standards have remarkably improved and people are getting more benefits. In 2013, disposable income per capita of the urban residents in the western area reached 22710 yuan and the net income per capita of rural residents amounted to 6,834 yuan.

3 从短缺匮乏到丰富充裕 商品和服务供给能力极大提高

Shift from a supply deficit to a rich abundance of goods and services.

新中国成立以来的65年，是我国农业基础日益巩固、农产品供给能力大幅提高的65年，是工业生产能力迅速扩张、制造业竞争力跃居世界前列的65年，也是服务业稳步发展、对经济社会发展的支撑和带动作用趋于上升的65年。

The 65 years since the founding of the PRC have seen 65 years of consolidation of the agricultural base and a substantial increase in the supply of agricultural products, 65 years of the rapid expansion of industrial capacity and the attainment of global leadership in manufacturing competitiveness, and 65 years of the steady development of the service industry, which has tended to positively affect the promotion and support of economic and social development.

（一）农业综合生产能力稳步提高，成功解决了占世界五分之一人口的吃饭问题。

建国 65 年来，农业在不断探索和制度创新中快速发展，从土地改革到农业合作化，从人民公社到家庭联产承包责任制，再到全面取消农业税、实施农业补贴，极大调动了农民生产积极性，农业综合生产能力稳步提高，抗风险能力不断增强，主要农产品产量大幅增长，农产品市场供应日益丰富，成功解决了占世界五分之一人口的吃饭问题，农业在国民经济中的基础地位日益巩固。

(1) Steady improvement in overall agricultural production capacity has successfully resolved the problem of providing food for one fifth of the world's population.

In the 65 years since the PRC's founding, agriculture rapidly developed by means through continuous exploration and institutional innovation. Measures ranging from agrarian reforms to agricultural cooperation, from people's communes to the household contract responsibility system, and the full cancellation of the agricultural tax and implementation of agricultural subsidies have greatly mobilized farmers' enthusiasm for production. This has led to steady improvements in overall agricultural production capacity, an increase in the agricultural economy's ability to resist risks, a significant increase in the volume of main agricultural production, the rich supply of agricultural production markets, and the successful resolution of the problem of providing food for one fifth of the global population, so that agriculture has consolidated its important position in the national economy.

中央一号文件

"中央一号文件"原指每年中共中央发布的第一份文件，内容并不固定，改革开放以来，"中央一号文件"逐渐被固定为"三农问题"，随着时间的推移，被社会和媒体用于代表中共中央一贯重视农村问题的专有名词，在国内外产生了广泛而深远的影响。

改革开放以来，共有两个集中出台"一号文件"的时期。一是1982-1986年，"一号文件"连续5年聚焦"三农"。1982年1月1日，中共中央批转《全国农村工作会议纪要》，肯定包产到户等各种生产责任制都是社会主义集体经济的组成部分，自此，连续5年中共中央"一号文件"均以农业、农村、农民为主题。这五个"一号文件"为改革开放初期家庭联产承包责任制的确立、完善和快速推广提供了政策依据和理论指导，调动了农民的生产积极性，激发了农业和农村经济的生机和活力，为工业化、城镇化发展奠定了坚实的物质基础。二是2004-2014年，"一号文件"连续11年锁定"三农"。为解决农业基础设施薄弱、农民增收困难、农村发展滞后问题，2004年中共中央一号文件《关于促进农民增加收入若干政策的意见》首次以促进农民增加收入为主题。自此开始，以农民稳定增收、农业稳定发展为目标，围绕社会主义新农村建设和发展现代化农业，一号文件着力解决农民最关心最直接最现实的利益问题，在提高农田基础设施建设、水利设施、农业科技创新、金融支持、土地承包经营权、农民社会保障等多个方面连续出台多项措施，全面深化农村改革，重农强农富农，牢牢夯实我国农业发展的基础地位。

the No.1 Document from the CPC Central Committee

The No.1 Document from the CPC Central Committee used to refer to the first document issued by the CPC Central Committee every year but with different topics. However, since the implementation of the Reform and Opening-up Policy, the No.1 Document from the Central Committee of the CPC has gradually focused on the "Three Rural Issues (issues of agriculture, farmer and rural areas)". With the passage of time, this phrase is exclusively used by the society and media to represent the CPC Central Committee's constant attention to the issues in China's rural areas, exerting extensive and profound influence both at home and abroad.

Since the Reform and Opening-up, there were primarily two periods when "No.1 Documents" were introduced quite intensively. One is from 1982 to 1986 when No.1 Documents were focused on "Three Rural Issues (issues of agriculture)" for 5 consecutive years. On January 1, 1982, the CPC Central Committee endorsed the "The National Rural Work Meeting Minutes", affirmed that fixing the farm output quotas on the household basis together with other production responsibility system was part of socialist collective economy. Since then, "No. 1 document" issued by the CPC Central Committee chose agriculture, rural areas and farmers as the themes for 5 consecutive years. These five "No.1 Documents" provided policy basis and theoretical guidance for the establishment, improvement and fast promotion of the household contract responsibility system with remuneration linked to output at the beginning of the Reform and Opening-up Age, mobilizing farmers' enthusiasm for production, stimulating the vitality and vigor of the agriculture and rural economy, and laying a solid material foundation for the industrialization and urbanization development. The second period is from 2004 to 2014 when "No.1 Document concentrated on "Three Rural Issues" for 11 consecutive years. In order to solve the problems like the weak agricultural infrastructure, farmers' poor ability to increase income, and the lagging rural development, the No.1 Document in 2004 several policy advices on increasing farmers' income took the growth of the farmers' income as the theme for the first time. Since then, the "No.1 Documents" have regarded the steady increase in farmers' incomes and steady development of agriculture as the targets, focusing on constructing and developing the new socialist countryside and modern agriculture. The "No.1 Documents" have exerted themselves to solve the most direct, concerned and realistic problems closely related to the interests of farmers, putting forward many measures in realms such as improving the agricultural infrastructure construction, water conservancy facilities, agricultural science and technology innovation, financial support, the reform of contractual right of land, the farmer social security, etc. These measures have deepened the rural reform, reinforced, prioritized, and enriched the agriculture, firmly tamping the fundamental position that agricultural development holds in China.

粮、棉、油、糖等基本农产品产量大幅增加。1949 年，我国粮食产量只有 11318 万吨，人均产量 209 公斤；1978 年粮食产量增长到 30477 万吨，人均产量增加到 319 公斤。改革开放以后，国家对农业的强力支持和农业科技的进步使粮食产量进入快速增长期，1984 年超过 4 亿吨，1996 年超过 5 亿吨，2013 年粮食产量达到 60194 万吨，比 1949 年增长 4.3 倍；人均粮食产量达到 443 公斤，比 1949 年增长 1.1 倍。与此同时，主要农产品产量增长迅速。棉花产量 1949 年只有 44.4 万吨，1978 年为 217 万吨，2013 年达到 630 万吨，比 1949 年增长 13.2 倍；油料产量 1949 年只有 256 万吨，1978 年为 522 万吨，2013 年达到 3517 万吨，比 1949 年增长 12.7 倍；糖料产量 1949 年只有 283 万吨，1978 年为 2382 万吨，2013 年达到 13746 万吨，比 1949 年增长 47.6 倍。与之相伴的是

A substantial increase in the production of grain, cotton, oil, sugar, and other basic agricultural products. In 1949, China's grain production was only 113.18 million tons, or 209 kg per capita; in 1978, total grain output had risen to 304.77 million tons, and per capita production increased to 319 kg. After the implementation of reform and opening up policy, China pushed strong support for agriculture and agricultural science and technology, which caused food production to enter a period of rapid growth. In 1984, food production exceeded 400 million tons; in 1996, it was more than 500 million tons; and in 2013, grain output reached 601.94 million tons, a 4.3-fold increase over the 1949 data; per capita grain production reached 443 kg, an increase of 1.1 times compared with 1949. At the same time, the volume of major agricultural products grew rapidly. Production of cotton in 1949 was only 444 thousand tons; in 1978, it grew to 2.17 million tons; in 2013, production reached 6.30 million tons, an increase of 13.2 times over 1949. Plant oils production in 1949 was only 2.56 million tons; in 1978 it reached 5.22 million tons; and in 2013 it increased to 35.17 million tons, an increase of 12.7 times compared with 1949. Sugar production in 1949 was only 2.83 million tons; in 1978, it reached 23.82 million tons; in 2013, it increased to 137.46 million tons, an

主要农产品人均产量也大幅提高。2013年，人均棉花、油料、糖料产量分别达到4.6公斤、25.9公斤和101.3公斤，分别比1949年增长4.7倍、4.5倍和18.4倍。

肉类、水果、水产品和牛奶等“菜篮子”日益丰富。猪牛羊肉类产量1952年只有339万吨，人均5.9公斤；1978年增加到865万吨，人均9.0公斤；2013年达到6574万吨，人均48.6公斤。水果产量1949年只有120万吨，人均2.2公斤；1978年增加到657万吨，人均6.9公斤；2013年达到25093万吨，人均184.9公斤。水产品产量1949年为44.8万吨，人均0.8公斤；1978年增加到465万吨，人均4.9公斤；2013年达到6172万吨，人均45.5公斤。牛奶产量1978年为88.3万吨，人均0.9公斤；2013年达到3531万吨，人均26.1公斤。

increase of 47.6 times compared with 1949. The output of main agricultural products per capita also greatly improved. In 2013, per capita production of cotton, oil-bearing seeds, and sugar reached 4.6 kg, 25.9 kg, and 101.3 kg respectively, increases of 4.7, 4.5 and 18.4 times respectively compared with 1949.

Increased abundance of meats, fruits, beverages and milk products in consumers“market baskets”. Pork, beef and lamb production in 1952 was only 3.39 million tons, or 5.9 kg per capita; in 1978, it increased to 8.65 million tons, or 9.0 kg per capita; and in 2013, it reached 65.74 million tons, or 48.6 kg per capita. Fruit production in 1949 was only 1.2 million tons, or 2.2 kg per capita; in 1978, it increased to 6.57 million tons, or 6.9 kg per capita; and in 2013, it reached 250.93 million tons, or 184.7 kg per capita. Beverage production in 1949 accounted for only 448 thousand tons, or 0.8 kg per capita; in 1978, it increased to 4.65 million tons, or 4.9 kg per capita; and in 2013, it reached 61.72 million tons, or 45.5 kg per capita. Outputs of milk products in 1978, increased to 883 thousand tons, or 0.9 kg per capita; and in 2013, it reached 35.31 million tons, or 26.1 kg per capita.

农业税成为历史

中国是传统的农业大国，农业税负一直在各朝各代中占据重要地位，唐朝的均田制、两税法，明朝的一条鞭法，清朝的摊丁入亩政策等都是农业税负的变化形式。封建历史中，偶尔有轻徭薄赋的时期，但始终未能跳出农民负担越减越重的"黄宗羲定律"，即中国历史上，封建王朝为减轻、规范农民的赋税而推出的新政策，初期起一定作用之后，最终往往会变本加厉地加重农民负担。

建国以来，农业各税是我国重要税种之一，建国初期农业各税约占我国各项税收的30%左右，之后逐渐下降。根据财政部科学研究所相关测算，1949–1976年我国农民的农业税实际负担率在9.1%左右；1976–2000年，农业税的负担不断下降，但"三提五统"等各项杂项负担不断增加，2000年农民人均税负负担占农民收入的10.2%–12.2%之间。新世纪以来，党中央、国务院开始了以减轻农民负担为中心，取消"三提五统"等税外收费、改革农业税收为主要内容的农村税费改革，农民的税费负担开始逐步下降，2006年1月1日起废止《农业税条例》，取消除烟叶以外的农业特产税、全部免征牧业税。几千年"皇粮国税"成为历史，在我国农业税负历史上具有划时代的意义，迈出了统筹城乡发展的新步伐。自此以后，农业生产不仅不需纳税，还开始享受到越来越多的各种补贴，是粮食生产连年丰收的重要原因之一。

Agricultural Tax Becomes History

Chinese is a traditionally agricultural country, with agricultural tax having long taken significant positions in various dynasties. The Juntianzhi and the Two-tax system in Tang Dynasty, the Yitiaobian Method in Ming Dynasty and the Tandingrumu policies in Qing Dynasty were all the changed form of agricultural taxes. During the history of the feudal society, there were occasional periods of the reduced corvee and taxes, but failed to jump out of "Huang Zongxi's law" that the burden of farmers continued to become heavy. In China's history, new policies were put forward to reduce and standardize the farmers' taxes. But the effect was invariably quite preliminary and the policies tended to aggravate farmers' burden.

Since the founding of New China, the agricultural tax is one of the important taxes in our country. The agricultural taxes accounted for about 30% of all tax revenues in China and gradually declined afterwards. According to the scientific research evaluation from the Ministry of Finance Science Institute, the years from 1949 to 1976 witnessed the actual agriculture burden of the tax rate reached 9.1% for our country's peasants; the years from 1976 to 2000, the agricultural tax burden has been declining, but "three increases and five unifications" and other miscellaneous burden have increased the burden of farmers in 2000. The farmers' per capita tax burden accounted for 10.2%-12.2% in farmers' incomes. Since the new century, the Central Committee of CPC and the State Council began to concentrate on relieving the burden of farmers. Efforts were also made to abolish the "three increases and five unifications" and other taxes, and to implement the taxes reform surrounding the agricultural taxes. As a result, the taxes burdens began to decrease gradually. January 1, 2006 witnessed the abolishment of "agricultural tax regulations", canceling all the agricultural special duties apart from tobaccos and all the taxes on animal husbandry. The agricultural taxes which lasted for thousands of years have become history. This has the epoch-making significance in the history of China's agricultural tax, striding new step of balancing the urban and rural developments. Since then, the agriculture production is not required to pay, it also begins to enjoy more and more subsidies, which is one of the important reasons of grain production harvests in successive years.

图 13　1949-2013 年粮食产量
Grain Output, 1949-2013

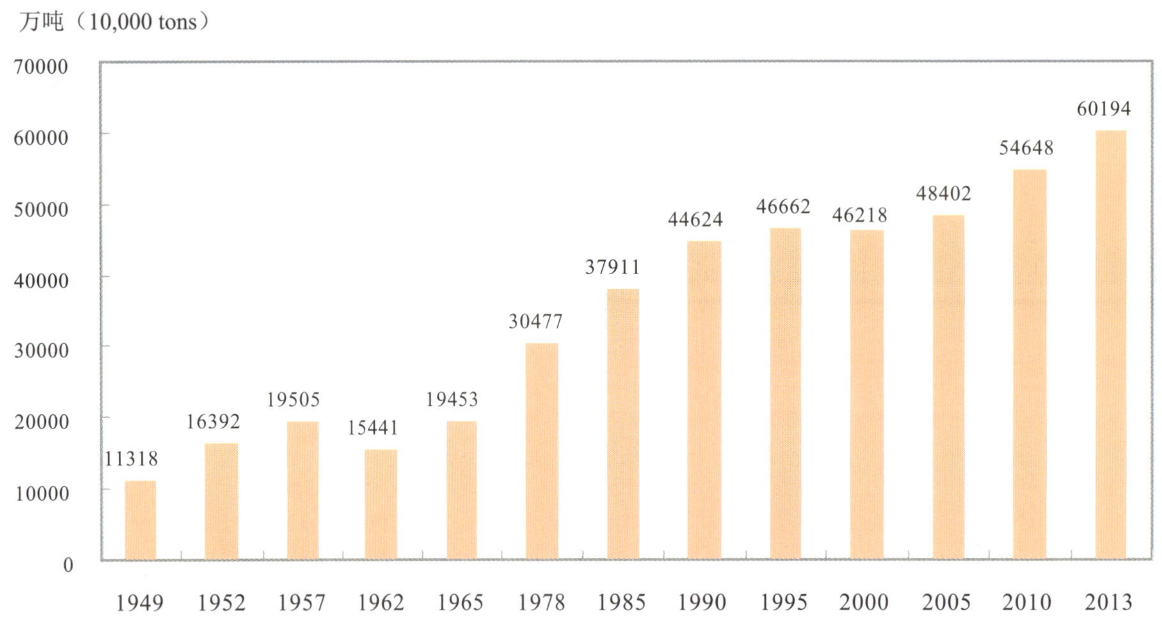

我国谷物生产能力登上万亿斤新台阶

改革开放以来，党中央、国务院坚持把"三农"作为全党和政府工作的重中之重，实行多项强农惠农政策扶持粮食生产，我国谷物产量2011年首次突破1万亿斤大关，达10388亿斤。2013年又突破1万1千亿斤大关，总产量达11054亿斤，比2008年增产1484亿斤，增长15.5%。从2009年到2013年，我国谷物平均年产量达到10357亿斤，表明生产能力已经达到1万亿斤水平。2013年稻谷产量达到4072亿斤，比2008年增产234亿斤，增长6.1%；小麦产量达到2439亿斤，比2008年增产189亿斤，增长8.4%；玉米产量达到4370亿斤，比2008年增产1051亿斤，增长31.7%。谷物生产能力登上万亿斤新台阶，自给率始终保持在95%以上，确保了"谷物基本自给，口粮绝对安全"的粮食安全目标的实现。

从增产因素看，一方面是受惠于国家持续粮食直补、良种补贴、农资综合补贴和农机购置补贴政策，同时国家对三大谷物实行最低价收购（临时收储）政策并逐年提高收购价格，农民种粮积极性空前高涨，千方百计扩大种植面积。另一方面，随着我国农业装备水平的提高，农业生产物质技术投入大幅度增加，农业生产条件得到大幅度改善。

New Step of 500 Billion Kilograms for Chinese Grain Production Capacity

Since the reform and opening up, the Party Central Committee and the State Council stick to the “Agriculture, Rural Areas and Farmers” policy, make it the top priority for the Party and the government work and implement a number of policies to strengthen agriculture and benefit farmers in order to support the grain production. In 2011, our grain output has topped 500 billion kilograms for the first time, reaching nearly 519.4 billion kilograms. In 2013, the total output grew to 552.7 billion kilograms, a 15.5% increase of 74.2 billion kilograms compared to 2008. From 2009 to 2013, the average annual grain output reached 517.85 billion kilograms, showing that our production capacity has reached the level of 500 billion kilograms. In 2013, rice output reached 20.36 billion kilograms, an increase of 11.7 billion kilograms to 2008, up by 6.1%; Wheat output reached 121.95 billion kilograms, an increase of 9.54 billion kilograms to 2008, up by 8.4%; Corn output reached 218.5 billion kilograms, an increase of 52.55 billion kilograms to 2008, up by 31.7%. The grain production capacity reached a new step of 500 billion kilograms. Self-sufficiency rate has been maintained at more than 95%, ensuring that the food safety goal of "basic self-sufficiency and absolute safety” can be realized.

From the production factors, on one side, due to the national sustainable food subsidies, seed subsidies, comprehensive agricultural subsidies and farm machinery purchase subsidy policy, and the implementation of the lowest bid for three grains (temporary storage) policy and increases in the purchase price year by year, the farmers' enthusiasm is all-time high, making every attempt to expand the planting area. On the other hand, with the improvement of China's agricultural equipments, material and technological input of agricultural production greatly increased. Agricultural production conditions have been greatly improved.

（二）工业生产能力迅速提升，工业品供给实现了从严重依赖进口到满足世界需求的历史性跨越。

解放初期，我国工业生产极为落后，不仅产品产量低，而且部门残缺不全，许多工业产品国内不能生产，完全依赖进口。党和政府从当时的国情出发，集中有限资源重点投向工业部门，一大批工业项目的开工建设拉开了中国工业化的序幕，我国工业发展驶入快车道。特别是改革开放后，我国工业发展迎来新的机遇，生产能力突飞猛进，技术水平和竞争力不断增强。

(2) A rapid increase in industrial production capacity has led to an historic leap from heavy dependence on imports for industrial supplies to satisfying world demand.

In the early days of liberation, China's industrial production was extremely far behind global levels. Not only was production output low, but the industrial sector's structure was also incomplete, and many industrial products could not be produced domestically, causing great dependence on imports. In order to alleviate this situation, the Party and government started to focus their limited resources on investment in key industrial sectors. The initiation of a large number of industrial construction projects opened the prologue for Chinese industrialization, putting China's industrial development on the fast track. Especially after the implementation of reform and opening up, China's industrial development ushered in new opportunities, advanced production capacity by leaps and bounds, and increased the country's level of technological ability and competitiveness.

主要工业产品供应由匮乏走向充裕。1949年，纱产量只有32.7万吨，2013年增加到3200万吨，增长96.9倍；布由18.9亿米增加到882.7亿米，增长45.7倍；原煤由0.32亿吨增加到36.8亿吨，增长114倍；粗钢由16万吨增加到77904万吨，增长4968倍。电视机、电冰箱、洗衣机、照相机、计算机、空调器等产品生产从无到有，在改革开放以后呈迅猛扩张之势。彩色电视机由1971年的0.02万台增加到2013年的12776万台，家用电冰箱由1956年的0.03万台增加到2013年的9261万台，房间空气调节器由1978年的0.02万台增加到2013年的13057万台。移动通信手持机和微型电子计算机从无到有，2013年产量分别达到14.6亿台和3.4亿台。

工业竞争力大幅提高。65年来，我国从一个落后的农业国成长为世界制造业大国，在能源、冶金、化工、建材、机械设备、电子设备和交通运输设备制造及各种消费品领域，形成了庞大的生产能力，“中国制造”的国际竞争力和影响力显著提高。根据联合国工业发展组织资料，目前我国工业竞争力指数在136个国家或地区中排名第七，制造业净出口居世界第一位。按照国际标准工业分类，在22个大类中，我国在7个大类中名列第一，钢铁、水泥、汽车等220多种工业品产量居世界第一位。一批具有国际竞争力的大企业迅速成长起来。2013年我国大陆企业进入《财富》世界500强达89家（含香港），总数位列美国之后居世界第二位。近年来，在国家政策扶持和带动下，我国工业转型势头良好，新能源、新材料、新医药等战略性新兴产业蓬勃发展，成为经济增长新亮点。

From shortage to an abundance of major industrial products. In 1949, the production of yarn was only 327 thousand tons; in 2013, it reached 32 million tons, an increase of 96.9 times, and the amount of cloth produced rose from 1.89 billion meters of to 88.27 billion meters over the same period, a 45.7-fold increase. Coal production grew from 32 million tons to 3.68 billion tons, an increase of 114 times; and crude steel production grew from 160 thousand tons to 779.04 million tons, an increase of 4,968 times. After the implementation of reform and opening up policy, the production of TV sets, refrigerators, washing machines, cameras, computers, air conditioners, and other home appliances rapidly grew from zero. The production of TV sets grew from 200 units in 1971 to 127.76 million units in 2013; refrigerator production grew from 300 units in 1956 to 92.61 million units in 2013; air conditioning unit production grew from 200 units in 1978 to 130.57 million units in 2013; mobile phones and mini-computer production developed from scratch, and in 2013, annual output of these products reached 1.46 billion units and 340 million units respectively.

Industrial competitiveness greatly improved. In 65 years, China grew from a lagging agricultural country into the world's manufacturing powerhouse. China has formed an enormous production capacity in the fields of energy, metallurgy, industrial chemicals, construction materials, machinery and equipment, electronic devices, transportation equipment manufacturing, and the production of a variety of consumer goods, significantly increasing the international competitiveness and influence of the “Made in China” moniker. According to UNIDO data, China's industrial competitiveness index currently ranks seventh in the among 136 countries or regions. In 2011, the total value of manufactured exports reached first in the world. According to the International Standard Industrial Classification, China ranks first in seven out of 22 sections; in the manufacturing of 220 kinds of industrial products, including steel, cement, and automobiles, China is ranked first in the world. A number of China's internationally competitive large enterprises grew rapidly. In 2013, 89 Chinese (including Hong Kong) enterprises were included in Fortune's Global 500; China ranked the second after the United States in the number of enterprises in this list. In recent years, under the support and guidance of national policy, China has experienced strong momentum in industrial restructuring, and strategic emerging industries such as new energy, new materials, and new medicines have flourished and became a new bright spot of economic growth.

图 14 1949-2013 年粗钢产量
Crude Steel Output, 1949-2013

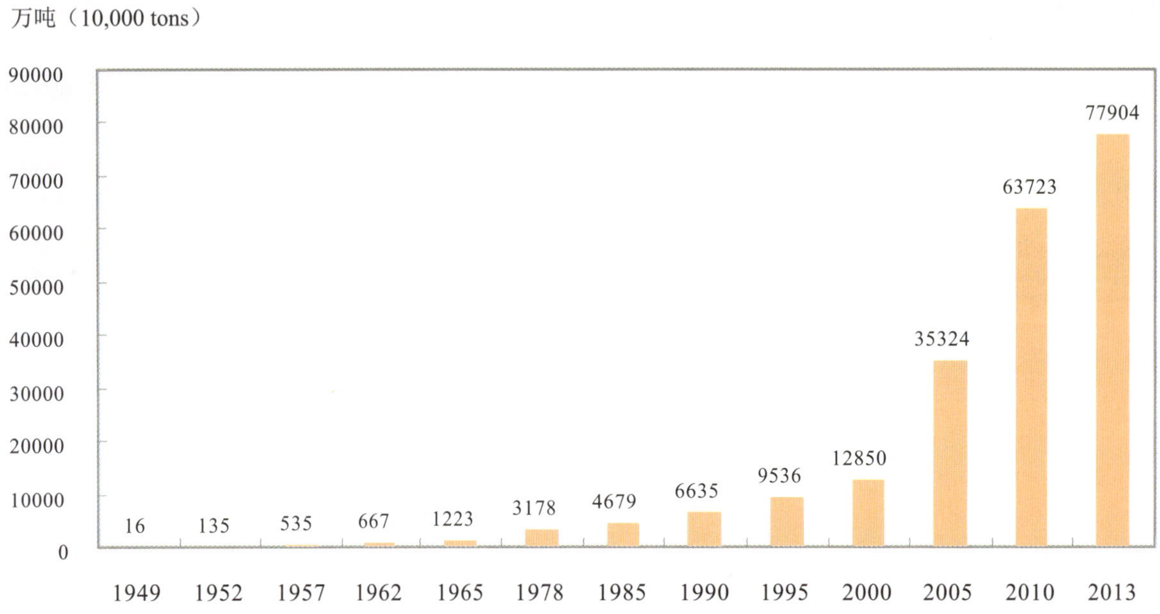

我国上榜世界 500 强企业的演变

美国《财富》杂志公布的数据显示，1996 年全球 500 强企业榜单中，中国内地（不包括香港和台湾地区，下同）仅有 2 家企业，分别位居 167 位和 338 位；2000 年，上榜企业数量上升到 9 家，最高位次为 58 位；2007 年，上榜企业超过 9 家，达到 22 家，最高位次为 17 位；2009 年后中国进入世界 500 强的企业数量迅速增加，2014 年，中国内地上榜的企业数量达到 91 家，并且首次有一家中国企业进入榜单前三甲。从数量来看，2014 年美国有 128 家，日本有 57 家，中国内地上榜企业数已经接近美国，远超日本。

Evolution of Chinese Enterprises on the List of World Top 500 Enterprises

According to the data published by the Fortune magazine in the US, in 1996's global top 500 enterprises list, Chinese mainland (excluding Hongkong and Taiwan area, the same below) only had 2 companies on the list, ranking 167 and 338 respectively. In 2000, the number of companies on the list rose to 9, the highest rank was 58. In 2007, more than 22 enterprises got on the list and number 17 at the highest. The number of the enterprises entering the top 500 worldwide increased dramatically. In 2014, the number of mainland enterprises on the list of the global top enterprises reached 91, and for the first time a Chinese enterprises successfully entered the top three. Statistically speaking, there are 128 American companies and 57 Japanese companies in 2014. The number of the Chinese mainland enterprises on the list is close to American counterparts, far more than the Japanese ones.

（三）服务业发展方兴未艾，对经济社会的支撑和带动作用日益突出。

建国以后，由于种种原因，第三产业一直是我国经济社会发展的一块“短板”。随着改革开放大幕拉开，我国工业化、城镇化进程快速推进，第三产业长期发展滞后的局面逐步得到改观，服务业体系不断完善，供给能力逐步提高，发展速度逐渐加快，目前已发展成为国民经济的第一大产业。

(3) Service industry development is rising, playing an increasingly prominent role in the support and promotion of economic and social development.

Since the PRC's founding, tertiary industry has always been a weak spot in economic and social development for various reasons. China's industrialization and urbanization process sped up with the beginning of reform and opening up, and China's tertiary industry's long-term lag gradually turned around. The service industry experienced continuous improvement, supply capacity gradually increased, and the pace of development accelerated, making tertiary industry the largest part of the national economy.

网络零售异军突起

自 1999 年 5 月〝中国电子商务第一人〞王峻涛创办〝8848〞涉水网络零售以来，在互联网、大数据、云计算等新一代信息技术的引领下，高效、便捷的网络零售异军突起，越来越成为消费者的普遍选择，到目前为止电子商务年交易规模突破 10 万亿元人民币，增速超过 30%，其中网络零售达到 1.85 万亿元，2013 年，中国网络购物用户规模达到 3.02 亿人，同比增长 24.7%，比 2006 年增长近 8 倍，年均增长率达到 36.9%，网购用户地域范围已从发达地区扩展到全国各地，我国已成为世界网络零售的第一大国。为应对网络零售的冲击，传统零售企业加快〝触网〞步伐，自建购物网站或加盟大型网购平台，开拓网络零售市场。苏宁云商推行〝一体两翼〞战略、万达集团拓展〝通用积分联盟〞，创新 O2O 模式，促进线上线下融合。展望未来，随着网络零售市场不断扩大，市场细分和多元化并重，火热的网络零售市场必将成为我国提振内需、扩大消费和解决就业的重要助力。

Online Retail as a Sudden New Rising Force

Since May, 1999 when "China's e-commerce founder" Wang Juntao launched the website of "8848" as a trial of online retail industry, the online retail, owing to its convenience and high efficiency has risen quickly as a new force. Under the guidance of the Internet, big data, cloud computing and other new generation of information technology, the online retail has increasingly become the popular choice for consumers. The trade volume has exceeded 10 trillion yuan up to now, with the annual growth rate of over 30%, among which the online retail reached 1.85 trillion yuan. In 2013, the users of the China's online shopping amounted to 302 million, an increase of 24.7% against the previous period, and an increase of nearly 8 times than the year of 2006, reaching an average annual growth rate at 36.9%. Online shopping users have expanded from developed regions to all parts of the country. China has become top in the world in terms of online retail. To deal with the impact of the online retail, the traditional retail enterprises accelerate the pace of "online access", by either building the shopping websites themselves or joining the large e-shopping platform to exploit the retail e-market. SuNing Electric Appliances puts forth "One body with two wings" strategy. Wanda Group expands "the overall integration alliance", creates the new O2O mode, and promotes the fusion of the online business with the offline business. Looking to the future, with the continuous development of network online retail market and the combination of the market segmentation and diversification, the hot online retail market will become an important driving force to boost China's domestic demand as well as create more jobs.

商业持续繁荣，市场规模不断扩大。经过 65 年的发展，我国已形成了多层次、多门类的商品市场体系和多种经济成份、多种市场流通渠道、多种经营方式并存的商品市场格局。2013 年，批发和零售业增加值 55672 亿元，比 1952 年实际增长 101.9 倍，年均增长 7.9%。社会消费品零售总额 237810 亿元，比 1952 年名义增长 858 倍，年均增长 11.7%。商品市场规模不断扩大，商业网点遍及全国。2012 年底全国批发和零售业法人单位达到 263.1 万个，住宿和餐饮业法人单位 18.7 万个。商业业态多样化、现代化，大型购物中心、超市、专卖店、便利店、折扣店、特许加盟店等呈现百花齐放、百业竞争的良好格局，网上购物等新业态不断涌现，迅猛发展。2014 年上半年，全国网上零售额 11375 亿元，同比增长 48.3%，相当于社会消费品零售总额的 9.2%。

Business continues to boom and markets have continued expanding. After 65 years of development, China has formed a multi-level market commodity system, as well as a commodity market with a variety of economic sectors and a variety of integrated market distribution channels.In 2013, the wholesale and retail industry's total added value was 5.5672 trillion yuan, showing a real increase of 101.9 times over 1952, with an average annual growth rate of 7.9 percent. Total retail sales of consumer goods reached 23.781 trillion yuan, an increase of 858 times compared with 1952, with an average annual growth rate of 11.7 percent. The scale of the commodity market continued to expand into business chains throughout the whole country. By the end of 2012, the number of wholesale and retail industry corporate units nationwide reached 2.631 million; the number of accommodation and catering industry units reached 187,000. Business formats have been diversified and modernized, and shopping malls, supermarkets, specialty stores, convenience stores, discount stores, franchise stores, and other retail outlets have flourished. A good pattern of better business competition emerged while online and other new shopping formats have rapidly developed. In the first half of 2014, the total sales volume of national-level brand online retail stores reached 1.1375 trillion yuan, showing an increase of 48.3 percent, accounting for 9.2 percent of total retail sales of consumer goods.

图 15　1952-2013 年社会消费品零售总额
Total Retail Sales of Consumer Goods, 1952-2013

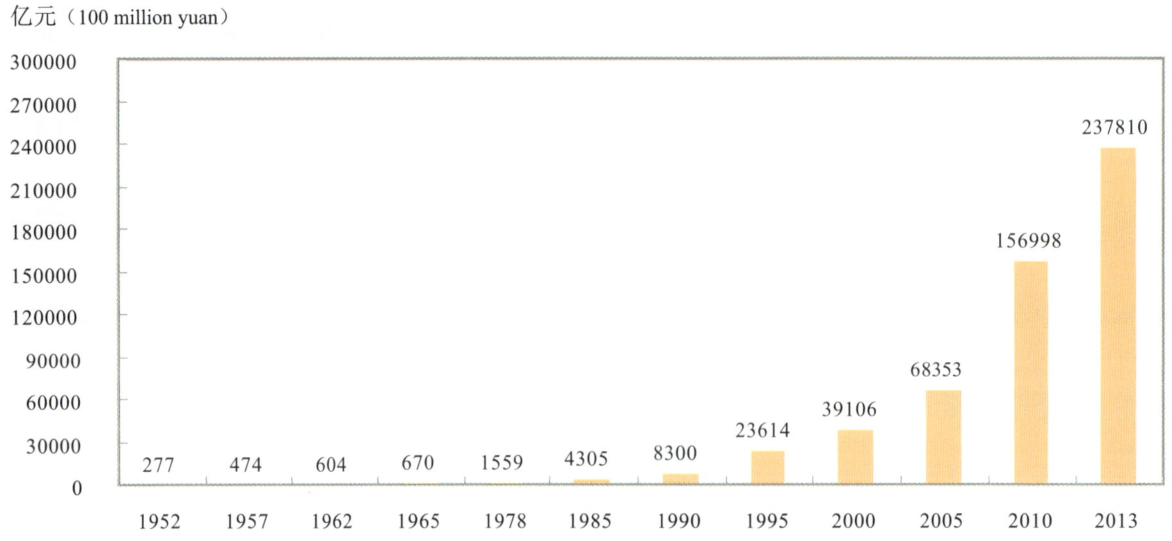

交通邮政服务能力迅速提高，保障了经济社会发展，方便了人民生活。2013年，交通运输、仓储和邮政业增加值27283亿元，比1952年实际增长159倍，年均增长8.7%。2013年，客运量212亿人，比1949年增长154倍，年均增长8.2%；旅客周转量27572亿人公里，增长176.9倍，年均增长8.4%；货运量410亿吨，增长218倍，年均增长8.8%；货物周转量168014亿吨公里，增长651.5倍，年均增长10.7%。近年来，随着网上购物和电子商务的兴起，邮政业快递业务迅猛发展。2013年，完成快递业务量91.9亿件，比1990年增长2675倍，年均增长40.9%，快递最高日处理量突破6000万件。

Transportation and postal service capabilities have been rapidly increasing, ensuring economic and social development and making people's lives easier. In 2013, the value added output of transportation, warehousing, and postal service industry was 2.7283 trillion yuan, showing a real increase of 159 times over the 1952 number, with average annual growth reaching 8.7 percent. In 2013, passenger traffic in China reached 21.2 billion people, 154 times more than the 1949 volume, with an average annual growth of 8.2 percent; revenue passenger-kilometers reached 2.7572 trillion, an increase of 176.9 times with an average annual growth rate of 8.4 percent; cargo volume amounted to 41 billion tons, an increase of 218 times with an average annual growth rate of 8.8 percent; freight turnover was 16.8014 trillion ton-kilometers, an increase of 651.5 times with an average annual growth rate of 10.7 percent. In recent years, with the rise of online shopping and e-commerce, the courier business has rapidly developed. In 2013, the number of packages sent via courier reached 9.19 billion, 2677 times more than the number sent in 1990, with an average annual growth of 40.9 percent. The highest daily delivery volume exceeded 60 million packages.

小快递，大民生

近几年，随着发展环境不断优化和电子商务迅速崛起，快递业务保持高速增长态势，成为国内发展潜力较大的新兴服务业之一。2006–2013 年，快递业务量年均增幅高达 36%，业务收入年均增幅达到 25%，其中，2013 年快递业务量连续十二个月以超过 60% 以上的增长速度高速发展，当年规模以上快递企业业务量累计完成 91.9 亿件，比上年增长 61.6%；快递企业完成业务收入 1441.7 亿元，增长 36.6% 。

从 2009 年开始，每年的 11 月 11 号，由于大型电子商务网站都会利用这一天来进行大规模的打折促销活动，电商企业的销售额呈现百倍增长态势，也成为监测我国快递行业服务能力的关键时点。国家邮政局监测数据显示，2013 年 11 月 11 日当天，主要电商企业共产生快递订单约 1.8 亿件，几家大型快递企业快递业务量均突破 1000 万件。11 日至 16 日短短 6 天时间里，全行业共揽投快件 3.46 亿件，比上年同期增长 73%，是日常处理量的 230%；最高日处理量达到 6517 万件，比上年增长 85%，是日常处理量的 260%。

Small Express Delivery, Vital People's Livelihood

In recent years, with the constant optimization of the development environment and the quick rise of e-commerce, the express delivery business keeps increasing rapidly, making it one of the new and emerging service industries with great development potential in China. From 2006 to 2013, the express business volume achieved an average annual growth rate as high as 36%, the business income reached an average annual increase of 25%, of which the express business' volume increased over 12 months by over 60%. The business volume of the enterprise above designated size totaled 9.19 billion, an increase of 61.6% over the previous year; the express delivery companies' business revenue achieved 144.17 billion yuan, with an increase of 36.6%.

From the beginning of 2009, the 11th of November every year, because of fact that the large e-commerce websites will use this day to carry out the large-scale discount promotion activities, the business enterprise sales has showed a hundred times growth, and has become a key point in monitoring the service capacity of China express delivery industry. From the State Postal Bureau's monitoring data show that on November 11, 2013, the main e-commerce companies achieved a total express order of about 180 million pieces, the business volume of several large express delivery enterprises achieved a breakthrough of 10 million pieces. During the short span of 6 days from 11st to 16th, the whole industry handled 346 million pieces, increasing by 73% than the same period in last year, and the daily processing capacity is 230% than the usual; the maximum daily processing volume reached 65.17 million, an increase of 85% over the previous year, and 260% of the daily processing volume.

图 16　1990–2013 年快递包裹件数

Pieces of Express Mail Services, 1990-2013

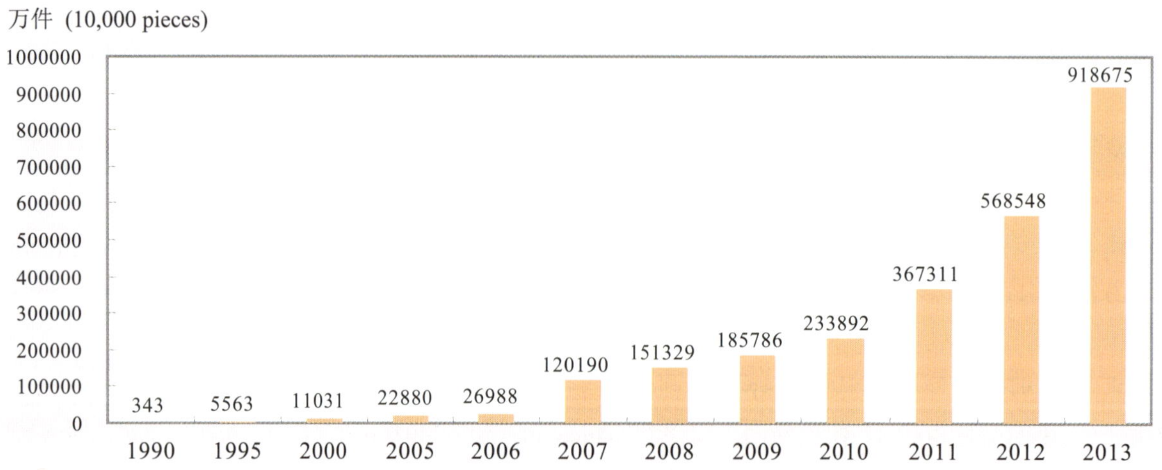

金融、房地产等新兴服务业迅速发展壮大，成为经济发展的新引擎。2013年，金融业增加值33535亿元，比1952年实际增长389.8倍，年均增长10.3%。2013年底，金融机构人民币各项贷款余额71.9万亿元，比1952年增长6656倍；保险公司原保险保费收入17222亿元，比1994年增长44.8倍。2013年，房地产业增加值33295亿元，比1952年实际增长143.4倍，年均增长8.5%。1981-2013年，全社会房屋竣工面积总计604亿平方米，商品房供给能力显著增强。近年来，伴随着我国新型工业化进入新的发展时期，研发设计、营销售后、法律服务、检验检测、会计、广告等生产性服务业蓬勃发展，旅游、文化、养老、教育、医疗、家政等生活性服务业发展方兴未艾，服务业日益成为带动我国经济增长的新引擎。

The rapid growth of financial, real estate and other new services has become a new engine of economic development. In 2013, the value added of the financial industry amounted to 3.3535 trillion yuan, 389.8 times more than the industry's value in 1952, with an average annual growth rate of 10.3 percent. By the end of 2013, financial institutions' RMB loans had reached 71.9 trillion yuan, 6,656 times more than in 1952; insurance companies' income from premiums accounted for 1.7222 trillion yuan, 44.8 times more than in 1994. In 2013, the value added of the real estate industry was 3.3295 trillion yuan, 143.4 times more than in 1952, with an average annual growth rate of 8.5 percent. The total area of residential housing completed between 1981 and 2013 was 60.4 billion square meters, significantly enhancing commercial housing supply capacity. In recent years, as China's new industrialization process has entered a new period of development, research and development, marketing, sales, legal services, inspection, accounting, advertising, and other producion services have boomed. Consumer services in fields such as tourism, culture, pensions, education, healthcare, and housekeeping have continued to expand, making the service industry the new engine driving China's economic growth.

图 17　1981-2013 年全社会房屋竣工面积
Floor Space of Buildings Completed of the Whole Country , 1981-2013

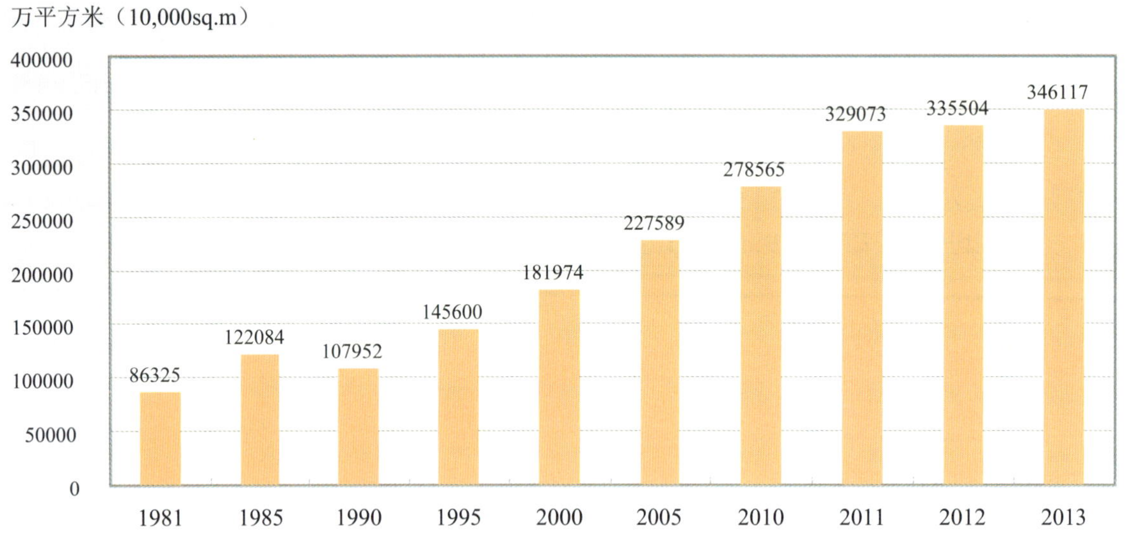

图 18　1991-2013 年股票发行筹资额
Raised Capital by Share-Issued, 1991-2013

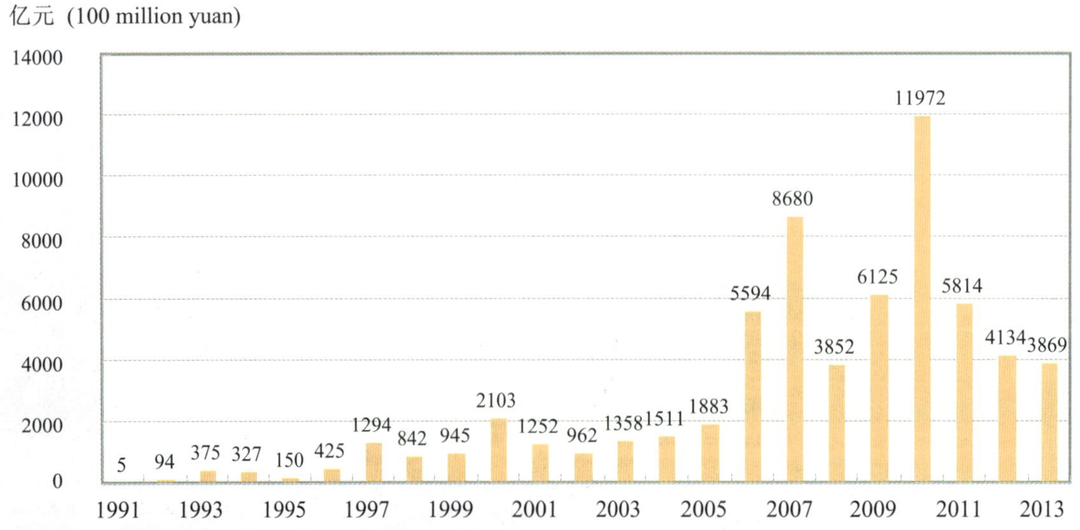

图 19 1994-2013 年保费收入

Premium of Insurance Companies, 1994-2013

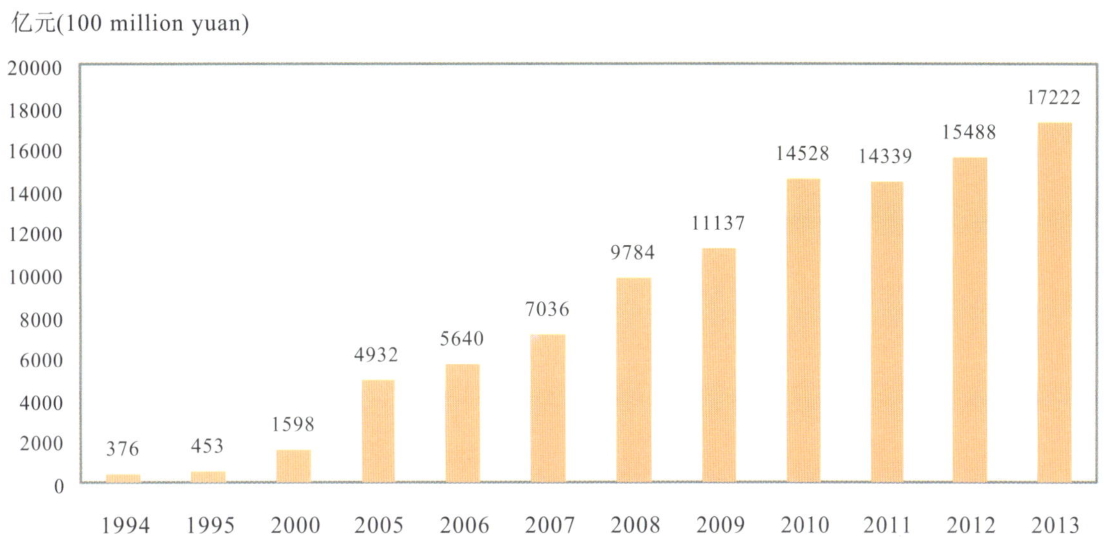

图 20 1952-2013 年金融机构人民币存贷款余额

Deposit and Loan of Financial Institutions, 1952-2013

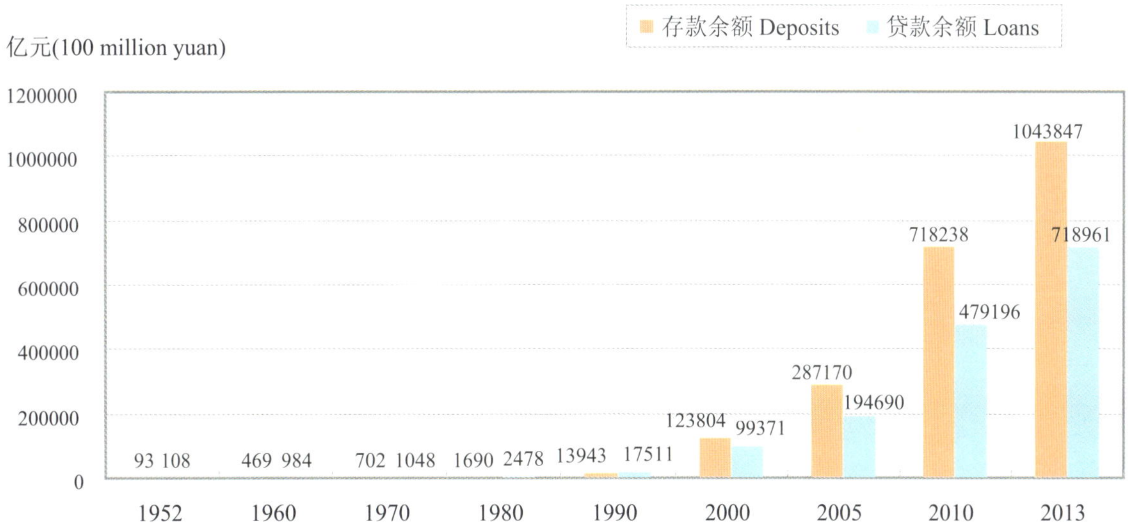

保障房建设

中国政府坚持不懈的民生工程。它通常是政府为中低收入住房困难家庭提供限定标准、限定价格或租金的住房，一般由廉租住房、经济适用住房和政策性租赁住房等构成，这些住房有别于完全由市场形成价格的商品房。截至 2012 年底，全国累计开工建设城镇保障性安居工程 3400 多万套，基本建成 2100 多万套；累计支持农村危房改造及游牧民定居工程 1100 多万户。2013 年，全国共开工建设城镇保障性安居工程 666 万套，基本建成 544 万套；实施农村危房改造 281 万户、游牧民定居工程 5.1 万户、渔民上岸工程 2.8 万户。保障性安居工程，对于促进经济增长、改善民生、扩大消费等都具有重要意义。一是有利于改善城市低收入居民的居住条件，促进社会和谐稳定。二是有利于改善城乡居民消费环境，扩大消费。三是有利于增加住房有效供应，分流商品住房市场需求，促进房地产市场健康发展。

Security Housing Construction

The Chinese government persists in the Security Housing Construction. It is usually the houses with reasonable standards and limited price or rentals that the government provides for the low-incomers of housing difficulties. They are generally composed of low-cost housing, affordable housing and policy-oriented rental housing, etc. These are different from the commercial residential buildings fully controlled by the market price of commercial housing. By the end of 2012, the number of the total town supportability projects under construction has reached over 340 million sets nationwide, basically 210 million of them almost finished. The number of the accumulation to support rural reconstruction of the dangerous houses and the settlement project of the nomads reached about 110 million. In 2013, China started the construction of urban housing projects of more than 6.66 million sets, and 5.44 million sets of them are already completed; implementing the rural reconstruction of the dangerous houses for more than 2.81 million, 51 thousand settlement projects for nomads and 28 thousands fishermen returning to the homeland. The protection housing construction is of great significance to promote the economic growth, improve people's livelihood, and expand consumption etc. Firstly, it is conducive to improving the living conditions of low-income residents and promoting the social harmony and stability. Secondly, it is helpful to improve the consumption environment of urban and rural residents, and expand consumption. The third point is to increase the effective supply of housing, diversifying the commercial housing market demand streaming to promote the healthy development of the real-estate market.

4 从"瓶颈"制约到优势支撑 基础设施和基础产业实现跨越式大发展

From "bottleneck" constraints to the advantages of support, infrastructure and foundational industries achieved huge leaps in development

新中国成立以来的65年，是农业、能源、交通、邮电通信等瓶颈制约不断缓解的65年，是基础产业体系逐步建立完善并形成比较优势的65年，也是我国基础设施和基础产业发展取得质的飞跃的65年。

The 65 years since the founding of the People's Republic of China have seen 65 years of the continuous easing of bottleneck constraints in agriculture, energy, transportation, mail and telecommunications, 65 years of gradual improvements in the basic industrial system and the formation of comparative advantages, and 65 years of making qualitative leaps in infrastructure and the development of basic industries.

（一）农业基础设施投入增加，农业生产条件不断改善。

新中国成立时，我国的农田水利设施十分薄弱，根本无法抵御频发的自然灾害，农业发展机械化水平较低，主要靠人畜力开展农业生产。面对困难局面，国家不断加大投入，大力兴建农田水利工程，改善农业生产条件，提高农业机械化水平，夯实农业发展基础，推动了农业生产稳定增长。

(1) Increase in investments in agricultural infrastructure and improvements in agricultural production conditions.

When the PRC was founded, the country's agricultural irrigation facilities were very weak and were unable to withstand frequent natural disasters. Agricultural mechanization was also very low, and agricultural production was mainly dependent on human and animal power. Faced with such difficulties, the state continuously increased investment, vigorously building agricultural irrigation facilities, improving agricultural production conditions, and raising the level of agricultural mechanization in order to create a solid foundation for agricultural development and to promote the steady growth of agricultural production.

农田水利基础设施建设不断加强。建国之初，我国仅有22座大中型灌溉水库、7.1万千瓦的机械排灌动力、2.4亿亩的灌溉面积，农业基础十分薄弱。政府积极兴建中小型水利设施，形成了遍布全国多数农村的以中小型水库、机井（水塘）以及灌溉渠网为主的水利基础设施体系。改革开放以来，继续对农田水利进行重点安排、常抓不懈，支持引水调水、骨干水源、江河湖泊治理、高效节水灌溉等重点项目，我国农田水利建设得到了跨越式发展，防洪、防涝、抵御自然灾害的能力明显增强。2013年，我国共有大中型水库4461座，水库总库容量8298亿立方米，堤防长度27.5万公里，堤坊保护面积4031.7万公顷。全国有效灌溉面积由1952年的1996万公顷扩大到2013年的6347万公顷。

Construction of agricultural irrigation infrastructure continued to strengthen. At the time of the founding of the PRC, China only had 22 large and medium-sized irrigation reservoirs, 71,000 kilowatts of mechanical power devoted to irrigation, and 240 million Mus of irrigated area, so the country's agricultural base was very weak.

The government built small and medium-sized irrigation facilities and formed an irrigation infrastructure system with small and medium-sized reservoirs, motor-pumped wells, and a primary network of irrigation channels. Since the adoption of reform and opening up policy, key aspects of the irrigation water conservation system were maintained, persistently supporting water drawing and transfer, maintenance of backbone water courses, rivers and lakes administration, efficient water-saving irrigation and other key projects. China's agricultural irrigation construction experienced a leap forward in development, significantly enhancing the country's ability to prevent floods and resist natural disasters. In 2013, China had a total of 4,461 medium and large-sized water reservoirs with a total capacity of 829.8 billion cubic meters, the length of dikes reached 275,000 km, and the total area of land protected by dikes was 40.317 million hectares. The total amount of effectively irrigated land expanded from 19.96 million hectares in 1952 to 63.35 million hectares in 2013.

图21 有效灌溉面积，1952-2013

Irrigated Area, 1952-2013

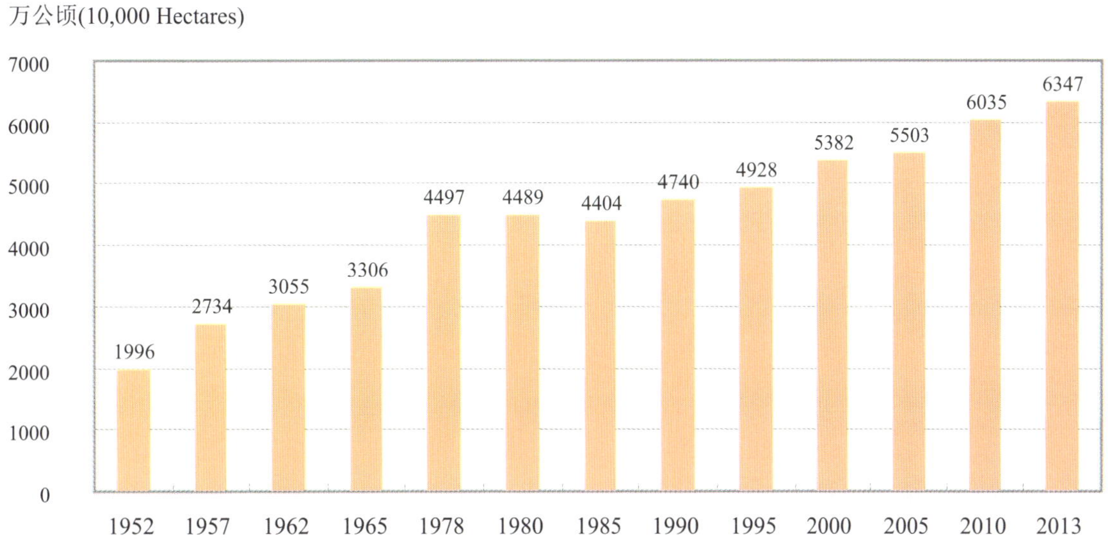

农业机械化程度不断提高。农业机械化是由传统农业向现代农业转变的必由之路，有利于提高土地产出率、资源利用率、劳动生产率，增强农业综合生产能力。65年来，我国农业机械化从无到有，发展很快。1952年农业机械总动力只有18万千瓦，2013年增加到103907万千瓦。大中型拖拉机、联合收割机等分别从1978年的55.7万台、1.9万台提高到2013年的527万台和142万台。2013年，耕种收综合机械化水平59%左右，基本实现了农业生产方式从人畜力为主向机械化为主的历史性转变。“三夏”期间，全国小麦机收率超过92%，黄淮海地区夏玉米机播水平达90.8%。

The level of agricultural mechanization continues increasing. Mechanization is the only way to transition into a modern agricultural system which improves land productivity, resource utilization, labor productivity, and overall agricultural production capacity. In the past 65 years, China's agricultural mechanization grew rapidly from scratch. In 1952, the total power used by agricultural machinery was only 180 thousand kilowatts, but by 2013 this level had increased to 1,039.07 million kilowatts. The number of large and medium-sized tractors and combines increased from 557 thousand units and 19 thousand units respectively in 1978 to 5.27 million units and 1.42 million units in 2013. In 2013, over 59 percent of agricultural operations had undergone mechanization, making a historical change from agricultural production dependent on people and animal power to mechanized agricultural production. In the "three summer" period, the proportion of China's wheat yield harvested by machine reached 92 percent; in Huanghe-Huaihe-Haihe area, the proportion of summer corn sown by machine reached 90.8 percent.

图22 1952-2013年农业机械总动力
Total Power of Agricultural Machinery, 1952-2013

（二）能源产品产量大幅增加，基础保障作用显著增强。

65年来，我国能源生产能力由弱变强，不仅终结了"贫油"、"缺电"历史，而且一跃成为世界第一大能源生产国；能源生产结构不断优化，清洁能源和可再生能源生产量在能源生产总量中的比重逐步提高；能源运输建设取得突出成绩，能源供给保障能力明显提高。

主要能源产品产量大幅度增加。1949年，我国能源生产总量只有2374万吨标准煤，2013年达到34亿吨标准煤，比1949年增长142倍，年均增长8.1%。同期，我国能源消费总量年均增长6.8%，略低于能源生产增速，能源总自给率达到90%。原煤产量由1949年的0.32亿吨扩大到2013年的36.8亿吨，增长114倍，居世界第一位；

(2) Energy production output sharply increased, basic safety functions significantly enhanced.

Over the past 65 years, China's energy production capacity has grown from weak to strong, not only ending its history of "oil insufficiencies" and "electricity shortages," but also becoming the world's largest energy producer. The energy production structure continued to be optimized, and the proportion of clean energy and renewable energy in total energy production gradually increased. Outstanding achievements have been made in energy transfer infrastructure, significantly improving the security of the country's energy supply.

Substantial increase in primary energy production output. In 1949, China's total energy production was limited to 23.74 million tons of standard coal; by 2013, it reached 3.4 billion tons of standard coal, 142 times more than in 1949, with an average annual growth rate of 8.1 percent. In the same period, China's energy consumption grew at an average of 6.8 percent annually, slightly lower than the energy production growth rate, and the country's energy self-sufficiency rate reached 90 percent. China's coal production output expanded from 32 million tons in 1949 to 3.68 billion tons in 2013, a 114-fold increase, ranking first in the world; crude oil production

原油产量由 12 万吨扩大到 2.09 亿吨，增长 1741 倍，居世界第四位；发电装机容量由 185 万千瓦扩大到 12.5 亿千瓦，增长 673 倍，发电量由 43 亿千瓦小时增加到 53976 亿千瓦小时，增长 1254 倍，居世界第一位。

能源生产初步形成了以煤炭为主体、电力为中心、石油天然气和可再生能源全面发展的新格局。我国是以煤炭为主要能源的国家，煤炭工业在国民经济中占有非常重要的地位，建国以来原煤占能源生产总量的比重基本保持在 70% 以上。随着经济和技术水平提高，我国煤炭工业勘探、开采技术和装备水平显著提高，煤炭产量连续多年稳居世界第一。与此同时，我国石油和天然气工业快速发展，逐渐成为具备先进科技装备、专业配套的现代化能源生产部门，形成了较为完整的勘探开发技术体系，复杂段块勘探开发、提高油田采收率等方面的技术已达国际领先水平。改革开放后，我国的水电、核电、

increased from 120,000 tons to 209 million tons, a 1,745-fold increase, ranking fourth in the world; power generators' capacity expanded from 1.85 million kilowatts to 1.25 billion kilowatts, an increase of 673 times. Generating capacity increased from 4.3 billion kilowatt-hours to 5.3976 trillion kilowatt-hours, an increase of 1,254 times, ranking first in the world.

Initial patterns of energy production formed around coal and electricity generation at the center, but new patterns give prevalence to oil, natural gas, and the comprehensive development of renewable energy. China is a country where coal is the main source of energy, so the coal industry has a very important position in the national economy. Since the country's founding, coal proportion has continuously accounted for more than 70 percent of total national energy production. With improvements in the country's economic and technological development, China's coal exploration, mining technology, and coal-mining equipment have significantly improved, leading to China ranking first in the world in coal production for many years; China's oil and gas industry also rapidly developed, gradually forming a modernized energy production sector with advanced technological equipment and professional support. A relatively complete exploration and technology development system has formed, rolling out

风电、太阳能等新能源、可再生能源和清洁能源得到迅速发展。先后建成葛洲坝、三峡等大型水电站，核电从无到有，建立浙江秦山、广东大亚湾、江苏田湾三个核电基地，风电、太阳能发电等近年来增长较快，水电、核电、风电等清洁能源和可再生能源生产量在能源生产总量中的比重大幅提高，由1978年的3.1%提高到2013年的10.9%。

能源运输大动脉建设取得巨大成就。我国能源资源主要集中分布在中西部地区，能源运输建设成为能源供应保障的重要环节，重载铁路、港口建设、西气东输、西电东送等重点工程极大缓解了地区经济发展与能源需求之间的矛盾。1988

exploration and development innovations, increasing oilfield output rates and other aspects of mining and exploration technology to reach an advanced international level. After the adoption of reform and opening up policy, China's hydropower, nuclear energy, wind energy, solar energy, and other renewable and clean energy sectors rapidly developed. Gezhouba and Three Gorges, etc. large hydropower stations have been built in succession; the nuclear energy developed from scratch and has culminated in the building of three nuclear energy power plants in Qinshan in Zhejiang province, Daya Bay in Guangdong province, and Tianwan in Jiangsu province. The growth of wind and solar power has greatly increased in recent years; total energy production from hydropower, nuclear power, wind power and other clean and renewable energy sources increased from 3.1 percent of total energy production in 1978 to 10.9 percent in 2013.

Great achievements have been made in the construction of energy transportation arteries. China's energy resources are mainly scattered throughout its central and western regions. Energy transport infrastructure thus became an important part of energy supply security, and heavy rail, port construction, western natural gas transfer to the east, western electric power transfer to the east, and other key projects greatly eased the imbalances between regional economic development and energy demand. After the construction of China's first electrified heavy railway

图23　1949-2013年能源生产总量
Total Production of Energy, 1949-2013

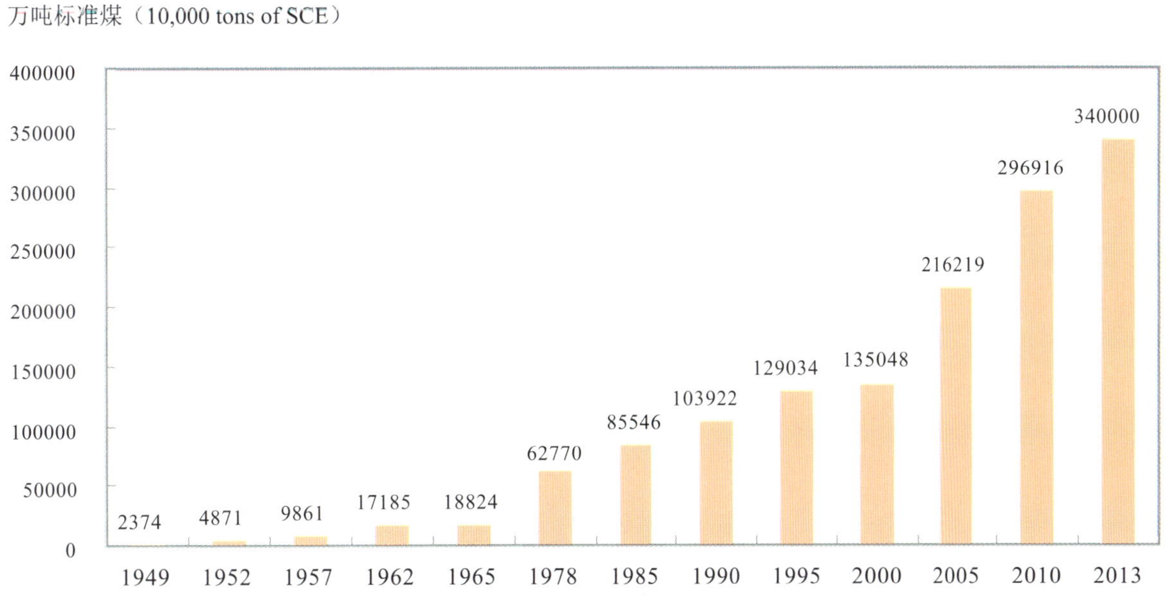

页岩气革命

页岩气是指赋存于富有机质泥页岩及其夹层中，以吸附和游离状态为主要存在方式的非常规天然气，成分以甲烷为主，是一种清洁、高效的能源资源。目前，页岩气在全球油气资源领域异军突起，形成勘探开发的新亮点。加快页岩气勘探开发，已经成为包括美国在内的世界主要页岩气资源大国和地区的共同选择。美国由于率先在开采技术上取得突破并快速形成生产能力，推动了美国原油和天然气产量大幅增长，降低了美国对进口能源的依赖程度，并引发了对美国能源独立前景的探讨，被称为"页岩气革命"。据统计，2000 年，美国页岩气产量仅占天然气总量的 1%。而到 2010 年，因为水力压裂、水平钻井等技术的进步，页岩气所占的比重已超过 20%。美国能源信息局预测，到 2035 年，美国 46% 的天然气供给将来自页岩气。加拿大是第二个对页岩气进行勘探开发的国家，除供应本国外，还可以增加对欧洲和亚太地区的供应；在欧洲，波兰、德国、奥地利、匈牙利、波兰、西班牙等国家页岩气的勘探开发已取得重大进展；亚太地区，印度、印尼、澳大利亚以及南美洲的阿根廷和哥伦比亚，还有非洲的南非等国也在积极开展页岩气勘探开发，都取得了明显的进展。

我国页岩气资源潜力巨大。2011 年，国土资源部完成了首次页岩气资源潜力评价，结果表明，我国页岩气可采资源潜力为 25 万亿立方米（不含青藏区），与我国陆域常规天然气相当，与美国的 24 万亿立方米相近。加快发展页岩气，对改变我国油气资源格局，甚至改变整个能源结构、缓解我国油气资源短缺、保障国家能源安全、促进经济社会发展，都有十分重要的意义。 2013 年 10 月，国家能源局发布了《页岩气产业政策》，引起了广泛的积极响应。总的来看，虽然我国页岩气勘探开发起步较晚，与美国差距较大，存在诸多不利因素，但开局良好，呈现出了积极的发展态势。

Shale Gas Revolution

Shale gas is an unconventional natural gas in organic-rich shale and interlayers in absorbed and free forms. As methane is the main component, shale gas is a clean and efficient energy resource. At present, shale gas has sprung up rapidly in global oil and gas resources, and shale gas exploration becomes a new highlight in exploration and development. Accelerating the exploration and development of shale gas has become the common choice of the world's major shale gas resource-rich countries and regions including the U.S. The United States has made breakthroughs in exploitation technology and developed high production capacity and the crude oil and natural gas production grew substantially. The United Stated was less dependent on imported energy. It initiated a heated discussion named "shale gas revolution" on the prospect of US energy independence. It's estimated that, in 2000, the US shale gas production only accounted for 1% of the natural gas. While in 2010, thanks to the technological advances in hydro fracture and horizontal drilling, the proportion has been over 20%. According to the US Energy Information Administration, by 2035, 46% of the natural gas supply will come from shale gas. Canada is the second country to explore and develop shale gas, which not only serves domestic needs, but also increases supplies to Europe and Asia-Pacific region. Many countries, such as European countries, Poland, Germany, Austria, Hungary, and Spain have made significant progress in the exploration and development of the shale gas. India, Indonesia, Australia in Asia-Pacific region and Argentina, Columbia in South America, and South Africa are also active in the exploration and development. Remarkable progress has been made in this regard.

The shale gas resources in China have great potential. In 2011, Ministry of Land and Resources evaluated the shale gas resources recoverable potential for the first time. As the result shows that, the shale gas resources recoverable potential amount to 25 trillion cubic meters (the Qinghai Tibet Region not included), which is equivalent with our land conventional gas, and close to the US 24 trillion cubic meters. Accelerating the development of shale gas is of great significance for upgrading the structure of oil and gas resources, and even changing the whole energy structure, alleviating the oil and gas resources shortage, safeguarding the national energy safety and promoting the economic and social development. In October 2013, the National Energy Administration released "Shale Gas Industrial Policy" which has sparked a wide range of positive responses. In general, although China started late in shale gas exploration, lagged far behind US, and there were many unfavorable factors, we have made a good start and seen a positive development trend.

年修建完成的西起山西大同东至秦皇岛港的我国第一条电气化重载铁路，是我国重要的煤炭运输线。秦皇岛港是我国“北煤南运”大通道的主枢纽和国家能源进出口重要港口，是迄今为止世界最大煤炭输出港和散货港，也是世界上最大的现代化生态型煤炭码头群，年吞吐量超过 2 亿吨。西气东输一线工程全长 4200 公里，是我国目前建成的距离最长、管道最大、压力最高、输气量最大、技术含量最多输气管道工程，年输气量 120 亿立方米。电网建设进入大规模跨省跨区送电和全国互联的新阶段，总投资超过 5000 亿元的西电东送工程，是在我国电力建设史上投资规模最大的电源、电网建设工程，极大地提高了我国电力输配能力。

was completed from Datong in western China's Shanxi province to Qinhuangdao port in the east in 1988, it became an important coal transport line. Port Qinhuangdao is the main hub of China's largest north- south coal shipping channel and the country's most important energy export and import port. It is by far world's largest coal export port and bulk cargo port, and also has one of the largest clean coal docks in the world with an annual loading and unloading volume of 200 million tons. A 4200 kilometer pipeline for the transfer of western gas to the east is currently China's largest gas pipeline project, covering the longest distance and having the largest volume of pipelines, the highest pressure, the biggest volume of gas transmission, and the most advanced technological content. The annual capacity of the pipeline is 12 billion cubic meters. Electrical network construction entered a new stage of large-scale cross-provincial and trans-regional power transmission and national interconnection, and 500 billion yuan has been invested in a project intended to transfer western-generated electricity to the east. It is the biggest project in China's history of electrical power construction, and electrical network construction projects have greatly improved China's electricity transmission and distribution capacity.

西部大开发的标志性建设工程——西气东输

“西气东输”工程是拉开西部大开发序幕的标志性建设工程，投资规模仅次于长江三峡工程。它主要运用天然气管道将我国西部地区的塔里木、柴达木、陕甘宁和四川盆地蕴藏着的丰富天然气资源运送到需求量较大的东部地区，实现优势互补。

“西气东输”工程共分为三线，一线工程全长4200公里，西起新疆塔里木油田，依次经过新疆、甘肃、宁夏、陕西、山西、河南、安徽、江苏和浙江，最终到达上海，途经10个省区市共66个县区。项目投资为1200亿元，上游气田开发、主干管道铺设和城市管网总投资超过3000亿元。一线工程已于2004年建成投产，年供气能力迄今已逾120亿立方米。二线工程是我国首条引进境外天然气资源的战略通道工程，西起新疆的霍尔果斯，途经全国15个省区市、192个县级单位，止于香港，工程全长8704公里，于2010年全部建成投产，年输气量300亿立方米。三线工程包括1条干线、8条支线，配套建设3座储气库和1座液化天然气应急调峰站，沿线经新疆、甘肃、宁夏、陕西、河南、湖北、湖南、江西、福建和广东10个省区，总长度为7378公里，设计年输气量300亿立方米。工程建设总投资1250亿元，计划2015年全线贯通。

西气东输工程把西部地区的资源优势转化为经济优势，促进和加快了西部及沿线地区的经济发展，有效保护了东部地区的生态环境，经济和社会效益十分显著。

West-East Gas Transmission-- the Landmark Construction Project of West Development

"West-East Gas Transmission" is the landmark project to open the prologue of the West Development project. The scale of investment only ranks after the Three Gorges Project. It mainly uses natural gas pipeline to transport the natural gas from China's western gas-rich regions such as Tarim, Qaidam, Shaanxi Gansu and Sichuan Basin to the eastern regions in much energy demand, thus realizing the complementary advantages.

"West-East Gas Transmission" project is divided into three lines, the first line project has the full-length of 4200 kilometers, starting from the west of Xinjiang Tarim Oilfield, followed by Xinjiang, Gansu, Ningxia, Shaanxi, Shanxi, Henan, Anhui, Jiangsu and Zhejiang, to the final end in Shanghai. It goes through a total of 66 counties in 10 provinces and municipalities. The investment of the project is 120 billion yuan, with the upstream gas field development, the main pipeline and piping in city accounting for a total investment of over 300 billion yuan. The first-line project has been completed and put into production in 2004. The annual gas transmission capacity so far is more than 12 billion cubic meters. The second project is the first strategic passage project of offshore natural gas resources in China's introduction of the foreign natural gas resources. It starts from Huoerguosi in Xinjiang, passing through 15 provinces and 192 county-level units, ending in Hong Kong. The total length reaches 8704 kilometers. 2010 marked the completion and production. The annual gas transmission capacity is 30 billion cubic meters. The third-line project consists of 1 main lines and 8 branches, with 3 supporting gas reservoirs and 1 liquefied natural gas emergency peak shaving station, along the Xinjiang, Gansu, Ningxia, Shaanxi, Henan, Hubei, Hunan, Jiangxi, Fujian and Guangdong 10 provinces with a total length of 7378 kilometers. The designed annual gas transmission has the capacity of 30 billion cubic meters. The total investment is 125 billion yuan. The project is planned to finish in 2015.

West-East gas pipeline project transforms the resource advantages in the western region into economic advantages, promoting and accelerating the economic development of the areas along the western region and the effectively protecting the ecological environment of the eastern area. The economic and social benefits are very significant.

西电东送工程

西电东送工程是西部大开发的重点骨干工程和标志性工程之一。实施西电东送是由我国能源资源和电力负荷的不均衡性决定的。我国地域辽阔，能源资源分布极不均匀，煤炭资源的69% 集中在〝三西〞地区（即山西、陕西和内蒙古西部）和云南、贵州，水能资源的 77% 分布在西南和西北地区。经济较发达的东部沿海地区能源资源匮乏，用电负荷却相对集中。开发西部的水电和煤炭资源，实施西电东送是变西部资源优势为经济优势，满足东部地区电力需求，促进东、西部地区协调发展的重要举措。

西电东送工程主要由南、中、北三大通道构成：南部通道主要将贵州乌江、云南澜沧江和桂、滇、黔 3 省区交界处的南盘江、北盘江、红水河的水电资源，以及黔、滇两省坑口火电厂的电能开发出来送往广东；中部通道则主要将三峡和金沙江干支流水电送往华东地区；北部通道主要将黄河上游水电和山西、内蒙古坑口火电送往京津唐地区。截至 2008 年底，西电东送三大通道送电能力已达 6318 万千瓦，其中，南通道 2018 万千瓦，中通道 1750 万千瓦，北通道 2550 万千瓦。

West-East Power Transmission Project

West-east power transmission project is one of the major western development project and a key project at the same time. The implementation of power transmission from west to east is determined by the imbalance of energy resources and electric power in our country. Our country is vast in territory, but the resources distribution is extremely uneven. 69% of the coal resources is concentrated in "3 West" areas (Shanxi, Shaanxi and West Inner Mongolia) and Yunnan, Guizhou. 77% of the water resource is concentrated in the southwest and northwest regions. East areas along the eastern coast are strong in economy but weak in resources, and electricity load is relatively concentrated. The development of the Western hydropower and coal resources, the implementation of power transmission from west to cast aims at changing resource advantages to economic advantages in order to meet the demand for electricity demand of the east and west. This is an important measure to promote the coordinated development of regions.

West-east power transmission project is mainly composed of the south, middle and north channels. The south channel mainly directs the hydropower from Wu River in Guizhou and Lancang River in Yunnan as well as the hydropower from the Nanpan River and Beipan River, Hongshui River which are located in the joint areas of Guangxi, Yunan and Guizhou.

The electricity produced from pithead power plants from Guizhou and Yunan will also be transmitted to eastern part of China. The central channel mainly transmits the water electricity produced from the Three Gorges and Jinsha River to East China. The North Channel mainly transmits the hydropower from upper Yellow River and the thermal electricity from Shanxi, Inner Mongolia pithead power plants to the Beijing, Tianjin and Tangshan. By the end of 2008, three major channels of the West-east power transmission's capacity has reached 63.18 million kilowatts, of which the south channel transmits 20.18 million kw, the central 17.50 million kw and the north 25.50 million kw.

（三）交通运输建设突飞猛进，由铁路、公路、民用航空、水运和管道组成的综合运输网络四通八达。

建国初期我国交通运输非常落后，民间运输工具主要以畜力车和木帆船为主，广大内地处于十分封闭的状态。65 年来，我国交通运输状况发生了翻天覆地的变化，多种运输方式组成的综合运输网络逐步形成，运输装备技术水平显著提高，不仅满足了经济持续快速增长的需要，也大大方便了人民群众的生活。

以铁路为骨干，公路、水运、民用航空和管道组成的综合运输网日益完善。1949 年，全国公路里程仅为 8.08 万公里，其中铺有路面的仅占 40%；铁路营业里程仅 2.18 万公里；内河航道 7.36 万公里，其中等级航道仅 2.42 万公里；民航线路 1.13 万公里，仅

(3) The transportation network has advanced by leaps and bounds with an integrated network of railways, highways, civil airways, waterways, and pipelines.

In the early days after the founding of PRC, China's transportation system was very backward. Civil transportation mainly consisted of animal-drawn vehicles and wooden sailboats, while most inland areas were closed off. Over the past 65 years, transportation in China has undergone a tremendous change: an integrated transportation network comprised of a variety of transport modes has gradually formed, significantly improving the level of transportation equipment and technology to not only meet the needs of rapid and sustained economic growth, but also to greatly improve living standards.

With railways as the backbone, an integrated transportation network of highways, waterways, civil airways and pipelines has emerged. In 1949, the number of kilometers of national highway totaled 80,800, only 40 percent of which was paved. There were only 21,800 kilometers of rail. There were 73,600 kilometers of inland waterways, but only 24,200 kilometers of rating waterways. The entire

图 24 1949-2013 年铁路营业里程
Length of National Railways in Operation, 1949-2013

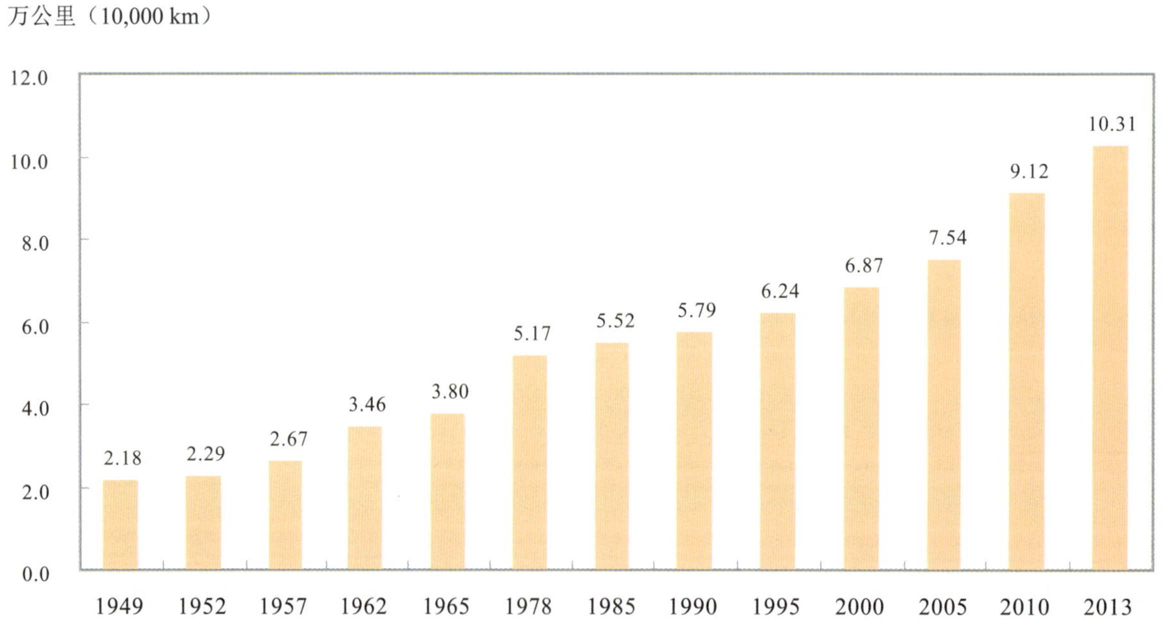

有 12 架小型飞机、12 条短程航线和 30 多个只能起降小型飞机的简易机场。经过 65 年的发展，我国交通网络不断完善，运输能力明显增强，运输效率显著提高，有力地支撑了经济发展。2013 年，铁路营业里程达到 10.31 万公里，比 1949 年增长 3.7 倍，居世界第二位；公路里程 435.62 万公里（不含村道），增长 53.0 倍，其中高速公路从无到有，迅速发展，总长度已达到 10.4 万公里，位居世界第二；内河航道通航里程 12.6 万公里，增长 71.2%。民用航空已开通 2876 条国际国内航线，航线里程达到 410.6 万公里。输油（气）管道里程由 1958 年的 0.02 万公里增加到 2013 年的 9.85 万公里。沿海主要港口货物吞吐量由 1985 年的 3.1 亿吨增加到 2013 年的 72.8 亿吨，增长 22.5 倍，连续多年居世界第一。

country had just 12 small aircraft operating 12 short-haul flights covering a total distance of 11,300 kilometers, while there were only 30 or so very basic airports only equipped to handle small aircraft. Over the past 65 years, China's transportation network has been continuously improved, transportation capacity significantly increased and efficiency improved, which has greatly supported the country's economic development. By 2013, the national railway increased 3.7 times in length compared to 1949 to 103.1 thousand kilometers, also ranking second in the world. The length of China's national highways had increased 53 times over 1949 to 4.3562 million kilometers, including 104 thousand kilometers of new highways, ranking second in the world. The aggregate length of inland waterways totaled 126 thousand kilometers in length, an increase of 71.2 percent over 1949 figures, while civil aviation has boomed to 2,876 international and domestic routes covering 4.106 million kilometers. Oil and gas pipelines increased from 200 kilometers in 1958 to 98.5 thousand kilometers in 2013. Volume of freight handled at China's coastal ports increased from 310 million tons in 1985 to 7.28 billion tons in 2013, an increase of 22.5 times, to rank first in the world.

图 25　1952–2013 年民航航线里程

Length of Civil Aviation Routes, 1952-2013

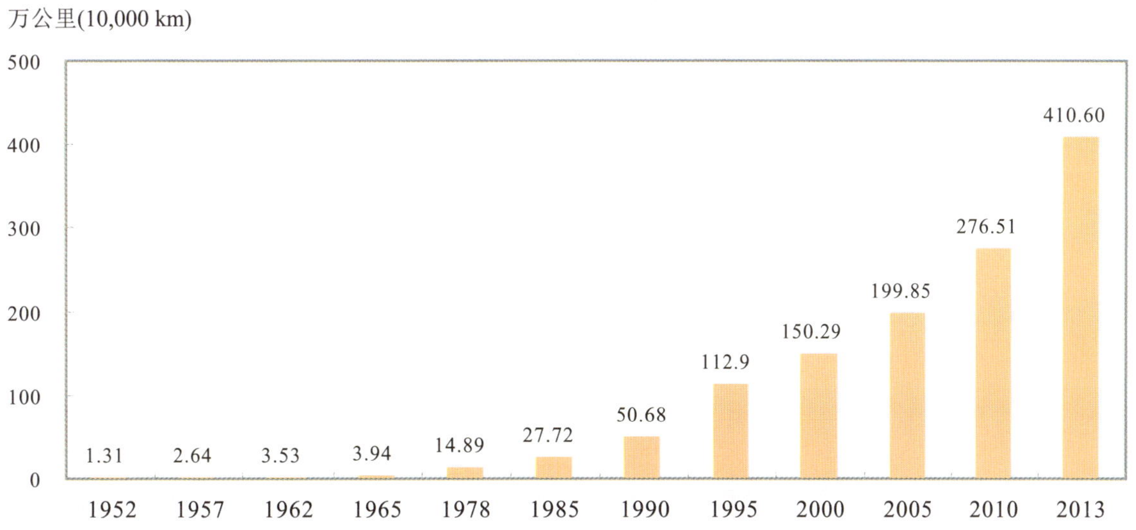

图 26 1949-2013 年公路里程
Length of Highways, 1949-2013

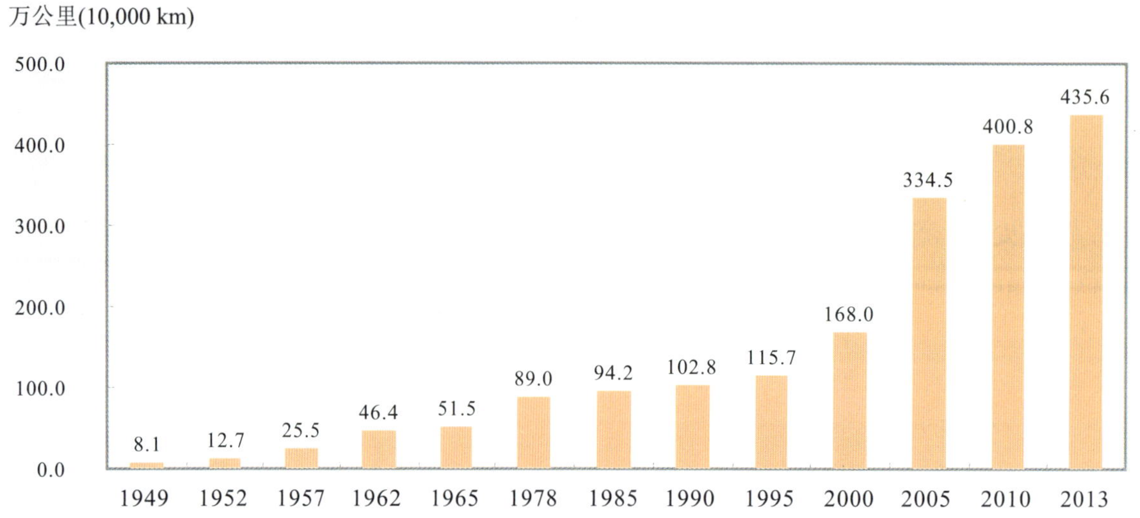

图 27 1990-2013 年高速公路里程
Length of Expressway, 1990-2013

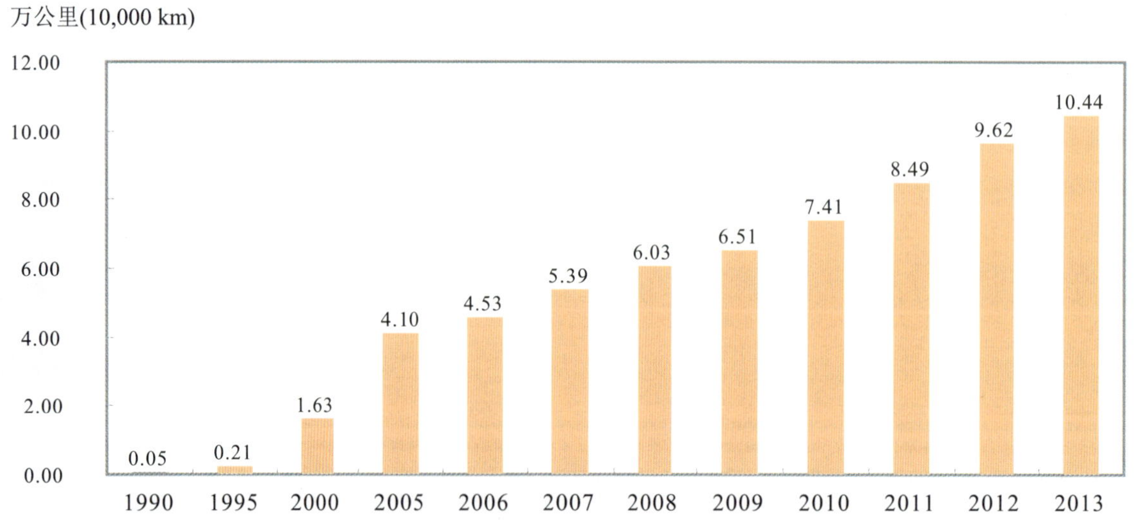

中国铁路跨入高铁时代

2013 年，随着宁杭、厦深、西宝、武咸、柳南、郫彭等高铁线路建成投产，我国已运营高铁达 34 条，总里程突破 11000 公里，覆盖北京、上海、天津、广州、黑龙江、陕西、四川、海南等 21 个省市，是目前世界上高铁运营里程最长的国家。

2003 年 5 月 29 日，铁道部向国家发展和改革委员会上报了《中长期铁路网规划方案建议(2003—2020 年)》，计划到 2020 年，我国新建高速铁路达 1.6 万公里以上，形成以"四纵四横"高铁为主骨架，由客运专线、城际铁路和快速客货线路构成的快速客运网总规模达到 5 万公里以上，基本覆盖 50 万以上人口城市。照此规划，从 2002 年 12 月 31 日我国第一条速度 250km/h 秦沈客专开通到 2013 年十年时间，我国高铁实现了从 0 到 10000 公里的跨越；特别是 2009 年以来的五年，高铁里程以年均 75.0% 的增长速度快速发展，到 2013 年末达到 11028 公里，占世界高铁总里程一半多，覆盖了 160 多个地级以上城市。长三角、珠三角、环渤海三大城市群高铁已连片成网，规划中的四纵已经全部贯通。

高速铁路作为现代化交通出行工具，具有安全可靠、方便快捷、运力强大、节约能源和绿色环保等优势，随着高铁大面积的投入运营，为铁路运输、旅客出行、时间效益等多方面带来深刻变化。截至 2013 年底，铁路每天开行固定旅客列车 2358 对，其中高铁动车组列车 1235 对，占旅客列车开行总量的 52%；高铁客运量 52962 万人，占全国铁路客运量的 25%。高速铁路的开通不仅便利了旅客的出行，也有效缓解了货运能力长期紧张的局面。此外，高铁让新时代的"中国制造"绽放出耀眼光辉，彰显了我国的经济和技术实力。我国高铁建设正走出国门、走向世界，得到越来越多国家和世界人民的广泛认可，为世界经济建设及发展做出贡献。

Chinese Railway into the High-Speed Rail Era

In 2013, with Ningbo-Hangzhou, Xiamen-Shenzhen, Xi'an-Baoji, Wuhan-Xianning, Liuzhou-Nanning, Pixian-Pengzhong and other High-speed Rail lines were completed and put into production, China had 34 high-speed rails in operation. The total mileage has reached 11000 kilometers, covering Beijing, Shanghai, Tianjin, Guangzhou, Heilongjiang, Shanxi, Sichuan, Hainan and other 21 provinces and cities. Now China is the nation with the world's longest operation mileages of High-speed Rails.

In May 29, 2003, the railway ministry reported "medium and long-term railway network plan (year 2003-2020)" to the national development and Reform Commission, planning that by 2020, China's new high-speed railway will have reached more than 16000 kilometers, that with the "four verticals and four horizontals" high-speed rails as the main skeleton, the high-speed fast passenger transport network which is consisted of passenger lines, inter-city railways and fast passenger lines will have reached above 50,000 kilometers in scale and basically covered cities with over 500,000 residents. According to this plan, in the past 10 years from Dec. 31, 2002 when China's first passenger line with its speed over 250 km/h—Qinhuangdao-Shenyang Passengers Railway was opened, to 2013, the number of China's high-speed rails have leaped from 0 to 10,000 kilometers. Especially in the past five years since 2009, the high-speed rail mileages developed rapidly at an average annual growth rate of 75%, reaching 11028 kilometers at the end of 2013, which is over half of that in the world. It covered over 160 cities at the prefecture level or above. The High-speed Rails in the three big city groups of the Yangtze River Delta, the Pearl River Delta, and the Bohai Rim have already connected into a network. The planned "four verticals" have been all through.

As a modern transportation tool, high-speed railways are safe, reliable, convenient, fast, strong in capacity, energy-saving and clean. With the high-speed railway put into general use, it has brought profound changes to many aspects, such as railway transportation, passenger travel, time efficiency, etc. By the end of 2013, the railway have run 2358 fixed passenger train daily, including 1235 High-speed Rails, 52% of the total passenger trains; with a passenger volume of 529.62 million people, accounting for 25% of the national railway passenger volume. The high-speed rail can not only facilitate passenger's travel, but also effectively alleviate the tense situation of freight capacity for a long time. Besides, high-speed rail makes "Made in China" shine with radiance, and highlights our country's economic and technological power. High-speed Rail construction in China is going out of the country, to the world. It has been widely recognized by more and more countries and people of the world, making contributions to the construction and development of the world economy.

交通运输设施和装备水平步入世界先进行列。上海磁悬浮示范运营线路的成功投产，标志着我国交通正在迅速向以高技术集成为显著特征的现代运输方式迈进。高速铁路飞速发展，2013 年高铁运营里程突破 1 万公里，居世界第一位。客车、货车和机车的制造水平大幅提升，生产出时速高达 350 公里的动车组列车，标志着我国铁路运输达到国际先进水平，从根本上扭转了我国铁路列车运行速度长期在低水平徘徊、不适应市场需求的局面。铁路重载技术取得突破，达到世界先进水平，铁路主要干线普遍开行了 5000-6500 吨货物列车，极大提高了我国铁路货物运输能力。

（四）邮电通信业快速发展，现代信息通信基础网络初步建成。

建国初期，我国邮电通信网络规模小、设备陈旧、技术落后，工作效率极低。经过 65

Transport facilities and equipment have approached world-class levels. The successful demonstration of the maglev line in Shanghai is representative of China's rapid advancement into modern transportation through high-tech features. The national high-speed rail system has developed rapidly, and in 2013 it had a total length of 10,000 kilometers, the largest system of its type in the world. The manufacture of passenger cars, vans, and locomotives has also dramatically increased, with the production of EMU trains capable of speeds up to 350 km marking the fact that China's rail transport system has reached an advanced world-class level able to meet market demand. China's freight rail technology has also reached an advanced level, and China's main trunk railway lines generally handle 5,000 to 6,500 tons of cargo trains, greatly improving China's rail cargo capacity.

(4) The rapid development of a postal and telecommunications industry forms the beginnings of a modern information and communications network.

In the early days after the founding of the People's Republic, China's postal and telecommunications network was small and inefficient and used outdated equipment and

年特别是改革开放以来的大规模投资建设，我国邮电通信能力迅速增强，网络规模容量、技术层次、服务水平都实现了跨越式发展，全国邮电业务总量从1949年的2.58亿元增加到2013年的18432亿元，年均增长高达17.0%，有力推动了国家工业化和信息化发展，有效满足了广大人民群众的通信需求。

邮政基础设施水平全面提升。建国初期，全国（除西藏）只有26328处邮电局所，邮路总长度仅70.6万公里，而且这些设施大都设在城市，广大农村地区用邮极为困难。1978年，邮政营业网点达到49623处，比1949年增长88.5%。改革开放后，邮政业发展突飞猛进，形成了沟通城乡、覆盖全国、连通世界的现代邮政网络，成为世界规模最大的邮政网络之一。2013年底，我国邮政营业网点达到

backward technologies. After 65 years of large-scale investment and construction and particularly since economic reform and opening up, China's postal and telecommunications capabilities grew rapidly, and its network capacity, technical level and service level leap-frogged. National postal and telecommunications services increased from 258 million yuan in 1949 to 1.8432 trillion yuan in 2013, with an average annual growth rate of 17.0 percent, strongly promoting national industrialization and the development of information technology and effectively meeting the country's communications needs.

Postal infrastructure has improved. After the founding of the People's Republic, China (excluding Tibet) had only 26,328 post offices and 706,000 kilometers of postal routes. Most of these facilities were located in cities, so it was extremely difficult to find post offices in rural areas. By 1978, the number of post offices had grown to 49,623, an increase of 88.5 percent over the 1949 number. Following economic reforms, China's postal industry developed by leaps and bounds into a modern postal network for communication in both urban and rural areas, domestically and internationally, and it became one of the world's largest postal networks. By the end of 2013, the number of post offices in China totaled 125,000, 3.8 times the number there were in 1949. Postal routes now total 5.897 million kilometers in length, an increase of

12.5 万处，比 1949 年增长 3.8 倍；邮路总长度 589.7 万公里，增长 7.4 倍；全国平均每一营业网点服务面积 76.7 平方公里，比 1949 年下降 79%；每一营业网点服务人口 1.09 万人，比 1949 年下降 48.1%。

电信业综合通信能力迅速提高。我国已建成包括光纤、数字微波、卫星、程控交换、移动通信、数据通信等覆盖全国、通达世界的公用电信网。2013 年电话普及率 109.9 部／百人，长途光缆线路长度达到 89 万公里，全国局用交换机容量达到 41089 万门，比 1949 年增长 1317 倍。固定电话用户达到 26699 万户，比 1949 年增长 1224 倍。移动电话用户从无到有，由 1988

7.4 times, while the average coverage of each office decreased by 79 percent compared to the 76.7 square kilometers covered by each office in 1949. Each post office now serves 10900 people on average, 48.1 percent less than in 1949.

Integrated telecommunications capabilities rapidly increased. China has built a public telecommunications network with national and global coverage incorporating optical fiber, digital microwaves, satellites, program-controlled exchange, mobile and data communications. In 2013, telephone penetration reached 109.9 phones per 100 people, and long-distance fiber optic lines totaled 890,000 kilometers. National bureaus using switchboards reached 410.89 million, 1,317 times the 1949 number. The number of fixed-line telephone subscribers reached 266.99 million, an increase of 1,224 times over 1949. The number of mobile phone users grew from 3,000 in 1988 to 1.22911 billion in 2013, of which 401.61 million were using 3G. Mobile phone switchboard capacity also reached 1.97 billion. Since the start

图 25　1949-2013 年电话普及率（含移动）
Telephone Penetration Rate (including Mobile Phone), 1949-2013

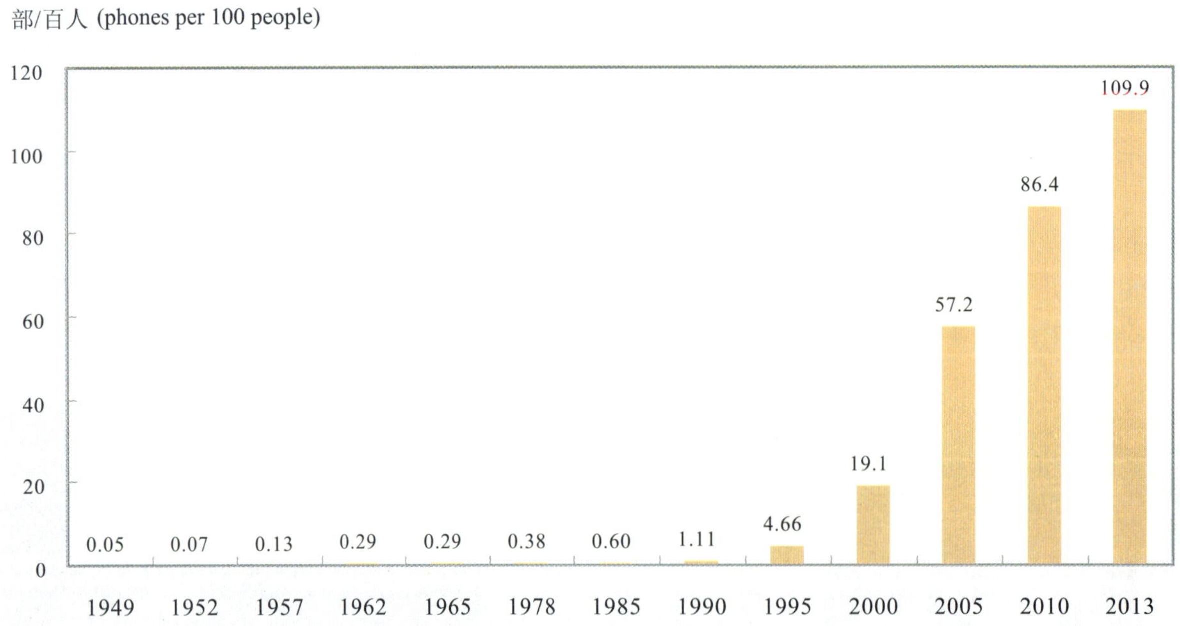

年的 0.3 万户增加到 2013 年末的 122911 万户，其中 3G 移动电话用户 40161 万户，移动电话交换机容量达到 19.7 亿户。新世纪以来多媒体通信飞速发展，互联网规模不断壮大，信息化进程明显加快。2013 年，互联网宽带接入端口 35945 万个，比 2003 年增长 18.9 倍，年均增长 34.9%。我国互联网上网人数达到 6.18 亿人，居世界第一位，手机上网人数 5.0 亿人，互联网普及率达到 45.8%。

of the 21st century, multimedia communications have developed rapidly, internet use has grown continuously, and the informatization process has significantly accelerated. In 2013, the number of internet broadband connection access ports reached 359.45 million, 18.9 times more than in 2003, amounting to an average annual growth rate of 34.9 percent. The number of internet users reached 618 million, ranking first in the world, while the number of internet users on mobile phones reached 500 million. The internet penetration rate was 45.8 percent.

图 29 1997-2013 年互联网上网人数
Number of Internet Users, 1997-2013

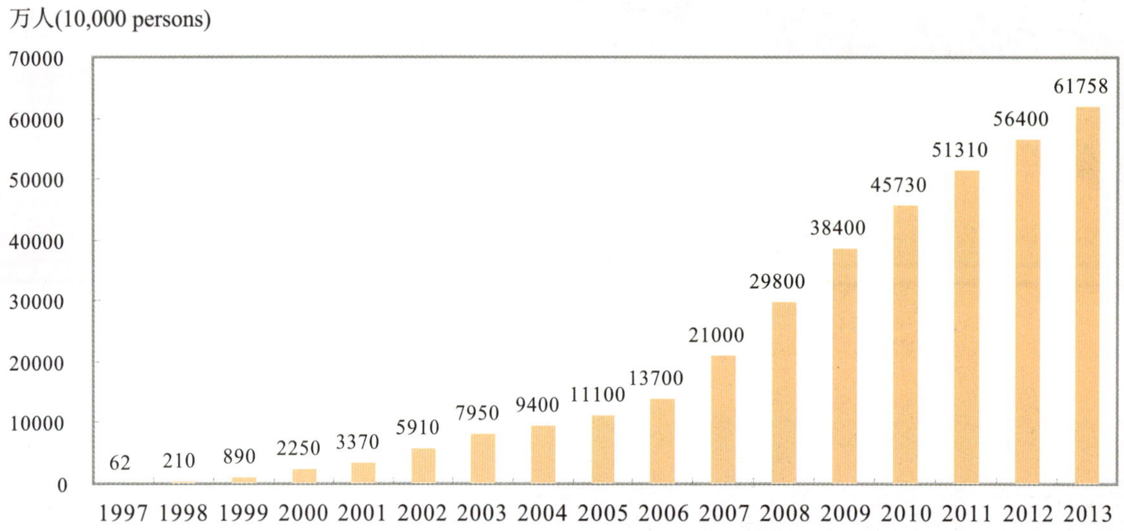

“宽带中国”战略

2013 年 8 月 1 日，国务院发布了《关于印发“宽带中国”战略及实施方案的通知》，宽带网络首次成为国家战略性公共基础设施，标志着“宽带战略”从部门行动上升为国家战略。“宽带中国”战略旨在加强战略引导和系统部署未来 8 年宽带发展目标及路径，推动我国宽带基础设施快速健康发展。按照“宽带中国”战略确定的发展目标，到 2015 年，初步建成适应经济社会发展需要的下一代国家信息基础设施；到 2020 年，我国宽带网络基础设施发展水平与发达国家之间的差距大幅缩小，国民充分享受宽带带来的经济增长、服务便利和发展机遇。发展宽带网络对拉动有效投资和促进信息消费、推进发展方式转变和小康社会建设具有重要支撑作用。

“Broadband China” Strategy

On August 1, 2013, the State Council released “Notice on the Issuance of ‘Broadband China’ Strategy and Implementation plan”. The broadband network has become the national strategic infrastructure for the first time, indicating that the “Broadband Strategy” has risen from a departmental move to a national strategy. “Broadband China” Strategy is aimed at strengthening strategic guidance, systematically deploying the goals and paths of broadband development in the next 8 years and promoting the healthy and rapid development of the broadband infrastructure in China. The “Broadband China” strategy sets the goals that by 2015, the preliminary next-generation national information infrastructure fit for economic and social development will have been set up; by 2020, the development gap between developed countries in the broadband network infrastructure will have been narrowed greatly. Citizens will have enjoyed the economic growth, convenient services and development opportunities brought by the broadband. Developing broadband network has significant supporting role in promoting effective investment, information consumption, and the transformation in development mode and the building of a well-off society.

从封闭半封闭到全方位开放 对外开放取得举世公认的伟大成就

5 China has made universally-acknowledged achievements on its path from a closed and semi-closed economy to one open to the outside world.

新中国成立以来的65年，是我国对外贸易规模持续扩大、质量不断提升的65年，是积极参与全球化进程、从大规模“引进来”到大踏步“走出去”的65年，也是对外经济合作步伐明显加快、与世界共同发展的65年。

（一）货物贸易规模不断扩大，进出口总额跃居世界第一。

建国之初，我国对外贸易规模小，贸易

In the 65 years since the founding of the People's Republic of China, the country has upgraded both the scale and quality of its foreign trade, adopting “drawing in” and “moving outwards” strategies in its active participation in globalization, quickening the pace of its international economic cooperation and collaborative development.

(1) Scale of trade in goods expanded, and import and export volumes rank first in the world

China's foreign trade was small in scale, and featured a small number of trade partners that often traded in a single

伙伴少，贸易方式和贸易商品单一，基本上处于封闭半封闭状态。随着我国加强同第三世界国家的联系和经贸往来，贸易规模缓慢增长。70 年代，我国在联合国合法席位得到恢复，与西方发达国家全面建交，对外经贸发展加快。1978 年改革开放以来，特别是 2001 年我国正式加入世界贸易组织（WTO）后，对外贸易总量迅速增长，在世界贸易中的位次持续提升。

货物进出口总额快速增长。1950 年，我国货物进出口贸易总额仅为 11.3 亿美元，1973 年突破百亿美元，1978 年为 206.4 亿美元，1988 年突破千亿美元，增长不断加快。特别是 2001 年加入世界贸易组织后，我国参与世界经济的深度和广度不断拓展，对外贸易总量连上新台阶，2001 年突破 5000 亿美元，2004 年突破 1 万亿美元，2007 年突破 2 万亿美元。近年来尽管受到国际金融危机冲击的

direction or in a single commodity in 1949 at the founding of the People's Republic of China, when China had a closed or semi-closed economy. China's foreign trade developed slowly as the country increased its trading contacts and its economic exchanges with other developing countries. In the 1970s, when China was restored to its legitimate seat in the United Nations, the country established full diplomatic relations with Western countries, and subsequently saw a rapid growth in foreign trade. The country has embraced the rapid development of foreign trade, and it has ranked high in foreign trade volume globally since the nation's adoption of reform and opening up policy in 1978, especially after China joined the WTO in 2001.

The total volume of imported and exported goods has risen swiftly. The total value of China's imports and exports was only US$1.13 billion in 1950, but it exceeded US$10 billion in 1973, US$20.64 billion in 1978, and it surpassed US$100 billion in 1988. Foreign trade reached new heights as China strengthened its integration into the world's economy after it became a WTO member in 2001. Its foreign trade volume surpassed US$500 billion in 2001, US$1 trillion in 2004 and US$2 trillion in 2007. The country's foreign trade retains its stable growth despite the global financial crisis in

图 30　1952–2013 年进出口总额
Total Value of Import and Export of Commodities, 1952-2013

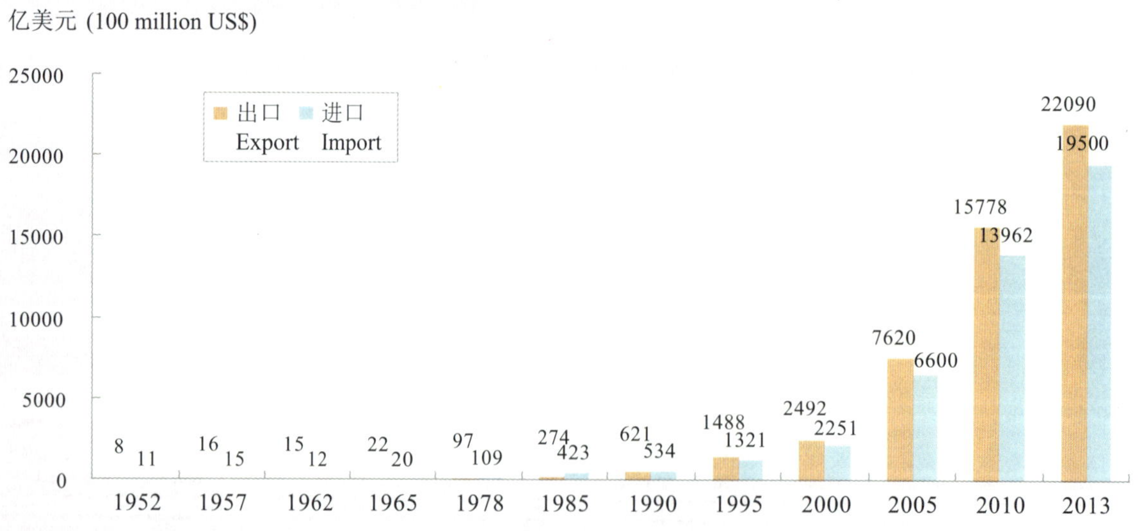

不利影响，我国对外贸易总体上仍保持稳定增长，2011 年突破 3 万亿美元，2013 年突破 4 万亿美元，达到 41590 亿美元。1951-2013 年，货物进出口总额年均增长 13.9%，其中 1979-2013 年年均增长 16.4%，2001-2013 年年均增长 18.2%。

货物贸易总额跃居世界第一。1978 年，我国货物贸易进出口额占世界贸易总额的比重仅为 0.8%，在世界贸易中居第 29 位。改革开放以来，随着货物贸易额稳步增加，居世界的位次逐步提高，特别是加入世界贸易组织后，我国货物贸易规模相继超越英国、法国、德国和日本，2010 年占世界贸易总额的比重为 9.7%，仅次于美国居世界第二位；2013 年比重进一步上升为 11.0%，超过美国跃居世界第一位，其中出口额比重为 11.7%，居世界第一位，进口额比重为 10.3%，居世界第二位。

recent years, with a total volume of more than US$3 trillion in 2011 and US$4 trillion in 2013, reaching US$4.159 trillion. The volume of imported and exported goods rose by 13.9 percent annually between 1951 and 2013, by 16.4 percent from 1979 to 2013 and by 18.2 percent from 2001 to 2013.

Total trade volume in goods ranks first in the world. In 1978, China's total trade volume in goods accounted for only 0.8 percent of the world's total, ranking 29th globally. But China's foreign trade in goods rose gradually through the world's rankings as imports and exports of goods grew stably in the wake of the country's reform and opening up, especially after China joined the WTO. China's scale of trade in goods surpassed those of the UK, France, Germany, and Japan, and China became the world's second largest trader, behind only the United States. China's trade volume accounted for 9.7 percent of the world's total trade volume in 2010. In 2013, China overtook the USA to become the world's biggest goods trader, with its trade volume accounting for 11 percent of the world's total. China's exports and imports accounted for 11.7 percent and 10.3 percent of the respective world totals, ranking the first and second in the world, respectively.

图 31　我国贸易总额占世界比重及居世界位次

The Value of Foreign Trade in Goods and the Proportion of World's Trade

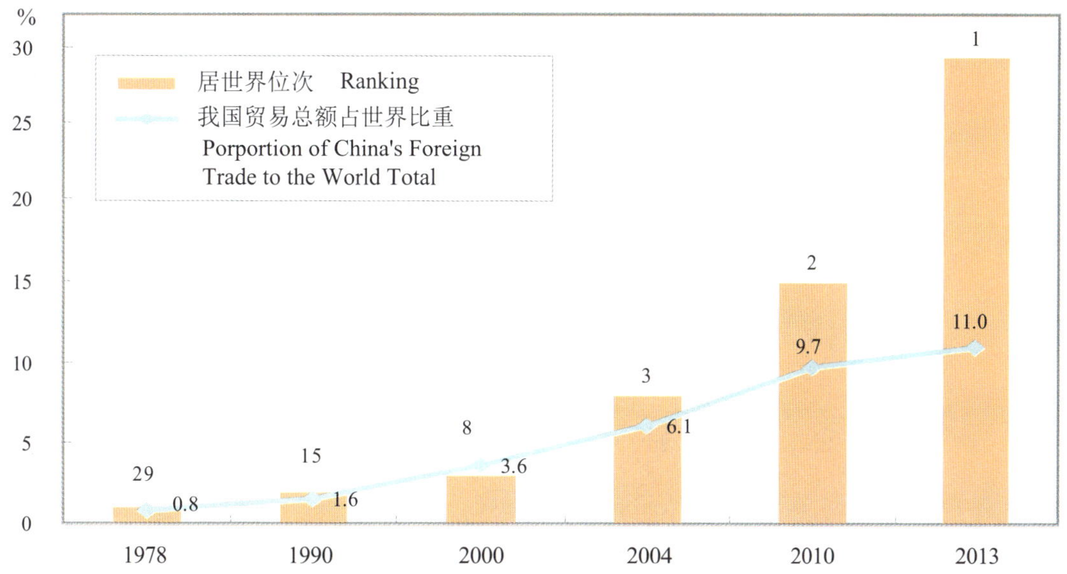

我国正式加入 WTO

我国是世界贸易组织（WTO）的前身——关贸总协定的创始缔约国，1986 年 7 月，我国正式提出复关申请，但未能如愿。1995 年，世界贸易组织取代关贸协定，我国复关谈判也转为入世谈判。1995 年世界贸易组织决定接纳中国为观察员，2001 年 7 月 3 日世界贸易组织就中国正式入世问题达成一致，同年 9 月 13 日我国完成了与所有世贸组织成员的双边市场准入谈判。2001 年 11 月 10 日，在卡塔尔多哈举行的世界贸易组织第四届部长级会议通过了我国加入世贸组织的法律文件，标志着经过 15 年的艰苦努力，我国终于成为世贸组织新成员。

加入世界贸易组织，是我国全面分析国内外形势、为加快推进改革开放和社会主义现代化作出的重大战略决策。加入世界贸易组织以来，我国坚持享受权利和履行义务相结合、实现自身发展和促进世界共同发展相结合，在更大范围、更高水平上参与国际经济合作和竞争，大力发展开放型经济。入世以来，我国贸易和投资自由化便利化程度显著提高。关税总水平由 15.3% 降至 9.8%，达到并超过了世界贸易组织对发展中国家的要求。服务贸易开放部门达到 100 个，接近发达国家水平。出口额跃居世界第一，进口额跃居世界第二，为贸易伙伴创造了大量就业岗位和投资机会。

China's Official Entry into WTO

China is the founding member of the WTO's predecessor-- GATT. In July 1986, China formally proposed to rejoin the GATT, but failed. In 1995, WTO replaced GATT. Our negotiations to rejoin GATT turned into WTO accession negotiations. In 1995, WTO decided to accept China as observer country. On July 3, 2001, WTO reached consensus on China's entry. Sep. 13, 2001, China finished all the bilateral market access negotiations related with WTO. On Nov.10, 2001, the Fourth WTO Ministerial Level Conference held in Doha Qatar passed the legal documents of China's accession to WTO, marking that through 15 years of hard efforts, China has finally become a new member of WTO.

Since China joined WTO, we have enjoyed rights and perform our duties at the same time, achieved our own development and promoted the common development at the same time, participated in global economic operation and competition in a wider range and in a higher level and vigorously pursued an open economy. Since China joined WTO, our trade and investment liberalization and facilitation have significantly increased. Tariff level reduced from 15.3% to 9.8%, met and exceeded the requirements of WTO to developing countries. Open departments in the service sector reached 100, approaching the level of developed countries. Export volume ranked first and imports ranked at the second place in the world, creating a lot of jobs and investment opportunities for trading partners.

图 32　2013 年中国十大贸易伙伴

China's Top Ten Trading Partners, 2013

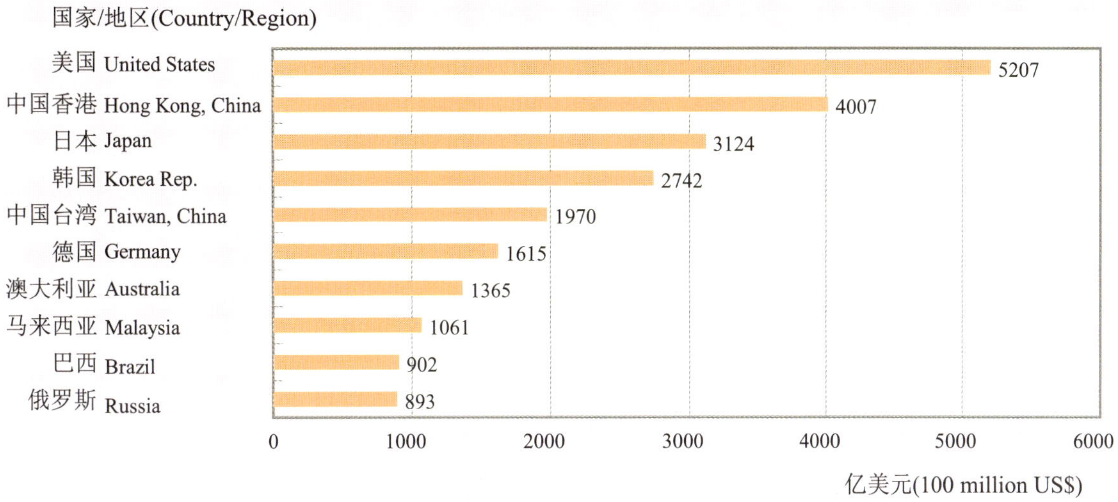

贸易结构不断优化。改革开放之初，我国出口商品主要以初级产品为主，随着经济发展水平的提高，工业制成品比重持续上升，出口商品附加值大幅度增加。初级产品出口额占全部出口的比重由 1978 年的 53.5% 下降到 2013 年的 4.9%，工业制成品出口比重则由 46.5% 上升至 95.1%。与此同时，机电产品和高新技术产品出口保持快速增长，占比不断上升。1979-2013 年，机电产品出口额年均增长 24.1%，占出口总额的比重由 1978 年的 6.8% 提高到 2013 年的 57.3%。高新技术产品出口额占出口总额的比重由 1998 年的 11% 提高到 2013 年的 29.9%。贸易伙伴日益多元。目前我国贸易伙伴已由 1978 年的 40 多个增加至 220 多个。我国在不断巩固同美国、欧盟和日本等传统主要贸易伙伴关系的基础上，与东盟、金砖国家等新兴经济体贸易往来也取得较大进展。2013 年，我国对欧盟、美国和日本的进出口额占比分别为 13.4%、12.5% 和 7.5%，对东盟和其他金砖国家的进出口额占比也分别达到 10.7% 和 7.5%。

Trade structure has been optimized step by step. Raw materials and unprocessed agricultural products were China's primary export commodities at the beginning of China's period of reform and opening up. Along with economic growth and the increasing production of manufactured goods, China's export began to gain added value. The proportion of raw materials in China's total exports dropped from 53.5 percent in 1978 to 4.9 percent in 2013, while the proportion of manufactured goods increased from 46.5 percent to 95.1 percent. Mechanical and electrical products, as well as high-tech products, also saw their proportions of total exports grow. The export volume for mechanical and electrical products increased by 24.1 percent annually from 1979 to 2013, while the proportion of these products in total exports increased from 6.8 percent in 1978 to 57.3 percent in 2013. The proportion of high-tech products in China's total exports also saw an increase from 11 percent in 1998 to 29.9 percent in 2013. China has also gained more and more trading partners, from just over 40 in 1978 to 220 currently. China has enjoyed rapid trade development with newly emerging markets, including the Association of Southeast Asian Nations (ASEAN) and BRICS countries, while it has consolidated trade exchanges with its three largest partners: the European Union (EU), the United States, and Japan. In 2013, China's trade volumes with the EU, the US, and Japan accounted for 13.4 percent, 12.5 percent, and 7.5 percent of the China's total trade volume, respectively. China's trade with ASEAN and BRICS countries respectively reached 10.7 percent and 7.5 percent of China's total trade volume in 2013.

图 33　1980 年、2013 年出口货物类型
Composition of Export Commodities, 1980 and 2013

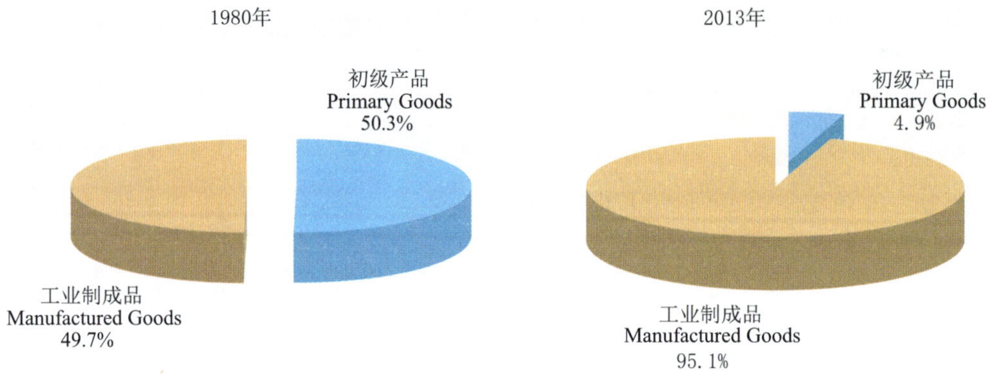

图 34　1980 年、2013 年进口货物类型
Composition of Import Commodities, 1980 and 2013

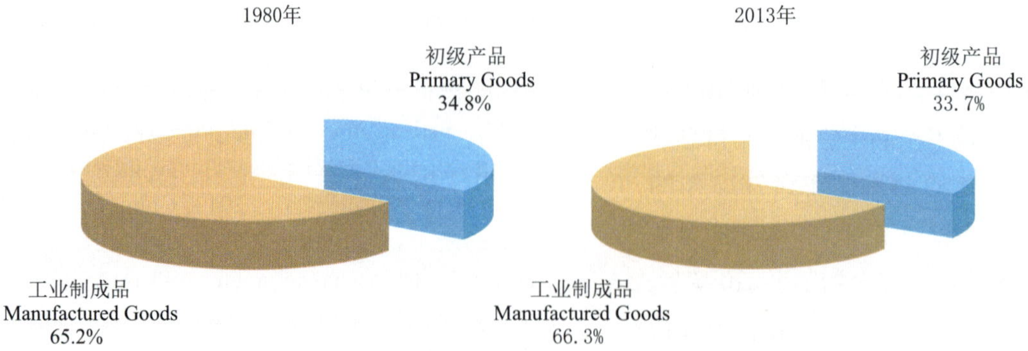

（二）服务贸易从无到有，成为对外贸易的重要组成部分。

改革开放前，除对外援建项目和少数外国友人来华旅游外，我国服务贸易基本上属于空白。改革开放以来，我国服务贸易从无到有，逐步发展壮大，初步形成了以旅游、运输服务为基础，以通讯、保险、金融、计算机信息服务、咨询和广告等新兴服务贸易为增长点的服务贸易发展新格局。

服务贸易规模稳步扩大。1982 年，我国服务贸易进出口总额仅为 44 亿美元，居世界第 34 位；其中出口 25 亿美元，进口 19 亿美元。加入世界贸易组织后，我国服务贸易发展步伐明显加快。2013 年，服务贸易进出口总额 5396 亿美元，居世界第三位；其中，出口 2106 亿美

(2) Trade in services grows from nothing to become an important part of China's foreign trade

Before the country's reform and opening up, China's trade in services was almost non-existent, except for foreign aid projects and tourism by a small amount of foreign travelers. But in the wake of China's adoption of reform and opening up, the country's trade in services developed from near zero to flourish rapidly. A new pattern of services trade has taken shape, featuring trade in tourism, transport, communications, insurance, finance, computers and information, and consulting and advertising.

Trade in services expands stably. In 1982, the volume of China's services imports and exports was only US$4.4 billion, ranking 34th globally Services exports stood at US$2.5 billion and imports at US$1.9 billion. Trade in services saw remarkable growth after the country became a WTO member. In 2013, the value of China's services trade was US$539.6 billion, the third highest in the world. Services exports stood at US$210.6 billion, services imports

图 35　1982-2013 年服务贸易进出口总额
Imports and Exports of Trade in Services, 1982-2013

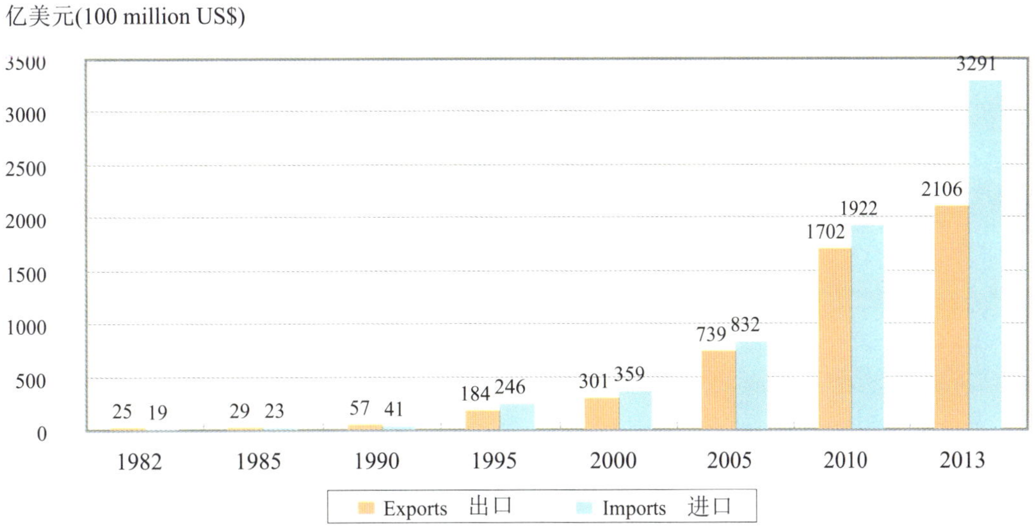

元，进口3291亿美元。从增速看，1983-2013年，服务贸易进出口额年均增长16.8%，快于同期对外货物贸易总额增速0.8个百分点；其中出口年均增长15.4%，进口年均增长18.1%。

服务贸易结构逐步改进。改革开放初期，我国服务贸易出口以旅游、运输、建筑等传统服务贸易为主，传统服务贸易出口占比达80%以上。随着改革开放的不断深入，保险、计算机和信息服务、咨询等高附加值服务贸易出口显现出强劲的增长势头，在服务贸易出口中的比重不断提高。1998年到2013年，计算机和信息服务出口额由1.3亿美元提高到154.3亿美元，年均增长34.8%，占服务贸易出口总额的比重由0.6%提高至7.3%；咨询服务出口额由5.2亿美元提高到405.4亿美元，年均增长31.3%，占比由2.2%提高到19.2%。而传统的运输和旅游业两大行业出口额占比由1998年的62.4%下降至2013年的42.4%。

hit US$329.1 billion. The trade in services grew at an annual rate of 16.8 percent from 1983 to 2013, 0.8 percentage points higher than overall foreign trade growth, with services exports rising by 15.4 percent annually and services imports rising by18.1 percent annually.

Services trade patterns are improved. At the beginning of China's period of reform and opening up, the country's trade in services was comprised mainly of tourism, transport and construction, and these traditional services accounted for over 80 percent of China's services trade. As the country deepened its process of reform and opening up, trade in services with high added value, such as insurance, computer and information services, and consulting, showed strong growth and increased their proportion in the overall services trade. The trade value of computer and information exports climbed from US$130 million to 15.43 billion US dollars, rising by 34.8 percent annually from 1998 to 2013. The export value of consulting services increased from US$520 million to 40.54 billion, with an annual growth rate of 31.3, and its proportion increased from 2.2 percent to 19.2 percent. The proportion of traditional construction and tourism services in the overall services trade dropped from 62.4 percent in 1998 to 42.4 percent in 2013.

图36 我国服务贸易总额及占世界服务贸易的比重
The Value of Service Trade and the Proportion of World's Service Trade

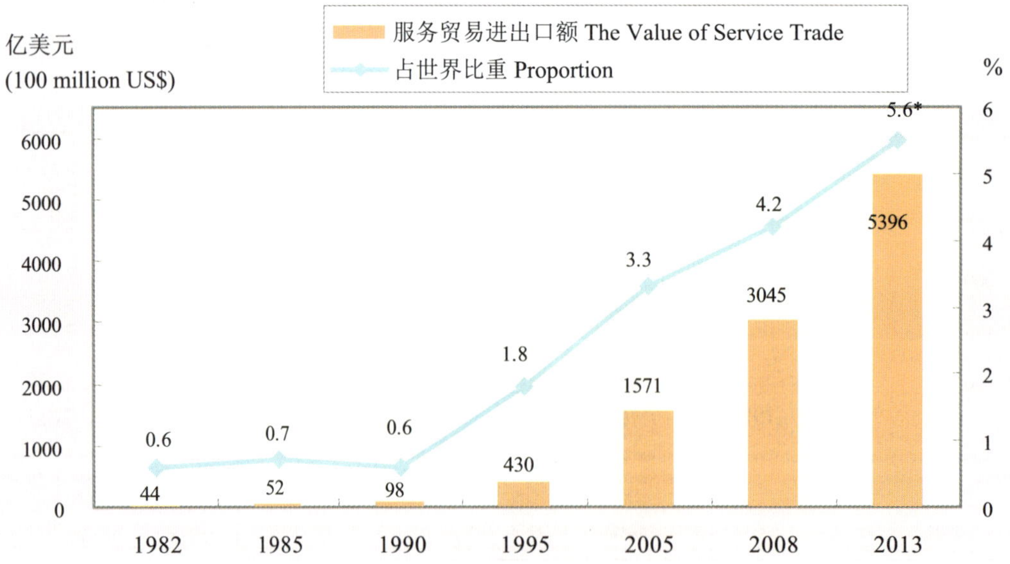

注：2013年服务贸易总额及占世界服务贸易的比重为2012年数据。
Note: The proportion of the value of service trade to the world's service trade is the 2012's data.

（三）积极参与经济全球化进程，从大规模“引进来”到大踏步“走出去”。

改革开放前，我国利用外资和对外投资均很少。改革开放后，我国投资环境不断改善，利用外资规模不断扩大。经过 20 多年的发展，在积累了一定的经济和技术实力并初步具备主动参与全球化分工能力的基础上，2000 年开始我国逐步探索实施“走出去”战略，通过采取对外投资、对外承包工程和对外劳务合作等多种方式走出国门。“引进来”和“走出去”相结合，我国参与国际分工合作的能力进一步提升。

(3) China adopts "drawing in" and "moving outward" strategies to guide its active participation in economic globalization

China initially saw small amounts of both foreign and outbound investment, but the country expanded the scale of its utilization of foreign investment as the it improved the investment environment after adopting reform and opening up policy. In 2000, China began to adopt a "moving outward" strategy, which used overseas investment, overseas contracting projects, and foreign labor cooperation to help the country sharpen its global competitiveness after two decades of economic and technological development. China beefed up its international cooperation and division of labor by combining "drawing in" and "moving outward" strategies.

“走出去”战略

2000年，在世纪之交，以对外投资合作为内涵和基础的“走出去”上升为国家战略。《中共中央关于制定国民经济和社会发展第十个五年计划的建议》指出，“十五”时期我国对外开放将进入新的阶段。实行对外开放的基本国策，在“十五”期间乃至更长的一段时期，一个很重要的内容，就是要实施“走出去”的开放战略。2002年，十六大报告明确提出，要坚持“引进来”和“走出去”相结合，全面提高对外开放水平。“走出去”战略的制定和实施，标志着我国对外开放战略的重大转变。

“走出去”战略又称国际化经营战略，是我国企业充分利用国内外“两个市场、两种资源”，通过对外直接投资、对外工程承包、对外劳务合作等形式积极参与国际竞争，实现我国经济可持续发展的现代化强国战略。在“走出去”战略不断完善和深化的过程中，我国对外投资和对外经济合作规模不断扩大，方式不断创新，企业全球化经营程度不断提高，也有效促进了中外双方互利共赢，扩大我国与投资合作东道国的共同利益，为其带去人才、资金、技术和生产能力，增加了当地税收，部分解决了当地就业，增强了当地自主发展能力。

2014年，在政府工作报告中，进一步提出了“在走出去中提升竞争力”的工作目标，要求健全金融、法律、领事等服务保障，规范走出去秩序，促进产品出口、工程承包与劳务合作；抓紧规划建设丝绸之路经济带、21世纪海上丝绸之路，推进孟中印缅、中巴经济走廊建设，推出一批重大支撑项目，加快基础设施互联互通，拓展国际经济技术合作新空间。这是适应国内外形势深刻变化，推动新一轮对外开放，倒逼深层次改革和结构调整，加快培育国际竞争新优势的重要举措。

“Going Out” Strategy

In 2000, at the turn of the century, “going out” strategy with foreign investment and cooperation as its connotation and basis has risen to a national strategy. "Suggestions of Tenth Five Year Plan of CPC Central Committee on national economic and Social Development" points out that "the tenth five year" period of China's opening up will enter a new stage. To carry out the basic national policy--reform and opening up, in the “tenth five year” period and in a rather long period of time, a very important content is to carry out “going out” strategy. In 2002, the Sixteenth National Congress of CPC report clearly stated that we should stick to the principle of “bringing in” and “going out”, and improve the level of opening up comprehensively.

“Going out” strategy is also known as international business strategy. Chinese enterprises make full use of domestic and foreign "two markets, two kinds of resources", and actively participate in international competition through foreign direct investment, foreign project contracting, and labor cooperation and in other forms. “Going Out” strategy is a modernization strategy to realize the economic sustainable development of our country. In the process of improving and deepening the “Going Out” strategy, China’s outward investment and economic cooperation have been expanding, and renovating. Business globalized operation has been deepening. The strategy effectively promoted the mutual benefit and win-win results, expanded mutual interests of China and investment and cooperation countries, brought talents, capital, technology, and production capacity, increased local taxes, provided job opportunities and strengthened local self-development ability.

In 2014, the report on the work of the government further put forward the work objective of “improving competitiveness through going out strategy”, required to improve financial, legal and consular and other services and assurances, to standardize going out order, promote product exports, project contraction, and labor cooperation, pay close attention to the planning and construction of the Silk Road Economic Belt, 21 Century Maritime Silk Road, accelerate the construction of BCIM, China Brazil Economic Corridor, introduce a number of major supporting projects, speed up the infrastructure inter connectivity, and explore new area of global economic and technological cooperation. This is a significant measure to fit with the profound changes in domestic and foreign situations, promote a new round of opening up, push for deeper level reform and structural adjustment, and accelerate to develop new international competitive advantages.

利用外资规模和领域不断扩大。改革开放初期，我国利用外资的规模较小，且主要形式是对外借款特别是政府贷款。1983 年，我国实际使用外资 22.6 亿美元，其中外商直接投资 9.2 亿美元。1990 年，实际使用外资上升至 102.9 亿美元，其中外商直接投资 34.9 亿美元。上世纪 90 年代以来，外商直接投资进入高速发展时期。1991-2000 年，实际使用外商直接投资 3277 亿美元，年均增长 27.9%。加入世界贸易组织后，利用外资规模进一步扩大。2013 年末，外商投资企业达到 44.6 万户；2001-2013 年实际使用外商直接投资 10454 亿美元，年均增长 8.5%。1979-2013 年，我国吸引外商直接投资累计达 13937 亿美元，是吸引外商直接投资最多的发展中国家。从结构上看，外商投资重点从一般制造业延伸到高新技术产业、基础产业、基础设施建设，近几年在研发中心、集成电路、计算机和通信产品等高技术项目的外商投资明显增加，商业、外贸、电信、金融、保险等服务业也逐渐成为外商投资的新热点。

The scale and areas of foreign investment usage have been enlarged and expanded. The initial stage of China's reform and opening up saw small scale foreign investment utilization, mainly foreign borrowing, especially government loans. In 1983, China used US$2.26 billion of foreign investment funds, of which US$920 million came from foreign direct investment (FDI). In 1990, actual foreign investment in China hit US$10.29 billion, with FDI accounting for US$3.49 billion. FDI in China has undergone rapid growth since the 1990s. The actual FDI used between 1991 and 2000 was US$327.7 billion, with an annual growth rate that reached 27.9 percent. China also expanded its foreign investment after becoming a WTO member. There were 446,000 foreign-invested enterprises in China at the end of 2013. Actual FDI use from 2001 to 2013 was US$1,045.4 billion, with an annual growth rate of 8.5 percent. China attracted a total of US$1,393.7 billion in FDI from 1979 to 2013, making the country the world's largest FDI recipient. Key foreign-invested industries include manufacturing, high-tech and basic industries, and infrastructure construction. There have been marked increases in foreign investment in the areas of research and development, integrated circuit, computers, and communication. The services trade in commerce, foreign trade, telecoms, finance and insurance has also become a new magnet for foreign investment.

图 37　1983-2013 年实际利用外商直接投资
Actual Utilization of Foreign Direct Investment, 1983-2013

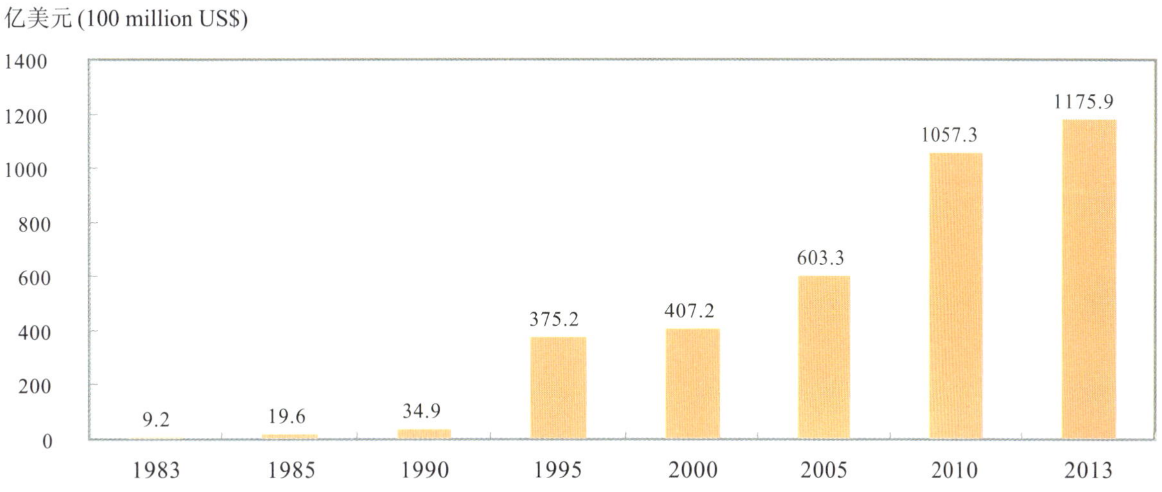

图 38　2013 年中国外商直接投资前十大来源地
China's Top Ten Sources of Foreign Direct Investment Flows, 2013

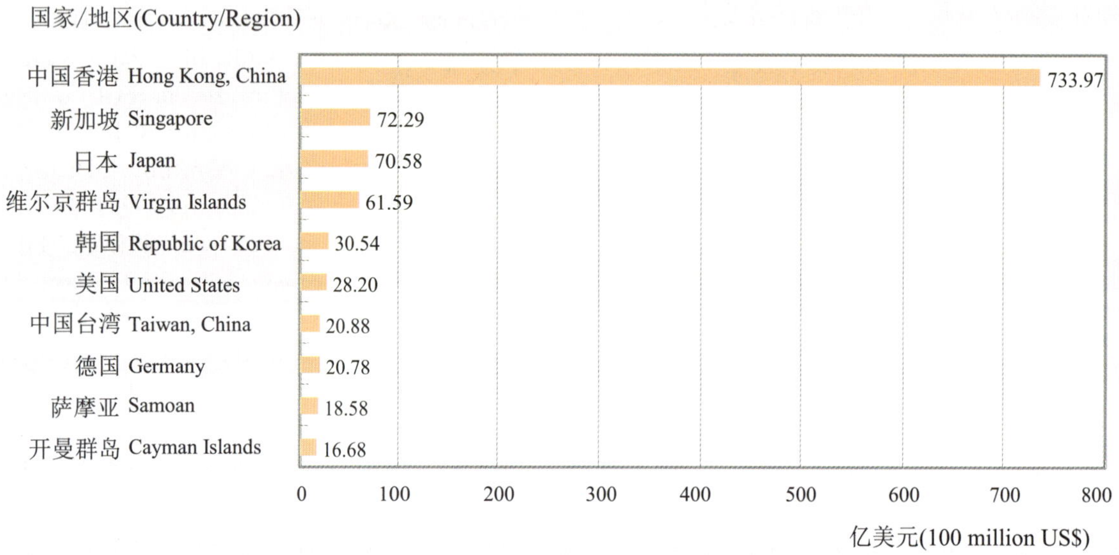

图 39　非金融类对外直接投资
China's Outward FDI of Non-financial Sector

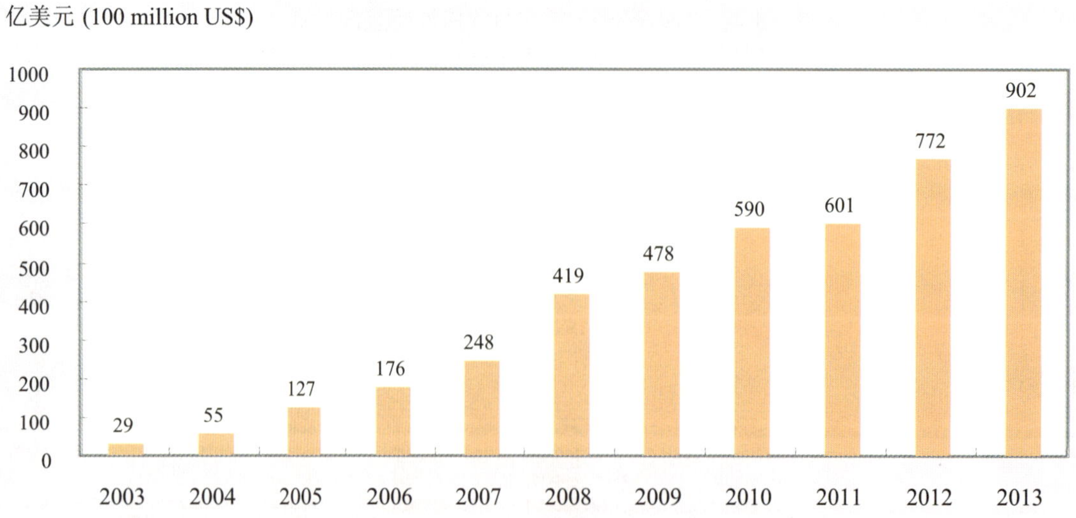

对外投资层次和水平不断提升。改革开放初期，我国只有少数国有企业走出国门，开办代表处或设立企业。加入世界贸易组织以后，我国企业对外投资进入快速发展时期。2013 年，我国非金融类对外直接投资为 927 亿美元，比 2003 年增长 31.5 倍，年均增长 41.7%。截至 2013 年底，国内 1.53 万家境内投资主体在全球 184 个国家和地区设立境外直接投资企业超过 2.54 万家。对外投资形式逐步多样化，由单一的绿地投资向跨国并购、参股、境外上市等多种方式扩展，跨国并购已经成为对外投资的重要方式。2013 年，通过跨国并购实现对外投资约 337.9 亿美元，占同期对外投资总量的 31.3%。对外投资领域也不断拓宽，从资源、电讯及石油化工等向金融、商务服务等领域延伸。

The level and quality of China's investments overseas increases. Only a small amount of state-owned enterprises established overseas representative offices and overseas enterprises at the beginning of China's period of reform and opening up. Chinese enterprises began rapid overseas investment after China's WTO entry. In 2013, China's outbound direct investment in non-finance sectors was US$92.7 billion, 31.5 times higher than it was in 2003, with an annual growth rate of 41.7 percent. So far, some 15300 Chinese enterprises have set up more than 25000 direct-invested enterprises in 184 countries and regions. In addition, The forms of China's outbound investments have been diversified from investment in a single area to transnational mergers and acquisitions, shareholding, and overseas stock listing. Of these transnational mergers and acquisitions are a major channel for Chinese outbound investment. Outbound investment in cross-border mergers and aqcuisitions reached US$33.79 billion between 2003 and 2013, accounting for 31.3 percent of China's total outbound investment. Fields for overseas investment have also expanded from natural resources, telecoms, and the petrochemical industry to finance and business services.

图 40　2013 年中国对外投资十大目的地

Top Ten Destinations of China's Outward FDI Flows, 2013

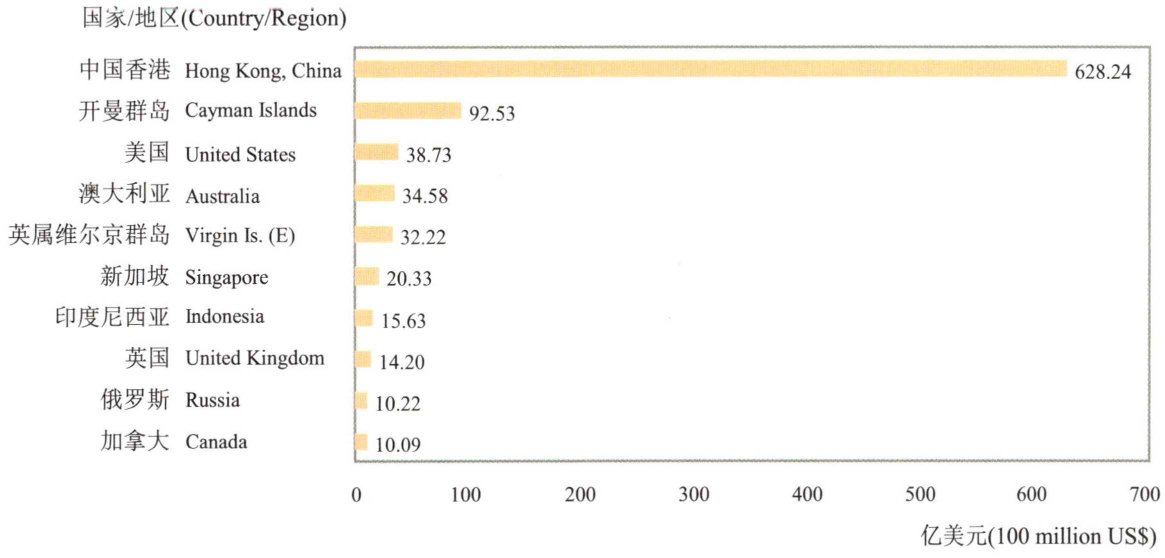

对外承包工程和劳务合作范围不断拓展。改革开放前，对亚非拉等第三世界国家的援建项目是我国参与对外经济合作的重要形式。1976 年，我国对外承包劳务队伍第一次走向国际舞台。1995 年起，我国开展了对外设计咨询服务，对外合作领域进一步拓宽。目前我国对外经济合作业务已经遍及全球 200 多个国家和地区，电力、冶金、石化、轨道交通和电子通讯等资金技术密集行业成为我国对外经济合作的主要领域。1979 年，我国签订对外承包工程合同数仅 27 份，2013 年增加至 11578 份；1979 年合同金额仅 0.3 亿美元，2013 年达到 1716.3 亿美元。

China has expanded the range of its overseas project contracting and labor service cooperation. Foreign aid projects were the major form of China's foreign economic cooperation with developing countries in Asia, Africa, and Latin America before China launched its reform and opening up policy. In 1976, China sent its first workers overseas for a contracting project, and in 1995, China launched its foreign designing consultation service. So far, China has conducted foreign economic cooperation in 200 countries and regions, primarily in capital-and-technology-intensive industries like electricity generation, metallurgy, petrochemical processing, transportation infrastructure, and electronic communications. China signed only 27 foreign economic cooperation contracts with a total value of US$300 million in 1979; it signed 11578 contracts in 2013 with a total value of US$171.63 billion.

图 41　1979-2013 年对外承包工程合同金额
Contracted Value of Foreign Economic Cooperation, 1979-2013

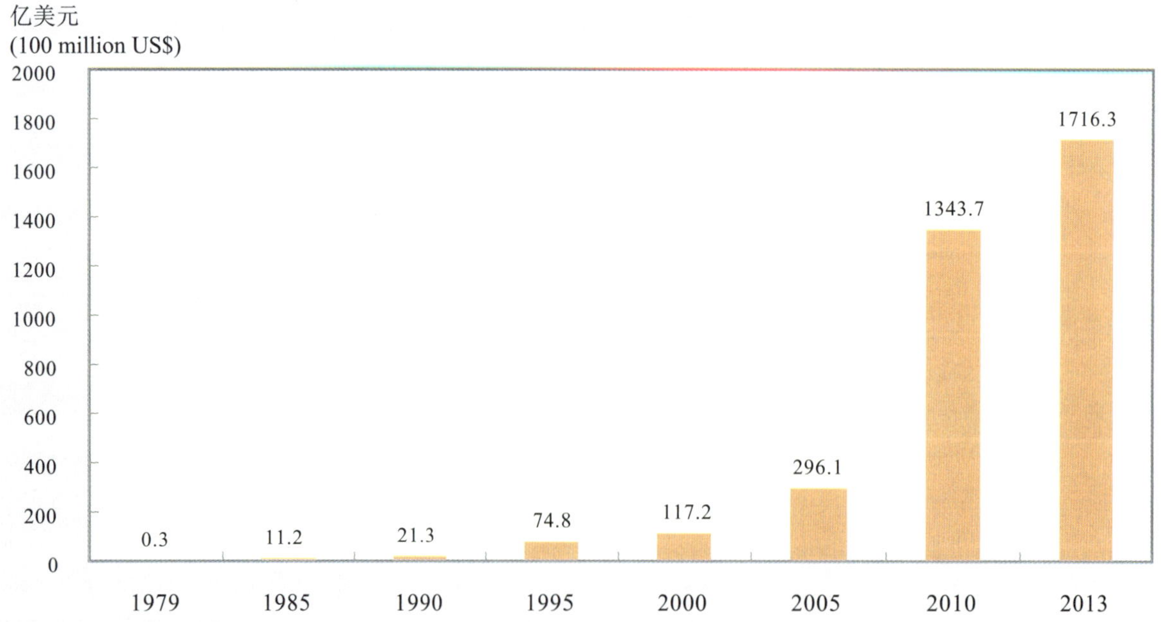

建设丝绸之路经济带、21世纪海上丝绸之路的构想

2013年9月、10月间，国家主席习近平在访问哈萨克斯坦和印度尼西亚时，分别提出共建"丝绸之路经济带"和"21世纪海上丝绸之路"的战略构想。"一路一带"构想成为我国深化改革开放和推进周边外交的新手笔，并写入2014年政府工作报告等政策文件，受到国内外高度重视。

建设"一带一路"，是以习近平同志为总书记的党中央主动应对全球形势深刻变化、统筹国内国际两个大局作出的重大战略决策，对推进我国新一轮对外开放和沿线国家共同发展意义重大。"一带一路"是世界上跨度最长的经济大走廊，发端于中国，贯通中亚、东南亚、南亚、西亚乃至欧洲部分区域，东牵亚太经济圈，西系欧洲经济圈。沿线大多是新兴经济体和发展中国家，总人口约44亿，经济总量约21万亿美元，分别约占全球的63%和29%。"一带一路"将构筑新一轮对外开放的"一体两翼"，在提升向东开放水平的同时加快向西开放步伐，助推内陆沿边地区由对外开放的边缘迈向前沿。

"一路一带"不是一个新的机制，而是合作发展的理念和倡议，将充分依靠我国与有关国家既有的双多边机制，借助既有的、行之有效的区域合作平台，如上海合作组织、欧亚经济联盟、中国—东盟（10+1）等，并注入新的内涵和活力。习近平主席提出，共同建设丝绸之路经济带，是一项造福沿途各国人民的大事业，可以从加强政策沟通、加强道路联通、加强贸易畅通、加强货币流通、加强民心相通等几个方面先做起来，以点带面，从线到片，逐步形成区域大合作。

The Conception of Constructing Silk Road Economic Belt and 21st Century Maritime Silk Road

In Sept. and Oct. 2013, President Xi Jinping visited Kazakhstan and Indonesia. During this visit, the strategic vision of building a "Silk Road Economic Belt" and "21st Century Maritime Silk Road" was proposed. "One Belt and One Road" vision has become a new highlight in China's deepening of reform and opening up, and promotion of peripheral diplomacy. The vision has been written into the 2014 report on the work of government, attracting great attention at home and abroad.

The construction of "One Belt and One Road" is a significant strategic decision made by the CPC Central Committee with Comrade Xi Jinping as the general secretary to respond to the profound changes in the global situation, coordinate the domestic and international situation. It is of great importance to promote China's a new round of opening up and the common development of the countries along the route. "One Belt and One Road" is the world's longest economic corridor, originates in China, runs through Middle Asia, Southeast Asia, South Asia, Western Asia and even some areas in the Europe, and connects the Asia Pacific economic belt in the east with the European economic belt in the west. Along the routes, most countries are new emerging economies and developing countries, with more than 4.4 billion people, and 21 trillion dollars of economic output, accounting for 63 percent and 29 percent of the world. "One Belt and One Road" will serve as "one body and two wings" of a new round of opening up. While improving the level of opening to the East, we should accelerate the opening to the west and boost the development of interior border area through opening up.

"One Belt and One Road" is not a new mechanism, but a new idea and initiative of cooperation and development. It will fully rely on the multi-lateral mechanisms of China and related countries make use of the existing and effective regional cooperative platforms, such as OECD, Eurasian Economic Union, China--Asean(10+1) and others and infuse new meanings and vitality. President Xi Jinping said that the common construction of Silk Road Economic Belt is a big undertaking which benefits the people all over the world. We can start from several aspects, such as strengthening the policy communication, road connections, trade facilitation, currency circulation and people's exchanges, promote work in all areas by drawing upon the experience gained on key points, and gradually develop regional cooperation.

（四）国际经济文化交流与合作日趋多样化，互利共赢新格局初步形成。

建国初期，在西方发达国家的封锁下，我国的国际交往受到很多限制。70 年代初，随着中美、中日建交和恢复联合国合法地位，我国的国际交往有所扩大。改革开放以来，我国主动参与国际经济文化交往，认真履行大国义务，积极倡导和推动区域经济合作和自由贸易，国际化水平不断提高。

广泛参与国际性、区域性经济合作。1980 年 4 月和 5 月，我国先后恢复了在国际货币基金组织和世界银行的合法席位。2001 年，我国加入世界贸易组织，以更加积极的姿态参与国际经济合作，通过积极兑现“入世”承诺，不断扩大市场开放范围，为自由贸易的发展起到了良好示范效应，同时积极

(4) A win-win framework has been established thanks to increasingly diverse international economic and cultural exchange and cooperation.

In the early days of the People's Republic of China, the country's international exchange was greatly restricted by Western countries' blockade. In the early 1970s, China was able to expand its international contacts when it established diplomatic relations with the US and Japan, and the country was restored to a legitimate seat in the UN. Ever since its reform and opening up, China has taken the initiative to participate in international economic and cultural exchange, fulfilling its obligations as a big power by advocating and promoting regional economic cooperation and free trade. As a result, the country has seen a rising level of internationalization.

China has participated widely in international and regional economic cooperation. The country was restored to its legitimate seats in the International Monetary Fund and the World Bank in April and May of 1980. China strengthened its international economic cooperation after its entry into the WTO in 2001 by keeping its promise to more widely open

参与多边谈判，在多边贸易体制中发挥了建设性作用。上世纪90年代以来，参与了亚太经合组织、上海合作组织、亚欧会议和大湄公河次区域经济合作等区域性合作，发挥了重要作用。2003年以来，我国自贸区建设从无到有，迄今已与亚洲、大洋洲、拉美、欧洲、非洲的多个国家和地区建设多个自贸区，内地与港澳更紧密经贸关系安排，中国－东盟自贸区、中国－智利自贸区、中国－巴基斯坦自贸区、中国－新西兰自贸区等等，促进了双边与多边贸易的大幅度增长。2013年，我国在上海设立了首个区域性自由贸易园区，积极探索负面清单管理模式，致力于培育面向全球的竞争新优势，构建与各国合作发展的新平台，将进一步促进国际经济合作。

its markets. The country has provided an excellent model for the development of free trade. The country has also actively participated in multi-lateral negotiations and has played a constructive role in the multi-lateral trade system. China has participated in regional economic cooperation through APEC, the Shanghai Cooperation Organization, the Asia-Europe Conference and the Greater Mekong sub region since the 1990s. Since 2003, China has established many free trade zones with many countries and regions in Asia, Oceania, Latin America, Europe and Africa, which accounted for more than many percent of China's total foreign trade volume in 2013. Bilateral and multi-lateral trade have risen rapidly thanks to the Closer Economic Partnership Arrangement (CEPA) between Mainland China and Hong Kong and the establishment of the China-ASEAN free trade zone (FTZ), China-Chile FTZ, China-Pakistan FTZ, and China-New Zealand FTZ. In 2013, the Shanghai FTZ was established as the first regional FTZ in China, which is exploring a negative-list administration model in an attempt to build a new platform for multi-national cooperation, for sharpening China's global competitiveness, and for furthering the cause of international economic cooperation.

教育和文化间的国际交流日益密切。教育是我国最早对外开放的领域之一，实现了主要向国外学习和借鉴国外经验的单向需求转为世界各国与我国之间的双向需求、合作共赢，世界各国对中国教育合作需求也从学习语言转向学生交流、科研合作等更多元化的层次。1978 年到 2013 年，我国出国留学人数由 860 人猛增到 41 万人，其中学成回国的由 248 人增长到 35 万人，各类出国留学人员总数达到 306 万人，学成回国人员总数达到 144 万人。同时，我国也逐渐发展成为一个新兴的留学目的地国家，来华留学人数快速增长。2013 年，来华留学人数由 1978 年仅 1200 人左右增加到来自 200 个国家和地区共 35.6 万人。此外，我国积极推进文化“走出去”，文化产品和服务项目出口的种类日益增多，已经培育推出一批具有民族特色、自主知识产权和原创性的知名文化品牌，中华文化在国际上的影响力日益提升。

International exchanges in education and culture are becoming closer. Education was one of the first areas of Chinese society to open up to the outside world. China has shifted from learning from foreign countries to mutual learning, developing a win-win model of educational exchange with the outside world. Foreign countries have expanded their educational cooperation with China from simple language learning to student exchange and cooperation in scientific research. The annual number of Chinese students who went abroad to study increased from 860 in 1978 to 410,000 in 2013, and the number of students who returned to China after their studies also increased from 248 to 350,000. Over this 35-year period, a total of 3.06 million Chinese went abroad to study, and 1.44 million returned to the country after studying in foreign countries. China has also become a favored destination for foreign students. The number of foreign students in China increased from 1,200 students in 1978 to 356,000 students from 200 countries and regions in 2013. Meanwhile, China promoted the strategy of “Chinese culture going out” by expanding the export of cultural products and service projects. China has developed some well-known cultural brands that exemplify national characteristics and which hold their own intellectual property rights. Chinese culture has seen a rise in its international influence as a result of these factors.

图 42 1978-2013 年出国留学人数
Number of Students Going Abroad, 1978-2013

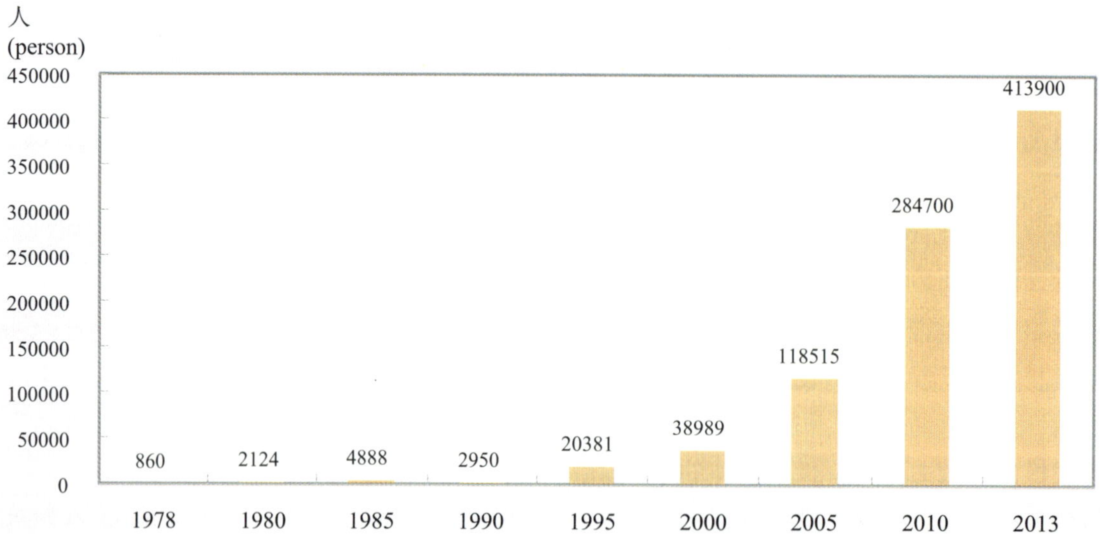

孔子学院

自2004年开始，为推动汉语加快走向世界，提升中国语言文化影响力，我国在借鉴英、法、德等国推广本民族语言经验的基础上，探索在海外设立以教授汉语和传播中国文化为宗旨的非营利性教育机构"孔子学院"。随着我国经济的发展和国际交往的日益广泛，世界各国对汉语学习的需求急剧增长，孔子学院也获得了长足发展的源动力。近年来，孔子学院建设快速发展，已成为世界各国人民学习汉语和了解中华文化的园地、中外文化交流的平台，中国人民与世界各国人民友谊合作的桥梁，受到广泛欢迎。

2010–2013年，孔子学院的发展呈现多元化趋势。除了以汉语言文化推广为主的普通孔子学院之外，还创建了各种各样的特色孔子学院，传播中国文化，如中医孔子学院、商务孔子学院、旅游孔子学院、音乐孔子学院、舞蹈和表演孔子学院、饮食文化孔子学院、茶文化孔子学院等。

截至2013年年底，全球已建立440所孔子学院和646个孔子课堂，分布在120个国家和地区。孔子学院设在115国（地区），共440所。其中，亚洲32国（地区）93所，非洲27国37所，欧洲37国149所，美洲16国144所，大洋洲3国17所。孔子课堂设在48国共646个，其中，亚洲13国50个，非洲8国10个，欧洲18国153个，美洲6国384个，大洋洲2国49个。

Confucius Institutes

Since 2004, to promote Chinese language in the world, and elevate the influences of Chinese language and culture, China has set up non-profit educational institutions—"Confucius Institute" on the basis of the experiences of Britain, France and Germany in promoting their national languages. With the development of China's economic development, and more extensive international exchanges, more and more foreigners have a desire to learn Chinese, thus the Confucius Institute has gained sustained momentum of development. In recent years, the Confucius Institute developed rapidly. It has become a platform for people all around the world to learn Chinese language and know the Chinese culture, to exchange Chinese and foreign cultures, and strengthen the friendship between Chinese people and people from all countries. The Institute has received wide welcome.

Between 2010 and 2013, the Confucius institute has had a diversified trend of development. Besides ordinary Confucius institute with the purpose of promoting Chinese language and culture, we have set up various special Confucius Institutes to spread Chinese culture, such as Chinese Medicine, Business, Tourism, Music, Dancing, Acting, food culture, and tea culture Confucius Institute and others.

As of the end of 2013, there have been 440 Confucius Institutes and 646 Confucius classes in 120 countries and regions. 440 Confucius Institutes have been set up in 115 countries (regions). 93 in 32 Asian countries (regions), 37 in 27 African countries, 149 in 37 European countries, 144 in 16 American countries, and 17 in 3 Oceanian countries. 646 Confucius classed have been set up in 48 countries, in which, 50 in 13 Asian countries, 10 in 8 African countries, 153 in 18 European countries, 384 in 6 American countries, and 49 in 2 Oceanian countries.

6 从温饱不足到向全面小康迈进，人民生活水平发生翻天覆地的变化

China makes the leap from a society lacking basic necessities to a peaceful and prosperous society. People's living standards see earth-shaking changes.

新中国成立以来的 65 年，是农村富余劳动力向城市转移、就业稳步增加的 65 年，是贫困人口大幅下降、人民群众生活保障水平不断提高的 65 年，也是城乡居民生活实现由温饱不足到总体小康并向全面小康迈进、发生翻天覆地变化的 65 年。

In the 65 years since the People's Republic of China was founded, the surplus rural labor force has moved to cities, employment has increased steadily, China's population in poverty has decreased, and people's living security standards have gradually improved. The past 65 years have seen the Chinese people transition from having inadequate basic necessities to leading prosperous lives. People's living standards also saw earth-shaking changes.

从总体小康迈向全面小康

“小康”一词，源于《礼记》，是古代思想家描绘的理想社会，意指比较宽裕、殷实的理想生活。在 20 世纪 70 年代末，邓小平提出了小康社会的概念——所谓小康社会，就是虽不富裕，但日子好过。为规划中国现代化建设的战略构想，党的十三大提出了中国经济建设分三步走的总体战略部署：第一步，从 1981 年到 1990 年，实现国民生产总值比 1980 年翻一番，解决人民的温饱问题；第二步，从 1991 年到 20 世纪末，国民生产总值再增长一倍，人民生活达到小康水平；第三步，到 21 世纪中叶，人均国民生产总值达到中等发达国家水平，人民生活比较富裕，基本实现现代化。

中国社会主义现代化建设发展过程中有不同的阶段，小康水平有一个从低到高的发展过程。总体小康是一个低水平、不全面、发展很不平衡的小康，全面小康是以总体小康为基点，需要进一步发展的、高水平的、均衡的小康。

随着中国特色社会主义建设事业的深入，“小康”内涵和意义不断地得到丰富和发展。党的十六大报告明确提出，到 2020 年，把我国建成全面小康的社会。党的十八大报告又进一步指出，全面小康社会是经济、政治、文化、社会、生态文明全面发展的小康社会。

20 世纪末，我们已经实现了“三步走”战略的第一步和第二步，我国人民生活水平总体上已经达到了小康水平，即实现了总体小康。现在，我们正在为实现全面小康社会而奋斗。

From Fairly Well-off Society Towards Overall Well-off Society

Originated from "Book of the Rites", "Xiao Kang" is the ideal society pictured by ancient thinkers, meaning a relatively well-off and prosperous life. At the end of 1970's, Deng Xiaoping put forward the idea of well-off society. The so called well-off society is not affluent, but people enjoy a happy life. To plan for Chinese modernization construction, the 13th National Congress of CPC put forward the overall strategies to build Chinese economy in three steps: the first step, from 1981 to 1990, double the GDP in 1980, and solve the problem of food and clothing of the people; the second step, from 1991 to the end of 20 century, double the GDP once more, strive for a well-off standard of living; the third step, by the mid 21 Century, GNP per capita will have reached the level of middle developed countries; people will have had a relatively affluent life and basically realized modernization.

China's socialist modernization construction has different development phases. The well-off society develops from a lower level to a higher level. The overall well-off society is a low level, unbalanced and incomplete society. Based on the overall well-off society, the comprehensive well-off society is a higher level and balanced society which needs further developing.

With the deepening of the course of building Chinese socialist society with Chinese characteristics, the connotation and meaning of "well-off society" has been enriched and developed. The 16th National Congress of CPC report has clearly pointed out that by 2020, we will have built a comprehensive well-off society. The 18th National Congress of CPC report further pointed out that the comprehensive well-off society pursues the common development of economy, politics, culture, society and ecological civilization.

At the end of 20th Century, we have realized the first and the second step of the "three step" strategy. People's living standard has reached the well-off level in the whole, meaning that the overall well-off society has been achieved. Now, we are striving for a comprehensive well-off society.

（一）就业规模不断扩大，就业结构逐步改善。

建国初期到改革开放前，我国城镇就业经历了由快速增长到徘徊不前的变化。改革开放以来，党和政府坚持以经济建设为中心，采取多种措施创造就业岗位，城乡分割的劳动力市场逐渐被打破，就业规模不断扩大，结构逐步改善。

就业规模持续扩大。1949 年末，全国城镇就业人员只有 1533 万人，城镇失业者高达 474.2 万人，失业率为 23.6%。1978 年末，全国就业人员增加到 40152 万人，其中城镇就业人员 9514 万人。改革开放以来，就业政策的不断完善和经济的快速发展，促进了我国就业规模的不断扩大。2010 年末，全国就业人员达到 76105 万人，

(1) The scope of employment has widened and employment structure has been optimized

Between the founding of the People's Republic of China and the country's adoption of reform and opening up policy, urban employment in China experienced sharp growth followed by stagnation. The Communist Party of China (CPC) and the Chinese government have focused on the central task of economic development and adopted various measures to create jobs since the country's reform and opening up. The initial division of the urban and rural labor markets has been gradually broken down, the scope of employment has expanded, and the employment structure has improved gradually.

Employment scope has been widened. At the end of 1949, the number of urban employed was only 15.33 million while the number of unemployed urbanites was as high as 4.742 million, amounting to a 23.6 percent unemployment rate. The total employed population rose to 401.52 million by the end of 1978, of which 95.14 million were urbanites. China's improved employment policies and fast economic growth helped to raise the country's overall employment scale after the country's reform and opening up. The number of employed people

图 43　1949–2013 年末城镇就业人员
Number of Employed Persons in Urban Areas, 1949-2013

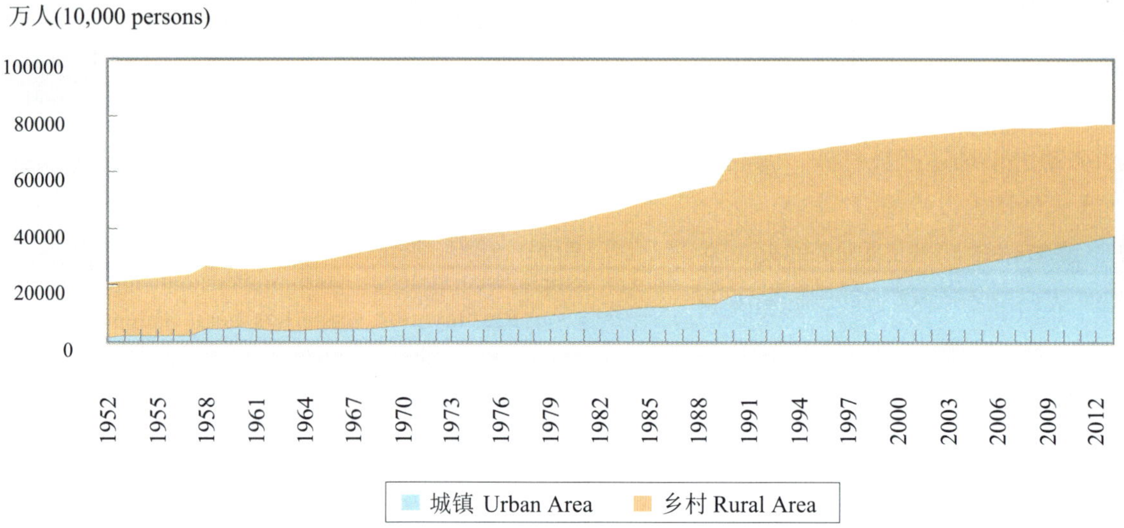

图 44　1952–2013 年城乡就业人员数
Employed Persons by Urban and Rural Areas, 1952-2013

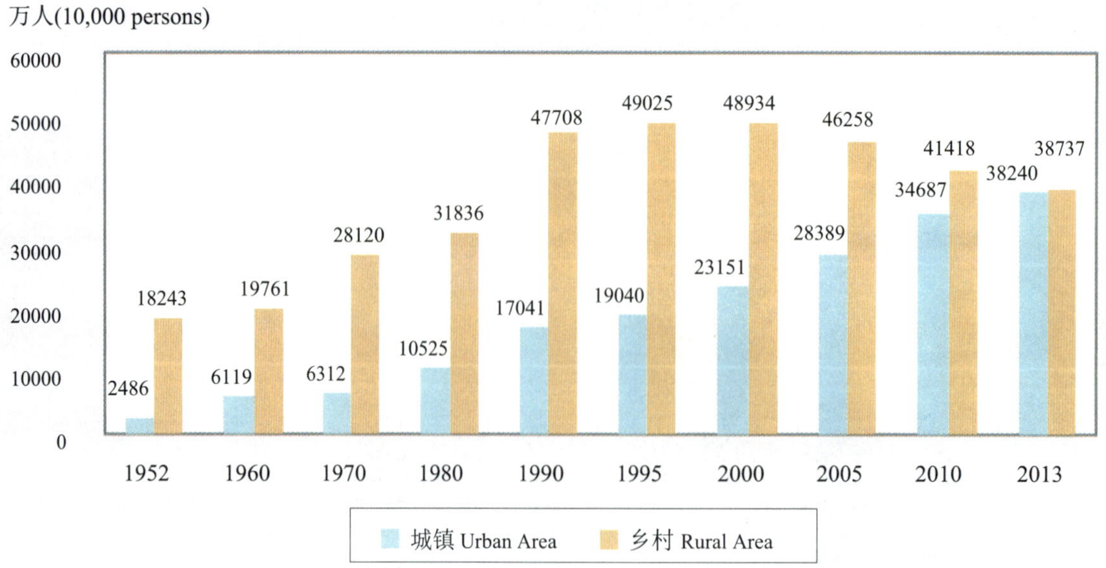

比1978年末增长了89.5%，年均增长2.0%；其中，城镇就业人员达到34687万人，增长了2.6倍，年均增长4.1%。近年来随着我国进入转型发展新阶段，经济增长有所放缓，但由于经济结构的调整以及就业方式的多样化，就业人数继续增加。2013年末，全国就业人员达到76977万人，比2010年末增加872万人，增长1.1%；其中城镇就业人员38240万人，增加3553万人，增长10.2%，年均增长3.3%。大量农村富余劳动力向非农产业有序转移。2013年，农民工数量达到26894万人，比上年增长2.4%。

就业结构深刻变化，第三产业成为吸纳就业的主渠道。新中国成立之初，我国绝大部分劳动者以务农为生。1952年，第一产业就业人员占比高达83.5%，第二、三产业就业人员仅占7.4%和9.1%。随着我国产业结构的调整，1978年，第一产业就业人员占比下降到70.5%，第二、三产业就业人员占比分别上升到17.3%和12.2%。改革开放以来，我国经济发展和结构调整进一步加快，大量农村富余劳动力向城镇和第二、三产业转移。由于第三产业多为劳动密集型产业，就业需求大，就业弹性高，逐渐成为吸纳就业的主渠道。2013年，第三产业就业人员29636万人，比1978年增长5.1倍，年均增长5.3%；第二产业就业人员23170万人，比1978年增长2.3倍，年均增长3.5%；第一产业就业人员24171万人，比1978年下降14.6%。1994年，第三产业就业人员占比达到23.0%，首次超过第二产业；2011年占比达到35.7%，超过第一产业成为吸纳就业最多的产业；2013年占比进一步上升到38.5%，比第一、二产业就业人员占比分别高7.1和8.4个百分点。

nationwide hit 761.05 million at the end of 2010, an 89.5 percent increase over the 1978 number and a 2.0 percent increase over the 2009 number. Of those employed in 2010, 346.87 million were urban employees, 2.6 times the 1978 number and 4.1 percent higher than the 2009 number. Although the Chinese economy has grown more slowly recently due to economic transformation, the overall number of employed people has still risen thanks to economic structural adjustment and diverse types of employment. In 2013, 769.77 million people were employed, a 1.1 percent from 2010, or an increase of 8.72 million. Of that number, 382.40 million were urban employees, a 10.2 percent increase over 2010, or an increase of 35.53 million, reaching an annual growth rate of 3.3 percent. The surplus rural labor force moved to non-agricultural industries, and in 2013, the number of migrant workers reached 268.94 million, a 2.4 percent increase over the previous year.

The employment structure has changed dramatically and tertiary industry has become the main sector to absorb surplus labor. In the early days of the People's Republic of China, most of the labor force in the country was comprised of peasants. In 1952, primary, secondary, and tertiary industries accounted for 83.5 percent, 7.4 percent, and 9.1 percent of employment, respectively. But after China restructured its industrial system, primary industry accounted for only 70.5 percent of overall employment in 1978, while the share of employment in secondary and tertiary industries rose to 17.3 percent and 12.2 percent respectively. As China accelerated economic growth and restructuring in its adoption of reform and opening up, a large amount of surplus labor from the rural labor force began to flow into cities and transfer to secondary and tertiary industries. Tertiary industry became the main industry to absorb surplus labor due to its labor intensiveness, large demand, and flexibility. In 2013, the number of employees in tertiary industry saw an annual growth rate of 5.3 percent and had reached 296.36 million, 5.1 times the number of people employed in this sector in 1978. The number of employees in secondary industry saw an annual growth rate of 3.5 percent in 2013 and reached 231.70 million, 2.3 times more than the number employed in secondary industry in 1978. Also in 2013, the number of employees in primary industry was 241.71 million, 14.6 percent down from the figure in 1978. In 1994, employees in tertiary industry accounted for 23.0 percent of total employment, exceeding secondary industry for the first time. In 2011, this figure rose to 35.7 percent, and tertiary industry replaced primary industry as the main employing industry in China. In 2013, employees in tertiary industries accounted for 38.5 percent of the employed labor force, 7.1 percent more than primary industries and 8.4 percent more than secondary industries.

图 45　1952-2013 年三次产业就业结构
Structure of the Employment of Three Industries, 1952-2013

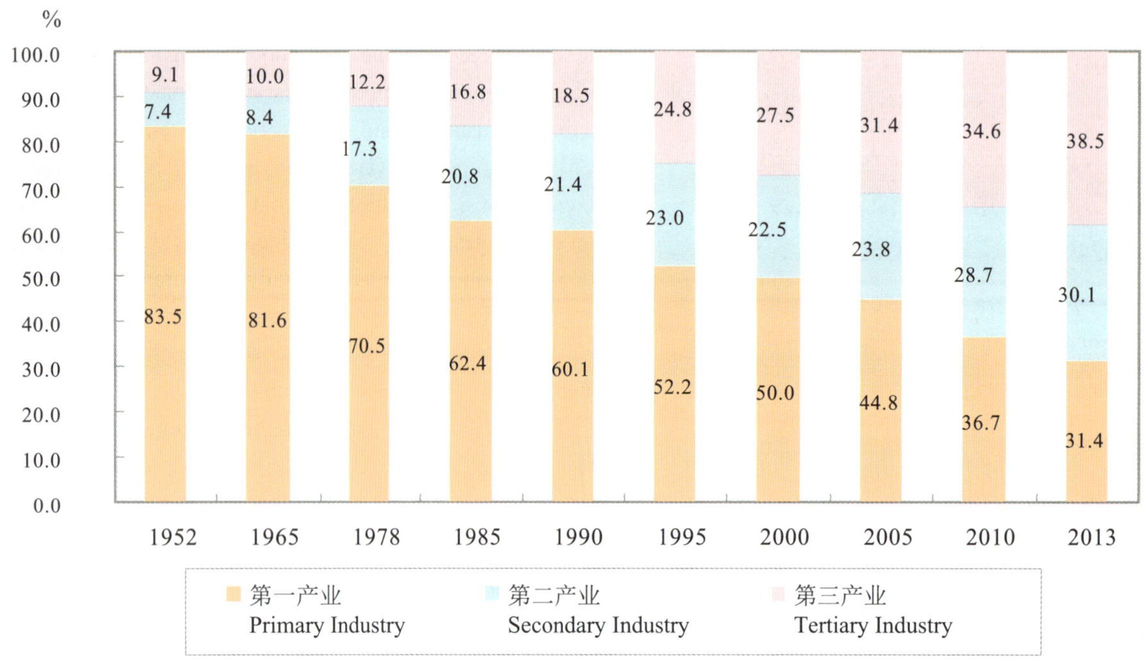

农民工

农民工是我国城乡二元体制下出现的一个特殊的社会群体，指在本地乡镇企业或者进入城镇务工的农业户口人员，具体指户籍仍在农村，在本地从事非农产业或外出从业 6 个月及以上的劳动者。改革开放以来，农民工规模不断扩大，为中国经济腾飞特别是成为世界制造业大国作出了重要贡献。

根据国家统计局抽样调查，2013 年全国农民工总量 26894 万人，占农村从业劳动力的 49.7%。其中，在本地从业的农民工有 10284 万人，占农民工总数 38.2%，外出从业的农民工 16610 万人，占农民工总数 61.8%。

农民工主要来自东、中部，分别为 1.05 亿人、0.93 亿人。农民工主要集中在东部，为 1.62 亿人，占全国 60%。东部地区外出农民工以省内流动为主，中西部地区外出农民工主要向东部地区跨省流动。农民工在东部地区就业以从事制造业为主，在中部地区就业从事建筑业与制造业并重，在西部地区就业以从事建筑业为主。

随着世代更替，老一代农民工开始逐年退出就业市场，新生代农民工开始大量出现。2013 年，1980 年及以后出生的新生代农民工 12528 万人，占农民工总量的 46.6%，占 1980 年及以后出生的农村从业劳动力的比重为 65.5%。与老一代农民工不同，新生代农民工受教育程度较高，主要选择外出务工，主要集中在东部地区及大中城市，并以从事制造业为主，消费倾向更趋城市化。

Migrant Workers

Migrant workers are a special group of people under the urban-rural dual system, referring to people with agricultural residence registration, who work in local township or urban enterprises. To be more specific, migrant workers are those whose registered residence is in rural area, yet work in local non-agricultural industries or work outside rural areas for six months and above. Since China's reform and opening-up, migrant workers are growing in size, having made significant contribution to China's economic development especially in terms of manufacturing.

According to the sampling survey of National Bureau of Statistics, in 2013, China's migrant workers reached 268.94 million, taking up 49.7% of rural total labor. In which, migrant workers working locally were 102.84 million, 38.2% of total migrant labor; migrant workers working outside rural areas reached 166.1 million, 61.8% of the total.

Migrant workers mainly come from eastern and middle China, the former is 105 million and the later is 93 million. Moreover, most of migrant workers, 162 million, 60% of total migrant workers work in eastern China. Migrant workers of eastern China mainly move within provinces, while migrant workers from central and western regions move to eastern provinces. Migrant workers at eastern regions mainly engage in manufacturing industries; middle regions engage in construction and manufacturing industry; western regions engage in construction industry.

As generation changes, migrant workers of older generation gradually leave the job market, and new generation grow like mushrooms after rain. In 2013, migrant workers who were born after 1980 came to 125.28 million, occupying 46.6% of total migrant workers, 65.5% of rural labor born after 1980. Different from migrant workers of older generation, new generation have higher education, therefore most of them choose to work outside rural regions, primarily in eastern China, big and middle cities, in manufacturing industries, with urbanized consumption propensity.

（二）城乡居民收入大幅增加，生活水平显著提高。

建国初期，我国城乡居民收入水平极其低下。在国家发展生产、恢复经济、增加收入的政策措施作用下，居民收入水平逐步提高。改革开放后，随着经济的快速增长与收入分配制度改革的深化，居民收入进入较快增长时期，人民生活水平得到极大改善。

城乡居民收入大幅增长。1949 年，城镇居民家庭人均现金收入不足 100 元，农村居民人均纯收入仅为 44 元。1978 年，城镇居民人均可支配收入达到 343 元，农村居民人均纯收入达到 134 元，分别比 1949 年名义增长 2.4 倍和 2.0 倍，年均增长 4.3%

(2) The income of urban and rural residents sees sharp increase and people's living standards improve by a large margin.

The incomes of urban and rural residents were rather low in the early days of the People's Republic of China. They rose gradually as the nation developed its economy and adopted proactive policies to increase people's income. Income has been increasing rapidly, and people's living standards have seen big improvements in the wake of fast economic development and the deepening of income distribution reform since the country's reform and opening up.

Urban and rural residents' incomes see rapid increase. In 1949, the per-capita cash income of urban households was less than 100 yuan, and the per-capita net income of rural residents was only 44 yuan. In 1978, the per capita disposable incomes of urbanites was 343 yuan, and the per-capita net income of rural residents was 134 yuan, a norminal growth of 2.4 times and 2.0 times over 1949, adjusted for inflation, amounting to annual growth rates of 4.3 percent and 3.9 percent,

图 46　1978–2013 年城镇居民人均可支配收入
Per Capita Annual Disposable Incomes of Urban Residents, 1978-2013

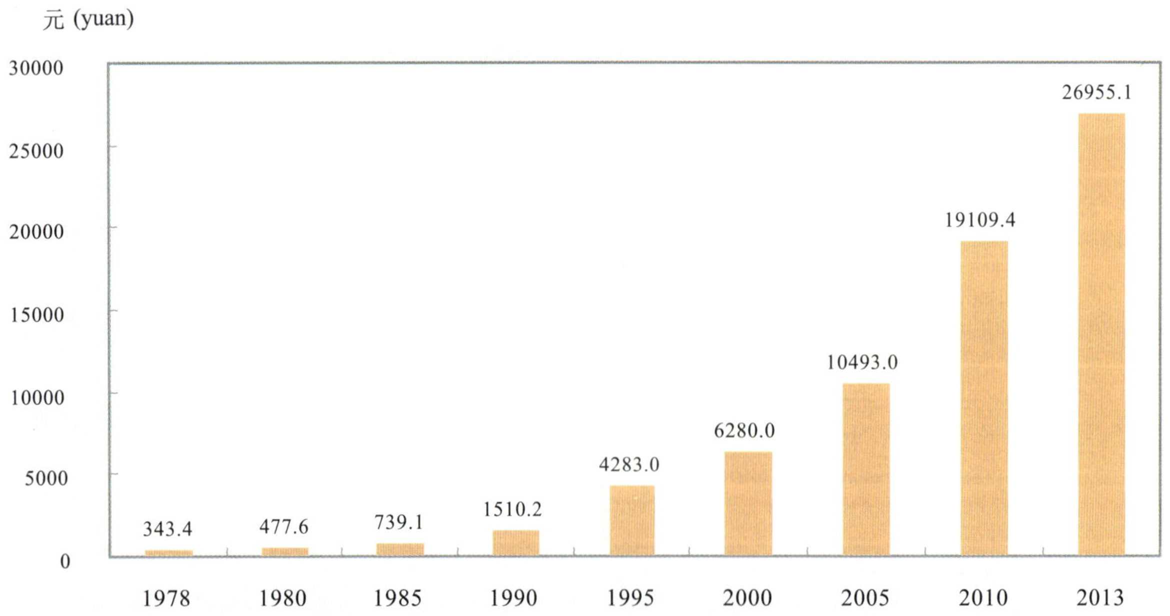

和 3.9%。党的十一届三中全会后，随着农村家庭联产承包责任制的推行、城市扩大企业经营自主权、扩大私营经济发展空间、提升开放水平以及发展市场经济等，城乡居民收入均实现快速增长。2013 年，城镇居民人均可支配收入 26955 元，扣除价格因素，比 1978 年实际增长 11.3 倍，年均增长 7.4%；农村居民人均纯收入 8896 元，扣除价格因素，实际增长 11.9 倍，年均增长 7.6%。伴随收入的快速增长，城乡居民财富成倍增长。1952 年末，城乡居民储蓄存款余额仅为 8.6 亿元，1978 年末增加到 211 亿元，2013 年末达到 447602 亿元，比 1978 年末增长 2124 倍，年均增长 24.5%。近年来居民拥有的股票、债券等金融资产规模不断扩大，住房等实物型财产也大幅增加。

respectively. After the Third Plenary Session of the 11th Central Committee of the Communist Party of China (CPC) in 1978, China began using the household contract responsibility system, enlarged the decision-making powers of enterprises in the cities, expanded room for the private economy in the national economic structure, upgraded its opening up, and developed a market economy. As a result, the incomes of urban and rural residents realized swift growth. In 2013, urbanites' per capita disposable income saw an annual growth rate of 7.4 percent and stood at 26,955 yuan, an 11.3-fold real increase over 1978. The per capita net income of rural residents saw an annual growth rate of 7.6 percent and stood at 8,896 yuan, an 11.9-fold real increase over 1978. Urban and rural residents have seen their wealth grow considerably because of increasing income. The savings deposits of urban and rural residents increased from 860 million yuan at the end of 1952 to 21.1 billion yuan in 1978, and the figure rose to 44.7602 trillion yuan in 2013, reaching an annual growth rate of 24.5 percent and a 2,124-fold increase over 1978. In recent years, China's people have accumulated more and more financial assets like stocks and bonds as well as physical assets, such as housing assets.

图 47 1978-2013 年农村居民人均纯收入

Per Capita Annual Net Income of Urban Residents, 1978-2013

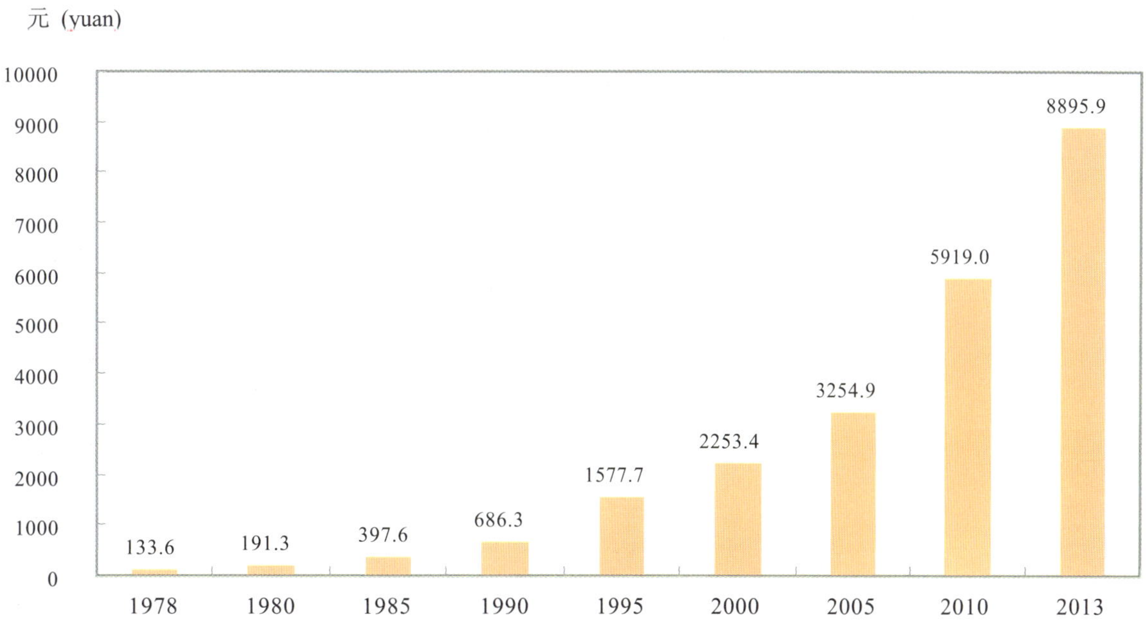

图 48　1952-2013 年城乡居民储蓄存款余额
Savings Deposit of Urban and Rural Residents, 1952-2013

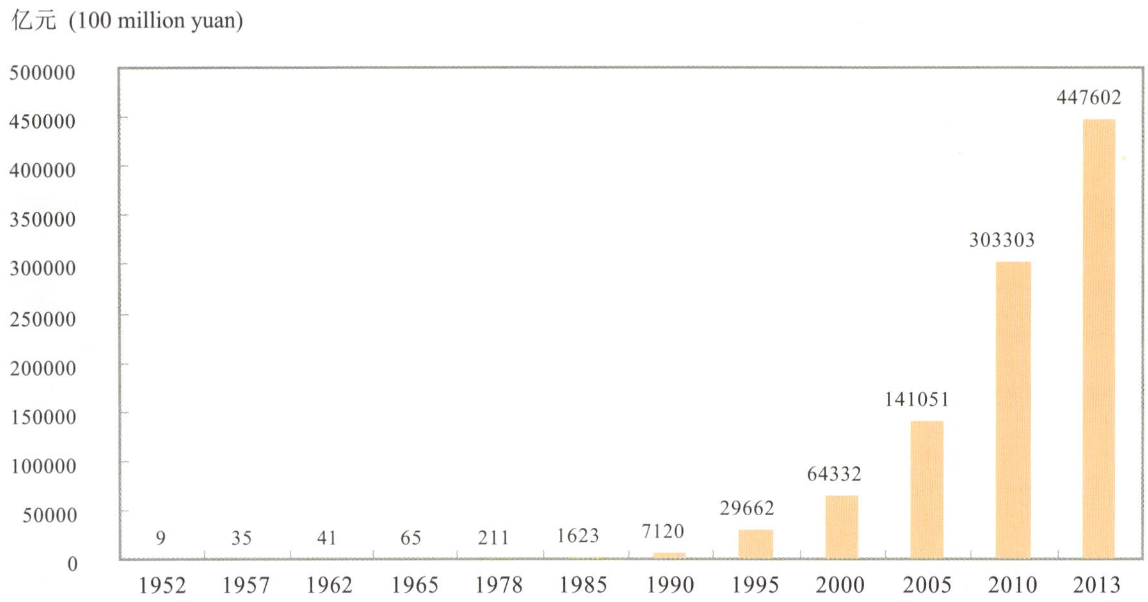

居民消费水平不断提升。1949 年到 1978 年，农村居民家庭人均消费支出从 40 元左右提高到 116 元，名义增长 1.9 倍，年均增长 3.7%。1952 年到 1978 年，城镇居民家庭人均现金消费支出从 168 元提高到 311 元，名义增长 85.1%，年均增长 2.4%。改革开放以来，城乡居民消费支出增长明显加快。2013 年，农村居民家庭人均消费支出为 6626 元，扣除价格因素，比 1978 年实际增长 9.0 倍，年均增长 6.8%；城镇居民家庭人均现金消费支出提高到 18023 元，扣除价格因素，实际增长 8.1 倍，年均增长 6.5%。

Chinese consumption levels have gradually risen. The annual per capita living expenditures of rural residents increased from 40 yuan in 1949 to 116 yuan in 1978, a nominal increase of 1.9 times adjusted for inflation, representing an annual growth rate of 3.7 percent. The annual per capita household living expenditures of urbanites increased from 168 yuan in 1952 to 311 yuan in 1978, a real increase of 85.1 percent adjusted for inflation, representing an annual growth rate of 2.4 percent. The consumption expenditures of urban and rural residents have both seen an obvious increase since China adopted reform and opening up policy. In 2013, the per capita household consumption expenditure of rural residents was 6,626 yuan, a real increase of 9.0 times over 1978 adjusting for inflation, amounting to an annual growth rate of 6.8 percent. The per capita cash consumption expenditure of urban households in 2013 was 18,023 yuan, a real increase of 8.1 times over 1978 adjusted for inflation, amounting to an annual growth rate of 6.5 percent.

图 49　2013 年全国居民人均消费支出构成

Composition of Per Capita Annual Expenditure of Nationwide Resident, 2013

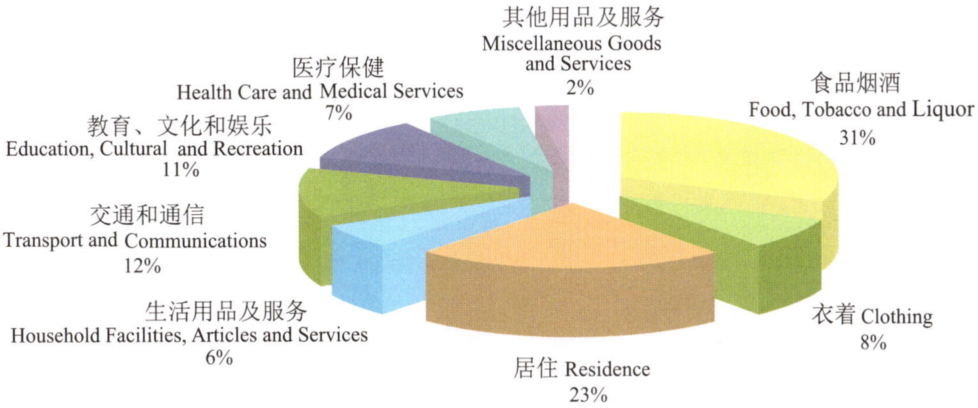

“舌尖上”的恩格尔系数

恩格尔系数是指家庭或个人食品支出金额占其全部消费支出总额的比重。这一指数是由 19 世纪德国统计学家恩格尔最先提出的。他在研究家庭消费支出结构时发现，一个家庭收入越少，家庭收入中（或总支出中）用来购买食物的支出所占的比例就越大；随着家庭收入的增加，食物的支出比例则会下降。推而广之，一个国家或地区越穷，每个国民的平均收入中（或平均支出中）用于购买食物的支出所占比例就越大，反之，国家变得富裕，这个比例呈下降趋势。

恩格尔系数是衡量一个家庭或一个国家富裕程度的主要标准之一。联合国根据恩格尔系数的大小，对世界各国的生活水平设定了一个划分标准：一个国家平均家庭恩格尔系数大于 60% 为贫穷；50%-60% 为温饱；40%-50% 为小康；30%-40% 属于相对富裕；20%-30% 为富足；20% 以下为极其富裕。按此划分标准，20 世纪 90 年代，恩格尔系数在 20% 以下的只有美国，达到 16%；欧洲、日本、加拿大一般在 20-30% 之间，是富足状态。我国城镇和农村居民家庭恩格尔系数已由 1978 年的 57.5% 和 67.7% 分别下降到 2013 年的 35.0% 和 37.7%。

恩格尔系数反映的是一种长期趋势，时间越长趋势越明显。在进行历史比较、国际（或区域）比较时，要注意不同政策、习俗及统计口径等方面的可比性。

A Bite of Engel's Coefficient

The Engel's coefficient refers to the proportion of household or personal expenditure on food on the total expenditure This coefficient was first proposed by Engel, German Statistician, in 19th century. When he studied on the structure of household expenditure, he found that the less a family is in income, the greater proportion of food expenditure on that household income (or total expenditure); and as the income increases, the proportion of food expenditure decreases. In that sense, the poorer a country or a region is, the larger the proportion of food expenditure is. On the contrary, the richer a country or a region is, the less the proportion is.

The Engel's coefficient is one of the major criteria of measuring how rich a family or a country is. The United Nations classifies the living standard of countries in the world according to their Engel’s coefficient. When in a country, the average household Engel’s coefficient exceeds 60%, then the country is poor; between 50% and 60%, in subsistence level; between 40% and 50%, fairly-well-off; between 30% and 40%, relatively rich; between 20% and 30%, rich; below 20%, extremely rich. According to this standard, during 1990s, only the Engel’s coefficient of the United States was under 20%, at 16%; while Europe, Japan, and Canada were rich, with their Engel’s coefficient between 20% and 30%. In China, the Engel’s coefficient of urban households decreased from 57.5% in 1978 to 35.0% in 2013; the Engel’s coefficient of rural households decreased from 67.7% in 1978 to 37.7% in 2013.

The Engel’s coefficient reflects a secular trend. The longer the time is, the more obvious it is. However, when comparing historically and internationally (or regionally), scholars should pay attention to the comparability of different policies, customs, and statistical caliber.

居民生活质量显著改善。新中国成立初期，人们普遍在贫困线上挣扎，城乡居民绝大部分消费都用于食品。1956 年，城镇居民家庭恩格尔系数为 42.6%；1954 年，农村居民家庭恩格尔系数为 68.6%。经过 65 年的发展，居民在发展和享受方面的支出不断上升，生存型消费支出不断下降。2013 年，城镇居民家庭恩格尔系数为 35.0%，比 1978 年下降 22.5 个百分点；交通通信、文教娱乐和医疗保健支出占比分别为 15.2%、12.7% 和 6.2%，比 1982 年分别上升 11.8、5.5 和 5.1 个百分点。农村居民家庭恩格尔系数为 37.7%，比 1978 年下降 30.0 个百分点，交通通信、文教娱乐和医疗保健的消费支出占比分别为 12.0%、7.3% 和 9.3%，比 1980 年分别上升 11.6、2.2 和 7.2 个百分点。城乡居民住

People's quality of life has improved considerably. In the early days of the founding of the PRC, most of China's people lived in poverty, and most of their expenditures were spent on food. In 1956, the Engel coefficient per urban and per rural household was 42.6 percent and 68.6 percent respectively. After 65 years of development, the Chinese people now spend more on development-and-enjoyment-oriented consumption and less on basic living consumption. In 2013 the Engel coefficient per urban household was 35.0 percent, down 22.5 percent from 1978. Urban households' expenditures on communications, culture-education-recreation, and healthcare accounted for 15.2 percent, 12.7 percent and 6.2 percent respectively, up by 11.8, 5.5 and 5.1 percentage points, respectively. The Engel coefficient per rural household was 37.7 percent, a decline of 30.0 percentage points from 1978. Rural households' expenditures on communications, culture-education-recreation, and healthcare accounted for 12.0 percent, 7.3 percent and 9.3 percent respectively, up by 11.6, 2.2 and 7.2

图 50　1978-2013 年城乡居民家庭恩格尔系数
Engel's Coefficient of Urban and Rural Residents, 1978-2013

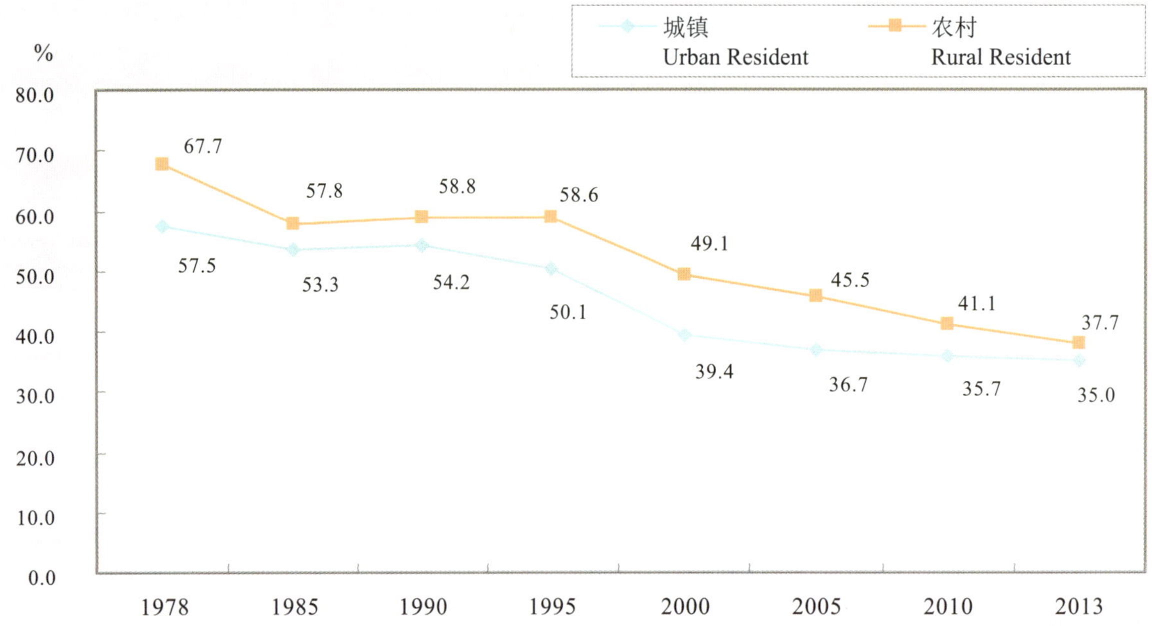

房条件明显改善。2012 年，城镇居民人均住房建筑面积 32.9 平方米，农村居民人均住房面积达到 37.1 平方米，分别比 1978 年增长 3.9 和 3.6 倍。彩电、电冰箱、空调、电话等耐用消费品逐步普及，汽车、电脑等高档耐用消费品拥有量大幅提高。2012 年末，城镇居民家庭平均每百户移动电话、计算机和家用汽车拥有量分别为 212.6 部、87.0 台和 21.5 辆，分别比 1997 年末增加 210.9 部、84.4 台和 21.3 辆；农村居民家庭平均每百户彩色电视机、洗衣机、电冰箱、空调、计算机和移动电话拥有量分别为 116.9 台、67.2 台、67.3 台、25.4 台、21.4 台和 197.8 部，分别比 2000 年末增加 68.2 台、38.6 台、55.0 台、24.1 台、20.9 台和 193.5 部。

percentage points respectively. The housing conditions of urban and rural residents have also improved. In 2012 the per capita floor space of urban and rural residents living space was 32.9 and 37.1 square meters, 3.9 times and 3.6 times the per capita floor space for urban and rural residents in 1978. The consumption of durable goods such as color TV sets, refrigerators, air-conditioners, and phones has been on the rise. Consumption of high-grade durable goods including sedans and computers has also increased by a large margin. By the end of 2012, every 100 urban households owned 212.6 mobile phones, 87.0 computers, and 21.5 cars, an increase of 210.9, 84.4 and 21.3 since 1997; every 100 rural households owned 116.9 colored TV sets, 67.2 washing machines, 67.3 fridges, 25.4 air-conditioners, 21.4 computers and 197.8 mobile phones, an increase of 68.2, 38.6, 55.0, 24.1, 20.9 and 193.5 compared with the end of 2000.

图 51　1981-2012 年每百户城乡居民家庭洗衣机拥有量

Number of Washing Machine Per 100 Urban and Rural Households, 1981-2012

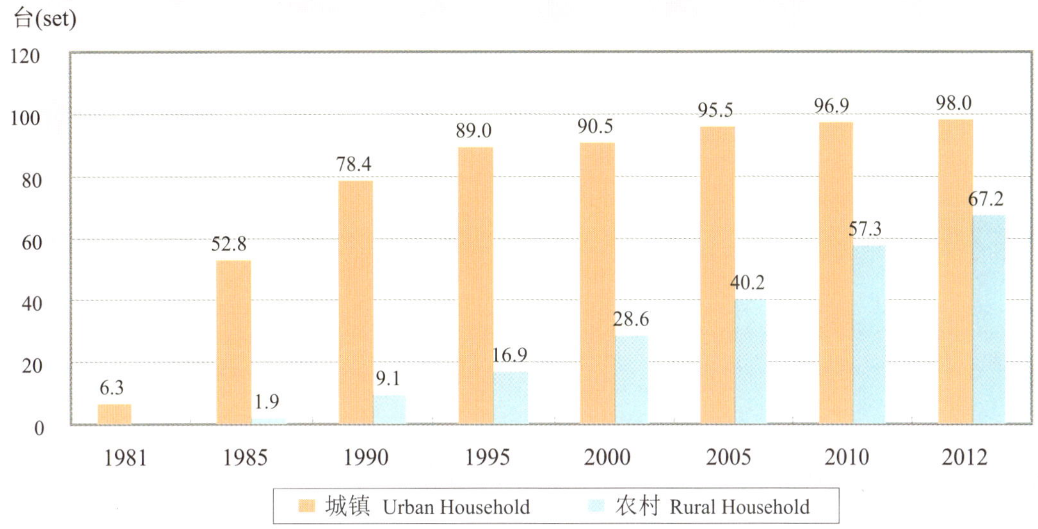

图 52　1985-2012 年每百户城乡居民家庭电冰箱拥有量

Number of Refrigerator Per 100 Urban and Rural Households, 1985-2012

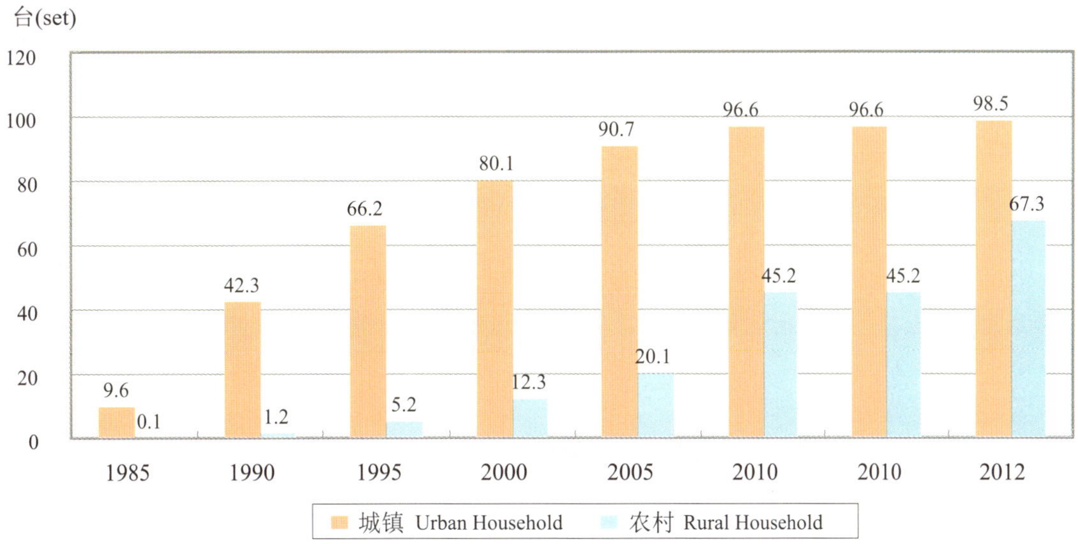

图 53　1981-2012 年每百户城乡居民家庭彩色电视机拥有量
Number of Colour TV Set Per 100 Urban and Rural Households, 1981-2012

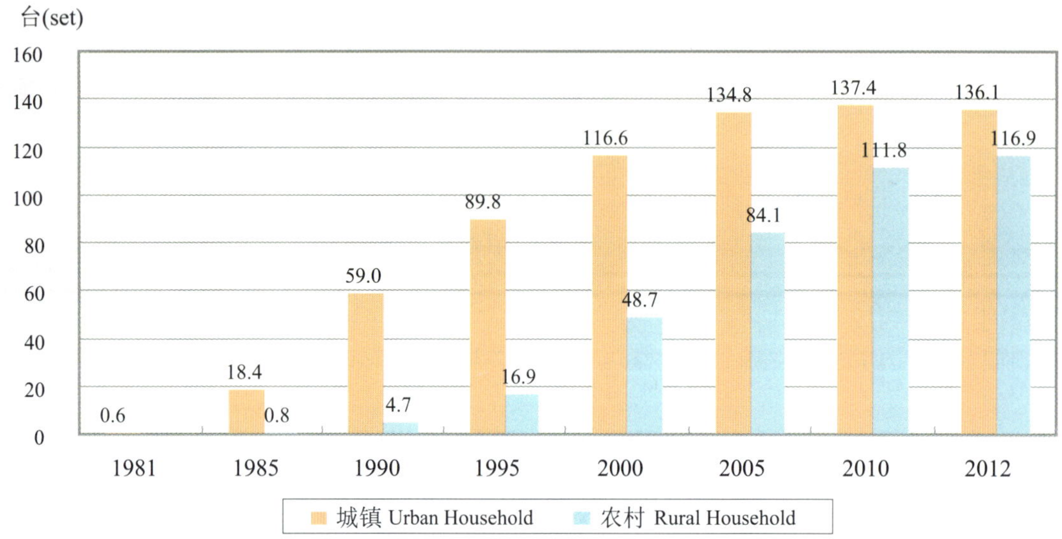

图 54　1997-2012 年每百户城乡居民家庭计算机拥有量
Number of Computer Per 100 Urban and Rural Households, 1997-2012

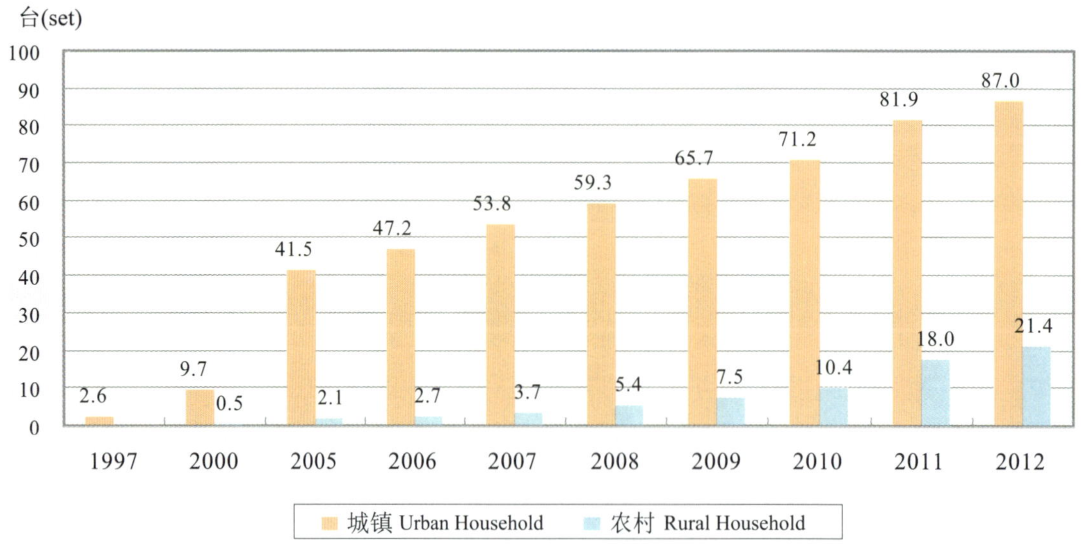

图 55 1985-2012 年每百户城乡居民家庭空调器拥有量
Number of Air Conditioner Per 100 Urban and Rural Households, 1985-2012

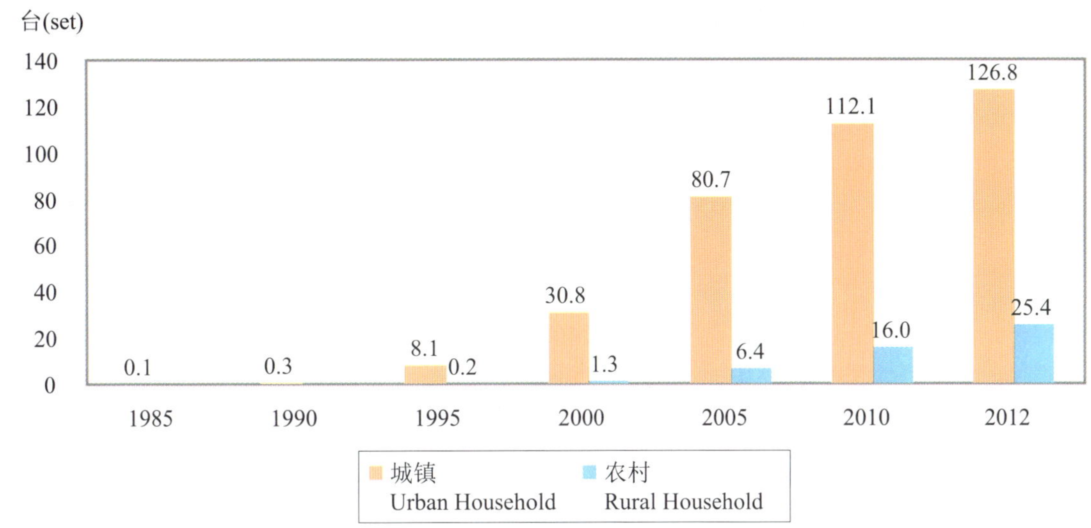

图 56 1997-2012 年每百户城乡居民家庭移动电话拥有量
Number of Mobile Phone Per 100 Urban and Rural Households, 1997-2012

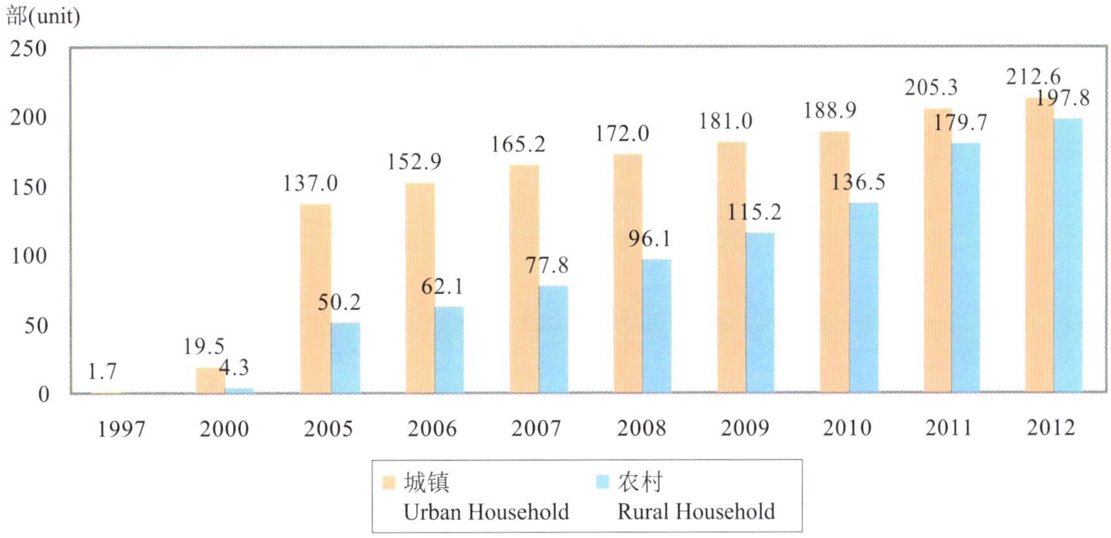

图 57　2000-2012 年每百户城镇居民家庭汽车拥有量
Number of Automobile Per 100 Urban Households, 2000-2012

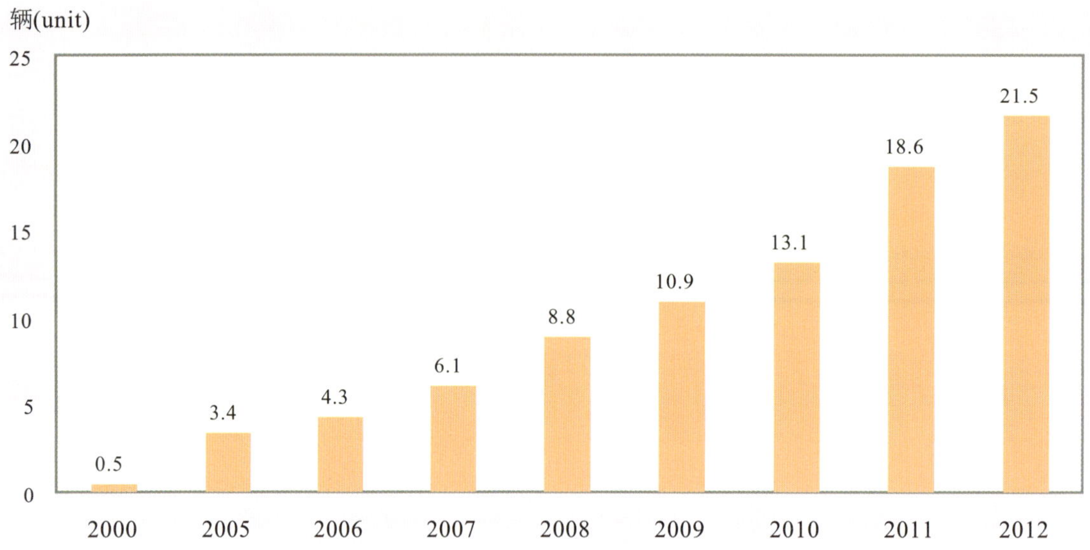

图 58　2001-2012 年城乡居民家庭住房情况
Floor Space of Residential Buildings of Urban and Rural Households, 2001-2012

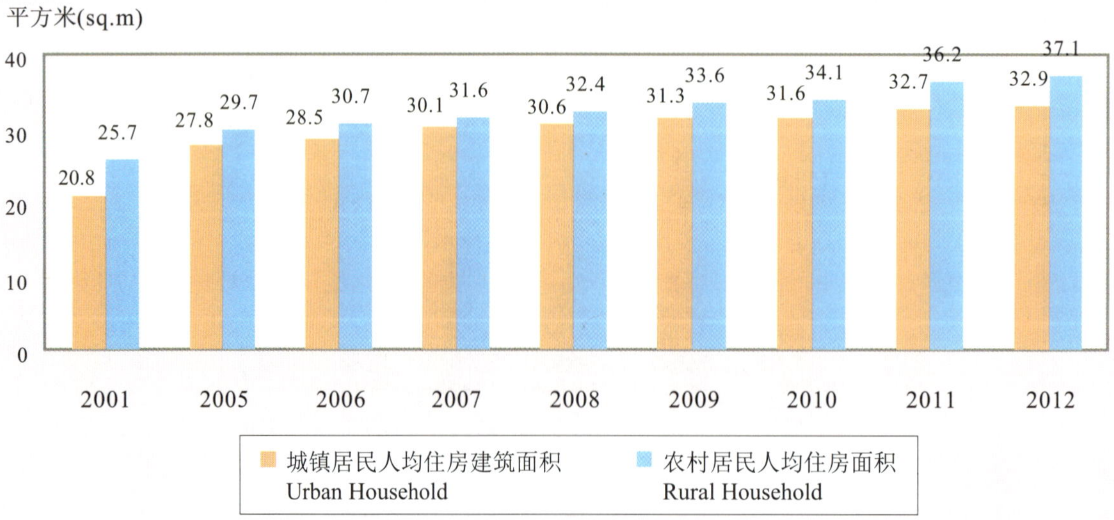

城乡住户调查一体化

长期以来，我国住户收支调查一直按照城镇和农村分别组织实施。城镇住户统计的是居民可支配收入，农村住户统计的是居民纯收入。从 2012 年起，国家统计局进行了一体化改革，统一了城乡居民收入指标名称、分类和统计标准，建立了城乡统一的住户调查制度。

改革后的住户调查对象为我国境内的住户，包括家庭户和集体户。无论户口性质和户口登记地，所有居民均以户为单位，在常住地参加调查。调查内容主要是城乡居民的收入和消费情况，同时也收集反映居民就业、社会保障参与、住房状况、家庭经营和生产投资以及收入分配影响因素的内容。

在进行样本抽选时，以省为总体，采用分层、多阶段、与人口规模大小成比例的概率抽样方法，随机抽选调查住宅，确定调查户。全国共抽选出 1650 个县（市、区）的 1.6 万个调查小区的 200 多万个住户进行全面摸底调查，在此基础上随机等距抽选出约 16 万住户参加记账调查。数据采集主要采用调查户日记账的方式，同时辅之以统一的调查问卷。所有调查、数据处理均由国家统计局及其派出机构组织实施。国家统计局还会采取电话回访、现场抽查等多种方式进行质量控制，确保数据真实可靠。

The Integration of Urban and Rural Household Survey

For a long time, the household budget surveys are organized separately in accordance with urban and rural areas. Urban household statistics is calibrated by the disposable income of residents, while rural household statistics by the net income. Since 2012, the National Bureau of statistics has conducted the integration reform, unifying the standards of the income of urban and rural residents' index names, classification and statistical standards. A unified urban and rural household survey system is thus established.

After the reform, the targets of the household survey changed into China's domestic households, including the family households and collective households. No matter from the accounts' nature or the place of household's registration, all residents share households as units and participate in the survey in the permanent residence. The investigation is mainly about the income and consumption of urban and rural residents. It also reflects the employment, social security, housing situation, family management as well as the production investment and income distribution factors.

In selecting the samples, the provinces are categorized as a whole. The probability sampling method that stratification, division of different stages, and the selection in accordance with the population size is employed with randomly surveying the residential to determine the surveyed households. A total of 1650 counties (cities and districts) over 2 million households are surveyed thoroughly. Based on random equidistance, about 160 thousand households are investigated. Data collection mainly uses the method of the daily bookkeeping of the surveyed households, supplemented by the unified questionnaire. All the surveys, data processing are implemented by the National Bureau of statistics and its dispatched institutions. The National Bureau of Statistics will make phone calls, spot checks and other methods for quality control, ensuring that the data is true and reliable.

（三）社会保障不断完善，扶贫工作取得举世瞩目的成就。

建国初期到改革开放前，我国社会保障主要依靠国家，保障水平较低。改革开放以来，在多方共同努力下，我国社会保障事业发展迅速，基本建立了以社会保险、社会救助、社会福利为基础，以基本养老、基本医疗和最低生活保障制度为重点，以慈善事业、商业保险为补充的多层次社会保障体系，满足了人民群众多样化的社会保障需求。与此同时，我国在扶贫工作方面取得了举世瞩目的成绩，为全世界的扶贫事业做出了突出贡献。

(3) China has improved its social security and attained poverty relief achievements that have attracted world-wide attention.

Social security was mainly provided by the government at rather low levels during the period from the founding of the PRC to the country's initiation of reform and opening up. The social security undertaking has developed swiftly due to concerted efforts since the adoption of reform and opening up policy. A multi-level social security system has taken shape, with social insurance, social assistance and social welfare as the basis, basic pension, with basic healthcare and minimum standard of living as the emphasis, and with charity and commercial insurance as supplements. The system caters to the dynamic social security requirements of the masses. Meanwhile, China has attained tremendous achievements in poverty relief and made outstanding contributions to world poverty reduction.

图 58　1989–2013 年社会保障参加保险人数
Number of Social Security Contributors, 1989-2013

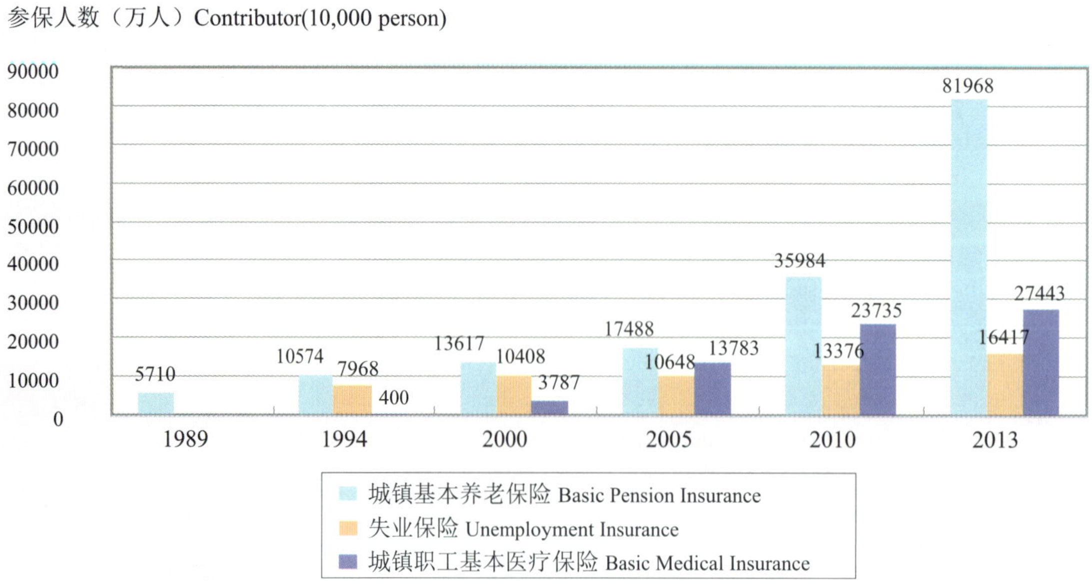

社会保障体系建设稳步推进。近年来，党中央、国务院按照全覆盖、保基本、多层次、可持续方针，以增强公平性、适应流动性、保证可持续性为重点，积极发展社会保障事业，城乡基本养老保险制度全面建立，全民医保基本实现，社会救助体系基本形成，社会保障基本实现全覆盖。2013 年末，全国参加城镇职工基本养老保险人数 32218 万人，比 1989 年末增加 26508 万人；参加城镇职工基本医疗保险人数 27443 万人，比 1994 年末增加 27043 万人；参加失业保险人数 16417 万人，增加 8449 万人；参加工伤保险的人数 19917 万人，增加 18095 万人；参加生育保险的人数 16392 万人，增加 15476 万人。城乡居民社会养老保险参保人数达到 49750 万人。2013 年末，2489 个县（市、区）实施了新型农村合作医疗制度，新型农村合作医疗参合人数达到 80209 万人，参合率为 98.7%。2064 万城市居民和5388 万农村居民得到政府最低生活保障。

The construction of a social security system is moving steadily forward. In recent years, the CPC Central Committee and the State Council have actively developed a social security undertaking guided by the principles of sustainable development, fairness, full coverage, and flexibility. A multi-level system incorporating basic pension insurance for urban and rural residents and nationwide medical insurance and social assistance has been established. The social security system basically covers the whole nation. By the end of 2013, the basic pension insurance system for workers in cities and towns covered 322.18 million, an increase of 265.08 million since 1989; the basic medical insurance system for workers in cities and towns covered 274.43 million, an increase of 270.43 million since 1994. The insurance systems for unemployment, work-related injury, and childbirth covered 164.17 million, 199.17 million and 163.92 million, an increase of 84.49 million, 180.95 million and 154.76 million respectively. The social pension insurance system for urban and rural residents covered 497.50 million. At the end of 2013, 2489 counties adopted new rural cooperative medical insurance which covered 802.09 million and had 98.7 percent coverage. Around 20.64 million urbanites and 53.88 million rural residents also received subsistence allowances.

扶贫工作成效卓著。消除贫困一直是党和政府工作的重点。新中国成立之初，国家首先对因老弱病残、丧失或缺少劳动能力而不能保障基本生活的农民进行社会救济，并建立了“五保”制度。新中国的扶贫工作就是在农村救济和救灾工作基础上逐步发展起来的。这一时期，虽然我国经济保持了一定速度的发展，但由于人口迅速增加，加上长期实行平均主义分配方式对生产积极性的抑制，农村贫困状况仍然十分严重。1978 年，全国农村贫困人口高达 2.5 亿人，贫困发生率为 30.7%。改革开放以后，大规模的全国性的扶贫工作正式开始实施，在长期的扶贫实践中逐渐探索出“输血”与“造血”相结合的扶贫办法，先后实施“国家八七扶贫攻坚计划”和 2001-2010 年的“中国农村扶贫开发纲要”，通过体制改革、经济发展、专项扶贫、城乡统筹等，农村的贫困状况得到了极大的缓解，扶贫事业取得举世瞩目的成就。2007 年，贫困人口下降为 1479 万人，1979-2007 年平均每年脱贫 811 万人。2008 年以来，为了更好地改善人民生活水平，多次提高贫困标准。按照 2008 年标准，2007 年农村贫困人口为 4320 万人，2010 年下降为 2688 万人，平均每年脱贫 544 万人。按照 2010 年制定的新标准，2010 年农村贫困人口为 16567 万人，2013 年下降为 8249 万人，平均每年脱贫 2773 万人。扶贫工作不仅有效推动了贫困地区经济增长，明显改善了贫困地区的生产生活条件，也极大提高了贫困地区社会事业的发展水平。联合国和世界银行认为，在消灭贫困方面，中国做出了巨大努力，为全人类的扶贫事业做出了突出贡献，是发展中国家的典范。

China has made tremendous progress in poverty alleviation. Poverty elimination has long been one of the major tasks of the CPC and the Chinese government. In the early days of the PRC, the country offered its first social relief programs to peasants who couldn't make ends meet due to old age, weakness, and/or work disability by setting up the Rural Five Guarantees System. China's poverty relief work developed from rural relief and disaster relief. During that period, rural poverty was still rather serious due to the sharp increase in the population, in addition to the suppression of enthusiasm for the long-term application of egalitarian distribution of income and production, though the national economy maintained its momentum. In 1978, the rural poverty-stricken population numbered 250 million, approximately 30.7 percent of the total rural population. A large-scale poverty relief campaign was launched nationwide after the initiation of reform and opening up. China integrated two measures in its long-term poverty alleviation efforts: "blood transfusion" (outside support) and "creating blood" (self-reliance). China implemented the Seven-Year Priority Poverty Alleviation Program (a program designed to lift 80 million people out of absolute poverty in the seven years from 1994 to 2000) and the Outline for Development-Oriented Poverty Reduction for China's Rural Areas (2001-2010). The country has made outstanding achievements in rural poverty reduction through system reform, economic development, establishing special work units, and balancing urban and rural development. The number of people living in poverty in China shrank to 14.79 million in 2007, and 8.11 million people rose out of poverty every year from 1979 to 2007. China began applying its new criteria for poverty in 2008 to further improve people's lives. According to the new criteria, the impoverished rural population was 43.20 million in 2007 and declined to 26.88 million in 2010, with 5.44 million people brought out of poverty each year. The new 2010 poverty-alleviation criteria show that China's impoverished rural population was 165.67 million in 2010, and the figure declined to 82.49 million in 2013, with 27.73 million pulled out of poverty each year. China's poverty elimination has not only boosted the economy in poor areas, but it has also improved the living and production conditions in those areas. The UN and the World Bank have both applauded China's huge efforts and its marked contributions to world poverty alleviation, holding up China as a model for other developing countries.

社会保障制度

社会保障制度是国家制定的社会保险、救助、补贴等一系列制度的总称，其作用在于保障全社会成员基本生存与生活需求，特别是保障公民在年老、疾病、伤残、失业、生育、死亡、遭遇灾害、面临生活困难时的特殊需要。目前，我国的社会保障制度主要包括社会保险、社会救济、社会福利、优抚安置、和社会互助五大类。

社会保险是政府为工薪劳动者在年老、疾病、生育、失业以及遭受职业伤害的情况下，提供必要的物质帮助的制度，分为养老保险、失业保险、医疗保险、工伤保险和生育保险。社会保险的保障对象是全体劳动者，资金主要来源是用人单位和劳动者个人的缴费，政府给予资助。

社会救济是政府对生活在社会基本生活水平以下的贫困地区或贫困居民给予的基本生活保障，是基础的、最低层次的社会保障。城乡居民最低生活保障制度就属于社会救济范畴。

社会福利是政府为社会成员举办的各种公益性事业及为各类残疾人、生活无保障人员提供生活保障的事业。目前，我国有社会福利院、敬老院、疗养院、儿童福利院等福利机构。

优抚安置是政府对军属、烈属、复员转业军人、残废军人予以优待抚恤的制度。

社会互助是指在政府鼓励和支持下，社会团体和社会成员自愿组织和参与的扶弱济困活动。其主要形式有工会、妇联、慈善救助机构等。

Social Security System

Social security system is a combination of a series of system of the national social insurance, assistance, subsidies and, its function is to guarantee the social member's basic survival and living needs, especially to protect citizens' special need when they are in old age, sickness, disability, unemployment, birth, death, disaster or facing difficulties in life. At present, China's social security system includes five categories, namely the social insurance, social relief, social welfare, social mutual aid, the special care and placement.

Social insurance is a material assistance system which is provided by government for salaried workers when they are in old age, disease, unemployment, maternity and suffer the occupation injury cases, including old-age insurance, unemployment insurance, medical insurance, work-related injury insurance and maternity insurance. The beneficiaries of social insurance are all labor, with the main capital source from the employing unit and the laborer individual payment, government grants.

As the lowest level of social security, Social relief is the basic life safeguard provided by government for the people lived in impoverished area or under the basic social living standard. The minimum livelihood guarantee system for rural residents belongs to the category of social relief

Social welfare is a public welfare undertaking to provide life insurance, which is held by the government for its social members, disability, and non-security personnel business. At present, China established social welfare, nursing homes, nursing homes, children's welfare homes and welfare institutions.

The special care and placement is the system provides preferential treatment to military' families, the martyr's family member, demobilized servicemen, disabled veterans.

Social mutual aid refers to the charitable activities, which social organizations and members of the community voluntarily organized and participate with encouragement and support of the government. The main forms of social mutual aid include trade unions, women's federations, and charity organizations.

贫困线

贫困线是用来划分贫困人口的标准。世界每个国家都存在贫困人口。贫困可分为绝对贫困和相对贫困，绝对贫困指低于维持身体有效活动的最低指标的一种贫困，相对贫困是指相对于中等社会生活而言的贫困。与此对应，绝对贫困标准是在一定的时间、空间和社会发展阶段的条件下，维持人们的基本生存所必需消费的物品和服务的最低费用。

绝对贫困标准是按最低营养标准来测定的。20 世纪 80 年代初期，我国根据国际规范来测算贫困线标准。首先，我国将营养标准确定为每人每天 2100 大卡；然后，根据 20% 的最低收入人群的消费结构来测定出满足这一营养标准所需要的各种食物量；再按照食物的价格计算出相应的货币价值。根据这一原则，1985 年我国确定的贫困线为人均年纯收入 200 元。世界银行则将每人每日 1.25 美元（2008 年前为 1 美元）作为极端贫困线。

相对贫困标准是按收入来计算的。经济合作与发展组织（OECD）将一个国家或地区的中位收入或平均收入的 50% 作为这个国家或地区的贫困线。

在 2000 年前，我国只有绝对贫困标准，2000 年后制定了低收入标准。到 2008 年，我国把绝对贫困标准与低收入标准合二为一。2008 年的贫困标准为 1067 元，2011 年调整为 2300 元。

Poverty Line

The poverty line is the standard used to divide the poverty groups. There are poor people in every country around the world. Poverty can be divided into absolute and relative poverty. Absolute poverty refers to a kind of poverty that people cannot sustain the effective body activities. Relative poverty is defined in relation to the society's middle class. In accordance with this, absolute poverty standard is positioned during certain period of time, in certain space and social development conditions to sustain the essential consumer goods and services to maintain the people's basic survival.

Absolute poverty standard is calculated according to the minimum standard of nutrition. In early 1980s, China measured the poverty line standard in line with the international standards. First of all, our country designated nutrition standards set for every person every day at 2100 calories; the amount of the food are calculated by the consumption structure of 20% of the lowest income groups' consumption structure. Then according to the price of food, the value of money was calculated. According to this principle, in 1985 China established poverty line of farmers at the net income of 200 yuan per capita. The World Bank assigned $1.25 per capita every day (based on the 1 US dollar before 2008) as the extreme poverty line.

Relative poverty standard is calculated by the income calculation. The Organization for Economic Cooperation and Development (OECD) selects the median income of a country or an area or 50% of the average income as the poverty line.

Before 2000, China has only absolute poverty standard. After 2000, low income standard is formulated. By 2008, China's absolute poverty standard and low income standards were united. The standard of poverty in 2008 was 1067 yuan, In 2011, it was adjusted to 2300 yuan.

最低生活保障

最低生活保障是国家对家庭人均收入低于当地政府公告的最低生活标准的人口给予一定现金资助，以保证该家庭成员基本生活所需的社会保障制度。由于二元体制，我国最低生活保障制度也是分城乡分别实施的。

城市最低生活保障制度所保障的对象是城市低于最低生活保障标准的非农业户口居民。1999 年 9 月，国务院颁布了《城市居民生活最低保障条例》，标志着城市居民最低生活保障制度在全国范围内全面施行。城市居民最低生活保障标准，按照当地维持城市居民基本生活所必需的衣、食、住费用，并适当考虑水电燃煤（燃气）费用以及未成年人的义务教育费用确定。

农村最低生活保障制度所保障的对象是农村人均纯收入低于最低生活保障标准的农业户口居民。2007 年，国务院发布《关于在全国建立农村最低生活保障制度的通知》，在全国范围内全面推行农村最低生活保障制度。农村最低生活保障标准，按照能够维持当地农村居民全年基本生活所必需的吃饭、穿衣、用水、用电等费用确定。在大多数地区，采用农村绝对贫困线作为农村最低生活保障标准。

Minimum Subsistence Allowances

The minimum subsistence allowance is a social system that the cash assistance are designated by the country to those whose per capita income in the households and living standards are lower than the minimum living standards of local government's stipulation to ensure that the family members' basic needs are met. Because of the system of two, the minimum living guarantee system in China is also implemented in urban and rural areas separately.

The targets of the subsistence allowance are the non-agriculture residents whose living standards are below the thresholds in the city's minimum living security standard. In September 1999, the State Council promulgated the city residents minimum living security regulations, marking the minimum living security system of city residents being fully implemented throughout the country. City residents' minimum living standards are made in accordance to maintain the basic livelihood of the local city residents clothing, food, lodging, and proper consideration of power coal (gas) costs and expenses of compulsory education for the children.

The objectives of the rural minimum living security system are the agricultural residence whose net income per capita is lower than the minimum living standard. In 2007, the State Council issued the notice on the establishment of rural minimum living security system to fully implement the rural minimum living security system throughout the country. The rural minimum living security standard are determined in order to sustain the local rural residents' annual basic eating, dressing, water, electricity and other costs. In most areas, the rural absolute poverty line adopts the rural minimum living security standard.

7 从文盲大国到人力资源大国，从受制于人到引领未来，教育和科技事业成就辉煌

Transformed from a largely illiterate country to a nation rich in human resources, China has become a leader of the future, no longer restricted by others. China has made splendid achievements in its educational, scientific, and technological undertakings.

新中国成立以来的65年，是我国教育事业大发展、实现从文盲大国到人力资源大国历史性转变的65年，是科技事业创造辉煌、科技创新硕果累累的65年，也是中华民族的科学文化素质逐渐提高、核心竞争力不断增强的65年。

China has witnessed a rapid growth in education 65 years after the founding of the PRC and has transformed itself from a largely illiterate country into a nation rich in human resources. Over the past 65 years, the country embraced a splendid period of scientific and technological advancement and entered an era of fruitful scientific and technological innovation. The quality of scientific knowledge, literacy, and core competencies of the Chinese people has been enhanced, too.

（一）教育事业取得巨大进步，人口素质大幅提高。

新中国成立之初，我国人口素质十分低下，全国 80% 的人口是文盲，农村的文盲率更是高达 95% 以上，适龄儿童小学入学率不足 20%。新中国成立后特别是改革开放以来，党和政府着眼百年大计，坚持教育优先发展的重大战略，教育事业取得了举世瞩目的伟大成就，中华民族的文化素质得到显著提升，实现了由文盲大国向人力资源大国的历史性转变。

人口受教育水平不断提高。党和政府高度重视教育事业，不断增加教育投入。1992 年，国家财政性教育经费为 729 亿元，占国内生产总值的比重为 2.71%。2013 年，国家财政性教育经费达到 24552 亿元，比 1992 年增长 32.7 倍，年均增长 18.2%，占国内生产总值的比重提高到 4.31%。15 岁及以上人口平均受教育年限由 1982 年的 5.3 年提高到 2013 年的 9.3 年，劳动年龄人口的平均受教育年限达到 9.3 年，其中受过高等教育

(1) Tremendous progress has been made in education and the basic skills of the population have greatly improved.

The basic skills of the Chinese population were rather low when the PRC was founded in 1949. 80 percent of the entire population was illiterate, the rural illiteracy rate was more than 95 percent, and less than 20 percent of children of school age went to school. The Party and the Chinese government have given priority to the development of education, an undertaking of vital and lasting importance, and have made great achievements since the founding of the PRC, especially after the country's reform and opening up. As a result, the education level of the Chinese people improved remarkably and China saw an historic turn from a largely illiterate country to a nation rich in human resources.

Chinese citizens' education level has continued to rise. The Party and the government put a high value on education and have increase their input into education. The government appropriation for education was 72.9 billion yuan, accounting for the proportion of GDP was 2.71 percent in 1992. The government appropriation for education was 2.4552 trillion yuan, increasing 32.7 times, with an annual growth rate of 18.2 percent from 1992 to 2013, accounting for 4.31 percent of the country's GDP. The per capita years of schooling for people age 15 or above increased from 5.3 years in 1982 to 9.3 years in 2013, and the number of years of schooling among the working-age population reached 9.3 years, of which 12.77

图 59　国家财政性教育经费占国内生产总值比例（%）
Porportion of Government Appropriation for Education to GDP

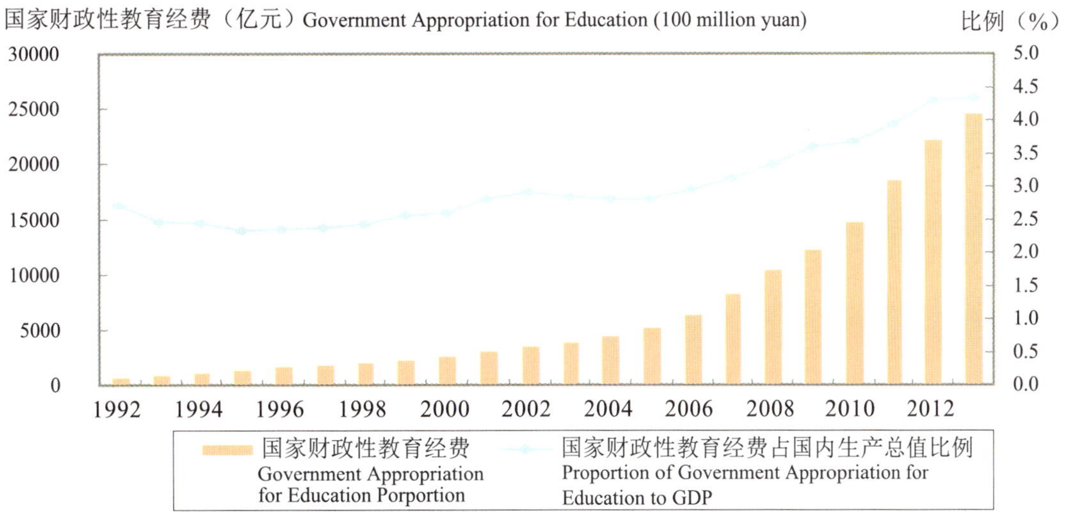

图 60 文盲人口及文盲率
Illiterate Population and Illiterate Rate

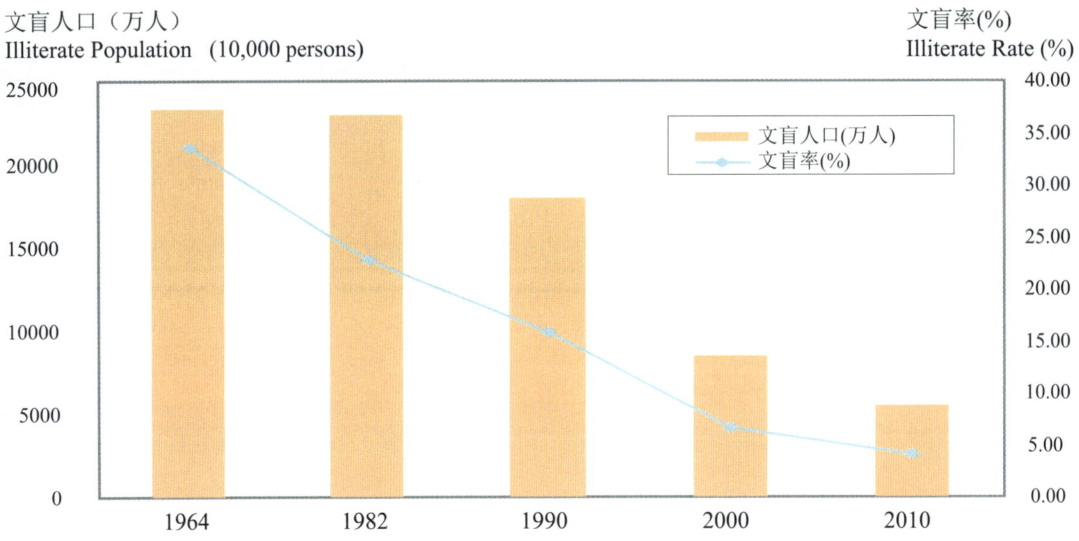

图 61 1982-2010 年全国 6 岁及以上人口平均受教育年限
Per Capita Years of Schooling for People Age 6 or Above, 1982-2010

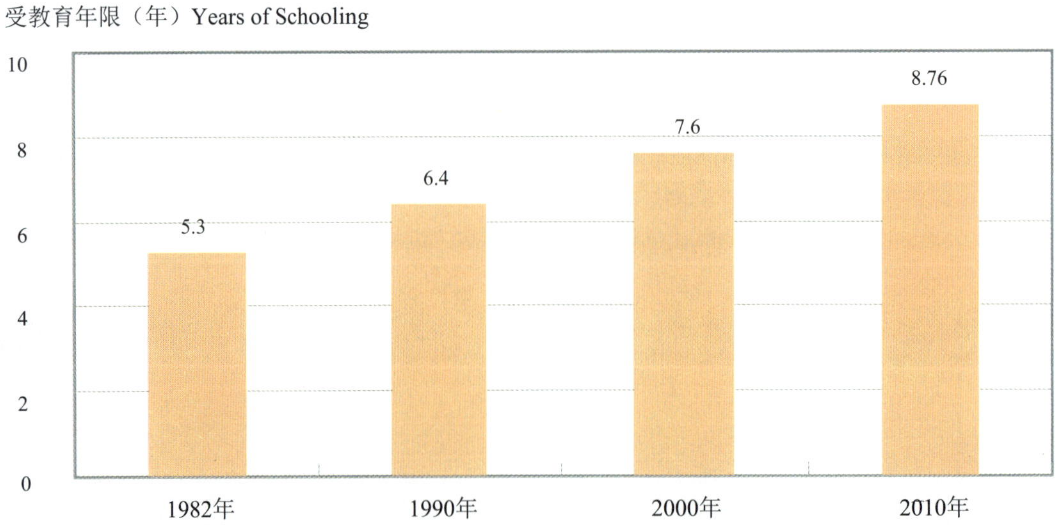

育的比例占 12.77%。从各种受教育程度人口比重看，2013 年大专及以上受教育程度人口比重为 10.54%，比 1982 年提高了 9.93 个百分点；小学文化程度人口占 24.56%，降低了 10.68 个百分点，而高中和初中文化程度人口比重均有不同程度提高，分别达到 15.39% 和 38.01%。

义务教育全面普及并不断巩固。1986 年我国颁布和实施了第一部义务教育法，经过 10 多年的艰苦努力，2000 年我国 85% 的人口地区实现了基本普及义务教育、基本扫除青壮年文盲的目标。2006 年起全面免除西部农村义务教育阶段学生学杂费，2008 年秋季，城市义务教育阶段学杂费全部免除，标志着我国免费九年义务教育已全面实现，我国普及义务教育工作得到了进一步的巩固和提高。2010 年，全国普及九年义务教育人口覆盖率达到 100%。全国小学学龄儿童净入学率由 1986 年的 96.4% 提高到 2013 年的 99.7%，小学毕业生升学率由 69.5% 提高到 98.3%，初中毕业生升学率由 40.6% 提高到 91.2%。

percent received higher education. In 2013, 10.54 percent of the population had attended junior college and and above, 9.93 percentage points higher than in 1982; 24.56 percent of the total population whose highest level of education was primary school, 10.68 percentage points down from 1982; while the population with a high school or middle school education climbed to 15.39 percent and 38.01 percent, respectively.

Compulsory education has become universal and is being constantly strengthened. China promulgated and implemented the compulsory education law, the first of its kind in the country, in 1986. After more than a decade of hard work, 85 percent population of China reached its goals of making nine years of compulsory education basically universal and eradicating adult illiteracy by 2000. In 2006, China waived tuition and fees for primary and middle school students in rural areas in the western region and waived tuition and fees for urban students pursuing compulsory education in the autumn of 2008, which marked China's full realization of a free, nine-year compulsory education system. China's compulsory education system has been improved and consolidated. By the end of 2010, 100 percent of the population was covered under the nine-year compulsory education system. The net enrollment rate of school-age children increased from 96.4 percent in 1986 to 99.7 percent in 2013; the progression rate for primary school graduates rose from 69.5 percent to 98.3 percent; the progression rate for middle school graduates also jumped from 40.6 percent to 91.2 percent.

图 62　1952-2013 年小学学龄儿童净入学率和各级学校毕业生升学率

Net Enrollment Rate of School-age Children and Progression Rates for Various School Graduates, 1952-2013

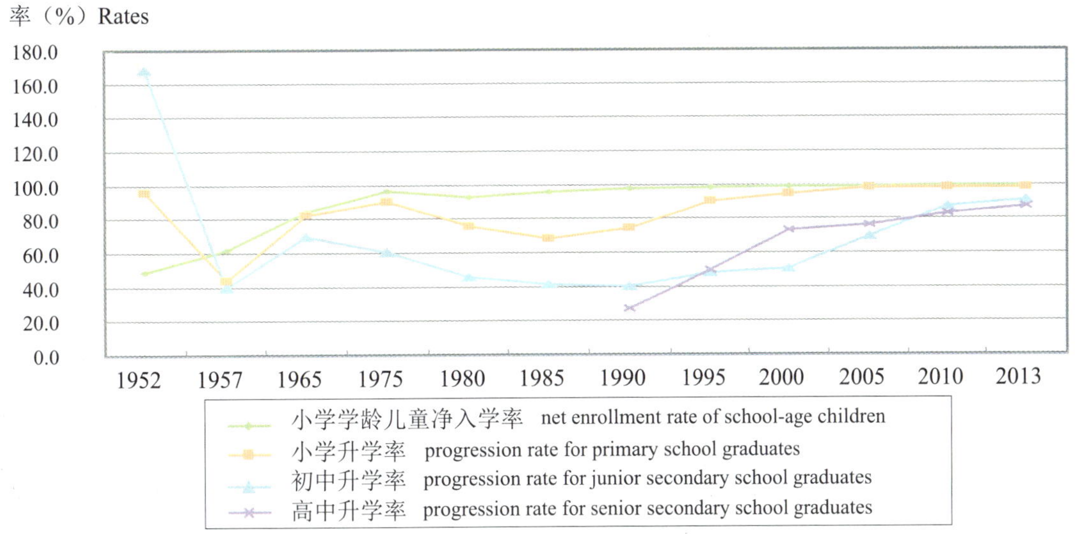

图 63　每十万人拥有的各种受教育人口

Population with Various Education Attainments Per 100,000 Persons

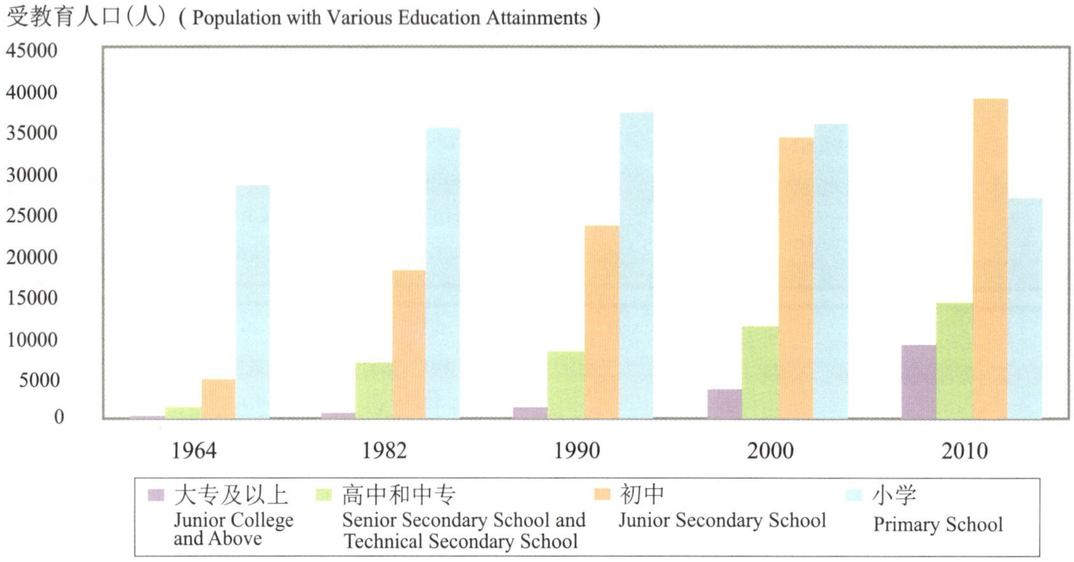

高等教育进入大众化阶段。2013 年，我国高等教育毛入学率达到 34.5%，在学总规模达到 3460 万人，位居世界第一。全国共招收普通本专科学生 700 万人，普通本专科在校生人数达到 2468 万人，分别比 1978 年增长 16.4 倍和 27.8 倍。自 1977 年恢复高考制度以来，普通高等学校共培养本专科毕业生 6518 万人，其中 2001-2013 年的毕业生占 81.1%。在本专科教育迅速发展的同时，研究生教育规模不断扩大。2013 年，高等学校和研究机构共招收研究生 61 万人，比 1978 年增长了 56.1 倍，年均增长 12.3%；在学研究生 179 万人，增长了 163.1 倍，年均增长 15.7%。高等教育为社会输送了大量的优秀毕业生，优化了劳动者队伍的素质结构。

Higher education has become accessible to the masses. In 2013 the gross enrollment rate in Chinese higher education reached 34.6 percent, and the total number of university students at school was 24.68 million, the highest number in the world. In 2013, China enrolled 7 million new college students, and the number of college students reached 24.68 million, 16.4 times and 27.8 times the numbers from 1978, respectively. China has 65.18 million college graduates, of which 81.1 percent graduated between 2001 and 2013, after the country reinstated the college entrance examination system. Along with the rapid growth of college education, postgraduate education also expanded. In 2013, 610 thousand postgraduates were enrolled in universities and research institutes, 56.1 times higher than the number enrolled in 1978, with an annual growth rate of 12.3 percent; the number of total postgraduates at school was 1.79 million, 163.1 times higher and with an annual growth rate of 15.7 percent. Higher education has generated a large number of excellent graduates and has upgraded the quality of the labor force.

图 64　1949-2013 年高等本专科招生人数

Number of New Students Enrollment of Higher Education, 1949-2013

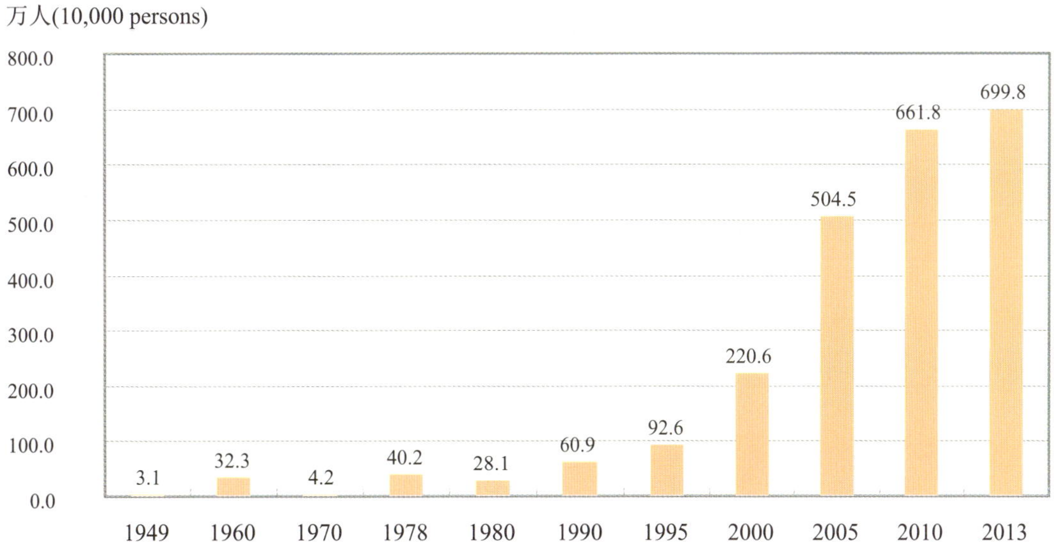

恢复高考制度

高考是"普通高等学校招生全国统一考试"的简称，高等学府以此次成绩为依据择优录取学生。

1977年，邓小平同志主持召开科学和教育工作座谈会，作出了当年恢复高考制度的决定。10月21日，国务院批转了教育部《关于1977年高等学校招生工作的意见》，规定从1977年起，对高等学校招生制度进行改革，恢复统一考试制度。

当年冬天，570万考生走进了曾被关闭10年之久的考场，其中27万余人成为"文革"后录取的第一批高等学校新生。高考制度的恢复是我国教育拨乱反正的一个重大举措，使中国的人才培养重新步入了健康发展的轨道，有力地推动了我国高等教育事业的恢复和发展，中国从此重新迎来了尊重知识、尊重人才的春天。

高考制度恢复后，各级各类高校为社会主义各行各业输送了大量的人才。从1978年到2013年，全国共有1.74亿人报名参加高考，其中0.87亿人被录取。

Resumption of College Entrance Examination System

College entrance examination referred to the "national higher education entrance examination", on which the institutions of higher learning admit students.

In 1977, Comrade Deng Xiaoping chaired a forum on work in science and education, and made the decision of the resumption of college entrance examination system. On October 21st, the State Council approved the Ministry of education "opinions about the 1977 enrollment work ", in which stipulated the reform of the enrollment system and restoral of the unified examination system from 1977 onwards.

In that winter, 5.7 million candidates entered the examination room which had been closed for 10 years, and among them more than 270 thousand people became the first batch of College freshmen after "Cultural Revolution". The resumption of college entrance examination system is an important measure for China's education to bring order out of chaos, making Chinese talent cultivation reentering into the track of healthy development, vigorously promoting the recovery and development of higher education in China, Chinese then reestablished a favorable environment of respecting knowledge and respecting talent.

After the resumption of college entrance examination system, Colleges and universities of all levels delivered a large number of talents to the socialist construction in all walks of life. From 1978 to 2013, a total of 174 million people enrolled in the college entrance examination, of which 87 million were admitted.

“211 工程”

"211 工程"，即面向 21 世纪、重点建设 100 所左右的高等学校和一批重点学科的建设工程。

1995 年 11 月，经国务院批准，原国家计委、原国家教委和财政部联合下发了《"211 工程"总体建设规划》，"211 工程"正式启动。

总体目标是：经过若干年的努力，使 100 所左右的高等学校以及一批重点学科在教育质量、科学研究、管理水平和办学效益等方面有较大提高，在高等教育改革特别是管理体制改革方面有明显进展，成为立足国内培养高层次人才、解决经济建设和社会发展重大问题的基地。

"211 工程"是中华人民共和国建国以来国家正式立项在高等教育领域进行的规模最大的重点建设工程，是国家"九五"期间提出的高等教育发展工程，也是高等教育事业的系统改革工程。是我国政府实施"科教兴国"战略的重大举措，是中华民族面对世纪之交的国内、国际形势而作出的发展高等教育的高瞻远瞩的重大决策。

"211 工程"建设大学现共有 112 所。

"211 Project"

The "211 Project" refers to the project constructed for twenty-first Century with about 100 colleges and universities and a number of key disciplines.

1995 November, approved by the State Council, the State Planning Commission, the former State Education Commission and the Ministry of Finance jointly issued the "" 211 Project "overall planning". "211" project officially started.

The overall objective is: after several years of efforts, the 100 schools of higher learning about as well as a number of key disciplines has great improvement in the quality of education, scientific research, management level and the school benefit, achieving the obvious progress in the reform of higher education, especially the reform of the management system, becoming the base for the domestic high level talents cultivation, solving the problems occurred in the economic construction and social development.

"211 Project" is the key construction project of the largest scale in the field of higher education since the founding of People's Republic of China , which also is the project of the development of higher education during national "The ninth five-year period" period, and also the system reform project of higher education . "211 Project" is a major measure for our government to implement the "rejuvenating the country through science and education" strategy, and a forward-looking decision to develop to higher education when facing the turn of the century, the international and domestic situation .

The university in construction of "211 Project"is now a total of 112.

“985 工程”

"985 工程"是我国政府为建设若干所世界一流大学和一批国际知名的高水平研究型大学而实施的高等教育建设工程。

1998 年 5 月 4 日，江泽民同志在庆祝北大建校 100 周年大会上向全社会宣告："为了实现现代化，我国要有若干所具有世界先进水平的一流大学。"为贯彻落实党中央科教兴国的战略和江泽民同志的号召，教育部决定在实施"面向 21 世纪教育振兴行动计划"中，重点支持北京大学、清华大学等部分高等学校创建世界一流大学和高水平大学，简称"985"工程。最初入选"985 工程"的高校有九所，被称九校联盟，截至 2011 年年末，"985 工程"共有 39 所高校。

“985 Project”

“985 Project” is a higher education construction project aimed at building several world class universities and a number of internationally famous high level research-based universities by Chinese government. On May 4, 1998, on the 100 anniversary of the founding of Peking University, Comrade Jiang Zemin declared to the society that to realize modernization, China needs several world’s class top universities. To implement the strategy of “rejuvenating the country through science and education” of the Central Party, and carry out the call of Comrade Jiang Zemin, the Ministry of Education decided that while implementing the “Action plan for educational vitalization facing the 21st century”, the ministry will focus on supporting the Peking University, Tsinghua University and some higher education universities to build world class and high level universities. Initially, 9 universities were selected into the “985 project” which were called nine school union. As of the end of 2011, the project has included 39 universities.

职业教育取得突破性进展。建国以来，我国职业教育获得了空前的发展。1949 年，我国中等职业教育在校生仅为 23 万人。改革开放以后我国职业教育得到恢复与发展。2002 年《国务院关于大力推进职业教育改革与发展的决定》颁布以来，我国职业教育的发展驶入快车道。2013 年，中等职业教育毕业生人数为 674 万人，比 2005 年增长了 61.3%；在校生人数达到 1923 万人，增长 20.2%。职业教育培养培训了大批中高级技能型人才，为提高劳动者素质、推动经济社会发展和促进就业作出了重要贡献。

（二）科技事业快速发展，科研成果硕果累累。

新中国的科技事业几乎是在一片空白的基础上起步的。65 年来，从向科学进军

Breakthrough progress has been made in vocational education. China's vocational education have attained unprecedented development since the founding of the PRC. In 1949, China's secondary vocational education students were only 230 thousand people. Vocational education has been restored and developed since China's reform and opening up, and its development has been fast tracked since China's promulgation of State Council's Decision to Vigorously Promote the Reform and Development of Vocational Education in 2002. The number of graduate students at secondary vocational schools was 6.74 million in 2013, an increase of 61.3 percent over the number in 2005; the number of students at all vocational schools reached 19.23 million, an increase of 20.2 percent. Vocational education has trained a large number of medium- and high-level technical professionals, improved the quality of the labor force, boosted economic and social development, and promoted employment.

(2) The pursuit of science and technology has moved ahead quickly and has seen many research achievements.

China's pursuit of science and technology basically started when the PRC was founded, but has advanced by leaps and bounds over the past 65 years. China has been building an

图 65 技工学校招生数
Number of Enrollment Skilled Workers Schools

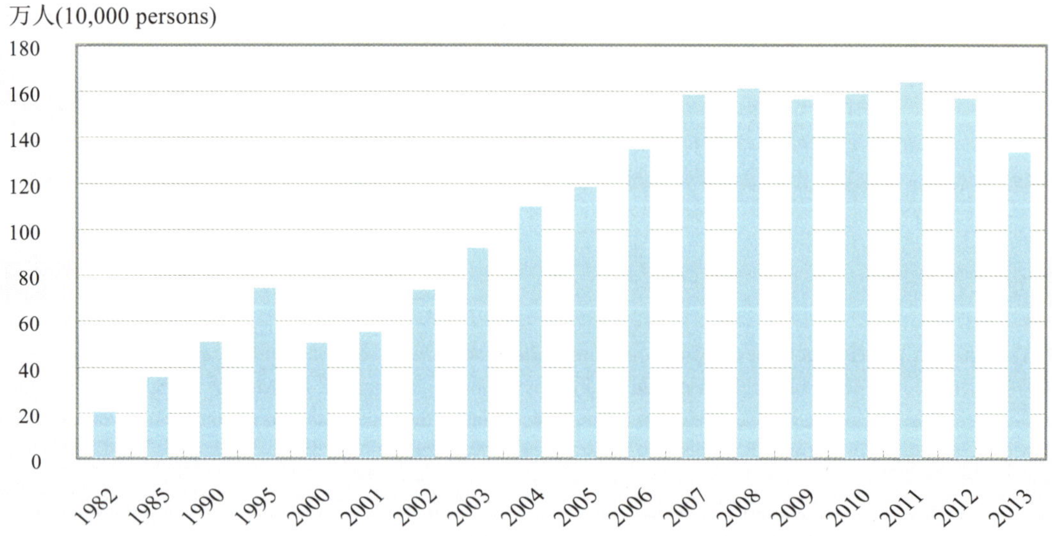

到建设创新型国家，我国科技事业实现了中华民族历史上最快的发展和最大的跨越，如今我国已经成为举世公认的科技大国，建立了比较完整的现代科技体系，形成了相当规模的科技队伍，科技已经承担起支撑发展、引领未来的重大历史使命。

科技投入快速增加。国家对科技创新的支持力度不断加大，对科技的财政投入逐年增加。2013 年，全社会研究与试验发展（R&D）经费支出达 11847 亿元，为 1995 年的 34 倍，年均增长 21.6%；R&D 经费支出占国内生产总值比重为 2.08%，比 1995 年提高 1.51 个百分点。国家中长期科技规划纲要实施以来，企业在科技活动中的主体地位日益显现，企业科研经费投入明显增加。在 2013 年全社会研究与试验发展(R&D)经费支出中，各类企业 R&D 经费支出 9076 亿元，为 2000 年的 16.9 倍，占全社会 R&D 支出的比重达 76.6%，比 2000 年提高 16.6 个百分点；其中起主导作用的大

innovative country, and is now recognized as a large scientific and technological power in the world. The country boasts a relatively complete modern science and technology system and a large talent pool that can fulfill important missions in the future.

Input in science and technology rises rapidly. China has increased its financial expenditures on science and technology while giving these undertakings swelling support. In 2013, research and development (R&D) expenditures reached 1.1847 trillion yuan, a 34-fold increase from 1999 with an annual growth rate of 21.6 percent. R&D expenditures constituted 2.08 percent of the country's GDP, 1.51 percentage points up over 1995. Enterprises have shown a bigger role in the country's scientific and technological development and have made increasing inputs into scientific research since the country promulgated and implemented the Outline of the National Program for Long- and Medium-Term Scientific and Technological Development. In 2013, R&D expenditures from enterprises amounted to 907.6 billion yuan, an increase of 16.9 times over 2000, accounting for 76.6 percent of China's total R&D

图 66 1995-2013 年 R&D 经费内部支出及占国内生产总值的比重
Intramural Expenditure on R&D and Percentage of GDP, 1995-2013

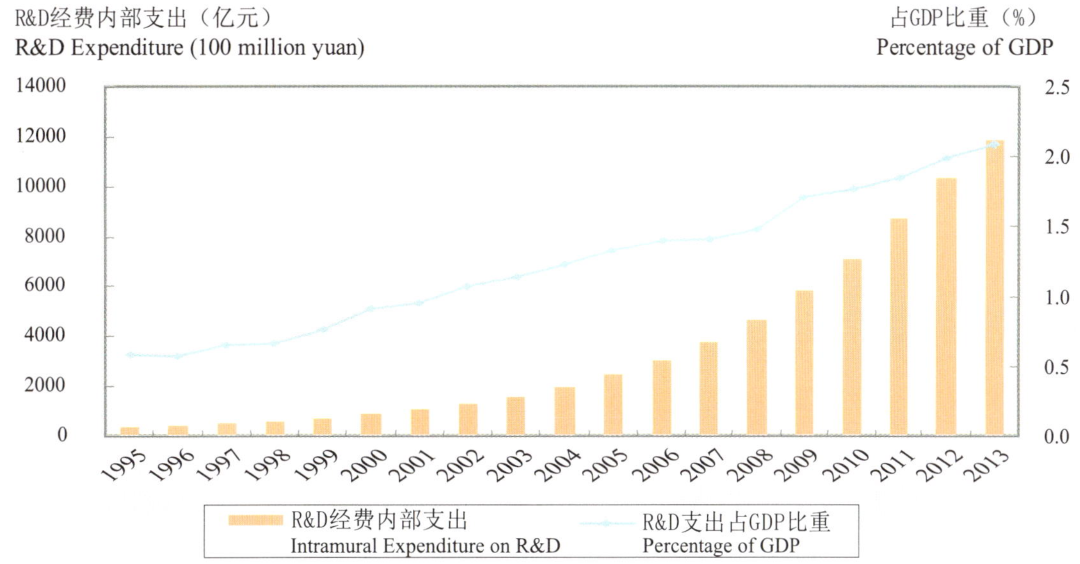

中型工业企业支出6744亿元，为1995年的47.6倍，占全社会R&D支出的比重达56.9%，比1995年提高16.3个百分点。

科技队伍不断壮大。建国初期，全国科技人员不超过5万人，其中专门从事科学研究的人员不足500人。随着科技人力投入不断增加，科技研发人员的水平与素质不断提高，初步形成了一支具有一定规模和较高水平的科技人才队伍。2013年，全国研究与试验发展（R&D）人次折合全时当量达353.3万人年，是1991年的5.3倍。目前，以折合全时当量计算的我国R&D人员和研究人员总量均位居世界第一。

科技领域硕果累累。经过65年的发展，我国整体科技发展水平已经处于发展中国家前列，部分科研领域达到国际先进水平，一些关键领域涌现出一系列重大科技成果。新

expenditures, 16.6 percentage points up over 2000. Medium and large industrial enterprises played a leading role — their expenditures in this field totaled 674.4 billion yuan, an increase of 47.6 times over 1995, accounting for 56.9 percent of total R&D expenditure, up 16.3 percentage points over 1995.

The contingent of scientific and technological personnel has steadily expanded. There were less than 50,000 scientific and technological personnel in the country when the PRC was founded, of which less than 500 were specially engaged in scientific research. A large-scale contingent of high-level scientific and technological personnel has been formed due to the increasing input and improved quality of scientific research personnel. In 2013, full-time equivalent of R&D personnel numbered 3.533 million man-years, an increase of 5.3 times over the number in 1991. China also has the world's first-highest number of equivalent of R&D personnel and scientific researchers.

Great achievements have been made in science and technology. China has ranked among the top developing countries in scientific and technological development after 65 years of concerted efforts. Scientific research in some fields is close to or has reached advanced international levels.

图67 1992-2013年科学研究与开发人员投入
Input of R&D Personnel, 1992-2013

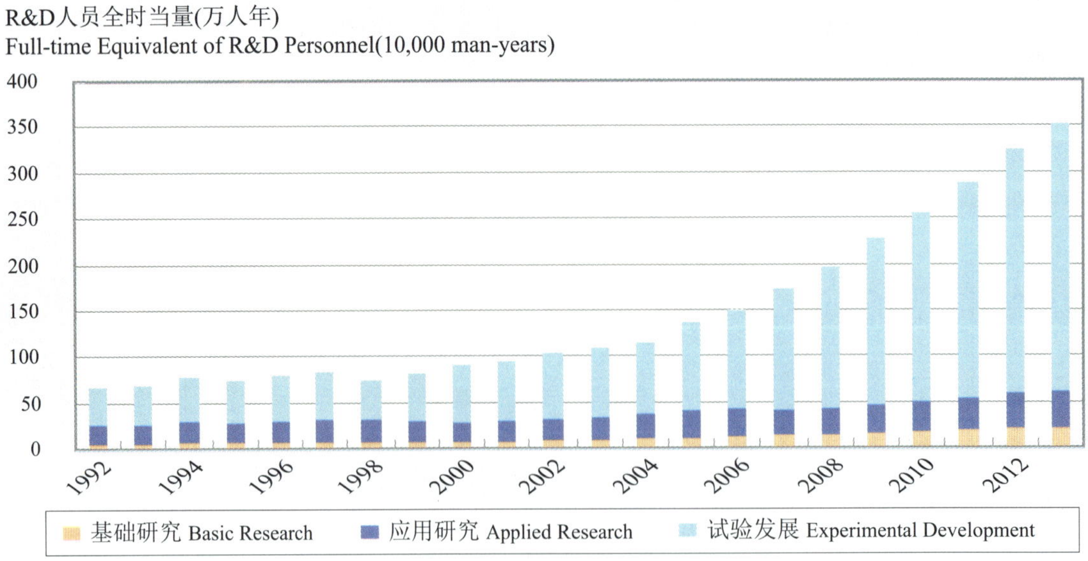

中国创新指数

中国创新指数是由国家统计局有关课题组对我国创新指标体系中的各项指标数据，按照综合评价方法测算得出的指数，旨在客观反映建设创新型国家进程中我国创新能力的发展情况。

中国创新指标体系和指数可以分成三个层次。第一个层次用以反映我国创新总体发展情况，通过计算创新总指数实现；第二个层次用以反映我国在创新环境、创新投入、创新产出和创新成效等 4 个领域的发展情况，通过计算分领域指数实现；第三个层次用以反映构成创新能力各方面的具体发展情况，通过上述 4 个领域所选取的 21 个评价指标实现。

测算结果显示，2012 年中国创新指数（CII）为 148.2（以 2005 年为 100），比上年增长 6.2%。创新环境指数、创新投入指数、创新产出指数和创新成效指数分别为 144.0、152.2、164.2 和 132.4，分别比上年增长 4.3%、8.2%、9.5% 和 2.2%。自 2005 年以来，中国创新指数（CII）持续稳步增长，年均增幅为 5.8%。创新环境指数、创新投入指数、创新产出指数、创新成效指数也均保持持续增长，年均增幅分别为 5.4%、6.2%、7.3% 和 4.1%。测算结果表明，我国创新环境继续优化，创新投入力度不断加大，创新产出能力明显提高，创新成效稳步增强。

China innovation index

China Innovation Index (CII) is the index determined by the National Bureau of Statistics according to the data of innovation index system in our country in the comprehensive evaluation method, and designed to objectively reflect the development of innovative ability in our country in the process of building an innovation-oriented country.

China innovation index system and index may be divided into three levels. The first level reflects the overall development of China innovation trough calculating the total innovation index. The second level reflects the development of innovation environment, innovation input, and innovation output and innovation effect through calculating the sub-domain index. The third level reflects the specific development of innovation ability through the selected 21 evaluation index in the above four areas.

According to the calculation results, in 2012, China Innovation Index (CII) was 148.2 (in 2005, it was 100.) which has an increase of 6.2% over the previous year. Innovation environment index, innovation input index, innovation output index and innovation effect index were 144.0, 152.2, 164.2 and 132.4 respectively which have an increase of 4.3%, 8.2%, 9.15% and 2.2% over the previous year. Since 2005, China Innovation Index (CII) continues to grow steadily in the average annual growth of 5.8%. Innovation environment index, innovation input index, innovation output index and innovation effect index are also keep growing in the average annual growth of 5.4%, 6.2%, 7.3% and 4.1% respectively. It turn out that China continues to optimize the innovation environment, to increase the innovation input, to promote the innovation output and to enhance the innovation effect.

中国成立后，我国相继在两弹一星、哥德巴赫猜想、反西格玛负超子、陆相成油理论、人工合成牛胰岛素结晶等方面取得了一批重要研究成果，接近或达到了同时代的国际先进水平。改革开放以来，又在高温超导、纳米材料、量子通讯、古生物考古、生命科学等领域取得了一批具有较大国际影响力的重要创新成果，在超级杂交水稻、高性能计算机、超大规模集成电路、第三代移动通信、深海载人潜水等前沿技术领域取得重要突破。随着载人航天与探月工程的实施，我国已成为少数几个独立掌握空间先进技术的国家之一。一系列关键技术难关的攻克，确保了三峡工程、青藏铁路等国家重大工程建设的成功实施，也为我国建设创新型国家奠定了良好基础。

专利事业取得长足进展。专利情况是反映创新能力和水平的重要指标。为保护知识产权、鼓励发明创造、促进技术交流，国家

Significant achievements have also been made in some key fields. China has obtained a series of research successes at an international advanced level after the PRC was founded, including two bombs and one satellite, advancements on the Goldbach conjecture, the negative anti sigma hyperon, the theory of continental oil, and the production of synthetic bovine insulin. China has also made great world-influencing innovative achievements in such fields as high temperature superconductors, nanometer materials, quantum communications, paleontology, and life sciences, since reform and opening up. The country has also made great breakthroughs in such frontier technological fields as super hybrid rice, high performance computers, VLSI, the third generation of mobile communication, and deep-sea manned submersibles. The success of China's manned space flight and lunar exploration project has made China one of the few countries to master advanced space technology. China has overcome difficulties in key technologies, which ensured the successful construction of key state projects such as the Three Gorges Project and Qinghai-Tibet Railway, which have laid a solid foundation on which to build an innovative country.

Great progress has been made in patent development. Patents are a significant index of a country's innovative level and capabilities. China implemented the

图 68　科技活动人员
Personnel Engaged in S&T Activities

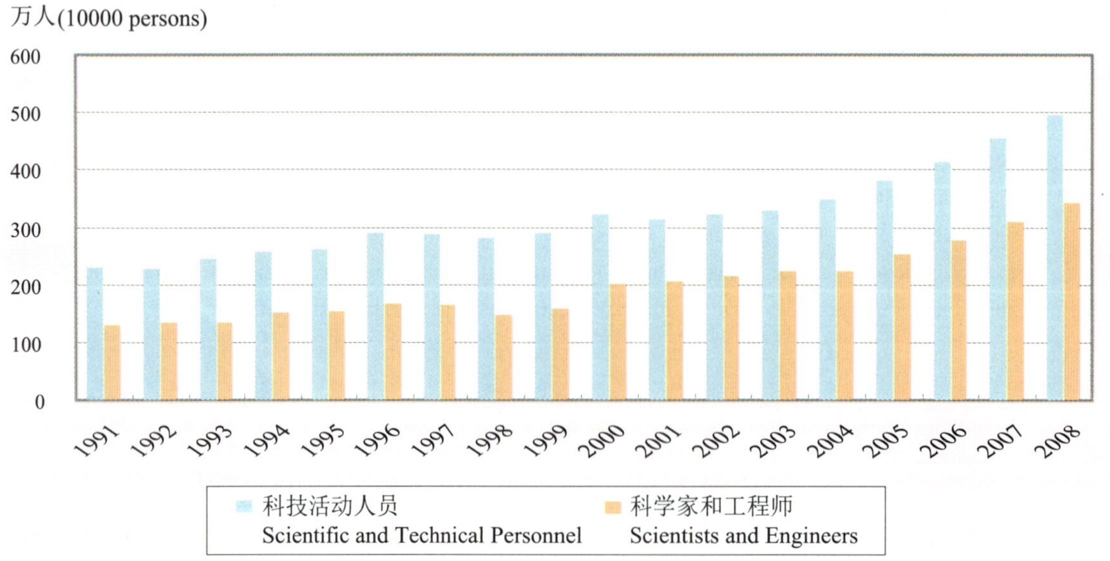

知识产权保护

是指公民、法人或者其他组织对其在科学技术和文学艺术等领域内，主要基于脑力劳动创造完成的智力成果所依法享有的专有权利。它是依照各国法律赋予符合条件的著作者、发明者或成果拥有者在一定期限内享有的独占权利，一般认为它包括版权（著作权）和工业产权。版权（著作权）是指创作文学、艺术和科学作品的作者及其他著作权人依法对其作品所享有的人身权利和财产权利的总称；工业产权则是指包括发明专利、实用新型专利、外观设计专利、商标、服务标记、厂商名称、货源名称或原产地名称等在内的权利人享有的独占性权利。

我国《中华人民共和国专利法》、《中华人民共和国商标法》、《中华人民共和国著作权法》等法律法规先后出台，为各个企业的知识产权保护提供了法律依据。2008 年 6 月 5 日，国务院印发了《国家知识产权战略纲要》，是中国运用知识产权制度促进经济社会全面发展的重要国家战略，也是今后较长一段时间内指导中国知识产权事业发展的纲领性文件，它对提升我国知识产权创造、运用、保护和管理能力，建设创新型国家，实现全面建成小康社会目标具有重要意义。

Intellectual Property Protection

It refers propriety right of citizens, legal person or the other organization, which based on mental work to create complete intellectual achievement in the field of science, technology, art and literature. It is to give eligible authors, inventors or owners the exclusive right in accordance with the national law within a certain period. It generally included copyright and industrial property right. Copyright refers to the general term of personal right and property right, which belongs to the author of creative literature, art and scientific work or other copyright owner according to law. Industrial property right refers to the exclusive right including patent for an invention, utility model patent, design patent, trademark, service mark, trade name, supplier name or appellation of origin and so on.

The laws such as The Patent Law of the People's Republic of China, The Trademark Law of the People's Republic of China, The Copyright Law of the People's Republic of China provide legal basis for the protection of intellectual property for each enterprise. On June 5, 2008, the state council issued the outline of the national intellectual property strategy. It is an important national strategy by which China use the intellectual property system to promote comprehensive economic and social development. It is also the programmatic document to guide the development of China's intellectual property rights in a long period of time in the future. It is significance to improve the ability to create, utilize, protect and manage intellectual property. It is also important in the process of building an innovation-oriented country and to realize the comprehensive construction of well-off society.

于 1985 年正式实施了《中华人民共和国专利法》。《专利法》实施以来，我国知识产权保护环境明显改善，科技人员知识产权意识普遍提高，专利申请量和授权量逐年增加。1987 年 -2013 年，我国专利申请量和授权量分别以年均 19.7% 和 25.2% 的速度增长。2013 年，国内专利申请量为 223.5 万件，1987-2013 年年均增长 20.8%；其中发明专利申请量为 70.5 万件，年均增长 21.7%；国内发明专利申请量占国内专利申请量的比重为 29.7%，比 1986 年提高 4.2 个百分点。2013 年，国内专利授权量为 122.8 万件，1987-2013 年年均增长 25.5%；其中，国内发明专利授权量为 14.4 万件，年均增长 34.1%；国内发明专利授权量占国内专利授权量的比重为 11.7%，比 1986 年提高 9.7 个百分点。大批的授权专利成果得到应用，取得了较好的经济效益和社会效益。

Patent Law of the People's Republic of China in 1985 in order to protect intellectual property rights (IPR), encourage invention and innovation, and promote technological exchange. The protected environment created by the IPR has remarkably improved the country as Chinese scientific and technological staff become more aware of IPR's protections, and more and more patent applications and patent grants are being filed. From 1987 to 2013, the number of patent applications and patent grants grew at an annual rate of 19.7 percent and 25.2 percent, respectively. In 2013, China handled 2.235 million domestic patent applications, with an annual growth rate of 20.8 percent from 1978 to 2013, of which 705 thousand were invention patent applications, with an annual growth rate of 21.7 percent, and accounting for 29.7 percent of the total application, 4.2 percentage points up over that of 1986. In 2013, China handled 1.228 million domestic patent grants, with an annual growth rate of 25.5 percent from 1987 to 2013, of which 144 thousand were invention patent grants, with an annual growth rate of 34.1 percent, and accounting for 11.7 percent of the total grants, 9.7 percentage points up over that of 1986. A large number of granted patents have been put into use and have generated good economic and social results.

图 69　1985-2013 年国内外三种专利申请授权数
Three Kinds of Patent Applications Granted, 1985-2013

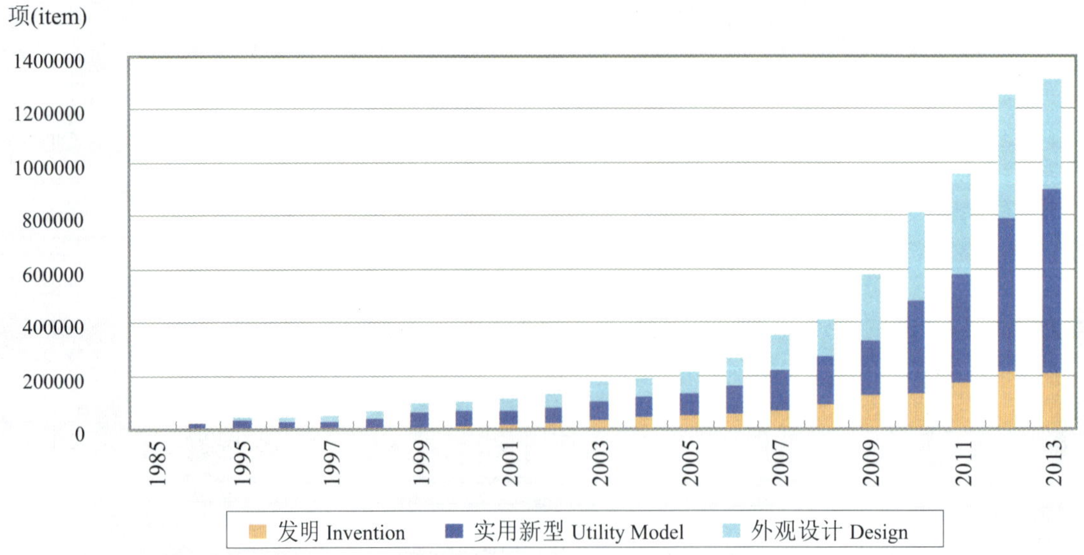

国家高技术研究发展计划（“863 计划”）

1986 年 3 月，面对世界高技术蓬勃发展、国际竞争日趋激烈的严峻挑战，邓小平同志在王大珩、王淦昌、杨嘉墀和陈芳允四位科学家提出的"关于跟踪研究外国战略性高技术发展的建议"上，做出"此事宜速作决断，不可拖延"的重要批示。在充分论证的基础上，党中央、国务院果断决策，于 1986 年 11 月启动实施了高技术研究发展计划，简称"863 计划"。

20 年多来，863 计划始终瞄准世界高技术发展前沿，按照有所为、有所不为的原则，在事关国家长远发展和国家安全的重要高技术领域，以提高我国自主创新能力为宗旨，坚持战略性、前沿性和前瞻性，以前沿技术研究发展为重点，统筹部署高技术的集成应用和产业化示范，充分发挥高技术引领未来发展的先导作用。

"863 计划"经过 20 多年的实施，为我国高技术的起步、发展和产业化奠定了坚实基础。目前，"863 计划"已经成为我国科学技术发展，特别是高技术研究发展的一面旗帜。更为重要的是，"863 计划"所取得的成就对于提升我国自主创新能力、提高国家综合实力、增强民族自信心等方面发挥了重要作用。

National High-tech Research and development Plan (“863 Plan”)

In Mar. 1986, faced with the severe challenges of the rapid development of world high technologies, and the increasingly fierce global competition, Comrade Deng Xiaoping made an important official reply on the “Suggestions on the Tracking Study of foreign Strategic High-Tech Development” proposed by four scientists--Wang Daxian, Wang Ganchang, Yang Jiachi and Chen Fangxun, The reply was “quick decision, no delay”. On the basis of adequate study, the Central Committee of CPC and the State Council made a quick decision to start carrying out the High-tech research and development Plan (“863 Plan” for short) in Nov. 1986.

In the past two decades, 863 plan has focused on the frontier of the world’s high-tech development in accordance with the principle of knowing what to do and not to do in important high-tech areas concerning China’s long-term development and national security. With the purpose of improving China’s ability of self innovation, the 863 plan stuck to the strategic, advanced and prospective nature, focused on the frontier technology researches and development, coordinate the integrated application and industrialization demonstration of high technologies, and give full play to the guiding role of high technologies in future development.

After 20 years of implementation, “863 plan” has laid a solid foundation for the start-up, development and industrialization of Chinese high technologies. At present, “863 plan” has become a banner for the development of Chinese science and technology, especially for the high-tech research and development. What’s more important, the achievements of “863 Plan” have played an important role in improving Chinese ability of independent innovation, the comprehensive national power, the national self-confidence.

超级计算机

超级计算机指能够执行一般个人电脑无法处理的大资料量与高速运算的电脑，其基本组成组件与个人电脑的概念无太大差异，但规格与性能则强大许多，是一种超大型电子计算机。是国家科技发展水平和综合国力的重要标志。

2009 年 10 月，中国国防科学技术大学研制出中国第一台千万亿次超级计算机——“天河一号”，使中国成为继美国之后世界上第二个能够研制千万亿次超级计算机的国家。2010 年 11 月 14 日，国际 TOP500 组织在网站上公布了最新全球超级计算机前 500 强排行榜，“天河一号”排名全球第一。

继天河一号之后，中国国防科学技术大学又研制出“天河二号”超级计算机系统，峰值计算速度每秒 5.49 亿亿次、持续计算速度每秒 3.39 亿亿次。2013 年 11 月 18 日，国际 TOP500 组织公布了最新全球超级计算机 500 强排行榜榜单，“天河二号”位居榜首，计算速度比第二名——美国的“泰坦”快近一倍。

Super Computer

Super computer can handle a large amount of data and high speed computing which can’t be handled by ordinary personal computer. Its components have no much difference with personal computer, but are much stronger in specification and quality. It is a super large electric computer and an important symbol of the development level of national science and technology, and comprehensive national power.

In Oct. 2009, China's National Defense University of Science and Technology invented China’s first petaflop super computer-- “Tian He 1”, making China the second country which has invented a petaflop computer, only after the US. On Nov. 14, 2010, the Global TOP500 Organization released the latest global super computer top 500 on its website, in which “Tian He 1” ranked first.

After “Tian He 1”, China’s National Defense University of Science and Technology again invented “Tian He 2” super computer system with 5.49 quadrillion computing speed per second at the peak and 3.39 quadrillion sustained double precision floating computing speed per second. On Nov. 18, 2013, the Global Top500 Organization released the latest Global Super Computer Top500 List, in which Tian He 2 took the first place with its speed nearly twice as fast as the second one-- “ Titan” of the US.

“蛟龙号”载人潜水器

为推动中国深海运载技术发展，为中国大洋国际海底资源调查和科学研究提供重要高技术装备，同时为中国深海勘探、海底作业研发共性技术，2002 年中国科技部将深海载人潜水器研制列为“国家高技术研究发展计划（863 计划）”重大专项，启动“蛟龙号”载人深潜器的自行设计、自主集成研制工作。经过 6 年努力，完成了载人潜水器本体研水面支持系统的研制和试验母船的改造以及潜航员的选拔和培训，从而使“蛟龙号”具备了开展海上试验的技术条件。2009 年至 2012 年，“蛟龙号”接连取得 1000 米级、3000 米级、5000 米级和 7000 米级海试成功。2012 年 7 月，“蛟龙号”在马里亚纳海沟试验海区创造了下潜 7062 米的中国载人深潜纪录，同时也创造了世界同类作业型潜水器的最大下潜深度纪录。这意味着中国具备了载人到达全球 99.8% 以上海洋深处进行作业的能力。2013 年，“蛟龙号”从冲击大深度转入试验性应用航次，开始了服务科考和资源勘探的业务化探索之旅。

Manned deep submergence vehicle “Jiaolong”

In order to promote the development of China’s deep-sea vehicle technology, provide important high-technology equipments for China’s investigations and researches on international submarine resources, and develop the generic technology for China’s deep-sea exploration and subbed operation, in 2000, the Ministry of Science and Technology listed the deep-sea manned submersible as the major project of the“ national high-technology research and development program (863 program)” and started the self-designed and integrated development of Manned deep submergence vehicle “Jiaolong”. After 6 years of hard work, China made a manned submersible to grind the water surface, the mother ship test and the pilot selection and training, so the Jiaolong met the technical requirement of the sea trial. From 2009 to 2012, the Jiaolong have successfully submerged at the undersea level of 1000 meters, 3000 meters, 5000 meters and 7000 meters. In July 2012, the Jiaolong created the record of Chinese manned deep submergence of 7062 meters in Mariana trench test area and also the record of the world maximum depth in the similar type submersible. It means that China could send men deep into the sea to do experiments in more than 99.8% of the world’s oceans. In 2013, Jiaolong turned from deep diving to experimental application and initiated the trip of exploring resources and serving the scientific researches.

神舟十号载人飞船

2013 年 6 月 11 日 17 时 38 分，神舟十号飞船在酒泉卫星发射中心成功发射。神舟十号飞船是中国"神舟"号系列飞船之一，它是中国第五艘搭载太空人的飞船。飞船由推进舱、返回舱、轨道舱和附加段组成。飞行乘组由男航天员聂海胜、张晓光和女航天员王亚平组成，聂海胜担任指令长。飞船先后与天宫一号进行一次自动交会对接和一次航天员手控交会对接。组合体飞行期间，航天员进驻天宫一号，并开展航天医学实验、技术试验及太空授课活动。完成组合体飞行后，飞船撤离并返回着陆场，天宫一号转至长期运营轨道。2013 年 6 月 26 日 08 时 07 分，神舟十号飞船成功地在内蒙古四子王旗着陆场着陆，随后 3 名航天员从飞船返回舱健康出舱。

神舟飞船系列的成功发射，标志着中国航天事业不断迈出新的步伐。它是中国自行研制，具有完全自主知识产权，达到或优于国际第三代载人飞船技术的飞船。神舟五号的载人发射，完成了和实现了中国载人航天工程第一步的计划和目标，神舟九号标志中国突破和掌握了载人交会对接技术，神舟十号进行载人天地往返运输系统的首次应用性飞行。神舟十号发射并完成与天宫一号空间交会对接等任务后，中国载人航天第二步任务第一阶段将完美收工，全面进入空间实验室和空间站研制阶段。

Manned Spacecraft Shenzhou 10

Seventeen thirty-eight on June 11, 2013, the Shenzhou 10 was successfully launched from the Jiuquan Satellite Launch Center. The spacecraft Shenzhou 10 was one of the Chinese "Shenzhou" spacecraft series and was the fifth manned spacecraft of China. The Shenzhou 10 was composed of the propelling module, the re-entry module, the orbital module and additional sections. The flight crew included the male astronaut Nie Haisheng, which served as the commander, Zhang Xiaoguang and the female astronaut Wang Yaping. Spacecraft Shenzhou 10 had an automatic docking and an astronaut hand control docking with Tiangong-1. During the assembly flight, the astronauts would enter Tiangong-1 and did aerospace medicine experiments, technology experiments and gave video lectures from the space. After the assembly flight, the spacecraft was evacuated and returned to the landing site. Tiangong-1 turned to the long-term operational orbit. At Eight Seven on June 26, 2013, spacecraft Shenzhou10 successfully landed on the landing site at Siziwang banner of Inner Mongolia. Three astronauts healthily descended from the re-entry module.

The successful launch of Shenzhou spacecraft series marks constant new strides of Chine aerospace undertakings. The Shenzhou series is developed by China itself, with completely independent intellectual property rights, having achieved or exceeded the international third generation manned spacecraft technology. The Shenzhou 5 manned launch achieved and implemented the first step and goal of Chinese manned aerospace project. Shenzhou 9 marks that China has broken through and mastered the manned rendezvous and docking technology. Shenzhou 10 first applied the manned round-trip transportation system. After Shenzhou 10 was launched and achieved the rendezvous and docking mission with Tiangong-1, the first stage of the second step in China's manned aerospace project has been completed perfectly. China will fully enter the stage for developing space laboratory and the space station.

8 从相对落后到全面繁荣，文化卫生体育环保等社会事业取得长足进步。

From relative backwardness to full prosperity, culture, health, sports, environmental protection and other social sectors have made a big step forward.

新中国成立以来的65年，是社会事业地位不断提升的65年，是文化卫生体育环保等社会事业全面繁荣的65年，也是自然、经济与社会发展协调性不断增强的65年。

The 65 years since the founding of the new China have seen the constant growth of the social status of different areas of society and the flourishing of all aspects of culture, health, sports, and environment, as well as the continued strengthening of the coordinated development of the economy, society and natural protection.

（一）文化事业繁荣发展，经济效益不断提高。

建国65年来，我国文化建设尽管经历曲折坎坷，但在党和政府的重视和支持下，取得了辉煌成就。特别是改革开放以来，伴随经济的快速发展和物质文化生活的极大丰富，我国文化事业进入快速发展期，公共文化服务设施建设加快推进，公共文化服务体系建设初具规模，文化事业的社会效益和经济效益不断提高。

覆盖城乡的公共文化服务网络逐步建成。建国初期，我国公共文化服务设施极其短缺，难以满足社会需求。1949年，全国公共图书馆仅有55个，文化馆站896个，博物馆21个。随着国家公共文化投入的增加，经过65年的发展，截至2013年底，全国共有公共图书馆3112个，为1949年的56.6倍；文化馆站44260个，为1949年的49.4倍，其中省地市级群众艺术馆385个，县市级文化馆2930个，乡镇（街道）文化站40945个；博物馆3473个，为1949年的165.5倍。2004年起，我国各级各类国有博物馆、纪念馆、美术馆、有条件的爱国主义教育基地等逐步实行优惠或者免费开放，2008年，全国文化、文物系统博物馆、纪念馆开始向社会免费开放。公共文化服务设施的不断完善，为丰富城乡群众文化活动提供了有力支撑。

文化产业蓬勃发展。随着我国改革开放和社会主义市场经济的发展，文化体制改革不断深入，文化市场不断壮大，文化产业发展方兴未艾。目前，我国基本形成了由娱乐市场、演出市场、音像市场、电影市场、网络文化市场、艺术品市场等组成的统一、开放、竞争、有序的文化市场体系，文艺表演团体和场馆不断增

(1) The prosperous development of the cultural sector and the constant improvement of economic efficiency.

During the 65 years since the founding of the PRC, despite twists and turns, cultural development has achieved excellent results with the help of the attention and support of the Party and the government. Especially since the beginning of reform and opening up, when rapid economic development and significant enrichment of material and cultural life took place, China's cultural life has entered a period of rapid development. The period since the adoption of reform and an opening up has witnessed the creation of a socio-cultural services infrastructure which has started to advance at an accelerated pace, and the social and economic efficiency of the cultural sector has been continuously improving.

A socio-cultural services network that covers urban areas and rural regions has been gradually established. When the PRC was first founded, there was a dearth of socio-cultural services infrastructure to meet society's demands. In 1949 there were only 55 public libraries, 896 cultural centers, 21 public museums in the entire country. During the past 65 years of development, the state has increasingly invested into the socio-cultural services infrastructure, and by the end of 2013, China had around 3,112 public libraries, that 56.6 times more than the number that existed in 1949; 42,260 culture centers, 49.4 times more than in 1949, of which, 385 art museums at the provincial, prefecture, and city levels, 2,930 country and city level cultural centers, 40,945 county and town(street) level cultural centers, 3,473 public libraries that 165.5 times more than in 1949. In 2004, China began to give away discount tickets and free tickets to different levels and types of state museums, including memorial museums and art galleries that meet the requirements to cultivate patriotism. In 2008, cultural museums, heritage museums, and memorials across the country became free to the public. The socio-cultural services infrastructure has been constantly improving and offers strong support for enriching cultural activities for the urban and rural masses.

The rapid development of the cultural industry. With the development of reforms, the adoption of an open door policy, and the introduction of a socialist market economy, the reform of the cultural system has continued to deepen, the cultural market has continued to expand, and the development of cultural industries has advanced. China has basically formed a unified, open, competitive, and orderly system in the cultural market that consists of entertainment, shows, audio and video, cinema, Internet culture, and works of art. The number of live bands and music halls has been constantly increasing. In 2013, there were 8,180 performing show groups of different types all across the

加。2013 年末，全国共有各类艺术表演团体 8180 个，为 1949 年末的 8.2 倍；艺术表演场馆 1344 个，为 1949 年末的 1.5 倍。文艺表演队伍和演出场次、收入持续增加。2013 年末，全国艺术表演团体从业人员 26.1 万人，全年演出 165.1 万场，国内演出观众人次 90064 万人次，全年演出收入 73.6 亿元。产业化发展方面，2013 年末，全国共有 8 个国家级文化产业示范园区，6 个国家级文化产业实验园区和 268 个国家文化产业示范基地；文化产业中长期本外币信贷余额 1574 亿元，185 家文化企业注册发行的债券余额 2878.5 亿元；77 家文化企业在沪深两地上市，各种类型文化产业股权投资基金 57 只，募集规模超过 1350 亿元。

country, 8.2 times the number there were in 1949, and 1,344 places for cultural performances, 1.5 times more than there were in 1949. The number of live musical performances and the level of income from performances have also been increasing. In 2013, performing groups had 261,000 employees who participated in 1.651 million performances for audiences which numbered 900.64 million people nation-wide, and which netted a total reported income of 7.36 billion yuan. As for industrial development, in late 2013, there were 8 exhibition parks and 6 experimental cultural industry demonstration parks of national importance throughout the country, as well as 286 cultural industry demonstration bases of national importance. The credit balance of cultural industries in medium and long-term local and foreign currency amounts to 157.4 billion yuan, and the balance of bonds authorized and issued by 185 cultural enterprises is 287.85 billion yuan. 77 cultural enterprises are listed on the Shanghai and Shenzhen Stock Exchange, and there are 57 mutual fund investment foundations of cultural industries of different kinds with capital of over 135 billion yuan.

图 70　1949-2013 年末公共图书馆个数
Number of Public Library, 1949-2013

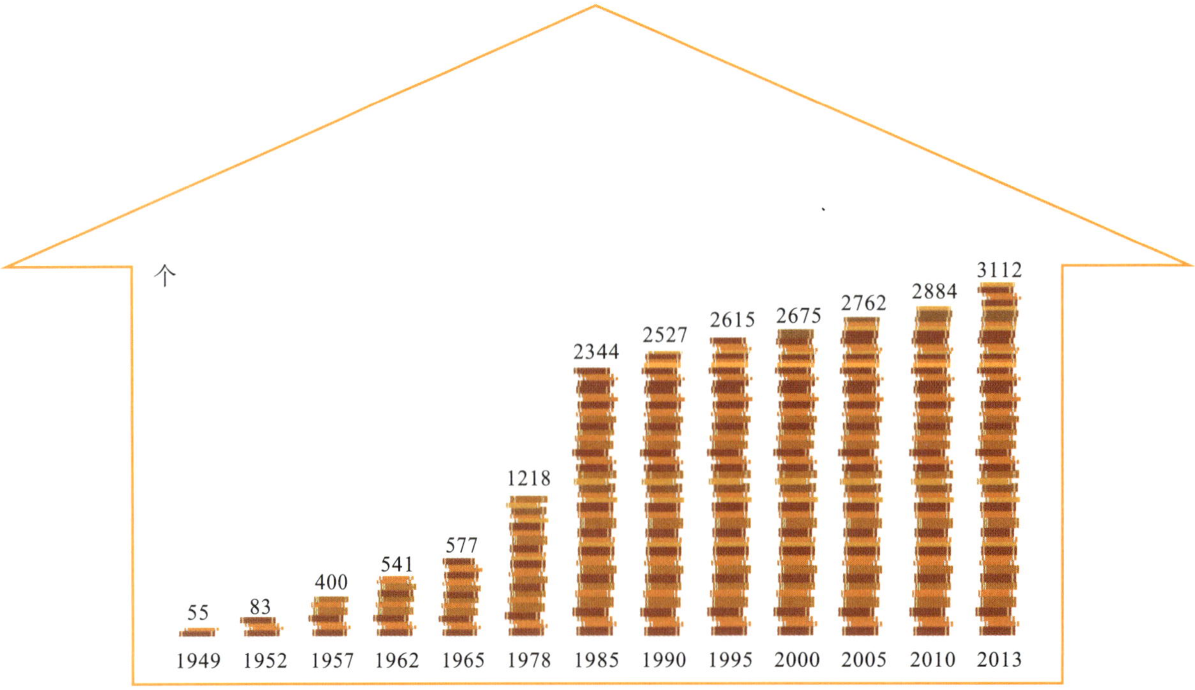

图 71　1949-2013 年末全国艺术表演团体数

Number of Art Performance Troupes, 1949-2013

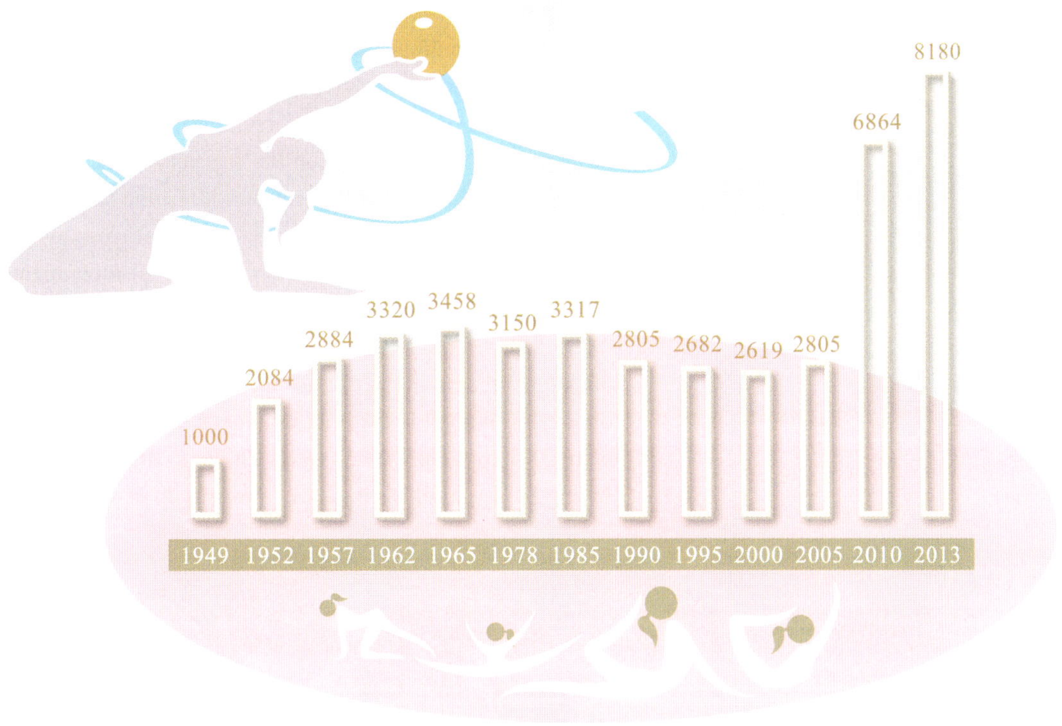

注：2007 年以前为文化部门系统内数据，2007 年起含非文化部门单位。

Note: Prior to 2007, the data are only those within the cultural system and include those of non-cultural sector units since 2007.

文化遗产保护成效突出。新中国成立以来，党中央、国务院高度重视文化遗产保护，出台一系列政策措施，并在改革开放以来进一步纳入法制化轨道。经过 65 年的努力，截至 2013 年底，全国共有文物机构 7737 个，从业人员 13.7 万人，重点文物保护单位总数达到 4295 处，我国世界遗产总数达到 45 项，位居世界第二。在非物质文化遗产方面，截至 2013 年底，全国共有国家级非遗项目保护单位 2658 家，入选联合国教科文组织人类非物质文化遗产代表作名录的项目总数达 38 个。

The outstanding results of the protection of cultural heritage. Since the founding of the PRC, the CPC Central Committee and the State Council have paid great attention to the protection of cultural heritage, introducing a series of political measures to support cultural preservation endeavors. Moreover, since the adoption of the reform and open door policy, they have put it these programs on the legislative track. Through the efforts made during this 65-year period, China had around 7,737 archaeological institutions with 137,000 employees by the end of 2013. The total number of important cultural monuments under state protection (Units of cultural relics protection) has reached 4,295. There are 45 World Heritage sites in China, the second-largest number in the world. By the end of 2013, there were 2,658 objects of intangible cultural heritage at the state level, and there were 38 items representative of Chinese culture on UNESCO's Intangible Cultural Heritage of Humanity list.

世界遗产

世界遗产是指被联合国教科文组织和世界遗产委员会确认的人类罕见的、目前无法替代的财富，是全人类公认的具有突出意义和普遍价值的文物古迹及自然景观。狭义的世界遗产包括〞世界文化遗产〞、〞世界自然遗产〞、〞世界文化与自然遗产〞和〞文化景观〞四类。广义概念，根据形态和性质，世界遗产分为文化遗产、自然遗产、文化和自然双重遗产、记忆遗产、人类口述和非物质遗产（简称非物质文化遗产）、文化景观遗产。

中国是世界上拥有世界遗产类别最齐全的国家之一，也是世界自然与文化遗产数量最多的国家。截至 2014 年，经联合国教科文组织审核被批准列入《世界遗产名录》的中国世界遗产共有 47 项，包括自然遗产 10 项，文化遗产 33 项，自然与文化遗产 4 项，数量居世界第二位。

World Heritage

World Heritage refers to the rare and irreplaceable treasuresin human history confirmed by UNESCO and the world heritage committee. World Heritage is cultural relics, historic sites and natural landscape which have prominent significance and universal value and have been recognized by all mankind around the world. The narrow sense of the World Heritage includes four types including the world cultural heritage, the world natural heritage, the world cultural and natural heritage and cultural landscape. According to the morphology and property, the broad sense refers to the cultural heritage, natural heritage, cultural and natural heritage, memory of the world, human oral history, intangible heritage (hereinafter referred to as intangible cultural heritage) and cultural landscape heritage.

China is one of the most complete countries with the World Heritage and one of the largest number of the world's natural and cultural heritages. As of 2014, China have 47 heritages, which were listed as World Heritage by UNESCO, including 10 natural heritages, 33 cultural heritages, 4 natural and cultural heritages, ranking the second in the world.

（二）医疗卫生事业成绩斐然，人民健康水平显著提高。

建国以来，我国医疗卫生投入快速增长，公共卫生体系和医疗服务体系不断完善，覆盖城乡的基本医疗保障制度逐步建立和完善，卫生事业发展成果丰硕，国民健康水平持续改善。

公共卫生服务机构不断加强。建国之初，我国公共卫生服务机构极为短缺。1949 年，全国各类公共卫生机构仅为 3670 个，其中医院卫生院 2600 个，门诊部、所 769 个，妇幼保健院 9 个，专科疾病防治院 11 个。随着公共卫生投入的增加，公共卫生服务机构数量大幅增加，在满足城乡居民卫生服务需求方面不断取得新成绩。2013 年末，全国

(2) Impressive achievements in medicine and health care have resulted in a significant increase in the level of human health.

Since the founding of the PRC, contributions to medicine and health care increased rapidly, the public health and medical care system continuously improved, the system of basic medical insurance was gradually established and improved to cover rural and urban areas, the results of the public health services development were fruitful, and residents' overall level of health continuously improved.

Public health institution has been constantly reinforced. There was a great shortage of public health institutions during the first years after the founding of the PRC. In 1949, there were only 3,670 public healthcare institutions, including 2,600 hospitals, 769 clinics, 9 maternal and child care service centers, and 11 special preventative clinics. With increases in investments into public health, the number of healthcare institutions has increased significantly. New results were consistently achieved in the meeting of urban and rural

图 72　1978-2013 年全国卫生总费用
Health Expenditure, 2000-2012

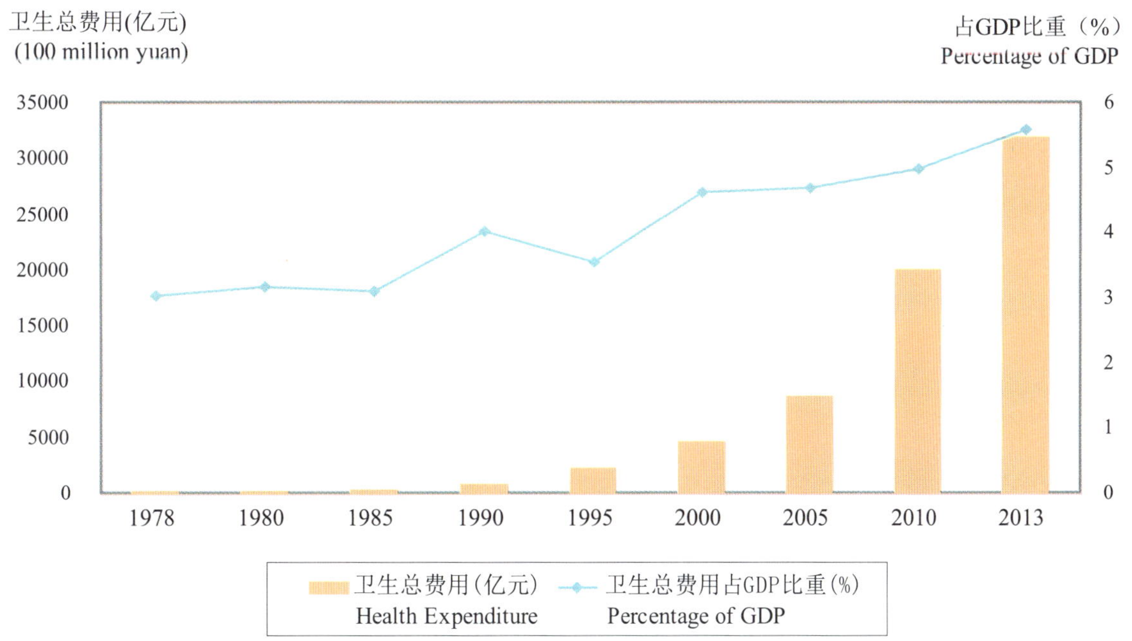

图 73　1949-2013 年末全国卫生机构数

Health Care Institutions, 1949-2013

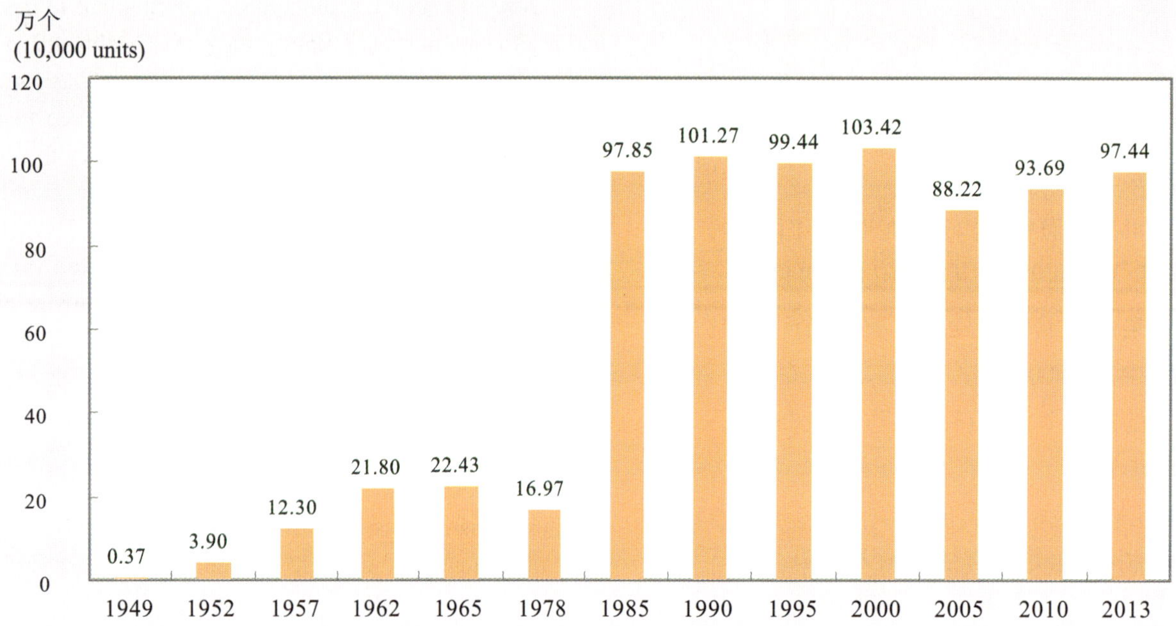

注：从 1985 年起村卫生室数计入医疗卫生机构数中。

a) Number of village clinics was included in health care institutions since 1985.

图 74　1949-2013 年全国卫生人员数

Medical Personnel, 2001-2012

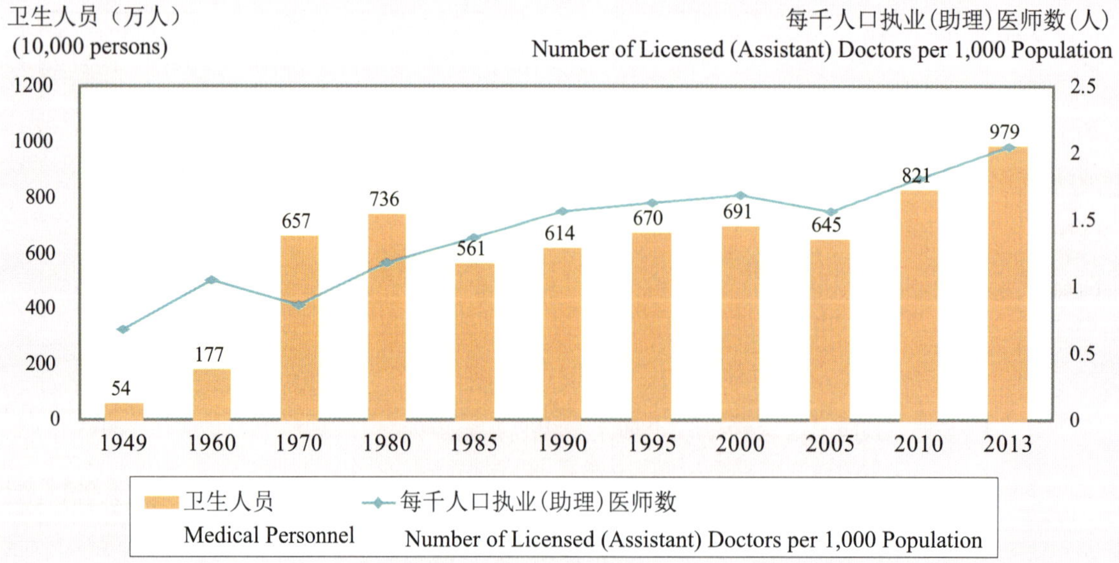

图 75 1949-2013 年末全国医疗卫生机构床位数

Number of Beds in Health Care Institutions at the Year-end, 1949-2013

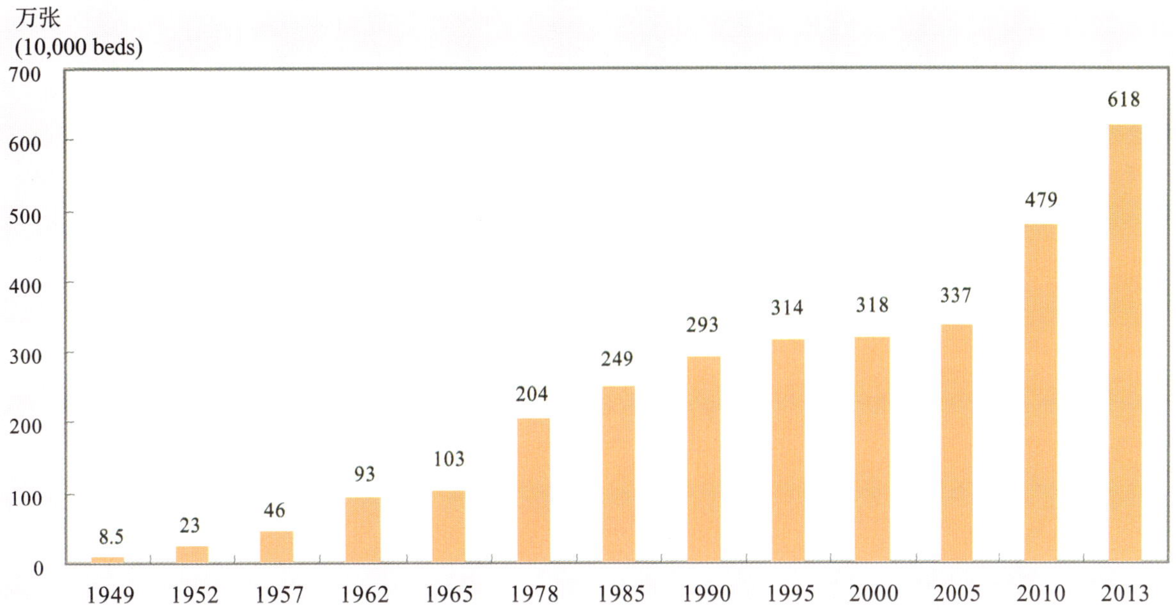

图 76 1991-2013 年 5 岁以下儿童和孕产妇死亡率

Mortality Rate of the Maternal and Children Aged under 5, 1991-2013

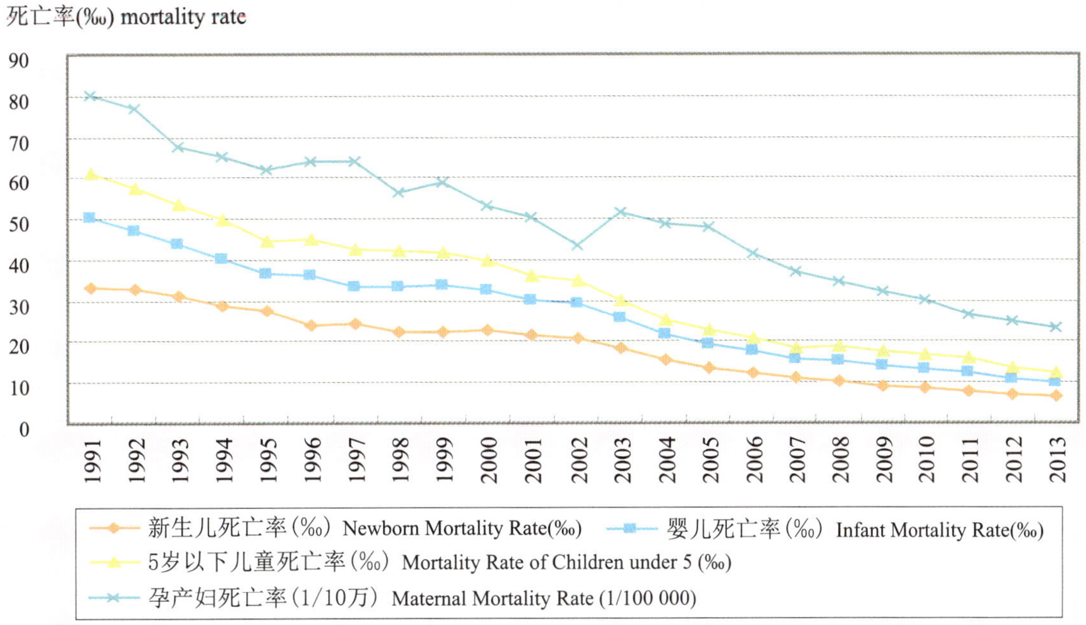

新型农村合作医疗

新型农村合作医疗，简称"新农合"，是指由政府组织、引导、支持，农民自愿参加，个人、集体和政府多方筹资，以大病统筹为主的农民医疗互助共济制度。采取个人缴费、集体扶持和政府资助的方式筹集资金。农村合作医疗是由我国农民自己创造的互助共济的医疗保障制度，在保障农民获得基本卫生服务、缓解农民因病致贫和因病返贫方面发挥了重要的作用。2002 年 10 月，《中共中央、国务院关于进一步加强农村卫生工作的决定》明确指出：要"逐步建立以大病统筹为主的新型农村合作医疗制度"，"到 2010 年，新型农村合作医疗制度要基本覆盖农村居民"，"从 2003 年起，中央财政对中西部地区除市区以外的参加新型合作医疗的农民每年按人均 10 元安排合作医疗补助资金，地方财政对参加新型合作医疗的农民补助每年不低于人均 10 元"，"农民为参加合作医疗、抵御疾病风险而履行缴费义务不能视为增加农民负担"。新型农村合作医疗制度从 2003 年起在全国部分县（市）试点，到 2010 年逐步实现基本覆盖全国农村居民。

New Rural Cooperative Medical System

New Rural Cooperative Medical System (hereinafter referred to as NRCMS) is an interdependent system of the medical aid of farmers, guided, organized and supported by the government and funded through multiple channels. Farmers attended NRCMS voluntarily. NRCMS takes individual contributions, collective support and government funding as ways to raise money. NRCMS is an interdependent system for the medical aid of farmers created by the farmers themselves. It plays an important role to protect farmers' access to basic healthcare services and alleviate farmers' "poverty due to illness" problem. In October 2002, Chinese Central Commission of Chinese Communist Party and State Council's Decision about Strengthening Rural Health Work pointed out that "gradually establish the New Rural Cooperative Medical System which takes comprehensive arrangement for serious diseases as the core", "By 2010, the New Rural Cooperative Medical System will basically have covered the rural resident.", "Since 2003, the central government will pay 10 Yuan medical subvention per capita to the Midwestern farmers except in the town who join the NRCMS and the local government pays 10 Yuan medical subvention per capita to the farmers.", " The fees of farmers to join the NRCMS for resisting disease risk cannot be seen as an increase of burden on farmers. ". Since 2003, NRCMS have launched pilot projects in some towns and cities. To 2010, it will gradually cover almost all the rural residents.

图 77　2007-2013 年新型农村合作医疗情况
New Rural Cooperative Medical System, 2007-2013

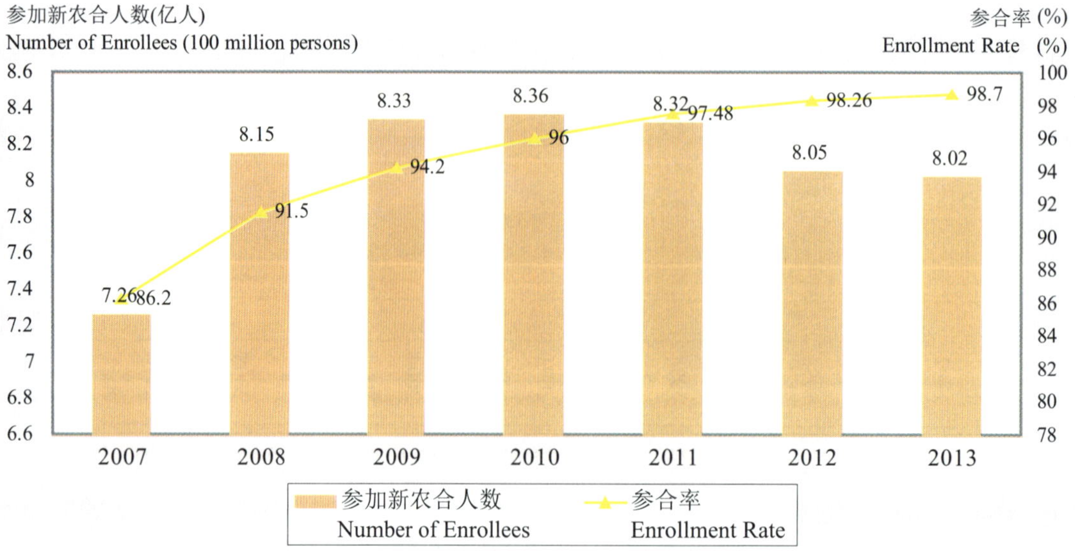

卫生机构数达到974398个，其中医院24709个，比1949年末增长8.5倍。卫生机构床位数增长较快。2013年末，全国医疗卫生机构床位数618万张，比1949年末增长71.7倍。其中医院床位数458万张，增长56.2倍。每千人口医疗卫生机构床位数由1949年0.16张增加到2013年4.55张，增长27.4倍，在解决看病难、住院难问题方面发挥了重要作用。

卫生服务人员数量大幅增加。2013年末，全国卫生机构人员总数达979.0万人，比1949年末增长17.1倍；其中卫生技术人员721.1万人，增长13.3倍。在卫生技术人员中，执业（助理）医师279.5万人（其中全科医生14.6万人），比1949年末增长6.7倍；注册护士278.3万人，增长83.3倍。2013年，每千人口执业（助理）医师2.04人，比1949年增长2.1倍；每千人口注册护士2.05人，增长33.2倍。卫生人员数量的增加及人员素质的提高为满足人民群众卫生服务需求提供了重要保障，为提高人民群众健康水平做出了重要贡献。

居民健康状况明显改善。随着医疗卫生事业的快速发展，传染病和重大疾病防治工作成效显著，妇幼保健水平不断提高，城乡居民健康状况显著改善。我国居民平均预期寿命由解放前的35岁提高到2010年的74.8岁，增加了39.8岁；婴儿死亡率由200‰下降至2013年的9.5‰；孕产妇死亡率由150/10万下降到23.2/10万。居民健康水平的提高为经济社会发展提供重要的人力资源保障，也极大地改善了居民生活质量。

residents' needs for health services. In 2013, the number of public health facilities across China reached 974,398, including 24,709 hospitals, an increase of 8.5 times over 1949. The number of beds in medical institutions is also rapidly growing. At the end of 2013, the figure reached 6.18 million throughout China, which is 71.7 times more than the number in 1949, induding 4.58 million beds, an increase of 56.2 times over 1949. The number of beds per thousand people in healthcare facilities increased from 0.16 units in 1949 to 4.55 units in 2013, an increase of 27.4 times. The difficult problem of hospitalization plays an important role in addressing the complexities of treatment.

The number of medical personnel significantly increases. At the end of 2013, China had around 9.79 million medical staff, 17.1 times more than in 1949, including 7.211 million technical personnel, a 13.3-fold increase. Among these technical personnel, the number of licensed (assistant) doctors is 2.795 million (including 146 thousand general practitioners), 6.7 times more than in 1949; the number of registered nurses is 2.783 million, an increase of 83.3 times over the number in 1949. In 2013, there were 2.04 licensed (assistant) doctors and 2.05 registered nurses for every thousand people, which is 2.1 times and 33.2 times more, respectively, than in 1949. Increasing the number of health care providers and improving the quality of personnel is necessary to meet the population's demand for health care services to make an important contribution to improving the overall health of the population.

Significant improvements in the health of the population. Programs to prevent critical and infectious diseases reached tangible results with the rapid development of medical and healthcare facilities. The level of health protection for mothers and children is constantly growing, and the health of urban and rural residents has greatly improved. The average life expectancy in China increased from 35 years at the time of liberation to 74.8 in 2010, an increase of 39.8 years. The infant mortality rate decreased by 200 to 9.5 in 2013, the maternal mortality rate decreased from 150 per 100,000 women to 23.2 per 100,000. Improving health not only improves the quality of people's lives, but it also guarantees that Chinese society can have the human resources necessary for socio-economic development.

（三）体育事业全面进步，竞技体育不断取得历史性突破。

新中国成立以来，我国体育事业快速发展，体育场地设施不断增加，群众体育科学化、组织化水平不断提高，全民健身活动蓬勃开展，竞技体育不断取得历史性突破，体育产业从无到有，市场效益和社会效益持续提升。

群众体育蓬勃发展。建国之初，党和国家领导人高度重视群众体育发展，颁布和实施国家体育锻炼标准制度、广播体操制度等，促进群众体育发展。改革开放之后，1995 年，全国人大颁布《体育法》，国务院批准下发了《全民健身计划纲要》；2009 年 9 月，国务院公布了《全民健身条例》，

3. Physical education gets all-round development, and historic breakthroughs have continually been reached in physical fitness and athletics.

Since the founding of PRC, the rapid development of China's sports undertakings. The sports facilities have increased, mass sports have been more scientific, organizational level have continued to increase, mass fitness activities have flourished, athletics sports have achieved a historic breakthrough continually, the sports industry has gradually developed and grown from scratch, market and social benefits have improved continually.

The rapid development of mass sports. In the initial period after the founding of the new China, the Party and state leaders paid great attention to the development of mass sports, promulgated and implemented national standards for a physical training system, and broadcasted gymnastics radio shows. After the implementation of reform and open door policy, in 1995, the National People's Congress promulgated the "Law on Sport" and the State Council approved and issued "Basis for national programs in physical training." In September 2009, the State Council announced the "Rules of national physical fitness" and started to promote construction and improvement of various kinds of sports facilities. There has been a steady growth of

图 78　1959-2013 年我国运动员获世界冠军数
World Championships Won by Chinese Athletes, 1959-2013

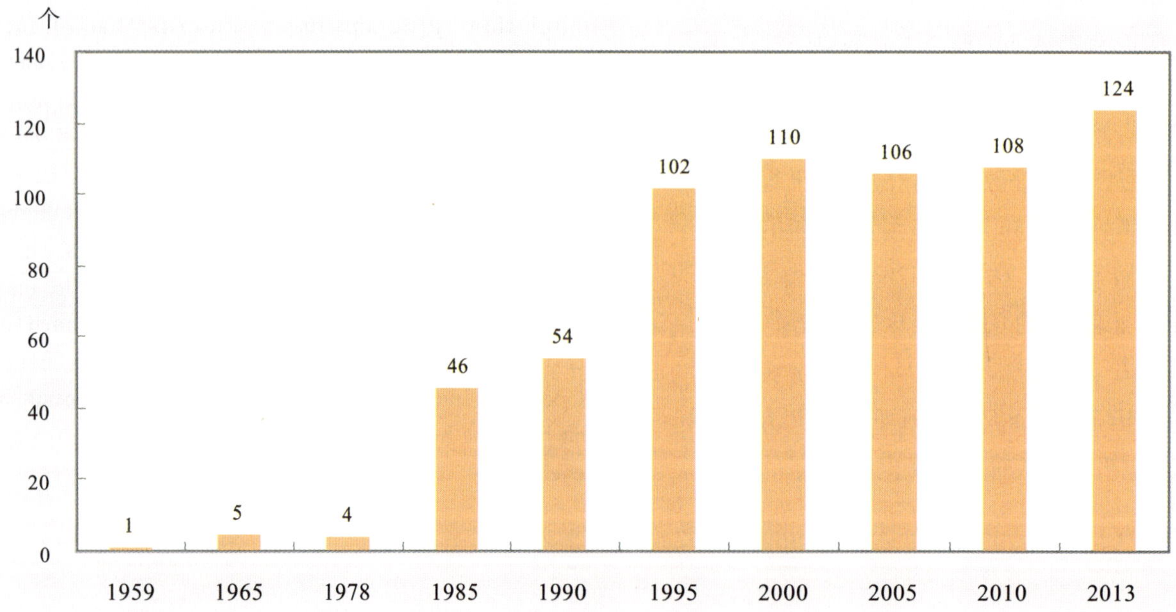

推动了各类体育设施的建设和完善，群众体育活动稳步扩大。目前，我国各类体育场地已超过 100 万个，是建国初期的 240 倍以上。健体强身的体育运动和锻炼参加人数持续增加，国民体质不断加强。2010 年，全国达到《国民体质测定标准》“合格”以上标准的人数比例为 88.9%。

竞技体育成绩显著。建国以前，我国的竞技体育水平低下，在新中国成立后特别是改革开放后，竞技体育连续取得历史性突破。1956 年，陈镜开打破了最轻量级挺举世界纪录，成为我国第一个创造世界纪录的运动员；1959 年，容国团在第 25 届世界乒乓球锦标赛中成为中国历史上第一个世界冠军；1984 年，中国在洛杉矶夏季奥运会上实现了奥运金牌“零”的突破；2008 年，北京成功举办了第 29 届夏季奥运会，实现了中华民族的百年梦想，中国代表团取得了 51 枚金牌、100 枚奖牌的优异成绩，位列金牌榜第一，创造了中国体育代表团参加奥运会以来最好成绩。据统计，1949-2013 年，我国运动员共获得世界冠军 2902 个，其中 1978-2013 年共获得世界冠军 2876 个，占建国以来总数的 99.1%。

体育产业从无到有逐步发展壮大。体育健身服务业快速发展，各种健身场所迅速兴起；竞赛表演业日益活跃，具有中国特色的篮球、排球、乒乓球等国内联赛初具规模，大型综合性运动会的市场开发取得了良好的效益。国务院自 1994 年起批准发行体育彩票。到 2013 年底，体育彩票销售累计超过 7000 亿元，筹集公益金超过 2000 亿元。

mass sport events. Currently, China has more than a million playgrounds, about 240 times more than there were in the initial period after the founding of the state. Physical training and the number of people involved in sports continue to grow, and the overall physical condition of the population is being strengthened. In 2010, during the "Definitions of Body Standards of the Population," it was revealed that 88.9 percent of Chinese residents meet or exceed the national standards.

Significant achievements in athletic sports. Before the founding of the PRC, the level of athletic sports in China was low. But after the founding of the PRC, especially since the beginning of reform and the open door policy, athletic sports continuously achieved historic breakthroughs. In 1956, Chen Jingkai – a lightest weight weightlifter – broke the world record, becoming the first athlete from China to set a world record; in 1959, Rong Guotuan became the first Chinese world champion at the 25th World Championships in table tennis; and in 1984, China made a historic breakthrough in the number of gold medals at the Summer Olympics in Los Angeles. In 2008, Beijing successfully hosted the 29th Summer Olympics, realizing an age-old dream of the Chinese people. The Chinese team won 51 gold medals and a total of 100 awards, winning first place in the number of gold medals, showing the best results in the history of the Chinese team's participation in the Olympics. According to statistics, 2,902 Chinese athletes became world champions between 1949 and 2013, including 2,876 people in the period from 1978 to 2013, accounting for a 99.1% increase since the founding of PRC.

The sports industry has gradually developed and grown from scratch. The sports and fitness industry is growing rapidly, and there has been a high rate increase in the number of sports centers. The industry that has developed around the performance of sporting events gains vitality day by day. Chinese leagues in basketball, volleyball, and table tennis have begun to take initial shape, and the market development of complex large-scale sport games has achieved excellent results. The State Council approved the issuance of the sports lottery in 1994. By the end of 2013, cumulative sales in the sports lottery amounted to 700 billion yuan, increasing the public welfare fund by 200 billion yuan.

国民体质测定标准

2003年10月，国家体育总局会同教育部、国家民委、民政部等有关部门制定的《国民体质测定标准》及《国民体质测定标准施行办法》正式颁布并实施。制定《国民体质测定标准》，是国家和各级政府部门了解和掌握国民体质状况的科学依据，是国民了解自身体质水平，激励群众参加体育健身的积极性，指导群众科学健身的有效方法。

《国民体质测定标准》的适应对象年龄为3至69岁，根据不同年龄人群在体质方面的特征，分为幼儿、儿童青少年、成年和老年四个部分。测试指标包括身体形态、身体机能、身体素质这三个方面。具体来说，以20至39岁的成年人为例，反映身体形态的指标是身高标准体重，即一定的身高所对应的体重范围；反映身体机能的指标是反映人体肺的容积和扩张能力的肺活量，以及反映人体心血管系统机能水平的台阶试验；反映身体素质的指标是反映力量素质的握力、俯卧撑（男）、1分钟仰卧起坐（女）、纵跳，反映柔韧素质的坐位体前屈，反映灵敏素质的选择反应时，反映平衡能力的闭眼单脚站立。而幼儿的情况则有所不同，测试指标只包括身体形态和素质两类，其中反映身体形态的指标是身高和身高标准体重，反映身体素质的指标有10米折返跑、立定跳远、网球掷远、双脚连续跳、坐位体前屈、走平衡木等6项。

National Physical Fitness Evaluation Standard

In October 2003, National Physical Fitness Evaluation Standard and the Implement Measures of National Physical Fitness Evaluation Standard which were formulated by General Administration of Sport of China jointly with Ministry of Education, State Ethnic Affairs Commission and Ministry of Civil Affairs, etc. National Physical Fitness Evaluation Standard is the scientific evidence for the country and government to know the national physical fitness situation. It is an effective method for the citizens to know their physical fitness level, inspiring the citizens to participate in sports fitness and guide them the scientific fitness method.

National Physical Fitness Evaluation Standard is applicable to people between 3 to 69 years of age. According to the physical characteristics of different age groups, four groups are divided including infant, preschool, children and adolescents, adult and agedness. Test index includes the body shape, body function and physical fitness. Specifically, for example, for adult from 20 to 39 years of age, the weight-for-height index reflects body shape, since the weight range correspondeds to a certain height; the vital capacity index reflects the body function, showing the human lung volume and expansion ability. The step test shows the function of human cardiovascular system; the grip strength, press-up for male, sit-up for female, vertical jump reflect the physical fitness, showing the physical fitness. Sit-and-reach test shows the flexibility; Choice reflection time shows the sensitivity; One-leg standing with eye-closed test balance capacity. While the situation of infant is different, text indexes only include the body shape reflected by the height and weight for height as well as the fitness function reflected by six index including 10 meters shuttle run, standing long jump, tennis throwing away, jump with two feet, sit-and-reach, balance beam.

中国奥运之路

从 1896 年的第一届奥运会，一直到 2008 年的第 29 届北京奥运会；从 1896 年清政府接到国际奥委会发出的邀请书而不知为何物，到 1932 年著名男子短跑运动员刘长春代表中国首次参加了第 10 届洛杉矶奥运会；从毫无斩获到 1984 年实现了中国在奥运会历史上金牌零的突破。漫漫奥运之路，不仅再现了近代百年来的世界变化、体育发展，不仅见证了伟大中国的体育事业的由弱变强，也见证了伟大中国的苍桑巨变、由发展到振兴。

20 世纪初，成为奥林匹克大家庭的一员仍只是中国人的一个梦想。1949 年以前，中国运动员曾参加过三届奥运会，均无功而返。自新中国成立以来，我国政府派代表团先后参加了九届夏季奥运会、十届冬奥会。我国健儿在夏季奥运会赛场上总计获 201 枚金牌 474 枚奖牌。在 1984 年美国洛杉矶奥运会开赛的第一天，射击选手许海峰在男子自选手枪慢射比赛中勇夺冠军，从而实现了中国在奥运会历史上金牌零的突破。此后，我国奥运健儿屡创佳绩，尤其是在 2008 年北京奥运会上，以 51 枚金牌的骄人战绩力压美国和俄罗斯，位列金牌榜第一。在冬季奥运会赛场上，总计获得 12 枚金牌，53 枚奖牌。其中，在 2002 年盐湖城冬奥会上，我国选手杨扬先后在女子 500 米与 1000 米短道速滑中两度夺冠，实现了我国冬奥会金牌零的突破。

China's Olympic Path

From the first Olympic Games in 1986 to the 29th Beijing Olympic Games in 2008, from when the Qing government received the invitation letter from the International Olympic Committee in 1896 but did not know what it was to when the famous sprinter Liu Changchun participated the 10th Los Angeles Olympic Games on behalf of China in 1932, from fruitlessness to the first gold medal in the history of China in 1984, China's Olympic Path not only reflected the world changes and the sports development in the recent hundred years, and witnessed the development of China's sports undertakings, and also the Chinese nation.

At the start of 20th century, it was still a dream for Chinese people to become a member of the Olympic family. Before 1949, Chinese athletes have participated in the Olympic Games for three times and returned without accomplishing anything. Since the founding of New China, our government has sent a delegation to participate in the 9th Summer Olympic Games and the 10th Winter Olympic Games. China's athletes gained 201 gold medals and 474 medals in total in the Summer Olympic Games. On the first day of the 1984 Olympic Game in Los Angeles, the shooter Xu Haifeng won the championship on the optional male pistol slow fire, getting the first gold medal in the history of China. Since then, China's athletes competed aggressively. Especially in the 2008 Beijing Olympic Games, China won 51 gold medals, exceeding the United States and Russia, and topping the gold medal list. In the Winter Olympic Games, China won a total of 12 gold medals and 53 medals. In 2002 Salt Lake City Winter Olympic Games, our athlete Yang Yang won the champion successively in the 500 meters and 1000 meters short tracking skating and won the first gold medal in the Winter Olympic Games.

（四）环境保护稳步推进，成效逐渐显现。

新中国成立以来，特别是改革开放以来，我国对环境保护的认识逐步深化，党和政府对环境保护的重视程度不断提高，环境保护事业在艰难中起步，并实现稳步发展。

环境法制法规建设持续推进。1972年6月，我国政府代表团参加了联合国人类环境会议，会议通过了《人类环境宣言》，环境保护开始摆上国家议事日程。1973年8月，国务院召开第一次全国环境保护工作会议，审议通过了《关于保护和改善环境的若干规定》，成为我国环保事业的第一个里程碑。1979年颁布的《中华人民共和国环境保护法（试

(4) Nature and environmental protection steadily improve and gradually begin to show results.

Since the founding of the new China, and especially since the implementation of reform and the open door policy, China has gradually deepened awareness of the need to protect the environment, and the degree of attention that the Party and the government have paid to nature and environmental protection has continuously increased. Environmental protection begins to develop in difficult conditions, yet achieves sustainable development.

Legislation and regulations in the field of ecology continue to advance. In June 1972, the Chinese government's delegation took part in the United Nations Conference on the Problems of the Environment, which adopted the "Declaration on the Human Environment," and the issue of environmental protection was placed on the government agenda. In August 1973, the State Council convened the first national conference on environmental protection, and considered and adopted "Some of the provisions for the protection and improvement of the environment," which was the first milestone for the protection of the environment in China. In 1979, "The Law of the PRC on the Protection of the Environment

行）》使环境保护工作步入法制轨道，加快了环境保护事业的发展。之后，国家陆续颁布多项环境保护法规、条例等，在污染防治、资源和生态保护、防灾减灾等涉及环境保护的多个方面起到了重要的促进作用。

环境保护投入大幅增加。新中国成立后特别是改革开放以来，国家对环境污染的防治力度逐步加大。在加大财政投入的同时，国家积极引导社会资金投向环保事业和环保产业，带动了全社会环保投入较快增长。上世纪 80 年代初期，全国环境保护治理投资每年仅为 30 亿元左右，约占同期国内生产总值的 0.51%；2013 年，全国环境污染治理投资总额为 9516.5 亿元，比 2000 年增长 8.4 倍；环境污染治

(test version)" was published, which put the work of ecological protection into the legal system and accelerated the development of the industry surrounding environmental protection. Since that time, the state has consistently promulgated a series of laws, regulations and rules on the protection of the environment, which has played an important role in helping to prevent pollution, protect resources and the environment, manage disaster prevention and mitigation, as well as other aspects related to the protection of the environment.

A significant increase in investment in environmental protection. Since the founding of the PRC, and especially since the beginning of the reform and open door policy, the State's pollution prevention and environment improvement efforts have been constantly increasing. Along with the increase in financial investments, the state actively directs social capital toward investment in the environmental protection industry, which has led to the rapid growth in environmental investments throughout the whole society. In the early 1980s, the state's total investments in environmental protection amounted to 3 billion yuan each year, accounting for 0.51 percent of GDP in the period. In 2013,

理投资占GDP比重为1.67%，比2000年提高0.65个百分点。污染治理投入的大幅增加，对我国环境污染防治发挥了重要作用。

主要污染物排放初步得到控制。随着我国的污染防治和节能减排工作稳步推进，环保专项行动积极开展，环境违法行为查处力度不断加大，环境保护工作取得了积极进展，特别是近年来主要化学污染物排放总量明显下降。2013年，工业化学需氧量排放总量为319.5万吨，比2005年下降42.4%；二氧化硫排放总量为2043.9万吨，下降19.8%；全国一般工业固体废物产生量为327701.9万吨，综合利用量（含利用往年贮存量）为205916.3万吨，综合利用率为62.3%，提高6.2个百分点。

回首新中国65年，在中国共产党的正确领导下，在全国各族人民的共同努力下，我国国民经济和各项社会事业实现了跨越性发展，取得了举世瞩目的辉煌成就。站在新的历史起点上，展望未来，前景依然光明，工业化、信息化、城镇化、农业现代化持续推进，我国发展仍处在大有可为的重要战略机遇期；挑战也前所未有，我国进入转型发展的新阶段，结构调整和转型升级刻不容缓，深层次矛盾凸显。我们相信，只要我们把握机遇，直面挑战，紧密团结在以习近平同志为总书记的党中央周围，坚定信心，迎难而上，砥砺奋进，锐意进取，始终不渝地沿着党的基本方针和路线指引的方向奋勇前行，就一定能够夺取全面建成小康社会的新胜利，实现中华民族伟大复兴的中国梦！

state investment in environmental protection amounted to 951.65 billion yuan, an increase of 8.4 times compared to 2000, and the share of investment in the fight against environmental pollution accounted for 1.67 percent of GDP, an increase of 0.65 percent compared to 2000. The amount of investment in the fight against pollution has significantly increased, which plays an important role in environmental protection and improvement.

Initial controls of major pollutants and emissions have been carried out. Along with China's steady progress in the work of pollution prevention and energy efficiency, environmental protection is becoming more active and investigations and punishment of illegal actions in relation to the environment are gaining strength. The work of environmental protection has achieved positive progress, particularly through the significant decrease in the total amount of main chemical pollutants and emissions in recent years. In 2013, the chemical oxygen demand due to emissions was 3.195 million tons, a decrease of 42.4 percent compared to 2005; sulfur dioxide emissions amounted to 20.439 million tons with a decrease of 19.8 percent; the amount of solid waste across the country amounted to 3.277019 billion tons, and the total volume of waste utilization (including stocks of previous years) reached 2.059163 billion tons, a utilization rate of 62.3 percent, an increase of 6.2 percent.

During the 65 years of the PRC's history, under the thorough leadership of Chinese Communist Party and the combined efforts of all the country's ethnic groups, the Chinese national economy and different social initiatives made a huge leap in development and achieved excellent results that have attract the whole world's attention. Standing at a new starting point in history and looking to the future, we see that the outlook remains bright. Industrialization, information technology, urbanization, and the modernization of agriculture continue to advance. China's development is still in a period of important strategic opportunities, and the challenges the country faces are also unprecedented. China is entering a new period of transitional development, restructuring, transformation, and modernization, and many urgent, deep contradictions remain visible. We believe that if we grasp the opportunities and meet the challenges and closely unite around the CPC Central Committee, led by Chairman Xi Jinping; and if we strengthen our faith to face the difficulties, become stronger, and gradually forge ahead tirelessly along with the general line of the Communist Party's policy in the direction of the indicated itinerary, we are sure to achieve a new victory in building a middle income society, a Chinese dream, to resurrect the Chinese nation.

表1 全国自然状况和自然资源
Basic Condition and Natural Resources

项　　目	Item	2013
国土	**Territory**	
国土面积（万平方公里）	Area of Territory (10 000 sq.km)	960
海域面积（万平方公里）	Area of Sea (10 000 sq.km)	473
岸线总长度（公里）	Length of Coastline (km)	32000
大陆岸线长度	Mainland Shore	18000
岛屿岸线长度	Island Shore	14000
气候	**Climate**	
气候带面积比例(国土面积=100)	Percentage of Climatic Zones to Total Area of Territory	
湿润地区（干燥度<1.0）	Humid Zone (aridity<1.0)	32
半湿润地区(干燥度=1.0-1.5)	Semi-Humid Zone (aridity 1.0-1.5)	15
半干旱地区(干燥度=1.5-2.0)	Semi-Arid Zone (aridity 1.5-2.0)	22
干旱地区（干燥度>2.0）	Arid Zone (aridity>2.0)	31
土地状况　（按特征分，万公顷）	**Land Characteristics by Use (10 000 hectares)**	
#耕地面积	Cultivated Land	12172
内陆水域面积	Water Area in Land	1747
草地面积	Area of Grassland	40000
森林资源	**Forest Resources**	
森林面积（万公顷）	Forest Area (10 000 hectares)	20769
森林覆盖率（%）	Forest-coverage Rate (%)	21.63
活立木总蓄积量（万立方米）	Total Standing Stock Volume (10 000 cu.m)	1643281
森林蓄积量（万立方米）	Stock Volume of the Forest (10 000 cu.m)	1513730
水利资源	**Water Resources**	
水资源总量（亿立方米）	Total Water Resources Volume (100 million cu.m)	27958
地表水资源量	Surface Water Volume	26839
地下水资源量	Ground Water Volume	8081
水力资源蕴藏量（亿千瓦）	Hydropower Resources (100 million kw)	6.76
内陆水域总面积（万公顷）	Inland Water Area (10 000 hectares)	1747
海水可养殖面积（万公顷）	Cultivatable Area in Marine Areas (10 000 hectares)	260
#已养殖面积（万公顷）	Cultivated Area (10 000 hectares)	109
主要矿产基础储量	**Major Mineral Basic Reserves**	
石油（万吨）	Petroleum (10 000 tons)	336732.81
天然气（亿立方米）	Natural Gas (100 million cu.m)	46428.84
煤炭（亿吨）	Coal (100 million tons)	2362.90
铁矿（矿石，亿吨）	Iron (Ore, 100 million tons)	199.17
锰矿（矿石，万吨）	Manganese (Ore, 10 000 tons)	21547.74
铬矿（矿石，万吨）	Chromite (Ore, 10 000 tons)	401.47
钒矿（矿石，万吨）	Vanadium (Ore, 10 000 tons)	909.91
原生钛铁矿（矿石，万吨）	Titanium (Ore,10000 tons)	21957.03

注：1.耕地面积数据来源于国土资源部；森林资源为2009-2013年清查数；草地资源为1991年调查数；水面资源为1988年数；水利资源为1985年评价数。
2.水资源总量等于地表水资源量加地下水资源量减两者之间的重复计算水量。
3.本表除国土面积、海域面积和森林资源外,其余指标均未包括香港、澳门特别行政区和台湾省数据。

a) Figures on area of cultivated land come from Ministry of Land and Resources.Figures on forest resource were taken from the 2009-2013's Forest Census.Figures on area of grassland was the figure of 1991's survey.Figures on water area were taken from 1988's survey.Water resources were the estimated figures in 1985.

b) Total amount of water resources is equal to surface water plus ground water and minus the repeat-calculated part between them.

c) Data in this table except Area of Terrritory and Area of Sea don't include that of Hong Kong Special Administrative Region, Macao Special Administrative Region and Taiwan Province.

表2 全国行政区划（年底数）
Divisions of Administrative Areas in China (at Year-end)

单位：个 (unit)

年份 Year	省级区划数 Number of Regions at Province Level	地级区划数 Number of Regions at Prefecture Level	#地级市 Cities at Prefecture Level	县级区划数 Number of Regions at County Level	市辖区 Districts under the Jurisdiction of Cities	县级市 Cities at County Level	县(旗) County (Qi)
1949	50	295	56	2741	394	61	2286
1950	53	282	64	2668	331	66	2271
1951	53	283	69	2765	414	78	2273
1952	45	259	67	2762	432	74	2256
1953	47	265	75	2786	474	74	2238
1954	32	284	82	2813	471	80	2262
1955	29	288	83	2649	421	78	2150
1956	29	287	88	2676	336	86	2254
1957	30	287	92	2664	336	81	2247
1958	29	236	68	2278	271	114	1893
1959	29	242	75	2153	274	102	1777
1960	29	244	88	2099	296	109	1694
1961	29	262	80	2403	312	126	1965
1962	29	268	81	2533	322	111	2100
1963	29	268	78	2524	321	97	2106
1964	29	272	75	2536	310	90	2136
1965	29	287	76	2550	288	90	2172
1966	29	294	79	2559	291	90	2178
1967	30	293	79	2561	308	90	2163
1968	30	291	79	2544	308	90	2146
1969	30	289	80	2567	331	93	2143
1970	30	291	79	2582	342	95	2145
1971	30	292	82	2594	349	96	2149
1972	30	294	82	2604	358	97	2149
1973	30	296	83	2589	360	95	2134
1974	30	300	87	2599	372	91	2136
1975	30	310	96	2617	380	86	2151
1976	30	311	96	2629	388	89	2152
1977	30	311	97	2639	396	90	2153
1978	30	340	99	2637	408	91	2138
1979	30	313	104	2766	520	109	2137
1980	30	316	107	2761	511	113	2137
1981	30	318	110	2830	581	113	2136

表2 续表 continued

单位：个 (unit)

年份 Year	省级区划数 Number of Regions at Province Level	地级区划数 Number of Regions at Prefecture Level	#地级市 Cities at Prefecture Level	县级区划数 Number of Regions at County Level	市辖区 Districts under the Jurisdiction of Cities	县级市 Cities at County Level	县(旗) County (Qi)
1982	30	319	109	2793	527	133	2133
1983	30	320	137	2835	599	141	2095
1984	30	323	148	2813	595	149	2069
1985	30	327	162	2825	620	159	2046
1986	30	325	166	2830	629	184	2017
1987	30	326	170	2817	623	208	1986
1988	31	334	183	2831	647	248	1936
1989	31	336	185	2829	648	262	1919
1990	31	336	185	2833	651	279	1903
1991	31	338	187	2833	650	289	1894
1992	31	339	191	2833	662	323	1848
1993	31	335	196	2835	669	371	1795
1994	31	333	206	2845	697	413	1735
1995	31	334	210	2849	706	427	1716
1996	31	335	218	2858	717	445	1696
1997	33	332	222	2862	727	442	1693
1998	33	331	227	2863	737	437	1689
1999	34	331	236	2858	749	427	1682
2000	34	333	259	2861	787	400	1674
2001	34	332	265	2861	808	393	1660
2002	34	332	275	2860	830	381	1649
2003	34	333	282	2861	845	374	1642
2004	34	333	283	2862	852	374	1636
2005	34	333	283	2862	852	374	1636
2006	34	333	283	2860	856	369	1635
2007	34	333	283	2859	856	368	1635
2008	34	333	283	2859	856	368	1635
2009	34	333	283	2858	855	367	1636
2010	34	333	283	2856	853	370	1633
2011	34	332	284	2853	857	369	1627
2012	34	333	285	2852	860	368	1624
2013	34	333	286	2853	872	368	1613

表3 全国人口状况
Population

本表各年人口未包括香港、澳门特别行政区和台湾省的人口数据。
Data in this table exclude the population of Hong Kong SAR, Macao SAR and Taiwan Province.

年份 Year	年底总人口（万人） Total Population (year-end) (10 000 persons)	按性别分（万人） By Sex (10 000 persons) 男 Male	女 Female	按城乡分（万人） By Residence (10 000 persons) 城镇 Urban	乡村 Rural	人口出生率（‰） Birth Rate (‰)	人口死亡率（‰） Death Rate (‰)	人口自然增长率（‰） Natural Growth Rate (‰)
1949	54167	28145	26022	5765	48402	36.00	20.00	16.00
1950	55196	28669	26527	6169	49027	37.00	18.00	19.00
1951	56300	29231	27069	6632	49668	37.80	17.80	20.00
1952	57482	29833	27649	7163	50319	37.00	17.00	20.00
1953	58796	30468	28328	7826	50970	37.00	14.00	23.00
1954	60266	31242	29024	8249	52017	37.97	13.18	24.79
1955	61465	31809	29656	8285	53180	32.60	12.28	20.32
1956	62828	32536	30292	9185	53643	31.90	11.40	20.50
1957	64653	33469	31184	9949	54704	34.03	10.80	23.23
1958	65994	34195	31799	10721	55273	29.22	11.98	17.24
1959	67207	34890	32317	12371	54836	24.78	14.59	10.19
1960	66207	34283	31924	13073	53134	20.86	25.43	-4.57
1961	65859	33880	31979	12707	53152	18.13	14.33	3.80
1962	67295	34517	32778	11659	55636	37.22	10.08	27.14
1963	69172	35533	33639	11646	57526	43.60	10.10	33.50
1964	70499	36142	34357	12950	57549	39.34	11.56	27.78
1965	72538	37128	35410	13045	59493	38.06	9.55	28.51
1966	74542	38189	36353	13313	61229	35.21	8.87	26.34
1967	76368	39115	37253	13548	62820	34.12	8.47	25.65
1968	78534	40226	38308	13838	64696	35.75	8.25	27.50
1969	80671	41289	39382	14117	66554	34.25	8.06	26.19
1970	82992	42686	40306	14424	68568	33.59	7.64	25.95
1971	85229	43819	41410	14711	70518	30.74	7.34	23.40
1972	87177	44813	42364	14935	72242	29.92	7.65	22.27
1973	89211	45876	43335	15345	73866	28.07	7.08	20.99
1974	90859	46727	44132	15595	75264	24.95	7.38	17.57
1975	92420	47564	44856	16030	76390	23.13	7.36	15.77
1976	93717	48257	45460	16341	77376	20.01	7.29	12.72
1977	94974	48908	46066	16669	78305	19.03	6.91	12.12
1978	96259	49567	46692	17245	79014	18.25	6.25	12.00
1979	97542	50192	47350	18495	79047	17.82	6.21	11.61
1980	98705	50785	47920	19140	79565	18.21	6.34	11.87
1981	100072	51519	48553	20171	79901	20.91	6.36	14.55
1982	101654	52352	49302	21480	80174	22.28	6.60	15.68
1983	103008	53152	49856	22274	80734	20.19	6.90	13.29
1984	104357	53848	50509	24017	80340	19.90	6.82	13.08
1985	105851	54725	51126	25094	80757	21.04	6.78	14.26

表3 续表 continued

年份 Year	年底总人口（万人） Total Population (year-end) (10 000 persons)	按性别分（万人） By Sex (10 000 persons)		按城乡分（万人） By Residence (10 000 persons)		人口出生率（‰） Birth Rate (‰)	人口死亡率（‰） Death Rate (‰)	人口自然增长率（‰） Natural Growth Rate (‰)
		男 Male	女 Female	城镇 Urban	乡村 Rural			
1986	107507	55581	51926	26366	81141	22.43	6.86	15.57
1987	109300	56290	53010	27674	81626	23.33	6.72	16.61
1988	111026	57201	53825	28661	82365	22.37	6.64	15.73
1989	112704	58099	54605	29540	83164	21.58	6.54	15.04
1990	114333	58904	55429	30195	84138	21.06	6.67	14.39
1991	115823	59466	56357	31203	84620	19.68	6.70	12.98
1992	117171	59811	57360	32175	84996	18.24	6.64	11.60
1993	118517	60472	58045	33173	85344	18.09	6.64	11.45
1994	119850	61246	58604	34169	85681	17.70	6.49	11.21
1995	121121	61808	59313	35174	85947	17.12	6.57	10.55
1996	122389	62200	60189	37304	85085	16.98	6.56	10.42
1997	123626	63131	60495	39449	84177	16.57	6.51	10.06
1998	124761	63940	60821	41608	83153	15.64	6.50	9.14
1999	125786	64692	61094	43748	82038	14.64	6.46	8.18
2000	126743	65437	61306	45906	80837	14.03	6.45	7.58
2001	127627	65672	61955	48064	79563	13.38	6.43	6.95
2002	128453	66115	62338	50212	78241	12.86	6.41	6.45
2003	129227	66556	62671	52376	76851	12.41	6.40	6.01
2004	129988	66976	63012	54283	75705	12.29	6.42	5.87
2005	130756	67375	63381	56212	74544	12.40	6.51	5.89
2006	131448	67728	63720	58288	73160	12.09	6.81	5.28
2007	132129	68048	64081	60633	71496	12.10	6.93	5.17
2008	132802	68357	64445	62403	70399	12.14	7.06	5.08
2009	133450	68647	64803	64512	68938	11.95	7.08	4.87
2010	134091	68748	65343	66978	67113	11.90	7.11	4.79
2011	134735	69068	65667	69079	65656	11.93	7.14	4.79
2012	135404	69395	66009	71182	64222	12.10	7.15	4.95
2013	136072	69728	66344	73111	62961	12.08	7.16	4.92

注：1.1981年及以前数据为户籍统计数，1982年、1990年、2000年和2010年数据为当年人口普查数据推算数，1987年、1995年和2005年数据根据全国1%人口抽样调查数据推算，其余年份数据为人口变动情况抽样调查推算数。

2.总人口和按性别分人口中包括中国人民解放军现役军人，按城乡分人口中现役军人计入城镇人口。

a) Data in 1981 and before were taken from the statistics of household registration. Data in 1982,1990,2000 and 2010 were from national population census. Data in 1987, 1995 and 2005 were estimated on the National 1% Population Sample Survey, and were estimated on the National Sample Survey on Population Changes in other years.

b) Total population and population by sex include the military personnel of Chinese People's Liberation Army, the military personnel are classified as urban population in the item of population by residence.

表4 人口年龄结构和抚养比
Age Composition and Dependency Ratio of Population

单位：万人 (10 000 persons)

年份 Year	总人口(年末) Total Population (year-end)	0-14岁 Aged 0-14		15-64岁 Aged 15-64		65岁及以上 Aged 65 and Over		总抚养比(%) Gross Dependency Ratio	少儿抚养比 Children Dependency Ratio	老年抚养比 Old Dependency Ratio
		人口数 Population	比重(%) Proportion	人口数 Population	比重(%) Proportion	人口数 Population	比重(%) Proportion			
1953	58796	21331	36.3	34872	59.3	2593	4.4	68.6	61.2	7.4
1964	70499	28686	40.7	39303	55.8	2510	3.6	79.4	73.0	6.4
1982	101654	34146	33.6	62517	61.5	4991	4.9	62.6	54.6	8.0
1987	109300	31347	28.7	71985	65.9	5968	5.4	51.8	43.5	8.3
1990	114333	31659	27.7	76306	66.7	6368	5.6	49.8	41.5	8.3
1995	121121	32218	26.6	81393	67.2	7510	6.2	48.8	39.6	9.2
1996	122389	32311	26.4	82245	67.2	7833	6.4	48.8	39.3	9.5
1997	123626	32093	26.0	83448	67.5	8085	6.5	48.1	38.5	9.7
1998	124761	32064	25.7	84338	67.6	8359	6.7	47.9	38.0	9.9
1999	125786	31950	25.4	85157	67.7	8679	6.9	47.7	37.5	10.2
2000	126743	29012	22.9	88910	70.1	8821	7.0	42.6	32.6	9.9
2001	127627	28716	22.5	89849	70.4	9062	7.1	42.0	32.0	10.1
2002	128453	28774	22.4	90302	70.3	9377	7.3	42.2	31.9	10.4
2003	129227	28559	22.1	90976	70.4	9692	7.5	42.0	31.4	10.7
2004	129988	27947	21.5	92184	70.9	9857	7.6	41.0	30.3	10.7
2005	130756	26504	20.3	94197	72.0	10055	7.7	38.8	28.1	10.7
2006	131448	25961	19.8	95068	72.3	10419	7.9	38.3	27.3	11.0
2007	132129	25660	19.4	95833	72.5	10636	8.1	37.9	26.8	11.1
2008	132802	25166	19.0	96680	72.7	10956	8.3	37.4	26.0	11.3
2009	133450	24659	18.5	97484	73.0	11307	8.5	36.9	25.3	11.6
2010	134091	22259	16.6	99938	74.5	11894	8.9	34.2	22.3	11.9
2011	134735	22164	16.5	100283	74.4	12288	9.1	34.4	22.1	12.3
2012	135404	22287	16.5	100403	74.1	12714	9.4	34.9	22.2	12.7
2013	136072	22329	16.4	100582	73.9	13161	9.7	35.3	22.2	13.1

注：本表数据来源为《2014中国统计年鉴》，1981年及以前数据为户籍统计数，1982年、1990年、2000年和2010年数据为当年人口普查数据推算数，2001-2004年、2006-2009年和2011-2013年数据为人口变动情况抽样调查推算数；1987年、1995年和2005年数据根据全国1%人口抽样调查数据推算。

a) Data come from China Statistical Yearbook-2014, before 1981 were from the statistics of household registrationin. Data in 1982, 1990, 2000 and 2010 were estimates of National Population Census, Data in 2001-2004, 2006-2009 and 2011-2013 have been estimated on the basis of the annual national sample surveys on population changes. Data in 1987, 1995 and 2005 are estimated on the National 1% Population Sample Survey.

表5 全国就业人员和城镇登记失业人员

Employment and Unemployment

单位：万人 (10 000 persons)

年份 Year	就业人员 Total Number of Employed Persons	按城乡分 By Residence		按三次产业分 By Three Industries			城镇登记失业人员 Urban Registered Unemployment	城镇登记失业率(%) Unemployment Rate (%)
		城镇 Urban Area	乡村 Rural Area	第一产业 Primary Industry	第二产业 Secondary Industry	第三产业 Tertiary Industry		
1952	20729	2486	18243	17317	1531	1881		
1953	21364	2754	18610	17747	1715	1902		
1954	21832	2744	19088	18151	1882	1799		
1955	22328	2802	19526	18592	1913	1823		
1956	23018	2993	20025	18544	2468	2006		
1957	23771	3205	20566	19309	2142	2320		
1958	26600	5300	21300	15490	7076	4034		
1959	26173	5389	20784	16271	5402	4500		
1960	25880	6119	19761	17016	4112	4752		
1961	25590	5336	20254	19747	2856	2987		
1962	25910	4537	21373	21276	2059	2575		
1963	26640	4603	22037	21966	2038	2636		
1964	27736	4828	22908	22801	2183	2752		
1965	28670	5136	23534	23396	2408	2866		
1966	29805	5354	24451	24297	2600	2908		
1967	30814	5446	25368	25165	2661	2988		
1968	31915	5630	26285	26063	2743	3109		
1969	33225	5825	27400	27117	3030	3078		
1970	34432	6312	28120	27811	3518	3103		
1971	35620	6868	28752	28397	3990	3233		
1972	35854	7200	28654	28283	4276	3295		
1973	36652	7388	29264	28857	4492	3303		
1974	37369	7687	29682	29218	4712	3439		
1975	38168	8222	29946	29456	5152	3560		
1976	38834	8692	30142	29443	5611	3780		
1977	39377	9127	30250	29340	5831	4206		
1978	40152	9514	30638	28318	6945	4890	530.0	5.3
1979	41024	9999	31025	28634	7214	5177	567.6	5.4
1980	42361	10525	31836	29122	7707	5532	541.5	4.9
1981	43725	11053	32672	29777	8003	5945	439.5	3.8
1982	45295	11428	33867	30859	8346	6090	379.4	3.2
1983	46436	11746	34690	31151	8679	6606	271.4	2.3
1984	48197	12229	35968	30868	9590	7739	235.7	1.9
1985	49873	12808	37065	31130	10384	8359	238.5	1.8

表5 续表 continued

单位：万人 (10 000 persons)

年份 Year	就业人员 Total Number of Employed Persons	按城乡分 By Residence		按三次产业分 By Three Industries			城镇登记失业人员 Urban Registered Unemployment	城镇登记失业率(%) Unemployment Rate (%)
		城镇 Urban Area	乡村 Rural Area	第一产业 Primary Industry	第二产业 Secondary Industry	第三产业 Tertiary Industry		
1986	51282	13292	37990	31254	11216	8811	264.4	2.0
1987	52783	13783	39000	31663	11726	9395	276.6	2.0
1988	54334	14267	40067	32249	12152	9933	296.2	2.0
1989	55329	14390	40939	33225	11976	10129	377.9	2.6
1990	64749	17041	47708	38914	13856	11979	383.2	2.5
1991	65491	17465	48026	39098	14015	12378	352.2	2.3
1992	66152	17861	48291	38699	14355	13098	363.9	2.3
1993	66808	18262	48546	37680	14965	14163	420.1	2.6
1994	67455	18653	48802	36628	15312	15515	476.4	2.8
1995	68065	19040	49025	35530	15655	16880	519.6	2.9
1996	68950	19922	49028	34820	16203	17927	552.8	3.0
1997	69820	20781	49039	34840	16547	18432	576.8	3.1
1998	70637	21616	49021	35177	16600	18860	571.0	3.1
1999	71394	22412	48982	35768	16421	19205	575.0	3.1
2000	72085	23151	48934	36043	16219	19823	595.0	3.1
2001	72797	24123	48674	36399	16234	20165	681.0	3.6
2002	73280	25159	48121	36640	15682	20958	770.0	4.0
2003	73736	26230	47506	36204	15927	21605	800.0	4.3
2004	74264	27293	46971	34830	16709	22725	827.0	4.2
2005	74647	28389	46258	33442	17766	23439	839.0	4.2
2006	74978	29630	45348	31941	18894	24143	847.0	4.1
2007	75321	30953	44368	30731	20186	24404	830.0	4.0
2008	75564	32103	43461	29923	20553	25087	886.0	4.2
2009	75828	33322	42506	28890	21080	25857	921.0	4.3
2010	76105	34687	41418	27931	21842	26332	908.0	4.1
2011	76420	35914	40506	26594	22544	27282	922.0	4.1
2012	76704	37102	39602	25773	23241	27690	917.0	4.1
2013	76977	38240	38737	24171	23170	29636	926.0	4.05

注：1.全国就业人员1990年及以后的数据根据劳动力调查、人口普查推算，2001年及以后数据根据第六次人口普查数据重新修订(下表同)。
2.本表城镇登记失业资料由劳动和社会保障部门提供。

a) From 1990 to 2000, the total number of employed persons were estimated according to Labour Force Survey and Population Census, since 2001, were revised according to the 6th National Population Census. The same applies to the following tables.

b) Figures of urban registered unemployment in this table are provided by the Ministry of Labour and Social Security.

表6 全国城镇单位就业人员数和平均工资

Number of Staff and Workers and Average Wage

年份 Year	就业人员数（万人） Number of Employees (10 000 persons)				平均货币工资（元） Average Money Wage (yuan)				平均实际工资指数（上年=100） Average Real Wage Indices (preceding year=100)			
	合计 Total	国有 State-owned	城镇集体 Urban Collective-owned	其他 Other	合计 Total	国有 State-owned	城镇集体 Urban Collective-owned	其他 Other	合计 Total	国有 State-owned	城镇集体 Urban Collective-owned	其他 Other
1952	1603	1580	23		445	446	348					
1953	1856	1826	30		495	496	415					
1954	2002	1881	121		517	519	464					
1955	2162	1908	254		527	534	453					
1956	2977	2423	554		601	610	547					
1957	3101	2451	650		624	637	571					
1958	5194	4532	662		536	550	470					
1959	5275	4561	714		512	524	430					
1960	5969	5044	925		511	528	409					
1961	5171	4171	1000		510	537	380					
1962	4321	3309	1012		551	592	405					
1963	4372	3293	1079		576	641	371					
1964	4601	3465	1136		586	661	358					
1965	4965	3738	1227		590	652	398					
1966	5198	3934	1264		583	636	423					
1967	5305	4006	1299		587	630	455					
1968	5504	4170	1334		577	621	441					
1969	5714	4335	1379		575	618	439					
1970	6216	4792	1424		561	609	405					
1971	6787	5318	1469		560	597	429					
1972	7134	5610	1524		588	622	465					
1973	7337	5758	1579		587	614	489					
1974	7651	6007	1644		584	622	441					
1975	8198	6426	1772		580	613	453					
1976	8673	6860	1813		575	605	464					
1977	9112	7196	1916		576	602	478					
1978	9499	7451	2048		615	644	506		106.0	106.2	105.1	
1979	9967	7693	2274		668	705	542		106.6	107.4	105.1	
1980	10444	8019	2425		762	803	623		106.1	106.0	106.9	
1981	10940	8372	2568		772	812	642		98.8	98.7	100.5	
1982	11281	8630	2651		798	836	671		101.3	100.9	102.5	
1983	11515	8771	2744		826	865	698		101.5	101.4	102.0	
1984	11890	8637	3216	37	974	1034	811	1048	114.8	116.4	113.1	
1985	12358	8990	3324	44	1148	1213	967	1436	105.3	104.8	106.6	122.5
1986	12809	9333	3421	55	1329	1414	1092	1629	108.2	108.9	105.5	106.0

表6 续表 continued

年份 Year	就业人员数（万人） Number of Employees (10 000 persons)				平均货币工资（元） Average Money Wage (yuan)				平均实际工资指数（上年=100） Average Real Wage Indices (preceding year=100)			
	合计 Total	国有 State-owned	城镇集体 Urban Collective -owned	其他 Other	合计 Total	国有 State-owned	城镇集体 Urban Collective -owned	其他 Other	合计 Total	国有 State-owned	城镇集体 Urban Collective -owned	其他 Other
1987	13214	9654	3488	72	1459	1546	1207	1879	100.9	100.5	101.6	106.0
1988	13608	9984	3527	97	1747	1853	1426	2382	99.2	99.3	97.9	105.0
1989	13742	10108	3502	132	1935	2055	1557	2707	95.2	95.4	93.9	97.7
1990	14059	10346	3549	164	2140	2284	1681	2987	109.2	109.7	106.6	108.9
1991	14508	10664	3628	216	2340	2477	1866	3468	104.0	103.2	105.6	110.5
1992	14792	10889	3621	282	2711	2878	2109	3966	106.7	107.0	104.1	105.3
1993	14849	10920	3393	536	3371	3532	2592	4966	107.1	105.7	105.9	107.9
1994	14849	10890	3211	747	4538	4797	3245	6303	107.7	108.7	100.2	101.5
1995	15301	11261	3147	894	5348	5553	3934	7728	101.8	100.4	103.7	102.6
1996	15221	11244	3016	962	5980	6207	4312	8521	102.8	102.7	100.7	101.3
1997	15036	11044	2883	1109	6444	6679	4516	9092	104.5	104.4	101.6	103.5
1998	12696	9058	1963	1675	7446	7579	5314	9241	116.2	114.2	118.4	102.3
1999	12130	8572	1712	1846	8319	8443	5758	10142	113.2	112.9	109.8	111.2
2000	11612	8102	1499	2011	9333	9441	6241	11238	111.3	110.9	107.5	109.9
2001	11166	7640	1291	2235	10834	11045	6851	12437	115.3	116.2	109.0	109.9
2002	10985	7163	1122	2700	12373	12701	7636	13486	115.4	116.2	112.6	109.5
2003	10970	6876	1000	3094	13969	14358	8627	14843	111.9	112.0	112.0	109.1
2004	11099	6710	897	3492	15920	16445	9723	16519	110.3	110.9	109.1	107.7
2005	11404	6488	810	4106	18200	18978	11176	18362	112.5	113.6	113.1	109.4
2006	11713	6430	764	4519	20856	21706	12866	21004	112.9	112.7	113.4	112.7
2007	12024	6424	718	4882	24721	26100	15444	24271	113.4	115.0	114.8	110.6
2008	12193	6447	662	5084	28898	30287	18103	28552	110.7	109.8	111.0	111.4
2009	12573	6420	618	5535	32244	34130	20607	31350	112.6	113.7	114.8	110.8
2010	13052	6516	597	5938	36539	38359	24010	35801	109.8	108.9	112.9	110.7
2011	14413	6704	603	7106	41799	43483	28791	41323	108.6	107.7	113.9	109.6
2012	15236	6839	590	7808	46769	48357	33784	46360	109.0	108.3	114.3	109.2
2013	18108	6365	566	11177	51483	52657	38905	51453	107.3	106.1	112.3	108.2

注：1.本表数据不含私营单位。
2.1994年及以前数据为职工人数和平均工资。
3.2013年就业人员数变动较大，系将原属于乡镇企业的规模以上法人单位纳入劳动工资统计范围所致。

a) Data in this table do not include private enterprises.
b) Data before 1994 were data of staff and workers and average wages.
c) Number of employees in 2013 changes relatively greatly, because legal persons above designated size which originally belonged to township and village enterprises were included in labor and wages statistics.

表7 国内生产总值

Gross Domestic Product

本表按当年价格计算。

Data in this table are calculated at current prices.

单位：亿元 (100 million yuan)

年份 Year	国民总收入 Gross National Income	国内生产总值 Gross Domestic Product	第一产业 Primary Industry	第二产业 Secondary Industry			第三产业 Tertiary Industry			人均国内生产总值（元/人） Per-Capita GDP (yuan/person)
					工业 Industry	建筑业 Construction		#交通运输、仓储和邮政业 Transport, Storage and Post	#批发和零售业 Wholesale and Retail Trade	
1952	679.0	679.0	346.0	141.8	119.8	22.0	191.2	29.0	70.1	119
1953	824.2	824.2	381.4	192.5	163.5	29.0	250.3	35.0	102.4	142
1954	859.4	859.4	395.5	211.7	184.7	27.0	252.2	38.0	106.6	144
1955	910.8	910.8	424.8	222.2	191.2	31.0	263.8	39.0	104.9	150
1956	1029.0	1029.0	447.9	280.7	224.7	56.0	300.4	46.0	115.3	166
1957	1069.3	1069.3	433.9	317.0	271.0	46.0	318.4	49.0	116.1	168
1958	1308.2	1308.2	449.9	483.5	414.5	69.0	374.8	71.0	120.9	200
1959	1440.4	1440.4	387.2	615.5	538.5	77.0	437.6	94.0	129.3	216
1960	1457.5	1457.5	343.8	648.2	568.2	80.0	465.5	104.0	120.3	218
1961	1220.9	1220.9	445.1	388.9	362.1	26.8	387.0	69.2	96.4	185
1962	1151.2	1151.2	457.2	359.3	325.4	33.9	334.8	57.4	67.6	173
1963	1236.4	1236.4	502.0	407.6	365.6	42.0	326.8	55.0	64.5	181
1964	1455.5	1455.5	564.0	513.5	461.1	52.4	378.0	58.4	81.7	208
1965	1717.2	1717.2	656.9	602.2	546.5	55.7	458.1	77.4	104.6	240
1966	1873.1	1873.1	708.5	709.5	648.6	60.9	455.1	85.1	132.1	255
1967	1780.3	1780.3	720.6	602.8	544.9	57.9	456.9	72.3	138.6	236
1968	1730.2	1730.2	732.8	537.3	490.3	47.0	460.0	70.5	126.1	223
1969	1945.8	1945.8	742.8	689.1	626.1	63.0	513.9	84.9	149.0	244
1970	2261.3	2261.3	800.4	912.2	828.1	84.1	548.7	100.2	162.8	276
1971	2435.3	2435.3	833.7	1022.8	926.6	96.2	578.7	108.4	162.5	290
1972	2530.2	2530.2	834.8	1084.2	989.9	94.3	611.2	122.9	176.6	294
1973	2733.4	2733.4	915.6	1173.0	1072.5	100.5	644.7	131.0	192.0	310
1974	2803.7	2803.7	953.7	1192.0	1083.6	108.4	658.1	132.2	188.2	311
1975	3013.1	3013.1	979.8	1370.5	1244.9	125.6	662.8	148.3	160.2	329
1976	2961.5	2961.5	975.7	1337.2	1204.6	132.6	648.6	147.1	134.4	318
1977	3221.1	3221.1	950.6	1509.1	1372.4	136.7	761.4	165.2	195.1	341
1978	3645.2	3645.2	1027.5	1745.2	1607.0	138.2	872.5	182.0	242.3	381
1979	4062.6	4062.6	1270.2	1913.5	1769.7	143.8	878.9	193.7	200.9	419
1980	4545.6	4545.6	1371.6	2192.0	1996.5	195.5	982.0	213.4	193.8	463
1981	4889.5	4891.6	1559.5	2255.5	2048.4	207.1	1076.6	220.7	231.1	492
1982	5330.5	5323.4	1777.4	2383.0	2162.3	220.7	1163.0	246.9	171.4	528
1983	5985.6	5962.7	1978.4	2646.2	2375.6	270.6	1338.1	274.9	198.7	583
1984	7243.8	7208.1	2316.1	3105.7	2789.0	316.7	1786.3	338.5	363.5	695

表7 续表 continued

单位：亿元 (100 million yuan)

年份 Year	国民总收入 Gross National Income	国内生产总值 Gross Domestic Product	第一产业 Primary Industry	第二产业 Secondary Industry	工业 Industry	建筑业 Construction	第三产业 Tertiary Industry	#交通运输、仓储和邮政业 Transport, Storage and Post	#批发和零售业 Wholesale and Retail Trade	人均国内生产总值（元/人） Per-Capita GDP (yuan/person)
1985	9040.7	9016.0	2564.4	3866.6	3448.7	417.9	2585.0	421.7	802.4	858
1986	10274.4	10275.2	2788.7	4492.7	3967.0	525.7	2993.8	498.8	852.6	963
1987	12050.6	12058.6	3233.0	5251.6	4585.8	665.8	3574.0	568.3	1059.6	1112
1988	15036.8	15042.8	3865.4	6587.2	5777.2	810.0	4590.3	685.7	1483.4	1366
1989	17000.9	16992.3	4265.9	7278.0	6484.0	794.0	5448.4	812.7	1536.2	1519
1990	18718.3	18667.8	5062.0	7717.4	6858.0	859.4	5888.4	1167.0	1268.9	1644
1991	21826.2	21781.5	5342.2	9102.2	8087.1	1015.1	7337.1	1420.3	1834.6	1893
1992	26937.3	26923.5	5866.6	11699.5	10284.5	1415.0	9357.4	1689.0	2405.0	2311
1993	35260.0	35333.9	6963.8	16454.4	14188.0	2266.5	11915.7	2174.0	2816.6	2998
1994	48108.5	48197.9	9572.7	22445.4	19480.7	2964.7	16179.8	2787.9	3773.4	4044
1995	59810.5	60793.7	12135.8	28679.5	24950.6	3728.8	19978.5	3244.3	4778.6	5046
1996	70142.5	71176.6	14015.4	33835.0	29447.6	4387.4	23326.2	3782.2	5599.7	5846
1997	78060.9	78973.0	14441.9	37543.0	32921.4	4621.6	26988.1	4148.6	6327.4	6420
1998	83024.3	84402.3	14817.6	39004.2	34018.4	4985.8	30580.5	4660.9	6913.2	6796
1999	88479.2	89677.1	14770.0	41033.6	35861.5	5172.1	33873.4	5175.2	7491.1	7159
2000	98000.5	99214.6	14944.7	45555.9	40033.6	5522.3	38714.0	6161.0	8158.6	7858
2001	108068.2	109655.2	15781.3	49512.3	43580.6	5931.7	44361.6	6870.3	9119.4	8622
2002	119095.7	120332.7	16537.0	53896.8	47431.3	6465.5	49898.9	7492.9	9995.4	9398
2003	134977.0	135822.8	17381.7	62436.3	54945.5	7490.8	56004.7	7913.2	11169.5	10542
2004	159453.6	159878.3	21412.7	73904.3	65210.0	8694.3	64561.3	9304.4	12453.8	12336
2005	183617.4	184937.4	22420.0	87598.1	77230.8	10367.3	74919.3	10666.2	13966.2	14185
2006	215904.4	216314.4	24040.0	103719.5	91310.9	12408.6	88554.9	12183.0	16530.7	16500
2007	266422.0	265810.3	28627.0	125831.4	110534.9	15296.5	111351.9	14601.0	20937.8	20169
2008	316030.3	314045.4	33702.0	149003.4	130260.2	18743.2	131340.0	16362.5	26182.3	23708
2009	340320.0	340902.8	35226.0	157638.8	135239.9	22398.8	148038.0	16727.1	28984.5	25608
2010	399759.5	401512.8	40533.6	187383.2	160722.2	26661.0	173596.0	19132.2	35746.1	30015
2011	468562.4	473104.0	47486.2	220412.8	188470.2	31942.7	205205.0	22432.8	43445.2	35198
2012	518214.7	519470.1	52373.6	235162.0	199670.7	35491.3	231934.5	24660.0	49394.4	38459
2013	566130.2	568845.2	56957.0	249684.4	210689.4	38995.0	262203.8	27282.9	55671.9	41908

注：国民总收入与国内生产总值的差额为国外净要素收入。
a) The difference between the Gross Domestic Product and the Gross National Income has been the net factor income from abroad.

表8 国内生产总值构成
Composition of Gross Domestic Product

本表按当年价格计算。
Data in this table are calculated at current prices.

单位：% (%)

年份 Year	国内生产总值 Gross Domestic Product	第一产业 Primary Industry	第二产业 Secondary Industry	工业 Industry	建筑业 Construction	第三产业 Tertiary Industry	#交通运输、仓储和邮政业 Transport, Storage and Post	#批发和零售业 Wholesale and Retail Trade
1952	100.0	51.0	20.9	17.6	3.2	28.2	4.3	10.3
1953	100.0	46.3	23.4	19.8	3.5	30.4	4.2	12.4
1954	100.0	46.0	24.6	21.5	3.1	29.3	4.4	12.4
1955	100.0	46.6	24.4	21.0	3.4	29.0	4.3	11.5
1956	100.0	43.5	27.3	21.8	5.4	29.2	4.5	11.2
1957	100.0	40.6	29.6	25.3	4.3	29.8	4.6	10.9
1958	100.0	34.4	37.0	31.7	5.3	28.7	5.4	9.2
1959	100.0	26.9	42.7	37.4	5.3	30.4	6.5	9.0
1960	100.0	23.6	44.5	39.0	5.5	31.9	7.1	8.3
1961	100.0	36.5	31.9	29.7	2.2	31.7	5.7	7.9
1962	100.0	39.7	31.2	28.3	2.9	29.1	5.0	5.9
1963	100.0	40.6	33.0	29.6	3.4	26.4	4.4	5.2
1964	100.0	38.7	35.3	31.7	3.6	26.0	4.0	5.6
1965	100.0	38.3	35.1	31.8	3.2	26.7	4.5	6.1
1966	100.0	37.8	37.9	34.6	3.3	24.3	4.5	7.1
1967	100.0	40.5	33.9	30.6	3.3	25.7	4.1	7.8
1968	100.0	42.4	31.1	28.3	2.7	26.6	4.1	7.3
1969	100.0	38.2	35.4	32.2	3.2	26.4	4.4	7.7
1970	100.0	35.4	40.3	36.6	3.7	24.3	4.4	7.2
1971	100.0	34.2	42.0	38.0	4.0	23.8	4.5	6.7
1972	100.0	33.0	42.8	39.1	3.7	24.2	4.9	7.0
1973	100.0	33.5	42.9	39.2	3.7	23.6	4.8	7.0
1974	100.0	34.0	42.5	38.6	3.9	23.5	4.7	6.7
1975	100.0	32.5	45.5	41.3	4.2	22.0	4.9	5.3
1976	100.0	32.9	45.2	40.7	4.5	21.9	5.0	4.5
1977	100.0	29.5	46.9	42.6	4.2	23.6	5.1	6.1
1978	100.0	28.2	47.9	44.1	3.8	23.9	5.0	6.6
1979	100.0	31.3	47.1	43.6	3.5	21.6	4.8	4.9
1980	100.0	30.2	48.2	43.9	4.3	21.6	4.7	4.3
1981	100.0	31.9	46.1	41.9	4.2	22.0	4.5	4.7
1982	100.0	33.4	44.8	40.6	4.1	21.8	4.6	3.2

表8　续表　continued

单位：%　　(%)

年份 Year	国内生产总值 Gross Domestic Product	第一产业 Primary Industry	第二产业 Secondary Industry	工业 Industry	建筑业 Construction	第三产业 Tertiary Industry	#交通运输、仓储和邮政业 Transport, Storage and Post	#批发和零售业 Wholesale and Retail Trade
1983	100.0	33.2	44.4	39.8	4.5	22.4	4.6	3.3
1984	100.0	32.1	43.1	38.7	4.4	24.8	4.7	5.0
1985	100.0	28.4	42.9	38.3	4.6	28.7	4.7	8.9
1986	100.0	27.1	43.7	38.6	5.1	29.1	4.9	8.3
1987	100.0	26.8	43.6	38.0	5.5	29.6	4.7	8.8
1988	100.0	25.7	43.8	38.4	5.4	30.5	4.6	9.9
1989	100.0	25.1	42.8	38.2	4.7	32.1	4.8	9.0
1990	100.0	27.1	41.3	36.7	4.6	31.5	6.3	6.8
1991	100.0	24.5	41.8	37.1	4.7	33.7	6.5	8.4
1992	100.0	21.8	43.5	38.2	5.3	34.8	6.3	8.9
1993	100.0	19.7	46.6	40.2	6.4	33.7	6.2	8.0
1994	100.0	19.9	46.6	40.4	6.2	33.6	5.8	7.8
1995	100.0	20.0	47.2	41.0	6.1	32.9	5.3	7.9
1996	100.0	19.7	47.5	41.4	6.2	32.8	5.3	7.9
1997	100.0	18.3	47.5	41.7	5.9	34.2	5.3	8.0
1998	100.0	17.6	46.2	40.3	5.9	36.2	5.5	8.2
1999	100.0	16.5	45.8	40.0	5.8	37.8	5.8	8.4
2000	100.0	15.1	45.9	40.4	5.6	39.0	6.2	8.2
2001	100.0	14.4	45.2	39.7	5.4	40.5	6.3	8.3
2002	100.0	13.7	44.8	39.4	5.4	41.5	6.2	8.3
2003	100.0	12.8	46.0	40.5	5.5	41.2	5.8	8.2
2004	100.0	13.4	46.2	40.8	5.4	40.4	5.8	7.8
2005	100.0	12.1	47.4	41.8	5.6	40.5	5.8	7.6
2006	100.0	11.1	47.9	42.2	5.7	40.9	5.6	7.6
2007	100.0	10.8	47.3	41.6	5.8	41.9	5.5	7.9
2008	100.0	10.7	47.4	41.5	6.0	41.8	5.2	8.3
2009	100.0	10.3	46.2	39.7	6.6	43.4	4.9	8.5
2010	100.0	10.1	46.7	40.0	6.6	43.2	4.8	8.9
2011	100.0	10.0	46.6	39.8	6.8	43.4	4.7	9.2
2012	100.0	10.1	45.3	38.4	6.8	44.6	4.7	9.5
2013	100.0	10.0	43.9	37.0	6.9	46.1	4.8	9.8

表9 国内生产总值指数
Indices of Gross Domestic Product

本表按不变价格计算。
Data in this table are calculated at constant prices.

(上年=100) (preceding year=100)

年份 Year	国民总收入 Gross National Income	国内生产总值 Gross Domestic Product	第一产业 Primary Industry	第二产业 Secondary Industry	工业 Industry	建筑业 Construction	第三产业 Tertiary Industry	#交通运输、仓储和邮政业 Transport, Storage and Post	#批发和零售业 Wholesale and Retail Trade	人均国内生产总值 Per-Capita GDP
1953	115.6	115.6	101.9	135.8	135.7	136.4	124.9	124.1	140.0	113.1
1954	104.2	104.2	101.7	115.7	119.3	96.7	99.6	110.8	101.7	101.8
1955	106.8	106.8	107.9	107.6	106.6	113.8	104.8	102.5	98.8	104.5
1956	115.0	115.0	104.7	134.5	128.6	170.0	113.3	121.8	108.7	112.7
1957	105.1	105.1	103.1	108.0	111.4	92.9	104.7	107.2	98.4	102.4
1958	121.3	121.3	100.4	152.9	153.4	150.0	118.1	146.7	105.0	118.3
1959	108.8	108.8	84.1	125.8	129.1	105.7	115.6	131.0	106.1	106.7
1960	99.7	99.7	83.6	105.6	106.1	101.4	105.0	110.4	92.9	99.5
1961	72.7	72.7	101.4	57.9	61.0	34.6	74.2	65.0	70.3	73.4
1962	94.4	94.4	104.5	89.2	86.7	123.8	90.7	81.1	92.5	93.6
1963	110.2	110.2	111.3	114.5	113.3	125.9	104.4	98.4	109.3	107.5
1964	118.3	118.3	112.9	125.6	125.6	125.6	115.5	105.4	116.1	115.5
1965	117.0	117.0	109.7	124.2	125.8	110.6	115.8	134.5	101.2	114.3
1966	110.7	110.7	107.2	122.4	123.8	109.4	98.1	110.3	121.5	107.7
1967	94.3	94.3	101.9	85.7	84.9	95.0	100.5	86.0	105.4	91.9
1968	95.9	95.9	98.4	90.8	91.8	81.1	100.7	97.7	91.2	93.4
1969	116.9	116.9	100.8	133.1	133.0	134.5	113.4	122.7	119.5	113.7
1970	119.4	119.4	107.7	134.8	135.2	130.4	107.1	116.8	109.8	116.1
1971	107.0	107.0	101.9	112.3	112.3	112.1	105.8	108.3	99.6	104.1
1972	103.8	103.8	99.1	106.7	107.6	97.9	105.1	115.1	108.5	101.2
1973	107.9	107.9	109.0	108.3	108.8	103.4	105.5	106.3	109.2	105.4
1974	102.3	102.3	104.1	101.4	101.0	106.2	101.5	100.7	98.0	100.2
1975	108.7	108.7	102.0	115.8	116.0	113.8	104.9	111.2	99.9	106.8
1976	98.4	98.4	98.2	97.5	96.9	104.3	100.4	98.8	96.5	96.9
1977	107.6	107.6	97.8	113.3	114.4	101.7	109.6	112.4	113.4	106.2
1978	111.7	111.7	104.1	115.0	116.4	99.4	113.8	108.9	123.1	110.2
1979	107.6	107.6	106.1	108.2	108.7	102.0	107.9	108.3	108.7	106.1
1980	107.8	107.8	98.5	113.6	112.7	126.7	106.0	104.3	98.1	106.5
1981	105.2	105.2	107.0	101.9	101.7	103.2	110.4	101.9	129.5	103.9
1982	109.2	109.1	111.5	105.6	105.8	103.4	113.0	111.4	99.3	107.5
1983	111.1	110.9	108.3	110.4	109.7	117.1	115.2	109.5	121.2	109.3

表9 续表 continued

(上年=100) (preceding year=100)

年份 Year	国民总收入 Gross National Income	国内生产总值 Gross Domestic Product	第一产业 Primary Industry	第二产业 Secondary Industry	工业 Industry	建筑业 Construction	第三产业 Tertiary Industry	#交通运输、仓储和邮政业 Transport, Storage and Post	#批发和零售业 Wholesale and Retail Trade	人均国内生产总值 Per-Capita GDP
1984	115.3	115.2	112.9	114.5	114.9	110.9	119.3	114.9	124.7	113.7
1985	113.2	113.5	101.8	118.6	118.2	122.2	118.2	113.8	133.5	111.9
1986	108.5	108.8	103.3	110.2	109.6	115.9	112.0	113.9	109.4	107.2
1987	111.5	111.6	104.7	113.7	113.2	117.9	114.4	109.6	114.7	109.8
1988	111.3	111.3	102.5	114.5	115.3	108.0	113.2	112.5	111.8	109.5
1989	104.2	104.1	103.1	103.8	105.1	91.6	105.4	104.2	89.3	102.5
1990	104.1	103.8	107.3	103.2	103.4	101.2	102.3	108.3	94.7	102.3
1991	109.1	109.2	102.4	113.9	114.4	109.6	108.9	110.6	105.2	107.7
1992	114.1	114.2	104.7	121.2	121.2	121.0	112.4	110.1	110.5	112.8
1993	113.7	114.0	104.7	119.9	120.1	118.0	112.2	112.5	108.6	112.7
1994	113.1	113.1	104.0	118.4	118.9	113.7	111.1	108.5	108.2	111.8
1995	109.3	110.9	105.0	113.9	114.0	112.4	109.8	111.0	108.2	109.7
1996	110.2	110.0	105.1	112.1	112.5	108.5	109.4	111.0	107.6	108.9
1997	109.6	109.3	103.5	110.5	111.3	102.6	110.7	109.2	108.8	108.2
1998	107.3	107.8	103.5	108.9	108.9	109.0	108.4	110.6	106.5	106.8
1999	107.9	107.6	102.8	108.1	108.5	104.3	109.3	112.2	108.7	106.7
2000	108.6	108.4	102.4	109.4	109.8	105.7	109.7	108.6	109.4	107.6
2001	108.1	108.3	102.8	108.4	108.7	106.8	110.3	108.8	109.1	107.5
2002	109.5	109.1	102.9	109.8	110.0	108.8	110.4	107.1	108.8	108.4
2003	110.5	110.0	102.5	112.7	112.8	112.1	109.5	106.1	109.9	109.3
2004	110.5	110.1	106.3	111.1	111.5	108.1	110.1	114.5	106.6	109.4
2005	110.8	111.3	105.2	112.1	111.6	116.0	112.2	111.2	113.0	110.7
2006	113.3	112.7	105.0	113.4	112.9	117.2	114.1	110.0	119.5	112.0
2007	114.6	114.2	103.7	115.1	114.9	116.2	116.0	111.8	120.2	113.6
2008	110.1	109.6	105.4	109.9	109.9	109.5	110.4	107.3	115.9	109.1
2009	108.3	109.2	104.2	109.9	108.7	118.6	109.6	104.2	112.1	108.7
2010	110.2	110.4	104.3	112.3	112.1	113.5	109.8	109.8	114.3	109.9
2011	108.7	109.3	104.3	110.3	110.4	109.7	109.4	109.9	112.6	108.8
2012	108.4	107.7	104.5	107.9	107.7	109.3	108.1	106.8	110.4	107.1
2013	107.4	107.7	104.0	107.8	107.6	109.5	108.3	107.2	110.3	107.1

表10 国内生产总值指数

Indices of Gross Domestic Product

本表按不变价格计算。
Data in this table are calculated at constant prices.

(1952年=100) (year of 1952=100)

年份 Year	国民总收入 Gross National Income	国内生产总值 Gross Domestic Product	第一产业 Primary Industry	第二产业 Secondary Industry	工业 Industry	建筑业 Construction	第三产业 Tertiary Industry	#交通运输、仓储和邮政业 Transport, Storage and Post	#批发和零售业 Wholesale and Retail Trade	人均国内生产总值 Per-Capita GDP
1952	100.0	100.0	100.0	100.0	100.0	100.0	100.0	100.0	100.0	100.0
1953	115.6	115.6	101.9	135.8	135.7	136.4	124.9	124.1	140.0	113.1
1954	120.5	120.5	103.6	157.1	161.9	131.8	124.4	137.6	142.5	115.1
1955	128.7	128.7	111.8	169.0	172.6	150.0	130.4	141.0	140.7	120.3
1956	148.1	148.1	117.0	227.3	222.0	255.0	147.7	171.7	153.0	135.6
1957	155.6	155.6	120.6	245.5	247.2	236.8	154.6	184.1	150.6	138.9
1958	188.6	188.6	121.1	375.4	379.2	355.2	182.6	270.2	158.2	164.3
1959	205.3	205.3	101.9	472.3	489.7	375.3	211.0	354.0	168.0	175.3
1960	204.6	204.6	85.2	498.6	519.8	380.5	221.5	390.8	156.0	174.5
1961	148.7	148.7	86.5	288.8	316.8	131.8	164.3	254.0	109.7	128.1
1962	140.4	140.4	90.4	257.8	274.7	163.2	149.0	205.9	101.5	119.9
1963	154.7	154.7	100.6	295.2	311.3	205.4	155.5	202.6	111.0	129.0
1964	182.9	182.9	113.6	370.8	391.0	257.9	179.6	213.4	128.8	149.0
1965	214.1	214.1	124.6	460.6	492.0	285.2	208.1	287.1	130.3	170.3
1966	237.1	237.1	133.6	564.0	608.9	312.0	204.1	316.8	158.3	183.4
1967	223.6	223.6	136.1	483.3	516.7	296.5	205.2	272.4	166.8	168.6
1968	214.4	214.4	134.0	438.7	474.1	240.4	206.5	266.1	152.2	157.5
1969	250.6	250.6	135.1	584.0	630.5	323.3	234.3	326.6	181.9	179.1
1970	299.3	299.3	145.5	787.3	852.5	421.6	250.9	381.4	199.7	208.1
1971	320.4	320.4	148.2	884.2	957.5	472.8	265.5	413.2	199.0	216.7
1972	332.4	332.4	146.9	943.6	1030.4	462.8	279.1	475.5	215.9	219.4
1973	358.5	358.5	160.1	1022.1	1120.9	478.4	294.3	505.5	235.7	231.3
1974	366.8	366.8	166.7	1036.4	1131.9	508.0	298.8	508.8	231.0	231.8
1975	398.7	398.7	170.1	1200.2	1312.9	578.2	313.5	565.9	230.8	247.5
1976	392.2	392.2	167.1	1170.3	1272.1	602.8	314.7	559.2	222.6	239.8
1977	422.1	422.1	163.4	1325.8	1455.5	612.9	345.0	628.3	252.5	254.5
1978	471.4	471.4	170.1	1525.2	1694.0	609.4	392.7	684.0	310.7	280.5
1979	507.1	507.1	180.6	1650.2	1840.7	621.4	423.5	740.5	337.8	297.7
1980	546.8	546.8	177.9	1874.1	2073.7	787.6	448.9	772.3	331.6	317.1
1981	575.3	575.5	190.3	1909.1	2109.7	812.5	495.7	786.8	429.4	329.4
1982	628.5	627.6	212.3	2015.3	2231.5	840.3	560.0	876.1	426.2	354.0

表10 续表 continued

(1952年=100) (year of 1952=100)

年份 Year	国民总收入 Gross National Income	国内生产总值 Gross Domestic Product	第一产业 Primary Industry	第二产业 Secondary Industry	工业 Industry	建筑业 Construction	第三产业 Tertiary Industry	#交通运输、仓储和邮政业 Transport, Storage and Post	#批发和零售业 Wholesale and Retail Trade	人均国内生产总值 Per-Capita GDP
1983	698.4	695.8	229.9	2224.2	2448.4	983.7	645.0	959.3	516.8	386.8
1984	805.3	801.3	259.6	2546.2	2812.1	1090.5	769.8	1102.1	644.5	439.7
1985	911.7	909.2	264.3	3019.0	3324.2	1332.6	909.6	1254.1	860.7	492.2
1986	989.6	989.7	273.1	3327.6	3644.7	1544.1	1019.1	1428.2	942.0	527.8
1987	1103.6	1104.3	286.0	3783.3	4127.4	1820.1	1165.5	1565.4	1080.6	579.6
1988	1228.4	1228.9	293.2	4332.6	4756.9	1965.5	1318.8	1761.4	1207.8	634.6
1989	1279.5	1278.8	302.3	4495.8	4997.4	1799.5	1389.5	1835.4	1078.4	650.4
1990	1331.5	1327.9	324.4	4638.3	5164.9	1820.9	1422.0	1988.6	1021.6	665.5
1991	1452.8	1449.8	332.2	5280.9	5908.2	1995.0	1548.1	2198.5	1074.5	716.7
1992	1657.1	1656.3	347.8	6398.0	7158.9	2414.5	1740.8	2419.6	1187.5	808.8
1993	1883.6	1887.6	364.2	7669.1	8597.1	2849.1	1952.9	2723.0	1289.3	911.3
1994	2130.5	2134.5	378.7	9077.1	10223.0	3238.7	2169.5	2955.1	1394.9	1018.9
1995	2329.4	2367.7	397.7	10336.6	11658.5	3640.2	2383.0	3279.4	1509.7	1118.0
1996	2566.8	2604.6	417.9	11587.9	13116.5	3950.0	2607.6	3641.4	1625.0	1217.0
1997	2813.9	2846.8	432.6	12802.2	14601.3	4053.4	2887.0	3976.4	1767.5	1316.6
1998	3019.7	3069.8	447.7	13943.0	15900.8	4418.9	3128.8	4397.5	1882.5	1406.2
1999	3259.6	3303.7	460.2	15077.3	17255.0	4608.1	3420.7	4932.8	2046.5	1500.3
2000	3538.4	3582.2	471.3	16499.0	18943.6	4869.3	3754.1	5356.0	2239.2	1614.0
2001	3823.4	3879.6	484.5	17891.8	20586.0	5199.6	4139.2	5827.7	2442.9	1735.4
2002	4188.4	4231.9	498.5	19650.4	22638.5	5656.6	4571.4	6243.0	2658.1	1880.3
2003	4627.2	4656.2	511.0	22140.5	25525.1	6340.1	5005.9	6625.5	2922.2	2056.0
2004	5112.1	5125.8	543.2	24600.8	28463.1	6855.5	5509.3	7584.6	3114.1	2249.9
2005	5664.8	5705.5	571.6	27573.2	31758.1	7952.1	6183.1	8434.4	3519.8	2489.7
2006	6416.6	6428.8	600.2	31265.5	35847.3	9322.0	7057.2	9275.1	4204.9	2789.7
2007	7356.1	7339.2	622.7	35975.2	41191.0	10830.9	8185.3	10369.7	5055.0	3168.2
2008	8097.2	8046.3	656.1	39528.6	45281.4	11860.0	9036.8	11129.2	5856.2	3455.7
2009	8772.7	8787.7	683.6	43457.9	49234.8	14060.7	9901.0	11594.0	6565.0	3755.4
2010	9663.4	9705.8	712.8	48781.6	55174.4	15954.5	10866.6	12729.2	7503.3	4127.8
2011	10506.6	10608.4	743.1	53798.6	60900.9	17504.7	11889.8	13985.6	8449.4	4490.1
2012	11392.6	11420.2	776.9	58057.5	65580.3	19137.4	12847.6	14937.8	9329.0	4810.2
2013	12237.6	12296.3	808.0	62612.8	70539.6	20963.8	13910.3	16016.9	10293.9	5153.7

表11 支出法国内生产总值
Gross Domestic Product by Expenditure Approach

本表按当年价格计算。
Data in this table are calculated at current prices.

单位：亿元 (100 million yuan)

年份 Year	支出法国内生产总值 Gross Domestic Product by Expenditure Approach	最终消费支出 Final Consumption Expenditure	居民消费支出 Household Consumption Expenditure	政府消费支出 Government Consumption Expenditure	资本形成总额 Gross Capital Formation	固定资本形成总额 Gross Fixed Capital Formation	存货变动 Changes in Inventories	货物和服务净出口 Net Export of Goods and Services
1952	692.2	546.3	453.0	93.3	153.7	80.7	73.0	-7.8
1953	834.3	644.4	529.2	115.2	198.3	115.3	83.0	-8.4
1954	878.3	654.1	550.0	104.1	226.9	140.9	86.0	-2.7
1955	934.9	722.3	602.6	119.7	221.5	145.5	76.0	-8.9
1956	1034.2	772.6	646.8	125.8	257.6	219.6	38.0	4.0
1957	1101.9	816.4	686.6	129.8	280.0	187.0	93.0	5.5
1958	1291.2	852.6	724.0	128.6	432.0	333.0	99.0	6.6
1959	1451.3	821.5	691.2	130.3	621.7	435.7	186.0	8.1
1960	1508.0	932.6	741.7	190.9	575.0	473.0	102.0	0.4
1961	1275.2	995.1	816.7	178.4	274.6	227.6	47.0	5.5
1962	1176.4	985.7	838.7	147.0	178.1	175.1	3.0	12.6
1963	1293.1	1014.3	844.2	170.1	265.3	215.3	50.0	13.5
1964	1441.8	1078.6	889.6	189.0	350.3	290.3	60.0	12.9
1965	1629.2	1158.6	951.5	207.1	462.1	350.1	112.0	8.5
1966	1827.3	1251.3	1021.1	230.2	569.8	406.8	163.0	6.2
1967	1707.7	1275.7	1081.5	194.2	425.7	323.7	102.0	6.3
1968	1708.7	1269.1	1076.6	192.5	432.2	300.2	132.0	7.4
1969	1857.7	1359.4	1127.7	231.7	485.9	406.9	79.0	12.4
1970	2207.0	1459.7	1206.8	252.9	744.9	545.9	199.0	2.4
1971	2392.5	1557.9	1262.0	295.9	819.0	603.0	216.0	15.6
1972	2453.8	1644.3	1334.2	310.1	791.1	622.1	169.0	18.4
1973	2669.6	1751.3	1432.5	318.8	903.5	664.5	239.0	14.8
1974	2738.7	1809.6	1467.0	342.6	936.1	748.1	188.0	-7.0
1975	2950.4	1887.4	1528.5	358.9	1062.3	880.3	182.0	0.7
1976	2968.3	1969.5	1588.5	381.0	990.1	865.1	125.0	8.7
1977	3166.0	2057.8	1647.8	410.0	1098.1	911.1	187.0	10.1
1978	3605.6	2239.1	1759.1	480.0	1377.9	1073.9	304	-11.4
1979	4092.6	2633.7	2011.5	622.2	1478.9	1153.1	325.8	-20
1980	4592.9	3007.9	2331.2	676.7	1599.7	1322.4	277.3	-14.7
1981	5008.8	3361.5	2627.9	733.6	1630.2	1339.3	290.9	17.1
1982	5590.0	3714.8	2902.9	811.9	1784.2	1503.2	281.0	91.0

表11 续表 continued

单位：亿元 (100 million yuan)

年份 Year	支出法国内生产总值 Gross Domestic Product by Expenditure Approach	最终消费支出 Final Consumption Expenditure	居民消费支出 Household Consumption Expenditure	政府消费支出 Government Consumption Expenditure	资本形成总额 Gross Capital Formation	固定资本形成总额 Gross Fixed Capital Formation	存货变动 Changes in Inventories	货物和服务净出口 Net Export of Goods and Services
1983	6216.2	4126.4	3231.1	895.3	2039.0	1723.3	315.7	50.8
1984	7362.7	4846.3	3742.0	1104.3	2515.1	2147.0	368.1	1.3
1985	9076.7	5986.3	4687.4	1298.9	3457.5	2672.0	785.5	-367.1
1986	10508.5	6821.8	5302.1	1519.7	3941.9	3139.7	802.2	-255.2
1987	12277.4	7804.6	6126.1	1678.5	4462.0	3798.7	663.3	10.8
1988	15388.6	9839.5	7868.1	1971.4	5700.2	4701.9	998.3	-151.1
1989	17311.3	11164.2	8812.6	2351.6	6332.7	4419.4	1913.3	-185.6
1990	19347.8	12090.5	9450.9	2639.6	6747.0	4827.8	1919.2	510.3
1991	22577.4	14091.9	10730.6	3361.3	7868.0	6070.3	1797.7	617.5
1992	27565.2	17203.3	13000.1	4203.2	10086.3	8513.7	1572.6	275.6
1993	36938.1	21899.9	16412.1	5487.8	15717.7	13309.2	2408.5	-679.5
1994	50217.4	29242.2	21844.2	7398.0	20341.1	17312.7	3028.4	634.1
1995	63216.9	36748.2	28369.7	8378.5	25470.1	20885.0	4585.1	998.6
1996	74163.6	43919.5	33955.9	9963.6	28784.9	24048.1	4736.8	1459.2
1997	81658.5	48140.6	36921.5	11219.1	29968.0	25965.0	4003.0	3549.9
1998	86531.6	51588.2	39229.3	12358.9	31314.2	28569.0	2745.2	3629.2
1999	91125.0	55636.9	41920.4	13716.5	32951.5	30527.3	2424.2	2536.6
2000	98749.0	61516.0	45854.6	15661.4	34842.8	33844.4	998.4	2390.2
2001	109028.0	66933.9	49435.9	17498.0	39769.4	37754.5	2014.9	2324.7
2002	120475.6	71816.5	53056.6	18759.9	45565.0	43632.1	1932.9	3094.1
2003	136613.4	77685.5	57649.8	20035.7	55963.0	53490.7	2472.3	2964.9
2004	160956.6	87552.6	65218.5	22334.1	69168.4	65117.7	4050.7	4235.6
2005	187423.4	99357.5	72958.7	26398.8	77856.8	74232.9	3624.0	10209.1
2006	222712.5	113103.8	82575.5	30528.4	92954.1	87954.1	5000.0	16654.6
2007	266599.2	132232.9	96332.5	35900.4	110943.2	103948.6	6994.6	23423.1
2008	315974.6	153422.5	111670.4	41752.1	138325.3	128084.4	10240.9	24226.8
2009	348775.1	169274.8	123584.6	45690.2	164463.2	156679.8	7783.4	15037.0
2010	402816.5	194115.0	140758.6	53356.3	193603.9	183615.2	9988.7	15097.6
2011	472619.2	232111.5	168956.6	63154.9	228344.3	215682.0	12662.3	12163.3
2012	529399.2	261993.6	190584.6	71409.0	252773.2	241756.8	11016.4	14632.4
2013	586673.0	292165.6	212187.5	79978.1	280356.1	269075.4	11280.7	14151.3

注：支出法国内生产总值不等于国内生产总值是由于计算误差的影响。
a) The gross domestic production by expenditure approach is not equal to gross domestic product due to statistical discrepancies.

表12 全国居民消费水平及指数

Household Consumption and Its Indices

本表绝对数按当年价格计算，指数按不变价格计算。

Absolute figures in this table are calculated at current prices, while indices are calculated at constant prices.

年份 Year	绝对数(元) Value (yuan)			指数(上年=100) Index (preceding year=100)			指数(1952=100) Index(1952=100)		
	全国居民 All Households	农村居民 Rural Households	城镇居民 Urban Households	全国居民 All Households	农村居民 Rural Households	城镇居民 Urban Households	全国居民 All Households	农村居民 Rural Households	城镇居民 Urban Households
1952	80	65	154				100.0	100.0	100.0
1953	91	72	188	107.5	102.8	115.1	107.5	102.8	115.1
1954	92	73	191	100.6	101.2	100.7	108.1	104.0	115.9
1955	99	80	198	106.8	108.7	103.7	115.5	113.1	120.2
1956	104	81	212	105.0	101.3	107.0	121.3	114.6	128.6
1957	108	82	222	102.7	102.0	102.4	124.5	116.8	131.7
1958	111	86	212	101.6	102.5	95.8	126.5	119.8	126.2
1959	104	70	224	91.7	80.8	100.8	116.0	96.8	127.2
1960	111	73	236	94.7	95.5	89.4	109.9	92.4	113.7
1961	124	87	248	93.7	101.3	87.2	103.0	93.6	99.1
1962	126	93	248	103.7	106.9	102.8	106.8	100.1	101.9
1963	124	94	240	109.4	107.5	116.3	116.8	107.6	118.5
1964	127	99	253	105.6	105.8	111.3	123.4	113.8	131.9
1965	133	104	259	109.8	110.0	109.3	135.4	125.2	144.2
1966	139	111	262	103.1	104.1	101.6	139.6	130.3	146.5
1967	143	115	268	103.3	104.2	102.4	144.2	135.8	150.0
1968	139	111	266	96.8	95.9	99.1	139.6	130.2	148.7
1969	142	113	272	102.7	103.0	102.9	143.4	134.2	153.0
1970	147	119	281	104.0	104.8	103.5	149.1	140.6	158.3
1971	150	121	287	101.3	101.2	102.2	151.1	142.3	161.8
1972	155	121	315	102.8	99.7	109.4	155.3	141.9	177.0
1973	162	128	325	104.7	105.4	103.3	162.6	149.5	182.9
1974	163	128	334	99.9	99.1	102.2	162.4	148.2	186.9
1975	167	130	349	102.2	101.5	103.9	166.0	150.4	194.2
1976	171	131	365	102.1	100.7	104.6	169.5	151.4	203.1
1977	175	130	390	101.3	99.8	103.7	171.7	151.1	210.6
1978	184	138	405	104.1	104.3	103.3	178.7	157.6	217.6
1979	208	159	425	106.9	106.5	102.8	191.0	167.8	223.7
1980	238	178	489	109.0	108.4	107.2	208.2	181.9	239.8
1981	264	201	521	108.3	109.8	104.0	225.5	199.8	249.4
1982	288	223	536	106.8	109.1	100.7	240.8	218.0	251.1

表12 续表 continued

年份 Year	绝对数(元) Value (yuan)			指数(上年=100) Index (preceding year=100)			指数(1952=100) Index(1952=100)		
	全国居民 All Households	农村居民 Rural Households	城镇居民 Urban Households	全国居民 All Households	农村居民 Rural Households	城镇居民 Urban Households	全国居民 All Households	农村居民 Rural Households	城镇居民 Urban Households
1983	316	250	558	108.1	110.6	102.1	260.3	241.1	256.4
1984	361	287	618	112.0	112.9	107.9	291.6	272.2	276.7
1985	446	349	765	113.5	113.3	111.1	331.0	308.3	307.4
1986	497	378	872	104.7	102.3	106.7	346.5	315.4	328.0
1987	565	421	998	106.0	104.9	105.6	367.3	330.9	346.3
1988	714	509	1311	107.8	105.2	109.7	395.9	348.1	379.9
1989	788	549	1466	99.8	98.3	100.7	395.2	342.2	382.6
1990	833	560	1596	103.7	99.2	108.5	409.8	339.4	415.1
1991	932	602	1840	108.6	105.4	110.7	445.0	357.8	459.5
1992	1116	688	2262	113.3	108.5	116.1	504.2	388.2	533.5
1993	1393	805	2924	108.4	104.3	110.4	546.6	404.9	589.0
1994	1833	1038	3852	104.6	103.1	104.4	571.7	417.4	614.9
1995	2355	1313	4931	107.8	106.8	107.2	616.3	445.8	659.2
1996	2789	1626	5532	109.4	114.5	103.4	674.2	510.5	681.6
1997	3002	1722	5823	104.5	103.1	102.2	704.6	526.3	696.6
1998	3159	1730	6109	105.9	101.2	105.9	746.1	532.6	737.7
1999	3346	1766	6405	108.3	105.1	107.0	808.1	559.8	789.3
2000	3632	1860	6850	108.6	104.5	107.8	877.6	585.0	850.9
2001	3887	1969	7161	106.1	104.5	103.9	930.0	611.6	882.8
2002	4144	2062	7486	107.0	105.2	104.9	995.0	643.2	926.0
2003	4475	2103	8060	107.1	100.3	107.0	1065.2	645.4	991.1
2004	5032	2319	8912	108.1	104.2	106.9	1151.5	672.7	1059.6
2005	5596	2657	9593	108.2	110.8	105.0	1245.9	745.3	1112.2
2006	6299	2950	10618	109.8	108.2	108.0	1367.7	806.5	1201.0
2007	7310	3347	12130	110.9	106.9	109.7	1516.7	861.9	1317.2
2008	8430	3901	13653	109.0	108.5	106.9	1653.1	935.5	1407.7
2009	9283	4163	14904	110.3	107.7	109.1	1823.8	1007.7	1535.2
2010	10522	4700	16546	108.2	108.0	105.9	1973.8	1088.1	1626.0
2011	12570	5870	19108	110.3	112.6	107.3	2176.7	1225.4	1745.5
2012	14110	6632	21035	109.4	109.3	107.5	2381.4	1339.2	1876.4
2013	15632	7409	22880	108.0	108.7	106.1	2571.3	1455.1	1990.0

表13 全社会固定资产投资
Total Investment in Fixed Assets

单位：亿元 (100 million yuan)

年份 Year	全社会固定资产投资总额 Total Investment	城镇 Urban	#房地产 Real Estate Development	农村 Rural	比上年增长(%) Increase over Preceding Year(%)
1981	961.00	711.10		249.90	5.5
1982	1230.40	900.50		329.90	28.0
1983	1430.10	1014.40		415.70	16.2
1984	1832.90	1279.00		553.90	28.2
1985	2543.20	1865.50		677.70	38.8
1986	3120.60	2300.40	101.00	820.20	22.7
1987	3791.70	2730.60	149.90	1061.10	21.5
1988	4753.80	3431.90	257.20	1321.90	25.4
1989	4410.40	3134.00	272.70	1276.40	-7.2
1990	4517.00	3274.40	253.30	1242.60	2.4
1991	5594.50	4057.90	336.20	1536.60	23.9
1992	8080.10	6079.70	731.20	2000.40	44.4
1993	13072.30	10303.40	1937.50	2768.90	61.8
1994	17042.10	13534.30	2554.10	3507.80	30.4
1995	20019.30	15643.70	3149.02	4375.60	17.5
1996	(22974.00)	(17627.70)	(3216.40)	(5346.30)	14.8
	22913.50	17567.20	3216.40	5346.30	
1997	24941.10	19194.20	3178.37	5746.90	8.8
1998	28406.20	22491.40	3614.23	5914.80	13.9
1999	29854.70	23732.00	4103.20	6122.70	5.1
2000	32917.73	26221.80	4984.10	6695.90	10.3
2001	37213.49	30001.20	6344.11	7212.30	13.0
2002	43499.91	35488.80	7790.92	8011.10	16.9
2003	55566.61	45811.70	10153.80	9754.90	27.7
2004	70477.44	59028.19	13158.25	11449.25	26.6

表13 续表 continued

单位：亿元 (100 million yuan)

年份 Year	全社会固定资产投资总额 Total Investment	城镇 Urban	#房地产 Real Estate Development	农村 Rural	比上年增长(%) Increase over Preceding Year(%)
2005	88773.62	75095.10	15909.20	13678.51	26.0
2006	109998.20	93368.70	19422.90	16629.50	23.9
2007	137323.94	117464.47	25288.84	19859.47	24.8
2008	172828.40	148738.30	31203.19	24090.10	25.9
2009	224598.77	193920.39	36241.81	30678.38	30.0
2010	(278121.9)	(241430.9)	(48259.4)	(36691.0)	23.8
	251683.77	243797.79	48259.40	7885.97	
2011	311485.13	302396.06	61796.89	9089.07	23.8
2012	374694.74	364854.15	71803.79	9840.59	20.3
2013	446294.09	435747.43	86013.38	10546.66	19.1

注：1.1995-1996年，除房地产投资、农村集体投资、个人投资以外，投资统计的起点为5万元；自1997年起，除房地产投资、农村集体投资、个人投资以外，投资统计的起点由5万元提高到50万元；自2011年起，除房地产投资、农村个人投资外，固定资产投资的统计起点由50万元提高至500万元；城镇固定资产投资数据发布口径改为固定资产投资(不含农户)，固定资产投资(不含农户)等于原口径的城镇固定资产投资加上农村企事业组织的项目投资。同时农村固定资产投资口径改变为农村住户口径，不包含农村企事业组织的项目投资。

2.为便于比较，对1996年、2010年的相应数据作了调整，这两年数据中括号内为原口径数，未加括号的为调整后的新口径数。新口径数据中，1996年为50万元起点以上数；2010年为500万元起点以上数，同时其中的城镇固定资产投资数据发布口径改为固定资产投资(不含农户)。

3.增长速度未扣除价格因素。

4.受经济普查影响，2004年投资额与上年有不可比因素，增长速度按可比口径计算。

a) From 1995 to 1996, statistical points of investment were 50 000 yuan, except real estate investment, rural collective investment, private investment; Since 1997, statistical points of investment rosed to 500 000 yuan, except real estate investment, rural collective investment, private investment; Since 2011, statistical points of investment rosed to 5 million yuan, except real estate investment, rural private investment; Statistical coverage of urban fixed assets investment changed to fixed assets investment (expcept rural households), which equals to original urban fixed assets investment plus projects investment of rural enterprises. And coverage of rural fixed assets investment changed to rural households investment, not including projects investment of rural enterprises.

b) For comparation, data of 1996 and 2010 was adjusted accordingly, data in brackets were original data, data without brackets were new coverage. Of new coverage, statistical points of 1996 were 500 000 yuan; of 2010 were 5 million yuan, and coverage of urban fixed assets investment changed to fixed assets investment(except rural households).

c) Growth rate are calculated without removing the factor of price.

d) As National Economic Census, investment in 2004 was not comparable with preceding year, growth rate was calcuated at comparable coverage.

表14　按资金来源分全社会固定资产投资和房屋建筑面积
Total Investment in Fixed Assets by Source of Funds and Floor Space of Buildings

年份 Year	按资金来源分（亿元） By Source of Funds (100 million yuan)				房屋建筑面积（万平方米） Floor Space of Buildings (10 000 sq.m)			
	国家预算内资金 State Budgetary Appropriation	国内贷款 Domestic Loans	利用外资 Foreign Investment	自筹和其他资金 Fundraising and Others	施工面积 Floor Space of Under Construction	#住宅 Residential Buildings	竣工面积 Floor Space of Completed	#住宅 Residential Buildings
1981	269.76	122.00	36.36	532.89			86325.00	69444.00
1982	279.26	176.12	60.51	714.51	109510.30		90289.00	71459.00
1983	339.71	175.50	66.55	848.30	129187.90		111610.00	86540.00
1984	421.00	258.47	70.66	1082.74	126407.20		106587.00	75820.00
1985	407.80	510.27	91.48	1533.64	148858.90		122084.00	90972.00
1986	455.62	658.46	137.31	1869.19	188183.70		154621.00	120516.00
1987	496.64	871.98	181.97	2241.11	174597.30		145425.00	110641.00
1988	431.96	977.84	275.31	2968.69	168951.00		140190.00	108418.00
1989	366.05	762.98	291.08	2990.28	131788.00		110557.00	87267.00
1990	393.03	885.45	284.61	2954.41	137171.00		107952.00	86425.00
1991	380.43	1314.73	318.89	3580.44	152813.08		120093.00	94685.00
1992	347.46	2214.03	468.66	5049.95	172173.10		116153.00	85880.00
1993	483.67	3071.99	954.28	8562.36	183449.00	98844.00	124949.00	78965.00
1994	529.57	3997.64	1768.95	11530.96	200830.00	126486.00	136550.00	97510.00
1995	621.05	4198.73	2295.89	13409.19	215084.62	140451.91	145600.12	107433.09
1996	(629.72)	(4576.53)	(2747.41)	(15465.35)	(236308.48)	(155849.32)	(162849.30)	(122204.48)
	625.88	4573.69	2746.60	15412.40	235258.57	155508.90	161965.70	121913.40
1997	696.74	4782.55	2683.89	17096.49	230490.98	149658.07	166057.13	121100.96
1998	1197.39	5542.89	2617.03	19359.61	245755.73	167600.83	170904.75	127571.61
1999	1852.14	5725.93	2006.78	20169.80	263294.25	181236.44	187357.07	139305.93
2000	2109.45	6727.27	1696.30	22577.40	265293.53	180634.32	181974.44	134528.83
2001	2546.42	7239.79	1730.73	26470.04	276025.40	182767.05	182437.05	130419.64
2002	3160.96	8859.07	2084.98	30941.91	304428.15	193730.96	196737.87	134002.10
2003	2687.82	12044.36	2599.35	41284.76	343741.65	205286.68	202643.73	130160.75
2004	3254.91	13788.04	3285.68	54236.30	376495.06	217580.48	207019.08	124881.12
2005	4154.29	16319.01	3978.80	70138.75	431123.04	239769.60	227588.65	132835.95
2006	4672.00	19590.47	4334.31	90360.20	462677.05	265565.31	212542.15	131408.19
2007	5857.06	23044.20	5132.69	116769.67	548542.04	315629.80	238425.31	146282.71
2008	7954.75	26443.74	5311.94	143204.86	632260.99	364354.38	260306.98	159404.62
2009	12685.73	39302.82	4623.73	193617.42	754189.40	431463.18	302116.53	184209.52
2010	(14677.79)	(47258.01)	(4986.76)	(244041.67)	(885173.43)	(492763.57)	(304306.12)	(183172.27)
	13012.75	44020.83	4703.64	224042.03	844056.90	480772.89	278564.54	174603.86
2011	14843.29	46344.51	5061.99	279734.38	1035518.88	574909.86	329073.26	197452.24
2012	18958.66	51593.50	4468.78	334654.71	1167238.42	614990.59	335503.55	195102.89
2013	22305.26	59442.04	4319.44	405545.78	1336287.60	673163.29	349895.79	193328.47

注：1993年及以后的资金来源为财务拨款数。

a) Since 1993, the source of funds refers to financial appropriation.

表15 全国房地产开发情况

Floor Space of Buildings and Real Estate Development of China

年份 Year	本年完成投资（亿元） Investment Made This Year (100 million yuan)	本年实际到位资金小计（亿元） Actual Funds for Investment This Year (100 million yuan)	房屋施工面积（万平方米） Floor Space of Buildings under Construction (10 000 sq.m)	房屋竣工面积（万平方米） Floor Space of Buildings Completed (10 000 sq.m)	商品房销售额（亿元） Total Sales of Commercial House (100 million yuan)	商品房销售面积（万平方米） Floor Space of Commercialized Buildings Sold (10 000 sq.m)	#住宅 Residential Buildings
1986							1835.0
1987					110.1	2697.2	2376.7
1988					147.2	2927.3	2549.1
1989					163.8	2855.4	2491.4
1990					201.8	2871.5	2544.6
1991					237.9	3025.5	2745.2
1992					426.6	4288.9	3812.2
1993					863.7	6687.9	6035.2
1994					1018.5	7230.4	6118.0
1995	3149.0				1257.7	7905.9	6787.0
1996	3216.4				1427.1	7900.4	6898.5
1997	3178.4	3817.1	44985.5	15819.7	1799.5	9010.2	7864.3
1998	3614.2	4414.9	50770.1	17566.6	2513.3	12185.3	10827.1
1999	4103.2	4795.9	56857.6	21410.8	2987.9	14556.5	12997.9
2000	4984.1	5997.6	65896.9	25104.9	3935.4	18637.1	16570.3
2001	6344.1	7696.4	79411.7	29867.4	4862.8	22411.9	19938.8
2002	7790.9	9750.0	94104.0	34975.8	6032.3	26808.3	23702.3
2003	10153.8	13196.9	117526.0	41464.1	7955.7	33717.6	29778.9
2004	13158.3	17168.8	140451.4	42464.9	10375.7	38231.6	33819.9
2005	15909.2	21397.8	166053.3	53417.0	17576.1	55486.2	49587.8
2006	19422.9	27135.6	194786.4	55830.9	20826.0	61857.1	55422.9
2007	25288.8	37478.0	236318.2	60606.7	29889.1	77354.7	70135.9
2008	31203.2	39619.4	283266.2	66544.8	25068.2	65969.8	59280.4
2009	36241.8	57799.0	320368.2	72677.4	44355.2	94755.0	86184.9
2010	48259.4	72944.0	405356.4	78743.9	52721.2	104764.7	93376.6
2011	61796.9	85688.7	506775.5	92619.9	58588.9	109366.7	96528.4
2012	71803.8	96536.8	573417.5	99425.0	64455.8	111303.6	98467.5
2013	86013.4	122122.5	665571.9	101435.0	81428.3	130550.6	115722.7

表16　国家财政收支总额及增长速度

Government Revenue and Expenditure and Their Increase Rates

年份 Year	财政收入（亿元） Government Revenue (100 million yuan)	财政支出（亿元） Government Expenditure (100 million yuan)	收支差额（亿元） Balance (100 million yuan)	增长速度（%）Increase Rates(%) 财政收入 Government Revenue	增长速度（%）Increase Rates(%) 财政支出 Government Expenditure	财政收入占国内生产总值的比重(%) Percentage of Government Revenue to GDP (%)
1950	62.17	68.05	-5.88			
1951	124.96	122.07	2.89	101.0	79.4	
1952	173.94	172.07	1.87	39.2	41.0	25.6
1953	213.24	219.21	-5.97	22.6	27.4	25.9
1954	245.17	244.11	1.06	15.0	11.4	28.5
1955	249.27	262.73	-13.46	1.7	7.6	27.4
1956	280.19	298.52	-18.33	12.4	13.6	27.3
1957	303.20	295.95	7.25	8.2	-0.9	28.4
1958	379.62	400.36	-20.74	25.2	35.3	29.0
1959	487.12	543.17	-56.05	28.3	35.7	33.9
1960	572.29	643.68	-71.39	17.5	18.5	39.3
1961	356.06	356.09	-0.03	-37.8	-44.7	29.2
1962	313.55	294.88	18.67	-11.9	-17.2	27.3
1963	342.25	332.05	10.20	9.2	12.6	27.8
1964	399.54	393.79	5.75	16.7	18.6	27.5
1965	473.32	459.97	13.35	18.5	16.8	27.6
1966	558.71	537.65	21.06	18.0	16.9	29.9
1967	419.36	439.84	-20.48	-24.9	-18.2	23.6
1968	361.25	357.84	3.41	-13.9	-18.6	21.0
1969	526.76	525.86	0.90	45.8	47.0	27.2
1970	662.90	649.41	13.49	25.8	23.5	29.4
1971	744.73	732.17	12.56	12.3	12.7	30.7
1972	766.56	765.86	0.70	2.9	4.6	30.4
1973	809.67	808.78	0.89	5.6	5.6	29.8
1974	783.14	790.25	-7.11	-3.3	-2.3	28.1
1975	815.61	820.88	-5.27	4.1	3.9	27.2
1976	776.58	806.20	-29.62	-4.8	-1.8	26.4
1977	874.46	843.53	30.93	12.6	4.6	27.3
1978	1132.26	1122.09	10.17	29.5	33.0	31.1
1979	1146.38	1281.79	-135.41	1.2	14.2	28.2
1980	1159.93	1228.83	-68.90	1.2	-4.1	25.5
1981	1175.79	1138.41	37.38	1.4	-7.4	24.0
1982	1212.33	1229.98	-17.65	3.1	8.0	22.8
1983	1366.95	1409.52	-42.57	12.8	14.6	22.9
1984	1642.86	1701.02	-58.16	20.2	20.7	22.8
1985	2004.82	2004.25	0.57	22.0	17.8	22.2
1986	2122.01	2204.91	-82.90	5.8	10.0	20.7

表16 续表 continued

年份 Year	财政收入 (亿元) Government Revenue (100 million yuan)	财政支出 (亿元) Government Expenditure (100 million yuan)	收支差额 (亿元) Balance (100 million yuan)	增长速度(%) Increase Rates(%) 财政收入 Government Revenue	增长速度(%) Increase Rates(%) 财政支出 Government Expenditure	财政收入占国内生产总值的比重(%) Percentage of Government Revenue to GDP (%)
1987	2199.35	2262.18	-62.83	3.6	2.6	18.2
1988	2357.24	2491.21	-133.97	7.2	10.1	15.7
1989	2664.90	2823.78	-158.88	13.1	13.3	15.7
1990	2937.10	3083.59	-146.49	10.2	9.2	15.7
1991	3149.48	3386.62	-237.14	7.2	9.8	14.5
1992	3483.37	3742.20	-258.83	10.6	10.5	12.9
1993	4348.95	4642.30	-293.35	24.8	24.1	12.3
1994	5218.10	5792.62	-574.52	20.0	24.8	10.8
1995	6242.20	6823.72	-581.52	19.6	17.8	10.3
1996	7407.99	7937.55	-529.56	18.7	16.3	10.4
1997	8651.14	9233.56	-582.42	16.8	16.3	11.0
1998	9875.95	10798.18	-922.23	14.2	16.9	11.7
1999	11444.08	13187.67	-1743.59	15.9	22.1	12.8
2000	13395.23	15886.50	-2491.27	17.0	20.5	13.5
2001	16386.04	18902.58	-2516.54	22.3	19.0	14.9
2002	18903.64	22053.15	-3149.51	15.4	16.7	15.7
2003	21715.25	24649.95	-2934.70	14.9	11.8	16.0
2004	26396.47	28486.89	-2090.42	21.6	15.6	16.5
2005	31649.29	33930.28	-2280.99	19.9	19.1	17.1
2006	38760.20	40422.73	-1662.53	22.5	19.1	17.9
2007	51321.78	49781.35	1540.43	32.4	23.2	19.3
2008	61330.35	62592.66	-1262.31	19.5	25.7	19.5
2009	68518.30	76299.93	-7781.63	11.7	21.9	20.1
2010	83101.51	89874.16	-6772.65	21.3	17.8	20.7
2011	103874.43	109247.79	-5373.36	25.0	21.6	22.0
2012	117253.52	125952.97	-8699.45	12.9	15.3	22.6
2013	129209.64	140212.10	-11002.46	10.2	11.3	22.7

注：1.在国家财政收支中，价格补贴1985年及以前冲减财政收入，1986年起列为财政支出。为了可比，本表将1985年及以前冲减财政收入的价格补贴改列在财政支出中。

2.国家财政收入中不包括国内外债务收入。从2000年起,财政支出中包括国内外债务付息支出，以下各表中涉及财政支出和中央财政支出数据的均为此口径。

a) Government price subsidies were listed as negative revenue items in 1985 and before, but they have been listed as expenditure items in government accounts since 1986. For comparison purpose,budgetary price subsidies in 1985 and before were adjusted, and listed as expenditure items.

b) Government revenue from both domestic and foreign borrowings are excluded in this table. Government expenditures include the payment for interest of domestic and foreign debts from 2000, and other tables which concern the government expenditure of the central government are consistent with this definition.

表17 全国各项税收
Taxes

单位：亿元 (100 million yuan)

年份 Year	合计 Total	#国内增值税 Value-added Tax	#营业税 Business Tax	#国内消费税 Consumption Tax	#关税 Tariffs	#个人所得税 Individual Income Tax	#企业所得税 Company Income Tax
1950	48.98				3.56		
1951	81.13				6.94		
1952	97.69				4.81		
1953	119.67				5.05		
1954	132.18				4.12		
1955	127.45				4.66		
1956	140.88				5.42		
1957	154.89				5.79		
1958	187.36				6.40		
1959	204.71				7.03		
1960	203.65				6.00		
1961	158.76				6.23		
1962	162.07				4.82		
1963	164.31				4.15		
1964	182.00				4.38		
1965	204.30				5.70		
1966	221.96				6.50		
1967	196.63				3.92		
1968	191.56				6.33		
1969	235.44				6.36		
1970	281.20				7.00		
1971	312.56				5.00		
1972	317.02				5.00		
1973	348.95				9.00		
1974	360.40				14.00		
1975	402.77				15.00		
1976	407.96				15.00		
1977	468.27				26.23		
1978	519.28				28.76		
1979	537.82				26.00		
1980	571.70				33.53		
1981	629.89				54.04		
1982	700.02				47.46		
1983	775.59				53.88		
1984	947.35				103.07		
1985	2040.79	147.70	211.07		205.21		696.06

表17 续表 continued

单位：亿元 (100 million yuan)

年份 Year	合 计 Total	#国内增值税 Value-added Tax	#营业税 Business Tax	#国内消费税 Consumption Tax	#关 税 Tariffs	#个人所得税 Individual Income Tax	#企业所得税 Company Income Tax
1986	2090.73	232.19	261.07		151.62		692.40
1987	2140.36	254.20	302.00		142.37		664.71
1988	2390.47	384.37	397.92		155.02		676.04
1989	2727.40	430.83	487.30		181.54		700.43
1990	2821.86	400.00	515.75		159.01		716.00
1991	2990.17	406.36	564.00		187.28		731.13
1992	3296.91	705.93	658.67		212.75		720.78
1993	4255.30	1081.48	966.09		256.47		678.60
1994	5126.88	2308.34	670.02	487.40	272.68		708.49
1995	6038.04	2602.33	865.56	541.48	291.83		878.44
1996	6909.82	2962.81	1052.57	620.23	301.84		968.48
1997	8234.04	3283.92	1324.27	678.70	319.49		963.18
1998	9262.80	3628.46	1575.08	814.93	313.04		925.54
1999	10682.58	3881.87	1668.56	820.66	562.23	413.66	811.41
2000	12581.51	4553.17	1868.78	858.29	750.48	659.64	999.63
2001	15301.38	5357.13	2064.09	929.99	840.52	995.26	2630.87
2002	17636.45	6178.39	2450.33	1046.32	704.27	1211.78	3082.79
2003	20017.31	7236.54	2844.45	1182.26	923.13	1418.03	2919.51
2004	24165.68	9017.94	3581.97	1501.90	1043.77	1737.06	3957.33
2005	28778.54	10792.11	4232.46	1633.81	1066.17	2094.91	5343.92
2006	34804.35	12784.81	5128.71	1885.69	1141.78	2453.71	7039.60
2007	45621.97	15470.23	6582.17	2206.83	1432.57	3185.58	8779.25
2008	54223.79	17996.94	7626.39	2568.27	1769.95	3722.31	11175.63
2009	59521.59	18481.22	9013.98	4761.22	1483.81	3949.35	11536.84
2010	73210.79	21093.48	11157.91	6071.55	2027.83	4837.27	12843.54
2011	89738.39	24266.63	13679.00	6936.21	2559.12	6054.11	16769.64
2012	100614.28	26415.51	15747.64	7875.58	2783.93	5820.28	19654.53
2013	110530.70	28810.13	17233.02	8231.32	2630.61	6531.53	22427.20

注：1.2001年以前企业所得税只包括国有及集体企业所得税，从2001年起还包括除国有企业和集体企业外的其他所有制企业所得税。
2.国内增值税不包括进口产品增值税；国内消费税不包括进口产品消费税。

a) Company income tax only includes those of state-owned and collective-owned enterprises before 2001, since 2001, other ownership enterprises are also included.

b) Dometic value-added tax do not include imported production value-added tax; domestic consumption tax do not include imported production consumption tax.

表18 国家财政主要支出项目

Main Government Expenditure by Item

单位：亿元 (100 million yuan)

年份 Year	基本建设支出 Expenditure for Capital Construction	增拨企业流动资金 Additional Appropriation for Circulating Capital of Enterprises	挖潜改造资金和科技三项费用 Innovation Funds and Science and Technology Promotion Funds	地质勘探费 Geological Prospecting Expenses	工、交、流通部门事业费 Operating Expenses of Industrial, Transport and Commerce	支农支出 Expenditure for Supporting Agricultural Production
1950	12.50					1.99
1951	27.03					3.67
1952	46.68	18.56				2.69
1953	70.34	13.78		0.68	6.39	2.99
1954	84.28	26.30	1.82	0.75	6.91	3.98
1955	88.53	30.81	3.09	3.66	10.08	5.82
1956	139.58	10.79	2.48	5.17	10.80	7.70
1957	123.71	20.82	2.29	6.27	12.36	7.99
1958	229.38	25.66	0.83	6.90	16.25	9.34
1959	302.34	54.28	2.20	8.96	14.98	22.05
1960	354.45	67.47	2.55	10.25	19.58	33.73
1961	110.18	29.39	2.67	6.47	13.54	31.01
1962	55.65	47.78	14.65	4.79	10.29	19.29
1963	80.21	36.65	18.28	4.68	7.89	22.19
1964	123.83	23.35	20.86	6.43	12.71	20.92
1965	158.49	27.55	25.23	7.71	15.91	17.29
1966	191.04	40.28	27.54	7.95	16.40	19.11
1967	161.25	29.10	10.32	7.71	12.01	16.12
1968	117.85	12.03	5.66	6.35	6.80	12.89
1969	206.22	26.61	10.74	8.07	6.37	14.87
1970	298.36	31.23	14.78	8.76	6.58	15.91
1971	309.56	35.30	26.40	10.30	6.49	19.65
1972	309.09	42.95	25.46	11.29	7.55	25.10
1973	317.17	53.82	25.49	12.20	8.90	35.49
1974	312.83	44.76	27.20	13.09	10.09	38.23
1975	326.96	41.84	31.47	14.16	12.76	42.53
1976	311.25	45.36	34.34	15.96	13.12	46.01
1977	300.88	65.68	39.45	17.26	14.43	50.68
1978	451.92	66.60	63.24	20.15	17.79	76.95
1979	443.68	52.05	71.79	21.67	20.90	89.97
1980	346.36	36.71	80.45	22.57	22.85	82.12
1981	257.55	22.84	65.30	21.85	23.68	73.68
1982	269.12	23.63	69.02	23.05	23.83	79.88
1983	344.98	12.89	78.71	23.60	27.88	86.66
1984	454.12	9.96	111.77	26.22	30.66	95.93
1985	554.56	14.30	103.42	29.58	35.16	101.04
1986	596.08	9.94	129.85	30.60	36.56	124.30

表18 续表 1 continued

单位: 亿元 (100 million yuan)

年份 Year	基本建设支出 Expenditure for Capital Construction	增拨企业流动资金 Additional Appropriation for Circulating Capital of Enterprises	挖潜改造资金和科技三项费用 Innovation Funds and Science and Technology Promotion Funds	地质勘探费 Geological Prospecting Expenses	工、交、流通部门事业费 Operating Expenses of Industrial, Transport and Commerce	支农支出 Expenditure for Supporting Agricultural Production
1987	521.64	12.06	124.93	30.29	33.13	134.16
1988	494.76	9.59	151.01	32.51	38.95	158.74
1989	481.70	12.09	146.30	33.16	45.01	197.12
1990	547.39	10.90	153.91	36.19	46.93	221.76
1991	559.62	13.08	180.81	38.34	52.41	243.55
1992	555.90	10.63	223.62	44.07	64.58	269.04
1993	591.93	18.48	421.38	49.06	76.22	323.42
1994	639.72	17.33	415.13	64.13	100.77	399.70
1995	789.22	34.80	494.45	66.32	102.76	430.22
1996	907.44	42.93	523.02	68.56	120.41	510.07
1997	1019.50	52.20	643.20	73.37	136.41	560.77
1998	1387.74	42.36	641.18	83.13	121.56	626.02
1999	2116.57	56.41	766.05	83.69	128.07	677.46
2000	2094.89	71.06	865.24	88.12	150.07	766.89
2001	2510.64	22.71	991.56	99.01	200.12	917.96
2002	3142.98	18.97	968.38	102.89	232.38	1102.70
2003	3429.30	11.95	1092.99	106.94	285.23	1134.86
2004	3437.50	12.44	1243.94	115.45	368.21	1693.79
2005	4041.34	18.17	1494.59	132.70	444.15	1792.40
2006	4390.38	16.58	1744.56	141.82	581.25	2161.35

表18 续表 2 continued

单位: 亿元 (100 million yuan)

年份 Year	一般公共服务 General Public Services	国防 National Defense	教育 Education	科学技术 Science & Technology	社会保障和就业 Social Security and Employment	医疗卫生与计划生育 Public Health and Family Planning	环境保护 Environment Protection	交通运输 Transport	城乡社区事务 Community Affairs
2007	8514.24	3554.91	7122.32	1783.04	5447.16	1989.96	995.82	1915.38	3244.70
2008	9795.92	4178.76	9010.21	2129.21	6804.29	2757.04	1427.42	2354.00	4206.14
2009	9164.21	4951.10	10437.54	2744.52	7606.68	3994.19	1934.04	4647.59	5107.66
2010	9337.16	5333.37	12550.02	3250.18	9130.62	4804.18	2441.98	5488.47	5987.38
2011	10987.78	6027.91	16497.33	3828.02	11109.40	6429.51	2640.98	7497.80	7620.55
2012	12700.46	6691.92	21242.10	4452.63	12585.52	7245.11	2963.46	8196.16	9079.12
2013	13755.13	7410.62	22001.76	5084.30	14490.54	8279.90	3435.15	9348.82	11165.57

注：1.2007年起实施《政府收支分类科目》，本表所列财政支出项目按照支出功能分类科目重新设置。
2.2011年起，"环境保护"更名为"节能环保"；2013年起，"医疗卫生"更名为"医疗卫生与计划生育"。

a) Since 2007, Public Income and Expenditure to Budgetary Accounting is performed, expenditure subject listed in this table was adjusted accordingly.
b) Since 2011, the indicator of Environment Protection have changed to Energy Saving and Environment Protection. Since 2013, the indicator of Public Health changed to Public Health and Family Planning.

表19 国家财政债务还本付息支出
Government Payment for the Principal and Interest of Debts

单位：亿元 (100 million yuan)

年份 Year	合计 Total	国内债务还本付息 Payment for the Principal and Interest of Domestic Debts	国外债务还本付息 Payment for the Principal and Interest of Foreign Debts	归还向人民银行借款的利息 Payment of the Interest of Loans from People's Bank	债务收入大于支出部分增列偿债基金 Sinking Fund from the Excessive Part of the Revenue from Borrowings minus the Expenditure for Debts
1950	0.03	0.03			
1951	0.42	0.40	0.01	0.01	
1952	3.92	0.58	0.23	3.11	
1953	0.91	0.65	0.26		
1954	2.21	0.89	1.32		
1955	6.56	1.58	4.98		
1956	7.22	1.25	5.97		
1957	8.26	2.18	6.08		
1958	9.04	1.81	7.23		
1959	9.69	2.58	7.11		
1960	10.46	3.73	6.73		
1961	10.93	4.35	6.58		
1962	10.37	3.95	6.42		
1963	7.58	4.72	2.86		
1964	5.23	4.27	0.96		
1965	6.36	5.66	0.70		
1966	3.91	3.91			
1967	2.01	2.01			
1968	2.00	2.00			
1969					
1970					
1971					
1972	0.50	0.50			
1973	0.50	0.50			
1974	0.50	0.50			
1975					
1976					
1977					
1978					
1979					
1980	28.58		24.40	4.18	
1981	62.89		57.89	5.00	
1982	55.52		49.62	5.90	
1983	42.47		36.56	5.91	
1984	28.90		22.73	6.17	
1985	39.56		32.59	6.97	
1986	50.17	7.98	34.50	7.69	
1987	79.83	23.18	51.96	4.69	

表19　续表　continued

单位：亿元　(100 million yuan)

年份 Year	合　计 Total	国内债务还本付息 Payment for the Principal and Interest of Domestic Debts	国外债务还本付息 Payment for the Principal and Interest of Foreign Debts	归还向人民银行借款的利息 Payment of the Interest of Loans from People's Bank	债务收入大于支出部分增列偿债基金 Sinking Fund from the Excessive Part of the Revenue from Borrowings minus the Expenditure for Debts
1988	76.76	28.44	42.59	5.73	
1989	72.37	19.30	45.84	7.23	
1990	190.07	113.42	68.21	8.44	
1991	246.80	156.69	80.22	9.89	
1992	438.57	342.42	80.26	15.89	
1993	336.22	224.30	89.22	22.70	
1994	499.36	364.96	107.17	27.23	
1995	882.96	784.06	71.69	27.21	
1996	1355.03	1266.29	60.76	27.98	
1997	1918.37	1820.40	70.76	27.21	
1998	2352.92	2245.79	76.60	30.53	
1999	1910.53	1792.33	90.99	27.21	12.90
2000	1579.82	1552.21	27.61		3.41
2001	2007.73	1923.42	84.31		
2002	2563.13	2467.71	95.42		19.00
2003	2952.24	2876.58	75.66		3.61
2004	3671.59	3542.42	129.17		7.99
2005	3923.37	3878.51	44.86		

注：1.本表2000年起为债务还本支出。
2.2006年起实行债务余额管理，国家财政预决算不再反映债务还本支出。
a) In this table, expenditure refers to payment for the principal of debts since 2000.
b) Since 2006, balance of debts was perfomed, national government budgetary and final accounting do not reflect expenditure on interest and principal of debts.

表20　中央财政债务余额情况
Balance of Debts of National Government Finance

单位：亿元　(100 million yuan)

年份 Year	合计 Total	国内债务 Domestic Debts	国外债务 Foreign Debts
2005	32614.21	31848.59	765.52
2006	35015.28	34380.24	635.02
2007	52074.65	51467.39	607.26
2008	53271.54	52799.32	472.22
2009	60237.68	59736.95	500.73
2010	67548.11	66987.97	560.14
2011	72044.51	71410.80	633.71
2012	77565.70	76747.91	817.79
2013	86746.91	85836.05	910.86

表21 全国外债余额
Balance of Foreign Debts

单位：亿美元 (USD 100 million)

年份 Year	外债余额总计 Total	按债务类型分 By Type of Debt: 外国政府贷款 Loans from Foreign Governments	国际金融组织贷款 Loans from International Financial Institutions	国际商业贷款 International Commercial Loans	贸易信贷 Trade Loans	按偿还期限分 By Repayment Terms: 长期债务 Balance of Long-term Debts	短期债务 Balance of Short-term Debts
1985	158.3					94.1	64.2
1986	214.8					167.1	47.7
1987	302.0					244.8	57.2
1988	400.0					326.9	73.1
1989	413.0					370.3	42.7
1990	525.5	83.9	62.9	291.9		457.8	67.7
1991	605.6	95.1	70.7	315.9		502.6	103.0
1992	693.2	115.0	84.2	354.8		584.7	108.5
1993	835.7	143.2	104.6	410.8		700.2	135.5
1994	928.1	195.9	129.4	473.4		823.9	104.2
1995	1065.9	220.6	148.0	526.3		946.7	119.2
1996	1162.8	221.6	167.4	569.4		1021.7	141.1
1997	1309.6	207.8	192.1	647.7		1128.2	181.4
1998	1460.4	224.1	229.5	682.2		1287.0	173.4
1999	1518.3	265.6	251.4	653.8		1366.5	151.8
2000	1457.3	246.1	263.5	947.7		1326.5	130.8
2001	2033.0	237.0	275.7	972.3	548.0	1195.3	837.7
2002	2026.3	244.2	277.0	929.1	576.0	1155.6	870.8
2003	2193.6	254.2	264.7	1051.7	623.0	1165.9	1027.7
2004	2629.9	322.1	251.0	1247.8	809.0	1242.9	1387.0
2005	2965.5	272.0	267.9	1362.6	1063.0	1249.0	1716.5
2006	3385.9	276.7	278.1	1635.1	1196.0	1393.6	1992.3
2007	3892.2	300.6	283.7	1820.9	1487.0	1535.3	2356.9
2008	3901.6	324.7	270.5	2010.3	1296.0	1638.8	2262.8
2009	4286.5	349.2	333.8	1986.5	1617.0	1693.9	2592.6
2010	5489.4	320.8	355.5	2701.1	2112.0	1732.4	3757.0
2011	6950.0	333.0	350.0	3775.0	2492.0	1941.0	5009.0
2012	7369.9	310.5	341.0	3803.4	2915.0	1960.6	5409.3
2013	8631.7	265.2	332.8	4668.7	3365.0	1865.4	6766.3

注：2001年起外债余额增加3个月以内贸易项下的对外融资余额。

a) Foreign debts since 2001 are collected by the new standard, the figures increase the foreign loans under the item of international trade loans within 3 months than the debts before 2001.

表22 各种价格总指数
Price Indices

(上年价格=100) (Preceding year=100)

年份 Year	居民消费价格指数 Consumer Price Index	城市居民消费价格指数 Urban Areas	农村居民消费价格指数 Rural Areas	商品零售价格指数 Retail Price Index	城市商品零售价格指数 Urban Areas	农村商品零售价格指数 Rural Areas	农业生产资料价格指数 Price Index of Agricultural Production	工业生产者出厂价格指数 Producer Price Index of Industrial Products	工业生产者购进价格指数 Purchasing Price Index for Industrial Producer	固定资产投资价格指数 Price Index for Investment in Fixed Assets
1951		112.5		112.2						
1952		102.7		99.6						
1953		105.1		103.4						
1954		101.4		102.3						
1955		100.3		101.0						
1956		99.9		100.0						
1957		102.6		101.5						
1958		98.9		100.2						
1959		100.3		100.9						
1960		102.5		103.1						
1961		116.1		116.2						
1962		103.8		103.8						
1963		94.1		94.1						
1964		96.3		96.3						
1965		98.8		97.3						
1966		98.8		99.7						
1967		99.4		99.3						
1968		100.1		100.1						
1969		101.0		98.9						
1970		100.0		99.8						
1971		99.9		99.3						
1972		100.2		99.8						
1973		100.1		100.6						
1974		100.7		100.5						
1975		100.4		100.2						
1976		100.3		100.3						
1977		102.7		102.0						
1978		100.7		100.7	102.5	100.1	99.9			
1979		101.9		102.0	101.9	102.0	100.4			
1980		107.5		106.0	108.1	104.4	101.0			
1981		102.5		102.4	102.7	102.1	101.7			
1982		102.0		101.9	102.1	101.7	101.9			
1983		102.0		101.5	101.9	101.2	103.0			
1984		102.7		102.8	102.5	103.0	108.9			

表22　续表　continued

(上年价格=100)　　(Preceding year=100)

年份 Year	居民消费价格指数 Consumer Price Index	城市居民消费价格指数 Urban Areas	农村居民消费价格指数 Rural Areas	商品零售价格指数 Retail Price Index	城市商品零售价格指数 Urban Areas	农村商品零售价格指数 Rural Areas	农业生产资料价格指数 Price Index of Agricultural Production	工业生产者出厂价格指数 Producer Price Index of Industrial Products	工业生产者购进价格指数 Purchasing Price Index for Industrial Producer	固定资产投资价格指数 Price Index for Investment in Fixed Assets
1985	109.3	111.9	107.6	108.8	112.2	107.0	104.8	108.7		
1986	106.5	107.0	106.1	106.0	107.0	105.0	101.1	103.8	109.5	
1987	107.3	108.8	106.2	107.3	109.1	106.3	107.0	107.9	111.0	
1988	118.8	120.7	117.5	118.5	121.3	117.1	116.2	115.0	120.2	
1989	118.0	116.3	119.3	117.8	116.0	118.8	118.9	118.6	126.4	
1990	103.1	101.3	104.5	102.1	100.2	103.2	105.5	104.1	105.6	
1991	103.4	105.1	102.3	102.9	104.5	102.0	102.9	106.2	109.1	109.5
1992	106.4	108.6	104.7	105.4	107.7	103.9	103.7	106.8	111.0	115.3
1993	114.7	116.1	113.7	113.2	114.2	112.6	114.1	124.0	135.1	126.6
1994	124.1	125.0	123.4	121.7	120.9	122.9	121.6	119.5	118.2	110.4
1995	117.1	116.8	117.5	114.8	113.5	116.4	127.4	114.9	115.3	105.9
1996	108.3	108.8	107.9	106.1	105.8	106.4	108.4	102.9	103.9	104.0
1997	102.8	103.1	102.5	100.8	100.8	100.7	99.5	99.7	101.3	101.7
1998	99.2	99.4	99.0	97.4	97.4	97.6	94.5	95.9	95.8	99.8
1999	98.6	98.7	98.5	97.0	97.0	97.1	95.8	97.6	96.7	99.6
2000	100.4	100.8	99.9	98.5	98.5	98.5	99.1	102.8	105.1	101.1
2001	100.7	100.7	100.8	99.2	98.9	99.6	99.1	98.7	99.8	100.4
2002	99.2	99.0	99.6	98.7	98.5	99.1	100.5	97.8	97.7	100.2
2003	101.2	100.9	101.6	99.9	99.6	100.5	101.4	102.3	104.8	102.2
2004	103.9	103.3	104.8	102.8	102.1	104.2	110.6	106.1	111.4	105.6
2005	101.8	101.6	102.2	100.8	100.5	101.4	108.3	104.9	108.3	101.6
2006	101.5	101.5	101.5	101.0	100.9	101.4	101.5	103.0	106.0	101.5
2007	104.8	104.5	105.4	103.8	103.3	104.9	107.7	103.1	104.4	103.9
2008	105.9	105.6	106.5	105.9	105.5	106.7	120.3	106.9	110.5	108.9
2009	99.3	99.1	99.7	98.8	98.7	99.0	97.5	94.6	92.1	97.6
2010	103.3	103.2	103.6	103.1	102.8	103.6	102.9	105.5	109.6	103.6
2011	105.4	105.3	105.8	104.9	104.7	105.5	111.3	106.0	109.1	106.6
2012	102.6	102.7	102.5	102.0	101.9	102.2	105.6	98.3	98.2	101.1
2013	102.6	102.6	102.8	101.4	101.3	101.8	101.4	98.1	98.0	100.3

注：1.本表1985年前城市居民消费价格指数为职工生活费用价格总指数。
2.从2011年起，原工业品出厂价格指数改称为工业生产者出厂价格指数，原材料、燃料、动力购进价格指数改称为工业生产者购进价格指数。

a) Urban areas consumer price indices remain with price indices of cost of living of workers and employees before 1985.

b) The original Ex-Factory price Indices of Industrial Produts since 2011 Changed its name to the Indices of Industrial Producer, price purchasing Indices of Raw Material, Fuel and power changed its name to the Purchasing Price Indices of Industrial Producer.

表23 各种价格定基指数
Fixed-base Price Indices

年份 Year	居民消费价格指数 Consumer Price Index (1978=100)	城市居民消费价格指数 Urban Areas (1978=100)	农村居民消费价格指数 Rural Areas (1985=100)	商品零售价格指数 Retail Price Index (1978=100)	农业生产资料价格指数 Price Index of Agricultural Production (1978=100)	工业生产者出厂价格指数 Producer Price Index of Industrial Products (1985=100)	工业生产者购进价格指数 Purchasing Price Index for Industrial Producer (1990=100)	固定资产投资价格指数 Price Index for Investment in Fixed Assets (1990=100)
1978	100.0	100.0		100.0	100.0			
1979	101.9	101.9		102.0	100.4			
1980	109.5	109.5		108.1	101.4			
1981	112.2	112.2		110.7	103.1			
1982	114.4	114.4		112.8	105.1			
1983	116.7	116.7		114.5	108.3			
1984	119.9	119.9		117.7	117.9			
1985	131.1	134.2	100.0	128.1	123.6	100.0		
1986	139.6	143.6	106.1	135.8	125.0	103.8		
1987	149.8	156.2	112.7	145.7	133.8	112.0		
1988	177.9	188.5	132.4	172.7	155.5	128.8		
1989	209.9	219.2	157.9	203.4	184.9	152.8		
1990	216.4	222.0	165.1	207.7	195.1	159.0	100.0	100.0
1991	223.8	233.3	168.9	213.7	200.8	168.9	109.1	109.5
1992	238.1	253.4	176.8	225.2	208.2	180.4	121.1	126.3
1993	273.1	294.2	201.0	254.9	237.6	223.7	163.6	159.8
1994	339.0	367.8	248.0	310.2	288.9	267.3	193.4	176.5
1995	396.9	429.6	291.4	356.1	368.1	307.1	222.9	186.9
1996	429.9	467.4	314.4	377.8	399.0	316.0	231.6	194.3
1997	441.9	481.9	322.3	380.8	397.0	315.0	234.6	197.6
1998	438.4	479.0	319.1	370.9	375.2	302.1	224.7	197.3
1999	432.2	472.8	314.3	359.8	359.4	294.8	217.3	196.5
2000	434.0	476.6	314.0	354.4	356.2	303.1	228.4	198.6
2001	437.0	479.9	316.5	351.6	353.0	299.2	227.9	199.4
2002	433.5	475.1	315.2	347.0	354.8	292.6	222.7	199.8
2003	438.7	479.4	320.2	346.7	359.8	299.3	233.4	204.2
2004	455.8	495.2	335.6	356.4	397.9	317.6	260.0	215.7
2005	464.0	503.1	343.0	359.3	430.9	333.2	281.6	219.1
2006	471.0	510.6	348.1	362.9	437.4	343.2	298.5	222.4
2007	493.6	533.6	366.9	376.7	471.1	353.8	311.6	231.1
2008	522.7	563.5	390.7	398.9	566.7	378.2	344.3	251.8
2009	519.0	558.4	389.5	394.1	552.5	357.8	317.2	245.8
2010	536.1	576.3	403.5	406.3	568.5	377.5	347.7	254.6
2011	565.0	606.8	426.9	426.2	632.7	400.2	379.3	271.4
2012	579.7	623.2	437.6	434.7	668.1	393.4	372.5	274.4
2013	594.8	639.4	449.9	440.8	677.5	385.9	365.1	275.2

表24　全国城乡居民人均收支和恩格尔系数

Per Capita Annual Income, Expenditure and Engel Coefficient of Urban and Rural Households

年份 Year	城镇居民家庭平均每人 Urban Households				农村居民家庭平均每人 Rural Households			
	可支配收入（元）Per Capita Annual Disposable Income (yuan)	可支配收入指数（1978=100）Per Capita Annual Disposable Income Index (1978=100)	消费支出（元）Living Expenditure (yuan)	恩格尔系数（%）Engel Coefficient (%)	纯收入（元）Net Income (yuan)	纯收入指数（1978=100）Net Income Index (1978=100)	消费支出（元）Living Expenditure (yuan)	恩格尔系数（%）Engel Coefficient (%)
1957			222.0		73.0		70.9	65.7
1964			220.7		102.3		93.6	67.1
1965					107.2		95.1	68.5
1977					117.1			
1978	343.4	100.0	311.2	57.5	133.6	100.0	116.1	67.7
1979	405.0	115.7			160.2	119.2	134.5	64.0
1980	477.6	127.0	412.4	56.9	191.3	139.0	162.2	61.8
1981	500.4	129.9	456.8	56.7	223.4	160.4	190.8	59.9
1982	535.3	136.3	471.0	58.6	270.1	192.3	220.2	60.7
1983	564.6	141.5	505.9	59.2	309.8	219.6	248.3	59.4
1984	652.1	158.7	559.4	58.0	355.3	249.5	273.8	59.2
1985	739.1	160.4	673.2	53.3	397.6	268.9	317.4	57.8
1986	900.9	182.7	799.0	52.4	423.8	277.6	357.0	56.4
1987	1002.1	186.8	884.4	53.5	462.6	292.0	398.3	55.8
1988	1180.2	182.3	1104.0	51.4	544.9	310.7	476.7	54.0
1989	1373.9	182.5	1211.0	54.5	601.5	305.7	535.4	54.8
1990	1510.2	198.1	1278.9	54.2	686.3	311.2	584.6	58.8
1991	1700.6	212.4	1453.8	53.8	708.6	317.4	619.8	57.6
1992	2026.6	232.9	1671.7	53.0	784.0	336.2	659.2	57.6
1993	2577.4	255.1	2110.8	50.3	921.6	346.9	769.7	58.1
1994	3496.2	276.8	2851.3	50.0	1221.0	364.3	1016.8	58.9
1995	4283.0	290.3	3537.6	50.1	1577.7	383.6	1310.4	58.6
1996	4838.9	301.6	3919.5	48.8	1926.1	418.1	1572.1	56.3
1997	5160.3	311.9	4185.6	46.6	2090.1	437.3	1617.2	55.1
1998	5425.1	329.9	4331.6	44.7	2162.0	456.1	1590.3	53.4
1999	5854.0	360.6	4615.9	42.1	2210.3	473.5	1577.4	52.6
2000	6280.0	383.7	4998.0	39.4	2253.4	483.4	1670.1	49.1
2001	6859.6	416.3	5309.0	38.2	2366.4	503.7	1741.1	47.7
2002	7702.8	472.1	6029.9	37.7	2475.6	527.9	1834.3	46.3
2003	8472.2	514.6	6510.9	37.1	2622.2	550.6	1943.3	45.6
2004	9421.6	554.2	7182.1	37.7	2936.4	588.0	2184.7	47.2
2005	10493.0	607.4	7942.9	36.7	3254.9	624.5	2555.4	45.5
2006	11759.5	670.7	8696.6	35.8	3587.0	670.7	2829.0	43.0
2007	13785.8	752.5	9997.5	36.3	4140.4	734.4	3223.9	43.1
2008	15780.8	815.7	11242.9	37.9	4760.6	793.2	3660.7	43.7
2009	17174.7	895.4	12264.6	36.5	5153.2	860.6	3993.5	41.0
2010	19109.4	965.2	13471.5	35.7	5919.0	954.4	4381.8	41.1
2011	21809.8	1046.3	15160.9	36.3	6977.3	1063.2	5221.1	40.4
2012	24564.7	1146.7	16674.3	36.2	7916.6	1176.9	5908.0	39.3
2013	26955.1	1227.0	18022.6	35.0	8895.9	1286.4	6625.5	37.7

注：收入指数按可比价格计算。

a) The indices in this table are calculated at constant prices.

表25 全国城乡居民住房面积和储蓄存款余额
Resident Buildings, Savings Deposit in Urban and Rural Areas

年份 Year	城市人均 住宅建筑面积 (平方米) Per Capita Building Space in City Areas (sq.m)	农村人均 住房面积 (平方米) Per Capita Living Space in Rural Area (sq.m)	城乡居民人民币 储蓄存款年底余额 (亿元) Total Outstading Amount of Savings Deposit in Urban and Rural Areas (100 million yuan)	定期 Time Deposits	活期 Demand Deposits	人均储蓄 存款余额 (元) Per Capita Amount of Savings Deposit in Urban and Rural Areas (yuan)
1952			8.6	4.8	3.8	1.5
1953			12.3	6.8	5.5	2.1
1954			15.9	9.8	6.1	2.6
1955			19.9	13.3	6.6	3.2
1956			26.7	15.6	11.1	4.3
1957			35.2	19.6	15.6	5.4
1958			55.2	23.9	31.3	8.4
1959			68.3	31.6	36.7	10.2
1960			66.3	37.3	29.0	10.0
1961			55.4	29.7	25.7	8.4
1962			41.1	25.6	15.5	6.1
1963			45.7	29.4	16.3	6.6
1964			55.5	37.0	18.5	7.9
1965			65.2	43.4	21.8	9.0
1966			72.3	46.9	25.4	9.7
1967			73.8	48.9	24.9	9.7
1968			78.3	50.3	28.0	10.0
1969			75.9	49.4	26.5	9.4
1970			79.5	53.8	25.7	9.6
1971			90.3	61.4	28.9	11.0
1972			105.2	69.6	35.6	12.1
1973			121.2	77.7	43.5	13.6
1974			136.4	86.7	49.7	15.0
1975			149.7	94.5	55.2	16.2
1976			159.1	100.6	58.5	17.0
1977			181.6	111.7	69.9	19.1
1978	6.7	8.1	210.6	128.9	81.7	21.9
1979	6.9	8.4	281.0	166.4	114.6	28.8
1980	7.2	9.4	395.8	304.9	90.9	40.1
1981	7.7	10.2	523.4	396.4	127.0	52.3
1982	8.2	10.7	675.4	519.3	156.1	66.5
1983	8.7	11.6	892.9	682.4	210.5	86.9
1984	9.1	13.6	1214.7	900.9	313.8	117.0
1985	10.0	14.7	1622.6	1225.2	397.4	154.5

表25 续表 continued

年份 Year	城市人均住宅建筑面积(平方米) Per Capita Building Space in City Areas (sq.m)	农村人均住房面积(平方米) Per Capita Living Space in Rural Area (sq.m)	城乡居民人民币储蓄存款年底余额(亿元) Total Outstading Amount of Savings Deposit in Urban and Rural Areas (100 million yuan)	定期 Time Deposits	活期 Demand Deposits	人均储蓄存款余额(元) Per Capita Amount of Savings Deposit in Urban and Rural Areas (yuan)
1986	12.4	15.3	2237.8	1729.2	508.6	210.1
1987	12.7	16.0	3083.4	2357.8	725.6	285.2
1988	13.0	16.6	3819.1	2845.3	973.8	348.5
1989	13.5	17.2	5184.5	4208.5	976.0	466.2
1990	13.7	17.8	7119.6	5909.4	1210.2	622.9
1991	14.2	18.5	9244.9	7634.9	1610.0	798.3
1992	14.8	18.9	11757.3	9445.0	2312.3	1003.2
1993	15.2	20.7	15203.5	12108.3	3095.2	1281.9
1994	15.7	20.2	21518.8	16838.7	4680.1	1794.7
1995	16.3	21.0	29662.3	23778.2	5884.1	2447.4
1996	17.0	21.7	38520.8	30873.2	7647.6	3147.1
1997	17.8	22.5	46279.8	36226.7	10053.1	3744.3
1998	18.7	23.3	53407.5	41791.6	11615.9	4280.8
1999	19.4	24.2	59621.8	44955.1	14666.7	4739.9
2000	20.3	24.8	64332.4	46141.7	18190.7	5075.8
2001	20.8	25.7	73762.4	51434.9	22327.5	5779.5
2002	24.5	26.5	86910.6	58788.9	28121.7	6765.9
2003	25.3	27.2	103617.7	68498.7	35119.0	8018.3
2004	26.4	27.9	119555.4	78138.9	41416.5	9197.4
2005	27.8	29.7	141051.0	92263.5	48787.5	10787.3
2006	28.5	30.7	161587.3	103011.4	58575.9	12292.9
2007	30.1	31.6	172534.2	104934.5	67599.7	13058.0
2008	30.6	32.4	217885.4	139300.2	78585.2	16406.8
2009	31.3	33.6	260771.7	160230.4	100541.3	19540.8
2010	31.6	34.1	303302.5	178413.9	124888.6	22619.2
2011	32.7	36.2	343635.9			25504.6
2012	32.9	37.1	399551.0			29508.1
2013			447601.6			32894.5

注：1978–2001年城市人均住宅建筑面积由建设部提供，2002–2012年城镇居民人均住房建筑面积为城镇住户抽样调查数据(不含集体户)。
2.2011年后，人民银行的居民储蓄存款统计取消了定期与活期的分类。

a) Data of per capita building space in city areas were provided by the Ministry of Construction from 1978 to 2001, per capita building space in urban and town areas were sample survey of urban and town household(not including collective households) from 2002 to 2012.

b) Since 2011, statistics of savings deposit of Central Bank of China do not classify time deposit and demand deposit.

表26 全国城乡居民平均每百户年末主要耐用消费品拥有量
Durable Consumer Goods Owned Per 100 Households at Year-end

年份 Year	洗衣机（台） Washing Machine(unit)		电冰箱（台） Refrigerator(unit)		彩色电视机（台） Color Television Set(set)		计算机（台） Computer (set)	
	城镇 Urban Households	农村 Rural Households	城镇 Urban Households	农村 Rural Households	城镇 Urban Households	农村 Rural Households	城镇 Urban Households	农村 Rural Households
1978								
1979								
1980								
1981	6.3		0.2		0.6			
1982	16.1		0.7		1.1			
1983	29.1	0.4	1.7		2.6			
1984	40.1	1.0	3.2	0.0	5.4			
1985	52.8	1.9	9.6	0.1	18.4	0.8		
1986	59.7	3.2	12.7	0.2	27.4	1.5		
1987	66.8	4.8	19.9	0.3	34.6	2.3		
1988	73.4	6.8	28.1	0.6	43.9	2.8		
1989	76.2	8.2	36.5	0.9	51.5	3.6		
1990	78.4	9.1	42.3	1.2	59.0	4.7		
1991	80.6	11.0	48.7	1.6	68.4	6.4		
1992	83.4	12.2	52.6	2.2	74.9	8.1		
1993	86.4	13.8	56.7	3.1	79.5	10.9		
1994	87.3	15.3	62.1	4.0	86.2	13.5		
1995	89.0	16.9	66.2	5.2	89.8	16.9		
1996	90.1	20.5	69.7	7.3	93.5	22.9		
1997	89.1	21.9	73.0	8.5	100.5	27.3	2.6	
1998	90.6	22.8	76.1	9.3	105.4	32.6	3.8	
1999	91.4	24.3	77.7	10.6	111.6	38.2	5.9	
2000	90.5	28.6	80.1	12.3	116.6	48.7	9.7	0.5
2001	92.2	29.9	81.9	13.6	120.5	54.4	13.3	0.7
2002	92.9	31.8	87.4	14.8	126.4	60.5	20.6	1.1
2003	94.4	34.3	88.7	15.9	130.5	67.8	27.8	1.4
2004	95.9	37.3	90.2	17.8	133.4	75.1	33.1	1.9
2005	95.5	40.2	90.7	20.1	134.8	84.1	41.5	2.1
2006	96.8	43.0	91.8	22.5	137.4	89.4	47.2	2.7
2007	96.8	45.9	95.0	26.1	137.8	94.4	53.8	3.7
2008	94.7	49.1	93.6	30.2	132.9	99.2	59.3	5.4
2009	96.0	53.1	95.4	37.1	135.7	108.9	65.7	7.5
2010	96.9	57.3	96.6	45.2	137.4	111.8	71.2	10.4
2011	97.1	62.6	97.2	61.5	135.2	115.5	81.9	18.0
2012	98.0	67.2	98.5	67.3	136.1	116.9	87.0	21.4

表26 续表 continued

年份 Year	照相机（架） Camera(set)		空调器（台） Air conditioner(unit)		固定电话（部） Fixed Telephone(unit)		移动电话（部） Mobile Telephone(unit)	
	城镇 Urban Households	农村 Rural Households	城镇 Urban Households	农村 Rural Households	城镇 Urban Households	农村 Rural Households	城镇 Urban Households	农村 Rural Households
1978								
1979								
1980								
1981	4.3							
1982	5.6							
1983	7.3							
1984	8.9							
1985	12.1	0.2	0.1					
1986	11.9	0.3	0.1					
1987	14.3	0.5	0.1					
1988	16.0	0.6	0.2					
1989	17.3	0.8	0.3					
1990	19.2	0.7	0.3					
1991	21.3	0.9	0.7					
1992	24.3	1.0	1.2					
1993	26.5	1.0	2.3	0.1				
1994	29.8	1.2	5.0	0.1				
1995	30.6	1.4	8.1	0.2				
1996	32.1	1.9	11.6	0.3				
1997	33.6	2.1	16.3	0.4			1.7	
1998	36.3	2.2	20.0	0.6			3.3	
1999	38.1	2.7	24.5	0.7			7.1	
2000	38.4	3.1	30.8	1.3		26.4	19.5	4.3
2001	39.8	3.2	35.8	1.7		34.1	34.0	8.1
2002	44.1	3.3	51.1	2.3	93.7	40.8	62.9	13.7
2003	45.4	3.4	61.8	3.5	95.4	49.1	90.1	23.7
2004	47.0	3.7	69.8	4.7	96.4	54.5	111.4	34.7
2005	46.9	4.1	80.7	6.4	94.4	58.4	137.0	50.2
2006	48.0	4.2	87.8	7.3	93.3	64.1	152.9	62.1
2007	45.1	4.3	95.1	8.5	90.5	68.4	165.2	77.8
2008	39.1	4.4	100.3	9.8	82.0	67.0	172.0	96.1
2009	41.7	4.8	106.8	12.2	81.9	62.7	181.0	115.2
2010	43.7	5.2	112.1	16.0	80.9	60.8	188.9	136.5
2011	44.5	4.5	122.0	22.6	69.6	43.1	205.3	179.7
2012	46.4	5.2	126.8	25.4	68.4	42.2	212.6	197.8

表27　全国城市公用事业
Basic Statistics on Urban Public Utilities

年份 Year	日供水综合生产能力（万立方米/日） Integrated Production Capacity of Tap Water (10 000 cu.m/day)	供水管道长度（公里） Length of Water Supply Pipelines (km)	全年供水总量（万立方米） Total Annual Volume of Water Supply (10 000 cu.m)	#生活用 For Residential Use	#生产用 For Productive Use	人均日生活用水量（升） Daily Water Consumption Per Capita (liter)
1949	240.7	6587				
1952	266.9	8132	45806	25093		38.2
1953	292.5	9175	56791	31853	19404	42.0
1954	316.9	10170	64502	37244	25319	42.0
1955	352.3	10700	70019	41506	27884	43.4
1956	381.5	11597	83176	47218	36460	43.0
1957	450.3	12564	95602	54948	44842	44.3
1958	615.3	14617	126345	64138	51584	43.7
1959	748.5	15457	184632	78860	91102	47.4
1960	1020.8	15889	250813	99150	139326	57.4
1961						
1962	982.7	17545	223409	110814	110660	65.6
1963	951.3	17480	229221	104477	106143	62.2
1965	1077.3	19028	262802	103423	136188	54.0
1972	1722.8	27635	491004	173202	296331	
1973	1775.0	27026	521745	194479	314347	
1974	1853.0	29918	560321	207916	329365	
1975	2081.5	30692	616548	227471	367951	
1976	2202.0	31944	642661	246950	385248	
1977	2350.0	34276	697867	259396	415642	118.5
1978	2530.4	35984	787507	275854	438501	120.6
1979	2714.0	39406	832201	309206	462066	121.8
1980	2979.0	42859	883427	339130	479935	127.6
1981	3258.0	46966	969943	367823	518428	130.4
1982	3424.9	51513	1011319	391422	537290	132.4
1983	3539.0	56852	1065956	421968	556188	138.1
1984	3960.9	62892	1176474	465651	612353	143.3
1985	4019.7	67350	1280238	519493	653427	151.0
1986	10407.9	72557	2773921	706971	1916119	161.9
1987	11363.6	77864	2984697	759702	2063356	164.1

表27 续表 1 continued

年份 Year	日供水综合生产能力 (万立方米/日) Integrated Production Capacity of Tap Water (10 000 cu.m/day)	供水管道长度 (公里) Length of Water Supply Pipelines (km)	全年供水总量 (万立方米) Total Annual Volume of Water Supply (10 000 cu.m)	#生活用 For Residential Use	#生产用 For Productive Use	人均日生活用水量 (升) Daily Water Consumption Per Capita (liter)
1988	12715.8	86231	3385847	873800	2345634	170.4
1989	12821.1	92281	3936648	930619	2830377	172.4
1990	14220.3	97183	3823425	1001021	2597906	175.7
1991	14584.0	102299	4085073	1159929	2701161	196.0
1992	16036.4	111780	4298437	1172929	2856051	186.0
1993	16927.9	123007	4502341	1282543	2915384	188.6
1994	18215.1	131052	4894620	1422453	3136099	194.0
1995	19250.4	138701	4815653	1581451	2736256	195.4
1996	19990.0	202613	4660652	1670673	2618145	208.1
1997	20565.8	215587	4767788	1757157	2575176	213.5
1998	20991.8	225361	4704732	1810355	2496452	214.1
1999	21551.9	238001	4675076	1896225	2364756	217.5
2000	21842.0	254561	4689838	1999960	2279239	220.2
2001	22900.0	289338	4661194	2036492	2209878	216.0
2002	23546.0	312605	4664574	2131919	2085609	213.0
2003	23967.1	333289	4752548	2246665	2069345	210.9
2004	24753.0	358410	4902755	2334625	2113633	210.8
2005	24719.8	379332	5020601	2437374	2098008	204.1
2006	26965.6	430426	5405246	2220459	2217048	188.3
2007	25708.4	447229	5019488	2263676	1828530	178.4
2008	26604.1	480084	5000762	2274266	1776630	178.2
2009	27046.8	510399	4967467	2334082	1668009	176.6
2010	27601.5	539778	5078745	2371488	1678125	171.4
2011	26668.7	573774	5134222	2476520	1596521	170.9
2012	27177.3	591872	5230326	2572473	1592723	171.8
2013	28373.4	646413	5373022	2676463	1617412	173.5

注：2006年住房和城乡建设部《城市建设统计报表制度》修订，范围、口径及部分指标计算方法有调整。

a) Statistical Reporting Form System on Urban Construction of Ministry of Housing and Urban-Rural Development was revised in 2006, the scope and coverage and calculating of some indicators was adjusted.

表27　续表 2 continued

年份 Year	全年供气总量 Total Gas Supply			供气管道长度 (公里) Length of Gas Pipelines (km)	集中供热面积 (万平方米) Heated Area (10 000 sq.m)	城市道路 Roads	
	人工煤气 (万立方米) Coal Gas (10 000 cu.m)	液化石油气 (吨) Liquefied Petroleum Gas (ton)	天然气 (万立方米) Natural Gas (10 000 cu.m)			长度 (公里) Length of Roads (km)	面积 (万平方米) Area of Roads (10 000 sq.m)
1949	3820			1039		11129	8432
1952	9914			1580		12291	8979
1953	11912			1814		13272	9767
1954	14284			1886		14178	11037
1955	15680			1972		14929	11774
1956	18672			2108		16404	13030
1957	20475			2137		18259	14422
1958	25401			1921			
1959	39159			1964			
1960	47444			2075			
1961	53417			2119			
1962	49410			2229			
1963	54711			2374		18374	
1965	69628			2412		24000	21000
1972	124639	23458		2978		23311	20106
1973	136903	31676		3142		24318	21464
1974	139183	50128		3309		25203	21329
1975	148253	82071		4059		26021	21756
1976	152413	137590	21790	4247		26489	21588
1977	160901	138857	79538	4599		26773	23238
1978	172541	194533	69078	4717		26966	22539
1979	182748	243576	68489	5197		28391	24069
1980	195491	290460	58937	5619		29485	25255
1981	199466	330987	93970	5889	1167	30277	26022
1982	208819	388596	90421	6356	1451	31934	27976
1983	214009	456192	49071	7116	1841	33934	29962
1984	231351	535289	168568	9318	2445	36410	33019
1985	244754	601803	162099	10567	2742	38282	35872

表27 续表 3 continued

年份 Year	全年供气总量 Total Gas Supply			供气管道长度 (公里) Length of Gas Pipelines (km)	集中供热面积 (万平方米) Heated Area (10 000 sq.m)	城市道路 Roads	
	人工煤气 (万立方米) Coal Gas (10 000 cu.m)	液化石油气 (吨) Liquefied Petroleum Gas (ton)	天然气 (万立方米) Natural Gas (10 000 cu.m)			长度 (公里) Length of Roads (km)	面积 (万平方米) Area of Roads (10 000 sq.m)
1986	337745	1011308	435887	10399	9907	71886	69856
1987	686518	1149116	501093	17115	15282	78453	77885
1988	667927	1730261	573983	19214	13883	88634	91355
1989	841297	1898003	591169	21297	19386	96078	100591
1990	1747065	2190334	642289	23628	21263	94820	101721
1991	1258088	2423988	754616	26235	27651	88791	99135
1992	1495531	2996699	628914	29418	32832	96689	110526
1993	1304130	3150296	637207	32841	44164	104897	124866
1994	1262712	3664948	752436	37282	50992	111058	137602
1995	1266894	4886528	673354	44000	64645	130308	164886
1996	1348076	5758374	637832	60000	73433	132583	179871
1997	1268944	5786023	663001	67764	80755	138610	192165
1998	1675571	7972947	688255	72612	86540	145163	206136
1999	1320925	7612684	800556	81482	96775	152385	222158
2000	1523615	10537147	821476	89458	110766	159617	237849
2001	1369144	9818313	995197	100479	146329	176016	249431
2002	1989196	11363884	1259334	113823	155567	191399	277179
2003	2020883	11263475	1416415	130211	188956	208052	315645
2004	2137225	11267120	1693364	147949	216266	222964	352955
2005	2558343	12220141	2104951	162109	252056	247015	392166
2006	2964500	12636613	2447742	189491	265853	241351	411449
2007	3223512	14667692	3086365	221083	300591	246172	423662
2008	3558287	13291072	3680393	257846	348948	259740	452433
2009	3615507	13400303	4050996	273461	379574	269141	481947
2010	2799380	12680054	4875808	308680	435668	294443	521322
2011	847256	11658326	6787997	348965	473784	308897	562523
2012	769686	11148032	7950377	388941	518368	327081	607449
2013	627989	11097298	9009904	432377	571677	336304	644155

表27　续表 4 continued

年份 Year	桥梁 (座) Number of Bridges (unit)	排水管道长度 (公里) Length of Drainage Pipelines (km)	污水日处理能力 (万立方米) Treatment Capacity of Waste Water (10 000 cu.m)	年末公共汽(电)车运营数(辆) Number of Public Vehicles of Bus, Trolley Bus at the year-end (unit)	出租汽车数量 (辆) Number of Taxis (unit)	建成区园林绿地面积 (公顷) Built District Area of Parks and Green Land (hectare)	生活垃圾清运量 (万吨) Volume of Garbage Disposal (10 000 tons)
1949		6035		2292			
1952		7028		3515			
1953		7642		4144			
1954		8169		4642			
1955		8542		4947			
1956		9168		5458			
1957		10107		6174			
1958				7763			
1959				8853	1010		
1960				9838	834		
1961				10106			
1962				9881			
1963		12666		10153			
1965		12855		11060			
1972	5287	15876		15831			
1973	5662	16181		18880			
1974	5616	17158		18814			
1975	5690	18290		21338			
1976	5610	18269		22581			
1977	5358	18619		23733	1714		
1978	5376	19556		25839	1628		
1979	5302	20432		29912			2508
1980	5477	21860		32098	3807		3132
1981	5726	23183		34189	4674	110037	2606
1982	6624	24638		36251	5962	121433	3125
1983	6373	26448		38616	5437	135304	3452
1984	6849	28775		41282	10425	146625	3757
1985	7436	31556		42993	25346	159291	4477

表27 续表 5 continued

年份 Year	桥梁 (座) Number of Bridges (unit)	排水管道长度 (公里) Length of Drainage Pipelines (km)	污水日处理能力 (万立方米) Treatment Capacity of Waste Water (10 000 cu.m)	年末公共汽(电)车运营数(辆) Number of Public Vehicles of Bus, Trolley Bus at the year-end (unit)	出租汽车数量 (辆) Number of Taxis (unit)	建成区绿地面积 (公顷) Built District Area of Parks and Green Land (hectare)	生活垃圾清运量 (万吨) Volume of Garbage Disposal (10 000 tons)
1986		42549		49460	54712	153235	5009
1987		47107		52504	61525	161444	5398
1988	17989	50678		56818	82010	180144	5751
1989	20306	54510	1022.1	59671	98508	196256	6292
1990	21747	57787	1301.9	62215	110697		6767
1991	19914	61601	1724.4	66093	128281		7636
1992	24085	67672	1726.0	77093	190345		8262
1993	25454	75207	1791.9	88950	286207		8791
1994	28706	83647	1902.9	100848	393315		9952
1995	32123	110293	2463.3	136922	504040		10671
1996	29491	112812	2932.7	148109	585369	385056	10825
1997	31354	119739	3276.5	169121	683687	427766	10982
1998	31496	125943	3769.1	189002	754247	466197	11302
1999	32516	134486	4421.1	209884	791411	495696	11415
2000	34739	141758	4741.0	225993	824931	531088	11819
2001	38911	158128	6215.5	230918	870023	582952	13470
2002	47341	173042	6153.1	246129	884195	670131	13650
2003	50732	198645	6626.4	264338	903381	771730	14857
2004	51092	218881	7387.2	281516	903734	842865	15509
2005	52123	241056	7989.7	310932	936973	927064	15577
2006	54643	261379	9734.0	312812	928647	1040823	14841
2007	48100	291933	10336.5	344489	959668	1110330	15215
2008	49840	315220	11172.5	367292	968811	1208448	15438
2009	51068	343892	12183.9	365161	971579	1338133	15734
2010	52548	369553	13392.9	374876	986190	1443663	15805
2011	53386	414074	13304.1	402645	1002306	1545985	16395
2012	57601	439080	13692.9	419410	1026678	1635240	17081
2013	59530	464878	14652.7	446604	1053580	1719361	17239

表28 全国城市设施水平
Level of National Municipal Public Facilities

年份 Year	城市人口密度 (人/平方公里) Population Density (person/sq.km)	城市用水普及率 (%) Water Coverage Rate (%)	城市燃气普及率 (%) Gas Coverage Rate (%)	每万人拥有公共交通车辆 (标台) Motor Vehicle for Public Traffic per 10 000 Persons (standard unit)	人均拥有道路面积 (平方米) Road Surface Area per Capita (sq. m)
1978					
1979					
1980					
1981	697	53.7	11.6		1.8
1982	426	56.7	12.6		2.0
1983	435	52.5	12.3		1.9
1984	374	49.5	13.0		1.8
1985	466	45.1	13.0		1.7
1986	284	51.3	15.2	2.5	3.1
1987	280	50.4	16.7	2.4	3.1
1988	281	47.6	16.5	2.2	3.1
1989	274	47.4	17.8	2.1	3.2
1990	279	48.0	19.1	2.2	3.1
1991	302	54.8	23.7	2.7	3.4
1992	317	56.2	26.3	3.0	3.6
1993	325	55.2	27.9	3.0	3.7
1994	324	56.0	30.4	3.0	3.8
1995	322	58.7	34.3	3.6	4.4
1996	367	60.7	38.2	3.8	5.0
1997	440	61.2	40.0	4.5	5.2
1998	459	61.9	41.8	4.6	5.5
1999	462	63.5	43.8	5.0	5.9
2000	442	63.9	45.4	5.3	6.1
2001	588	72.3	60.4	6.1	7.0
2002	754	77.9	67.2	6.7	7.9
2003	847	86.2	76.7	7.7	9.3
2004	865	88.9	81.5	8.4	10.3
2005	870	91.1	82.1	8.6	10.9
2006	2238	86.7	79.1	9.1	11.0
2007	2104	93.8	87.4	10.2	11.4
2008	2080	94.7	89.6	11.1	12.2
2009	2147	96.1	91.4	11.1	12.8
2010	2209	96.7	92.0	11.2	13.2
2011	2228	97.0	92.4	11.8	13.8
2012	2307	97.2	93.2	12.1	14.4
2013	2362	97.6	94.3	12.8	14.9

表28 续表 continued

年份 Year	污水处理率(%) Wastewater Treatment Rate (%)	园林绿化 Landscaping			每万人拥有公共厕所(座) Number of Public Lavatories per 10 000 Persons (unit)
		人均公共绿地面积(平方米) Public Green Space Per Capita (sq. m)	建成区绿地率(%) Green Space Rate of Built District (%)	建成区绿化覆盖率(%) Green Coverage Rate of Built District (%)	
1978					
1979					
1980					
1981		1.5			3.8
1982		1.7			4.0
1983		1.7			4.0
1984		1.6			3.6
1985		1.6			3.3
1986		1.8		16.9	3.6
1987		1.9		17.1	3.5
1988		1.8		17.0	3.1
1989		1.7		17.8	3.1
1990		1.8		19.2	3.0
1991	14.9	2.1		20.1	3.4
1992	17.3	2.1		21.0	3.1
1993	20.0	2.2		21.3	2.9
1994	17.1	2.3		22.1	2.7
1995	19.7	2.5		23.9	3.0
1996	23.6	2.8	19.1	24.4	3.0
1997	25.8	2.9	20.6	25.5	3.0
1998	29.6	3.2	21.8	26.6	2.9
1999	31.9	3.5	23.0	27.6	2.9
2000	34.3	3.7	23.7	28.2	2.7
2001	36.4	4.6	24.3	28.4	3.0
2002	40.0	5.4	25.8	29.8	3.2
2003	42.4	6.5	27.3	31.2	3.2
2004	45.7	7.4	27.7	31.7	3.2
2005	51.9	7.9	28.5	32.5	3.2
2006	55.9	8.3	30.9	35.1	2.9
2007	62.9	9.0	31.3	35.3	3.0
2008	70.2	9.7	33.3	37.4	3.1
2009	75.3	10.7	34.2	38.2	3.1
2010	82.3	11.2	34.5	38.6	3.0
2011	83.6	11.8	35.3	39.2	2.9
2012	87.3	12.3	35.7	39.6	2.9
2013	89.3	12.6	35.8	39.7	2.8

表29 全国环境保护基本情况
Basic Statistics on Environmental Protection

年份 Year	工业废水排放总量(万吨) Industrial Waste Water Discharge (10 000 tons)	工业废水排放达标量(万吨) Industrial Waste Water Meeting Discharge Standards (10 000 tons)	工业废气排放量(亿标立方米) Industrial Waste Gas Emission (100 million standard cu.m)	工业烟尘排放量(万吨) Emission of Soot (10 000 tons)	工业固体废物产生量(万吨) Industrial Solid Wastes Generated (10 000 tons)	自然保护区面积(万公顷) Area of Nature Reserves (10 000 hectares)
1978						
1979						
1980	2335512				48725	
1981	2379272	700376			43055	
1982	2394396	820711			40501	
1983	2387744	886604	63167		41185	
1984	2513637	940679	68501		45211	
1985	2574009	987015	73972		48409	
1986	2602380	1105937	69679		60364	2939
1987	2637531	1207153	77270		53541	
1988	2683886	1238928	82382		56132	4818
1989	2520945	1203299	83062		57173	
1990	2486861	1246092	85380		57797	
1991	2358687	1182722	84653	845	58759	5692
1992	2338534	1236216	90308	870	61884	
1993	2194919	1204858	93423	880	61708	6618
1994	2155111	1196969	97463	807	61704	
1995	2218943	1228680	107478	838	64474	7185
1996	2058881	1217033	111196	758	65897	
1997	1883296	1164623	113378	1565	65750	7698
1998	2004658	1232203	121203	1179	80068	
1999	1973036	1316043	126807	953	78442	8815
2000	1942405	1493277	138145	953	81608	9821
2001	2026282	1727185	160863	852	88840	12989
2002	2071885	1830394	175257	804	94509	13295
2003	2122527	1892891	198906	846	100428	14398
2004	2211424	2005680	237696	887	120030	14823
2005	2431121	2217093	268988	949	134449	14995
2006	2401946	2178461	330990	865	151541	15154
2007	2466493	2260719	388169	771	175632	15188
2008	2416511	2233986	403866	671	190127	14894
2009	2343857	2208743	436064	604	203943	14775
2010	2374732	2263587	519168	603	240944	14944
2011	2308743		674509		326204	14971
2012	2216000		635519		332509	14979
2013	2098398		669361		330859	14631

注：1.从1997年起，工业"三废"排放及处理的统计范围由原来的对县及县以上有污染物排放的工业企业，扩大到对有污染排放的乡镇工业企业的统计。
2.2011年环境保护部对统计制度中的指标体系、调查方法及相关技术规定等进行了修订，统计范围扩展为工业源、农业源、城镇生活源、机动车、集中式污染治理设施5个部分。

a) From 1997, statistical coverage of emission of industrial waste water, waste gas and solid waste are widened, from industrial enterprises with pollution emission at county level and above to those at township level.

b) In 2011, Ministry of Environmental Protection revised indicator system, survey method and relevant technical regulation in statistical system, statistical coverage expanded to 5 parts: industrial sources, agricultural sources, urban living sources, motor vehicle, centralized pollution treatment facilities.

表30 全国农林牧渔业总产值和构成
Gross Output Value and Composition of Farming, Forestry, Animal Husbandry and Fishery

本表绝对数按当年价格计算。2003年执行新国民经济行业分类标准，总产值包括农林牧渔服务业产值。
Data in value terms in this table are calculated at current prices. Service value for farming forestry, animal husbandry and fishery has been included since 2003.

年份 Year	农林牧渔业总产值(亿元) Gross Output Value of Farming, Forestry, Animal Husbandry and Fishery(100 million yuan)					构成（总产值=100) Composition (Total=100)			
	总产值 Total	农业 Farming	林业 Forestry	牧业 Animal Husbandry	渔业 Fishery	农业 Farming	林业 Forestry	牧业 Animal Husbandry	渔业 Fishery
1949	326								
1950	384								
1951	420								
1952	461	396	7	52	6	85.9	1.6	11.2	1.3
1953	510								
1954	535								
1955	575								
1956	610								
1957	537	444	18	65	10	82.7	3.3	12.2	1.9
1958	566								
1959	497								
1960	457								
1961	559								
1962	584	495	13	64	13	84.7	2.2	10.9	2.2
1963	642								
1964	720								
1965	833	684	22	112	15	82.2	2.7	13.4	1.8
1966	910								
1967	924								
1968	928								
1969	948								
1970	1021	838	29	137	17	82.1	2.8	13.4	1.7
1971	1068								
1972	1075								
1973	1173								
1974	1215								
1975	1260	1020	39	178	22	81.0	3.1	14.2	1.7
1976	1258								
1977	1253								
1978	1397	1118	48	209	22	80.0	3.4	15.0	1.6
1979	1698	1325	61	286	26	78.1	3.6	16.8	1.5
1980	1923	1454	81	354	33	75.6	4.2	18.4	1.7
1981	2181	1636	99	402	44	75.0	4.5	18.4	2.0

表30 续表 continued

年份 Year	农林牧渔业总产值(亿元) Gross Output Value of Farming, Forestry, Animal Husbandry and Fishery(100 million yuan)					构成（总产值=100) Composition (Total=100)			
	总产值 Total	农业 Farming	林业 Forestry	牧业 Animal Husbandry	渔业 Fishery	农业 Farming	林业 Forestry	牧业 Animal Husbandry	渔业 Fishery
1982	2483	1865	110	457	51	75.1	4.4	18.4	2.1
1983	2750	2074	127	485	63	75.4	4.6	17.6	2.3
1984	3214	2380	162	587	85	74.1	5.0	18.3	2.6
1985	3619	2506	189	798	126	69.2	5.2	22.1	3.5
1986	4013	2772	201	876	164	69.1	5.0	21.8	4.1
1987	4676	3160	222	1068	225	67.6	4.7	22.8	4.8
1988	5865	3667	275	1601	322	62.5	4.7	27.3	5.5
1989	6535	4101	285	1800	349	62.8	4.4	27.6	5.3
1990	7662	4954	330	1967	411	64.7	4.3	25.7	5.4
1991	8157	5146	368	2159	483	63.1	4.5	26.5	5.9
1992	9085	5588	423	2461	613	61.5	4.7	27.1	6.8
1993	10996	6605	494	3014	882	60.1	4.5	27.4	8.0
1994	15750	9169	611	4672	1298	58.2	3.9	29.7	8.2
1995	20341	11885	710	6045	1701	58.4	3.5	29.7	8.4
1996	22354	13540	778	6016	2020	60.6	3.5	26.9	9.0
1997	23788	13853	818	6835	2283	58.2	3.4	28.7	9.6
1998	24542	14242	851	7026	2423	58.0	3.5	28.6	9.9
1999	24519	14106	886	6998	2529	57.5	3.6	28.5	10.3
2000	24916	13874	937	7393	2713	55.7	3.8	29.7	10.9
2001	26180	14463	939	7963	2815	55.2	3.6	30.4	10.8
2002	27391	14932	1033	8455	2971	54.5	3.8	30.9	10.8
2003	29692	14870	1240	9539	3138	50.1	4.2	32.1	10.6
2004	36239	18138	1327	12174	3606	50.1	3.7	33.6	9.9
2005	39451	19613	1426	13311	4016	49.7	3.6	33.7	10.2
2006	40811	21522	1611	12084	3971	52.7	3.9	29.6	9.7
2007	48893	24658	1862	16125	4458	50.4	3.8	33.0	9.1
2008	58002	28044	2153	20584	5203	48.4	3.7	35.5	9.0
2009	60361	30778	2193	19468	5626	51.0	3.6	22.8	9.3
2010	69320	36941	2595	20826	6422	53.3	3.7	30.0	9.3
2011	81304	41989	3121	25771	7568	51.6	3.8	31.7	9.3
2012	89453	46940	3447	27189	8706	52.5	3.9	30.4	9.7
2013	96995	51497	3902	28435	9635	53.1	4.0	29.3	9.9

表31 全国农林牧渔业总产值指数

Indices of Gross Output Value of Farming, Forestry, Animal Husbandry and Fishery

年份 Year	农林牧渔业总产值指数(上年=100) Indices of Gross Output of Farming,Forestry, Animal Husbandry and Fishery(preceding year=100)					农林牧渔业总产值指数(1952=100) Indices of Gross Output of Farming,Forestry, Animal Husbandry and Fishery(1952=100)				
	总产值 Total	#农业 Farming	#林业 Forestry	#牧业 Animal Husbandry	#渔业 Fishery	总产值 Total	#农业 Farming	#林业 Forestry	#牧业 Animal Husbandry	#渔业 Fishery
1953	102.4	100.7	103.4	112.1	107.7	102.4	100.7	103.4	112.1	107.7
1954	103.3	102.9	113.3	105.8	114.3	105.7	103.6	117.2	118.6	123.1
1955	108.4	110.9	135.3	90.7	131.3	114.6	114.9	158.6	107.5	161.5
1956	106.4	105.5	191.3	106.6	81.0	121.9	121.3	303.4	114.6	130.8
1957	105.6	102.9	105.7	125.7	170.6	128.7	124.8	320.7	144.1	223.1
1958	102.5	102.6	150.5	94.3	175.9	131.9	128.0	482.8	135.9	392.3
1959	86.4	85.4	108.6	64.1	176.5	113.9	109.4	524.1	87.1	692.3
1960	87.4	87.8	91.4	59.7	126.7	99.5	96.0	479.3	52.0	876.9
1961	97.6	98.8	50.4	128.1	68.4	97.1	94.9	241.4	66.6	600.0
1962	106.2	103.3	104.3	139.5	98.7	103.2	98.0	251.7	92.9	592.3
1963	111.6	107.5	126.0	143.6	114.3	115.2	105.4	317.2	133.4	676.9
1964	113.5	113.4	113.0	118.8	104.5	130.8	119.5	358.6	158.5	707.7
1965	108.1	111.2	115.4	109.0	109.8	141.4	132.9	413.8	172.7	776.9
1966	108.7	105.9	104.2	109.8	105.0	153.7	140.8	431.0	189.6	815.4
1967	101.6	101.9	104.0	100.8	99.1	156.2	143.5	448.3	191.0	807.7
1968	97.4	97.1	103.8	97.5	92.4	152.2	139.4	465.5	186.2	746.2
1969	101.2	100.2	103.7	98.9	110.3	153.9	139.6	482.8	184.1	823.1
1970	111.6	117.0	114.3	105.0	101.9	171.8	163.3	551.7	193.3	838.5
1971	103.0	96.6	101.3	108.0	109.2	176.9	157.7	558.6	208.8	915.4
1972	99.8	97.3	109.0	103.5	109.2	176.6	153.4	608.9	216.1	999.7
1973	108.4	109.5	109.6	102.4	102.4	191.4	168.1	667.1	221.3	1023.8
1974	104.2	103.8	109.3	101.3	108.8	199.3	174.4	729.4	224.3	1114.1
1975	104.6	102.8	102.2	103.5	103.2	208.6	179.4	745.5	232.2	1150.3
1976	102.5	98.1	115.6	102.2	101.0	213.8	176.0	862.0	237.4	1162.3
1977	101.7	99.0	98.1	100.3	105.2	217.4	174.2	846.0	238.0	1222.5
1978	94.9	109.8	105.5	104.9	100.0	206.2	191.3	892.2	249.8	1222.5
1979	107.6	106.7	101.3	114.6	96.6	221.8	204.2	904.2	286.3	1180.4
1980	101.4	99.7	112.2	107.0	107.7	224.9	203.6	1014.8	306.4	1270.7
1981	106.5	106.8	104.1	105.9	104.4	239.5	217.4	1056.6	324.4	1326.4
1982	111.3	110.9	108.5	113.4	112.3	266.5	241.2	1146.8	368.0	1490.1
1983	107.8	108.5	110.2	103.9	108.6	287.2	261.7	1263.9	382.5	1617.8

表31 续表 continued

年份 Year	农林牧渔业总产值指数(上年=100) Indices of Gross Output of Farming,Forestry, Animal Husbandry and Fishery(preceding year=100)					农林牧渔业总产值指数(1952=100) Indices of Gross Output of Farming,Forestry, Animal Husbandry and Fishery(1952=100)				
	总产值 Total	#农业 Farming	#林业 Forestry	#牧业 Animal Husbandry	#渔业 Fishery	总产值 Total	#农业 Farming	#林业 Forestry	#牧业 Animal Husbandry	#渔业 Fishery
1984	112.3	111.5	119.0	113.4	117.6	322.4	291.7	1504.4	433.6	1902.8
1985	103.4	99.8	104.5	117.2	118.9	333.4	291.2	1572.1	508.2	2263.0
1986	103.4	102.7	96.4	105.6	120.6	344.7	299.1	1516.2	536.6	2728.1
1987	105.8	106.4	99.7	103.2	118.1	364.7	318.3	1512.3	553.8	3221.0
1988	103.9	101.3	102.3	112.6	111.6	379.0	322.4	1547.5	623.8	3595.3
1989	103.1	102.5	100.4	105.5	107.2	390.8	330.4	1553.0	658.3	3852.7
1990	107.6	108.0	103.1	107.0	110.0	420.5	356.7	1601.1	704.4	4238.2
1991	103.7	100.9	108.0	108.8	107.6	436.0	360.1	1728.5	766.5	4562.1
1992	106.4	104.2	107.7	108.8	115.3	463.0	375.3	1861.1	834.1	5260.5
1993	107.8	105.2	108.0	110.8	118.4	500.0	394.9	2010.4	923.8	6222.5
1994	108.6	103.2	108.9	116.7	120.0	543.0	407.5	2189.3	1078.1	7467.0
1995	110.9	107.9	105.0	114.8	119.4	602.2	439.7	2298.8	1237.7	8915.6
1996	109.4	107.8	105.7	111.4	114.0	658.9	474.0	2428.1	1379.0	10161.8
1997	106.7	104.5	103.3	110.1	111.5	703.2	495.2	2508.7	1518.3	11331.4
1998	106.0	104.9	102.9	107.4	108.8	745.0	519.6	2582.0	1629.9	12328.6
1999	104.7	104.3	103.2	104.6	107.2	779.7	542.0	2664.6	1704.0	13215.0
2000	103.6	101.4	105.4	106.3	106.5	807.8	549.6	2808.5	1811.4	14074.0
2001	104.2	103.6	99.3	106.3	103.9	842.0	569.4	2788.4	1924.8	14622.3
2002	104.9	103.9	107.1	106.0	106.1	883.6	591.6	2985.6	2040.5	15518.0
2003	104.0	100.5	106.9	107.3	105.3	918.9	591.6	3194.6	2183.3	16293.9
2004	107.5	108.5	102.0	107.2	106.0	987.8	641.9	3258.5	2340.5	17271.5
2005	105.7	104.1	103.2	107.8	106.5	1044.1	668.2	3362.8	2523.1	18394.1
2006	105.4	105.4	105.6	105.0	106.0	1100.7	704.2	3550.5	2649.3	19496.5
2007	103.9	104.0	106.9	102.3	104.8	1143.2	731.7	3795.6	2718.2	20451.8
2008	105.7	104.8	108.1	106.8	106.0	1208.7	766.7	4102.1	2901.7	21671.7
2009	104.6	103.8	107.1	105.8	105.8	1264.3	796.0	4395.3	3069.9	22927.1
2010	104.4	104.1	106.5	104.1	105.5	1320.2	828.3	4681.9	3195.5	24198.4
2011	104.5	105.6	107.6	101.7	104.5	1379.0	875.0	5037.5	3250.2	25286.6
2012	104.9	104.4	106.7	105.2	105.1	1446.8	913.5	5374.0	3420.0	26588.4
2013	104.0	104.4	107.3	102.0	105.2	1504.2	953.5	5768.5	3488.6	27971.3

表32 全国农业生产条件
Production Condition for Agriculture

年份 Year	耕地面积 (千公顷) Cultivated Land (1 000 hectares)	农作物总播种面积 (千公顷) Total Sown Area (1 000 hectares)	#粮食面积 Grain Crops	农业机械总动力 (万千瓦) Total Power of Agricultural Machinery (10 000 kw)	有效灌溉面积 (千公顷) Irrigated Area (1 000 hectares)	化肥施用量 (万吨) Consumption of Chemical Fertilizers (10 000 tons)	农村用电量 (亿千瓦小时) Electricity Consumed in Rural Areas (100 million kwh)
1949	97881.3	124286.0	109959.0				
1950	100356.0	128826.0	114406.0				
1951	103671.3	132860.0	117769.0				
1952	107918.7	141256.0	123979.0	18.4	19959.0	7.8	0.5
1953	108528.7	144035.3	126637.0				
1954	109354.7	147925.3	128995.0				
1955	110156.7	151081.3	129839.0				
1956	111824.7	159172.7	136339.0				
1957	111830.0	157244.0	133633.0	121.4	27339.0	37.3	1.4
1958	106900.7	151994.7	127613.0		32791.0	54.6	2.4
1959	104579.3	142404.7	116023.0		35010.0	53.8	3.8
1960	104861.3	150642.0	122429.0		35083.0	66.2	6.9
1961	103310.7	143214.0	121443.0		32078.0	44.8	10.3
1962	102903.3	140228.7	121621.0	757.0	30545.0	63.0	16.1
1963	102726.7	140218.0	120741.0		30060.0	104.3	24.3
1964	103312.0	143531.3	122103.0		31518.0	129.0	27.8
1965	103594.0	143290.7	119627.0	1098.8	33055.0	194.2	37.1
1966	102958.0	146828.7	120988.0				
1967	102564.0	144942.7	119230.0				
1968	101553.3	139827.3	116157.0				
1969	101460.0	140944.0	117604.0				
1970	101134.7	143487.3	119267.0	2165.3	36000.0	351.2	95.7
1971	100699.3	145684.0	120846.0		36441.0	364.7	104.5
1972	100614.7	147918.7	121209.0		38005.0	420.7	132.8
1973	100212.7	148547.3	121156.0	4782.9	39223.0	511.1	139.9
1974	99912.0	148635.3	120976.0	5930.3	41269.0	485.8	156.1
1975	99708.0	149545.3	121062.0	7478.6	43284.0	536.9	183.1
1976	99388.0	149722.7	120743.0	8629.6	44981.0	582.8	204.8
1977	99247.3	149333.3	120400.0	10261.7	44999.0	648.0	221.9
1978	99389.3	150104.1	120587.2	11749.9	44965.0	884.0	253.1
1979	99498.0	148476.9	119262.7	13379.5	45003.1	1086.3	282.7
1980	99305.3	146379.5	117234.3	14745.7	44888.1	1269.4	320.8
1981	99037.3	145157.1	114957.7	15680.1	44573.8	1334.9	369.9
1982	98606.0	144754.6	113462.4	16614.2	44176.9	1513.4	396.9
1983	98359.3	143993.5	114047.2	18021.9	44644.1	1659.8	435.2
1984	97854.0	144221.3	112883.9	19497.2	44453.0	1739.8	464.0

表32 续表 continued

年份 Year	耕地面积 (千公顷) Cultivated Land (1 000 hectares)	农作物总播种面积 (千公顷) Total Sown Area (1 000 hectares)	#粮食面积 Grain Crops	农业机械总动力 (万千瓦) Total Power of Agricultural Machinery (10 000 kw)	有效灌溉面积 (千公顷) Irrigated Area (1 000 hectares)	化肥施用量 (万吨) Consumption of Chemical Fertilizers (10 000 tons)	农村用电量 (亿千瓦小时) Electricity Consumed in Rural Areas (100 million kwh)
1985	96846.0	143625.9	108845.1	20912.5	44035.9	1775.8	508.9
1986	96230.0	144204.0	110932.6	22950.0	44225.8	1930.6	586.7
1987	95888.7	144956.5	111267.8	24836.0	44403.0	1999.3	658.8
1988	95722.0	144868.9	110122.6	26575.0	44375.9	2141.5	712.0
1989	95656.0	146553.9	112204.7	28067.0	44917.2	2357.1	790.5
1990	95672.7	148362.3	113465.9	28707.7	47403.1	2590.3	844.5
1991	95653.3	149585.8	112313.6	29388.6	47822.1	2805.1	963.2
1992	95426.0	149007.1	110559.7	30308.4	48590.1	2930.2	1107.1
1993	95101.3	147740.7	110508.7	31816.6	48727.9	3151.9	1244.9
1994	94906.7	148240.6	109543.7	33802.5	48759.1	3317.9	1473.9
1995	94970.9	149879.3	110060.4	36118.1	49281.2	3593.7	1655.7
1996	130039.2	152380.6	112547.9	38546.9	50381.4	3827.9	1812.7
1997	130039.2	153969.2	112912.1	42015.6	51238.5	3980.7	1980.1
1998	130039.2	155705.7	113787.4	45207.7	52295.6	4083.7	2042.1
1999	130039.2	156372.8	113161.0	48996.1	53158.4	4124.3	2173.4
2000	130039.2	156299.8	108462.5	52573.6	53820.3	4146.4	2421.3
2001	130039.2	155707.9	106080.0	55172.1	54249.4	4253.8	2610.8
2002	130039.2	154635.5	103890.8	57929.9	54354.9	4339.4	2993.4
2003	130039.2	152415.0	99410.4	60386.5	54014.2	4411.6	3432.9
2004	130039.2	153552.5	101606.0	64027.9	54478.4	4636.6	3933.0
2005	130039.2	155487.7	104278.4	68397.8	55029.3	4766.2	4375.7
2006	121735.6	152149.5	104957.7	72522.1	55750.5	4927.7	4895.8
2007	121735.2	153463.9	105638.4	76589.6	56518.3	5107.8	5509.9
2008	121715.9	156265.7	106792.6	82190.4	58471.7	5239.0	5713.2
2009		158613.5	108985.7	87496.1	59261.4	5404.4	6104.4
2010		160674.8	109876.1	92780.5	60347.7	5561.7	6632.3
2011		162283.2	110573.0	97734.7	61681.6	5704.2	7139.6
2012		163415.7	111204.6	102559.0	62490.5	5838.8	7508.5
2013	135157.3	164626.9	111955.6	103906.8	63473.3	5911.9	8549.5

注：1996-2005年耕地面积（总资源)来源于国土资源部、国家统计局、全国农业普查办公室“关于土地利用现状调查数据成果的公报”，数据为1996年10月31日时点数，2006年起为国土资源部数据。

a) Data of cultivated land(total area) come from the "Communique of Main Data on Land Use Survey" issued by the Ministry of Land and Resources, National Bureau of Statistics, and National Agricultural Census Office of China from 1996 to 2005. Data are at Oct.31,1996. Data are from the Ministry of Land and Resources since 2006.

表33 全国主要农业产品产量

Yield of Major Farm Crops, Forest Products, Livestock Products and Aquatic Products

单位：万吨 (10 000 tons)

年份 Year	粮食 Grain	棉花 Cotton	油料 Oil-Bearing Crops	黄红麻 Jute and Ambary Hemp	糖料 Sugar	茶叶 Tea	水果 Fruits	蔬菜 Vegetable
1949	11318.0	44.4	256.4	3.7	283.3	4.1	120.0	
1950	13212.5	69.2	297.2	7.9	337.8	6.5	132.5	
1951	14368.5	103.1	362.0	25.0	498.9	7.9	156.4	
1952	16391.5	130.4	419.3	30.6	759.5	8.2	244.3	
1953	16683.0	117.5	385.6	13.8	771.4	8.5	296.9	
1954	16951.5	106.5	430.5	13.7	958.1	9.2	297.8	
1955	18393.5	151.8	482.7	25.7	970.6	10.8	255.0	
1956	19274.5	144.5	508.6	25.8	1030.1	12.1	310.5	
1957	19504.5	164.0	419.6	30.1	1189.3	11.2	324.7	
1958	19765.0	196.9	477.0	26.7	1563.1	13.5	390.0	
1959	16968.0	170.9	410.4	22.6	1214.7	15.2	425.0	
1960	14384.5	106.3	194.1	20.2	985.5	13.6	397.7	
1961	13650.0	80.0	181.4	12.3	506.5	7.9	284.1	
1962	15441.0	75.0	200.3	13.2	378.2	7.4	271.2	
1963	17000.0	120.0	245.8	19.8	832.0	8.4	287.6	
1964	18750.0	166.3	336.8	23.5	1346.5	9.2		
1965	19452.5	209.8	362.5	27.9	1537.5	10.1	323.9	
1966	21400.0	233.7	391.9	34.9	1403.5	10.6		
1967	21782.0	235.4	398.5	39.8	1524.1	11.3		
1968	20905.5	235.4	343.2	39.6	1249.6	11.8		
1969	21097.0	207.9	333.1	34.4	1288.3	12.2		
1970	23995.5	227.7	377.2	34.1	1556.0	13.6	374.5	
1971	25014.0	210.5	411.3	30.4	1526.4	15.3	386.3	
1972	24048.0	195.8	411.8	37.9	1873.8	17.0	444.2	
1973	26493.5	256.2	418.6	55.8	1964.3	18.2	518.2	
1974	27527.0	246.1	441.4	63.0	1872.1	19.8	515.3	
1975	28451.5	238.1	452.1	69.9	1914.3	21.1	538.1	
1976	28630.5	205.5	400.8	73.1	1956.3	23.3	540.4	
1977	28272.5	204.9	401.7	86.1	2020.8	25.2	568.5	
1978	30476.5	216.7	521.8	108.8	2381.9	26.8	657.0	
1979	33211.5	220.7	643.5	108.9	2461.3	27.7	701.5	
1980	32055.5	270.7	769.1	109.8	2911.3	30.4	679.3	
1981	32502.0	296.8	1020.5	126.0	3602.8	34.3	780.1	
1982	35450.0	359.8	1181.7	106.0	4359.4	39.7	771.3	

注：2003年起水果总产量包括种植业中的瓜果类产量。

a) Data of output of fruit after 2003 include yield of melon and fruit.

表33 续表 1 continued

单位：万吨 (10 000 tons)

年份 Year	粮食 Grain	棉花 Cotton	油料 Oil-Bearing Crops	黄红麻 Jute and Ambary Hemp	糖料 Sugar	茶叶 Tea	水果 Fruits	蔬菜 Vegetable
1983	38727.5	463.7	1055.0	101.9	4032.3	40.1	948.7	
1984	40730.5	625.8	1191.0	149.2	4780.4	41.4	984.5	
1985	37910.8	414.7	1578.4	411.9	6046.8	43.2	1163.9	
1986	39151.2	354.0	1473.8	142.0	5852.5	46.0	1347.7	
1987	40297.7	424.5	1527.8	113.7	5550.4	50.8	1667.9	
1988	39408.1	414.9	1320.3	107.8	6187.5	54.5	1666.1	
1989	40754.9	378.8	1295.2	66.0	5803.8	53.5	1831.9	
1990	44624.3	450.8	1613.2	72.6	7214.5	54.0	1874.4	
1991	43529.3	567.5	1638.3	51.3	8418.7	54.2	2176.1	
1992	44265.8	450.8	1641.2	61.9	8808.0	56.0	2440.1	
1993	45648.8	373.9	1803.9	67.2	7624.2	60.0	3011.2	
1994	44510.1	434.1	1989.6	35.5	7345.2	58.8	3499.8	
1995	46661.8	476.8	2250.3	37.1	7940.1	58.8	4214.6	25726.7
1996	50453.5	420.3	2210.6	36.5	8360.2	59.3	4652.8	30123.1
1997	49417.1	460.3	2157.4	43.0	9386.5	61.3	5089.3	35962.4
1998	51229.5	450.1	2313.9	24.8	9790.4	66.5	5452.9	38491.9
1999	50838.6	382.9	2601.2	16.4	8334.1	67.6	6237.6	40513.5
2000	46217.5	441.7	2954.8	12.6	7635.3	68.3	6225.1	44467.0
2001	45263.7	532.4	2864.9	10.6	8655.1	70.2	6658.0	48422.4
2002	45705.8	491.6	2897.2	15.9	10292.7	74.5	6952.0	52860.6
2003	43069.5	486.0	2811.0	10.0	9641.6	76.8	14517.4	54032.3
2004	46946.9	632.4	3065.9	8.7	9570.7	83.5	15340.9	55064.7
2005	48402.2	571.4	3077.1	8.3	9451.9	93.5	16120.1	56451.5
2006	49804.2	753.3	2640.3	8.7	10460.0	102.8	17102.0	53953.1
2007	50160.3	762.4	2568.7	9.9	12188.2	116.5	18136.3	56452.0
2008	52870.9	749.2	2952.8	8.4	13419.6	125.8	19220.2	59240.3
2009	53082.1	637.7	3154.3	7.5	12276.6	135.9	20395.5	61823.8
2010	54647.7	596.1	3230.1	6.9	12008.5	147.5	21401.4	65099.4
2011	57120.8	659.8	3306.8	7.5	12516.5	162.3	22768.2	67929.7
2012	58958.0	683.6	3436.8	6.8	13485.4	179.0	24056.8	70883.1
2013	60193.8	629.9	3517.0	6.1	13746.1	192.4	25093.0	73512.0

表33 续表 2 continued

年份 Year	木材 (万立方米) Lumber (10 000 cu.m)	肉类产量 (万吨) Output of Meat (10 000 tons)	#猪牛羊肉 Output of Pork,Beef and Mutton	奶类 (万吨) Milk (10 000 tons)	#牛奶 Cow Milk	禽蛋 (万吨) Poultry Eggs (10 000 tons)	水产品产量 (万吨) Total Aquatic Products (10 000 tons)	海水产品 Seawater Aquatic Products	淡水产品 Freshwater Aquatic Products
1949							44.8		
1950							91.0	55.0	36.0
1951							133.0	81.0	52.0
1952			338.5				166.6	106.0	60.6
1953							190.0	122.0	68.0
1954							229.0	139.0	90.0
1955							252.0	166.0	86.0
1956							265.0	171.0	94.0
1957			398.5				311.6	193.7	117.9
1958							281.0	171.0	110.0
1959							309.0	186.0	123.0
1960							304.0	187.0	117.0
1961							231.0	143.0	88.0
1962			194.0				228.3	149.8	78.5
1963							261.0	176.0	85.0
1964							280.0	188.0	92.0
1965			551.0				298.4	201.4	97.0
1966							310.0	218.0	92.0
1967							305.0	219.0	86.0
1968							271.0	192.0	79.0
1969							290.0	205.0	85.0
1970			596.5				318.5	228.1	90.4
1971							350.0	256.0	94.0
1972							384.0	291.0	93.0
1973							393.0	291.0	102.0
1974							428.0	325.0	103.0
1975			797.0		88.9		441.2	334.7	106.5
1976			780.5				448.0	342.0	106.0
1977			780.0				470.0	362.0	108.0
1978	5162		865.3		88.3		465.4	359.5	105.9
1979	5439	1062.4	797.0		106.5		430.5	318.9	111.6
1980	5359	1205.4	1205.4		114.1		449.7	325.7	124.0
1981	4942	1260.9	1260.9		129.1		460.6	323.2	137.3

表33 续表 3 continued

年份 Year	木材 (万立方米) Lumber (10 000 cu.m)	肉类产量 (万吨) Output of Meat (10 000 tons)	#猪牛羊肉 Output of Pork,Beef and Mutton	奶类 (万吨) Milk (10 000 tons)	#牛奶 Cow Milk	禽蛋 (万吨) Poultry Eggs (10 000 tons)	水产品产量 (万吨) Total Aquatic Products (10 000 tons)	海水产品 Seawater Aquatic Products	淡水产品 Freshwater Aquatic Products
1982	5041	1350.8	1350.8		161.8	280.9	515.5	359.3	156.2
1983	5232	1402.1	1402.1		184.5	332.3	545.8	361.7	184.1
1984	6385	1540.6	1540.6		218.6	431.6	619.3	394.4	225.0
1985	6323	1926.5	1760.7	289.4	249.9	534.7	705.2	419.7	285.4
1986	6502	2112.4	1917.1	332.9	289.9	555.0	823.6	475.4	348.2
1987	6408	2215.5	1986.0	378.8	330.1	590.2	955.3	548.2	407.2
1988	6218	2479.5	2193.6	418.9	366.0	695.5	1060.9	605.7	455.2
1989	5802	2628.5	2326.2	435.8	381.3	719.8	1151.7	661.2	490.5
1990	5571	2857.0	2513.5	475.1	415.7	794.6	1237.0	713.3	523.7
1991	5807	3144.4	2723.8	524.3	464.6	922.0	1350.8	800.1	550.7
1992	6174	3430.7	2940.6	563.9	503.1	1019.9	1557.1	933.7	623.5
1993	6392	3841.5	3225.3	563.7	498.6	1179.8	1823.0	1076.0	747.0
1994	6615	4499.3	3692.7	608.9	528.8	1479.0	2143.2	1241.5	901.7
1995	6767	4076.4	3304.0	672.8	576.4	1676.7	2517.2	1439.1	1078.1
1996	6710	4584.0	3694.7	735.8	629.4	1965.2	3288.1	2012.9	1275.2
1997	6395	5268.8	4249.9	681.1	601.1	1897.1	3118.6	1888.1	1230.5
1998	5966	5723.8	4598.2	745.4	662.9	2021.3	3382.7	2044.5	1338.1
1999	5237	5949.0	4762.3	806.9	717.6	2134.7	3570.1	2145.3	1424.9
2000	4724	6013.9	4743.2	919.1	827.4	2182.0	3706.2	2203.9	1502.3
2001	4552	6105.8	4832.1	1122.9	1025.5	2210.1	3795.9	2233.5	1562.4
2002	4436	6234.3	4928.4	1400.4	1299.8	2265.7	3954.9	2298.5	1656.4
2003	4759	6443.3	5089.8	1848.6	1746.3	2333.1	4077.0	2332.8	1744.2
2004	5197	6608.7	5234.3	2368.4	2260.6	2370.6	4246.6	2404.5	1842.1
2005	5560	6938.9	5473.5	2864.8	2753.4	2438.1	4419.9	2465.9	1954.0
2006	6612	7089.0	5591.0	3302.5	3193.4	2424.0	4583.6	2509.6	2074.0
2007	6977	6865.7	5283.8	3633.4	3525.2	2529.0	4747.5	2550.9	2196.6
2008	8108	7278.7	5614.0	3731.5	3555.8	2702.2	4895.6	2598.3	2297.3
2009	7068	7649.7	5915.7	3677.7	3518.8	2742.5	5116.4	2681.6	2434.8
2010	8090	7925.8	6123.1	3748.0	3575.6	2762.7	5373.0	2797.5	2575.5
2011	8146	7965.1	6101.0	3810.7	3657.8	2811.4	5603.2	2908.0	2695.2
2012	8175	8387.2	6405.9	3875.4	3743.6	2861.2	5907.7	3033.3	2874.3
2013	8438	8535.0	6574.4	3649.5	3531.4	2876.1	6172.0	3138.8	3033.2

表34 全国受灾和成灾面积
Areas Covered and Affected by Natural Disaster

单位：千公顷 (1 000 hectares)

年份 Year	受灾面积 Areas Covered	成灾面积 Areas Affected	成灾面积占受灾面积% Percentage of Disaster Areas Affected to Areas Covered(%)	水灾 Flood 受灾面积 Areas Covered	水灾 Flood 成灾面积 Areas Affected	旱灾 Drought 受灾面积 Areas Covered	旱灾 Drought 成灾面积 Areas Affected
1950	10637	5122	48.2	6559	4710	2398	412
1951	14240	3775	26.5	4173	1476	7829	2299
1952	9137	4433	48.5	2794	1844	4236	2589
1953	23415	7079	30.2	7409	3198	8616	675
1954	21451	12593	58.7	16131	11305	2988	259
1955	19993	7869	39.4	5247	3073	13433	4139
1956	22191	15329	69.1	14377	10991	3127	2063
1957	29149	14983	51.4	8083	6032	17205	7400
1958	30963	7821	25.3	4279	1441	22361	5031
1959	44629	13728	30.8	4813	1817	33807	11173
1960	65455	24977	38.2	10155	4975	38125	16177
1961	61749	28834	46.7	8871	5395	37847	18654
1962	37175	17286	46.5	9810	6318	20808	8691
1963	32651	20023	61.3	14071	10479	16865	9021
1964	21639	12635	58.4	14933	10038	4219	1423
1965	20804	11223	53.9	5587	2813	13631	8107
1966	24207	9757	40.3	2513	950	20015	8106
1967	6441	895	13.9	1885	333	4076	533
1970	9974	3295	33.0	3129	1234	5723	1931
1971	31051	7445	24.0	3989	1481	25049	5319
1972	40458	17177	42.5	4083	1259	30699	13605
1973	36493	7618	20.9	6235	2577	27202	3928
1974	38647	6526	16.9	6399	2296	25553	2737
1975	35379	10239	28.9	6817	3467	24832	5318
1976	42499	11437	26.9	4197	1327	27492	7848
1977	52021	15159	29.1	9095	4989	29852	7006
1978	50807	24457	48.1	3109	2012	32641	16564
1979	39367	15790	40.1	6757	2868	24646	9316
1980	50025	29777	59.5	9687	6070	21901	14174
1981	39786	18743	47.1	8625	3973	25693	12134
1982	33133	16117	48.6	8361	4397	20697	9972

表34 续表 continued

单位：千公顷 (1 000 hectares)

年份 Year	受灾面积 Areas Covered	成灾面积 Areas Affected	成灾面积占受灾面积% Percentage of Disaster Areas Affected to Areas Covered(%)	水灾 Flood 受灾面积 Areas Covered	水灾 Flood 成灾面积 Areas Affected	旱灾 Drought 受灾面积 Areas Covered	旱灾 Drought 成灾面积 Areas Affected
1983	34713	16209	46.7	12162	5747	16089	7586
1984	31887	15607	48.9	10632	5395	15819	7015
1985	44365	22705	51.2	14197	8949	22989	10063
1986	47135	23656	50.2	9155	5601	31042	14765
1987	42086	20393	48.5	8686	4104	24920	13033
1988	50874	24503	48.2	11949	6128	32904	15303
1989	46991	24449	52.0	11328	5917	29358	15262
1990	38474	17819	46.3	11804	5605	18175	7805
1991	55472	27814	50.1	24596	14614	24914	10559
1992	51332	25893	50.4	9422	4463	32981	17047
1993	48827	23134	47.4	16390	8608	21097	8656
1994	55046	31382	57.0	17328	10744	30423	17050
1995	45824	22268	48.6	12734	7604	23455	10402
1996	46991	21234	45.2	18147	10855	20152	6247
1997	53427	30307	56.7	11415	5839	33516	20012
1998	50145	25181	50.2	22292	13785	14236	5060
1999	49980	26734	53.5	9020	5071	30156	16614
2000	54688	34374	62.9	7323	4321	40541	26784
2001	52215	31793	60.9	6042	3614	38472	23698
2002	46946	27160	57.9	12288	7388	22124	13174
2003	54506	32516	59.7	19208	12289	24852	14470
2004	37106	16297	43.9	7314	3747	17253	8482
2005	38818	19966	51.4	10932	6047	16028	8479
2006	41091	24632	59.9	8003	4569	20738	13411
2007	48992	25064	51.2	10463	5105	29386	16170
2008	39990	22283	55.7	6477	3656	12137	6798
2009	47214	21234	45.0	7613	3162	29259	13197
2010	37426	18538	49.5	17525	7024	13259	8987
2011	32471	12441	38.3	6863	2840	16304	6599
2012	24962	11475	46.0	7730	4145	9340	3509
2013	31350	14303	45.6	8757	4859	14100	5852

表35 全国工业企业主要经济指标
Main Indicators of Industrial Enterprises

年 份 Year	工业企业单位数 (万个) Number of Industrial Enterprises (10 000 units)	资产合计 (亿元) Total Assets (100 million yuan)	出口交货值 (亿元) Total Export (100 million yuan)	主营业务收入 (亿元) Revenue from Principal Business (100 million yuan)	利润总额 (亿元) Total Profits (100 million yuan)	税金总额 (亿元) Total Tax (100 million yuan)
1978	34.84				599	
1979	35.50	3964		3999	654	
1980	37.73	4233		4459	692	367
1981	38.15	4538		4644	682	399
1982	38.86	4905		5059	704	437
1983	39.25	5299		5585	772	464
1984	43.72	5783		6379	852	534
1985	46.32	6972		7899	944	727
1986	49.93	8149		8963	878	788
1987	49.36	9490		10890	1005	888
1988	50.00	11149		14001	1190	1099
1989	50.54	13553		15847	1000	1275
1990	50.44	15953		16793	560	1386
1991	50.48	18804		20597	643	1591
1992	50.21	28321		25866	972	1828
1993	52.01	46601		38084	1603	2321
1994	53.18	62583		42399	1797	3139
1995	59.21	79234		52936	1635	3415
1996	57.88	90016		57970	1490	3657
1997	53.44	103400		63451	1703	4037
1998	16.51	108822	10842	64149	1458	4064
1999	16.20	116969	11545	69852	2288	4414
2000	16.29	126211	14575	84152	4393	5119
2001	17.13	135403	16245	93733	4733	5572
2002	18.16	146218	20055	109486	5784	6238

表35 续表 continued

年 份 Year	工业企业单位数 (万个) Number of Industrial Enterprises (10 000 units)	资产合计 (亿元) Total Assets (100 million yuan)	出口交货值 (亿元) Total Export (100 million yuan)	主营业务收入 (亿元) Revenue from Principal Business (100 million yuan)	利润总额 (亿元) Total Profits (100 million yuan)	税金总额 (亿元) Total Tax (100 million yuan)
2003	19.62	168808	26942	143172	8337	7537
2004	21.95	195262	36841	187815	11342	8864
2005	27.18	244784	47741	248544	14803	11518
2006	30.20	291215	60560	313592	19504	14454
2007	33.68	353037	73393	399717	27155	18422
2008	42.61	431306	82498	500020	30562	23968
2009	43.44	493693	72052	542522	34542	26486
2010	45.29	592882	89910	697744	53050	33656
2011	32.56	675797	99612	841830	61396	38972
2012	34.38	768421	106610	929292	61910	44029
2013	35.25	850626	113471	1029150	62831	45748

注：1.本表统计范围：1997年及以前年份为乡及乡以上独立核算工业企业；1998-2006年为全部国有及年产品销售收入在500万元及以上非国有工业企业；2007-2010年为年主营业务收入在500万元及以上的工业企业；2011年及以后年份为年主营业务收入在2000万元及以上工业企业。
2.资产合计一栏，1992年及以前年份为资金总额。
3.主营业务收入一栏，2003年及以前年份为产品销售收入。
4.2013年为统计快报数据。

a) Statistical coverage of this table: industrial enterprises of independence accounting at county level and above before 1997, all state-owned and non-state owned industrial enterprises with sales revenue over 5 million yuan from 1998 to 2006, and industrial enterprises with principal business over 5 million yuan from 2007 to 2010, and industrial enterprises with principal business over 20 million yuan since 2011.
b) Total assets referred to total funds before 1992.
c) Revenue from principal business referred to sales revenue of products before 2003.
d) Data of 2013 are preliminary statistics.

表36 全国工业企业主要经济效益指标

Main Indicators on Economic Benefit of Industrial Enterprises

年份 Year	总资产贡献率 (%) Ratio of Assets to Industrial Output Value (%)	资产负债率 (%) Assets-Liability Ratio (%)	流动资产周转次数 (次/年) Turnover of Working Capital (times/year)	成本费用利润率 (%) Ratio of Profits to Industrial Cost (%)
1998	7.1	63.7	1.4	2.4
1999	7.45	61.83	1.47	3.42
2000	9.00	60.81	1.62	5.56
2001	8.91	58.97	1.66	5.35
2002	9.45	58.72	1.80	5.62
2003	10.50	58.96	2.00	6.28
2004	11.01	57.97	2.19	6.43
2005	11.82	57.81	2.35	6.42
2006	12.74	57.46	2.50	6.74
2007	14.09	57.48	2.63	7.43
2008	13.96	57.71	2.67	6.61
2009	13.44	57.88	2.43	6.91
2010	15.68	57.41	2.50	8.31
2011	16.09	58.10	2.62	7.71
2012	15.11	57.96	2.57	7.11
2013	15.00	57.81	2.67	6.60

表37　全国主要工业产品产量
Output of Major Industrial Products

年份 Year	原煤（亿吨）Coal (100 million tons)	原油（万吨）Crude Oil (10 000 tons)	天然气（亿立方米）Natural Gas (100 million cu.m)	原盐（万吨）Salt (10 000 tons)	成品糖（万吨）Refined Sugar (10 000 tons)	卷烟（亿支）Cigarettes (100 million pieces)	纱（万吨）Yarn (10 000 tons)	布（亿米）Cloth (100 million m)	机制纸及纸板（万吨）Machine-made Paper and Paperboards (10 000 tons)
1949	0.32	12	0.07	299.00	20.00	160.00	32.70	18.90	11.00
1950	0.43	20	0.07	246.00	24.00	185.00	43.70	25.20	14.00
1951	0.53	31	0.03	435.00	30.00	200.00	48.70	30.60	24.00
1952	0.66	44	0.08	495.00	45.00	265.00	65.60	38.30	37.00
1953	0.70	62	0.11	357.00	64.00	355.00	74.50	46.90	43.00
1954	0.84	79	0.15	489.00	69.00	373.00	83.40	52.30	52.00
1955	0.98	97	0.17	754.00	72.00	357.00	72.00	43.60	58.00
1956	1.10	116	0.26	494.00	81.00	391.00	95.20	57.70	73.00
1957	1.31	146	0.70	828.00	86.00	446.00	84.40	50.50	91.00
1958	2.70	226	1.10	1040.00	90.00	475.00	126.20	64.60	122.00
1959	3.69	373	2.90	1106.00	110.00	550.00	153.10	75.70	170.00
1960	3.97	520	10.40	1287.00	44.00	449.00	109.30	54.50	180.00
1961	2.78	531	14.70	1113.00	39.00	254.00	66.90	31.10	110.00
1962	2.20	575	12.10	994.00	34.00	244.00	54.80	25.30	112.00
1963	2.17	648	10.20	1056.00	44.00	323.00	67.80	33.40	128.00
1964	2.15	848	10.60	501.00	107.00	413.00	97.00	47.10	145.00
1965	2.32	1131	11.00	1147.00	146.00	478.00	130.00	62.80	173.00
1966	2.52	1455	13.40	998.00	159.00	540.00	156.50	73.10	209.00
1967	2.06	1388	14.60	1043.00	148.00	490.00	135.20	65.60	196.00
1968	2.20	1599	14.00	1325.00	151.00	521.00	137.70	64.40	177.00
1969	2.66	2174	19.60	966.00	121.00	677.00	180.50	82.10	217.00
1970	3.54	3065	28.70	1109.00	135.00	783.00	205.20	91.50	241.00
1971	3.92	3941	37.40	1235.00	141.00	701.00	190.00	84.20	263.00
1972	4.10	4567	48.40	1386.00	155.00	745.00	188.60	83.50	282.00
1973	4.17	5361	59.80	1076.00	191.00	846.00	196.70	87.10	313.00
1974	4.13	6485	75.30	1456.00	184.00	872.00	180.30	80.80	299.00
1975	4.82	7706	88.50	1481.00	174.00	992.00	210.80	94.00	341.00

注：1.原煤包括无烟煤、烟煤、褐煤,不包括石煤。
2.原油包括天然原油和人造原油。
3.成品糖1997年及以前名称为糖，产量包括土糖，1998-2004年名称为机制糖。
4.卷烟2003年及以前计量单位为万箱。

a) Coal includes anthracite, bituminous coal and lignite, but does not include stone coal.
b) Crude oil includes natural and synthetic crude oil.
c) Machined-made sugar was called sugar in 1997 and before, in which the homemade sugar was included.1998-2004 was called machine-made sugar.
d) Unit of cigarettes in 2003 and before was 10 000 boxes.

表37 续表 1 continued

年份 Year	原煤 （亿吨） Coal (100 million tons)	原油 （万吨） Crude Oil (10 000 tons)	天然气 （亿立方米） Natural Gas (100 million cu.m)	原盐 （万吨） Salt (10 000 tons)	成品糖 （万吨） Refined Sugar (10 000 tons)	卷烟 （亿支） Cigarettes (100 million pieces)	纱 （万吨） Yarn (10 000 tons)	布 （亿米） Cloth (100 million m)	机制纸及纸板 （万吨） Machine-made Paper and Paperboards (10 000 tons)
1976	4.83	8716	101.00	1401.00	165.00	982.00	196.00	88.40	341.00
1977	5.50	9364	121.20	1710.00	182.00	1211.00	223.00	101.50	377.00
1978	6.18	10405	137.30	1953.00	227.00	1182.00	238.20	110.30	439.00
1979	6.35	10615	145.10	1477.00	250.00	1303.00	263.50	121.50	493.00
1980	6.20	10595	142.70	1728.00	257.00	1520.00	292.60	134.70	535.00
1981	6.22	10122	127.40	1832.00	317.00	1704.00	317.00	142.70	540.00
1982	6.66	10212	119.30	1638.00	338.00	1885.00	335.40	153.50	589.00
1983	7.15	10607	122.10	1613.00	377.00	1938.00	327.00	148.80	661.00
1984	7.89	11461	124.30	1642.00	380.00	2132.00	321.90	137.00	756.00
1985	8.72	12490	129.30	1479.00	451.00	2370.00	353.50	146.70	911.00
1986	8.94	13069	137.60	1766.00	525.00	2596.00	397.80	164.70	998.00
1987	9.28	13414	138.90	1764.00	506.00	2881.00	436.80	173.10	1141.00
1988	9.80	13705	142.60	2264.00	461.00	3096.00	465.70	187.90	1270.00
1989	10.54	13764	150.50	2829.00	501.00	3195.00	476.70	189.20	1333.00
1990	10.80	13831	152.98	2023.00	582.00	3298.00	462.60	188.80	1372.00
1991	10.87	14099	160.73	2410.00	640.00	3226.00	460.80	181.70	1479.00
1992	11.16	14210	157.88	2838.00	829.00	3285.00	501.70	190.70	1725.00
1993	11.50	14524	167.65	2943.00	771.00	3376.00	501.50	203.00	1914.00
1994	12.40	14608	175.59	2996.00	592.00	3432.00	489.50	211.30	2138.00
1995	13.61	15005	179.47	2977.72	558.64	3485.02	542.20	260.18	2812.30
1996	13.97	15733	201.14	2903.57	640.20	3401.92	512.21	209.10	2638.20
1997	13.88	16074	227.03	3082.66	702.58	3377.42	559.83	248.79	2733.20
1998	13.32	16100	232.79	2242.52	826.00	3374.00	542.00	241.00	2125.63
1999	13.64	16000	251.98	2812.36	861.00	3340.00	567.00	250.00	2159.30
2000	13.84	16300	272.00	3128.00	700.00	3397.00	657.00	277.00	2486.94
2001	14.72	16396	303.29	3410.51	653.10	3402.10	760.68	290.00	3777.07
2002	15.50	16700	326.61	3602.43	926.00	3467.08	850.00	322.39	4666.99
2003	18.35	16960	350.15	3437.70	1083.94	3580.86	983.58	353.52	4849.33
2004	21.23	17587	414.60	4043.44	1033.70	18736.35	1291.34	482.10	5413.27
2005	23.50	18135	493.20	4661.06	912.37	19389.08	1450.54	484.39	6205.42
2006	25.29	18477	585.53	5663.13	949.07	20218.13	1742.96	598.55	6863.02
2007	26.92	18632	692.40	6166.97	1271.38	21438.84	1958.42	675.26	7792.43
2008	28.02	19043	802.99	6664.43	1432.61	22199.20	2055.72	723.05	8404.30
2009	29.73	18949	852.69	6662.79	1338.35	22901.50	2266.45	753.42	8965.13
2010	32.35	20241	948.48	7037.76	1117.59	23752.60	2572.82	800.00	9832.63
2011	35.20	20288	1026.89	6742.16	1187.43	24474.00	2717.86	814.14	11010.89
2012	36.50	20571	1070.35	6911.78	1409.47	25160.90	2984.00	848.94	10956.54
2013	36.80	20947	1170.46	6460.30	1589.73	25604.00	3200.00	882.66	11368.18

表37　续表 2 continued

年份 Year	焦炭 (万吨) Coke (10 000 tons)	硫酸 (万吨) Sulfuric Acid (10 000 tons)	烧　碱 (万吨) Caustic Soda (10 000 tons)	纯　碱 (万吨) Caustic Soda (10 000 tons)	乙烯 (万吨) Ethylene (10 000 tons)	化肥 (万吨) Chemical Fertilizers (10 000 tons)	化学纤维 (万吨) Chemical Fiber (10 000 tons)	水泥 (万吨) Cement (10 000 tons)	平板玻璃 (万重量箱) Plate Glass (10 000 weight cases)
1949	54	4.0	1.5	8.8		0.60		66	108
1950	150	6.9	2.3	16.0		1.50		141	135
1951	203	14.9	4.8	18.5		2.80		249	181
1952	289	19.0	7.9	19.2		3.90		286	213
1953	355	26.0	8.8	22.3		5.00		388	242
1954	450	34.4	11.5	30.9		6.70		460	315
1955	548	37.5	13.7	40.5		7.90		450	333
1956	637	51.7	15.6	47.6		11.10		639	308
1957	830	63.2	19.8	50.6		15.10	0.02	686	462
1958	2174	74.4	27.4	64.7		19.40	0.03	930	527
1959	4504	106.1	37.2	80.8		26.60	0.54	1227	600
1960	5647	133.0	40.7	81.5	0.07	40.50	1.06	1565	670
1961	2809	90.4	27.7	48.6	0.01	29.70	0.53	621	332
1962	1342	96.8	29.0	51.9	0.08	46.40	1.36	600	399
1963	1106	130.6	33.8	66.4	0.18	64.80	1.89	806	497
1964	1113	170.4	41.1	69.5	0.20	100.80	3.21	1209	539
1965	1333	234.0	55.6	88.0	0.30	172.60	5.01	1634	599
1966	1634	290.9	69.3	106.6	0.54	240.90	7.58	2015	719
1967	1102	198.3	57.8	91.5	0.36	164.10	5.22	1462	578
1968	1098	141.5	49.6	70.1	0.37	110.90	3.60	1262	573
1969	1676	234.3	70.4	89.4	0.51	174.90	6.66	1829	807
1970	2330	291.4	89.2	107.7	1.51	243.50	10.09	2575	928
1971	3023	357.9	105.5	115.5	3.19	299.40	11.99	3258	1051
1972	3437	400.5	111.5	119.7	4.44	370.10	13.73	3547	1048
1973	3451	468.1	121.0	120.4	5.10	459.20	14.88	3731	1042
1974	3104	442.7	112.6	110.6	6.10	422.20	14.26	3709	1024
1975	3680	484.7	128.9	124.3	6.47	524.70	15.48	4626	1262
1976	3570	450.8	121.5	111.7	13.35	524.40	14.61	4670	1261
1977	3929	537.5	138.6	107.7	30.27	723.80	18.98	5565	1481
1978	4690	661.0	164.0	132.9	38.03	869.30	28.46	6524	1784
1979	4583	699.8	182.6	148.6	43.49	1065.40	32.63	7390	2083

表37 续表 3 continued

年份 Year	焦炭 (万吨) Coke (10 000 tons)	硫酸 (万吨) Sulfuric Acid (10 000 tons)	烧 碱 (万吨) Caustic Soda (10 000 tons)	纯 碱 (万吨) Caustic Soda (10 000 tons)	乙烯 (万吨) Ethylene (10 000 tons)	化肥 (万吨) Chemical Fertilizers (10 000 tons)	化学纤维 (万吨) Chemical Fiber (10 000 tons)	水泥 (万吨) Cement (10 000 tons)	平板玻璃 (万重量箱) Plate Glass (10 000 weight cases)
1980	4343	764.3	192.3	161.3	48.99	1232.10	45.03	7986	2466
1981	3895	780.7	192.3	165.2	50.48	1239.00	52.73	8290	2701
1982	4019	817.5	207.3	173.5	56.49	1278.10	51.70	9520	3154
1983	4220	869.6	212.3	179.3	65.37	1378.90	54.07	10825	3647
1984	4557	817.2	222.2	188	64.80	1460.20	73.49	12302	4190
1985	4802	676.4	235.3	201.1	65.21	1322.20	94.78	14595	4942
1986	5276	763.1	251.8	214.6	69.52	1395.70	101.73	16606	5202
1987	5795	983.3	273.9	236.3	93.72	1672.20	117.50	18625	5803
1988	6108	1111.3	300.5	260.9	123.21	1740.20	130.12	21014	7293
1989	6624	1153.3	321.1	304.2	139.57	1802.50	148.09	21029	8442
1990	7328	1196.9	335.4	379.5	157.20	1879.70	165.42	20971	8067
1991	7352	1332.9	354.1	393.6	176.10	1979.50	191.03	25261	8712
1992	7984	1408.7	379.5	455.0	200.30	2047.90	213.04	30822	9359
1993	9320	1336.5	395.4	534.9	202.70	1956.30	237.37	36788	11086
1994	11477	1536.5	429.6	581.4	212.90	2272.80	280.33	42118	11925
1995	13510	1811.0	531.8	597.7	240.10	2548.14	341.17	47561	15732
1996	13643	1883.6	573.8	669.3	304.00	2809.04	375.45	49119	16069
1997	13731	2036.9	574.4	725.8	358.60	2820.96	471.62	51174	16631
1998	12806	2171.0	539.4	744.0	377.30	3010.00	510.00	53600	17194
1999	12074	2356.0	580.1	766.0	435.00	3251.00	600.00	57300	17420
2000	12184	2427.0	667.9	834.0	470.00	3186.00	694.00	59700	18352
2001	13131	2696.3	788.0	914.4	480.60	3383.01	841.38	66104	20964
2002	14280	3050.4	878.0	1033.2	543.02	3791.00	991.20	72500	23446
2003	17776	3371.2	945.3	1133.6	611.77	3881.31	1181.15	86208	27703
2004	20619	3928.9	1041.1	1334.7	629.85	4804.82	1699.80	96682	37026
2005	25412	4544.7	1240.0	1421.1	755.54	5177.86	1664.79	106885	40210
2006	29768	5033.2	1511.8	1560.0	940.51	5345.05	2073.18	123676	46575
2007	33553	5412.6	1759.3	1765.0	1027.80	5824.98	2413.78	136117	53918
2008	32031	5098.0	1926.0	1854.6	987.58	6028.05	2453.29	142356	59890
2009	35510	5960.9	1832.4	1944.8	1072.62	6385.01	2747.28	164398	58574
2010	38864	7090.5	2228.4	2034.8	1421.34	6337.86	3090.00	188191	66331
2011	43271	7482.7	2473.5	2294.0	1527.50	6419.39	3390.07	209926	79108
2012	44779	7876.6	2696.8	2395.9	1486.80	6832.10	3837.37	220984	75051
2013	47932	8122.6	2859.0	2435.0	1622.60	7036.96	4121.94	241614	77898

表37　续表 4 continued

年份 Year	生铁 (万吨) Pig Iron (10 000 tons)	粗钢 (万吨) Steel (10 000 tons)	成品钢材 (万吨) Steel Products (10 000 tons)	金属切削机床 (万台) Metal-cutting Machine Tools (10 000 units)	汽车 (万辆) Motor Vehicles (10 000 sets)	#轿车 Cars	家用电冰箱 (万台) Household Refrigerators (10 000 units)	房间空气调节器 (万台) (10 000 units)	家用洗衣机 (万台) (10 000 units)
1949	25.0	16.0	13.0	0.16					
1950	98.0	61.0	37.0	0.33					
1951	145.0	90.0	67.0	0.59					
1952	193.0	135.0	106.0	1.37					
1953	223.0	177.0	147.0	2.05					
1954	311.0	223.0	172.0	1.59					
1955	387.0	285.0	216.0	1.37	0.01				
1956	483.0	447.0	314.0	2.59	0.17		0.03		
1957	594.0	535.0	415.0	2.80	0.79		0.16		
1958	1369.0	800.0	591.0	8.00	1.60		0.26		
1959	2191.0	1387.0	897.0	11.55	1.96		0.34		
1960	2716.0	1866.0	1111.0	15.35	2.26		0.36		
1961	1281.0	870.0	613.0	5.67	0.36		0.11		
1962	805.0	667.0	455.0	2.25	0.97		0.09		
1963	741.0	762.0	533.0	2.22	2.06		0.14		
1964	902.0	964.0	688.0	2.81	2.81		0.17		
1965	1077.0	1223.0	881.0	3.96	4.05		0.30		
1966	1334.0	1532.0	1035.0	5.49	5.59		0.54		
1967	963.0	1029.0	718.0	4.07	2.04		0.59		
1968	857.0	904.0	666.0	4.64	2.51		0.67		
1969	1280.0	1333.0	926.0	8.56	5.31		0.66		
1970	1706.0	1779.0	1188.0	13.89	8.72		0.52		
1971	2100.0	2132.0	1389.0	14.57	11.10		0.61		
1972	2355.0	2338.0	1561.0	16.22	10.82		0.76		
1973	2490.0	2522.0	1684.0	18.33	11.62		1.00		
1974	2062.0	2112.0	1466.0	16.45	10.48		1.34		
1975	2449.0	2390.0	1622.0	17.49	13.98		1.80		
1976	2233.0	2046.0	1466.0	15.70	13.52		2.12		
1977	2505.0	2374.0	1633.0	19.87	12.54		2.46		
1978	3479.0	3178.0	2208.0	18.32	14.91		2.80	0.02	0.04
1979	3673.0	3448.0	2497.0	13.96	18.57		3.18	0.86	1.81
1980	3802.0	3712.0	2716.0	13.36	22.23	0.54	4.90	1.32	24.53
1981	3417.0	3560.0	2670.0	10.26	17.56	0.34	5.56	1.40	128.08

表37 续表 5 continued

年份 Year	生铁 (万吨) Pig Iron (10 000 tons)	粗钢 (万吨) Steel (10 000 tons)	成品钢材 (万吨) Steel Products (10 000 tons)	金属切削机床 (万台) Metal-cutting Machine Tools (10 000 units)	汽车 (万辆) Motor Vehicles (10 000 sets)	#轿车 Cars	家用电冰箱 (万台) Household Refrigerators (10 000 units)	房间空气调节器 (万台) (10 000 units)	家用洗衣机 (万台) (10 000 units)
1982	3551.0	3716.0	2902.0	9.98	19.63	0.51	9.99	2.44	253.26
1983	3738.0	4002.0	3072.0	12.10	23.98	0.60	18.85	3.45	365.86
1984	4001.0	4347.0	3372.0	13.35	31.64	0.65	54.74	6.12	578.06
1985	4384.0	4679.0	3693.0	16.72	43.72	0.90	144.81	12.35	887.20
1986	5064.0	5220.0	4058.0	16.37	36.98	1.17	225.02	9.65	893.40
1987	5503.0	5628.0	4386.0	17.22	47.18	1.79	401.34	13.22	990.20
1988	5704.0	5943.0	4689.0	19.17	64.47	2.96	757.63	25.91	1046.80
1989	5820.0	6159.0	4859.0	17.87	58.35	3.58	670.79	37.47	825.40
1990	6238.0	6635.0	5153.0	13.45	51.40	3.50	463.06	24.07	662.68
1991	6765.0	7100.0	5638.0	16.39	71.42	6.87	469.94	63.03	678.20
1992	7589.0	8094.0	6697.0	22.87	106.67	16.17	485.76	158.03	707.93
1993	8739.0	8956.0	7716.0	26.20	129.85	22.29	596.66	346.41	895.85
1994	9741.0	9261.0	8428.0	20.65	136.69	26.87	768.12	393.42	1094.24
1995	10529.3	9536.0	8979.8	20.34	145.27	33.70	918.54	682.56	948.41
1996	10722.5	10124.1	9338.0	17.74	147.52	38.29	979.65	786.21	1074.72
1997	11511.4	10894.2	9978.9	18.65	158.25	48.60	1044.43	974.01	1254.48
1998	11863.7	11559.0	10737.8	11.91	163.00	50.71	1060.00	1156.87	1207.31
1999	12539.2	12426.0	12109.8	14.22	183.20	57.10	1210.00	1337.64	1342.17
2000	13101.5	12850.0	13146.0	17.66	207.00	60.70	1279.00	1826.67	1442.98
2001	15554.3	15163.4	16067.6	25.58	234.17	70.36	1351.26	2333.64	1341.61
2002	17084.6	18236.6	19251.6	30.86	325.10	109.20	1598.87	3135.11	1595.76
2003	21366.7	22233.6	24108.0	30.58	444.39	207.08	2242.56	4820.86	1964.46
2004	26831.0	28291.1	31975.7	48.72	509.11	227.63	3007.59	6390.33	2533.41
2005	34375.2	35324.0	37771.1	51.14	570.49	277.01	2987.06	6764.57	3035.52
2006	41245.2	41914.9	46893.4	57.30	727.89	386.94	3530.89	6849.42	3560.50
2007	47651.6	48928.8	56560.9	64.69	888.89	479.78	4397.13	8014.28	4005.10
2008	47824.4	50305.8	60460.3	71.73	930.59	503.81	4799.95	8147.37	4447.00
2009	55283.5	57218.2	69405.4	58.55	1379.53	748.48	5930.45	8078.25	4973.63
2010	59733.3	63723.0	80276.6	69.73	1826.53	957.59	7295.72	10887.47	6247.73
2011	64050.9	68528.3	88619.6	88.68	1841.64	1012.67	8699.20	13912.50	6715.94
2012	66354.4	72388.2	95577.8	88.23	1927.62	1077.00	8427.00	12398.72	6791.12
2013	70897.0	77904.1	106762.2	72.30	2211.72	1210.42	9261.02	13057.20	7201.90

表37 续表 6 continued

年份 Year	移动通信手持机（万部） Mobile Telephones (10 000 uints)	彩色电视机（万台） Television Sets (10 000 uints)	微型电子计算机（万台） Micro-computer (10 000 uints)	集成电路（万块） Integrated Circuit (10 000 uints)	复印和胶版印制设备（万台） Copying Machines (10 000 units)	程控交换机（万线） Program Controlled Switchboards (10 000 lines)	传真机（万台） Fax Machines (10 000 units)	电话单机（万部） Telephone Sets (10 000 units)	发电量（亿千瓦小时） Electricity (100 million kwh)
1949									43.00
1950									46.00
1951									57.00
1952									73.00
1953									92.00
1954									110.00
1955									123.00
1956									166.00
1957									193.00
1958									275.00
1959									423.00
1960									594.00
1961									480.00
1962									458.00
1963									490.00
1964									560.00
1965									676.00
1966									825.00
1967				2					774.00
1968				8					716.00
1969				78					940.00
1970				423					1159.00
1971		0.02		406					1384.00
1972		0.01		264					1524.00
1973		0.07		186					1668.00
1974		0.24		388					1668.00
1975		0.29		579					1958.00
1976		0.28							2031.00
1977		0.25							2234.00
1978		0.38		3041					2566.00
1979		0.95							2820.00
1980		3.21		1684					3006.00
1981		15.21		1279					3093.00

表37 续表 7 continued

年份 Year	移动通信手持机（万部） Mobile Telephones (10 000 uints)	彩色电视机（万台） Television Sets (10 000 uints)	微型电子计算机（万台） Micro-computer (10 000 uints)	集成电路（万块） Integrated Circuit (10 000 uints)	复印和胶版印制设备（万台） Copying Machines (10 000 units)	程控交换机（万线） Program Controlled Switchboards (10 000 lines)	传真机（万台） Fax Machines (10 000 units)	电话单机（万部） Telephone Sets (10 000 units)	发电量（亿千瓦小时） Electricity (100 million kwh)
1982		28.81		1352					3277.00
1983		53.11		2604					3514.00
1984		133.95		4148					3770.00
1985		435.28		6385	2.37			274.10	4107.00
1986		414.6	4.21	5720	1.80			471.68	4495.00
1987		672.72	5.12	9544	1.81			451.96	4973.00
1988		1037.66	11.61	13160				721.64	5452.00
1989		940.02	7.54	13156				880.00	5848.00
1990		1033.04	8.21	10838				880.00	6212.00
1991		1205.06	16.25	17049				1482.00	6775.00
1992		1333.08	12.62	16099	4.38			1982.27	7539.00
1993		1435.76	14.66	20101	6.06			2663.59	8395.00
1994		1689.15	24.57	48462	4.10			5722.92	9281.00
1995		2057.74	83.57	551686	21.75	2091.60	136.1	9956.36	10070.30
1996		2537.60	138.83	388987	63.87	2274.80	137.9	7960.82	10813.10
1997		2711.33	206.55	255455	107.75	2787.30	162.5	8653.71	11355.53
1998		3497.00	291.40	262577	117.93	4219.90	128.7	6520.48	11670.00
1999		4262.00	405.00	415000	210.29	4726.00	160.0	7139.93	12393.00
2000	5247.90	3936.00	672.00	588000	156.63	7136.00	196.3	9597.99	13556.00
2001	8031.70	4093.70	877.65	636288	144.12	7223.50	318.2	10302.74	14808.02
2002	12146.35	5155.00	1463.51	963101	207.39	5860.70	297.3	11892.42	16540.00
2003	18231.37	6541.40	3216.70	1483101	264.17	6549.10	746.6	12935.90	19105.75
2004	23751.58	7431.83	5974.90	2355100	324.57	7625.22	851.2	19515.71	22033.09
2005	30354.21	8283.22	8084.89	2699729	403.56	7720.90	1068.2	18861.52	25002.60
2006	48013.79	8375.40	9336.44	3357499	467.80	7404.63	1188.6	18647.83	28657.26
2007	54857.86	8478.01	12073.38	4116200	452.36	5387.05	888.5	16516.46	32815.53
2008	55945.10	9187.14	15853.65	4387700	517.70	4583.95	749.4	18244.72	34957.61
2009	68193.37	9898.79	18215.07	4144000	421.02	4152.51	683.5	14537.70	37146.51
2010	99827.36	11830.03	24584.46	6525000	534.82	3137.97	181.1	16769.68	42071.60
2011	113257.71	12231.34	32036.93	7195200	655.05	3034.04	268.1	14017.91	47130.19
2012	118154.57	12823.52	31806.71	7796100	609.69	2829.08	263.6	12773.84	50210.41
2013	145560.99	12776.05	33660.98	8665400	635.40	3115.74	161.0	12540.40	53975.86

表38 全国能源生产总量及构成
Total Production of Energy and Its Composition

年份 Year	能源生产总量 (万吨标准煤) Total Energy Production (10 000 tons of SCE)	占能源生产总量的比重(%) As Percentage of Total Energy Production			
		原　煤 Coal	原　油 Crude Oil	天然气 Natural Gas	水电、核电、风电 Hydro-power,Nuclear Power, Wind Power
1949	2374	96.3	0.7		3.0
1950	3174	96.7	0.9		2.3
1951	3903	97.0	1.1		1.9
1952	4871	96.7	1.3		2.0
1953	5192	96.3	1.7		2.0
1954	6262	95.8	1.8		2.4
1955	7295	95.9	1.9		2.2
1956	8242	95.3	2.0		2.7
1957	9861	94.9	2.1	0.1	2.9
1958	19845	97.1	1.6	0.1	1.2
1959	27161	97.0	2.0	0.1	0.9
1960	29637	95.6	2.5	0.5	1.4
1961	21224	93.5	3.6	0.9	2.0
1962	17185	91.4	4.8	0.9	2.9
1963	17009	91.1	5.5	0.8	2.7
1964	17232	89.1	7.0	0.8	3.1
1965	18824	88.0	8.6	0.8	2.6
1966	20833	86.4	10.0	0.9	2.8
1967	17494	84.1	11.3	1.1	3.5
1968	18715	83.9	12.2	1.0	2.9
1969	23104	82.2	13.5	1.1	3.2
1970	30990	81.6	14.1	1.2	3.1
1971	35289	79.3	16.0	1.4	3.3
1972	37785	77.5	17.3	1.7	3.5
1973	40013	74.4	19.2	2.0	4.4
1974	41626	70.8	22.3	2.4	4.5
1975	48754	70.6	22.6	2.4	4.4
1976	50340	68.5	24.8	2.7	4.1
1977	56396	69.6	23.7	2.9	3.8
1978	62770	70.3	23.7	2.9	3.1
1979	64562	70.2	23.5	3.0	3.3
1980	63735	69.4	23.8	3.0	3.8
1981	63227	70.2	22.9	2.7	4.2
1982	66778	71.3	21.8	2.4	4.5
1983	71270	71.6	21.3	2.3	4.8

表38 续表 continued

年份 Year	能源生产总量 (万吨标准煤) Total Energy Production (10 000 tons of SCE)	占能源生产总量的比重(%) As Percentage of Total Energy Production			
		原 煤 Coal	原 油 Crude Oil	天然气 Natural Gas	水电、核电、风电 Hydro-power,Nuclear Power, Wind Power
1984	77855	72.4	21.0	2.1	4.5
1985	85546	72.8	20.9	2.0	4.3
1986	88124	72.4	21.2	2.1	4.3
1987	91266	72.6	21.0	2.0	4.4
1988	95801	73.1	20.4	2.0	4.5
1989	101639	74.1	19.3	2.0	4.6
1990	103922	74.2	19.0	2.0	4.8
1991	104844	74.1	19.2	2.0	4.7
1992	107256	74.3	18.9	2.0	4.8
1993	111059	74.0	18.7	2.0	5.3
1994	118729	74.6	17.6	1.9	5.9
1995	129034	75.3	16.6	1.9	6.2
1996	133032	75.0	16.9	2.0	6.1
1997	133460	74.2	17.2	2.1	6.5
1998	129834	73.3	17.7	2.2	6.8
1999	131935	73.9	17.3	2.5	6.3
2000	135048	73.2	17.2	2.7	6.9
2001	143875	73.0	16.3	2.8	7.9
2002	150656	73.5	15.8	2.9	7.8
2003	171906	76.2	14.1	2.7	7.0
2004	196648	77.1	12.8	2.8	7.3
2005	216219	77.6	12.0	3.0	7.4
2006	232167	77.8	11.3	3.4	7.5
2007	247279	77.7	10.8	3.7	7.8
2008	260552	76.8	10.5	4.1	8.6
2009	274619	77.3	9.9	4.1	8.7
2010	296916	76.6	9.8	4.2	9.4
2011	317987	77.8	9.1	4.3	8.8
2012	331848	76.5	8.9	4.3	10.3
2013	340000	75.6	8.9	4.6	10.9

注：电力折算标准煤的系数根据当年平均发电煤耗计算(下表同)。

a)The coefficient for conversion of electric power into SCE (standard coal equivalent) is calculated on the basic of the data on the average coal consumption in generating electric power in the same year. The same applies to the table following.

表39　全国能源消费总量及构成
Total Consumption of Energy and Its Composition

年份 Year	能源消费总量（万吨标准煤） Total Energy Consumption (10 000 tons of SCE)	占能源消费总量的比重(%) As Percentage of Total Energy Consumption			
		煤　炭 Coal	石　油 Crude Oil	天然气 Natural Gas	水电、核电、风电 Hydro-power,Nuclear Power, Wind Power
1953	5411	94.3	3.8		1.8
1954	6234	93.5	4.3		2.2
1955	6968	92.9	4.9		2.1
1956	8800	92.7	4.8		2.4
1957	9644	92.3	4.6	0.1	3.0
1958	17599	94.6	3.9	0.1	1.4
1959	23926	94.7	4.1	0.1	1.1
1960	30188	93.9	4.1	0.5	1.5
1961	20390	91.3	5.5	0.9	2.3
1962	16540	89.2	6.6	0.9	3.2
1963	15567	88.9	7.2	0.8	3.1
1964	16637	88.0	8.0	0.7	3.3
1965	18901	86.5	10.3	0.9	2.7
1966	20269	86.2	10.2	0.7	2.9
1967	18328	84.8	10.9	0.8	3.5
1968	18405	83.8	12.1	0.8	3.4
1969	22730	81.9	13.8	0.8	3.5
1970	29291	80.9	14.7	0.9	3.5
1971	34496	79.2	16.0	1.4	3.4
1972	37273	77.5	17.2	1.7	3.6
1973	39109	74.8	18.6	2.0	4.6
1974	40144	82.1	20.7	2.5	4.7
1975	45425	71.9	21.1	2.5	4.6
1976	47831	69.9	23.0	2.8	4.3
1977	52354	70.3	22.6	3.1	4.1
1978	57144	70.7	22.7	3.2	3.4
1979	58588	71.3	21.8	3.3	3.6
1980	60275	72.2	20.7	3.1	4.0
1981	59447	72.7	20.0	2.8	4.5
1982	62067	73.7	18.9	2.5	4.9
1983	66040	74.2	18.1	2.4	5.3

表39 续表 continued

年份 Year	能源消费总量 (万吨标准煤) Total Energy Consumption (10 000 tons of SCE)	占能源消费总量的比重(%) As Percentage of Total Energy Consumption			
		煤 炭 Coal	石 油 Crude Oil	天然气 Natural Gas	水电、核电、风电 Hydro-power,Nuclear Power, Wind Power
1984	70904	75.3	17.4	2.4	4.9
1985	76682	75.8	17.1	2.2	4.9
1986	80850	75.8	17.2	2.3	4.7
1987	86632	76.2	17.0	2.1	4.7
1988	92997	76.1	17.1	2.1	4.7
1989	96934	76.1	17.1	2.1	4.7
1990	98703	76.2	16.6	2.1	5.1
1991	103783	76.1	17.1	2.0	4.8
1992	109170	75.7	17.5	1.9	4.9
1993	115993	74.7	18.2	1.9	5.2
1994	122737	75.0	17.4	1.9	5.7
1995	131176	74.6	17.5	1.8	6.1
1996	135192	73.5	18.7	1.8	6.0
1997	135909	71.4	20.4	1.8	6.4
1998	136184	70.9	20.8	1.8	6.5
1999	140569	70.6	21.5	2.0	5.9
2000	145531	69.2	22.2	2.2	6.4
2001	150406	68.3	21.8	2.4	7.5
2002	159431	68.0	22.3	2.4	7.3
2003	183792	69.8	21.2	2.5	6.5
2004	213456	69.5	21.3	2.5	6.7
2005	235997	70.8	19.8	2.6	6.8
2006	258676	71.1	19.3	2.9	6.7
2007	280508	71.1	18.8	3.3	6.8
2008	291448	70.3	18.3	3.7	7.7
2009	306647	70.4	17.9	3.9	7.8
2010	324939	68.0	19.0	4.4	8.6
2011	348002	68.4	18.6	5.0	8.0
2012	361732	66.6	18.8	5.2	9.4
2013	375000	66.0	18.4	5.8	9.8

表40 全国分品种能源消费量
Consumption of Energy by Type

年份 Year	煤炭(万吨) Coal (10 000 tons)	焦炭(万吨) Coke (10 000 tons)	原油(万吨) Grude Oil (10 000 tons)	汽油(万吨) Gasoline Oil (10 000 tons)	柴油(万吨) Diesel Oil (10 000 tons)	燃料油(万吨) Fuel Oil (10 000 tons)	液化石油气(亿立方米) Liquefied Petroleum Gas (100 million (cu.m)	天然气(亿立方米) Natural Gas (100 million (cu.m)	电力(亿瓦小时) Electricity (100 million (kwh)
1982	64125.8	3997.2	8688.3	993.1	1587.0	2810.8	121.3	119.0	3280.1
1983	68713.0	4150.2	9079.8	1094.9	1647.1	2856.5	147.0	121.3	3518.7
1984	74968.3	4431.3	9210.0	1199.7	1725.7	2879.1	150.3	126.2	3777.6
1985	81603.0	4689.7	9509.5	1396.3	1939.4	2837.4	155.7	129.3	4117.6
1986	86015.1	5249.0	10210.6	1500.2	2116.7	3008.2	200.5	137.6	4507.0
1987	92799.0	5720.9	10685.5	1624.3	2314.0	3120.9	213.4	138.9	4985.2
1988	99353.9	6027.1	11201.9	1789.9	2575.2	3238.0	230.9	143.6	5466.8
1989	103427.0	6368.4	11607.1	1853.6	2748.0	3390.6	251.5	150.3	5865.3
1990	105523.0	6914.7	11762.2	1899.5	2691.7	3367.8	254.2	152.5	6230.4
1991	110432.0	7118.0	12356.1	2209.5	2895.9	3509.1	301.5	158.9	6804.0
1992	114084.8	7839.1	13225.8	2509.8	3373.0	3421.9	358.3	158.8	7589.2
1993	120919.5	8814.3	13832.5	2887.9	3948.2	3803.1	500.7	167.6	8426.5
1994	128532.2	9094.3	14024.6	2696.7	3803.0	3594.9	570.9	173.4	9260.4
1995	137676.5	10725.3	14886.4	2909.6	4321.4	3693.7	750.6	177.4	10023.4
1996	140065.3	11865.0	15865.0	3166.3	4825.1	3632.3	931.3	185.9	10764.3
1997	137748.4	10870.6	17367.2	3244.1	5278.5	3692.8	1009.7	196.4	11284.4
1998	135013.3	11447.8	17357.3	3306.8	5309.7	3828.6	1186.0	202.6	11598.4
1999	139336.5	10786.8	18949.5	3389.3	6204.1	3934.1	1178.5	214.9	12304.7
2000	141091.7	10840.8	21232.0	3504.6	6806.2	3872.8	1389.7	245.0	13472.4
2001	144528.1	11931.5	21342.7	3597.8	7158.0	3850.2	1411.2	274.3	14723.5
2002	152282.7	12343.6	22544.1	3749.3	7666.9	3873.9	1625.4	291.8	16465.5
2003	180587.0	15298.5	24922.0	4072.0	8409.4	4220.5	1796.6	339.1	19031.6
2004	207561.3	18067.0	28749.3	4695.7	9895.9	4783.5	2016.0	396.7	21971.4
2005	231851.1	25105.8	30086.2	4854.9	10972.2	4242.1	2046.5	467.6	24940.3
2006	255065.5	27892.8	32245.2	5242.5	11835.4	4368.3	2207.6	561.4	28588.0
2007	272745.9	29168.1	34031.6	5519.1	12496.7	4157.5	2327.9	705.2	32711.8
2008	281095.9	29900.2	35498.2	6145.5	13532.6	3237.1	2118.9	812.9	34541.4
2009	295833.1	31850.0	38128.6	6172.7	13756.6	2827.8	2153.1	895.2	37032.2
2010	312236.5	33687.8	42874.6	6886.2	14633.8	3758.0	2240.3	1069.4	41934.5
2011	342950.2	38163.3	43965.8	7396.0	15635.1	3662.8	2470.2	1305.3	47000.9
2012	352647.1	39373.0	46678.9	8140.9	16966.0	3683.3	2482.2	1463.0	49762.6

表41　全国人均生活能源消费量
Annual Per Capita Energy Consumption for Non-Production Purpose

年　份 Year	平均每人生活消费能源（千克标准煤） Annual Per Capita Consumption for Non-production Purpose (Kg of SCE)	煤　炭（千克） Coal (kg)	电　力（千瓦小时） Electricity (kwh)	煤　油（千克） Kerosene (kg)	液化石油气（千克） Liquefied Petroleum Gas (kg)	天然气（立方米） Natural Gas (cu.m)	煤　气（立方米） Coal Gas (cu.m)
1980	112.3	118.0	10.7	1.0	0.4	0.2	1.4
1981	101.3	121.6	11.9	1.2	0.5	0.2	1.4
1982	102.2	123.5	12.0	1.0	0.5	0.2	1.5
1983	106.6	127.7	13.4	1.2	0.6	0.1	1.5
1984	113.5	134.9	15.3	1.4	0.6	0.4	1.6
1985	126.7	148.7	21.2	1.2	0.9	0.4	1.3
1986	127.3	148.3	23.2	1.3	1.1	0.6	1.3
1987	132.1	152.1	26.4	1.2	1.1	0.7	1.6
1988	141.0	159.1	31.2	1.1	1.2	1.4	1.6
1989	139.3	152.4	35.3	1.1	1.4	1.5	2.4
1990	139.2	147.1	42.4	0.9	1.4	1.6	2.5
1991	139.0	143.0	47.2	0.8	1.8	1.6	3.2
1992	134.2	126.9	54.9	0.7	2.1	1.8	4.4
1993	133.5	123.2	62.5	0.6	2.5	1.5	4.6
1994	129.3	109.5	72.7	0.6	3.2	1.7	6.3
1995	130.7	112.3	83.5	0.5	4.4	1.6	4.7
1996	120.5	83.0	87.7	0.5	5.9	1.7	6.4
1997	119.3	77.2	98.6	0.5	6.2	1.7	8.9
1998	119.0	73.1	104.2	0.6	6.9	1.9	9.7
1999	121.8	69.9	108.6	0.6	6.8	2.1	9.3
2000	123.7	67.0	115.0	0.6	6.8	2.6	10.0
2001	127.2	66.1	126.5	0.6	6.7	3.3	9.4
2002	134.0	65.7	138.3	0.3	7.6	3.6	9.8
2003	153.4	69.9	159.7	0.3	8.6	4.0	10.2
2004	175.7	75.4	184.0	0.2	10.4	5.2	10.7
2005	194.1	77.0	221.3	0.2	10.2	6.1	11.1
2006	211.8	76.6	255.6	0.2	11.1	7.8	12.7
2007	233.8	74.1	308.3	0.1	12.4	10.9	14.1
2008	240.8	69.1	331.9	0.1	11.0	12.8	13.9
2009	254.2	68.5	365.9	0.1	11.2	13.3	12.5
2010	258.3	68.5	383.1	0.1	10.9	17.0	14.5
2011	278.3	68.5	418.1	0.2	12.0	19.7	10.9
2012	293.8	67.8	460.4	0.1	12.1	21.3	10.2

注：按年平均人口数计算。
a) Data in the table are calculated with the data on the annual average population in each year.

表42 全国建筑业企业概况

Main Indicators on Construction Enterprises

年份 Year	建筑业企业单位数(个) Number of Enterprises (unit)	#国有 State-owned	#集体 Collective-owned	建筑业企业从业人员(万人) Number of Persons Employed (10 000 persons)	#国有 State-owned	#集体 Collective-owned	建筑业企业总产值(亿元) Gross Output Value (100 million yuan)	#国有 State-owned	#集体 Collective-owned
1978									
1979									
1980	6604	1996	4608	648.00	481.80	166.20	286.93	220.90	66.03
1981	7327	2586	4741	685.20	509.30	175.90	282.30	213.70	68.60
1982	7884	2808	5076	733.00	523.90	200.10	345.33	258.03	87.30
1983	9653	2885	6768	802.60	544.50	258.10	419.54	298.54	121.00
1984	9741	3017	6724	847.70	554.20	293.50	517.15	371.56	145.59
1985	11150	3385	7765	911.50	576.70	334.80	675.10	474.51	200.59
1986	12585	3608	8977	993.70	617.30	376.40	808.07	566.83	241.24
1987	13625	3788	9837	1024.10	618.20	405.90	952.65	660.11	292.54
1988	14134	3798	10336	1044.80	623.50	421.30	1131.65	776.96	354.69
1989	13106	3927	9179	1004.80	614.70	390.10	1282.98	878.57	404.41
1990	13327	4275	9052	1010.70	621.00	389.70	1345.01	935.19	409.82
1991	13825	4638	9187	1058.30	638.90	419.40	1564.33	1062.48	501.85
1992	14536	4985	9551	1157.50	681.20	476.30	2174.44	1432.13	742.31
1993	20998	6363	14130	1096.70	631.50	455.70	3253.50	2054.83	1163.85
1994	23315	7251	15196	1445.85	818.16	601.93	4653.32	3033.66	1519.45
1995	24133	7531	15348	1497.87	824.31	631.89	5793.75	3670.25	1899.47
1996	41364	9109	29044	2121.87	855.93	1171.42	8282.25	4160.21	3695.68
1997	44017	9650	29872	2101.51	828.63	1148.24	9126.48	4526.52	3925.81
1998	45634	9458	28410	2029.99	738.36	1057.30	10061.99	4571.44	4012.01
1999	47234	9394	27197	2020.13	690.55	993.09	11152.86	4861.38	4081.79
2000	47518	9030	24756	1994.30	635.60	887.50	12497.60	5053.79	4035.84
2001	45893	8264	19096	2110.66	590.65	739.94	15361.56	5362.81	3775.89
2002	47820	7536	13177	2245.19	543.75	579.18	18527.18	5582.86	3338.50
2003	48688	6638	10425	2414.27	524.32	505.57	23083.87	6060.23	3270.73
2004	59018	6513	8959	2500.28	467.36	386.40	29021.45	7325.61	2756.12
2005	58750	6007	8090	2699.92	480.05	361.57	34552.10	8432.03	2815.20
2006	60166	5555	7051	2878.16	467.61	331.99	41557.16	9218.56	2904.48
2007	62074	5319	6614	3133.71	470.12	316.99	51043.71	10630.90	3153.65
2008	71095	5315	5843	3314.95	472.11	266.78	62036.81	12231.66	3216.43
2009	70817	5009	5352	3672.56	518.92	246.79	76807.74	15190.05	3281.75
2010	71863	4810	5026	4160.44	576.87	246.53	96031.13	18148.59	3655.27
2011	72280	4642	4847	3852.47	444.94	220.40	116463.32	20436.81	4306.49
2012	75280	4602	4640	4267.24	457.78	216.24	137217.86	22930.19	4919.00
2013	79528	4607	4572	4499.31	477.48	222.97	159312.95	26161.24	5543.33

注：1.本表1980—1992年数据为全民和集体所有制建筑业企业数据；1993—1995年数据为各种经济成分的建制镇以上建筑业企业数据；1996—2001年数据为资质等级(旧资质)四级及四级以上建筑业企业数据；2002年及以后数据为所有具有资质等级的施工总承包、专业承包建筑业企业（不含劳务分包建筑业企业)数据。
2.从业人员数1993—1997年为年平均人数。

a) Data from 1980 to 1992 are the figures of state-owned and collective-owned construction enterprises. Data from 1993 to 1995 are the figures of all economic types of construction enterprises above towns. The statistical coverage from 1996 to 2001 included the fourth and higher grades construction enterprises (old classification of grades), and that since 2002 included all grades construction enterprises, both general constructing contractors and professional contractors (excluding the construction enterprises of work subcontractors).

b) The number of employed persons refers to the annual average number from 1993 to 1997.

表42 续表 continued

年份 Year	建筑业企业增加值(亿元) Total Value-added of Construction Enterprises (100 million yuan)	资产合计 (亿元) Total Assets (100 million yuan)	利润总额 (亿元) Total Profits (100 million yuan)	税金总额 (亿元) Total Tax (100 million yuan)	按总产值计算劳动生产率 (元/人) Overall Labor Productivity in Term of Gross Output Value (yuan/person)	房屋建筑面积(万平方米) Floor Space of Building Construction (10 000 sq.m)	
						施工面积 Under Construction	竣工面积 Completed
1978							
1979							
1980							
1981							
1982							
1983							
1984							
1985						35491.80	17072.70
1986			31.65	8.82	8070	37773.90	18601.00
1987			28.00	8.47	10345	39856.60	19437.90
1988			31.80	19.44	12168	42735.20	19060.70
1989			38.60	36.10	12505	40649.90	19723.40
1990			25.70	42.69	13109	37923.00	19552.50
1991	464.70		28.50	50.60	14741	41054.20	20256.30
1992	614.60		46.00	66.20	18238	51885.40	24045.50
1993	840.70	3719.50	64.13	96.20	24214	65374.20	28684.80
1994	1322.11	5404.68	72.52	135.75	32184	78032.20	32383.30
1995	1668.64	6718.70	74.20	168.04	38679	89862.80	35666.30
1996	2405.62	9242.85	109.35	218.00	39033	129087.00	60047.90
1997	2540.54	10592.78	109.92	271.70	43428	128680.30	62244.00
1998	2783.79	11870.42	117.33	301.93	48255	137593.60	65682.60
1999	3022.26	13144.29	154.80	339.61	53328	147262.47	73924.94
2000	3341.09	14578.37	192.06	387.16	59585	160141.10	80714.90
2001	4023.57	16967.61	294.39	499.03	67275	188328.68	97699.00
2002	3822.42	20390.11	370.35	599.43	76171	215608.70	110217.05
2003	4654.71	23541.90	519.87	758.65	86666	259377.13	122827.61
2004	5615.78	28564.62	719.24	936.20	107942	310985.70	147364.00
2005	6899.71	31485.73	906.66	1159.79	117317	352744.67	159406.20
2006	8116.39	36008.78	1193.07	1401.49	131800	410154.41	179672.96
2007	9944.35	43029.27	1561.12	1714.27	148101	482005.52	203992.68
2008	12488.95	51711.93	2201.84	2264.98	161805	530518.63	223591.62
2009	15619.82	62164.39	2718.76	2653.69	185087	588593.91	245401.64
2010	18983.54	75221.77	3409.07	3351.31	203962	708023.51	277450.22
2011	22070.98	93859.86	4168.20	3864.41	231917	851828.12	316429.28
2012	26583.31	111692.15	4776.14	4388.88	296424	986427.45	358736.23
2013	30768.47				324842	1129967.69	389244.93

表43 全国运输线路长度
Length of Transport Routes

单位：万公里 (10 000 km)

年份 Year	铁路营业里程 Length of Railways in Operation	#国家铁路电气化里程 National Electrified Railways	公路里程 Length of Highways	#高速公路 Expressway	内河航道里程 Length of Navigable Inland Waterways	定期航班航线里程 Length of Regular Civil Aviation Routes	#国际航线 International Routes	管道输油(气)里程 Length of Petroleum and Gas Pipelines
1949	2.18		8.08		7.36			
1950	2.22		9.96		7.36	1.14	0.69	
1951	2.23		11.44		7.36	1.12	0.69	
1952	2.29		12.67		9.50	1.31	0.51	
1953	2.38		13.71		9.50	1.40	0.50	
1954	2.45		14.61		9.50	1.52	0.50	
1955	2.56		16.73		9.99	1.55	0.30	
1956	2.65		22.63		10.36	1.91	0.49	
1957	2.67		25.46		14.41	2.64	0.43	
1958	3.02		42.18		15.20	3.30	0.44	0.02
1959	3.23		50.79		16.30	3.72	0.53	0.02
1960	3.39		51.95		17.39	3.81	0.53	0.02
1961	3.45		47.74		17.22	3.91	0.45	0.02
1962	3.46	0.01	46.35		16.19	3.53	0.44	0.02
1963	3.50		47.51		15.72	3.58	0.44	0.03
1964	3.69		47.92		15.69	3.85	0.44	0.03
1965	3.80	0.01	51.45		15.77	3.94	0.45	0.04
1966	3.93		54.36		14.72	3.94	0.45	0.07
1967	3.86		55.75		14.78	4.45	0.38	0.08
1968	3.88		57.17		14.78	4.01	0.44	0.09
1969	4.17		60.06		14.81	3.99	0.44	0.10
1970	4.37	0.03	63.67		14.84	4.06	0.44	0.12
1971	4.53	0.03	67.54		14.16	4.21	0.44	0.20
1972	4.63	0.04	69.99		14.06	4.25	0.44	0.23
1973	4.66	0.06	71.56		13.88	4.54	0.44	0.34
1974	4.75	0.06	73.79		13.74	8.13	3.71	0.42
1975	4.86	0.07	78.36		13.56	8.42	3.71	0.53
1976	4.91	0.07	82.34		13.74	9.78	4.09	0.63
1977	5.06	0.10	85.56		13.74	13.21	4.09	0.67
1978	5.17	0.10	89.02		13.60	14.89	5.53	0.83
1979	5.30	0.10	87.58		10.78	16.00	5.13	0.91
1980	5.33	0.17	88.83		10.85	19.53	8.12	0.87
1981	5.39	0.17	89.75		10.87	21.82	8.28	0.97
1982	5.33	0.18	90.70		10.86	23.27	9.99	1.04
1983	5.46	0.23	91.51		10.89	22.91	9.99	1.08
1984	5.48	0.30	92.67		10.93	26.02	10.74	1.10
1985	5.52	0.41	94.24		10.91	27.72	10.60	1.17

表43 续表 continued

单位：万公里 (10 000 km)

年份 Year	铁路营业里程 Length of Railways in Operation	#国家铁路电气化里程 National Electrified Railways	公路里程 Length of Highways	#高速公路 Expressway	内河航道里程 Length of Navigable Inland Waterways	定期航班航线里程 Length of Regular Civil Aviation Routes	#国际航线 International Routes	管道输油(气)里程 Length of Petroleum and Gas Pipelines
1986	5.58	0.44	96.28		10.94	32.31	10.76	1.30
1987	5.60	0.46	98.22		10.98	38.91	14.89	1.38
1988	5.62	0.57	99.96	0.01	10.94	37.38	12.83	1.43
1989	5.70	0.64	101.43	0.03	10.90	47.19	16.64	1.51
1990	5.79	0.69	102.83	0.05	10.92	50.68	16.64	1.59
1991	5.78	0.78	104.11	0.06	10.97	55.91	17.74	1.62
1992	5.81	0.84	105.67	0.07	10.97	83.66	30.30	1.59
1993	5.86	0.89	108.35	0.11	11.02	96.08	27.87	1.64
1994	5.90	0.90	111.78	0.16	11.02	104.56	35.19	1.68
1995	6.24	0.97	115.70	0.21	11.06	112.90	34.82	1.72
1996	6.49	1.01	118.58	0.34	11.08	116.65	38.63	1.93
1997	6.60	1.20	122.64	0.48	10.98	142.50	50.44	2.04
1998	6.64	1.30	127.85	0.87	11.03	150.58	50.44	2.31
1999	6.74	1.40	135.17	1.16	11.65	152.22	52.33	2.49
2000	6.87	1.49	167.98	1.63	11.93	150.29	50.84	2.47
2001	7.01	1.69	169.80	1.94	12.15	155.36	51.69	2.76
2002	7.19	1.74	176.52	2.51	12.16	163.77	57.45	2.98
2003	7.30	1.81	180.98	2.97	12.40	174.95	71.53	3.26
2004	7.44	1.86	187.07	3.43	12.33	204.94	89.42	3.82
2005	7.54	1.94	334.52	4.10	12.33	199.85	85.59	4.40
2006	7.71	2.34	345.70	4.53	12.34	211.35	96.62	4.81
2007	7.80	2.40	358.37	5.39	12.35	234.30	104.74	5.45
2008	7.97	2.50	373.02	6.03	12.28	246.18	112.02	5.83
2009	8.55	3.02	386.08	6.51	12.37	234.51	91.99	6.91
2010	9.12	3.27	400.82	7.41	12.42	276.51	107.02	7.85
2011	9.32	3.43	410.64	8.49	12.46	349.06	149.44	8.33
2012	9.76	3.55	423.75	9.62	12.50	328.01	128.47	9.16
2013	10.31	3.60	435.62	10.44	12.59	410.60	150.32	9.85

注：1.2004年起内河航道里程为内河航道通航里程数。
2.2005年起公路里程包括村道。
3.2011年起民航航线里程改为定期航班航线里程。
4.2013年，管道运输统计口径在原中国石油天然气集团公司、中国石油化工集团公司基础上增加中国海洋石油总公司,2012年管道数据按同口径调整(以下相关表同)。

a) Since 2004, length of navigable inland waterways refers to length of navigable.
b) Since 2005, length of highways includes village roads.
c) Since 2011, length of civil aviation routes changed to length of regular civil aviation routes.
d) In 2013, length of petroleum and gas pipelines includes that of China National Offshore Oil Corp. except for originally PetroChina Company Ltd., SinoPec Company Ltd. Data of 2012 were adjusted according. The same applies to the tables following.

表44 全国客运量
Passenger Traffic

单位：万人 (10 000 persons)

年份 Year	客运量总计 Total	铁路 Railways	国家 National Railways	地方 Local Railways	合资 Joint-venture Railways	公路 Highways	水运 Waterways	民用航空 Civil Aviation
1949	13695	10297	10297			1809	1562	27
1950	20370	15691	15691			2301	2377	1
1951	22334	16037	16037			3350	2945	2
1952	24518	16352	16352			4559	3605	2
1953	35627	22861	22861			7439	5324	3
1954	37465	23290	23290			8648	5523	4
1955	36764	20801	20801			10312	5646	5
1956	50621	25211	25211			18224	7177	9
1957	63821	31262	31262			23772	8780	7
1958	75136	34569	34569			31063	9492	12
1959	91183	47972	47972			32569	10626	16
1960	106700	61822	61822			32524	12333	21
1961	119835	77062	77062			27601	15152	20
1962	122154	75003	74067	936		30737	16397	17
1963	97538	51985	51478	507		32857	12678	18
1964	94300	45085	44618	467		37313	11878	24
1965	96334	41245	40708	537		43693	11369	27
1966	108656	41413	40830	583		54437	12780	26
1967	114067	46614	45982	632		53874	13548	31
1968	111182	49994	49308	686		47125	14038	25
1969	123859	52040	51296	744		56266	15531	22
1970	130056	52455	51646	809		61812	15767	22
1971	142931	56032	55182	850		71227	15638	34
1972	160828	62809	61220	1589		80676	17297	46
1973	174805	65704	64781	923		89771	19270	60
1974	182146	66924	66040	884		95481	19647	94
1975	192969	70465	69648	817		101350	21015	139
1976	201411	71249	70489	760		108718	21298	146
1977	225007	79471	78662	809		122919	22452	165
1978	253993	81491	80729	762		149229	23042	231
1979	289665	86389	85611	778		178618	24360	298
1980	341785	92204	91246	958		222799	26439	343
1981	384763	95219	94236	980		261559	27584	401
1982	428964	99922	98888	1034		300610	27987	445
1983	470614	106044	104946	1098		336965	27214	391
1984	530217	113353	112265	1088		390336	25974	554
1985	620206	112110	110913	1197		476486	30863	747
1986	688211	108579	107358	1221		544259	34377	996

表44 续表 continued

单位：万人 (10 000 persons)

年份 Year	客运量总计 Total	铁路 Railways	国家 National Railways	地方 Local Railways	合资 Joint-venture Railways	公路 Highways	水运 Waterways	民用航空 Civil Aviation
1987	746422	112479	111414	1065		593682	38951	1310
1988	809592	122645	121595	1050		650473	35032	1442
1989	791374	113805	112796	1009		644508	31778	1283
1990	772682	95712	94888	824		648085	27225	1660
1991	806048	95080	94208	872		682681	26109	2178
1992	860855	99693	98788	905		731774	26502	2886
1993	996634	105458	104580	878		860719	27074	3383
1994	1092882	108738	108009	729		953940	26165	4039
1995	1172596	102745	102081	664		1040810	23924	5117
1996	1245357	94797	93551	612	634	1122110	22895	5555
1997	1326094	93308	91919	659	730	1204583	22573	5630
1998	1378717	95085	92991	629	1465	1257332	20545	5755
1999	1394413	100164	97725	528	1911	1269004	19151	6094
2000	1478573	105073	101847	519	2707	1347392	19386	6722
2001	1534122	105155	101680	558	2917	1402798	18645	7524
2002	1608150	105606	101741	516	3349	1475257	18693	8594
2003	1587497	97260	93634	412	3214	1464335	17142	8759
2004	1767453	111764	107346	378	4040	1624526	19040	12123
2005	1847018	115583	110651	319	4613	1697381	20227	13827
2006	2024158	125656	119728	423	5505	1860487	22047	15968
2007	2227761	135670	128712	451	6507	2050680	22835	18576
2008	2867892	146193	144452	474	1267	2682114	20334	19251
2009	2976898	152451	150798	419	1234	2779081	22314	23052
2010	3269508	167609	164761	477	2371	3052738	22392	26769
2011	3526319	186226	179199	528	6498	3286220	24556	29317
2012	3804035	189337	187863	583	891	3557010	25752	31936
2013	2122992	210597	207541	690	2366	1853463	23535	35397

注：1.2008年起，国家铁路和合资铁路客货运输量及周转量统计口径调整，其中国家铁路包括国家控股合资铁路部分，合资铁路仅指非控股合资铁路(以下相关表同)。
2.2008年公路、水路运输量统计口径有调整(以下相关表同)。
3.2013年公路水路客货运输数据，源自2013年交通运输业经济统计专项调查，统计范围口径有所调整(以下相关表同)。

a) Since 2008, statistical coverage of passenger traffic and freight traffic of national railways and joint-venture railways is adjusted, national railways include state-holding joint-venture railways, joint-venture railways only refer to non state-holding joint-venture railways. The same applies to the tables following.

b) Statistical coverage of transport volume of highways, waterways is adjusted in 2008. The same applies to the tables following.

c) In 2013, transports and passenger traffic of highways and waterways come from statistical survey of transport, statistical coverage changed. The same applies to the tables following.

表45 全国旅客周转量
Passenger-Kilometers

单位：亿人公里 (100 million passenger-km)

年份 Year	旅客周转量总计 Total	铁路 Railways	国家 National Railways	地方 Local Railways	合资 Joint-venture Railways	公路 Highways	水运 Waterways	民用航空 Civil Aviation
1949	155.0	130.0	130.0			8.0	15.2	1.9
1950	239.9	212.4	212.4			12.8	14.7	0.1
1951	269.6	230.5	230.5			17.2	21.7	0.2
1952	248.0	200.6	200.6			22.6	24.5	0.2
1953	350.0	281.7	281.7			33.8	34.1	0.3
1954	370.9	294.7	294.7			41.3	34.4	0.5
1955	353.5	267.4	267.4			50.3	35.2	0.6
1956	465.3	343.8	343.8			78.2	42.3	1.0
1957	496.6	361.3	361.3			88.1	46.4	0.8
1958	572.3	409.2	409.2			116.1	45.8	1.2
1959	711.7	517.2	517.2			139.7	53.4	1.4
1960	883.6	674.0	674.0			146.0	61.9	1.6
1961	1105.3	895.6	895.6			128.8	79.5	1.4
1962	1085.6	859.0	857.3	1.8		141.5	83.9	1.2
1963	726.6	532.1	531.2	0.9		134.3	58.8	1.4
1964	685.8	486.2	485.2	0.9		146.3	51.3	2.0
1965	697.0	479.0	477.8	1.2		168.2	47.4	2.5
1966	778.8	504.9	503.6	1.3		207.5	64.2	2.2
1967	863.8	595.4	593.8	1.5		200.0	66.0	2.4
1968	936.3	680.6	678.8	1.7		185.8	67.8	2.1
1969	1070.7	772.1	770.1	2.0		222.2	74.7	1.7
1970	1031.1	718.2	715.9	2.3		240.1	71.0	1.8
1971	1106.9	762.5	760.1	2.4		268.1	73.4	3.0
1972	1235.7	851.9	849.0	2.9		302.5	77.1	4.2
1973	1325.2	902.6	899.9	2.7		333.3	83.6	5.7
1974	1376.6	925.5	922.8	2.7		354.9	86.9	9.3
1975	1434.6	954.1	952.6	1.5		374.5	90.6	15.4
1976	1469.6	957.1	954.7	2.4		402.5	94.3	15.7
1977	1586.7	1022.7	1020.2	2.6		448.1	97.5	18.3
1978	1743.1	1093.2	1090.8	2.4		521.3	100.6	27.9

表45 续表 continued

单位：亿人公里 (100 million passenger-km)

年份 Year	旅客周转量总计 Total	铁路 Railways	国家 National Railways	地方 Local Railways	合资 Joint-venture Railways	公路 Highways	水运 Waterways	民用航空 Civil Aviation
1979	1968.5	1216.2	1213.7	2.4		603.3	114.0	35.0
1980	2281.3	1383.2	1380.4	2.8		729.5	129.1	39.6
1981	2499.6	1472.6	1469.9	2.8		839.0	137.8	50.2
1982	2742.8	1574.8	1572.0	2.8		963.9	144.5	59.5
1983	3095.0	1776.5	1773.4	3.1		1105.6	153.9	59.0
1984	3620.0	2046.4	2043.2	3.2		1336.9	153.5	83.2
1985	4435.4	2416.1	2412.5	3.6		1724.9	178.7	115.7
1986	4896.5	2586.7	2583.1	3.6		1981.7	182.1	146.0
1987	5415.5	2843.1	2840.0	3.1		2190.4	195.9	186.1
1988	6209.4	3260.3	3257.3	3.0		2528.2	203.9	216.9
1989	6074.6	3037.4	3034.4	3.0		2662.1	188.3	186.8
1990	5628.3	2612.6	2610.1	2.5		2620.3	164.9	230.5
1991	6178.4	2828.1	2824.8	3.2		2871.7	177.2	301.3
1992	6949.4	3152.2	3148.3	4.0		3192.6	198.4	406.1
1993	7858.0	3483.3	3479.4	3.9		3700.7	196.4	477.6
1994	8591.4	3636.0	3632.8	3.2		4220.3	183.5	551.6
1995	9001.9	3545.7	3542.6	3.1		4603.1	171.8	681.3
1996	9164.8	3347.6	3322.0	3.4	22.2	4908.8	160.6	747.8
1997	10055.5	3584.9	3543.5	4.7	36.6	5541.4	155.7	773.5
1998	10636.7	3773.4	3691.0	5.0	77.4	5942.8	120.3	800.2
1999	11299.7	4135.9	4046.3	4.4	85.3	6199.2	107.3	857.3
2000	12261.1	4532.6	4414.7	4.6	113.3	6657.4	100.5	970.5
2001	13155.1	4766.8	4636.6	5.2	125.1	7207.1	89.9	1091.4
2002	14125.6	4969.4	4803.1	5.3	161.1	7805.8	81.8	1268.7
2003	13810.5	4788.6	4622.8	4.0	161.8	7695.6	63.1	1263.2
2004	16309.1	5712.2	5512.0	4.0	196.2	8748.4	66.3	1782.3
2005	17466.7	6062.0	5833.2	3.5	225.2	9292.1	67.8	2044.9
2006	19197.2	6622.1	6353.3	4.7	264.2	10130.8	73.6	2370.7
2007	21592.6	7216.3	6896.2	5.3	314.8	11506.8	77.8	2791.7
2008	23196.7	7778.6	7739.1	5.9	33.6	12476.1	59.2	2882.8
2009	24834.9	7878.9	7840.1	5.6	33.2	13511.4	69.4	3375.2
2010	27894.3	8762.2	8725.7	6.3	30.2	15020.8	72.3	4039.0
2011	30984.0	9612.3	9582.7	6.6	23.0	16760.2	74.5	4537.0
2012	33383.1	9812.3	9784.0	6.9	21.5	18467.5	77.5	5025.7
2013	27571.7	10595.6	10550.3	7.3	38.0	11250.9	68.3	5656.8

表46 全国货运量
Freight Traffic

单位：万吨 (10 000 tons)

年份 Year	货运量总计 Total	铁路 Railways	国家 National Railways	地方 Local Railways	合资 Joint-venture Railways	公路 Highways	水运 Waterways	民用航空 Civil Aviation	管道输油(气)量 Petroleum and Gas Pipelines
1949	18713	5589	5589			10579	2543		
1950	24396	9983	9983			11729	2684	0.1	
1951	28692	11083	11083			13749	3860	0.2	
1952	35605	13217	13217			17247	5141	0.2	
1953	49542	16131	16131			26174	7237	0.4	
1954	60286	19288	19288			30834	10163	0.5	
1955	65083	19376	19376			33991	11715	0.5	
1956	82002	24605	24605			43504	13892	0.8	
1957	89990	27421	27421			46762	15806	0.8	
1958	132377	38109	38109			71726	22540	1.5	
1959	206050	54410	54410			117300	34337	2.6	
1960	223052	67219	67219			117200	38630	3.2	
1961	132477	44988	44988			61583	25903	2.9	
1962	92185	35261	34598	663		38909	18013	1.8	
1963	94062	36418	35953	465		39983	17659	1.8	
1964	114168	41786	41230	556		51336	21044	2.0	
1965	133253	49100	48358	742		59995	24155	2.5	
1966	144289	54951	54150	801		64268	25067	3.1	
1967	123804	43089	42140	949		58843	21868	3.5	
1968	115053	42095	40970	1125		52979	19976	3.0	
1969	138238	53120	51787	1333		62311	22804	3.3	
1970	167913	68132	66552	1580		72929	26848	3.7	
1971	194469	76471	74190	2281		86611	30230	3.3	1154
1972	211877	80873	78833	2040		95823	32916	3.0	2262
1973	225473	83111	81294	1817		104171	35423	2.8	2765
1974	223860	78772	76973	1799		106095	35198	3.5	3791
1975	251593	88955	86746	2209		117633	38968	4.7	6032
1976	253967	84066	82116	1950		122119	39875	5.3	7902
1977	290254	95309	92711	2598		142302	43731	5.3	8907
1978	319431	110119	107492	2627		151602	47357	6.4	10347
1979	318258	111893	109495	2398		147935	47080	8.0	11342
1980	310841	111279	108584	2695		142195	46833	8.9	10525
1981	298642	107673	104836	2837		134499	45532	9.4	10929
1982	311937	113495	111048	2447		138634	48632	10.2	11166
1983	323956	118784	116070	2714		144051	49489	11.6	11620
1984	339995	124074	121215	2859		151835	51527	15.0	12544

表46 续表 continued

单位：万吨 (10 000 tons)

年份 Year	货运量总计 Total	铁路 Railways	国家 National Railways	地方 Local Railways	合资 Joint-venture Railways	公路 Highways	水运 Waterways	民用航空 Civil Aviation	管道输油(气)量 Petroleum and Gas Pipelines
1985	745763	130709	127516	3193		538062	63322	19.5	13650
1986	853557	135635	132219	3416		620113	82962	22.4	14825
1987	948229	140653	136949	3704		711424	80979	29.9	15143
1988	982195	144948	140555	4395		732315	89281	32.7	15618
1989	988435	151489	146805	4685		733781	87493	31.0	15641
1990	970602	150681	146209	4472		724040	80094	37.0	15750
1991	985793	152893	147898	4995		733907	83370	45.2	15578
1992	1045899	157627	152317	5310		780941	92490	57.5	14783
1993	1115902	162794	156791	6003		840256	97938	69.4	14845
1994	1180396	163216	157278	5938		894914	107091	82.9	15092
1995	1234938	165982	159473	6509		940387	113194	101.1	15274
1996	1298421	171024	161787	7125	2112	983860	127430	115.0	15992
1997	1278218	172149	162010	7854	2285	976536	113406	124.7	16002
1998	1267427	164309	153435	8035	2839	976004	109555	140.1	17419
1999	1293008	167554	157239	7296	3019	990444	114608	170.4	20232
2000	1358682	178581	166056	8369	4156	1038813	122391	196.7	18700
2001	1401786	193189	179201	9542	4446	1056312	132675	171.0	19439
2002	1483447	204956	187578	11241	6137	1116324	141832	202.1	20133
2003	1564492	224248	199814	13064	11370	1159957	158070	219.0	21998
2004	1706412	249017	217816	14924	16277	1244990	187394	276.7	24734
2005	1862066	269296	231839	17802	19655	1341778	219648	306.7	31037
2006	2037060	288224	245476	19593	23154	1466347	248703	349.4	33436
2007	2275822	314237	262400	24390	27447	1639432	281199	401.8	40552
2008	2587413	330354	275243	27128	27983	1916759	294510	407.6	45382
2009	2825222	333348	277572	23873	31903	2127834	318996	445.5	44598
2010	3241807	364271	309541	19089	35641	2448052	378949	563.0	49972
2011	3696961	393263	329535	22179	41549	2820100	425968	557.5	57073
2012	4100436	390438	323559	22907	43971	3188475	458705	545.0	62274
2013	4098900	396697	322207	24999	49491	3076648	559785	561.3	65209

注：1.从1979年起公路运输包括社会车辆完成数量，从1984年起包括私营运输完成数量(下表同)。
2.1993年及以后年份铁路货物运输指标口径调整，增加了行包运量(下表同)。

a) Since 1979, the freight traffic by highways has included the quantities transported by trucks of non-highway departments. Since 1984, it has also included the quantities transported by private trucks. The same as the following table.

b) The indicator standard of railways freight has been adjusted since 1993, increased freight of package. The same as the following table.

表47　全国货物周转量
Freight Ton-Kilometers

单位：亿吨公里　　(100 million ton-km)

年份 Year	货物周转量总计 Total	铁路 Railways	国家 National Railways	地方 Local Railways	合资 Joint-venture Railways	公路 Highways	水运 Waterways	民用航空 Civil Aviation	管道输油(气)量 Petroleum and Gas
1949	257.9	184.0	184.0			10.5	63.1	0.21	
1950	457.3	394.1	394.1			11.9	51.3	0.01	
1951	634.3	515.6	515.6			15.2	103.5	0.02	
1952	767.0	601.6	601.6			19.6	145.8	0.02	
1953	997.2	781.4	781.4			30.1	185.6	0.04	
1954	1212.8	932.4	932.4			38.7	241.7	0.06	
1955	1329.9	981.5	981.5			44.3	304.0	0.05	
1956	1602.3	1203.5	1203.5			55.1	343.6	0.08	
1957	1825.8	1345.9	1345.9			62.4	417.4	0.08	
1958	2480.3	1855.3	1855.3			102.6	522.3	0.13	
1959	3346.9	2476.3	2476.3			166.2	704.1	0.22	
1960	3739.8	2766.9	2766.9			187.8	784.9	0.26	
1961	2665.4	2007.7	2007.7			103.0	554.5	0.24	
1962	2252.3	1721.1	1719.1	2.0		75.1	456.0	0.15	
1963	2362.9	1816.0	1814.6	1.4		75.6	471.2	0.17	
1964	2768.6	2126.0	2124.5	1.5		87.3	555.0	0.20	
1965	3485.4	2698.7	2696.4	2.3		110.0	676.4	0.25	
1966	3919.9	3018.9	3016.3	2.7		128.9	771.8	0.32	
1967	3068.8	2268.8	2265.7	3.0		113.2	686.4	0.38	
1968	3126.1	2238.8	2235.3	3.5		95.3	791.7	0.32	
1969	3774.4	2783.3	2779.3	4.0		123.4	867.3	0.33	
1970	4590.1	3496.0	3491.4	4.6		154.0	939.9	0.35	
1971	5235.5	3765.9	3759.6	6.4		175.0	1285.2	0.32	9
1972	5685.5	3913.2	3905.1	8.1		191.4	1523.6	0.29	57
1973	6342.1	4082.2	4074.8	7.4		206.8	1965.9	0.30	87
1974	6367.0	3812.9	3805.8	7.1		210.1	2180.6	0.42	163
1975	7594.2	4255.7	4246.1	9.5		248.1	2827.8	0.60	262
1976	6978.7	3869.5	3860.7	8.8		261.0	2490.4	0.73	357
1977	8063.1	4568.8	4557.3	11.5		318.6	2787.9	0.76	387
1978	9928.2	5345.2	5333.5	11.7		350.3	3801.8	0.97	430

表47 续表 continued

单位：亿吨公里 (100 million ton-km)

年份 Year	货物周转量总计 Total	铁路 Railways	国家 National Railways	地方 Local Railways	合资 Joint-venture Railways	公路 Highways	水运 Waterways	民用航空 Civil Aviation	管道输油(气)量 Petroleum and Gas
1979	11013.7	5598.7	5588.7	10.0		351.0	4586.7	1.23	476
1980	11629.3	5717.5	5707.3	10.2		342.9	5076.5	1.41	491
1981	11746.8	5712.0	5701.3	10.7		357.8	5176.3	1.70	499
1982	12539.6	6119.9	6109.0	10.8		411.5	5505.3	1.98	501
1983	13465.5	6646.5	6634.5	12.1		462.7	5820.0	2.29	534
1984	14919.6	7247.6	7234.8	12.9		527.4	6569.4	3.11	572
1985	18365.0	8125.7	8111.6	14.1		1903.0	7729.3	4.15	603
1986	20147.5	8764.8	8750.1	14.7		2118.0	8647.9	4.76	612
1987	22228.5	9471.5	9455.7	15.8		2660.4	9465.1	6.52	625
1988	23825.7	9877.6	9860.2	17.4		3220.4	10070.4	7.32	650
1989	25591.7	10394.2	10373.0	21.2		3374.8	11186.8	6.93	629
1990	26207.6	10622.4	10601.2	21.2		3358.1	11591.9	8.18	627
1991	27986.6	10972.0	10948.1	23.9		3428.0	12955.4	10.10	621
1992	29217.6	11575.6	11548.5	27.0		3755.4	13256.2	13.42	617
1993	30646.8	12090.9	12059.7	31.2		4070.5	13860.8	16.61	608
1994	33435.5	12632.0	12600.6	31.4		4486.3	15686.6	18.58	612
1995	35908.9	13049.5	13015.2	34.2		4694.9	17552.2	22.30	590
1996	36589.8	13106.2	12935.0	48.6	122.5	5011.2	17862.5	24.93	585
1997	38384.7	13269.9	13063.0	50.7	156.2	5271.5	19235.0	29.10	579
1998	38088.7	12560.1	12304.5	50.7	204.8	5483.4	19405.8	33.45	606
1999	40567.8	12910.3	12649.8	37.6	222.9	5724.3	21262.8	42.34	628
2000	44320.5	13770.5	13444.0	43.6	282.9	6129.4	23734.2	50.27	636
2001	47709.9	14694.1	14368.8	55.4	270.0	6330.4	25988.9	43.72	653
2002	50685.9	15658.4	15219.1	62.8	376.5	6782.5	27510.6	51.55	683
2003	53859.2	17246.7	16475.6	69.0	702.1	7099.5	28715.8	57.90	739
2004	69445.1	19288.8	18285.5	89.1	914.2	7840.9	41428.7	71.80	815
2005	80258.1	20726.0	19533.4	99.2	1093.5	8693.2	49672.3	78.90	1088
2006	88839.9	21954.4	20557.2	105.7	1291.6	9754.2	55485.7	94.28	1551
2007	101418.8	23797.0	22112.5	132.7	1551.8	11354.7	64284.8	116.39	1866
2008	110300.8	25106.3	23648.9	150.9	1306.5	32868.2	50262.7	119.60	1944
2009	122133.3	25239.2	23649.9	126.6	1462.7	37188.8	57556.7	126.23	2022
2010	141837.4	27644.1	25937.3	116.1	1590.7	43389.7	68427.5	178.90	2197
2011	159323.6	29465.8	27631.7	138.7	1695.4	51374.7	75423.8	173.91	2885
2012	173804.5	29187.1	27220.5	136.2	1830.4	59534.9	81707.6	163.89	3211
2013	168013.8	29173.9	26845.0	154.9	2173.9	55738.1	79435.7	170.29	3496

表48 全国民用汽车拥有量

Number of Civil Vehicles Owned

单位：万辆 (10 000 units)

年份 Year	民用汽车合计 Civil Vehicles	#载客汽车 Passenger Vehicles	#载货汽车 Trucks	营运汽车合计 Transport Vehicles	#载客汽车 Passenger Vehicles	#载货汽车 Trucks	私人汽车合计 Private-owned Transport Vehicles	#载客汽车 Passenger Vehicles	#载货汽车 Trucks
1949	5.09	1.71	3.25	2.59	0.31	2.28			
1950	5.43	1.73	3.57	2.63	0.34	2.29			
1951	6.19	1.93	4.06	2.62	0.36	2.26			
1952	6.63	1.97	4.42	2.75	0.35	2.40			
1953	7.81	2.35	5.14	2.90	0.38	2.52			
1954	8.95	2.60	5.97	3.28	0.41	2.87			
1955	10.14	2.75	6.94	3.71	0.42	3.29			
1956	11.74	3.24	7.96	4.12	0.51	3.61			
1957	12.60	3.44	8.62	4.40	0.55	3.85			
1958	17.26	3.89	12.70	5.60	0.60	5.00			
1959	21.07	4.41	15.89	6.44	0.64	5.80			
1960	22.38	4.34	17.31	6.92	0.64	6.28			
1961	24.00	4.50	18.58	6.78	0.65	6.13			
1962	24.80	4.70	19.13	6.76	0.65	6.11			
1963	26.13	4.87	20.02	7.08	0.71	6.37			
1964	27.61	5.27	20.86	7.13	0.79	6.34			
1965	29.95	5.98	22.31	7.52	0.96	6.56			
1966	31.92	6.36	23.56	8.29	1.11	7.18			
1967	33.21	6.51	24.58	8.78	1.18	7.60			
1968	34.80	6.64	26.66	9.08	1.22	7.86			
1969	37.16	6.80	27.82	9.75	1.35	8.40			
1970	42.41	7.53	32.04	10.65	1.53	9.12			
1971	49.44	8.38	37.64	11.29	1.76	9.53			
1972	57.74	10.02	43.74	12.02	2.00	10.02			
1973	67.31	11.97	50.52	12.78	2.23	10.55			
1974	78.57	14.28	58.61	13.35	2.29	11.06			
1975	91.77	17.31	68.03	14.81	2.56	12.25			
1976	106.70	20.31	78.54	16.01	2.78	13.23			
1977	119.93	22.64	88.36	17.04	3.03	14.01			
1978	135.84	25.90	100.17	18.15	3.34	14.81			
1979	155.43	29.63	114.33	18.98	3.56	15.42			
1980	178.29	35.08	129.90	19.95	4.07	15.88			
1981	199.14	40.57	144.09	22.17	4.97	17.20			
1982	215.74	44.18	156.75	24.17	5.62	18.50			
1983	232.63	47.78	169.44	25.45	6.18	19.27			
1984	260.41	56.28	188.37	26.11	6.96	19.15			
1985	321.12	79.45	223.20	27.73	8.32	19.41	28.49	1.93	26.48
1986	361.95	96.61	246.57	29.27	9.06	20.21	34.71	3.44	31.23
1987	408.07	111.46	281.21	30.32	9.63	20.25	42.29	7.34	34.91

表48 续表 continued

单位：万辆 (10 000 units)

年份 Year	民用汽车合计 Civil Vehicles	#载客汽车 Passenger Vehicles	#载货汽车 Trucks	营运汽车合计 Transport Vehicles	#载客汽车 Passenger Vehicles	#载货汽车 Trucks	私人汽车合计 Private-owned Transport Vehicles	#载客汽车 Passenger Vehicles	#载货汽车 Trucks
1988	464.38	130.38	317.85	30.69	10.16	19.93	60.42	15.29	45.06
1989	511.32	146.43	346.37	30.85	10.49	19.73	73.12	20.28	52.79
1990	551.36	162.19	368.48	31.30	10.76	20.22	81.62	24.07	57.48
1991	606.11	185.24	398.62	31.67	11.53	19.83	96.04	30.36	65.61
1992	691.74	226.16	441.45	30.87	12.70	18.17	118.20	41.78	76.15
1993	817.58	285.98	501.00	28.96	12.85	16.15	155.77	59.85	94.00
1994	941.95	349.74	560.33	27.97	13.05	14.87	205.42	78.62	123.29
1995	1040.00	417.90	585.43	27.49	13.73	13.75	249.96	114.15	131.83
1996	1100.08	488.02	575.03	28.81	15.41	13.40	289.67	143.04	142.78
1997	1219.09	580.56	601.23	29.89	17.01	12.88	358.36	191.27	163.19
1998	1319.30	654.83	627.89	31.88	19.40	12.48	423.65	230.65	192.03
1999	1452.94	740.23	676.95	501.77	92.14	409.62	533.88	304.09	228.68
2000	1608.91	853.73	716.32	702.82	216.81	486.02	625.33	365.09	259.09
2001	1802.04	993.96	765.24	764.39	255.12	509.27	770.78	469.85	298.95
2002	2053.17	1202.37	812.22	826.34	289.55	536.78	968.98	623.76	341.29
2003	2382.93	1478.81	853.51	924.64	352.19	572.45	1219.23	845.87	367.35
2004	2693.71	1735.91	893.00	1067.18	439.09	628.09	1481.66	1069.69	402.82
2005	3159.66	2132.46	955.55	733.22	128.40	604.82	1848.07	1383.93	452.11
2006	3697.35	2619.57	986.30	802.58	161.92	640.66	2333.32	1823.57	494.91
2007	4358.36	3195.99	1054.06	849.22	164.73	684.49	2876.22	2316.91	539.45
2008	5099.61	3838.92	1126.07	930.61	169.64	760.97	3501.39	2880.50	596.39
2009	6280.61	4845.09	1368.60	1087.35	180.79	906.56	4574.91	3808.33	753.40
2010	7801.83	6124.13	1597.55	1133.32	83.13	1050.19	5938.71	4989.50	931.52
2011	9356.32	7478.37	1787.99	1263.75	84.34	1179.41	7326.79	6237.46	1067.43
2012	10933.09	8943.01	1894.75	1339.89	86.71	1253.19	8838.60	7637.87	1175.63
2013	12670.14	10561.78	2010.62	1504.73	85.26	1419.48	10501.68	9198.23	1275.49

注：1.小轿车包括在载客汽车中。
2.运输汽车1999年以前数据为公路部门营运汽车，1999年为全国营运汽车；2000-2004年为全国运输汽车(含营运汽车和非营运汽车)；2005年起为全国营运汽车(不含非营运汽车)。
3.从2010年起，公路营运载客汽车不包括在公路运输管理部门管理并注册登记为公共汽车和出租汽车。
4.从2013年起，公路营运载货汽车包括货车、牵引车和挂车，统计口径发生调整，数据与上年同期不可比。

a) Passenger vehicles include cars.

b) Before 1999, number of vehicles for business transportation only included those owned by the department of highway transportation. That referred to all working vehicles for business transportation in 1999, and all vehicles for business transportation, including working and non-working vehicles from 2000 to 2004, and refers to national working vehicles(not including non-working) since 2005.

c) Since 2010, pasenger vehicles in operation was not included in highway transport department and registered as bus and taxi.

d) Since 2013, highway trucks in operation included freight car, tractor and trailor, so it was not comparable with preceding years.

表49 全国邮电业务量

Postal and Telecommunication Services

年份 Year	邮电业务总量（亿元） Business Volume of Postal and Telecommunication Services (100 million yuan)	营业网点（处） Number of Offices (unit)	邮路总长度（万公里） Length of Postal Routes (10 000 km)	函 件（亿件） Number of Letters (100 million pcs)	报刊期发数（万份） Issue of Newspapers and Magazines (10 000 copies)
1949	2.58	26328	70.60	5.99	
1950	2.89	36975	86.31	6.46	300
1951	3.95	43753	110.74	7.72	771
1952	4.36	49541	128.97	8.09	1363
1953	5.26	51649	151.47	9.46	1605
1954	5.80	48205	164.00	10.37	2087
1955	6.32	43774	173.94	11.50	2825
1956	7.90	44665	181.13	14.38	3423
1957	7.79	45375	222.26	16.41	3264
1958	11.08	60719	301.29	17.34	7922
1959	16.49	58621	420.61	23.15	5965
1960	21.20	61745	408.51	28.28	4009
1961	18.90	51751	318.80	25.55	2590
1962	16.92	44513	266.54	22.75	2492
1963	16.04	44022	286.55	20.21	3455
1964	16.28	43748	306.47	19.96	4689
1965	16.66	43787	349.28	21.76	5621
1966	17.25	44812	368.06	22.39	4385
1967	16.34	45081	367.31	21.69	3387
1968	15.20	44551	366.23	20.72	2672
1969	16.51	44626	371.32	22.68	2973
1970	18.21	45027	397.71	23.70	3307
1971	20.29	45949	428.80	24.38	4697
1972	21.92	46162	448.58	25.04	5285
1973	23.33	48495	451.14	26.35	5894
1974	24.04	48290	464.09	26.11	6917
1975	25.39	48707	479.63	27.34	7823

注：1.邮电业务总量2000年及以前按1990年不变单价计算，2001-2010年按2000年不变单价计算，2011年起按2010年不变价格计算。
2.营业网点1998年及以前为邮电局所,1999-2001年为邮政局所,2002-2006年为邮政局所和邮政代办点,2007年起为邮政企业和规模以上快递企业营业网点。
3.邮路总长度1981年及以前为邮路及农村投递路线总长度之和。

a) The business volume of postal and telecommunication services was calculated at 1990's constant prices before 2000 and at 2000's from 2001 to 2010, and at 2010's since 2011.

b) Number of postal offices refers to postal and telecommunication offices before 1998, and refers to postal offices form 1999 to 2001, and refers to postal offices and postal sub-stations from 2002 to 2006, and refers to postal enterprises and express mail enterprises above designated size since 2007.

c) Length of postal routes before 1981 included the length of postal routes and rural delivery routes.

表49 续表 1 continued

年份 Year	邮电业务总量 (亿元) Business Volume of Postal and Telecommunication Services (100 million yuan)	营业网点 (处) Number of Offices (unit)	邮路总长度 (万公里) Length of Postal Routes (10 000 km)	函件 (亿件) Number of Letters (100 million pcs)	报刊期发数 (万份) Issue of Newspapers and Magazines (10 000 copies)
1976	28.17	48931	483.60	27.79	8806
1977	29.55	49586	486.02	28.50	8707
1978	34.09	49623	486.33	28.35	11250
1979	33.29	49647	481.23	30.80	12680
1980	39.03	49471	473.71	33.13	16431
1981	37.18	49570	466.02	33.88	18124
1982	38.88	49727	130.63	33.94	19598
1983	42.41	50162	130.85	35.21	22933
1984	47.68	51463	133.63	39.48	28141
1985	62.21	53107	141.63	46.78	30172
1986	62.60	52777	153.59	49.59	28731
1987	73.99	52882	153.57	54.79	31005
1988	102.87	52881	155.78	59.77	27443
1989	123.46	53092	152.61	57.28	17704
1990	155.54	53629	161.82	54.87	20078
1991	204.38	54006	160.33	52.11	23277
1992	290.94	54891	164.69	57.18	25104
1993	462.71	57005	176.05	68.70	25511
1994	688.19	60447	178.18	76.50	24096
1995	988.85	61898	188.61	79.55	21689
1996	1342.04	72496	211.89	78.68	21157
1997	1773.29	79273	236.31	68.55	21875
1998	2431.21	102225	285.39	65.51	22989
1999	3330.82	66649	297.90	60.52	25035
2000	4792.70	58437	307.33	77.71	20090
2001	4556.26	57136	310.26	86.93	21811
2002	5695.80	76358	308.10	106.01	17620
2003	7019.79	63555	327.02	103.84	16594
2004	9712.29	66393	333.64	82.81	14789
2005	12028.54	65917	340.62	73.51	14601
2006	15325.87	62799	336.94	71.31	14373
2007	19805.06	70655	353.30	69.50	13031
2008	23649.52	69146	369.35	73.63	15658
2009	27193.46	65672	402.78	75.32	13910
2010	31978.48	75739	463.56	74.01	17158
2011	13333.49	78667	514.03	73.78	15008
2012	15019.28	95572	585.51	70.74	15402
2013	18432.24	125115	589.72	63.41	15141

表49 续表 2 continued

年份 Year	固定电话用户（万户） Number of Fixed Telephone Subscribers at Year-end (10 000 subscribers)	城市电话用户 Urban Fixed Telephone Subscribers	#住宅电话用户 Household Fixed Telephone Subscribers	农村电话用户 Rural Fixed Telephone Subscribers	#住宅电话用户 Household Fixed Telephone Subscribers	#公用电话用户（万户） Public Telephone (10 000 subscribers)	移动电话用户（万户） Number of Mobile Telephone Subscribers at Year-end (10 000 subscribers)
1949	21.8	21.8					
1950	22.5	22.5					
1951	31.9	27.4		4.6			
1952	35.4	29.5		5.8			
1953	40.1	33.2		6.9			
1954	43.9	35.6		8.3			
1955	47.9	37.5		10.4			
1956	61.4	44.4		17.0			
1957	66.5	46.5		20.0			
1958	90.7	51.5		39.1			
1959	129.3	59.2		70.1			
1960	157.8	65.9		91.9			
1961	161.6	70.3		91.3			
1962	155.2	70.0		85.3			
1963	151.6	72.2		79.5			
1964	121.6	74.8		46.8			
1965	126.3	77.1		49.2			
1966	130.9	79.9		51.0			
1967	131.8	80.6		51.1			
1968	125.9	75.8		50.2			
1969	126.4	75.8		50.7			
1970	131.1	78.4		52.7			
1971	135.1	81.2		53.9			
1972	145.6	88.4		57.2			
1973	153.8	93.6		60.2			
1974	160.5	98.0		62.5			
1975	169.2	103.3		65.9			
1976	176.1	107.9		68.2			
1977	183.4	112.7		70.7		1.1	
1978	192.5	119.2		73.4		1.2	
1979	203.3	127.0		76.3		1.3	
1980	214.1	134.2		79.9		1.4	
1981	222.1	142.6		79.5		1.5	
1982	234.3	153.9		80.4		1.8	
1983	250.8	168.9		81.9		2.0	

注：2002年起公用电话用户包括安装在街道等公共场所的智能网专线接入终端用户。

a) Number of subscirbers of public telephone since 2002 include the smart net special end-users which were installed at the public spatial, such as street.

表49 续表 3 continued

年份 Year	固定电话用户 (万户) Number of Fixed Telephone Subscribers at Year-end (10 000 subscribers)	城市电话用户 Urban Fixed Telephone Subscribers	#住宅电话用户 Household Fixed Telephone Subscribers	农村电话用户 Rural Fixed Telephone Subscribers	#住宅电话用户 Household Fixed Telephone Subscribers	#公用电话用户 Public Telephone	移动电话用户 (万户) Number of Mobile Telephone Subscribers at Year-end (10 000 subscribers)
1984	277.4	191.1		86.4		2.4	
1985	312.0	219.0		93.1		2.7	
1986	350.4	250.5		99.9		3.0	
1987	390.7	293.0		97.7		3.3	
1988	472.7	362.3		110.4		3.7	0.3
1989	568.0	439.6	89.6	128.4	21.3	4.0	1.0
1990	685.1	538.5	152.7	146.6	30.7	4.6	1.8
1991	845.1	670.8	239.0	174.2	49.5	5.4	4.8
1992	1146.9	920.6	415.4	226.3	79.0	8.4	17.7
1993	1733.2	1407.4	800.4	325.8	139.5	15.8	63.8
1994	2729.5	2246.8	1489.4	482.7	274.9	38.7	156.8
1995	4070.6	3263.6	2358.4	807.0	551.4	85.0	362.9
1996	5494.7	4277.8	3224.6	1216.9	907.3	138.0	685.3
1997	7031.0	5244.4	4057.2	1786.6	1406.6	193.9	1323.3
1998	8742.1	6259.8	4911.1	2482.3	2070.7	259.5	2386.3
1999	10871.6	7463.3	5894.4	3408.4	2949.2	297.4	4329.6
2000	14482.9	9311.6	7219.4	5171.3	4597.8	352.0	8453.3
2001	18036.8	11193.7	8535.3	6843.1	6197.7	346.2	14522.2
2002	21422.2	13579.1	10196.7	7843.1	7183.8	985.5	20600.5
2003	26274.7	17109.7	12533.9	9165.0	8389.7	1561.4	26995.3
2004	31175.6	21025.1	15246.5	10150.5	9240.5	2215.0	33482.4
2005	35044.5	23975.3	17201.2	11069.2	10023.9	2681.2	39340.6
2006	36778.6	25132.9	17697.6	11645.6	10561.5	2960.7	46105.8
2007	36563.7	24859.8	16988.2	11704.0	10533.1	2991.9	54730.6
2008	34035.9	23155.9	15588.3	10880.0	9612.2	2771.5	64124.5
2009	31373.2	21190.0	12969.5	10183.2	8813.3	2708.8	74721.4
2010	29434.2	19658.1	11973.4	9776.1	8325.0	2595.9	85900.3
2011	28509.8	19121.7	11411.6	9388.1	7861.2	2468.3	98625.3
2012	27815.3	18893.4	11013.2	8921.9	7315.8	2347.1	111215.5
2013	26698.5	18456.8	10474.3	8241.7	6643.4	2233.4	122911.3

表49 续表 4 continued

年份 Year	平均每一营业网点服务面积（平方公里） Average Area Served by Every Postal Office (sq.km)	平均每一营业网点服务人口（万人） Average People Served by Every Postal Office (10 000 persons)	平均每百人每年订报刊数（份） Annual Average Number of Newspaper and Magazine Subscribed per 100 Persons (piece)	已通固定电话的行政村比重（%） Percentage of Administrative Village with Fixed Telephone (%)	电话普及率（包括移动电话）（部/百人） Popularization Rate of Telephone (Include Mobile Telephone) (sets/100 persons)
1949	364.6	2.10			0.05
1950	259.6	1.50	0.5		0.05
1951	219.4	1.30	1.4		0.06
1952	193.8	1.20	2.4		0.07
1953	185.9	1.10	2.7		0.08
1954	199.1	1.30	3.5		0.08
1955	219.3	1.40	4.6		0.09
1956	214.9	1.40	5.4		0.11
1957	211.6	1.40	5.0		0.13
1958	158.1	1.10	2.7	58.8	0.19
1959	163.8	1.10	8.9	75.9	0.25
1960	155.5	1.10	6.1	86.9	0.31
1961	185.5	1.30	3.9	68.4	0.32
1962	215.7	1.50	3.7	59.5	0.29
1963	218.1	1.60	5.0	52.1	0.21
1964	219.4	1.60	6.7	50.8	0.29
1965	219.2	1.70	7.7	52.5	0.29
1966	214.2	1.70	5.9	54.8	0.29
1967	213.0	1.70	4.5	54.6	0.28
1968	215.5	1.80	3.4	55.3	0.27
1969	215.1	1.80	3.5	56.1	0.26
1970	213.2	1.80	4.0	58.1	0.27
1971	208.9	1.80	5.5	60.2	0.27
1972	208.0	1.90	6.1	60.6	0.28
1973	198.0	1.80	6.6	60.9	0.30
1974	198.8	1.90	7.7	61.6	0.32
1975	197.1	1.90	8.5	62.4	0.33
1976	196.2	1.90	9.4	65.4	0.35
1977	193.6	1.90	9.2	67.0	0.36
1978	193.5	1.94	11.7	67.8	0.38
1979	193.4	1.97	13.1	65.5	0.41
1980	194.1	1.98	16.7	62.8	0.43
1981	193.7	2.01	18.1	58.0	0.44
1982	193.1	2.04	19.3	53.9	0.46
1983	191.4	2.04	22.4	48.3	0.49

注：1.电话普及率1990年起含移动电话用户，以前为固定电话用户普及率。
2.已通固定电话的行政村比重2009年及以后为已通电话的行政村比重。

a) Popularization rate of telephone includes mobile phones since 1990, and only refers to fixed telephones before.

b) Percentage of Administrative Village with Fixed Telephone since 1990 refers percentage of administrative village with telephone.

表49 续表 5 continued

年份 Year	平均每一营业网点服务面积（平方公里） Average Area Served by Every Postal Office (sq.km)	平均每一营业网点服务人口（万人） Average People Served by Every Postal Office (10 000 persons)	平均每百人每年订报刊数（份） Annual Average Number of Newspaper and Magazine Subscribed per 100 Persons (piece)	已通固定电话的行政村比重（%） Percentage of Administrative Village with Fixed Telephone (%)	电话普及率（包括移动电话）（部/百人） Popularization Rate of Telephone (Include Mobile Telephone) (sets/100 persons)
1984	186.5	2.01	27.2	47.4	0.53
1985	180.8	1.97	28.8	45.4	0.60
1986	181.9	2.01	27.1	45.4	0.67
1987	181.5	1.99	25.0	44.8	0.75
1988	181.5	2.06	25.0	44.3	0.86
1989	180.8	2.09	14.6	43.6	0.98
1990	179.0	2.13	17.6	43.3	1.11
1991	177.8	2.14	20.1	43.4	1.29
1992	174.9	2.11	22.2	44.0	1.61
1993	168.4	2.08	21.8	44.7	2.20
1994	159.0	1.98	20.1		3.20
1995	155.1	1.95	18.0		4.66
1996	132.6	1.65	17.6	53.5	6.33
1997	122.3	1.56	17.7	55.6	8.11
1998	93.9	1.22	18.4	71.0	9.95
1999	144.0	1.87	20.1	77.9	13.12
2000	135.3	1.77	16.4	82.9	19.10
2001	168.0	2.20	17.2	85.3	26.55
2002	123.8	1.70	13.9	87.9	33.67
2003	148.8	2.03	12.9	89.9	42.16
2004	142.4	2.00	11.4	91.2	50.03
2005	145.6	1.97	11.2	94.4	57.22
2006	152.9	2.09	11.2	95.9	63.40
2007	135.9	1.90	9.9	96.7	69.45
2008	138.8	1.90	11.9	96.9	74.29
2009	146.2	2.03	10.4	99.9	79.89
2010	126.8	1.77	12.8	100.0	86.41
2011	122.0	1.71	11.1	100.0	94.81
2012	100.4	1.42	11.4	100.0	103.10
2013	76.7	1.09	11.0	100.0	109.95

表50 全国社会消费品零售总额
Total Retail Sale of Consumer Goods

年份 Year	社会消费品零售总额(亿元) Total Retail Sales of Consumer Goods (100 million yuan)	比上年增长(%) Increase Over Preceding Year (%)	年份 Year	社会消费品零售总额(亿元) Total Retail Sales of Consumer Goods (100 million yuan)	比上年增长(%) Increase Over Preceding Year (%)
1952	276.8		1983	2849.4	10.9
1953	348.0	25.7	1984	3376.4	18.5
1954	381.1	9.5	1985	4305.0	27.5
1955	392.2	2.9	1986	4950.0	15.0
1956	461.0	17.5	1987	5820.0	17.6
1957	474.2	2.9	1988	7440.0	27.8
1958	548.0	15.6	1989	8101.4	8.9
1959	638.0	16.4	1990	8300.1	2.5
1960	696.9	9.2	1991	9415.6	13.4
1961	607.7	-12.8	1992	10993.7	16.8
1962	604.0	-0.6	1993	14270.4	29.8
1963	604.5	0.1	1994	18622.9	30.5
1964	638.2	5.6	1995	23613.8	26.8
1965	670.3	5.0	1996	28360.2	20.1
1966	732.8	9.3	1997	31252.9	10.2
1967	770.5	5.1	1998	33378.1	6.8
1968	737.3	-4.3	1999	35647.9	6.8
1969	801.5	8.7	2000	39105.7	9.7
1970	858.0	7.0	2001	43055.4	10.1
1971	929.2	8.3	2002	48135.9	11.8
1972	1023.3	10.1	2003	52516.3	9.1
1973	1106.7	8.2	2004	59501.0	13.3
1974	1163.6	5.1	2005	68352.6	14.9
1975	1271.1	9.2	2006	79145.2	15.8
1976	1339.4	5.4	2007	93571.6	18.2
1977	1432.8	7.0	2008	114830.1	22.7
1978	1558.6	8.8	2009	132678.4	15.5
1979	1800.0	15.5	2010	156998.4	18.3
1980	2140.0	18.9	2011	183918.6	17.1
1981	2350.0	9.8	2012	210307.0	14.3
1982	2570.0	9.4	2013	237809.9	13.1

注：1992年及以前为社会商品零售总额。
a) Figures before 1992 refer to retail sales of commodities.

表51 全国货物进出口贸易总额
Total Value of Imports and Exports of Goods

年份 Year	人民币（亿元）(100 million yuan) 进出口总额 Total Imports & Exports	出口总额 Total Exports	进口总额 Total Imports	差额 Balance	美元（亿美元）(USD 100 million) 进出口总额 Total Imports & Exports	出口总额 Total Exports	进口总额 Total Imports	差额 Balance
1950	41.3	20.0	21.3	-1.3	11.3	5.5	5.8	-0.3
1951	59.5	24.2	35.3	-11.1	19.6	7.6	12.0	-4.4
1952	64.6	27.1	37.5	-10.4	19.4	8.2	11.2	-3.0
1953	80.9	34.8	46.1	-11.3	23.7	10.2	13.5	-3.3
1954	84.7	40.0	44.7	-4.7	24.4	11.5	12.9	-1.4
1955	109.8	48.7	61.1	-12.4	31.4	14.1	17.3	-3.2
1956	108.7	55.7	53.0	2.7	32.1	16.5	15.6	0.9
1957	104.5	54.5	50.0	4.5	31.0	16.0	15.0	1.0
1958	128.7	67.0	61.7	5.3	38.7	19.8	18.9	0.9
1959	149.3	78.1	71.2	6.9	43.8	22.6	21.2	1.4
1960	128.4	63.3	65.1	-1.8	38.1	18.6	19.5	-0.9
1961	90.7	47.7	43.0	4.7	29.4	14.9	14.5	0.4
1962	80.9	47.1	33.8	13.3	26.6	14.9	11.7	3.2
1963	85.7	50.0	35.7	14.3	29.2	16.5	12.7	3.8
1964	97.5	55.4	42.1	13.3	34.7	19.2	15.5	3.7
1965	118.4	63.1	55.3	7.8	42.5	22.3	20.2	2.1
1966	127.1	66.0	61.1	4.9	46.2	23.7	22.5	1.2
1967	112.2	58.8	53.4	5.4	41.6	21.4	20.2	1.2
1968	108.5	57.6	50.9	6.7	40.5	21.0	19.5	1.5
1969	107.0	59.8	47.2	12.6	40.3	22.0	18.3	3.7
1970	112.9	56.8	56.1	0.7	45.9	22.6	23.3	-0.7
1971	120.9	68.5	52.4	16.1	48.4	26.4	22.0	4.4
1972	146.9	82.9	64.0	18.9	63.0	34.4	28.6	5.8
1973	220.5	116.9	103.6	13.3	109.8	58.2	51.6	6.6
1974	292.2	139.4	152.8	-13.4	145.7	69.5	76.2	-6.7
1975	290.4	143.0	147.4	-4.4	147.5	72.6	74.9	-2.3
1976	264.1	134.8	129.3	5.5	134.3	68.5	65.8	2.7
1977	272.5	139.7	132.8	6.9	148.0	75.9	72.1	3.8
1978	355.0	167.6	187.4	-19.8	206.4	97.5	108.9	-11.4
1979	454.6	211.7	242.9	-31.2	293.3	136.6	156.7	-20.1
1980	570.0	271.2	298.8	-27.6	381.4	181.2	200.2	-19.0
1981	735.3	367.6	367.7	-0.1	440.3	220.1	220.2	-0.1
1982	771.3	413.8	357.5	56.3	416.1	223.2	192.9	30.3
1983	860.1	438.3	421.8	16.5	436.2	222.3	213.9	8.4
1984	1201.0	580.5	620.5	-40.0	535.5	261.4	274.1	-12.7

表51 续表 continued

年份 Year	人民币（亿元）(100 million yuan)				美元（亿美元）(USD 100 million)			
	进出口总额 Total Imports & Exports	出口总额 Total Exports	进口总额 Total Imports	差额 Balance	进出口总额 Total Imports & Exports	出口总额 Total Exports	进口总额 Total Imports	差额 Balance
1985	2066.7	808.9	1257.8	-448.9	696.0	273.5	422.5	-149.0
1986	2580.4	1082.1	1498.3	-416.2	738.5	309.4	429.1	-119.7
1987	3084.2	1470.0	1614.2	-144.2	826.5	394.4	432.1	-37.7
1988	3821.8	1766.7	2055.1	-288.4	1027.9	475.2	552.7	-77.5
1989	4155.9	1956.0	2199.9	-243.9	1116.8	525.4	591.4	-66.0
1990	5560.1	2985.8	2574.3	411.5	1154.4	620.9	533.5	87.4
1991	7225.8	3827.1	3398.7	428.4	1357.0	718.4	637.9	80.5
1992	9119.6	4676.3	4443.3	233.0	1655.3	849.4	805.9	43.5
1993	11271.0	5284.8	5986.2	-701.4	1957.0	917.4	1039.6	-122.2
1994	20381.9	10421.8	9960.1	461.7	2366.2	1210.1	1156.1	54.0
1995	23499.9	12451.8	11048.1	1403.7	2808.6	1487.8	1320.8	167.0
1996	24133.8	12576.4	11557.4	1019.0	2898.8	1510.5	1388.3	122.2
1997	26967.2	15160.7	11806.5	3354.2	3251.6	1827.9	1423.7	404.2
1998	26849.7	15223.6	11626.1	3597.5	3239.5	1837.1	1402.4	434.7
1999	29896.3	16159.8	13736.5	2423.3	3606.3	1949.3	1657.0	292.3
2000	39273.2	20634.4	18638.8	1995.6	4742.9	2492.0	2250.9	241.1
2001	42183.6	22024.4	20159.2	1865.2	5096.5	2661.0	2435.5	225.5
2002	51378.2	26947.9	24430.3	2517.6	6207.7	3256.0	2951.7	304.3
2003	70483.5	36287.9	34195.6	2092.3	8509.9	4382.3	4127.6	254.7
2004	95539.1	49103.3	46435.8	2667.5	11545.5	5933.2	5612.3	320.9
2005	116921.8	62648.1	54273.7	8374.4	14219.1	7619.5	6599.5	1020.0
2006	140974.0	77597.2	63376.9	14220.3	17604.4	9689.8	7914.6	1775.2
2007	166863.7	93563.6	73300.1	20263.5	21765.7	12204.6	9561.2	2643.4
2008	179921.5	100394.9	79526.5	20868.4	25632.6	14306.9	11325.6	2981.3
2009	150648.1	82029.7	68618.4	13411.3	22075.4	12016.1	10059.2	1956.9
2010	201722.1	107022.8	94699.3	12323.5	29740.0	15777.5	13962.4	1815.1
2011	236402.0	123240.6	113161.4	10079.2	36418.6	18983.8	17434.8	1549.0
2012	244160.2	129359.3	114801.0	14558.3	38671.2	20487.1	18184.1	2303.1
2013	258168.9	137131.4	121037.5	16094.0	41589.9	22090.0	19499.9	2590.1

注：1.本表1979年及以前为外贸业务统计数，1980年起为海关进出口统计数。
2.进出口差额负数为逆差。

a) Data in 1979 and before were obtained from the Ministry of Foreign Trade, and the data since 1980 have been obtained from the Customs statistics.

b) A negative balance indicates an unfavourable balance of foreign trade.

表52 按贸易方式和商品类别分全国进出口贸易总额

Total Value of Imports and Exports by Trading Form and by Category of Commodities

单位：亿美元 (USD 100 million)

年份 Year	按贸易方式分 By Trading Form						按商品类别分 By Category of Commodities			
	一般贸易 Conventional Trade		加工贸易 Processing Trade		其他贸易 Other Trading Forms		初级产品 Primary Goods		工业制成品 Manufactured Goods	
	出口 Exports	进口 Imports	出口 Exports	进口 Imports	出口 Exports	进口 Imports	出口 Exports	进口 Imports	出口 Exports	进口 Imports
1980							91.14	69.59	90.05	130.58
1981	208.00	203.66	11.31	15.04	0.79	1.40	102.48	80.44	117.59	139.71
1982	222.45	188.85	0.53	2.76	0.22	1.38	100.50	76.34	122.71	116.51
1983	201.60	187.68	19.44	22.72	1.26	3.50	96.20	58.08	126.06	155.82
1984	231.62	238.49	29.29	31.47	0.49	4.14	119.34	52.08	142.05	222.02
1985	237.30	372.72	33.16	42.74	3.04	7.04	138.28	52.89	135.22	369.63
1986	250.95	352.07	56.20	67.03	2.25	9.90	112.72	56.49	196.70	372.55
1987	296.43	287.72	89.94	101.91	8.03	42.47	132.31	69.15	262.06	363.01
1988	326.22	352.04	140.60	151.05	8.38	49.61	144.06	100.68	331.10	452.07
1989	315.52	356.14	197.85	171.64	12.03	63.62	150.78	117.54	374.60	473.86
1990	354.60	262.00	254.20	187.60	12.10	83.90	158.86	98.53	462.05	434.92
1991	381.20	295.40	324.30	250.30	13.60	92.20	161.45	108.34	556.98	529.57
1992	436.80	336.20	396.20	315.40	16.40	154.30	170.04	132.55	679.36	673.30
1993	432.00	380.50	442.50	363.70	43.00	295.40	166.66	142.10	750.78	897.49
1994	615.60	355.20	569.80	475.70	24.70	325.20	197.08	164.86	1012.98	991.28
1995	713.70	433.70	737.00	583.70	37.10	303.40	214.85	244.17	1272.95	1076.67
1996	628.40	393.60	843.30	622.70	38.80	372.00	219.25	254.41	1291.23	1133.92
1997	779.74	390.30	996.02	702.06	52.14	331.34	239.53	286.20	1588.39	1137.50
1998	742.35	436.80	1044.54	685.99	50.22	279.58	204.89	229.49	1632.20	1172.88
1999	791.35	670.40	1108.82	735.78	49.14	250.81	199.41	268.46	1749.90	1388.53
2000	1051.81	1000.79	1376.52	925.58	63.70	324.57	254.60	467.39	2237.43	1783.55
2001	1118.81	1134.56	1474.34	939.74	67.83	361.23	263.38	457.43	2397.60	1978.10
2002	1361.87	1291.11	1799.27	1222.00	94.82	438.59	285.40	492.71	2970.56	2458.99
2003	1820.34	1877.00	2418.49	1629.35	143.45	621.22	348.12	727.63	4034.16	3399.96
2004	2436.06	2481.45	3279.70	2216.95	217.50	913.89	405.49	1172.67	5527.77	4439.62
2005	3150.63	2796.33	4164.67	2740.12	304.23	1063.08	490.37	1477.14	7129.16	5122.39
2006	4162.33	3330.74	5103.55	3214.72	423.81	1369.15	529.19	1871.29	9160.17	6043.32
2007	5393.55	4286.64	6175.60	3684.75	623.20	1590.20	615.09	2430.85	11562.67	7128.65
2008	6628.62	5720.93	6751.14	3783.77	927.17	1820.92	779.57	3623.95	13527.36	7701.67
2009	5298.12	5344.70	5868.62	3222.91	849.37	1491.62	631.12	2898.04	11384.83	7161.19
2010	7206.12	7692.76	7402.79	4174.82	1168.63	2094.86	816.86	4338.50	14960.69	9623.94
2011	9170.34	10076.21	8352.84	4697.56	1460.64	2661.07	1005.45	6042.69	17978.36	11392.15
2012	9878.99	10223.86	8626.77	4812.75	1981.38	3147.43	1005.58	6349.34	19481.56	11834.71
2013	10873.26	11098.59	8600.40	4966.62	2616.38	3434.68	1072.68	6580.81	21017.36	12919.09

表53 全国实际利用外资
Uitilization of Foreign Capital

年份 Year	总计 Total		对外借款 Foreign Loans		外商直接投资 Direct Foreign Investments		外商其他投资额 (亿美元) Other Foreign Investments (USD 100 million)
	项目 (个) Number of Projects (unit)	金额 (亿美元) Value (USD 100 million)	项目 (个) Number of Projects (unit)	金额 (亿美元) Value (USD 100 million)	项目 (个) Number of Projects (unit)	金额 (亿美元) Value (USD 100 million)	
1979-1982	947	130.60	27	106.90	920	17.69	6.01
1983	690	22.61	52	10.65	638	9.16	2.80
1984	2204	28.66	38	12.86	2166	14.19	1.61
1985	3145	47.60	72	25.06	3073	19.56	2.98
1986	1551	76.28	53	50.14	1498	22.44	3.70
1987	2289	84.52	56	58.05	2233	23.14	3.33
1988	6063	102.26	118	64.87	5945	31.94	5.45
1989	5909	100.60	130	62.86	5779	33.92	3.81
1990	7371	102.89	98	65.34	7273	34.87	2.68
1991	13086	115.54	108	68.88	12978	43.66	3.00
1992	48858	192.03	94	79.11	48764	110.08	2.84
1993	83595	389.60	158	111.89	83437	275.15	2.56
1994	47646	432.13	97	92.67	47549	337.67	1.79
1995	37184	481.33	173	103.27	37011	375.21	2.85
1996	24673	548.05	117	126.69	24556	417.26	4.10
1997	21138	644.08	137	120.21	21001	452.57	71.30
1998	19850	585.57	51	110.00	19799	454.63	20.94
1999	17022	526.59	104	102.12	16918	403.19	21.28
2000	22347	593.56		100.00	22347	407.15	86.41
2001	26140	496.72			26140	468.78	27.94
2002	34171	550.11			34171	527.43	22.68
2003	41081	561.40			41081	535.05	26.35
2004	43664	640.72			43664	606.30	34.42
2005	44001	638.05			44001	603.25	34.80
2006	41473	670.76			41473	630.21	40.55
2007	37871	783.39			37871	747.68	35.72
2008	27514	952.53			27514	923.95	28.58
2009	23435	918.04			23435	900.33	17.71
2010	27406	1088.21			27406	1057.35	30.86
2011	27712	1176.98			27712	1160.11	16.87
2012	24925	1132.94			24925	1117.16	15.78
2013	22773	1187.21			22773	1175.86	11.34

表54 对外经济合作

Economic Cooperation with Foreign Countries or Regions

年 份 Year	对外承包工程 Foreign Engineering Projects 合同数（份） Contract Number (unit)	合同金额（亿美元） Contract Value (USD 100 million)	完成营业额（亿美元） Turnover (USD 100 million)	年末在外人数（万人） Persons Abroad by the End of Year (10000 persons)	对外劳务合作 Foreign Labour Services 派出劳务人数（万人） Dispatched Labor (10000 persons)	年末在外人数（万人） Persons Abroad by the End of Year (10000 persons)
1979	27	0.33				
1980	138	1.40	1.23 (1979-1981)			
1981	250	2.76				
1982	195	3.46	1.00			
1983	280	7.99	1.89			
1984	344	15.38	4.94	2.19		2.76
1985	465	11.16	6.63	3.06		2.49
1986	486	11.89	8.19	2.74		1.90
1987	616	16.48	11.14	3.13		3.19
1988	642	18.13	12.53	3.00		3.98
1989	776	17.81	14.84	2.40		4.31
1990	920	21.25	16.44	2.18		3.61
1991	1171	25.24	19.70	2.15		6.83
1992	1164	52.51	24.03	2.54		10.56
1993	1393	51.89	36.68	3.42		13.09
1994	1702	60.27	48.83	3.83		18.43
1995	1558	74.84	51.08	3.84		22.59
1996	1634	77.28	58.21	3.88		24.66
1997	2085	85.16	60.36	4.78		28.55
1998	2322	92.43	77.69	6.11		29.08
1999	2527	101.99	85.22	5.53		32.65
2000	2597	117.19	83.79	5.56		36.93
2001	5836	130.39	88.99	6.00		41.47
2002	4036	150.55	111.94	7.85		41.04
2003	3708	176.67	138.37	9.40		42.97
2004	6694	238.44	174.68	11.47	17.30	41.94
2005	9502	296.14	217.63	14.48	18.34	41.87
2006	12996	660.05	299.93	19.86	21.48	47.52
2007	6282	776.21	406.43	23.60	21.49	50.51
2008	5411	1045.62	566.12	27.16	22.49	46.71
2009	7280	1262.10	777.06	32.69	18.01	45.03
2010	9544	1343.67	921.70	37.65	18.68	47.01
2011	6381	1423.32	1034.24	32.40	20.91	48.84
2012	6710	1565.29	1165.97	34.46	27.84	50.56
2013	11578	1716.29	1371.43	37.01	25.57	48.26

表55 全国国际旅游情况
International Tourism

年份 Year	入境游客（万人次） Total Number of International Tourists (10 000 person-times)	#外国人 Foreigners	#港澳台同胞 Compatriots from Hong Kong, Macao and Taiwan	#过夜游客 Tourists (Overnight Visitors)	国际旅游收入（亿美元） International Tourism Earnings (100 million USD)	世界排名（位次） Rank	
						过夜游客者人数 Tourists (Overnight Visitors)	国际旅游收入 International Tourism Earnings
1978	180.9	23.0	156.2	71.6	2.63		
1979	420.4	36.2	382.1	152.9	4.49		
1980	570.3	52.9	513.9	350.0	6.17	18	34
1981	776.7	67.5	705.3	376.7	7.85	17	34
1982	792.4	76.4	711.7	392.4	8.43	16	29
1983	947.7	87.3	856.4	379.1	9.41	16	26
1984	1285.2	113.4	1167.0	514.1	11.31	14	21
1985	1783.3	137.0	1637.8	713.3	12.50	13	21
1986	2281.9	148.2	2126.9	900.1	15.31	12	22
1987	2690.2	172.8	2508.7	1076.0	18.62	12	26
1988	3169.5	184.2	2977.3	1236.1	22.47	10	26
1989	2450.1	146.1	2297.2	936.1	18.60	12	27
1990	2746.2	174.7	2562.3	1048.4	22.18	11	25
1991	3335.0	271.0	3050.6	1246.4	28.45	12	21
1992	3811.5	400.6	3394.3	1651.2	39.47	9	17
1993	4152.7	465.6	3670.5	1898.2	46.83	7	15
1994	4368.5	518.2	3838.7	2107.0	73.23	6	10
1995	4638.7	588.7	4038.4	2003.4	87.33	8	10
1996	5112.8	674.4	4422.9	2276.5	102.00	6	9
1997	5758.8	742.8	5006.1	2377.0	120.74	6	8
1998	6347.8	710.8	5625.0	2507.3	126.02	6	7
1999	7279.6	843.2	6425.5	2704.7	140.99	5	7
2000	8344.4	1016.0	7320.8	3122.9	162.24	5	7
2001	8901.3	1122.6	7778.7	3316.7	177.92	5	5
2002	9790.8	1344.0	8446.9	3680.3	203.85	5	5
2003	9166.2	1140.3	8025.9	3297.1	174.06	5	7
2004	10903.8	1693.3	9210.6	4176.1	257.39	4	7
2005	12029.2	2025.5	10003.7	4680.9	292.96	4	6
2006	12494.2	2221.0	10273.2	4991.3	339.49	4	5
2007	13187.3	2611.0	10576.4	5472.0	419.19	4	5
2008	13002.7	2432.5	10570.2	5304.9	408.43	4	5
2009	12647.6	2193.8	10453.8	5087.5	396.75	4	5
2010	13376.2	2612.7	10763.5	5566.5	458.14	3	4
2011	13542.4	2711.2	10831.2	5758.1	484.64	3	4
2012	13240.5	2719.2	10521.4	5772.5	500.28	3	4
2013	12907.8	2629.0	10278.8	5568.6	516.64	4	4

注：本表资料由旅游部门提供。
a) Data in this table are provided by the department of tourism.

表56 全国国内旅游情况
Statistics of Domestic Tourism

年份 Year	国内游客（百万人次）Domestic Tourists (million person-times)	城镇居民 Urban Residents	农村居民 Rural Residents	旅游总花费（亿元）Tourism Expenditure (100 million yuan)	城镇居民 Urban Residents	农村居民 Rural Residents	人均花费（元）Per Capita Expenditure (yuan)	城镇居民 Urban Residents	农村居民 Rural Residents
1994	524	205	319	1023.5	848.2	175.3	195	415	55
1995	629	246	383	1375.7	1140.1	235.6	219	464	61
1996	640	256	383	1638.4	1368.4	270.0	256	534	70
1997	644	259	385	2112.7	1551.8	560.9	328	600	146
1998	695	250	445	2391.2	1515.1	876.1	345	607	197
1999	719	284	435	2831.9	1748.2	1083.7	394	615	250
2000	744	329	415	3175.5	2235.2	940.3	426	679	227
2001	784	375	409	3522.4	2651.7	870.7	450	708	213
2002	878	385	493	3878.4	2848.1	1030.3	442	740	209
2003	870	351	519	3442.3	2404.1	1038.2	396	685	200
2004	1102	459	643	4710.7	3359.0	1351.7	428	732	210
2005	1212	496	716	5285.9	3656.1	1629.7	436	737	228
2006	1394	576	818	6229.7	4414.7	1815.0	447	766	222
2007	1610	612	998	7770.6	5550.4	2220.2	483	907	223
2008	1712	703	1009	8749.3	5971.7	2777.6	511	849	275
2009	1902	903	999	10183.7	7233.8	2949.9	535	801	295
2010	2103	1065	1038	12579.8	9403.8	3176.0	598	883	306
2011	2641	1687	954	19305.4	14808.6	4496.8	731	878	471
2012	2957	1933	1024	22706.2	17678.0	5028.2	768	915	491
2013	3262	2186	1076	26276.1	20692.6	5583.5	806	947	519

表57 全国金融机构人民币业务基本情况
General Statistics of Financial Institutions of RMB

单位：亿元 (100 million yuan)

年份 Year	金融机构 Financial Institutions 存款余额 Deposits	金融机构 Financial Institutions 贷款余额 Loans	货币供应量余额 Money Supply 货币和准货币 (M_2)	货币供应量余额 Money Supply 狭义货币 (M_1)	货币供应量余额 Money Supply 流通中现金 (M_0)	货币供应量增速(%) Money Supply 货币和准货币 (M_2)	货币供应量增速(%) Money Supply 狭义货币 (M_1)	货币供应量增速(%) Money Supply 流通中现金 (M_0)
1952	93.3	108.0			27.5			
1953	107.7	134.8			39.4			
1954	154.1	185.8			41.2			
1955	141.9	206.6			40.3			
1956	136.8	239.2			57.3			
1957	168.3	283.0			52.8			
1958	304.0	498.2			67.8			
1959	407.5	814.7			75.1			
1960	468.5	983.9			95.9			
1961	491.1	814.8			125.7			
1962	411.8	691.7			106.5			
1963	414.9	576.5			89.9			
1964	439.3	588.8			80.0			
1965	481.7	656.7			90.8			
1966	554.8	766.9			108.5			
1967	582.5	807.0			121.9			
1968	621.6	902.6			134.1			
1969	641.2	959.1			137.1			
1970	702.4	1048.0			123.6			
1971	770.2	1130.8			136.2			
1972	781.6	1163.8			151.2			
1973	869.1	1287.1			166.1			
1974	903.1	1373.3			176.6			
1975	982.5	1487.0			182.6			
1976	993.2	1574.1			204.0			
1977	1080.4	1699.5			195.4			
1978	1155.0	1890.4			212.0			
1979	1362.6	2082.5			267.7			
1980	1689.7	2478.1			346.2			
1981	2097.2	2853.3			396.3			
1982	2449.1	3162.7			439.1			
1983	2883.3	3566.6			529.8			
1984	3735.3	4746.8			792.1			
1985	4560.0	6198.4			987.8			
1986	5933.9	8142.7			1218.4			
1987	7392.4	9814.1			1454.5			

表57 续表 continued

单位：亿元 (100 million yuan)

年份 Year	金融机构 Financial Institutions		货币供应量余额 Money Supply			货币供应量增速(%) Money Supply		
	存款余额 Deposits	贷款余额 Loans	货币和准货币 (M_2)	狭义货币 (M_1)	流通中现金 (M_0)	货币和准货币 (M_2)	狭义货币 (M_1)	流通中现金 (M_0)
1988	8810.4	11964.3			2134.0			
1989	10709.6	14248.8			2344.0			
1990	13942.9	17511.0	15293.4	6950.7	2644.4			
1991	17972.8	21116.4	19349.9	8633.3	3177.8	26.5	24.2	20.2
1992	23143.8	25742.8	25402.2	11731.5	4336.0	31.3	35.9	36.4
1993	29646.0	32955.8	34879.8	16280.4	5864.7			
1994	40502.5	39976.0	46923.5	20540.7	7288.6	34.5	26.2	24.3
1995	53882.1	50544.1	60750.5	23987.1	7885.3	29.5	16.8	8.2
1996	68595.6	61156.6	76094.9	28514.8	8802.0	25.3	18.9	11.6
1997	82392.8	74914.1	90995.3	34826.3	10177.6	17.3	16.5	15.6
1998	95697.9	86524.1	104498.5	38953.7	11204.2	14.8	11.9	10.1
1999	108778.9	93734.3	119897.9	45837.2	13455.5	14.7	17.7	20.1
2000	123804.4	99371.1	134610.3	53147.2	14652.7	12.3	16.0	8.9
2001	143617.2	112314.7	158301.9	59871.6	15688.8	14.4	12.7	7.1
2002	170917.4	131293.9	185007.0	70881.8	17278.0	16.8	16.8	10.1
2003	208055.6	158996.2	221222.8	84118.6	19746.0	19.6	18.7	14.3
2004	241424.3	178197.8	254107.0	95969.7	21468.3	14.7	13.6	8.7
2005	287169.5	194690.4	298755.7	107278.8	24031.7	17.6	11.8	11.9
2006	335459.8	225347.2	345603.6	126035.1	27072.6	17.0	17.5	12.7
2007	389371.2	261690.9	403442.2	152560.1	30375.2	16.7	21.1	12.2
2008	466203.3	303394.6	475166.6	166217.1	34219.0	17.8	9.1	12.7
2009	597741.1	399684.8	610224.5	221445.8	38247.0	27.7	32.4	11.8
2010	718237.9	479195.6	725851.8	266621.5	44628.2	19.7	21.2	16.7
2011	809368.3	547946.7	851590.9	289847.7	50748.5	13.6	7.9	13.8
2012	917554.8	629909.6	974148.8	308664.2	54659.8	13.8	6.5	7.7
2013	1043846.9	718961.5	1106525.0	337291.1	58574.4	13.6	9.3	7.1

注：1.1989年及以前金融机构存贷款余额为国家银行存贷款余额。

2.金融机构包括人民银行、政策性银行、国有独资商业银行、邮政储蓄机构、其他商业银行、城市合作银行、农村信用社、城市信用社、外资银行、信托投资公司、租赁公司、财务公司等。

3.2001年6月起货币供应量(M2)含证券公司客户保证金。

a) Data in 1989 and before were from central bank, and the rest are from financial institutions.

b) Financial Institutions include banks, savings deposit agencies of postal offices, housing saving banks, urban credit cooperative banks, rural credit cooperatives, urban credit banks, foreign-funded banks, financial trust investment agencies and financial companies etc.

c) Since June in 2001, the margin account of security companies are included in money supply (M2).

表58 全国金融机构法定存款利率
Official Deposits Rates in Financial Institutions

单位：年利率% %(annual rate)

日期 Date	活期 Demand Deposit	定期 Time Deposit					
		3个月 3-month	6个月 6-month	1年 1-year	2年 2-year	3年 3-year	5年 5-year
1990.04.15	2.88	6.30	7.74	10.08	10.98	11.88	13.68
1990.08.21	2.16	4.32	6.48	8.64	9.36	10.08	11.52
1991.04.21	1.80	3.24	5.40	7.56	7.92	8.28	9.00
1993.05.15	2.16	4.86	7.20	9.18	9.90	10.80	12.06
1993.07.11	3.15	6.66	9.00	10.98	11.70	12.24	13.86
1996.05.01	2.97	4.86	7.20	9.18	9.90	10.80	12.06
1996.08.23	1.98	3.33	5.40	7.47	7.92	8.28	9.00
1997.10.23	1.71	2.88	4.14	5.67	5.94	6.21	6.66
1998.03.25	1.71	2.88	4.14	5.22	5.58	6.21	6.66
1998.07.01	1.44	2.79	3.96	4.77	4.86	4.95	5.22
1998.12.07	1.44	2.79	3.33	3.78	3.96	4.14	4.50
1999.06.10	0.99	1.98	2.16	2.25	2.43	2.70	2.88
2002.02.21	0.72	1.71	1.89	1.98	2.25	2.52	2.79
2004.10.29	0.72	1.71	2.07	2.25	2.70	3.24	3.60
2006.08.19	0.72	1.80	2.25	2.52	3.06	3.69	4.14
2007.03.18	0.72	1.98	2.43	2.79	3.33	3.96	4.41
2007.05.19	0.72	2.07	2.61	3.06	3.69	4.41	4.95
2007.07.21	0.81	2.34	2.88	3.33	3.96	4.68	5.22
2007.08.22	0.81	2.61	3.15	3.60	4.23	4.95	5.49
2007.09.15	0.81	2.88	3.42	3.87	4.50	5.22	5.76
2007.12.21	0.72	3.33	3.78	4.14	4.68	5.40	5.85
2008.10.9	0.72	3.15	3.51	3.87	4.41	5.13	5.58
2008.10.30	0.72	2.88	3.24	3.60	4.14	4.77	5.13
2008.11.27	0.36	1.98	2.25	2.52	3.06	3.60	3.87
2008.12.23	0.36	1.71	1.98	2.25	2.79	3.33	3.60
2010.10.20	0.36	1.91	2.20	2.50	3.25	3.85	4.20
2010.12.26	0.36	2.25	2.50	2.75	3.55	4.15	4.55
2011.02.09	0.40	2.60	2.80	3.00	3.90	4.50	5.00
2011.04.06	0.50	2.85	3.05	3.25	4.15	4.75	5.25
2011.07.07	0.50	3.10	3.30	3.50	4.40	5.00	5.50
2012.06.08	0.40	2.85	3.05	3.25	4.10	4.65	5.10
2012.07.06	0.35	2.60	2.80	3.00	3.75	4.25	4.75

注：1.本表为个人人民币储蓄存款利率。
2.从2004年10月29日起，允许存款利率下浮，即所有存款类金融机构对其吸收的人民币存款利率，可在不超过各档次存款基准利率的范围浮动。存款利率不能上浮。

a) Effective from October 29, 2004, the PBC decided to allow all financial institutions to lower RMB deposit rates, not lower than the benchmark rates of different tranches. Deposit rates cannot be adjusted upward.

b) Data in this table are household RMB savings deposit rates.

表59 全国金融机构法定贷款利率

Official Lending Rates in Financial Institutions

单位：年利率%　　　　%(annual rate)

日期 Date	短期贷款 Short-term Loans		中长期贷款 Medium and Long-term Loans			
	6个月 6-month	1年 1-year	1年以内（含1年） 1-year and Below	1−3年（含3年） 1 to 3-year	3−5年（含5年） 3 to 5-year	5年以上 5-year and Above
1991.04.21	8.10	8.64	8.46	9.00	9.54	9.72
1993.05.15	8.82	9.36	9.18	10.80	12.06	12.24
1993.07.11	9.00	10.98	10.98	12.24	13.86	14.04
1995.01.01	9.00	10.98	11.70	12.96	14.58	14.76
1995.07.01	10.08	12.06	12.24	13.50	15.12	15.30
1996.05.01	9.72	10.98	11.52	13.14	14.94	15.12
1996.08.23	9.18	10.08	10.08	10.98	11.70	12.42
1997.10.23	7.65	8.64	8.64	9.36	9.90	10.53
1998.03.25	7.02	7.92	7.92	9.00	9.72	10.35
1998.07.01	6.57	6.93	6.93	7.11	7.65	8.01
1998.12.07	6.12	6.39	6.12-6.39	6.66	7.20	7.56
1999.06.10	5.58	5.85	5.58-5.85	5.94	6.03	6.21
2002.02.21	5.04	5.31		5.49	5.58	5.76
2004.10.29	5.22	5.58		5.76	5.85	6.12
2006.08.19	5.58	6.12		6.30	6.48	6.84
2007.03.18	5.67	6.39		6.57	6.75	7.11
2007.05.19	5.85	6.57		6.75	6.93	7.20
2007.07.21	6.03	6.84		7.02	7.20	7.38
2007.08.22	6.21	7.02		7.20	7.38	7.56
2007.09.15	6.48	7.29		7.47	7.65	7.83
2007.12.21	6.57	7.47		7.56	7.74	7.83
2008.9.16	6.21	7.20		7.29	7.56	7.74
2008.10.9	6.12	6.93		7.02	7.29	7.74
2008.10.30	6.03	6.66		6.75	7.02	7.20
2008.11.27	5.04	5.58		5.67	5.94	6.12
2008.12.23	4.86	5.31		5.4	5.76	5.94
2010.10.20	5.10	5.56		5.60	5.96	6.14
2010.12.26	5.35	5.81		5.85	6.22	6.40
2011.02.09	5.60	6.06		6.10	6.45	6.60
2011.04.06	5.85	6.31		6.40	6.65	6.80
2011.07.07	6.10	6.56		6.65	6.90	7.05
2012.06.08	5.85	6.31		6.40	6.65	6.80
2012.07.06	5.60	6.00		6.15	6.40	6.55

表60 全国证券市场基本情况
General Statistics on Securities Markets

年份 Year	境内上市公司(A、B股)(家) Number of Listed Companies (A and B Shares) in Mainland	境内上市外资股(B股)(家) Number of Listed Companies of Foreign Fund (B Shares) in Mainland	境外上市公司(H股)(家) Number of Listed Companies (H Shares) Overseas	股票总发行股本(亿股) Total Issued Capital (100 million shares)	#流通股本 Negotiable Capital	股票市价总值(亿元) Total Market Capitalization (100 million yuan)	#股票流通市值 Negotiable Market Capitalization	股票成交量(百万股) Stock Trading Volume (million shares)	股票成交金额(亿元) Total Stock Turnover (100 million yuan)
1990	10								
1991	14								
1992	53	18		68.87	21.18	1048.1		3795.4	681.3
1993	183	41	6	387.73	107.88	3531.0	861.6	23422.2	3667.0
1994	291	58	15	684.54	226.04	3690.6	968.9	201333.9	8127.6
1995	323	70	18	848.42	301.46	3474.3	938.2	70547.1	4036.5
1996	530	85	25	1219.54	429.85	9842.4	2867.0	253314.1	21332.2
1997	745	101	42	1942.67	671.44	17529.2	5204.4	256079.1	30721.8
1998	851	106	43	2526.79	861.94	19505.6	5745.6	215411.0	23544.3
1999	949	108	46	3088.95	1079.65	26471.2	8214.0	293238.9	31319.6
2000	1088	114	52	3791.71	1354.26	48090.9	16087.5	475840.0	60826.6
2001	1160	112	60	5218.01	1813.17	43522.2	14463.2	315228.8	38305.2
2002	1224	111	75	5875.45	2036.90	38329.1	12484.6	301619.5	27990.5
2003	1287	111	93	6428.46	2269.92	42457.7	13178.5	416308.4	32115.3
2004	1377	110	111	7149.43	2577.18	37055.6	11688.6	582773.3	42333.9
2005	1381	109	122	7629.51	2914.77	32430.3	10630.5	662373.2	31664.8
2006	1434	109	143	14926.35	5637.78	89403.9	25003.6	1614522.6	90468.9
2007	1550	109	148	22416.85	10331.52	327140.9	93064.4	3640376.0	460556.2
2008	1625	109	153	24522.85	12578.91	121366.4	45213.9	2413138.0	267112.6
2009	1718	108	159	26163.00	19760.00	243939.0	151259.0	5110699.0	535987.0
2010	2063	108	165	33184.00	25642.00	265423.0	193110.0	4215198.0	545634.0
2011	2342	108	171	36095.52	28850.26	214758.1	164921.3	3395751.0	421649.7
2012	2494	107	179	38395.00	31339.60	230357.6	181658.3	3288106.0	314667.4
2013	2489	106	182	40569.08	36744.16	239077.2	199579.5	4837268.0	468729.0

表61 全国保险业基本情况
General Statistics on Insurance

年份 Year	机构数（个） Number of Institution (unit)	职工人数（人） Employed Person (person)	保费（亿元） Premium (100 million yuan)	财产保险公司 Property Insurance Companies	人寿保险公司 Life Insurance Companies	赔款及给付（亿元） Claim and Payment (100 million yuan)	财产保险公司 Property Insurance Companies	人寿保险公司 Life Insurance Companies
1985								
1986								
1987								
1988								
1989								
1990								
1991								
1992								
1993								
1994			376					
1995			453					
1996			538					
1997			773	382	390	247	215	32
1998		172892	1256	506	750	532	290	242
1999		171865	1406	527	879	508	280	228
2000	34	166602	1598	608	990	526	308	218
2001	35	185502	2109	685	1424	597	333	264
2002	44	194383	3054	780	2274	707	403	304
2003	62	199705	3880	869	3011	841	476	365
2004	68	262429	4318	1125	3194	1004	579	426
2005	93	366559	4932	1283	3649	1137	691	446
2006	107	434001	5640	1579	4061	1438	825	614
2007	120	500441	7036	2087	4950	2265	1064	1201
2008	130	599344	9784	2446	7338	2971	1475	1496
2009	138	630734	11137	2993	8144	3126	1638	1487
2010	142	685856	14528	4027	10501	3200	1815	1385
2011	152	776258	14339	4779	9560	3929	2249	1680
2012	164	846504	15488	5530	9958	4716	2897	1819
2013	174	831303	17222	6481	10741	6213	3556	2657

表62 黄金和外汇储备
Gold and Foreign Exchange Reserves

年份 Year	黄金储备 (万盎司) Gold (10 000 fine troy ounce)	外汇储备 (亿美元) Foreign Exchange Reserve (USD 100 million)	年份 Year	黄金储备 (万盎司) Gold (10 000 fine troy ounce)	外汇储备 (亿美元) Foreign Exchange Reserve (USD 100 million)
1952	500	1.39	1983	1267	89.01
1953	500	1.14	1984	1267	82.20
1954	500	1.06	1985	1267	26.44
1955	500	1.93	1986	1267	20.72
1956	500	1.23	1987	1267	29.23
1957	500	1.28	1988	1267	33.72
1958	500	0.86	1989	1267	55.50
1959	400	1.30	1990	1267	110.93
1960	400	1.02	1991	1267	217.12
1961	400	1.27	1992	1267	194.43
1962	300	1.38	1993	1267	211.99
1963	300	1.73	1994	1267	516.20
1964	300	2.36	1995	1267	735.97
1965	500	2.81	1996	1267	1050.29
1966	500	4.20	1997	1267	1398.90
1967	500	3.50	1998	1267	1449.60
1968	700	3.32	1999	1267	1546.75
1969	700	4.98	2000	1267	1655.70
1970	700	1.91	2001	1608	2121.65
1971	900	2.02	2002	1929	2864.07
1972	900	5.43	2003	1929	4032.51
1973	900	0.83	2004	1929	6099.32
1974	1280	3.69	2005	1929	8188.72
1975	1280	8.99	2006	1929	10663.40
1976	1280	12.55	2007	1929	15282.49
1977	1280	23.45	2008	1929	19460.30
1978	1280	1.67	2009	3389	23991.52
1979	1280	8.40	2010	3389	28473.38
1980	1280	-12.96	2011	3389	31811.48
1981	1267	27.08	2012	3389	33115.89
1982	1267	69.86	2013	3389	38213.15

表63 国际收支概况

General Statistics on Balance of Payments

单位：百万美元 (USD million)

年份 Year	经常项目差额 Current Account Balance	货物和服务 Goods and Service Balance	收益 Income and Profit Balance	经常转移 Current Transfer Balance	资本和金融项目差额 Capital and Finance Account Balance	资本项目 Capital Account Balance	金融项目 Financial Account Balance	储备资产 Reserve Assets Balance	净误差与遗漏 Net Error and Omission Balance
1982	5674	4812	376	486	-1736		-1736	-4217	279
1983	4240	2571	1158	511	-1372		-1372	-2695	-173
1984	2030	54	1534	442	-3752		-3752	531	1191
1985	-11417	-12501	841	243	8485		8485	5422	-2490
1986	-7035	-7390	-23	378	6540		6540	1727	-1232
1987	300	291	-215	224	2731		2731	-1660	-1371
1988	-3803	-4061	-161	419	5269		5269	-455	-1011
1989	-4318	-4928	229	381	6428		6428	-2202	92
1990	11997	10668	1055	274	-2774		-2774	-6089	-3134
1991	13271	11601	840	830	4580		4580	-11091	-6760
1992	6401	4998	248	1155	-251		-251	2102	-8252
1993	-11904	-11792	-1284	1172	23474		23474	-1767	-9803
1994	7658	7357	-1036	1337	32644		32644	-30527	-9775
1995	1618	11958	-11774	1434	38675		38675	-22463	-17830
1996	7242	17550	-12437	2129	39967		39967	-31662	-15547
1997	36963	42823	-11004	5143	21015	-21	21036	-35724	-22254
1998	31471	43837	-16644	4278	-6321	-47	-6275	-6426	-18724
1999	21114	30641	-14470	4943	5180	-26	5205	-8505	-17788
2000	20519	28873	-14666	6311	1922	-35	1958	-10548	-11893
2001	17405	28086	-19173	8492	34775	-54	34829	-47325	-4856
2002	35422	37383	-14945	12984	32291	-50	32340	-75507	7794
2003	43052	35821	-10218	17449	54873	-48	54921	-106148	8224
2004	68941	51174	-5132	22898	108152	-69	108222	-190060	12967
2005	132378	124627	-16114	23865	95349	4102	91247	-250649	22921
2006	231843	208919	-5143	28068	49305	4020	45285	-284776	3628
2007	353183	308036	8044	37102	94232	3099	91132	-460704	13290
2008	420569	348833	28580	43156	40126	3051	37075	-479539	18844
2009	243257	220130	-8533	31659	198470	3939	194531	-400344	-41383
2010	237810	223024	-25899	40686	286865	4630	282234	-471739	-52936
2011	136097	181904	-70318	24511	265470	5446	260024	-387801	-13766
2012	215392	231845	-19887	3434	-31766	4272	-36038	-96552	-87074
2013	182807	235380	-43839	-8733	326203	3052	323151	-431379	-77631

注：本表数据来自国家外汇管理局。

a) Data in this table come from State Administration of Foreign Exchange.

表64 全国各级各类学校数
Number of School by Level and Type of School

单位：所 (unit)

年份 Year	普通高等学校 Regular Institutions of Higher Education	普通高中 Senior Secondary Schools	初中 Junior Secondary Schools	普通小学 Primary Schools	特殊教育学校 Special Schools	学前教育 Kinder-gartens
1949	205	1597	2448	346769		
1950	193	1541	2472	383647		1799
1951	206	1321	2673	501105		4833
1952	201	1181	3117	526964		6531
1953	181	1206	3227	512056	64	5469
1954	188	1249	3543	506105	57	6293
1955	194	1330	3790	504077	57	7129
1956	227	2029	4686	529043	62	18534
1957	229	2184	8912	547306	66	16420
1958	791	4144	24787	776769	91	695297
1959	841	4144	16691	737445	297	532043
1960	1289	4690	17115	726484	476	784905
1961	845	4431	14552	645170	341	60307
1962	610	4434	15087	668318	261	17564
1963	407	4303	15296	707959	253	16577
1964	419	4149	15065	1066036	254	17706
1965	434	4112	13990	1681939	266	19226
1966	434			1006965		
1967	434			964152		
1968	434			940608		
1969	434			915739		
1970	434			961131		
1971	328			968541		
1972	331	28029	64937	1009205		
1973	345	29365	67959	1031705	221	45528
1974	378	31589	69032	1053297	234	40267
1975	387	39120	84385	1093317	246	171749
1976	392	60535	131617	1044274	269	442650
1977	404	64903	136365	982291	286	261936
1978	598	49215	113130	949323	292	163952
1979	633	40289	103944	923532	289	165629
1980	675	31300	87077	917316	292	170419
1981	704	24447	82271	894074	302	130296

表64 续表 continued

单位：所 (unit)

年份 Year	普通高等学校 Regular Institutions of Higher Education	普通高中 Senior Secondary Schools	初中 Junior Secondary Schools	普通小学 Primary Schools	特殊教育学校 Special Schools	学前教育 Kinder-gartens
1982	715	20874	80775	880516	312	122107
1983	805	18876	77598	862165	319	136306
1984	902	17847	75867	853740	330	166526
1985	1016	17318	75903	832309	375	172262
1986	1054	17111	75856	820846	423	173376
1987	1063	16930	75927	807406	504	176775
1988	1075	16524	74968	793261	577	171845
1989	1075	16050	73525	777244	662	172634
1990	1075	15678	71953	766072	746	172322
1991	1075	15243	70608	729158	886	164465
1992	1053	14850	69171	712973	1027	172506
1993	1065	14380	68415	696681	1123	165197
1994	1080	14242	68116	682588	1241	174657
1995	1054	13991	67029	668685	1379	180438
1996	1032	13875	66092	645983	1428	187324
1997	1020	13880	64762	628840	1440	182485
1998	1022	13948	63940	609626	1535	181368
1999	1071	14127	63086	582291	1520	181136
2000	1041	14564	63898	553622	1539	175836
2001	1225	14907	66590	491273	1531	111706
2002	1396	15406	65645	456903	1540	111752
2003	1552	15779	64730	425846	1551	116390
2004	1731	15998	63757	394183	1560	117899
2005	1792	16092	62486	366213	1593	124402
2006	1867	16153	60885	341639	1605	130495
2007	1908	15681	59384	320061	1618	129086
2008	2263	15206	57914	300854	1640	133722
2009	2305	14607	56320	280184	1672	138209
2010	2358	14058	54890	257410	1706	150420
2011	2409	13688	54117	241249	1767	166750
2012	2442	13509	53216	228585	1853	181251
2013	2491	13352	52804	213529	1933	198553

表65 全国各级各类学校专任教师数
Number of Full-Time Teachers by Level and Type of School

单位：万人 (10 000 persons)

年 份 Year	普通高等学校 Regular Institutions of Higher Education	普通高中 Senior Secondary Schools	初 中 Junior Secondary Schools	普通小学 Primary Schools	特殊教育学校 Special Schools	学前教育 Kinder-gartens
1949	1.6	1.4	5.3	83.6		
1950	1.7	1.2	5.7	90.1		0.17
1951	2.3	0.9	6.4	122.2		0.44
1952	2.7	1.3	8.1	143.5		1.4
1953	3.4	1.7	9.6	155.4	0.04	1.6
1954	3.9	2.3	11.5	155.5	0.04	2.1
1955	4.2	2.6	12.3	159.4	0.04	2.6
1956	5.8	3.5	15.2	174.9	0.06	4.8
1957	7.0	4.0	19.4	188.4	0.07	5.0
1958	8.5	5.1	25.4	225.7	0.09	134.0
1959	10.0	6.3	28.7	250.3	0.18	95.8
1960	13.9	8.0	34.6	269.3	0.26	134.0
1961	15.9	8.3	33.5	255.4	0.23	11.7
1962	14.4	8.1	31.8	251.1	0.21	7.0
1963	13.8	8.0	34.0	260.1	0.22	6.8
1964	13.5	7.9	36.3	310.8	0.23	7.0
1965	13.8	7.8	37.9	385.7	0.26	6.2
1966	13.9	6.6	53.1	322.1		
1967	13.9	6.3	54.1	319.6		
1968	14.3	7.1	63.0	325.5		
1969	13.7	8.3	85.5	348.7		
1970	12.9	15.1	102.3	361.2		
1971	13.8	29.2	103.5	409.5		
1972	13.0	39.3	126.4	439.8		
1973	13.9	42.2	127.4	467.9	0.32	8.5
1974	14.8	45.8	132.4	494.4	0.33	10.5
1975	15.6	53.0	156.2	520.4	0.34	23.7
1976	16.7	69.4	203.5	528.9	0.38	51.4
1977	18.6	82.6	236.1	522.6	0.40	33.5
1978	20.6	74.1	244.1	522.6	0.42	27.7
1979	23.7	66.7	241.0	538.2	0.45	29.5
1980	24.7	57.1	244.9	549.9	0.48	41.1
1981	25.0	49.4	235.0	558.0	0.51	40.1

表65 续表 continued

单位：万人 (10 000 persons)

年 份 Year	普通高等学校 Regular Institutions of Higher Education	普通高中 Senior Secondary Schools	初 中 Junior Secondary Schools	普通小学 Primary Schools	特殊教育学校 Special Schools	学前教育 Kinder-gartens
1982	28.7	46.6	221.5	550.5	0.54	41.5
1983	30.3	45.1	241.6	542.5	0.56	43.3
1984	31.5	45.9	209.7	537.0	0.60	49.1
1985	34.4	49.2	216.0	537.7	0.73	55.0
1986	37.2	51.8	223.9	541.4	0.81	60.5
1987	38.5	54.4	232.7	543.4	0.95	65.1
1988	39.3	55.7	240.3	550.1	1.08	67.0
1989	39.7	55.4	242.7	554.4	1.22	70.9
1990	39.5	56.2	247.0	558.2	1.38	75.0
1991	39.1	57.3	251.7	553.2	1.60	76.9
1992	38.8	57.6	256.5	552.6	1.85	81.5
1993	38.8	55.9	260.8	555.2	2.04	83.6
1994	39.6	54.7	268.7	561.1	2.27	86.2
1995	40.1	55.1	278.4	566.4	2.52	87.5
1996	40.3	57.2	289.3	573.6	2.70	88.9
1997	40.4	60.5	298.2	579.4	2.85	88.4
1998	40.7	64.2	305.5	581.9	2.99	87.5
1999	42.6	69.2	314.8	586.0	3.14	87.2
2000	46.3	75.7	328.7	586.0	3.2	85.6
2001	53.2	84.0	338.6	579.8	2.9	54.6
2002	61.8	94.6	346.8	577.9	3.0	57.1
2003	72.5	107.1	349.8	570.3	3.0	61.3
2004	85.8	119.1	350.1	562.9	3.1	65.6
2005	96.6	129.9	349.2	559.2	3.2	72.2
2006	107.6	138.7	347.5	558.8	3.3	77.6
2007	116.8	144.3	347.3	561.3	3.5	82.7
2008	123.7	147.6	347.6	562.2	3.6	89.9
2009	129.5	149.3	351.8	563.3	3.8	98.6
2010	134.3	151.8	352.5	561.7	4.0	114.4
2011	139.3	155.7	352.5	560.5	4.1	131.6
2012	144.0	159.5	350.4	558.5	4.4	147.9
2013	149.7	162.9	348.1	558.5	4.6	166.3

表66 全国各级各类学校在校学生数

Number of Students Enrollment by Level and Type of School

单位：万人 (10 000 persons)

年份 Year	普通本专科 Regular Institutions of Higher Education	普通高中 Senior Secondary Schools	初中 Junior Secondary Schools	普通小学 Primary Schools	特殊教育学校 Special Schools	学前教育 Kinder-gartens
1949	11.7	20.7	83.2	2439.1		
1950	13.7	23.8	106.7	2892.4		14.0
1951	15.3	18.4	138.4	4315.4		38.2
1952	19.1	26.0	223.0	5110.0		42.4
1953	21.2	36.0	257.3	5166.4	0.5	43.0
1954	25.3	47.8	310.9	5121.8	0.5	48.4
1955	28.8	58.0	332.0	5312.6	0.5	56.2
1956	40.3	78.4	438.1	6346.6	0.7	108.1
1957	44.1	90.4	537.7	6428.3	0.8	108.8
1958	66.0	117.9	734.1	8640.3	1.0	2950.1
1959	81.2	143.6	774.3	9117.9	1.8	2172.2
1960	96.2	167.5	858.5	9379.1	2.7	2933.1
1961	94.7	153.3	698.5	7578.6	2.0	289.6
1962	83.0	133.9	618.9	6923.9	1.8	144.6
1963	75.0	123.6	638.1	7157.5	1.8	147.2
1964	68.5	124.7	729.4	9294.5	2.0	158.9
1965	67.4	130.8	803.0	11620.9	2.3	171.3
1966	53.4	137.3	1112.5	10341.7		
1967	40.9	126.5	1097.2	10244.3		
1968	25.9	140.8	1251.5	10036.3		
1969	10.9	189.1	1832.4	10066.8		
1970	4.8	349.7	2292.2	10528.0		
1971	8.3	558.7	2568.9	11211.2		
1972	19.4	858.1	2724.4	12549.2		
1973	31.4	923.3	2523.2	13570.4	2.5	245.0
1974	43.0	1002.7	2647.6	14481.4	2.6	263.8
1975	50.1	1163.7	3302.4	15094.1	2.7	620.0
1976	56.5	1483.6	4352.9	15005.5	2.9	1395.5
1977	62.5	1800.0	4979.9	14617.6	3.0	896.8
1978	85.6	1553.1	4995.2	14624.0	3.1	787.7
1979	102.0	1292.0	4613.0	14662.9	3.2	879.2
1980	114.4	969.8	4538.3	14627.0	3.3	1150.8
1981	127.9	715.0	4144.6	14332.8	3.3	1056.2

表66 续表 continued

单位：万人 (10 000 persons)

年份 Year	普通本专科 Regular Institutions of Higher Education	普通高中 Senior Secondary Schools	初 中 Junior Secondary Schools	普通小学 Primary Schools	特殊教育学校 Special Schools	学前教育 Kinder-gartens
1982	115.4	640.5	3888.0	13972.0	3.4	1113.1
1983	120.7	629.0	3768.8	13578.0	3.6	1140.3
1984	139.6	689.8	3864.3	13557.1	4.0	1294.7
1985	170.3	741.1	3964.8	13370.2	4.2	1479.7
1986	188.0	773.4	4116.6	13182.5	4.7	1629.0
1987	195.9	773.7	4174.4	12835.9	5.3	1807.8
1988	206.6	746.0	4015.5	12535.8	5.8	1854.5
1989	208.2	716.1	3837.9	12373.1	6.4	1847.7
1990	206.3	717.3	3868.7	12241.4	7.2	1972.2
1991	204.4	722.9	3960.6	12164.2	8.5	2209.3
1992	218.4	704.9	4065.9	12201.3	13.0	2428.2
1993	253.6	656.9	4082.2	12421.2	16.9	2552.5
1994	279.9	664.8	4316.9	12822.6	21.1	2630.3
1995	290.6	713.2	4657.8	13195.2	29.6	2711.2
1996	302.1	769.3	4970.4	13615.0	32.1	2666.3
1997	317.4	850.1	5167.8	13995.4	34.1	2519.0
1998	340.9	938.0	5363.0	13953.8	35.8	2403.0
1999	413.4	1049.7	5721.6	13548.0	37.2	2326.3
2000	556.1	1201.3	6256.3	13013.3	37.8	2244.2
2001	719.1	1405.0	6514.4	12543.5	38.6	2021.8
2002	903.4	1683.8	6687.4	12156.7	37.5	2036.0
2003	1108.6	1964.8	6690.8	11689.7	36.5	2003.9
2004	1333.5	2220.4	6527.5	11246.2	37.2	2089.4
2005	1561.8	2409.1	6214.9	10864.1	36.4	2179.0
2006	1738.8	2514.5	5958.0	10711.5	36.3	2263.9
2007	1884.9	2522.4	5736.2	10564.0	41.9	2348.8
2008	2021.0	2476.3	5585.0	10331.5	41.7	2475.0
2009	2144.7	2434.3	5440.9	10071.5	42.8	2657.8
2010	2231.8	2427.3	5279.3	9940.7	42.6	2976.7
2011	2308.5	2454.8	5066.8	9926.4	39.9	3424.4
2012	2391.3	2467.2	4763.1	9695.9	37.9	3685.8
2013	2468.1	2435.9	4440.1	9360.5	36.8	3894.7

表67 全国各级各类学校招生数
Number of New Students Enrollment by Level and Type of School

单位：万人 (10 000 persons)

年份 Year	普通本专科 Regular Institutions of Higher Education	普通高中 Senior Secondary Schools	初 中 Junior Secondary Schools	普通小学 Primary Schools	特殊教育学 校 Special Schools
1949	3.1	7.1	34.1	680.0	
1950	5.8	10.8	50.1	696.6	
1951	5.2	9.1	80.6	1086.2	
1952	7.9	14.1	124.2	1149.3	
1953	8.1	16.1	81.8	819.5	
1954	9.2	19.5	123.6	1054.5	
1955	9.8	22.1	128.2	1182.0	
1956	18.5	37.4	196.9	1592.3	
1957	10.6	32.3	217.0	1249.2	
1958	26.5	56.2	378.3	3000.5	
1959	27.4	65.6	318.3	2049.1	
1960	32.3	67.8	364.8	2494.3	
1961	16.9	44.7	221.8	1647.1	
1962	10.7	41.7	238.3	1586.3	
1963	13.3	43.4	263.5	1698.2	
1964	14.7	43.8	286.6	2968.9	
1965	16.4	45.9	299.8	3296.0	
1966		20.7	272.7	1879.2	
1967		13.6	198.3	1402.5	
1968		63.0	648.5	1753.2	
1969		103.6	1023.4	2205.7	
1970	4.2	239.0	1176.3	2831.8	
1971	4.2	321.3	1234.9	3387.5	
1972	13.4	479.0	1247.1	3603.6	
1973	15.0	452.0	1139.0	3369.3	0.55
1974	16.5	541.1	1345.1	3249.5	0.52
1975	19.1	633.1	1810.5	3352.1	0.51
1976	21.7	861.1	2344.3	3161.1	0.54
1977	27.3	993.1	2367.7	3111.5	0.56
1978	40.2	692.9	2006.0	3315.4	0.59
1979	27.5	614.1	1727.8	3101.7	0.60
1980	28.1	383.4	1550.9	2942.3	0.59
1981	27.9	327.8	1412.7	2749.2	0.60

表67　续表　continued

单位：万人 (10 000 persons)

年份 Year	普通本专科 Regular Institutions of Higher Education	普通高中 Senior Secondary Schools	初　中 Junior Secondary Schools	普通小学 Primary Schools	特殊教育学　校 Special Schools
1982	31.5	279.3	1363.1	2671.7	0.61
1983	39.1	259.8	1317.1	2544.0	0.64
1984	47.5	262.3	1302.5	2472.9	0.75
1985	61.9	257.5	1349.4	2298.2	0.92
1986	57.2	257.3	1386.6	2258.2	1.14
1987	61.7	255.2	1394.3	2094.6	1.18
1988	67.0	244.3	1340.5	2123.3	1.20
1989	59.7	242.1	1309.4	2151.5	1.36
1990	60.9	249.8	1369.9	2064.0	1.60
1991	62.0	243.8	1411.3	2072.7	1.98
1992	75.4	234.7	1465.0	2183.2	2.95
1993	92.4	228.3	1478.9	2353.5	3.35
1994	90.0	243.4	1616.4	2537.0	3.98
1995	92.6	273.6	1752.3	2531.8	5.63
1996	96.6	282.2	1760.7	2524.7	4.82
1997	100.0	322.6	1805.6	2462.0	4.61
1998	108.4	359.6	1961.4	2201.4	4.91
1999	159.7	396.3	2149.7	2029.5	5.01
2000	220.6	472.7	2295.6	1946.5	5.3
2001	268.3	558.0	2287.9	1944.2	5.6
2002	320.5	676.7	2281.8	1952.8	5.3
2003	382.2	752.1	2220.1	1829.4	4.9
2004	447.3	821.5	2094.6	1747.0	5.1
2005	504.5	877.7	1987.6	1671.7	4.9
2006	546.1	871.2	1929.5	1729.4	5.0
2007	565.9	840.2	1868.5	1736.1	6.3
2008	607.7	837.0	1859.6	1695.7	6.2
2009	639.5	830.3	1788.5	1637.8	6.4
2010	661.8	836.2	1716.6	1691.7	6.5
2011	681.5	850.8	1634.7	1736.8	6.4
2012	688.8	844.6	1570.8	1714.7	6.6
2013	699.8	822.7	1496.1	1695.4	6.6

表68 全国各级各类学校毕业生数

Number of Graduates by Level and Type of School

单位：万人 (10 000 persons)

年份 Year	普通本专科 Regular Institutions of Higher Education	普通高中 Senior Secondary Schools	初中 Junior Secondary Schools	普通小学 Primary Schools	特殊教育学校 Special Schools
1949	2.1	6.1	21.9	64.6	
1950	1.8	6.2	23.4	78.3	
1951	1.9	5.9	22.5	116.6	
1952	3.2	3.6	18.5	149.0	
1953	4.8	5.6	39.8	293.5	
1954	4.7	6.8	57.6	332.5	0.01
1955	5.5	9.9	87.0	322.9	0.05
1956	6.3	15.4	78.5	405.1	0.05
1957	5.6	18.7	111.2	498.0	0.02
1958	7.2	19.7	111.6	606.3	0.04
1959	7.0	29.9	149.1	547.3	
1960	13.6	28.8	142.2	734.0	
1961	15.1	37.9	189.2	580.8	
1962	17.7	44.1	158.4	559.0	
1963	19.9	43.3	152.3	476.8	0.12
1964	20.4	36.7	138.6	567.4	0.14
1965	18.6	36.0	173.8	667.6	0.15
1966	14.1	28.0	162.0	900.5	
1967	12.5	26.8	186.4	899.5	
1968	15.0	79.4	519.0	1428.2	
1969	15.0	38.0	361.4	1489.5	
1970	10.3	67.6	618.9	1652.5	
1971	0.6	100.4	835.0	1376.0	
1972	1.7	215.9	1035.5	1414.9	
1973	3.0	349.4	1129.4	1349.0	0.29
1974	4.3	417.9	1060.6	1521.0	0.34
1975	11.9	447.0	1047.7	1999.4	0.27
1976	14.9	517.2	1206.0	2489.5	0.27
1977	19.4	585.8	1558.6	2573.9	0.33
1978	16.5	682.7	1692.6	2287.9	0.31
1979	8.5	726.5	1657.9	2087.9	0.34
1980	14.7	616.2	964.8	2053.3	0.37
1981	14.0	486.1	1154.2	2075.7	0.37

表68　续表　continued

单位：万人　(10 000 persons)

年份 Year	普通本专科 Regular Institutions of Higher Education	普通高中 Senior Secondary Schools	初　中 Junior Secondary Schools	普通小学 Primary Schools	特殊教育学　校 Special Schools
1982	45.7	310.6	1032.1	2068.9	0.35
1983	33.5	235.1	960.3	1980.7	0.33
1984	28.7	189.8	950.4	1995.0	
1985	31.6	196.6	998.3	1999.9	0.40
1986	39.3	224.0	1057.0	2016.1	0.50
1987	53.2	246.8	1117.3	2043.0	0.40
1988	55.3	250.6	1157.2	1930.3	0.50
1989	57.6	243.2	1134.3	1857.1	0.50
1990	61.4	233.0	1109.1	1863.1	0.50
1991	61.4	222.9	1085.5	1896.7	0.60
1992	60.4	226.1	1102.3	1872.4	0.90
1993	57.1	231.7	1134.2	1841.5	1.20
1994	63.7	209.3	1152.6	1899.6	1.40
1995	80.5	201.6	1227.4	1961.5	1.90
1996	83.9	204.9	1279.0	1934.1	2.40
1997	82.9	221.7	1442.4	1960.1	2.80
1998	83.0	251.8	1580.2	2117.4	3.50
1999	84.8	262.9	1589.8	2313.7	3.81
2000	95.0	301.5	1633.5	2419.2	4.3
2001	103.6	340.5	1731.5	2396.9	4.6
2002	133.7	383.8	1903.7	2351.9	4.4
2003	187.8	458.1	2018.5	2267.9	4.5
2004	239.1	546.9	2087.3	2135.2	4.7
2005	306.8	661.6	2123.4	2019.5	4.3
2006	377.5	727.1	2071.6	1928.5	4.5
2007	447.8	788.3	1963.7	1870.2	5.0
2008	511.9	836.1	1868.0	1865.0	5.2
2009	531.1	823.7	1797.7	1805.2	5.7
2010	575.4	794.4	1750.4	1739.6	5.9
2011	608.2	787.7	1736.7	1662.8	4.4
2012	624.7	791.5	1660.8	1641.6	4.9
2013	638.7	799.0	1561.6	1581.1	5.1

表69 研究生和留学人员数
Number of Postgraduates and Students Studying Abroad

单位：人 (person)

年份 Year	研究生 Number of Postgraduates			出国留学人员 Number of Students Studying Abroad	学成回国留学人员 Number of Returned Students
	毕业生数 Graduates	招生数 New Student Enrollment	在校学生数 Student Enrollment		
1949	107	242	629		
1950	159	874	1261	35	
1951	166	1273	2168	380	
1952	627	1785	2763	231	
1953	1177	2887	4249	675	16
1954	660	1155	4753	1518	22
1955	1730	1751	4822	2093	104
1956	2349	2235	4841	2401	258
1957	1723	334	3178	529	347
1958	1113	275	1635	415	670
1959	727	1345	2171	576	1380
1960	589	2275	3635	441	2217
1961	179	2198	6009	124	1403
1962	1019	1287	6130	114	980
1963	1512	781	4938	32	426
1964	895	1240	4881	650	191
1965	1665	1456	4546	454	199
1966	1137		3409		
1967	852		2557		
1968	1240		1317		
1969	1317				
1972				36	
1973				259	
1974				180	70
1975				245	186
1976				277	189
1977			226	220	270
1978	9	10708	10934	860	248
1979	140	8110	18830	1777	231
1980	476	3616	21604	2124	162
1981	11669	9363	18848	2922	1143
1982	4058	11080	25847	2326	2116

表69 续表 continued

单位：人 (person)

年份 Year	研究生 Number of Postgraduates 毕业生数 Graduates	研究生 招生数 New Student Enrollment	研究生 在校学生数 Student Enrollment	出国留学人员 Number of Students Studying Abroad	学成回国留学人员 Number of Returned Students
1983	4497	15642	37166	2633	2303
1984	2756	23181	57566	3073	2920
1985	17004	46871	87331	4888	1424
1986	16950	41310	110371	4676	1388
1987	27603	39017	120191	4703	1605
1988	40838	35645	112776	3786	3000
1989	37232	28569	101339	3329	1753
1990	35440	29649	93018	2950	1593
1991	32537	29679	88128	2900	2069
1992	25692	33439	94164	6540	3611
1993	28214	42145	106771	10742	5128
1994	28047	50864	127935	19071	4230
1995	31877	51053	145443	20381	5750
1996	39652	59398	163322	20905	6570
1997	46539	63749	176353	22410	7130
1998	47077	72508	198885	17622	7379
1999	54670	92225	233513	23749	7748
2000	58767	128484	301239	38989	9121
2001	67809	165197	393256	83973	12243
2002	80841	202611	500980	125179	17945
2003	111091	268925	651260	117307	20152
2004	150777	326286	819896	114682	24726
2005	189728	364831	978610	118515	34987
2006	255902	397925	1104653	134000	42000
2007	311839	418612	1195047	144000	44000
2008	344825	446422	1283046	179800	69300
2009	371273	510953	1404942	229300	108300
2010	383600	538177	1538416	284700	134800
2011	429994	560168	1645845	339700	186200
2012	486455	589673	1719818	399600	272900
2013	513626	611381	1793953	413900	353500

表70 全国各级学校平均在校生数、升学率和入学率

Student Enrollment, Percentage of Graduates Entering Higher Level Schools by Level and Percentage of School-Age Children Enrolled

年份 Year	每十万人口平均在校生数(人) Number of Students Per 100 000 Population by Level (person)			毕业生升学率(%) Percentage of Graduates Entering Higher Level Schools(%)			小学学龄儿童净入学率(%) Percentage of School-age Children Enrolled (%)
	高等教育 Higher Education	高中阶段 Senior Secondary Education	小学 Primary Education	高中 Senior Secondary Schools	初中 Junior Secondary Schools	小学 Primary Schools	
1949							
1952					168.6	96.0	49.2
1957					39.7	44.2	61.7
1962					30.0	45.3	56.1
1965					70.0	82.5	84.7
1971					38.5	89.7	
1975					60.4	90.6	96.8
1978	89		15190		40.9	87.7	95.5
1979	105		15100		37.6	82.8	93.0
1980	116		14820		45.9	75.9	93.0
1981	128		14390		32.5	68.3	93.0
1982	114		13820		32.3	66.2	93.2
1983	118		13300		35.5	67.3	94.0
1984	135		13160		38.4	66.2	95.3
1985	161		12630		41.7	68.4	95.9
1986	175		12260		40.6	69.5	96.4
1987	179		11740		39.1	69.1	97.1
1988	186		11290		38.0	70.4	97.1
1989	185		10980		38.3	71.5	97.4
1990	326	1337	10707	27.3	40.6	74.6	97.8
1991	304	1355	10502	28.7	42.6	77.7	97.9
1992	313	1365	10413	34.9	43.4	79.7	97.2
1993	376	1448	10656	43.3	44.1	81.8	97.7

表70 续表 continued

年份 Year	每十万人口平均在校生数(人) Number of Students Per 100 000 Population by Level (person)			毕业生升学率(%) Percentage of Graduates Entering Higher Level Schools(%)			小学学龄儿童净入学率(%) Percentage of School-age Children Enrolled (%)
	高等教育 Higher Education	高中阶段 Senior Secondary Education	小学 Primary Education	高中 Senior Secondary Schools	初中 Junior Secondary Schools	小学 Primary Schools	
1994	433	1293	10819	46.7	47.8	86.6	98.4
1995	457	1610	11010	49.9	48.3	90.8	98.5
1996	470	1780	11273	51.0	48.8	92.6	98.8
1997	482	1905	11435	48.6	57.5	93.7	98.9
1998	504	1978	11287	46.1	50.7	94.3	98.9
1999	594	2032	10855	63.8	49.5	94.4	99.1
2000	723	2005	10335	73.2	51.1	94.9	99.1
2001	931	2021	9937	78.8	53.2	95.5	99.1
2002	1146	2283	9525	83.5	58.3	97.0	98.6
2003	1298	2523	9100	83.4	59.6	97.9	98.7
2004	1420	2824	8725	82.5	63.8	98.1	98.9
2005	1613	3070	8358	76.3	69.7	98.4	99.2
2006	1816	3321	8192	75.1	75.7	100.0	99.3
2007	1924	3409	8037	70.3	80.5	99.9	99.5
2008	2042	3463	7819	72.7	82.1	99.7	99.5
2009	2128	3495	7584	77.6	85.6	99.1	99.4
2010	2189	3504	7448	83.3	87.5	98.7	99.7
2011	2253	3495	7403	86.5	88.9	98.3	99.8
2012	2335	3411	7196	87.0	88.4	98.3	99.9
2013	2418	3227	6913	87.6	91.2	98.3	99.7

注：平均每十万人口在校生中高中阶段指标口径范围发生变化，故一些年份无数据。
a) Of number of students per 100 000 population by level, coverage of senior secondary education changed, so there are no data in some years.

表71　教育经费情况

Basic Statistics on Educational Funds

单位：亿元　　(100 million yuan)

年 份 Year	全国教育经费总投入 Total	#国家财政性教育经费 Government Appropriation for Education	#公共财政教育支出 Public Expenditure on Education	公共财政教育支出占公共财政支出比例(%) Public Expenditure on Education as Percentage	国家财政性教育经费占国内生产总值比例(%) Government Appropriation for Education as GDP
1992	867.05	728.75	564.94	15.10	2.71
1993	1059.94	867.76	676.61	14.57	2.46
1994	1488.78	1174.74	931.13	16.07	2.44
1995	1877.95	1411.52	1092.94	16.02	2.32
1996	2262.34	1671.70	1288.08	16.23	2.35
1997	2531.73	1862.54	1441.27	15.61	2.36
1998	2949.06	2032.45	1654.02	15.32	2.41
1999	3349.04	2287.18	1911.37	14.49	2.55
2000	3849.08	2562.61	2191.77	13.80	2.58
2001	4637.66	3057.01	2705.66	14.31	2.79
2002	5480.03	3491.40	3254.94	14.76	2.90
2003	6208.27	3850.62	3619.10	14.68	2.84
2004	7242.60	4465.86	4244.42	14.90	2.79
2005	8418.84	5161.08	4946.04	14.58	2.79
2006	9815.31	6348.36	6135.35	15.18	2.93
2007	12148.07	8280.21	8094.34	16.26	3.12
2008	14500.74	10449.63	10212.97	16.32	3.33
2009	16502.71	12231.09	11974.98	15.69	3.59
2010	19561.85	14670.07	14163.90	15.76	3.65
2011	23869.29	18586.70	17821.74	16.31	3.93
2012	27695.97	22236.23	20314.17	16.13	4.28
2013	30428.95	24552.45	21469.90	15.31	4.32

注：1.国家财政性教育经费：主要包括公共财政预算教育经费，各级政府征收用于教育的税费，企业办学中的企业拨款，校办产业和社会服务收入用于教育的经费等。
2.2012年对部分教育经费统计指标进行了修订。“公共财政教育支出”2012年以前包括教育事业费、科研经费、基建经费、其他经费和教育费附加；2012年包括教育事业费、基建经费和教育费附加。

a) Government Appropriation for Education mainly includes the public expenditures on education, taxes and fees collected for education by governments at all all levels, enterprise appropriation for enterprise-run schools, income from school-run enterprises and social services used for education.

b) Revisions were made in 2012 to the defitions of some indicators of the expenditures on education. Prior to 2012, the Public Expenditure on Education included the appropriated funds for education, for science research, capital construction, other funds, and education surcharges while it included the appropriated funds for education, capital construction and education surcharges in 2012.

表72　全国科技活动发展情况

Basic Statistics on Scientific and Technological Activities

年份 Year	科技活动人员(万人) Personnel Engaged in S&T Activities (10000 persons)	研究与试验发展经费支出(亿元) Expenditure on R&D (100 million yuan)	国家技术发明奖(项) National Invention Prizes Awarded (item)	国家科学技术进步奖(项) National Scientific and Technological Progress Prizes Awarded (item)	技术市场成交额(亿元) Transaction Value in Technical Market (100 million yuan)	专利申请受理量(件) Patent Applications Accepted (piece)	专利申请授权量(件) Patent Applications Granted (piece)
1978							
1979							
1980							
1981							
1982							
1983							
1984							
1985			185	1761			
1986			30			18509	3024
1987			225	806		26077	6811
1988			217	515	72	34011	11947
1989			150	504	81	32905	17129
1990			224	505	75	41469	22588
1991	228.6		209	502	95	50040	24616
1992	227.0		170	649	143	67135	31475
1993	245.2		175	441	208	77276	62127
1994	257.6				229	77735	43297
1995	262.5	348.7	131	607	268	83045	45064
1996	290.3	404.5	111	536	300	102735	43780
1997	288.6	509.2	100	475	351	114208	50992
1998	281.4	551.1	72	471	436	121989	67889
1999	290.6	678.9	69	506	523	134239	100156
2000	322.4	895.7	23	250	651	170682	105345
2001	314.1	1042.5	14	191	783	203573	114251
2002	322.2	1287.6	21	218	884	252631	132399
2003	328.4	1539.6	19	216	1085	308487	182226
2004	348.1	1966.3	28	244	1334	353807	190238
2005	381.5	2450.0	40	236	1551	476264	214003
2006	413.2	3003.1	56	241	1818	573178	268002
2007	454.4	3710.2	51	255	2227	693917	351782
2008	496.7	4616.0	55	254	2665	828328	411982
2009	637.2	5802.1	55	282	3039	976686	581992
2010	670.2	7062.6	46	273	3907	1222286	814825
2011	739.0	8687.0	55	283	4764	1633347	960513
2012	812.2	10298.4	77	212	6437	2050649	1255138
2013	865.3	11846.6	71	188	7469	2377061	1313000

表73 全国文化事业机构数
Number of Cultural Institutes

单位：个 (unit)

年份 Year	艺术表演团体 Art Performance Troupes	艺术表演场馆 Arts Centers	文化馆(站) Cultural Centers (Stations) and Mass Cultural Centers	公共图书馆 Public Libraries	博物馆 Museums	广播电台 Broadcasting Stations	电视台 Television Stations	广播电视台 Broadcasting and Television
1949	1000	891	896	55	21	49		
1950	1676	1083	1693	63	22	65		
1951	1855	1319	2226	66	31	74		
1952	2084	1510	2430	83	35	72		
1953	2267	1862	2455	93	49	63		
1954	2424	2064	2417	93	46	61		
1955	2414	2159	2437	96	50	58		
1956	2720	2173	2584	375	67	58		
1957	2884	2296	2748	400	72	61		
1958	3181	2573	2616	922	360	91	2	
1959	3504	2565	2699	1011	480	122	7	
1960	3309	2333	2480	1093	452	137	17	
1961	3233	2237	4767	873	300	135	20	
1962	3320	2249	3767	541	230	94	14	
1963	3428	2980	4069	490	215	89	13	
1964	3478	2902	4435	543	228	86	13	
1965	3458	2943	4785	577	214	87	12	
1966	3374	1785	4846	523	193	78	13	
1967	3223	1677	4681	470	187	78	13	
1968	3030	1651	4546	448	179	79	15	
1969	2683	1497	4239	400	171	81	19	
1970	2541	1432	4126	323	182	80	31	
1971	2514	1420	4375	392	184	81	32	
1972	2681	1407	4405	460	195	85	31	
1973	2731	1448	4716	523	210	86	32	
1974	2760	1430	5123	583	217	88	32	
1975	2836	1464	5387	629	242	88	32	
1976	2906	1458	5575	768	263	89	32	
1977	2941	1448	5743	851	300	90	32	
1978	3150	1095	4569	1218	349	93	32	
1979	3482	1255	25340	1651	344	99	38	
1980	3533	1444	28403	1732	365	106	38	
1981	3483	2302	31567	1787	383	114	42	
1982	3460	2469	39021	1889	409	118	47	
1983	3444	1818	45046	2038	467	122	52	
1984	3397	1779	53578	2217	618	167	93	

表73 续表 continued

单位：个 (unit)

年份 Year	艺术表演团体 Art Performance Troupes	艺术表演场馆 Arts Centers	文化馆(站) Cultural Centers (Stations) and Mass Cultural Centers	公共图书馆 Public Libraries	博物馆 Museums	广播电台 Broadcasting Stations	电视台 Television Stations	广播电视台 Broadcasting and Television
1985	3317	1377	8576	2344	711	168	143	
1986	3195	2058	8913	2406	777	278	292	
1987	3094	2148	8974	2440	827	386	366	
1988	2985	2081	9045	2485	903	461	422	
1989	2850	2050	9037	2512	967	531	469	
1990	2805	1955	9216	2527	1013	239	282	
1991	2772	2068	10507	2535	1075	246	298	
1992	2753	2037	9564	2558	1106	261	308	
1993	2707	2024	10155	2572	1130	282	324	
1994	2698	1998	11276	2589	1161	296	324	
1995	2682	1958	13487	2615	1194	312	336	
1996	2664	1934	45253	2620	1219	315	344	
1997	2663	1947	45449	2628	1282	318	347	
1998	2652	1929	45834	2662	1339	298	347	1304
1999	2632	1911	45837	2669	1363	296	357	1562
2000	2619	1900	45321	2675	1392	304	354	1446
2001	2605	1854	43379	2696	1461	301	357	1387
2002	2587	1829	42516	2697	1511	306	368	1526
2003	2601	1900	41816	2709	1515	277	317	1579
2004	2759	1928	41402	2720	1548	282	314	1913
2005	2805	1866	41588	2762	1581	273	302	1932
2006	2866	1839	40088	2778	1617	267	296	1935
2007	4512	1732	40601	2799	1722	263	287	1993
2008	5114	1662	41156	2820	1893	257	277	2069
2009	6139	1499	41959	2850	2252	251	272	2087
2010	6864	1461	43382	2884	2435	227	247	2120
2011	7055	1429	43675	2952	2650	197	213	2153
2012	7321	1279	43876	3076	3069	169	183	2185
2013	8180	1344	44260	3112	3473	153	166	2207

注：1.2007年以前艺术表演团体为文化系统内数据，2007年起含非文化部门单位。艺术表演场馆不含民营艺术表演场馆。
2.1996年以前文化站数据未包括其他部门所属乡镇文化站。1996—1998年包括其他部门所属文化站，1999年以后，其他部门所属文化站划归文化部门管理。

a) The Art performance troupes referred to those under the official cultural system before 2007 and expanded the coverage to those both under and outside the official cultural system starting from 2007. The Art Performace Places do not include those of non-state owned.

b) Culture stations did not include township culture stations of other department before 1996, and included culture stations of other department from 1996 to 1998. Since 1999, culture stations of other department was put under Culture Department's administration.

表74　图书、期刊和报纸出版
Number of Books, Magazines and Newspaper Published

年份 Year	图书 Books Published		期刊 Magazines Published		报纸 Newspapers Published	
	种数（种） Number of Publications (kind)	总印数（亿册，亿张） Printed Copies (100 million Copies)	种数（种） Number of Publications (kind)	总印数（亿册） Total Printed Copies (100 million Copies)	种数（种） Number of News Published (kind)	总印数（亿份） Total Printed Copies (100 million Copies)
1950	12153	2.7	295	0.4	382	8.0
1951	18300	7.0	302	1.8	390	12.6
1952	13692	7.9	354	2.0	296	16.1
1953	17819	7.5	295	1.7	265	16.7
1954	17760	9.4	304	2.0	253	17.1
1955	21071	10.8	370	2.9	285	19.5
1956	28773	17.8	484	3.5	347	26.1
1957	27571	12.8	634	3.2	364	24.4
1958	45495	23.9	822	5.3	491	39.1
1959	41905	20.9	851	5.3	463	49.0
1960	30797	18.0	442	4.7	396	50.9
1961	13529	10.2	410	2.3	260	30.8
1962	16548	10.9	483	2.0	273	25.8
1963	17266	12.9	681	2.3	289	33.0
1964	18005	17.1	856	3.5	329	41.4
1965	20143	21.7	790	4.4	343	47.4
1966	11055	35.0	191	2.3	49	36.7
1967	2925	32.3	27	0.9	43	34.9
1968	3694	25.0	22	0.3	42	35.8
1969	3964	19.1	20	0.5	42	41.1
1970	4889	17.9	21	0.7	42	46.5
1971	7771	24.2	72	1.6	195	84.0
1972	8829	23.9	194	2.3	185	97.6
1973	10372	28.0	320	3.2	192	100.5
1974	11812	29.9	382	4.0	189	101.4
1975	13716	35.8	476	4.4	180	109.7
1976	12842	29.1	542	5.6	182	124.3
1977	12886	33.1	628	5.6	180	123.7
1978	14987	37.7	930	7.6	186	127.8
1979	17212	40.7	1470	11.8		130.8
1980	21621	45.9	2191	11.3	188	140.4
1981	25601	55.8	2801	14.6	242	140.7

表74 续表 continued

年份 Year	图书 Books Published		期刊 Magazines Published		报纸 Newpapers Published	
	种数（种）Number of Publications (kind)	总印数（亿册，亿张）Printed Copies (100 million Copies)	种数（种）Number of Publications (kind)	总印数（亿册）Total Printed Copies (100 million Copies)	种数（种）Number of News Published (kind)	总印数（亿份）Total Printed Copies (100 million Copies)
1982	31784	58.8	3100	15.1	277	140.0
1983	35700	58.0	3415	17.7	340	155.1
1984	40072	62.5	3907	21.8	458	180.8
1985	45603	66.7	4705	25.6	1445	246.8
1986	51798	52.0	5248	24.0	1574	242.7
1987	60213	62.5	5687	25.9	1611	264.5
1988	65962	62.3	5865	25.5	1537	267.8
1989	74973	58.6	6078	18.4	1576	207.0
1990	80224	56.4	5751	17.9	1444	211.3
1991	89615	61.4	6056	20.6	1524	236.5
1992	92148	63.4	6486	23.6	1657	257.9
1993	96761	59.3	7011	23.5	1788	263.8
1994	103836	60.1	7325	22.1	1953	253.2
1995	101381	63.2	7583	23.4	2089	263.3
1996	112813	71.6	7916	23.1	2163	274.3
1997	120106	73.1	7918	24.4	2149	287.6
1998	130613	72.4	7999	25.4	2053	300.4
1999	141831	73.2	8187	28.5	2038	318.4
2000	143376	62.7	8725	29.4	2007	329.3
2001	154526	63.1	8889	28.9	2111	351.1
2002	170962	68.7	9029	29.5	2137	367.8
2003	190391	66.7	9074	29.5	2119	383.1
2004	208294	64.1	9490	28.3	1922	402.4
2005	222473	64.7	9468	27.6	1931	412.6
2006	233971	64.1	9468	28.5	1938	424.5
2007	248283	62.9	9468	30.4	1938	438.0
2008	274123	70.6	9549	31.0	1943	442.9
2009	301719	70.4	9851	31.5	1937	439.1
2010	328387	71.7	9884	32.2	1939	452.1
2011	369523	77.1	9849	32.9	1928	467.4
2012	414005	79.2	9867	33.5	1918	482.3
2013	444427	83.1	9877	32.7	1915	482.4

表75 运动员获世界冠军情况

World Championships Won by Chinese Athletes

单位：项、人、个

年份 Year	项 数 Number of Events	人 数 Number of Persons	个 数 Number of Times
1959	1	1	1
1961	3	6	3
1963	4	7	4
1965	5	9	5
1971	4	7	4
1973	3	4	3
1975	2	9	2
1977	4	11	4
1978	4	4	4
1979	12	20	12
1980	3	3	3
1981	25	53	25
1982	12	31	13
1983	37	50	39
1984	33	46	37
1985	42	70	46
1986	26	56	26
1987	64	72	69
1988	54	59	54
1989	80	83	82
1990	54	61	54
1991	88	86	93
1992	86	68	89
1993	101	106	103
1994	79	86	79
1995	98	187	102
1996	72	58	75
1997	87	96	92
1998	75	89	83
1999	91	129	92
2000	92	109	110
2001	79	138	90
2002	99	123	110
2003	17	94	84
2004	27	175	101
2005	22	159	106
2006	24	169	141
2007	22	217	123
2008	24	151	120
2009	30	223	142
2010	22	180	108
2011	24	198	138
2012	24	140	107
2013	22	164	124

注：男女混合运动项目，女子按半项和半个计算。
a) For mixed doubles champions, the score for women counts 0.5.

表76　全国各类医疗卫生机构数

Health Institutions by Kind

单位：个 (unit)

年份 Year	合计 Total	医院 Hospitals	基层医疗卫生机构 Health Care Institutions at Grass-root Level	社区卫生服务中心(站) Community Health Service Centers	乡镇卫生院 Urban Health Centers	村卫生室 Town-ship Health Centers	门诊部(所) Village Clinics	专业公共卫生机构数 Out-patient Depart-ment	疾病预防控制中心 Specialized Public Health Institutions	专科疾病防治院(所/站) Center for Disease Control and Prevention	妇幼保健院(所/站) Specialized Disease Prevention & Treatment Institution	卫生监督所(中心) Women and Children Care Agencies
1949	3670	2600					769			11	9	
1950	8915	2803					3356		61	30	426	
1951	16181	3065					8934		68	89	1270	
1952	38987	3442					29050		147	188	2477	
1953	52038	3482					38987		313	255	4144	
1954	56610	3563					42840		328	265	4034	
1955	67725	3648					51600		315	287	3944	
1960	261195	6020			24849		213823		1866	683	4213	
1961	269197	6339			31153		217568		2125	735	3070	
1962	217985	5203			28656		172708		2308	678	2733	
1963	215491	5138			27140		170717		2382	692	2967	
1964	215474	5244			31080		167715		2530	803	3077	
1965	224266	5330			36965		170430		2499	822	2910	
1966	206613	5479			35733		153730		2513	793	2793	
1967	196455	5604			45430		134725		2496	775	2440	
1968	171494	5734			50341		108090		1871	635	1639	
1969	153891	5773			51242		90744		1480	600	1124	
1970	149823	5964			56568		79600		1714	607	1124	
1971	131367	6600			54091		62457		2245	659	1065	
1972	135127	6908			55570		66067		2558	613	1071	
1973	143733	7271			56625		72117		2702	601	1536	
1974	149965	7472			57065		76988		2778	626	1843	
1975	151733	7654			54026		80739		2912	683	2128	
1976	157959	7850			54541		85616		2973	737	2341	
1977	164199	8868			54978		90285		2990	795	2459	
1978	169732	9293			55018		94395		2989	887	2571	
1979	176793	9646			55263		99643		3047	1066	2659	
1980	180553	9902			55413		102474		3105	1138	2745	
1981	800205	10252			55500	610079	111189		3202	1197	2789	
1982	801869	10471			55496	608431	113916		3271	1272	2827	
1983	870686	10901			55559	674669	115826		3274	1326	2851	
1984	905424	11381			55549	707168	117028		3339	1458	2955	
1985	978540	11955			47387	777674	126604		3410	1566	2996	

表76 续表 continued

单位：个 (unit)

年份 Year	合计 Total	医院 Hospitals	基层医疗卫生机构 Health Care Institutions at Grass-root Level	社区卫生服务中心(站) Community Health Service Centers	乡镇卫生院 Urban Health Centers	村卫生室 Town-ship Health Centers	门诊部(所) Village Clinics	专业公共卫生机构数 Out-patient Depart-ment	疾病预防控制中心 Specialized Public Health Institutions	专科疾病防治院(所/站) Center for Disease Control and Prevention	妇幼保健院(所/站) Specialized Disease Prevention & Treatment Institution	卫生监督所(中心) Women and Children Care Agencies
1986	999102	12442			46967	795963	127575		3475	1635	3059	
1987	1012804	12962			47177	807844	128459		3512	1697	3082	
1988	1012485	13544			47529	806497	128422		3532	1727	3103	
1989	1027522	14090			47523	820798	128112		3591	1747	3112	
1990	1012690	14377			47749	803956	129332		3618	1781	3148	
1991	1003769	14628			48140	794733	128665		3652	1818	3187	
1992	1001310	14889			46117	796523	125873		3673	1845	3187	
1993	1000531	15436			45024	806945	115161		3729	1872	3115	
1994	1005271	15595			51929	813529	105984		3711	1905	3190	
1995	994409	15663			51797	804352	104406		3729	1895	3179	
1996	1078131	15833			51277	755565	237153		3737	1887	3172	
1997	1048657	15944			50981	733624	229474		3747	1893	3180	
1998	1042885	16001			50071	728788	229349		3746	1889	3191	
1999	1017673	16678			49694	716677	226588		3763	1877	3180	
2000	1034229	16318	1000169		49229	709458	240934	11386	3741	1839	3163	
2001	1029314	16197	995670		48090	698966	248061	11471	3813	1783	3132	
2002	1005004	17844	973098	8211	44992	698966	219907	10787	3580	1839	3067	571
2003	806243	17764	774693	10101	44279	514920	204468	10792	3584	1749	3033	838
2004	849140	18393	817018	14153	41626	551600	208794	10878	3588	1583	2998	1284
2005	882206	18703	849488	17128	40907	583209	207457	11177	3585	1502	3021	1702
2006	918097	19246	884818	22656	39975	609128	212243	11269	3548	1402	3003	2097
2007	912263	19852	878686	27069	39876	613855	197083	11528	3585	1365	3051	2553
2008	891480	19712	858015	24260	39080	613143	180752	11485	3534	1310	3011	2675
2009	916571	20291	882153	27308	38475	632770	182448	11665	3536	1291	3020	2809
2010	936927	20918	901709	32739	37836	648424	181781	11835	3513	1274	3025	2992
2011	954389	21979	918003	32860	37295	662894	184287	11926	3484	1294	3036	3022
2012	950297	23170	912620	33562	37097	653419	187932	12083	3490	1289	3044	3088
2013	974398	24709	915368	33965	37015	648619	195176	31155	3516	1271	3144	2967

注：①村卫生室数计入医疗卫生机构数中；②2008年社区卫生服务中心(站)减少的原因是江苏省约5000家农村社区卫生服务站划归村卫生室；③2002年起，医疗卫生机构数不再包括高中等医学院校本部、药检机构、国境卫生检疫所和非卫生部门举办的计划生育指导站；④2013年起，医疗卫生机构数包括原计生部门主管的计划生育技术服务机构；⑤1996年以前门诊部(所)不包括私人诊所。

a) Number of village clinics was included in health care institutions. The reasons of decrease of community health centers(stations) in 2008 is that 5000 rural community health stations in Jiangsu is divided into village clinics. Since 2002, medical institutions did not include headquaters of higher education and specialized medical institutions, medicine inspection institutions, border medical quarantine institutions and family planning service station run by non medical department. Since 2013,medical institutions include family planning technical service institutions managed by original family planning department. Clincs before 1996 do not include private clinics.

表77 全国各类卫生机构人员数

Number of Employed Personnel in Health Institutions

单位：万人 (10 000 persons)

年份 Year	卫生人员 Medical Personnel	#卫生技术人员 Medical Technical Personnel	#执业(助理)医师 Licensed (Assistant) Doctors	#注册护士 Senior and Junior Nurses	每千人口执业(助理)医师数(人) Number of Doctors per 1000 Population (person)
1949	54.1	50.5	36.3	3.3	0.67
1950	61.1	55.5	38.0	3.8	0.69
1951	68.5	60.6	39.7	4.6	0.70
1952	81.9	69.0	42.4	6.1	0.74
1953	94.3	77.8	45.0	7.9	0.76
1954	103.8	85.4	47.6	9.4	0.79
1955	105.3	87.4	50.0	10.7	0.81
1956	120.1	98.8	52.5	11.8	0.84
1957	125.4	103.9	54.6	12.8	0.84
1958	152.9	132.9	54.4	13.8	0.82
1959	163.8	139.0	59.4	16.0	0.88
1960	176.9	150.5	59.6	17.0	1.04
1961	178.4	149.2	65.2	19.0	0.99
1962	168.5	141.4	68.8	20.0	1.02
1963	173.0	145.3	72.1	21.3	1.04
1964	176.7	147.9	73.9	22.5	1.05
1965	187.2	153.2	76.3	23.5	1.05
1966	182.7	148.4	70.7	24.4	0.95
1967	185.4	150.7	71.0	26.0	0.93
1968	183.4	149.1	70.0	28.3	0.90
1969	181.2	147.1	69.7	29.3	0.87
1970	657.2	145.3	70.2	29.5	0.85
1971	672.0	155.1	71.3	31.8	0.84
1972	654.2	170.8	73.8	33.1	0.85
1973	657.0	182.2	78.2	33.5	0.88
1974	694.2	193.2	83.0	35.7	0.92
1975	743.5	205.7	87.8	38.0	0.95
1976	806.5	220.6	93.0	41.3	1.00
1977	809.7	234.1	97.8	40.5	1.03
1978	788.3	246.4	97.8	40.5	1.08
1979	773.8	264.2	108.8	42.1	1.12
1980	735.5	279.8	115.3	46.6	1.17
1981	719.9	301.1	124.4	52.5	1.25

注：①卫生人员和卫生技术人员包括获得"卫生监督员"证书的公务员1万人；②2013年卫生人员数包括卫生计生部门主管的计划生育技术服务机构人员数，2013年以前不包括原人口计生部门主管的计划生育技术服务机构人员数；③执业(助理)医师数包括村卫生室执业(助理)医师数；④1985年以前乡村医生和卫生员系赤脚医生数。⑤2002年以前，执业(助理)医师数系医生，执业医师数系医师,注册护士数系护师(士)；⑥城市包括直辖市区和地级市辖区，农村包括县及县级市；⑦分母系常住人口数。

a) Medical Personnel and medical technical personnel include 10 000 civil servants obtained Medical Supervisor certificate. Medical personnel of 2013 include personnel of family planning technical service institutions managed by family planning department, which did not included it before 2013. Licensed (Assistant) Doctors include village clinic doctorss. Rural doctors before 1985 referred o bare foot doctors. Licensed (Assistant) Doctors before 2002 were doctors, Licensed Doctors referred to doctors, licensed nurses referred to nurses. City include municipality directly under the central government and cities at prefecture level, rural areas include county and city at county level. Denominator was usual residents.

表77 续表 continued

单位：万人 (10 000 persons)

年份 Year	卫生人员 Medical Personnel	#卫生技术人员 Medical Technical Personnel	#执业(助理)医师 Licensed (Assistant) Doctors	#注册护士 Senior and Junior Nurses	每千人口执业(助理)医师数(人) Number of Doctors per 1000 Population (person)
1982	695.4	314.3	130.7	56.4	1.29
1983	675.7	325.3	135.3	59.6	1.33
1984	662.3	334.4	138.1	61.6	1.34
1985	560.6	341.1	141.3	63.7	1.36
1986	572.6	350.7	144.4	68.1	1.37
1987	584.3	360.9	148.2	71.8	1.39
1988	592.5	372.4	161.8	82.9	1.49
1989	602.8	380.9	171.8	92.2	1.56
1990	613.8	389.8	176.3	97.5	1.56
1991	627.8	398.5	178.0	101.2	1.56
1992	640.9	407.4	180.8	104.0	1.57
1993	654.1	411.7	183.2	105.6	1.58
1994	663.1	419.9	188.2	109.4	1.60
1995	670.4	425.7	191.8	112.6	1.62
1996	673.5	431.2	194.1	116.3	1.62
1997	683.4	439.8	198.5	119.8	1.65
1998	686.3	442.4	200.0	121.9	1.65
1999	689.5	445.9	204.5	124.5	1.67
2000	691.0	449.1	207.6	126.7	1.68
2001	687.5	450.8	210.0	128.7	1.69
2002	652.9	427.0	184.4	124.7	1.47
2003	621.7	438.1	194.2	126.6	1.54
2004	633.3	448.6	199.9	130.8	1.57
2005	644.7	456.4	204.2	135.0	1.56
2006	668.1	472.8	209.9	142.6	1.60
2007	696.4	491.3	212.3	155.9	1.61
2008	725.2	517.4	220.2	167.8	1.66
2009	778.1	553.5	232.9	185.5	1.75
2010	820.8	587.6	241.3	204.8	1.80
2011	861.6	620.3	246.6	224.4	1.83
2012	911.6	667.6	261.6	249.7	1.94
2013	979.0	721.1	279.5	278.3	2.04

表78 全国医疗卫生机构床位

Number of Beds in Health Care Institutions

单位：万张 (10 000 beds)

年份 Year	合计 Total	#医院 Hospitals	#基层医疗卫生机构 Health Care Institutions at Grass-root Level	#社区卫生服务中心(站) Health Service Centers for Community (stations)	#乡镇卫生院 Township Health Centers	#专业公共卫生机构 Specialized Public Health Institutions	#妇幼保健院(所、站) Maternity and Child Care Centers (Institutions, Stations)	#专科疾病防治院(所、站) Specialized Prevention & Treatment Centers (Institutions, Stations)	每千人口医疗卫生机构床位 Beds of Medical Institutions (unit)
1949	8.5	8.0							
1950	11.9	9.7					0.27		
1951	15.9	12.1					0.31		
1952	23.1	15.6					0.43		
1953	27.3	17.6					0.49		
1954	32.9	19.9					0.54		
1955	36.3	21.5					0.57		
1956	41.4	25.5					0.62	0.84	
1957	46.2	28.8					0.66	0.87	
1958	67.2	41.8					0.85	1.35	
1959	81.0	51.3			3.02		0.86	1.94	
1960	97.7	59.1			4.63		0.88	1.74	
1961	91.6	62.7			1.86		0.90		
1962	93.3	56.8			10.00		0.84	1.56	
1963	93.4	56.5			9.95		0.86	1.37	
1964	97.2	58.2			10.90		0.90	1.50	
1965	103.3	61.2			13.25		0.92		
1966	111.8	65.7			16.49		0.88		
1967	113.0	66.4			21.67		0.87		
1968	112.3	65.6			25.71		0.84		
1969	115.4	67.2			29.69		0.68		
1970	126.2	70.5			36.80		0.70	1.90	
1971	133.1	75.0			42.62		0.62		
1972	147.2	82.2			49.37		0.64	2.63	
1973	156.4	86.1			52.89		0.81	2.52	
1974	166.2	89.7			57.66		0.89	2.70	
1975	176.4	94.0			62.03		0.97	2.88	
1976	186.2	97.8			66.92		1.02	3.02	
1977	195.4	104.1			71.37		1.09	2.56	
1978	204.2	110.0			74.73		1.16	2.63	
1979	212.8	114.7			77.12		1.50	2.70	
1980	218.4	119.6			77.54		1.64	2.73	2.19
1981	223.4	124.1			76.31		1.97	2.71	

表78 续表 continued

单位：万张 (10 000 beds)

年份 Year	合计 Total	#医院 Hospitals	#基层医疗卫生机构 Health Care Institutions at Grass-root Level	#社区卫生服务中心(站) Health Service Centers for Community (stations)	#乡镇卫生院 Township Health Centers	#专业公共卫生机构 Specialized Public Health Institutions	#妇幼保健院(所、站) Maternity and Child Care Centers (Institutions, Stations)	#专科疾病防治院(所、站) Specialized Prevention & Treatment Centers (Institutions, Stations)	每千人口医疗卫生机构床位 Beds of Medical Institutions (unit)
1982	228.03	128.52			75.32		2.33	2.73	
1983	234.16	134.53			74.62		2.75	2.85	
1984	241.24	141.24			73.14		3.18	2.96	
1985	248.71	150.86			72.06		3.46	2.95	2.33
1986	256.25	155.98			71.12		3.67	3.06	
1987	268.50	165.34			72.30		4.00	3.07	
1988	279.49	174.70			72.61		4.35	3.00	
1989	286.70	181.46			72.30		4.50	3.10	
1990	292.54	186.89			72.29		4.66	3.10	2.53
1991	299.19	192.61			72.92		4.80	3.17	
1992	304.94	197.66			73.28		5.00	3.22	
1993	309.90	203.64			73.08		4.50	3.03	
1994	313.40	207.04			73.24		4.80	2.98	
1995	314.06	206.33			73.31		5.13	3.07	2.55
1996	309.96	209.65			73.47		5.60	2.83	
1997	313.45	211.92			74.24		6.02	3.06	
1998	314.30	213.41			73.77		6.30	2.90	
1999	315.90	215.07			73.40		6.63	2.93	
2000	317.70	216.67	76.65		73.48	11.86	7.12	2.84	2.47
2001	320.12	215.56	77.14		74.00	12.02	7.40	2.70	
2002	313.61	222.18	71.05	1.20	67.13	12.37	7.98	3.18	2.49
2003	316.40	226.95	71.05	1.21	67.27	12.61	8.09	3.38	2.49
2004	326.84	236.35	71.44	1.81	66.89	12.73	8.70	3.12	2.56
2005	336.75	244.50	72.58	2.50	67.82	13.58	9.41	3.34	2.62
2006	351.18	256.04	76.19	4.12	69.62	13.50	9.93	2.80	2.70
2007	370.11	267.51	85.03	7.66	74.72	13.29	10.62	2.59	2.83
2008	403.87	288.29	97.10	9.80	84.69	14.66	11.73	2.64	3.05
2009	441.66	312.08	109.98	13.13	93.34	15.40	12.61	2.71	3.32
2010	478.68	338.74	119.22	16.88	99.43	16.45	13.44	2.93	3.58
2011	515.99	370.51	123.37	18.71	102.63	17.81	14.59	3.14	3.84
2012	572.48	416.15	132.43	20.32	109.93	19.82	16.16	3.57	4.24
2013	618.19	457.86	134.99	19.42	113.65	21.49	17.55	3.85	4.55

表79　养老机构及提供住宿的社会服务床位数

Institution for the Aged and Beds of Social Welfare Institutions with Accommodations

单位：个、万张　(unit, 10 000 beds)

年份 Year	机构数 Number of Institutions	床位数 Number of Beds	#老年及残疾人床位 The Aged and Disable	#智障和精神疾病床位 Mental Retardation and Mental Diseases	#儿童床位 Child
1978	8571	16.3	15.7	0.6	
1979	8988	22.6	20.1	2.1	0.4
1980	9669	24.2	21.3	2.4	0.5
1981	10031	25.3	22.2	2.5	0.6
1982	12275	28.2	24.8	2.8	0.6
1983	15807	32.4	29.0	2.8	0.6
1984	22796	42.5	39.0	2.9	0.6
1985	29100	49.1	45.5	2.9	0.5
1986	35008	58.7	54.7	3.1	0.6
1987	37372	64.9	60.7	3.3	0.6
1988	39030	69.5	65.3	3.4	0.6
1989	39743	73.8	69.3	3.6	0.7
1990	40583	78.0	73.5	3.7	0.8
1991	42264	82.8	78.3	3.8	0.7
1992	43319	89.8	85.2	3.8	0.8
1993	43681	92.7	87.4	4.0	0.9
1994	43240	95.5	90.1	4.0	0.9
1995	43074	97.6	91.9	4.0	1.1
1996	42829	100.8	95.0	4.0	1.2
1997	42385	103.1	97.2	4.0	1.3
1998	42131	105.8	99.6	4.1	1.5
1999	40430	108.9	102.4	4.1	1.6
2000	40491	113.0	104.5	4.1	1.8
2001	38785	140.7	114.6	4.2	2.3
2002	38200	141.5	114.9	4.3	2.5
2003	37294	142.9	120.6	4.5	2.7
2004	38593	157.2	139.5	4.5	3.0
2005	42487	180.7	158.1	4.4	3.2
2006	43187	204.5	179.6	4.4	3.2
2007	44958	269.6	242.9	4.7	3.4
2008	41099	300.3	267.4	5.4	4.3
2009	43944	326.5	293.5	5.9	4.8
2010	44482	349.6	316.1	6.1	5.5
2011	45973	396.4	353.2	6.5	6.8
2012	48078	449.3	416.5	6.7	8.7
2013	45977	526.9	493.9	7.5	9.9

表80 全国社会保障基本情况

Basic Statistics for Social Security of China

年份 Year	参加保险人数（万人） Active Contributors (10 000 persons)			社会保险基金（亿元） Social Insurance Funds (100 million yuan)			农村贫困人口（万人） Rural Population in Poverty (10 000 persons)
	基本养老保险 Basic Pension Insurance	失业保险 Unemployment Insurance	城镇职工基本医疗保险 Basic Medical Insurance	基金收入 Revenue	基金支出 Expenses	累计结余 Balance at the Year-end	
1978							25000
1979							
1980							22000
1981							15200
1982							14500
1983							13500
1984							12800
1985							12500
1986							13100
1987							12200
1988							9600
1989	5710			154	121	82	10200
1990	6166			187	152	117	8500
1991	6740			225	176	170	9400
1992	9456			377	327	253	8000
1993	9848			526	482	304	
1994	10574	7968	400	742	680	366	7000
1995	10979	8238	746	1006	877	517	6540
1996	11117	8333	856	1252	1082	696	
1997	11204	7961	1762	1458	1339	832	4962
1998	11203	7928	1878	1623	1637	791	4210
1999	12485	9852	2065	2212	2108	1010	3412
2000	13617	10408	3787	2645	2386	1328	9422
2001	14183	10355	7286	3102	2748	1623	9029
2002	14737	10182	9401	4049	3471	2423	8645
2003	15507	10373	10902	4883	4016	3314	8517
2004	16353	10584	12404	5780	4627	4493	7587
2005	17488	10648	13783	6975	5401	6074	6432
2006	18766	11187	15732	8643	6477	8256	5698
2007	20137	11645	18020	10812	7888	11237	4320
2008	21891	12400	19996	13696	9925	15226	4007
2009	23550	12715	21937	16116	12303	19007	3597
2010	35984	13376	23735	19276	15019	23408	16567
2011	61573	14317	25227	25153	18653	30233	12238
2012	78796	15225	26486	30739	23331	38107	9899
2013	81968	16417	27443	35253	27916	45588	8249

注：1.2010年开始，基本养老保险参保人数包含城乡居民基本养老保险。

2.农村贫困人口根据三种标准测算：①1978-1999年根据农村绝对贫困标准测算；②2000-2009年根据农村低收入标准(或称为农村贫困标准)测算；③2010年及以后根据新确定的农村扶贫标准测算。

a) Since 2010, active contributors of basic pension insurance included those of urban and rural basic pension insurance.

b) There are three kinds of standards to calculate rural population in poverty: rural absolute poverty standard from 1978 to 1999; rural low income standard (rural poverty standards) from 2000 to 2009; newly revised standard of rural population in poverty since 2010.